RSITY OF
NGHAM

Health Care

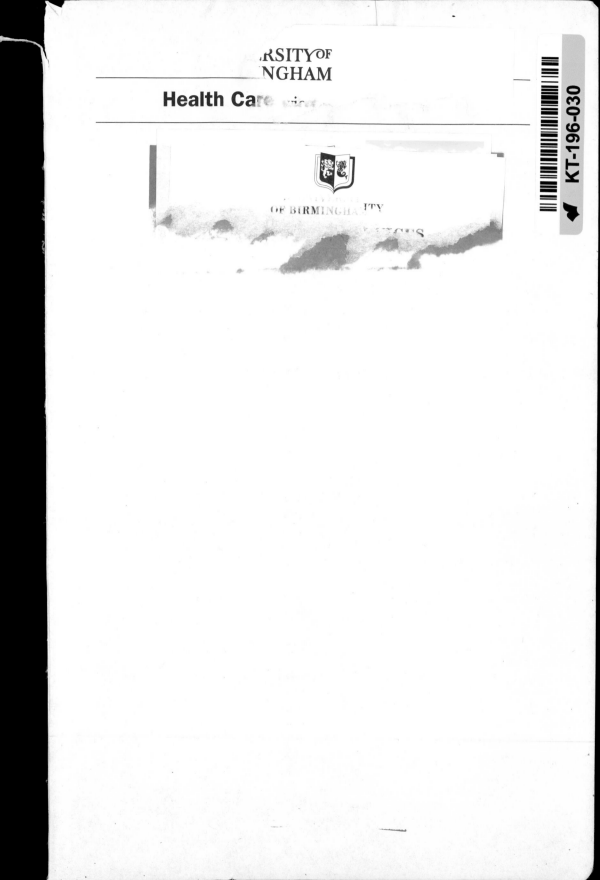

OF BIRMINGHAM

KT-196-030

1 +10
$12

HEALTH CARE LAW

Jonathan Montgomery

Oxford University Press
1997

Oxford University Press, Great Clarendon Street, Oxford OX2 6DP

Oxford New York
Athens Auckland Bangkok Bogota Bombay
Buenos Aires Calcutta Cape Town Dar es Salaam
Delhi Florence Hong Kong Istanbul Karachi
Kuala Lumpur Madras Madrid Melbourne
Mexico City Nairobi Paris Singapore
Taipei Tokyo Toronto
and associated companies in
Berlin Ibadan

Oxford is a trade mark of Oxford University Press

Published in the United States
by Oxford University Press Inc., New York

© Jonathan Montgomery 1997

All rights reserved. No part of this publication may be reproduced,
stored in a retrieval system, or transmitted, in any form or by any means,
without the prior permission in writing of Oxford University Press.
Within the UK, exceptions are allowed in respect of any fair dealing for the
purpose of research or private study, or criticism or review, as permitted
under the Copyright, Designs and Patents Act, 1988, or in the case of
reprographic reproduction in accordance with the terms of the licences
issued by the Copyright Licensing Agency. Enquiries concerning
reproduction outside these terms and in other countries should be
sent to the Rights Department, Oxford University Press,
at the address above

This book is sold subject to the condition that it shall not, by way
of trade or otherwise, be lent, re-sold, hired out or otherwise circulated
without the publisher's prior consent in any form of binding or cover
other than that in which it is published and without a similar condition
including this condition being imposed on the subsequent purchaser

British Library Cataloguing in Publication Data
Data available

Library of Congress Cataloging in Publication Data
Montgomery, Jonathan.
Health care law / Jonathan Montgomery.
p. cm.
1. Medical laws and legislation—Great Britain.
2. Medical Care—Law and legislation—Great Britain.
I. Title
KD3395.M66 1996 344.41'041—dc21 96–36931
ISBN 0–19–876260–7
ISBN 0–19–876259–3 (Pbk)

Typeset by Hope Services (Abingdon) Ltd.
Printed in Great Britain
on acid-free paper by
Biddles Ltd., Guildford and King's Lynn

Preface

Over the past few years, frequent requests for lectures and advice have convinced me of the need for a comprehensive text explaining the law that governs the delivery of health care. This book hopes to meet that need. It seeks to provide those who work in the health service, and those who advise them, with a detailed survey of the legal context of their work. It is also intended for use by students of law, medicine, nursing, midwifery, and the other health professions.

The title of the book marks a departure from the tradition established by its predecessors (and competitors). This work is about health care law, not law and medicine or nursing and the law. In part, this reflects themes in my earlier work exploring the role of law in promoting good health, and the legal position of health professionals other than doctors. More than this, though, I think the term 'health care law' best captures the content of the body of law that affects the day-to-day workings of the National Health Service.

Chapter 1 of the book explains the scope of health care law and introduces the main legal forms that are relevant to understanding how it works. It contains some material that will be familiar to lawyers, but needs introducing to health professionals who will know little of the workings of the law. However, I hope that even experienced lawyers will find that the discussion of the role of human rights law and quasi-legislation (including administrative circulars and professional rules) is of interest.

The main body of the book is divided into four parts. The first covers public health law, and the workings of the NHS (including the handling of complaints). The second explores the general framework for regulating health-care practice; the workings of the relevant professional bodies, malpractice law, and the law governing the use of medicines. The third part explores the legal status of patients. It covers the law of consent, confidentiality, and access to health records and considers the special problems arising in relation to child patients, those with mental illnesses, and those involved in research. The final part of the book examines particular areas of practice that throw up legal and ethical problems. There are chapters on abortion, fertility, maternity care, neonatal care, transplantation, and terminal care.

Throughout the book I have tried to explain the law as clearly and as accurately as I can (acknowledging that the current state of the law often makes certainty impossible). Like everyone, I have views on the ethical issues that arise, but I have sought here to provide a balanced account of the law, not a partisan case for its being the way I would like it to be. It is important to promote reform, but a legal textbook like this one is not the place to do so. This work provides the basis on which informed debate about the need for change can be built, and the footnotes identify literature which engages in the task. I have also tried to take account of socio-legal research on how the law actually affects health care. A true understanding of the position requires both knowledge of legal doctrine and an appreciation of how it works in practice.

Health-care law is a broad and rapidly developing field. This book has taken some years to write, and the manuscript has already been substantially rewritten even before publication to accommodate changes as they have occurred. To the best of my ability, I have described the law as in force on 10 October 1996. I have anticipated reforms to the constitution of the Committee of the General Medical Council which will come into effect on 1 January 1997.

JONATHAN MONTGOMERY

Southampton, October 1996.

Acknowledgements

Thanks to the many friends and colleagues who read and commented upon drafts of parts of this book, assisted with queries, helped me find materials, and kept people away when I needed time to work. Their help has improved the book. They include Priscilla Alderson, Kit Barker, Catherine Barnard, Margaret Brazier, David Carson, Gordon Dunstan, Jane Fortin, Stephen Gough, Andrew Halpin, David Hughes, Tim Jewell, Deidre Keeble, Alison Lampard, Jean McHale, Elsa Montgomery, Margaret Montgomery, Derek Morgan, John Murphy, Chris Newdick, Richard Nicholson, Winifred Phillips, Sarah Roch, Andrew Sharpe, Ann Sommerville, Jenny Steele, Rachel Trost, Dick Young, Catherine Watson, Nick Wikeley, and Tom Woodcock. I ask those whom I have forgotten to name to forgive me.

The early drafts of Chapters 3 to 8 were produced as part of project funded by the Economic and Social Research Council (ESRC award number L114251005) as part of the ESRC Contracts and Competition Research Programme. That support is gratefully acknowledged.

Thanks also to Richard Hart at Oxford University Press for not giving up on me during the long gestation of the book, and for Elissa Soave and Kate Elliott for their help in the production process.

Finally, the book would never have been finished were it not for the support of Elsa, Beth, and Rachel who 'had to be nice to me' until it was completed. I hope they will still be nice to me now that it is.

Contents

Table of Cases

Table of Cases before National Courts and Authorities

Table of Legislation

National Legislation

United States

1 The Scope and Sources of Health Care Law

The academic study of health care law is still a relatively young discipline and no consensus has yet been reached as to its proper scope. Kennedy and Grubb have argued that 'medical law' (as they call it)

> is essentially concerned with the relationship between doctors (and to a lesser extent hospitals and other institutions) and patients. . . . There are common issues which permeate all the problems which arise: respect for autonomy, consent, truth-telling, confidentiality, respect for personhood and persons, respect for dignity, and respect for justice.[1]

This is an approach which begins from the work of doctors and works outwards. It sees the clinical interaction between doctor and patient as the paradigm. This view influences both the content of the subject, individualizing its focus, and its underlying conceptual coherence, emphasizing the application of ethical principles.

While these are clearly important aspects of health care law, to restrict the subject's scope to issues raised in the clinical medical context would exclude a number of important areas of law. This is first because doctors are not the only health professionals, secondly because the delivery of health care in the United Kingdom is primarily the responsibility of the National Health Service, and thirdly because it underplays the increasing importance of public health issues (in which the health of communities and the whole population is the focus of concern).

The proper scope of a text on health care law needs to be assessed in the light of these considerations. This book defines the subject in terms of the United Kingdom's international obligations to tackle health problems and ensure that citizens have access to the health care that they need. The remainder of this Chapter is concerned with delineating the scope of the subject by examining those obligations, and describing the nature and sources of the legal regimes which are used to meet them.

[1] *Medical Law: Text with Materials* (London: Butterworths, 1994), 3, see also I. Kennedy, 'Emerging Problems of Medicine, Technology, and the Law' in I. Kennedy *Treat Me Right* (Oxford: Oxford University Press, 1988), 3.

A. The Scope of Health Care Law

Few would dispute the fact that good health is fundamental to a full and active life.[2] Securing it is therefore an important contribution to human well-being. In recognition of this the right to health appears in the international documents on human rights. The International Covenant on Economic, Social and Cultural Rights commits signatories, including the United Kingdom, to recognizing 'the right to enjoyment of the highest attainable standard of physical and mental health'.[3] The Universal Declaration states that '[e]veryone has the right to a standard of living adequate for the health and well-being of himself and his family, including food, clothing, housing and medical care and necessary social services'.[4]

The right to health is also included in the statements of rights for specific groups of people, such as children and women.[5] These international commitments enshrine noble aspirations and it is necessary to examine the idea of health rights more closely before its implications become clear.[6]

Such an examination immediately reveals that the concept of health is a problematic one. A contrast can be made between approaches which build on a social model of health and ill-health and those which use an engineering or mechanical model. Under the latter approach, health is concerned with the adequate functioning of the human body, preventing its breakdown and repairing it where necessary. The World Health Organization (WHO) has adopted the former and defined health as a 'state of complete physical, mental and social well-being and not merely the absence of infirmity'.[7] This is a definition which defines health in terms of an ultimate goal of perfection, and the WHO has also specified particular objectives to be reached on the way to this ideal.[8]

---

[2] L. Doyal, and I. Gough, *A Theory of Human Need* (London: Macmillan, 1991) explore the arguments.

[3] International Covenant on Economic, Social and Cultural Rights (1976), Art. 12.

[4] Universal Declaration of Human Rights (1948), Art. 25.

[5] UN Convention on the Rights of the Child, Art. 24; UN Convention on the Elimination of All Forms of Discrimination against Women, Arts. 11, 12, 14. These enshrine both the general right to health, and specific aspects of that right that governments are obliged to provide for members of the groups covered. For further discussion, see G. Van Bueren, *The International Law on the Rights of the Child* (London: Martinus Nijhoff, 1995), ch. 11, and R. Cook, *Women's Health and Human Rights* (Geneva: World Health Organization, 1994).

[6] J. Montgomery, 'Recognising a Right to Health' in R. Beddard and D. Hill, *Economic, Social and Cultural Rights: Progress and Achievement* (London: Macmillan, 1992).

[7] World Health Organization, *The Constitution* (Geneva: WHO, 1948).

[8] See, e.g., WHO, *Targets for Health for All: Targets in Support of the Regional Strategy for Health for All by the Year 2000* (Copenhagen: WHO 1985).

From the perspective of a social model of health, the potential scope of a book on health care law is vast. The state of our health is fundamentally affected by our diet, the condition of our environment, the way in which the society in which we live is organized, the lifestyles we adopt, and our own genetic heritage. Following this model of the causes of ill-health a text on health law would have to consider (at least) controls on the quality of food, environmental protection, the provision of public housing, and welfare benefits.

The focus of modern health care has been rather different. The emphasis has been on the impact of disease and the way in which it affects the human body conceived as a machine.[9] Thus scientific medicine emerged as the study of disease, with the patient seen as little more than the context in which this study could take place.[10] This concept of medical practice is superimposed on a more ancient tradition,[11] but much of the practice of modern medicine has become closely intertwined with a focus on disease and a concentration on 'engineering' issues. On this basis the scope of health care law will be largely confined to the control of disease and the provision of health care services. Given the influence of modern medicine on the development of health services it is not surprising that this more limited view dominates the modern English legal framework.

A more expansive concept of health care law would include protection from disease and accidents, protection from adverse environmental factors, the promotion of an environment which would foster improvements in health, and the provision of health care. So, too, it requires examination of the sharing of responsibility for health between private individuals (for their own health and that of others), the state and those who take on responsibility through their status as employers or health professionals.[12]

The most detailed exposition of the obligations of the United Kingdom Government to tackle health issues is found in the European Social Charter of 1961, to which it is a signatory. The Convention recognizes a number of important social rights. In particular, it declares that 'everyone has the right to benefit from any measures enabling him to enjoy the highest standard of health attainable' and that 'anyone without adequate resources has the right to social and medical assistance'.[13] The implications of these rights are fleshed out in Part II of the Convention. Under Article 11 of that Charter, the Government has undertaken

---

[9] T. McKeown, *The Role of Medicine* (Oxford: Blackwell, 1979).
[10] M. Foucault, *The Birth of the Clinic* (1963, tr. by A. Sheridan, London: Tavistock, 1976).
[11] J. Jacob, *Doctors and Rules: A Sociology of Professional Values* (London: Routledge, 1988).
[12] Montgomery, n. 6 above.
[13] European Social Charter, 1961, Part I, rights 11 and 13.

1. to remove so far as possible the cases of ill-health;
2. to provide advisory and educational facilities for the promotion of health and the encouragement of individual responsibility in matters of health;
3. to prevent as far as possible epidemic, endemic and other diseases.

Under Article 13, the United Kingdom has undertaken to ensure, so that the right to social and medical assistance can be effectively exercised, 'that any person who is without adequate resources and who is unable to secure such resources either by his own efforts or from other sources . . . be granted adequate assistance, and, in the case of sickness, the care necessitated by his condition.'

In the United Kingdom, the main Government responsibility for health lies with the Department of Health and is carried out principally through the National Health Service. Health promotion issues are pursued under an initiative known as 'Health of the Nation', under which targets have been set for the improvement of the health of the population.[14] The provision of health care is secured by obligations on the Secretary of State for Health, which are in practice met by the NHS Executive, by health authorities, and NHS trusts. To understand this picture, the legal structure of the NHS, including its internal standards, its duties, and its mechanisms for accountability, will all therefore need extensive treatment. Much of the day-to-day work within the Service is carried out by members of the health care professions, subject to their own ethical and legal disciplines. These, too, provide a substantial contribution to the concept of health care law.

This means that the subject of health care law is wider than medical law. It embraces not only the practice of medicine, but also that of the non-medical health care professions, the administration of health services and the law's role in maintaining public health. It also means that the concept of 'law' in this context must be examined carefully. Legal rules in a strict sense, as developed by Parliament and the courts, are not the only type of binding norm that is relevant to health care law. The next section considers the various types of law that impinge on health care practice.

B. Types of Health Care Law

There are many different ways of defining 'law'. Some argue that the word should only be used to describe the types of rule which are backed up by a sanction approved by a court, whether it be punishment, ordering financial

---

[14] *The Health of the Nation: A Strategy for Health in England* (London: HMSO, 1992, Cm 1986).

compensation for injuries caused when the rules are broken, or some sort of disqualification. Such an approach focuses on what happens when things go wrong and the rules are not followed. Others argue that the idea of law connotes rules which govern practice, and therefore covers those principles which people are bound to follow. On this basis there can be laws even if they are in practice unenforceable. They are laws because they are instructions given by a legitimate authority, not because they are backed up by force.

The concept of 'law' used here is broader than the first view would allow. If law is understood as describing only those rules whose breach may lead the involvement of the courts, then there is relatively little health care law in Britain. The bulk of the English law with which we are concerned sets out rules to guide the practice of health professionals. The very existence of such rules should prevent the courts needing to get involved, because they clarify in advance what should be done and reduce the occasions when there are disputes.

On the other hand, a more sophisticated version of the second concept of 'law' needs to be developed before it is satisfactory for our purposes. While it would be wrong to exclude all rules which are not backed up by some sort of sanction, it is nevertheless important to distinguish between different types of health care law. This can be most conveniently done by reference to the authorities which make the law. Law in the strict sense is made by the courts or Parliament, is binding on all citizens, and usually enforced in the courts. Professional law on the other hand is made and policed by regulatory bodies, set up by statute but left largely to their own devices. This type of law binds only the members of the profession but is backed up by significant sanctions. The third type of law, which will be discussed under the heading of 'quasi-law', describes rules which may be made without explicit legal authority and which are most important for the guidance they offer rather than the sanctions which follow if they are disregarded. Most professionals are more concerned to do what is right than to avoid punishment, and quasi-law is often used to advise them rather than to coerce them. Its force is therefore sometimes ethical rather than strictly legal. However, some forms of quasi-law may have direct or indirect legal consequences.

Health professionals need to be aware of more than the rules applied by the courts if they are to be able to abide by the expected canons of good practice. Health care lawyers need to appreciate the range of obligations to which health professionals are subject. This study of health care law takes this into account, but it is also careful to distinguish between those rules which must be obeyed on pain of punishment and those which merely provide an indication of good practice. Individuals may sometimes legitimately depart from the latter if they believe that ethical considerations require them to do so.

Should they ignore the former, they will usually be departing from the mandate which society has given them.

It should not be thought from the variety of sources of law that there is a coherent plan for allocating problems to be dealt with by the appropriate type of law. It is clear that, for the most part, the use of one variety rather than another is the result of accidents of history and politics rather than rational design.[15] Nevertheless, it is important to be aware of the differences between the various law-making processes both in order to understand the nature of the existing law and also to enable reform to occur.

C. General Law

The United Kingdom is not, for legal purposes, a single entity. This book deals with the law in England. Save in respect of the organization of the health service, the position in Wales is identical because the legal system is the same. However, Northern Ireland and Scotland are technically different legal jurisdictions, and while health care law is often very similar this is not always so. The courts will sometimes use the law in other parts of the United Kingdom (and indeed from other countries) as a guide to assist them, but it is not strictly binding.

There is no special exemption from English law for health professionals. This means that they, like any other citizens, must obey the criminal prohibitions and pay compensation when they are responsible for accidents. English law, in the strict sense, derives either from the practice of the courts ('common law') or from the legislative work of Parliament, and these two ways of law-making require separate treatment. It is also worth noting that each of these sources of law can provide for both 'civil' and 'criminal' rules.

Civil law governs the relationship between citizens; if its rules are broken then the victim has been wronged and will have some form of redress, usually resulting in compensation for any injury suffered. Victims may choose whether or not to make use of the legal process, waiving their rights to compensation if they do not wish to sue. Criminal law, on the other hand, is a matter for society as a whole. Crimes are wrongs, not just against the victims, but also against society. The appropriate sanction is punishment and the decision to bring in the courts is for society's agents (usually the Crown Prosecution Service). A third commonly used subdivision of law is 'public' law. This deals with the relationship between citizens and the state. It concerns the limits of

[15] I. Kennedy, and J. Stone, 'Making Public Policy on Medical-moral Issues' in P. Byrne (ed.), *Ethics and Law in Health Care and Research* (Chichester: Wiley, 1990).

government power, including that of public bodies such as the Department of Health, health authorities, and NHS trusts.

(i) Common Law

The phrase 'common law' is used to describe the rules which are extrapolated from the practice of the judges in deciding cases. Judges should take a consistent approach to recurring issues and are obliged to follow the decisions of earlier cases, at least when they have been given by the higher courts. Once a matter has been resolved by a judge it therefore sets a precedent which enshrines the legal rule. However, cases only come to court when there is a dispute and it follows that the development of the common law is haphazard rather than systematic. Distilling the common law principles is by no means an easy matter. Judges are reluctant to make sweeping statements of principle and will not usually go beyond the immediate circumstances of the case before them. Many decisions therefore shed little light on future cases unless their facts are very similar.

Judges do, however, sometimes explain their reasons for deciding a case in a particular way. Even where the facts of a case are not precisely the same as an earlier one there may be sufficient help from an earlier case to enable a court to resolve the matter. If there is not, the court will have to reason from fundamental principles, and if this happens the outcome can never be certain in advance. There are three states in which the common law may find itself in relation to a new dispute. It may be that there is an earlier case which is indistinguishable from the current one, in which case the earlier decision should be followed. It may be that the earlier case is not identical, but the judges expressed themselves in terms which make it reasonably clear what they would have done if faced by the new circumstances. If this is the case then the new court will usually follow their lead, but is not bound to do so. It may, however, be that the case is completely new and the judges must look to develop the law from general principles. The best way to do this is a matter of considerable controversy.[16]

Lawyers sometimes use two Latin tags to capture the distinction between aspects of an earlier decision that are binding in subsequent cases and those that are not. The former are described as being the *ratio decidendi* (reasons for the decision). These constitute firm decisions on rules of law. A contrast is drawn with *obiter dicta* (things said by the way) which were not strictly necessary for the court to consider, and are regarded as helpful, but not binding on later cases. A statement of law that was *obiter* is therefore a less secure guide

---

[16] For an introduction to the issues see R. Dworkin, *Law's Empire* (London: Fontana, 1986).

to the outcome of a future case than one that was an essential part of the decision (i.e. part of the *ratio*).

A significant amount of the law governing health care practice is still regulated by the common law. Consent to treatment is probably the single most common intersection between law and health care practice, and it is entirely a matter for the common law. This has resulted in the law on consent remaining relatively unsophisticated despite a considerable amount of judicial activity and academic commentary.[17]

(ii) Legislation

Legislation describes the creation and reform of the law under the authority of the Houses of Parliament. For present purposes a distinction should be made between two levels of legislation: primary and secondary.

(a) *Primary Legislation*

Primary legislation describes statutes passed by Parliament, that is both the Houses of Lords and Commons, and formally approved by the Queen. Once passed, these are described as Acts of Parliament. While they are under discussion in the Houses of Parliament they are known as bills. When judge-made rules and statutes conflict the statute law prevails. However, judges need to interpret the statutory provisions and their decisions as to the meaning of words in Acts of Parliament are themselves a source of law.

Although it is relatively recently that issues of health care ethics have been the subject of legislative activity, statute law plays an important part in the modern law. Organ transplantation, for example, is governed by the Human Tissue Act 1961 and the Human Organ Transplants Act 1989. The National Health Service is entirely the creature of statute. The professional bodies are established by statutes. Very often the legal rules governing an area of health care practice have a mixture of sources. This can be illustrated by the law governing health care records. The confidentiality of such records is established by judge-made law, but rights of access to records are created by statute law.[18]

Most Acts of Parliament are drafted by the Government. Although there is no necessity for statutes to be prepared by any particular process, it is common for major legislation to be presented to Parliament after public consultation on the Government's proposals. The usual procedure is for a 'Green Paper' to be published outlining the problems which need to be addressed, setting out possible ways forward, and inviting comments. Once these comments have been considered, the Government publishes a 'White Paper'

---

[17] See Ch. 10.   [18] See Ch. 11.

explaining what it proposes to do and then drafts a bill to do it. This is then introduced to Parliament.

Such is the process by which well-thought-out legislation is expected to emerge. Things do not always follow such a route, and the Government has sometimes been persuaded to act rather more hurriedly. Two recent examples are the Surrogacy Arrangements Act 1985 and the Human Organ Transplants Act 1989. Both Acts were passed in a climate of what has been called 'moral panic'.[19] The former was rushed through Parliament well before a considered response was formulated to the Warnock Committee's report on developments in human fertilization and embryology.[20] It was prompted by revulsion to an 'unnatural and unfortunate practice which has sickened so many decent and family loving people'[21] rather than reasoned policy. The comprehensive statute dealing with the area was not passed until 1990.[22]

Similarly, the Human Organ Transplants Act 1989 was passed as an immediate reaction to a public scandal. It was an example of 'public policy being made on the hoof' and resulted in a statute which diverged significantly from the general political philosophy of the Government.[23] It was also a reform which concentrated on a single, highly contentious aspect of transplantation law and ignored long-standing proposals for reform[24] and European initiatives.[25] Far from being the result of a long and careful process of consultation such legislation bears closer resemblance to reflex action. Once passed, however, the history behind a bill is irrelevant—all legislation is equally binding.

Once introduced into Parliament, a bill must go through a number of hurdles before it becomes an Act. The most important of these are the second reading, the Committee stage, and the report stage. At the first reading the title of the bill is read out. The second reading consists of debate on the principles of the bill. If the principles of a bill are approved it will be sent to a committee which has the task of examining its detailed wording and considering amendments. At the report stage amendments are put to the vote of the whole House. It is at this point that the final text of the bill is reached. Bills must be passed by both Houses, and will go through a similar process in both, although amendments are mostly made by the House into which they were originally introduced.

---

[19] The origin of this phrase is to be found in S. Cohen, *Folk Devils and Moral Panics: The Creation of the Mods and Rockers* (Oxford: Martin Robertson, 1972).

[20] D. Morgan, 'Who to Be or Not to Be: The Surrogacy Story' (1986) 49 *MLR* 358–68.

[21] P. Bruinvels MP, *Hansard*, HC, Vol. 77, col. 43. [22] See Ch. 16.

[23] Kennedy and Stone, n. 15 above.

[24] e.g. I. Kennedy, 'The Donation and Transplantation of Kidneys: Should the Law be Changed ?' reprinted in I. Kennedy, *Treat Me Right*, n. 1 above.

[25] Res. (78)29 of the Committee of Ministers, 'On Harmonisation of Legislations of Member States Relating to Removal, Grafting and Transplantation of Human Substances'.

In addition to government legislation there is provision for 'private members' bills'. These do not usually succeed in being passed because there is rarely sufficient Parliamentary time to allow them to pass through all the stages. The most important example of a private member's bill in health care is probably the Abortion Act 1967, which was a private member's bill introduced by David Steele. The Government chose to support it by making sure that sufficient Parliamentary time was made available. There were numerous attempts to amend the 1967 Act by private members' bills which failed for lack of time.[26] Reform was finally effected by the Human Fertilization and Embryology Act 1990, when the Government agreed to allow the issue to be added to its bill during the Parliamentary process.

(b) Secondary Legislation

The second type of legislative activity is the making of regulations by statutory instrument. Secondary legislation is approved by Parliament, but it is prepared by ministers and the details are not debated. Legislation of this type is often used to spell out the details of the plans which Parliament has approved in statutes. It takes up less Parliamentary time than specifying everything in the statute itself, and can be amended more easily if needs change. Powers to produce secondary legislation are conferred on the Secretary of State by much of the NHS primary legislation. They can be used to specify duties and standards and set out proper procedures. While such legislation is subject to Parliamentary scrutiny, it is mostly by 'negative resolution' procedure, so that this scrutiny is rarely rigorous. Once passed, statutory instruments have the full force of statute law. It is only the way in which they are prepared which makes them different from statutes.

In fact, more binding health service law is found in regulations made by statutory instrument than in the statutes themselves. For example, the terms and conditions under which general practitioners work are set out in this way in the NHS (General Medical Services) Regulations 1992 (as amended).[27] This is by far the most important source for the law governing GPs. The constitutions of professional bodies and the rules by which they operate are usually to be found in statutory instruments. Practitioners who are terminating a pregnancy will usually have more need to consult the Abortion Regulations 1991[28] than the Abortion Act 1967 because it is the Regulations which set out the forms on which terminations must be notified to the Department of Health.

---

[26] J. Keown, *Abortion, Doctors and the Law. Some Aspects of the Legal Regulation of Abortion in England from 1803 to 1982* (Cambridge: Cambridge University Press, 1988).

[27] SI 1992 No 635.   [28] SI 1991 No 499.

D. Professional Law

Many of the personnel working in health services will be subject to a regime of professional discipline. They will need to be entered on their professional register before they can practise and will be liable to being removed from that register if they fail to abide by the standards which the profession requires. In addition to the requirements of the general law, which apply to all citizens alike, professionals must therefore obey more onerous rules of behaviour set by their colleagues. If a breach of professional law is alleged, then the 'accused' will be judged by the professional body rather than by a court. This essentially means that their conduct will be assessed by their peers. If they are found guilty, the penalties will be professional penalties relating to their ability to continue practise. These matters are considered more fully in Chapter 6.

Two examples can illustrate the regulatory function of the professions. One of the problems facing those with HIV is the refusal of health care professionals to offer them care. While in the United States this has caused problems,[29] in the United Kingdom the medical and nursing professions have settled the matter by issuing statements to the effect that it would be considered professional misconduct to refuse to treat those with HIV.[30] This position threatens recalcitrant professionals with suspension from the register, with its probable consequence of loss of livelihood, and also establishes an ethical standard.

A second incident illustrating the disciplinary functions of the professions concerns the transplantation of sold human kidneys. The Government has now intervened and enacted the Human Organ Transplants Act 1989, but the General Medical Council acted in relation to doctors involved in kidney sales at a time when they were not illegal. It is interesting to consider which is the most effective form of regulation. The 1989 Act provided for a fine of £1,000 (now raised to £5,000). The General Medical Council is able to remove a doctor's right to practise. More significant, perhaps, is the power to regulate the type of practice by imposing conditions for the registration of a practitioner. This was done in the transplantation cases to prevent those concerned practising privately, and to ban their continuing to work on transplantation.

---

[29] Taunya Lovell Banks, "The Right to Medical Treatment" in H. L. Dalton, S. Burris, *et al., AIDS and the Law* (New Haven, Conn.: Yale University Press, 1987).

[30] General Medical Council statement, 26 May 1988, cited in Medical Defence Union, *AIDS: Medico-legal Advice* (rev. edn. London: MDU, 1989), 13; Sheila Mackie-Bailey, 'Abhorrent, Unethical and Impractical for Nurses to Refuse to Care for AIDS Patients', *Nursing Standard*, 6 Nov. 1986; see now UK Central Council for Nursing, Midwifery and Health Visiting, *Guidelines for Professional Practice* (London: UKCC, 1996), para. 49.

E. Quasi-law

The National Health Service is a mammoth bureaucratic organization, and there is a constant stream of communication from the NHS Executive giving guidance and instructions to health authorities and NHS trusts on how they should carry out their work. These generally take the form of circulars, guidance, and executive letters.[31] These documents are part of the growing body of what can be called quasi-law. The term quasi-law covers rules which are not usually legally binding, although they may have some legal force, but which will in practice determine they way in which people act.[32] There may be no legal sanction against failure to obey such laws, but in most circumstances they will be followed, and therefore any survey of the norms which govern practice must take them into account.

There is a great deal of quasi-law created in the health care context. Sometimes it must be obeyed because the statutory provisions state that instructions given under it are binding. Thus, the Secretary of State can issue 'directions' under the NHS Act 1977, sections 13 to 17, with which health authorities must comply. Once issued, the directions create legal duties. Failure to carry them out may lead to the use of default powers under section 85 of the 1977 Act.

It is more common, however, for the Department of Health to use guidance and encouragement than compulsion. A steady stream of circulars and notices offers explanation of legal requirements and guidance as to good practice. Two controversial examples have been the advice given on the participation by nurses in prostaglandin terminations of pregnancy[33] and the circular on contraceptive services for young people which aroused the wrath of Mrs Gillick.[34] Mrs Gillick objected because the circular envisaged that in exceptional circumstances a doctor might offer contraceptive advice and treatment to a child under 16 without parental consent. She sought a declaration that this advice was wrong in law.

---

[31] These have their own classification systems. Health circulars are given 'HC' attributions, guidance 'HSG'. Circulars were previously called 'notes' and were indicated by 'HN'. General executive instructions are indicated by the prefix 'EL' which is sometimes 'TEL' where only NHS trusts are addressed. These prefixes are followed by the last two digits of the year in brackets and the number of the document in the year's sequence. Thus a direction to NHS Trusts on the appointment of medical and dental consultants was issued with HSG(96)24, being the 24th guidance document of 1996.

[32] See G. Ganz, *Quasi-legislation: Recent Developments in Secondary Legislation* (London: Sweet & Maxwell, 1987). The NHS is specifically considered at 83–5.

[33] *RCN* v. *DHSS* [1981] 1 All ER 545.

[34] *Gillick* v. *W. Norfolk & Wisbech AHA* [1985] 3 All ER 402. The circular in question was HN(80)46 and it has now been replaced by HC(86)1.

What is most interesting is that the circular in fact contained a mixture of advice on the legal position and health care ethics. The legal advice, finally vindicated by the House of Lords, was tempered by ethical exhortations which in fact restricted the occasions on which offering lawful advice was recommended. Similarly, the new circular interprets the speeches of the House of Lords in a way which declines to recommend advising young people in circumstances which other commentators have suggested would be permissible.[35] The circular therefore creates standards of practice based on considerations of both law and ethics. Health professionals are likely to rely on the circular rather than primary legal sources for a statement of their legal responsibilities.

Guidance of this type exists in a large number of areas which are largely unregulated by 'law' in the strict sense. Research on human subjects remains virtually untouched by English law, but a significant amount of quasi-law exists on which the practice of those involved is based. Some of this emanates from the Department of Health or from the various statutory bodies charged with overseeing the professions, and could therefore be said to be in some sense 'official'. Other sources of quasi-law include non-statutory professional organizations and agreements on proper practice.

Many of the principles which guide practice come, however, from the work of professional organizations. There are Department of Health guidelines on the practice of local research ethics committees,[36] but the most detailed general guidance on the proper conduct of research and its approval by committees has come from the Royal College of Physicians.[37] Although established by the professions themselves rather than by state initiative, the royal colleges are recognized by Royal Charter and often by Act of Parliament. Other norms governing practice come from less official bodies. Consideration of the proper limits of research with children is likely, in practice, to include consideration of the guidelines produced by the British Paediatric Association—an entirely voluntary body.[38] Problems relating to the compensation of volunteers injured during drug trials are currently dealt with under a code agreed by the Association of the British Pharmaceutical Industry.[39] While in the strict sense

---

[35] e.g. J. Eekelaar, 'The Eclipse of Parental Rights' (1986) 102 *LQR* 4–9 at 7; J. Montgomery, 'Children as Property ?' (1988) 51 *MLR* 323–42 at 339.

[36] *Local Research Ethics Committees* (London: DoH, 1991) issued with HSG(91)5.

[37] Royal College of Physicians, *Research Involving Patients* (London: RCP, 1990); Royal College of Physicians, *Guidelines on the Practice of Ethics Committees in Medical Research Involving Human Subjects* (London: RCP, 1990).

[38] British Paediatric Association, *Guidelines for the Ethical Conduct of Research Involving Children* (London: BPA, 1992).

[39] APBI, 'Guidelines on Clinical Trials—Compensation for Medicine-induced Injury' (1983) 287 *BMJ* 675.

there is very little law governing research on humans, it can be seen that there are nevertheless detailed norms which inform practice.

A third type of quasi-law which is important in the health care context is the code of practice. Codes of practice may contain more extensive and detailed advice than will usually be included in circulars and may be produced by a number of bodies. Codes of practice will not usually be binding, but may have indirect force in a number of ways. Adherence to the code of practice drawn up by the Human Fertilization and Embryology Authority is not specifically required by the law, but those who depart from it are likely to lose their licences to practise in the areas which it covers because the Authority is entitled to take compliance into account when deciding whether to revoke them.[40] Codes of professional conduct will be taken into account under professional law. Codes of practice may also receive indirect force from providing the basis of a complaint to the Health Service Commissioners. The Commissioner investigates maladministration, and if a hospital failed to organize itself so that the Code of Practice could be followed it could well amount to maladministration.

F. Scrutinizing Professional and Quasi-law

It will have become clear that professional and quasi-law are very important in terms of setting the standards against which health care practice must operate. Yet the manner in which it is created militates against public discussion and thorough debate. The substance of some rules has not satisfied everybody, and there have been a number of attempts to challenge quasi-law in the courts through the process of 'judicial review'. This is a form of litigation in which the activities of public authorities are scrutinized by the courts. The courts may not strike down decisions merely because they believe them to be wrong, but can control abuses of power. The circumstances in which they may do this are strictly limited. Three hurdles need to be surmounted.

First, it is necessary for complainants to establish that they are personally affected by the decision in question. The law will not allow public authorities to be bothered by interfering busybodies and demands personal involvement to guard against this. Aggrieved parties have brought a number of health care issues to court by this route. One case involved a patient who said she had been refused infertility treatment because she did not come within rules based on the qualifications for adoptive parents, which, it was alleged, had been adopted

---

[40] Human Fertilization and Embryology Act 1990, s. 25.

as the criteria for access to care.[41] A doctor whose livelihood was threatened by the GMC's rules on advertising has challenged those rules in court,[42] as has a pharmaceutical company adversely affected by a similar rule.[43]

In the context of health care law the courts have been prepared to relax the usually stringent rules requiring a personal interest in the matter. They permitted Mrs Gillick to bring a matter to court on the basis that her interests as a parent might by involved. Yet, normally a mere possibility would not be sufficient.[44] The courts have also been prepared to countenance representative actions by the Royal College of Nursing despite the fact that it was unclear that the interests of any specific member were in issue.[45] In one case the Court of Appeal noted that the courts had never refused to hear a health care case on the basis that the applicant had an insufficient interest to bring it.[46]

Secondly, it is necessary to show that the body whose actions are being questioned is a public organization rather than a private one.[47] This has now been established in relation to the Department of Health when issuing circulars,[48] professional bodies giving guidance as they are required to do under the relevant statute,[49] a voluntary body recognized by the Department but not part of a statutory framework,[50] and an ethics committee set up purely as a local initiative.[51] On the basis of these decisions it should be possible to ask a court to consider the activities of most of the bodies who produce quasi-law.

Being able to ask does not guarantee that the court may do anything. The third requirement for a successful judicial review challenge is that it must be based on one of a limited list of types of abuse of power. Guidance may only be overturned where it is wrong as to the interpretation of the law,[52] is irrational in that no reasonable body could have issued such guidance,[53] or where it has been tainted by procedural impropriety.[54] If it can be shown that there has been an abuse of power, then the court can declare that the public body has acted unlawfully, quash the decision and force the matter to be reconsidered.[55] Examples of the application of these principles can be seen in the

---

[41] R. v. *Ethical Committee of St Mary's Hospital, ex p. Harriott* [1988] 1 FLR 512.

[42] R. v. *GMC, ex p. Colman* [1990] 1 All ER 489.

[43] R. v. *British Pharmaceutical Industry Association Code of Practice Committee, ex p. Professional Counselling Aids Ltd, Independent* 1 Nov. 1990.

[44] C. Harlow, 'Gillick: A Comedy of Errors?' (1986) 49 *MLR* 768–76.

[45] *RCN* v. *DHSS* [1981] 1 All ER 545.

[46] *Re S* [1995] 3 All ER 290, *per* Sir Thomas Bingham MR.

[47] R. v. *Panel on Takeovers and Mergers, ex p. Datafin* [1987] 1 All ER 564.

[48] *Gillick*, n. 34 above.   [49] R. v. *GMC, ex p. Colman*, n. 42 above.

[50] R. v. *British Pharmaceutical Industry Association Code of Practice Committee*, n. 43 above.

[51] R. v. *Ethical Committee of St Mary's Hospital*, n. 41 above.

[52] This was the issue in the unsuccessful challenge to the DHSS circular in *Gillick*, n. 34 above.

[53] *Associated Provincial Picture Houses* v. *Wednesbury Corp* [1947] 2 All ER 680 [1948] 1 KB 223.

[54] *Council of Civil Service Unions* v. *Minister for the Civil Service* [1984] 3 All ER 935.

[55] See generally P. Craig, *Administrative Law* (3rd edn., London: Sweet & Maxwell, 1994).

discussion of the enforcement of rights to health care under the NHS (Chapter 3).

G. Employment Law

A further way in which the activity of health workers is constrained is through their obligations as employees. Like all employees, health professionals are obliged to follow the lawful and reasonable instructions of their employers. Health service bodies frequently develop protocols and policies to guide practitioners. These indicate the way in which they are expected to carry out their work, and will usually constitute an employer's instruction, even if they have been developed by professional staff.

The sanctions for failing to comply with policies arise in a number of ways. Sometimes a departure from an agreed protocol may make it easier to show that there has been negligence.[56] Sometimes it may be used as part of an allegation of professional misconduct.[57] Most importantly, however, staff may be liable to disciplinary action for disobeying instructions. In serious cases, this may ultimately result in dismissal. Employers' policies therefore constitute an important constraint on the way in which staff work. They may sometimes conflict with a practitioner's clinical judgement, and it is important to note the way in which the law will treat health professionals who seek to justify their refusal to follow protocols by appealing to clinical freedom.

In *Owen* v. *Coventry HA* a registered mental nurse who had been dismissed for refusing to participate in electro-convulsive therapy (ECT) claimed that he had been unfairly dismissed.[58] The Court of Appeal upheld his dismissal, finding that he had been in breach of the implied contractual term of employment that he would obey his employer's instructions. Owen was not entitled to refuse to be involved in the treatment merely because he disapproved of it on clinical grounds. However, the Court indicated that there might be legitimate scope for a slightly different type of claim. He might have shown that, while he would normally co-operate with ECT even though he disapproved of its use, in the particular circumstances there were unusual factors that made it dangerous for his patient. If this were the case, then Owen might have been able to show that he was carrying out his primary professional (and contractual) duty to exercise his professional skills in caring for his patients. This could justify, in an individual case, disobeying what would otherwise be a lawful instruction. However, on the facts, the court did not accept that Owen's case fell into this category.

[56] See Ch. 7.   [57] Ch. 6.   [58] 19 Dec. 1986, unreported.

The implications of this decision are that health professionals have a *prima facie* obligation to follow the policies set down by NHS trusts and other employers. They may be disciplined for failing to follow them, and they therefore constitute a set of rules that are backed up by legal sanctions. Health professionals may sometimes exercise their professional judgement to depart from policies, but they need to be able to show that there were factors specific to the particular case which made it their professional responsibility to do so.

H. European Law

European Community law is an emerging source of rules governing the delivery of health care.[59] Legislation is proposed or made by the European Commission. It has powers to legislate directly, but it is essentially an executive body pursuing the policies approved by the Council of Ministers. It also formulates proposals for the Council to consider. The Council of Ministers approves or rejects proposals from the Commission after consultation with the European Parliament. The latter body does not itself legislate, but if it approves proposals, it becomes possible for the Council to pass legislation by a majority vote. Otherwise there must be unanimous approval from members of the Council.

There are four main sources of European law. The first is the Treaties under which the European Community is established and operates. Some of the treaty provisions have a direct impact in English law. This is where they impose precise and unconditional obligations.[60] Other Articles of the Treaties have an indirect effect, in that they oblige the United Kingdom Government to change the law. The second form of European law is regulations. These are made by the Council and by the Commission. They are binding in Member States and do not need to be incorporated into English law to have legal force.

The third source of European law is the directive. In principle, directives bind the Member States of the Community rather than individuals, and are not binding until incorporated into domestic law. However, directives have direct force in relation to state authorities, and health authorities have been held to be such bodies.[61] Thus the NHS is obliged to comply with the provisions of Community law even before they have been fully incorporated into English law. This would apply just as much to NHS trusts as to health

---

[59] For an introduction, see D. Medhurst, *A Brief and Practical Guide to EC Law* (Oxford: Blackwell, 1994).

[60] Case 41/74, *Van Duyn* v. *Home Office* [1974] ECR 1337.

[61] Case 152/84, *Marshall* v. *Southampton & SW Hampshire AHA* [1986] ECR 723.

authorities; even though they have a degree of independence, they are still providing a public service under the control of the state with special powers.[62]

A number of directives are important for health care law. Mutual recognition of the qualifications of practitioners who have qualified in other EC countries is required.[63] In relation to doctors and nurses, the relevant statutes have been amended to reflect this law and it is not necessary to examine the original directive.[64] However, in relation to chiropractors and osteopaths, European law is incorporated by reference.[65] Much of European law is concerned to ensure that economic activity within the Community is based on fair competition. Consequently, it plays an important role in the regulation of the pharmaceutical industry.[66] The procurement of public works and services generally has to be subject to open competition from all Member States, a matter that will need to be considered in the context of the NHS market.

The final source of Community law is the decisions of the European Court of Justice. This Court, based at Luxembourg, hears cases between Member States and Community institutions concerning alleged failures of governments to meet their obligations under European law. It also considers the legality of actions of the institutions of the Community. Finally, it can be asked by a domestic court to give preliminary rulings on problems of interpretation of European law.

I. Human Rights Law

The final source of health care law comes from the international agreements on human rights. For practical purposes, the most significant of these is the European Convention for the Protection of Human Rights and Fundamental Freedoms, originally drawn up by the Council of Europe in 1950.[67] That document is concerned with political rights, and social and economic rights are set out in the European Social Charter of 1961. The machinery for

---

[62] Case 188/89, *Foster* v. *British Gas* [1990] 3 CMLR 833.

[63] Council Directive of 21 Dec. 1988 on a general system for the recognition of higher-education diplomas awarded on completion of professional education and training of at least three years' duration, 89/48/EEC [1989] OJ L19/16; Council Directive of 18 June 1992 on a second general system for the recognition professional education and training to supplement Directive 89/48/EEC, 92/51/EEC, [1992] OJ L209/25.

[64] Medical Act 1983, s. 17, sch. 2; Nurses, Midwives and Health Visitors Act 1979, s. 10(3A); and the EEC Nursing and Midwifery Qualifications Designation Order 1983, SI 1983 No 921.

[65] Osteopaths Act 1993, s. 14; Chiropractors Act 1994, s. 14.   [66] See Ch. 9.

[67] For introductions, see R. Beddard, *Human Rights and Europe* (Cambridge: Grotius Publications, 1993); A. Robertson, and J. Merrills, *Human Rights in Europe* (Manchester: Manchester University Press, 1993).

protecting human rights, under the auspices of the Council of Europe, is quite separate from that of the European Community. Individuals who believe that they have been denied their rights under the Convention may petition the European Commission of Human Rights (not to be confused with the European Commission discussed above). They may only do this once they have exhausted the remedies available to them under the law of their own country. However, as the United Kingdom has no machinery for the vindication of human rights, petitions from the United Kingdom are relatively common. The Commission considers petitions to see whether they are admissible. This includes considering whether they have been brought within six months of the denial of a remedy in the domestic courts, whether a ruling under the Convention would constitute an effective remedy for the complainant, and whether the petition should be rejected as manifestly unfounded.

Where the Commission believes that there has been a possible breach of the Convention, it forwards the case to the European Court of Human Rights. The Court will then rule on whether there has been a breach of the Convention. Those states, including the United Kingdom, which are members of the Council of Europe have undertaken to abide by the decision of any case in which they are involved. Thus the usual result of a decision that there has been a breach of the Convention is that the law will be changed. There is also a limited power for the Court to order that damages be paid.

As already discussed, the European Social Charter of 1961 deals with rights to health: to disease prevention, health promotion, and access to health services. There are few specific references to health issues in the European Convention. Nevertheless, there may be rights that may be threatened by the activities of health professionals. However, the provisions of the Convention generally facilitate such activities rather than limit them. Thus, it expressly provides for the detention of those judged to be insane or threatening to infect others with disease.[68] Further, infringements of rights can often be justified on the basis of 'the public health': rights to personal and family privacy, freedom of assembly, expression, thought, conscience, and religion are limited in this way.[69] Nevertheless, the existence of the European Convention provides limits on the *way* in which matters such as infectious disease control and the detention of mental patients can be provided for by English law. Some substantive rights, such as the right to found a family,[70] are also significant in underpinning the reform of health care law.

[68] Art. 5(1)(e).   [69] European Convention on Human Rights, Arts. 8 to 11.
[70] Art. 12.

J. Conclusion

If law is understood as encompassing the norms that are binding upon health care workers, then the sources of health care law are extremely complex. The sanctions behind some rules may be only indirectly enforceable, but they are nevertheless important in understanding the legal framework in which health care operates. In some areas, the less formal types of legal rules may be more influential than the strict requirements of legislation or case law. It would be dangerous to disregard them.

The influence of human rights law and European law may still be small, compared to the intervention of English law on practice. However, it is far from marginal, and its significance is growing. Health services are a major economic activity, and European Community law impinges on them in a number of ways. The scope of health care law can be defined by the international obligations of the United Kingdom Government in relation to health matters. This is the way in which the content of health care law, the subject of this book, is determined.

In relation to medical law, more narrowly conceived, international aspects are also increasingly important. The European Parliament has committed itself to the production of a European Charter of Patients' Rights.[71] In a separate initiative, the Council of Europe is also working towards a Convention on Bioethics, whose purpose is to reflect the common values protected by the European Court of Human Rights.[72] The scope and sources of health care law are thus by no means fixed for all time.

[71] Res. passed by the European Parliament on 19 Jan. 1984.

[72] C. Byk, 'The European Convention on Bioethics' (1993) 19 *JME* 13–16; A. Rogers, and A. Durand de Bousingen, *Bioethics in Europe* (Strasbourg, Council of Europe, 1995).

Part I

Health and the Law

2   Public Health Law

As discussed in the previous Chapter, the United Kingdom Government is committed, by its international obligations, to take measures to improve the public health. Under Article 11 of the European Social Charter it must take steps to remove the causes of ill-health, prevent disease, and advise citizens on how to look after their health. These steps need not all take the form of legal intervention, but at a number of points the law plays an important role in promoting public health.

The law's involvement in public health emerged in the Nineteenth Century. However, the public health concerns of that century were quite different from those which exist today.[1] Many diseases which were then deadly are no longer widespread or dangerous. The sources of threats to ill-health were largely beyond individual control and public initiatives on sanitation, vaccination, and medical treatment were able to make a considerable impact on the rate and causes of death. In 1854 20,000 people died from cholera, a cause of death virtually unrecorded in modern Britain. The picture which presents itself today raises very different problems. While public health measures remain important, particularly in the eradication of inequalities in health,[2] it has been said that 'much of the responsibility for ensuring his own good health lies with the individual'.[3] Health care is therefore 'everybody's business' as the Department of Health and Social Security has put it.[4]

Consequently, the nature of public health medicine has changed drastically.[5] This is connected with three interrelated trends. The first concerns changes in mortality patterns (to do with deaths). The second is developments in morbidity (relating to the incidence of ill-health). The third is shifts in the understanding of the concept of health. In different ways, each of these has led to a change of emphasis away from collective and environmental work, towards a concentration on individual responsibility and lifestyle issues.

---

[1] DHSS, *Prevention and Health: Everybody's Business* (London: HMSO, 1976); A. Smith, and B. Jacobson (eds.), *The Nation's Health: A Strategy for the 1990s* ((London: King's Fund, 1988).

[2] P. Townsend, N. Davidson, and M. Whitehead, *Inequalities in Health* (London: Penguin, 1988).

[3] DHSS, n. 1 above, 95.   [4] *Ibid.*

[5] J. Ashton and H. Seymour, *The New Public Health* (Milton Keynes: Open University Press, 1988), esp. ch. 2.

Death rates have declined dramatically over the period for which statistics are available. Between 1841 and 1971, mortality figures, standardized to eliminate the effect of different age distributions, dropped from twenty-three per thousand to seven per thousand for males and from twenty-one per thousand to fewer than five per thousand for females.[6] Life expectancy has also increased. At the end of the Nineteenth Century at birth a girl could hope to live until 48 and a boy until 44. By 1992 the figures were 79 and 73 respectively.[7] In the face of high death rates public health officials naturally concentrated on tackling the causes of death. This necessarily indicates a different focus from modern work as the causes of death in Victorian England were very different from those that prevail today.

The reduction of death rates was largely due to the control and elimination of infectious diseases, and it has been estimated that over 90 per cent of the reduction in mortality achieved in the second half of the Nineteenth Century was due to the control of infections.[8] Even in 1931 infectious diseases accounted for 13 per cent of deaths, but by 1991 the Government White Paper, *The Health of the Nation* found that their contribution was not worth recording separately.[9] This success has resulted in the focus on new challenges. The Government recognizes that the strategies by which the old problems were overcome must not be neglected: 'safe water and effective disposal of waste, the supply of wholesome food, safety at work, controls on pollution and good housing remain as important as ever.'[10] However, the targets for further success focus on the main contemporary causes of death: coronary heart disease, strokes, and cancers. Tackling these diseases requires persuading individuals to examine their lifestyles, and raises new questions about the role of law.

The second factor that has led to a reorientation of public health concerns is the greater concern with the quality of people's health while alive.[11] With increased life expectancy this has become more pressing. Consequently, the mere fact of life is not enough and public health medicine has become concerned with making people healthier while alive as well as preventing them from dying prematurely. This focus is inextricably linked with developing understandings of the idea of health.[12] The focus of medicine on the human

[6] T. Mckeown, *The Role of Medicine* (Oxford: Blackwell, 1979), 31, Fig. 3.1.

[7] *The Health of the Nation* (London: HMSO, 1992, Cm 1986), 6–7.

[8] Mckeown, n. 6 above, 31, Table 3.1.

[9] N. 7 above, 10, Fig. 5. See the consultative document of the same name (1991 Cm 1523), 7, Fig. 6, for more detailed figures.

[10] *The Health of the Nation: A Consultative Document* (London: HMSO, 1991, Cm 1523), 5.

[11] Compare M. Whitehead, 'The Health Divide' (1987) with D. Black, J. N. Morris, C. Smith, and P. Townsend, 'The Black Report' (1982) published together in Townsend, Davidson, and Whitehead, n. 2 above.

[12] See DHSS, *Inequalities in Health: Report of a Research Working Group Chaired by Sir Douglas Black* (1980), published as 'The Black Report' in Townsend, Davidson, and Whitehead, n. 2 above.

body encouraged an understanding of ill-health in terms of the failure of the human machine to operate properly and health as freedom from clinically ascertainable disease. A broader social model of health has now developed, epitomized by the definition in the World Health Organization as 'a state of complete physical, mental and social well-being and not merely the absence of disease or infirmity'.[13] The social model of health has led to an expansion in the horizons of public health concerns.

The law has been involved in the protection and promotion of public health in a number of ways. The provisions cover a wide range, and it is beyond the scope of this work to provide a detailed discussion of them all. This Chapter outlines the role of the law in underpinning public health work through control of the environment and influencing the lifestyles of citizens. This overview is intended to provide an understanding of the potential for a legal contribution in public health strategy. Detailed analysis is reserved for the legal powers to control the spread of infectious disease, and in particular the legal response to HIV. Health professionals are directly involved with the day-to-day operation of these powers and therefore need to understand their precise scope.

A. Environmental and Collective Issues

Environmental factors have a significant effect on the health of the population.[14] The now considerable body of environmental law in the United Kingdom and the European Community can, therefore, be seen as part of the framework of health law in so far as it serves to reduce health hazards and secure the preconditions for good health. This book cannot hope to cover the whole area.[15] Instead it considers two areas in order to illustrate the role of the law. The first is air, the second is water; a third section considers pollution control more generally. These examples demonstrate the need for enforcement agencies to secure health rights that individuals could not themselves enforce.[16] They also show that the control of environmental pollution does not lie in the hands of health authorities, but in those of local authorities or specialist agencies.

---

[13] *Constitution of the World Health Organization* (Geneva: WHO, 1948).

[14] Department of Health and Social Security, n. 1 above, McKeown, n. 6 above.

[15] For more detailed general surveys, see S. Ball, and S. Bell, *Environmental Law* (London: Blackstone Press, 1991); N. Hawke, *Environmental Health Law* (London: Sweet & Maxwell, 1995); and D. Hughes, *Environmental Law* (2nd edn., London: Butterworths, 1992).

[16] See J. Montgomery, 'Rights to Health and Health Care' in A. Coote (ed.), *The Welfare of Citizens* (London: Rivers Oram/Institute for Public Policy Research, 1992), 89–90.

(i) Air

There has long been concern over the poor quality of air in England. Hughes reports that the first legal measure passed in London dates back to 1273.[17] London 'smog' was notorious in the mid-Twentieth Century. The Clean Air Act 1956 was passed after an inquiry prompted by five days of smog that reduced visibility in London to nil, and left the air barely breathable. The provisions of that Act have now been consolidated into the Clean Air Act 1993, which covers the emission of 'dark smoke' from chimneys and industrial and trade premises. It also enables the composition of motor fuels to be controlled. Responsibility for enforcing these provisions lies with local authorities. There is no provision for direct individual enforcement, although clearly individuals may complain to the relevant local authority and request that they take action. Local authorities may also declare 'smoke control areas' in which only authorized fuels may be burnt. Under the Environment Act 1995, a planning process to improve air quality has been established. This comprises a national air quality strategy, with local authorities required to review the need for local air quality management areas, and designate them where necessary.[18] Wider pollution control is discussed briefly below.

(ii) Water

There are two statutory regimes concerned with water. The Water Resources Act 1991 deals with the regulation of inland and coastal waters. It charges the National Rivers Authority (NRA) with ensuring the proper use of water resources in the United Kingdom. This includes responsibility for the quality of water, for which standards must be set under the Act. Those standards are recorded in pollution control registers, which are available for public scrutiny. Part III of the Act is concerned with water pollution and gives the NRA various enforcement powers. The Water Industry Act 1991 deals with the obligations of the privatized water companies. It covers the supply of drinking water and the sewerage system, both matters which have a significant impact on health. The great achievements of public health medicine in the Nineteenth Century were largely achieved by improving the quality of sanitation and drinking water. It is the duty of the water companies to maintain an efficient and economical supply of 'wholesome' water.[19] The Secretary of State for the Environment has the power to specify the definition of 'wholesomeness'.[20] Responsibility for ensuring that the water industry meets its obligations under the Act lies with the Director General of Water Services. These provi-

---

[17] Hughes, n. 15 above, 319.
[18] Environment Act 1995, Pt. IV.
[19] Water Industry Act 1991, ss. 37, 68.
[20] Water Industry Act 1991, s. 67.

sions ensure that the risk of exposure to water-borne disease is minimal. The part of the Water Industry Act concerning fluoridation of water, as a measure to improve public health, is considered later in the Chapter.

(iii) Pollution Control

A comprehensive system for the control of pollution was established by the Environmental Pollution Act 1990 and the Environment Act 1995. The latter statute provides for 'Integrated Pollution Control' under the auspices of the Environment Agency (in England and Wales). This approach brings together the responsibility for control of emissions to air, water, and land. Under the 1990 Act, certain prescribed processes can only take place if they have been specifically authorized: a system of licensing. The Agency has the power to issue enforcement and prohibition notices. The former identify breaches of the conditions under which authorization was given and specify the remedial steps which must be taken. The latter require the person on whom they are served to stop the process which risks causing serious pollution.

B. State Responsibility for Infectious Disease Control

Here, the concern is with the use by health professionals of powers to control people's activities in their own interests or in order to advance the public health. These powers have changed little since they were first introduced in the Nineteenth Century, and there has been no reasoned reform since 1945.[21] Consequently, they have been left largely untouched by modern ideas on civil rights, and present a stark contrast with the framework established by the Mental Health Act 1983 to protect against abuse. The main powers are those conferred by the National Assistance Acts of 1948 and 1951 and by the Public Health (Control of Diseases) Act 1984, but a number of miscellaneous other powers appear in specific regulations.[22] The statutory responsibilities for infectious disease control lie with local authorities, not health authorities. However, in practice, local authorities will usually appoint employees of the health authority to be their 'proper officers' for the purpose of exercising those powers.

[21] M. Gray, 'Forcing Old People to Leave Their Homes' (1979) *Community Care*, 8 Mar., 19–21; Department of Health, *Review of Law on Infectious Disease Control: Consultation Document* (London: HMSO, 1989), 1.3.
[22] Department of Health, n. 21 above, Annex A.

Part II of the Public Health Act 1984 provides a series of public health powers designed to control the spread of infectious diseases. The Act specifies five diseases: cholera, plague, relapsing fever, smallpox, and typhus, as 'notifiable diseases' to which all the provisions of Part II of the Act apply.[23] The Secretary of State has the power to extent the Act to other diseases and has done so, sometime with amendments, under the Public Health (Infectious Diseases) Regulations 1988.[24] These are set out in Table 1. The extension of the Act to HIV is discussed separately below. There is also provision for local authorities to extend the operation of the Act after advertising the fact in local newspapers. This is normally done only with the approval of the Secretary of State, but in an emergency an order can be made for one month without such prior approval. An emergency order of this type may be revoked by the Secretary of State.[25] It follows that the list of diseases to which the powers under the Act apply can vary geographically and through time, and the list set out in the Regulations may not be exhaustive for a particular time and place.

(i) Notification

Disease control powers can be divided into a number of categories. The first concerns reporting. Under the Public Health Act 1984, a doctor must notify 'forthwith' the relevant local authority officer of the identity, sex, and address of any person whom he suspects of having a notifiable disease or food poisoning.[26] Criminal penalties apply for failure to notify, but prosecutions are rare and only one doctor was prosecuted in 1987.[27] Specific obligations to notify the proper local authority officer of infectious diseases exist in relation to food handlers,[28] meat and dairy workers,[29] keepers of common lodging houses,[30] and under the law of health and safety at work.[31]

When notification is received, the local authority officer must send a copy to the Health Authority within forty-eight hours.[32] In certain cases the Government's Chief Medical Officer must be notified immediately. These are

[23] Public Health (Control of Disease) Act 1984, s. 10.
[24] SI 1988 No 1546, made under the Public Health (Control of Disease) Act 1984, s. 13.
[25] Public Health (Control of Disease) Act 1984, s. 16.   [26] Public Health Act 1984, s. 11.
[27] Public Health Act 1984, s. 11(4); DoH, n. 21 above, 4.6.
[28] Food Hygiene (General) Regulations 1970, SI 1970 No 1172, r. 13; Food Hygiene (Markets, Stalls and Delivery Vehicles) Regulations 1966, SI 1966 No 791, r. 11.
[29] Fresh Meat (Hygiene and Inspection) Regulations 1992, SI 1992 No 2037, r. 21(1)(iv); Milk and Dairies (General) Regulations 1959, SI 1959 No 277, r. 18.
[30] Public Health (Control of Disease) Act 1984, s. 39. The provisions relating to common lodging-houses are discussed below.
[31] Reporting of Injuries, Diseases and Dangerous Occurrences Regulations 1985, SI 1985 No 2023, r. 5.
[32] Public Health Act 1984, s. 11(3).

Table 1: *Diseases to which the Public Health Act 1984 has been extended.**

Diseases	Enactments applied
Acquired immune deficiency syndrome	Ss. 35, 37, 38 (as modified by regulation 5), 43 and 44.
Acute encephalitis Acute poliomyelitis Meningitis Meningococcal septicæmia (without meningitis)	Ss. 11, 12, 17 to 24, 26, 28 to 30, 33 to 35 (as modified by regulation 4), 37, 38, 44 and 45.
Anthrax	Ss. 11, 12, 17 to 22, 24, 26, 28 to 30, 33 to 35 (as modified by regulation 4), 37, 38 and 43 to 45.
Diphtheria Dysentery (amœbic or bacillary) Paratyphoid fever Typhoid fever Viral hepatitis	Ss. 11, 12, 17 to 24, 26, 28 to 30, 33 to 38, 44 and 45.
Leprosy	Ss. 11, 12, 17, 19 to 21, 28 to 30, 35 (as modified by regulation 4), 37, 38 and 44.
Leptospirosis Measles Mumps Rubella Whooping cough	Ss. 11, 12, 17 to 22, 24, 26, 28 to 30, 33 to 35 (as modified by regulation 4), 37, 38, 44 and 45.
Malaria Tetanus Yellow fever	Ss. 11, 12, 18 and 35 (as modified by regulation 4).
Ophthalmia neonatorum	Ss. 11, 12, 17, 24 and 26.
Rabies	Ss. 11, 12, 17 to 26, 28 to 30 and 32 to 38.
Scarlet fever	Ss. 11, 12, 17 to 22, 24, 26, 28 to 30, 33 to 38, 44 and 45.
Tuberculosis	Ss. 12, 17 to 24, 26, 28 to 30, 35 (as modified by regulation 4), 44 and 45; in addition—(a) s. 11 shall apply where the opinion of the registered medical practitioner that a person is suffering from tuberculosis is formed from evidence not derived solely from tuberculin tests, and (b) ss. 25, 37 and 38 shall apply to tuberculosis of the respiratory tract in an infectious state.
Viral hæmorrhagic fever	Ss. 11, 12, 17 to 38, 43 to 45 and 48.

Note: The modification to s. 35 introduced by regulation 4 prevents s. 35 being applied where a person does not have a disease, but merely carries an organism capable of causing it. The modification for AIDS introduced by regulation 5 is discussed in the text below.
* Taken from Public Health (Infectious Disease) Regulations 1988, SI 1988 No 1546.

cases of cholera, plague, smallpox and yellow fever, leprosy, viral hæmor-rhagic fever, malaria and rabies cases where the disease was contracted in Britain, and serious outbreaks of any disease.[33] Statistical returns are in any event made on a weekly and quarterly basis.[34] The Regulations specify that the reports must be sent in a manner that ensures confidentiality and may only be revealed in so far as is necessary to comply with the regulations or as the local authority officer thinks is necessary to prevent the spread of disease.[35] However, if a court order has been made under the 1984 Act and the time for challenging it has expired, then there is no power for the court to restrict the publication of the subject's name in the interests of confidentiality.[36]

(ii) Powers to Acquire Information

Where further information needs to be obtained, recourse can be had to a range of powers to investigate and duties to co-operate with the medical offi-cers. These include obligations on the occupiers of premises, employers, and head teachers to provide information that is reasonably required.[37] More drastic powers of entry and investigation are available,[38] and, more intrusive still, compulsory medical examination. Under section 35 of the 1984 Act, the local authority's nominated officer can issue a written certificate on the strength of which a justice of the peace can order a person to be medically examined.

The criteria for such an order are that there is reason to believe that the per-son is or has been suffering from a 'notifiable disease' or carries an organism capable of causing it,[39] and when it is in the interests of that person, the inter-ests of his or her family, or in the public interest that an examination be car-ried out. If a doctor is treating the person, then his or her consent is required. The JP can issue an examination order in *ex parte* proceedings, which means that the person concerned may have no opportunity to oppose the order being made. However, an appeal lies to the Crown Court.[40] A power to order the examination of a group of persons, one of whom is thought to have or

---

[33] Public Health Infectious Diseases (Regulations) 1988, n. 24 above, r 6.

[34] *Ibid.*, r. 8. The collated statistics are published annually by the Department of Health in the series *Health and Personal Social Services Statistics* (London: HMSO).

[35] Public Health Infectious Diseases (Regulations) 1988, n. 24 above, r. 12.

[36] *Birmingham Post & Mail* v. *Birmingham CC* (1993) 17 BMLR 116.

[37] Public Health (Control of Disease) Act 1984, ss. 18 (occupiers), 22 (head teachers); Health and Safety at Work Act 1974, s. 27 (employers).

[38] Public Health (Control of Disease) Act 1984, s. 61.

[39] The power to test those suspected of carrier status only has not been extended to all the diseases to which s. 35 applies, see Public Health (Infectious Diseases) Regulations, SI 1988 No 1546, r. 4 and Sch 1. See Table 1 for details.

[40] S. 67.

carry a notifiable disease, is conferred by section 36 of the 1984 Act, with the same criteria for its use. When an order is made under these sections it can also authorize the entry into private premises in order to carry out the examination.[41]

A number of provisions relate to specific categories of case. The inmates of a common lodging-house may also be examined on the authority of a magistrate, but there are no statutory criteria governing the issue of the warrant, which is wholly a matter for the magistrate's undefined discretion.[42] A power to require a medical examination also exists where dairy workers are suspected of presenting a risk of infection to milk.[43] Further, midwives may be required to undergo an examination by their supervisors if they deem it necessary for preventing the spread of infection, and must allow themselves to be examined.[44] Where those who prepare food may be the source of an infection that has caused food poisoning, their manager may be required to provide reasonable assistance in their being medically examined.[45] However, the Regulations do not provide for the person suspected of being infectious to be examined without their consent.

(iii) Powers to Remove, Isolate, and Detain

Public health powers to remove an unwilling person to hospital are provided by the National Assistance Act 1948, the National Assistance (Amendment) Act 1951, the Public Health (Control of Disease) Act 1984, and the Mental Health Act 1983. The Mental Health Act powers are discussed in Chapter 13.[46] The National Assistance Acts are concerned with protecting those unable to look after themselves, and are examined under the heading of compulsory care later in this Chapter. This section considers the powers under the 1984 Act.

Under section 37 of the 1984 Act, a magistrate may order that a person who is suffering from a notifiable disease, or any other disease to which the section has been extended (see Table 1), shall be removed to hospital. Before such an order can be made, the magistrate must be satisfied of three things. First, that proper precautions to prevent the spread of disease cannot be, or are not being, taken. Secondly, that the lack of precautions creates a serious risk of infection to others. It is not clear whether seriousness is to be judged only in relation to the probability of contagion, or whether the seriousness of the

---

[41] S. 35(2), 36(2).   [42] S. 40. See below for the definition of 'common lodging house'.
[43] Milk and Dairies Regulations 1959, n. 29 above, r. 19(1).
[44] Nurses, Midwives and Health Visitors Rules 1983, SI 1983 No 873, r. 39, as amended.
[45] Public Health (Infectious Diseases) Regulations 1988, n. 24 above, Sch. 4.
[46] For consideration of the relationship between the powers, see P. Fennell, 'The *Beverley Lewis* Case: Was the Law to Blame' (1989) 139 *NLJ* 1557–8.

disease itself may be taken into account. If the latter is possible, then a small risk of a lethal infection could constitute a 'serious' risk within the meaning of the section. The third requirement is that suitable hospital accommodation is available. Magistrates cannot order that people be removed to hospital unless the hospital authority agrees to accept them. An order under section 38 can be made *ex parte*, so those to be removed may have no opportunity to challenge the case made against them. However, an appeal lies to the Crown Court against any order made by a magistrate under the 1984 Act.[47]

A special provision permits the removal to hospital of a person lodging in a 'common lodging-house'.[48] A common lodging-house is a place for the overnight accommodation of the poor, not being a public assistance institution, in which people share the same room for sleeping or eating.[49] There is no need to show that precautions are not being taken, but otherwise the criteria for removal are the same as under section 37. However, there is no need to seek a magistrate's order, because the local authority itself may order a person's removal. A number of other sections of the 1984 Act deal specifically with common lodging-houses. Keepers of such places must notify local authorities if one of their clients is suffering from a notifiable disease.[50] All the inmates of a common lodging-house in which there is a person reasonably believed to have a notifiable disease may be medically examined, on the authority of a magistrate's warrant, to see if they are infected.[51] A magistrates' court may also order the closure of a common lodging-house until the medical officer of health certifies that it is free from infection.[52] The only way to challenge decisions of the local authority would seem to be judicial review.

It may also be necessary to require those who are not themselves sick to vacate premises so that they can be disinfected. Section 32 of the Public Health (Control of Disease) Act 1984 permits local authorities to provide alternative accommodation while this is done. This must be without charge. It also provides for a magistrate's order for compulsory removal of well people where she or he is satisfied that removal is 'necessary'. Such an order can be made *ex parte* (i.e. without the person to be removed being a party to the hearing). Disinfection is principally the financial responsibility of occupiers, and the local authority must give them time to make suitable arrangements before doing the work and charging for it.[53] It may, however, be paid for by the local authority if it believes that the occupier is unable to disinfect 'effectually',[54] and there is a discretion to pay compensation for any articles destroyed in the process.[55]

[47] S. 67.   [48] Public Health (Control of Disease) Act 1984, s. 41.
[49] Public Health (Control of Disease) Act 1984, s. 74.   [50] S. 39.   [51] S. 40.
[52] S. 42.   [53] S. 31(1).   [54] S. 31(3).   [55] S. 31(4).

Once people suffering from a notifiable disease are in hospital, they are subject to a power to detain them there. Under section 38 of the 1984 Act, a magistrate, acting *ex parte* if necessary, may order such detention if the patient would not be going to accommodation in which proper precautions could be taken to prevent the spread of the disease. An order under section 38 authorizes the staff of the hospital to do all that is 'necessary' to give effect to the order.[56]

People with infectious diseases may be isolated from those they might infect. Those suffering from a notifiable disease must not use public transport, public laundries, or public libraries.[57] Infected children may be excluded by the local authority from school, and from public places of entertainment and assembly such as fairs, swimming pools, cinemas, and skating rinks.[58] Individuals with diseases notifiable under the 1984 Act may be prevented from working, with compensation for any loss suffered as a result.[59] This provision is extended to enteric fever, dysentery, diphtheria, scarlet fever, acute inflammation of the throat, gastro-enteritis, and undulant fever.[60] The Public Health (Infectious Diseases) Regulations 1988 provide specific powers to stop people continuing to work preparing or handling food when a case of food poisoning has been reported.[61] Under the 1984 Act, the local authority may also prohibit certain types of work relating to making, cleaning and repairing clothes on premises where there has been a case of a notifiable disease.[62]

(iv) Vaccination

Immunization programmes are now widely accepted as an efficient form of preventive medicine, the most resounding success being the global eradication of smallpox. Over the past few years, where immunization rates have dropped as a result of public concern over the safety of the vaccines used, there has been a corresponding rise in the number of reported cases.[63] Some argue that the control of infectious diseases owes more to general improvement in environmental health and social conditions than to medical intervention,[64] and it is clear that social factors have a significant impact on the take up of vaccinations.[65] Nevertheless, immunization has become a key tool in disease control.

The World Health Organization's targets for European 'Health for All' by the year 2000 include that there should be no indigenous measles,

---

[56] S. 38(2).   [57] Ss. 33, 24, 25.   [58] Ss. 21, 23.   [59] S. 20.
[60] S. 20(1A) inserted by the Food Safety Act 1990, sch. 3.   [61] N. 24 above, Sch 4.
[62] S. 28.   [63] Smith, and Jacobson, n. 1 above, 171–81.
[64] McKeown, n. 6 above, 45–65.
[65] K. Jones, and G. Moon, *Health, Disease and Society: An Introduction to Medical Geography* (London: RKP, 1987), 179–85.

poliomyelitis, neonatal tetanus, congenital rubella, or diphtheria.[66] These diseases will need to be eliminated through vaccination programmes, which the United Kingdom Government intends to extend to mumps and whooping cough (pertussis). England and Wales has already achieved the eradication of indigenous poliomyelitis, diphtheria, and neonatal tetanus. Target immunization rates of 95 per cent are proposed to tackle the remaining diseases.[67]

A number of legal techniques might be used to realize this target. For example, in the United States school entry is dependent upon prior vaccination, and compulsory vaccination has been found to be consistent with the rights guaranteed by the US Constitution.[68] Compulsory vaccination was introduced in England in the Nineteenth Century and withdrawn in the face of widespread public opposition.[69] It is unlikely that compulsion would be used again after this experience. Even in relation to notifiable diseases, the Public Health (Infectious Diseases) Regulations 1988 provide for free vaccination and immunization, but only for those willing to accept it.[70] Coercive health measures are rarely permitted by English law. A lesser sanction might be to bring failure to vaccinate within the definition of child neglect, although this is implausible on the current English law.[71] The Government's chosen approach has been to bypass issues of patient choice and to introduce financial incentives for general practitioners to reach the target rates.[72] This approach has been successful and almost 90 per cent of doctors met the targets introduced in April 1990.[73] It appears, therefore, that if the doctors can be won over, their patients will follow.

(v) Conclusion

The Public Health (Control of Disease) Act 1984 consolidated a number of earlier statutes. Many of its provisions have remained essentially unchanged since the Nineteenth Century. In 1989 the Department of Health issued a consultation paper canvassing reform.[74] It proposed replacing the present range of specific powers with a single flexible 'infectious disease control order' which would inform infected individuals of what they could not do. However,

[66] World Health Organisation (European Region), *Targets for Health for All* (Copenhagen: WHO, 1985), Target 5.

[67] *The Health of the Nation*, n. 10 above, Annex L.

[68] *Jacobson* v. *Massachusetts*, 197 US 11 (1905).

[69] R. M. MacLeod, 'Law, Medicine and Public Opinion: The Resistance to Compulsory Health Legislation 1870–1907' [1967] *PL* 107–28, 189–211.

[70] N. 24 above, r. 10.   [71] Children and Young Person's Act 1933, s. 1. See Ch. 18.

[72] NHS (General Medical Services) Regulations 1992, SI 1992 No 635, r. 34.

[73] DoH Press Release H91/379, *GPs help to drive down diseases as they hit health targets in the first year of the GP contract*, 8 Aug. 1991.

[74] DoH, n . 21 above.

as yet nothing has been implemented. It is arguable that the United Kingdom Government is in breach of its obligations under human rights law in failing to provide better safeguards against the abuse of public health powers. This will be considered after the way in which the law has dealt with HIV/AIDs has been examined.

C. HIV and Public Health Law

The need for public health officials to tackle the spread of HIV raises a number of legal issues. The need for reliable data on the incidence of infection has led to calls for widespread testing. Where this is done with the consent of those tested, no legal issues arise. The Government's preferred approach has been to instigate from January 1990 anonymized non-consensual testing on leftover blood from those attending ante-natal and sexually-transmitted disease clinics.[75] The legality of non-consensual testing has been questioned by a number of commentators and is discussed in the context of the law governing consent in Chapter 10.

The only new legislation passed as a consequence of HIV is the AIDS (Control) Act 1987. Under this Act health authorities and NHS trusts are obliged to provide the Secretary of State with statistics on positive HIV tests, persons with AIDS, and deaths of those with AIDS.[76] The Act also requires those health service bodies to report on facilities and services they provide for those with HIV or AIDS. The reports must be made at least annually and must be published. Unlike reports in respect of diseases notifiable under section 11 of the 1984 Act these reports do not reveal the identities of the persons concerned.

In addition to passing the 1987 Act, Parliament has extended a number of the provisions of the Public Health Act 1984 to cover the condition, although AIDS has not been made a notifiable disease in the full sense.[77] The sections applied to AIDS allow for compulsory examination (section 35), removal to hospital (section 37), detention in hospital (section 38), and the removal and isolation of the body of a person who has died while suffering from AIDS (sections 43, 44). These are drastic interventions into the liberty of those who have or are suspected to have HIV, and the safeguards against abuse are

[75] DoH, Press release H91/226, 17 May 1991 contains a report on the first results from this programme.

[76] AIDS (Control) Act 1987, Sch., as amended by SI 1988 No 1047.

[77] See now the Public Health (Infectious Diseases) Regulations 1988, n. 24 above. These consolidate the original statutory instrument extending the 1984 Act to AIDS, SI 1985 No 434.

limited.[78] The main safeguard is that the first three powers may only be exercised on the order of a Justice of the Peace after an official application, but its effectiveness is reduced by the fact that orders can be made without any opportunity for representation by the person to be coerced. No case on the use of these powers in relation to HIV has appeared in the main law reports, but it appears that they have been employed to prevent a patient with AIDS who was 'bleeding copiously' discharging himself from hospital. By the time the appeal against the order was heard, it was no longer justified because the danger was past, but the initial order was not criticized.[79]

The terms of these public health powers have already been discussed, but two aspects of the extension to AIDS require further consideration. The first is the modification of the provisions of section 38; the second concerns the definition of AIDS. Section 38 of the 1984 Act generally allows detention only where the person suffering from the disease would otherwise go to premises where he or she would be *unable* to take precautions against its spread. When applied to AIDS, however, the requirement is that the person *would* not (as opposed to could not) take precautions. This amendment is required because the modes of transmission are such that all premises would allow precautions to be taken. Without it, there would be no scope for the application of section 38.

The meaning of 'AIDS' is not explained in the Regulations. It is possible to argue that the 1984 Act distinguishes between HIV infection and AIDS. Such a distinction is implied in section 35, which is expressed to cover both those 'suffering from a notifiable disease' and those 'carrying an organism that is capable of causing it'. On a strict reading of the provisions, this means that only section 35 would apply to those infected with HIV but not having AIDS.[80] However desirable this limitation of the powers under the Act, it is likely that the term AIDS in the Regulations would be interpreted by a court to include HIV infection and not merely the full manifestation of the syndrome. AIDS is not in fact a single disease in the sense in which cholera or typhus (two of the diseases for which the 1984 Act was designed) are clearly defined conditions. Instead, it is a term to describe a group of symptoms associated with HIV infection. There is no necessary uniformity in the way in which AIDS is manifested, no common factor which unites all cases other than the presence of the virus. Consequently, it will be difficult for the courts to define AIDS without reference to the presence of HIV. The risk of trans-

[78] For further discussion, see J. Montgomery, 'Victims or Threats ?—The Framing of HIV' (1990) XII *Liverpool Law Review* 25–53, and C. d'Eca, 'Medico-legal Aspects of AIDS' in D. Harris, and R. Haigh, *AIDS: A Guide to the Law* (London 1990), 7–27.

[79] 'Detaining Patients with AIDS' (1985) 291 *BMJ* 1102.

[80] For the ways in which the statute can be construed in order to minimize the application of the Act to those with HIV see d'Eca, n. 78 above, 14–17.

mission, which provides the justification for extending the Act, is common to those with HIV and AIDS. A purposive construction would therefore lead to an expansive definition of AIDS. It is probable, therefore, that all the provisions extended to AIDS will apply to persons infected with the virus, even if they show no symptoms.

D. Human Rights Issues

Any power to restrict the freedom of citizens to act as they wish is a *prima facie* breach of their civil rights.[81] This is especially true when the restriction is a physical one. Control powers therefore require justification in human rights law. It has been established that, for the purposes of human rights law, compulsory testing is an infringement of liberty.[82] The need for justification is consequently not confined to the restriction of the movements of infected persons. Procedural safeguards are also necessary to ensure that the powers are used properly.

Nevertheless, there can be no doubt that some control powers for public health purposes are acceptable in human rights law. First, the 'protection of public health' is recognized as a limitation on many of the freedoms recognized by the European Convention on Human Rights and Fundamental Freedoms, including the right to 'private and family life'.[83] Secondly, Article 5(1)(e), specifically permits 'lawful' detention for purpose of preventing spread of infectious diseases. The European Social Charter does not explicitly deal with control powers, but it does oblige governments to take appropriate measures to remove the causes of ill-health and to prevent disease as far as possible.[84] It can be argued that this implies that citizens at risk from infection have a right to a proper regime of control powers. This cannot negate the rights of individuals to be free from restrictions, but it provides a countervailing right with which they need to be balanced.

In order for control powers to be acceptable, a number of conditions must be satisfied. There must be a defined procedure for their use. Under Article 5 of the European Convention, detention for the prevention of the spread of infectious disease must be 'in accordance with a procedure prescribed by law'.

---

[81] For an authoritative account of human rights issues in relation to HIV disease, see P. Sieghart, *AIDS and Human Rights* (London: BMA, 1989). See also, I. Kennedy, and A. Grubb, 'HIV and AIDS: Discrimination and the Challenge for Human Rights' in A. Grubb (ed.), *Challenges in Medical Care* (Chichester: Wiley, 1992).

[82] *X* v. *Austria* (1979) 18 D&R 154; *Acmanne* v. *Belgium* (1984) 40 D&R 251.   [83] Art. 8.

[84] Art. 11.

This requirement cannot be satisfied if the detention is arbitrary.[85] A clear definition of the basis on which powers can be exercised is therefore necessary. This is not always the case with the existing legislation, in that no criteria are laid down for the exercise of certain powers.

The European Convention also requires that those detained have the opportunity to challenge the lawfulness of their detention before a court.[86] Habeas corpus proceedings are not sufficient.[87] This opportunity must be available 'speedily' and the court must order the person's release if the detention is not lawful. There is no precise meaning of the time requirement, although four months was found to be too great a delay in *Koendjbiharie* v. *The Netherlands*.[88] To constitute a court within this provision the decision-making body must be judicial in character. This implies independence from the government and those in dispute over the exercise of the power.[89] There must also be procedural safeguards appropriate to the nature of the deprivation of liberty involved.[90]

It is not necessary that a court in the traditional sense be involved. A tribunal will suffice if it has the necessary characteristics. However, where an administrative body originally exercised the power to deprive people of their liberty, they must have the right to have their case reviewed by a court. Thus a form of appeal is required. This is not necessary where the power was exercised by a court, because the right to challenge the legality of detention in a court will already have been satisfied.[91] This creates a difficulty in relation to powers exercised by local authorities without reference to a court, such as those concerning common lodging-houses.

A further important principle drawn from human rights law is that of proportionality. Even where an infringements of human rights can be justified under the European Convention in the interests of the public health, that infringement must be no more than necessary in a democratic society. The degree of infringement must be proportional to the overriding good. In *Acmanne* v. *Belgium*,[92] the Commission found that compulsory screening for tuberculosis was acceptable because the test was not detrimental to the patient and there was 'a social duty to defer to the general interest and not endanger the health of others where his life was not in danger'. Sieghart has argued that this would not justify mandatory screening for HIV because the test brings considerable disadvantages for the person tested with little benefit while there is no cure.[93]

---

[85] *Wintwerp* v. *Netherlands* (1979) 2 EHRR 387; *X* v. *United Kingdom* (1982) 4 EHRR 188.
[86] Art. 5(4).   [87] *B* v. *United Kingdom* (1984) 6 EHRR 204, 232–3.
[88] (1991) 13 EHRR 820.   [89] *Neumeister* v. *Austria* (1968) 1 EHRR 91, 132; *X* v. *UK*, n. 85 above.
[90] *Bouamar* v. *Belgium* (1989) 11 EHRR 1.   [91] *Luberti* v. *Italy* (1984) 6 EHRR 440.
[92] N. 82 above, 251.   [93] N. 81 above, 30–3.

The social usefulness of testing is also relevant to the test of proportionality. Where compulsory testing will discourage people from seeking medical assistance, it is likely to reduce rather than encourage responsible preventive practices. The United Kingdom experience of venereal disease control (especially the failure of the Contagious Diseases Acts 1864–9) suggests that with certain diseases voluntary co-operation and strict confidentiality provide greater protection for the public.

No application to the European Commission on Human Rights has yet required consideration of the Public Health (Control of Disease) Act 1984. The provisions have not, therefore, been measured up against the requirements of human rights law. However, it is apparent that certain provisions need to be tightened up so that clear criteria are established for the exercise of all control powers. There are also some areas where proper recourse to a court needs to be available, but is not at present. Reform of the law would need to take the requirements of human rights law into account. One area that is not dealt with by the current regime at all is the regular review of cases where there is prolonged detention. Human rights law requires that, where a detention order is of indefinite duration, provision is made for periodic judicial review.[94]

E. Employers' Responsibilities for Health and Safety at Work

In addition to the powers and obligations of the state authorities to protect the public health, there is also a body of law that deals with responsibility for health in the workplace. International human rights law recognizes that workers have the right to safe and healthy working conditions.[95] The principal piece of United Kingdom legislation that ensures that this entitlement is honoured is the Health and Safety at Work Act 1974. Under that Act, employers are obliged to ensure, so far as is reasonably practicable, the health and safety at work of their employees.[96] They must also ensure, so far as is reasonably practicable, that non-employees are not exposed to health and safety risks by the way that work is carried out.[97] There is also a specific obligation to prevent the emission of noxious or offensive substances into the atmosphere.[98] These obligations can only provide an effective guarantee of health and safety if the workforce is prepared to co-operate with the employers. The

---

[94] *Wintwerp*, n. 85 above; *X* v. *UK*, n. 85 above.   [95] European Social Charter 1961, Art. 3.
[96] S. 2.   [97] S. 3.   [98] S. 5.

Act obliges it to do so, and to take reasonable care for its own and its colleagues' safety.[99]

These general duties are supplemented by specific provisions created by regulations passed under the Act and guidance may be given on proper standards by Codes of Practice issued by the Health and Safety Commission. Amongst the most important of these are the Control of Substances Hazardous to Health Regulations 1988.[100] Regulations also provide for the notification of prescribed industrial diseases and accidents.[101] Proposals for regulations are made to the Secretary of State by the Health and Safety Commission. That body is also responsible for issuing or approving Codes of Practice, giving advice, and encouraging relevant research.

Enforcement of the Act and regulations is the task of the Health and Safety Executive. The Executive's inspectors have powers of entry to premises to check for compliance with the legislation. If breaches are found, then they can issue improvement notices, specifying the breaches and requiring them to be put right. They may also issue prohibition notices, which forbid the continuation of specified activities. Prosecutions may be brought for failure to comply with the requirements of the Act. Individual employees cannot bring actions for compensation under the Act,[102] but they may sue under the common law. Employers are bound to provide safe equipment, safe colleagues, and a safe system of work. They will be liable in negligence if they fail to take reasonable steps to meet these obligations. This may include a failure to have proper health-screening procedures in place.[103] A civil action can also be brought for breaches of the statutory duties which result in injury to individual employees.

F. Individual Responsibility for the Health of Others

In addition to the steps taken by public officials to control the spread of infectious diseases, the law may also provide an incentive for individuals to take responsibility for the prevention of infection. The possibility that individuals who infect others may be criminally or civilly liable to their 'victims' should deter them from putting others at risk. Liability in tort might provide some of those who contract disease with compensation to help them pay for treatment or overcome some aspects of disability that their condition might cause.[104]

---

[99] S. 7.   [100] SI 1988 No 1657.
[101] Reporting of Injuries, Diseases and Dangerous Occurrences Regulations 1985, n. 31 above.
[102] S. 47.   [103] *Stokes* v. *Guest Keen & Nettleford* [1968] 1 WLR 1776.
[104] J. Stapleton, 'Compensating the Victims of Disease' (1985) 5 *OJLS* 248.

Criminal liability would also reflect the seriousness of the threat presented by irresponsible behaviour to individual and public health.[105] However, it can also be argued that the implication that those already infected bear the responsibility for safeguarding the public health may not be the most effective message to give where everybody needs to be encouraged to take precautions to protect themselves. On this view, the regulatory public health powers under the 1984 Act are more appropriate than making individuals liable to punishment or to pay compensation.[106]

A number of criminal offences already exist which could be used to punish those who infect others. They will only catch those who know, or ought to have known, that they were infectious because criminal law requires there to be both a guilty mind and a guilty act. The Public Health (Control of Disease) Act 1984 creates a number of criminal offences in relation to notifiable diseases. The first of these covers those who, knowing that they are suffering from a notifiable disease, put others at risk of infection by their actions in a street, public place, place of entertainment, club, hotel, inn, or shop.[107] An offence would also be committed by anyone 'having the care of' an infected person who caused or permitted a risk to be run in the same manner.[108] A person who knowingly carries on working in an occupation which creates a risk of spreading a notifiable disease is also guilty of an offence.[109] It is criminal to allow clothing or bedding or other articles to create a risk of infection.[110] Placing such material in dustbins is specifically prohibited.[111] Those with a notifiable disease may not use public libraries,[112] or public transport.[113]

Other offences relating to diseases that are notifiable under the 1984 Act cover those with particular responsibilities. Children with notifiable diseases must be kept away from school, and those looking after them will commit an offence if they permit them to attend.[114] Those who let rooms to members of the public may not do so when someone with a notifiable disease has previously stayed there, until disinfection has been carried out.[115] Occupiers must take similar precautions when they leave.[116] Public transport drivers may not permit those with notifiable diseases to share their vehicles, and must disinfect them before other passengers are allowed to use them.[117] However, it

---

[105] K. Smith, 'Risking Death by Dangerous Sexual Behaviour and the Criminal Law' in R. Lee and D. Morgan (eds.), *Death Rites: Law and Ethics at the End of Life* (London: Routledge, 1994).

[106] P. Old and J. Montgomery, 'Law, Coercion and the Public Health' (1992) 304 *BMJ* 891–2.

[107] S. 17(1)(a).

[108] S. 17(1)(b). In *Tunbridge Wells Local Board* v. *Bisshopp* (1877) 2 CPD it was held that a doctor was not 'in charge of', within s. 126 of the Public Health Act 1875, an infectious patient whom he accompanied to hospital through the streets. It is not clear whether the same interpretation would be made of 'having the care of' a person.

[109] S. 19.   [110] Ss. 17(1),(2), 24.   [111] S. 26.   [112] S. 25.   [113] S. 33.
[114] S. 21.   [115] S. 29.   [116] S. 30.   [117] S. 34.

must be remembered that these provisions cover only the five statutory 'notifiable' diseases, and a small number of other specified disorders, not all contagious conditions.[118]

Punishment for the offences under the 1984 Act is a relatively small fine, and it has been argued that more serious sanctions are appropriate for those who pass on, or risk passing on, possibly lethal infections.[119] This might be achieved using a number of general criminal offences. It would take a degree of judicial innovation to interpret the provisions so as to cover such behaviour and the application of a wide range of offences has been considered in the academic literature[120] (although reported prosecutions have been exceedingly rare). The most likely offences to be used are homicide (including attempted murder), assault (which is in fact a group of statutory offences), administering dangerous substances, and public nuisance.

The first two offences are committed only when a victim has suffered harm as a result of the criminal conduct. This may lead to considerable difficulties of proof. In criminal proceedings, a causal link between the victim's injuries and the defendant's actions must be proved beyond all reasonable doubt. However, it might well be unclear whether victims already had the disease when they came into contact with the defendant. There might often be an alternative possible source of the infection.

The principal homicide offence is murder. That is committed when someone does an act which kills another, intending to do so, or intending to cause serious harm.[121] The concept of intention is sufficiently broad to include cases where the defendant knew that there was a risk of infection.[122] This could cover only those who were aware that they were infected by a contagious disease. The offence of manslaughter might go further and embrace those who recklessly put others at risk. This would cover people who, while not actually aware that they presented a risk of infection, showed an indifference to an obvious risk to health.[123] In principle, it is possible that people who knew that they were members of a group at high risk of being infected (perhaps, in relation to HIV, those who regularly shared dirty needles) would be found to be reckless if they chose not to establish that they were not infected, but failed to take precautions that would prevent the spread of the disease if they had it.

---

[118] Public Health (Control of Disease) Act 1984, s. 10; Public Health (Infectious Diseases) Regulations 1988, n. 24 above. See Table 1 above.

[119] Smith, n. 105 above.

[120] S. Bronitt, 'Spreading Disease and the Criminal Law' [1994] *Crim. LR* 21–34; A. Lynch, 'Criminal Liability for Transmitting Disease' [1978] *Crim. LR* 612–25; Smith, n. 105 above.

[121] *DPP v. Smith* [1960] 3 All ER 161.

[122] *R. v. Savage, R. v. Parmenter* [1991] 4 All ER 698.

[123] *R. v. Adomako* [1994] 2 All ER 79.

However, it seems unlikely that criminal sanctions would be applied to those who were not actually aware that they were infected.

Prosecutions for assault are perhaps more likely. An assault is committed where a person inflicts bodily harm on another. A range of crimes of assault may be relevant, dealing with different types of harm and degrees of seriousness.[124] The defendants would need to be aware that they were causing harm, or, in the case of simple assault under section 47 of the Act, reckless whether they did so. As with the homicide offences, it is unlikely that this would be the case unless the defendants actually knew that they were infected, and chose to take no precautions. The main difficulty with this group of offences is that it is unclear whether they can be committed when the victim consents to be involved in the activity during which the infection occurs. This might be merely meeting the defendant, or could be intimate behaviour such as sexual intercourse. In *R. v. Clarence* it was held that there was no assault because the victim had consented to sexual intercourse, even though the defendant had not told her that he was suffering from a venereal disease.[125] The fact that she had been misled about her partner's health did not invalidate her consent; only a mistake about his identity or the nature of the act to which she had consented would do that. The modern law does not apply precisely the same test, now requiring the infliction of a degree of force rather than physical contact without consent.[126] The problem still remains that it would be difficult to argue that any force was used on a willing partner. This makes the role of the criminal law in relation to sexually transmitted diseases uncertain.

It could also be argued that passing on a virus is a form of poisoning, which might come within the provisions of sections 23 and 24 of the Offences Against the Person Act 1861. These involve 'administering' a destructive or noxious thing. There is no reason why viruses could not be held to be 'noxious things' within the section. In *R. v. Clarence* one of the judges suggested that infection could be viewed as 'a kind of poisoning . . . the application of an animal poison'.[127] The poisoning offences may be committed even though actual infection cannot be proved, because they concern the administration of the substance which *endangers* the victim, not the actual infection. Thus if HIV-infected blood were placed into the victim's body, an offence would be committed even if she or he did not contract the disease.

Finally, on criminal matters, the common law offence of public nuisance may cover those who create a risk of infection in a public place. In one nineteenth-century case, it was held that carrying a child with smallpox through the streets, knowingly exposing others to a risk of infection, constituted a

---

[124] Offences against the Person Act 1861, ss. 18, 20, 47.
[126] *R. v. Wilson* [1983] 3 All ER 448.
[125] (1888) 22 QBD 23.
[127] N. 125 above, 42.

public nuisance.[128] However, where there is a legitimate reason for exposing the public to an infectious person, no offence would be committed. It has been said that this would include carrying sick people through a crowd to save them from a fire, or where there was no practicable means of isolating them.[129] It appears that the offence of public nuisance has been recently used to imprison a surgeon who continued to operate after contracting hepatitis B.[130] The essence of nuisance is that the public is exposed to an unacceptable risk, and it would not be necessary to show that anyone actually contracted the disease.

In addition to the possibility that a criminal offence may have been committed, there may also be civil liability for the transmission of disease. Once again, a number of possible causes of action have been discussed.[131] The most likely to succeed, trespass to the person and negligence, are considered here. An action for trespass to the person might be brought if there was direct or indirect physical contact with the victim. However, the consent of the victim provides a defence to a claim.[132] Thus, where victims have been willingly involved in the activity that has led to their infection, such as intercourse in relation to a sexually transmitted disease, they may not be able to sue. This raises a similar problem as that with the criminal law of assault discussed above. Nevertheless, the case law on consent to treatment has indicated that a consent obtained fraudulently or by misrepresentation in bad faith would be invalid.[133] Thus it may be easier to overcome the difficulties in the civil context. As the wrong committed in trespass is the violation of the right to physical integrity, there is no need to show that the victim contracted the disease, merely that he or she did not agree to the risky contact.

In contrast, plaintiffs suing in negligence have to prove that they have suffered damage, and would therefore need to show that the defendant's conduct had actually led to them being infected.[134] For reasons already discussed, this may be difficult. Further difficulties will arise in relation to establishing that the law imposes a duty on individuals to concern themselves with the health of others. Such a duty would normally be imposed where it is reasonably foreseeable that a risk of infection exists, but there may be public policy grounds on which a court could decide that it would be better to exclude the possibil-

---

[128] *R.* v. *Vantandillo* (1815) 4 M & S 73, 105 ER 762.

[129] *Metropolitan Asylum District* v. *Hill* (1881) 6 App. Cas. 193, 204–5.

[130] L. Hunt, 'Surgeon who Lied about Hepatitis B Jailed', *Independent*, 30 Sept. 1994.

[131] F. Kaganas, 'Compensation for AIDS Victims' (1988) 16 *AALR* 117–38; R. O'Dair, 'Liability in Tort for the Transmission of AIDS: Some Lessons from Afar and the Prospects for the Future' [1990] *CLP* 219–46.

[132] The rules are discussed in detail in relation to consent to treatment in Ch. 10.

[133] *Chatterton* v. *Gerson* [1981] 1 All ER 257; *Freeman* v. *Home Office* [1984] 1 All ER 1036.

[134] The rules of negligence are discussed in detail in the context of malpractice litigation in Ch. 7.

ity of legal liability.[135] This boils down to a policy issue: would the public health be better protected by encouraging individuals to take care not to infect others or not? It can be argued that those suffering from contagious diseases are better seen as victims requiring help than threats to others. However, it seems probable that the courts would hold that at least those who know they are infected have a duty of care to those they put at risk.[136] It is also possible that this duty would also apply to those who know that they might be infected, but have not been tested to make certain.

A third difficulty with liability in negligence for transmitting disease lies in determining the nature of the infected person's responsibility to protect others. This is fixed by reference to what a reasonable person in that position would do. This might include taking precautions to exclude, or at least minimize, the risks of infection. However, it would probably be necessary to balance the inconvenience of the infected person against the risk to others. It might not be reasonable to expect people to quarantine themselves for the rest of their lives when they have an incurable condition that is difficult to transmit, such as HIV/AIDS. On the other hand, it might be quite reasonable to require a brief period of isolation while the infectious stage of chicken pox passes. Reasonable people might also be expected to warn others of the risks that they present, although this would conflict with the expectation that medical details remain confidential.[137]

It can be seen from the above discussion that there is considerable uncertainty about the extent of duties to take care for the health of our fellow citizens. There is good reason to believe that the law is concerned with liability for the transmission of disease, but specific provision has been made only for a few specified conditions. Until the boundaries of liability are explored in litigation, it is difficult to be clear what the law requires.

G. Lifestyle Issues

The Government's 'Health of the Nation' targets for health improvement include a number that can only be achieved if citizens change their lifestyles. This is particularly true of the targets set to reduce the incidence of coronary heart disease, strokes, and cancers. Changes to diet are sought, including reductions in the amount of fat and alcohol consumed. It is also hoped that less tobacco will be smoked. These objectives have been set because fatty food,

---

[135] The principles on which the extent of the duty of care is determined are set out in Ch. 7.
[136] This has been accepted in the USA: see *Kathleen K* v. *Robert B*, 198 Cal. Rept. 273 (1984).
[137] This is discussed in O'Dair, n. 131 above.

alcohol, and tobacco have been identified as risk factors in relation to the modern diseases of affluence which provide the new challenge for public health medicine. A successful programme to combat the abuse of alcohol and tobacco requires a varied armoury of tools. The law has a limited, but not insignificant, role to play. The Government has committed itself to the use of legislation where appropriate,[138] and this section considers the ways in which law can contribute to promoting healthier lifestyles.[139]

Lifestyle questions raise different issues from the areas of public health law already considered. They raise acutely the problem of paternalism.[140] In a liberal society, it is generally thought to be wrong to force people to do what is good for them. Individual freedom may be restricted in order to protect others, but it should be for us to decide what is good for us. Seeking to influence a person's lifestyle can rarely be justified on the basis that it protects the interests of others. Rather, it seeks to make people healthier whether or not they wish to be. In addition, much of the behaviour that is sought to be changed is currently socially acceptable. This rules out prohibition as a strategy. Nevertheless, a number of techniques involving the law are brought to bear.

One of the these is the restriction of the availability of harmful products. Tobacco may not be sold to children under 16, and alcohol sales to those under 18 are prohibited.[141] Outlets selling alcohol must be licensed, and opening hours may be restricted. This makes it more difficult to obtain the substances, but does not prevent those adults who wish to drink or smoke doing so. A further disincentive is provided by the taxation of tobacco and alcohol. A significant amount of the price paid by consumers is made up of excise duties. These have been raised in recent years partly in order to influence consumption.

One major step towards reducing exposure to tobacco is restrictions on where smoking is permitted. The Health Education Authority has suggested that the obligations of employers under the Health and Safety at Work Act 1974 may require them to ban smoking, although this interpretation of the law has not been tested in the courts.[142] Employees who smoke have sought to argue that they have an implied right to smoke, but this has been rejected

---

[138] *The Health of the Nation*, n. 7 above, 21.

[139] See the report of the Working of the Faculty of Public Health Medicine of the Royal College of Physicians, *Alcohol and the Public Health* (Basingstoke: Macmillan, 1991) and M. Gray and C. Fletcher, 'Prevention through Legislation' in M. Vessey and M. Gray (eds.), *Cancer Risks and Prevention* (Oxford: Oxford University Press, 1985) 231–48.

[140] For discussion, see A. Yarrow, *Politics, Society and Preventive Medicine: A Review* (London: Nuffield Provincial Hospitals Trust, 1986).

[141] Children and Young Persons Act 1933, s. 7, as amended; Licensing Act 1964, s. 169.

[142] M. Jenkins, *Smoking Policies at Work* (London: Health Education Authority, 1987).

by industrial tribunals.[143] However, this does not mean that a no-smoking policy can be imposed by an employer without consultation, time to adjust to its requirements, and possibly the provision of facilities for smokers.[144]

The main strategy that is used, however, is education. It is thought that if the public is provided with information about the dangers of consuming tobacco and alcohol, they will recognize the need to cut back. This brings spending on health education into direct competition with the advertising budgets of the tobacco and alcohol industries. The focus on education does not prevent the law being important. Legal, and informal, regulation can set the basis on which these competing vested interests can sell their products, requiring health warnings,[145] and preventing advertising that associates the products with healthy activity such as sport.[146]

H. Compulsory Care

In general, English law does not force people to accept treatment. Thus, the Public Health (Infectious Disease) Regulations 1988 confer a power to provide immunization services, but not for mandatory immunization. Without specific authorization, treatment without consent would be unlawful (see Chapter 10). Mental illness presents particular difficulties because refusal of treatment may be part of the patient's health problems. The special regime dealing with this is discussed in Chapter 13. The general principle of English law is that patients are the best judges of what is good for them, and it is firmly set against paternalistic interference with autonomy on the grounds of good health.

Public health law, however, is not concerned with paternalistic treatment, but with imposing treatment in the interests of the health of other citizens. This may sometimes require autonomy to be limited. Arguably there may even be a need for compulsory care. Limited provision is made for this in relation to infectious diseases. Two other areas of law also deserve consideration in relation to the legitimacy of public health measures taken without the consent of all of those subject to them. The first is the powers of removal to

---

[143] *Rogers* v. *Wicks & Wilson Ltd* (1988) IDS Brief No 366 11.

[144] *Watson* v. *Cooke, Webb & Holton Ltd* (1984) IDS Brief No 294 4.

[145] Tobacco Products Labelling (Safety) Regulations 1991, SI 1991 No 1530, implementing EEC Council Directive 89/622/EEC.

[146] British Code of Advertising Practice (1988), Section C.XII, reproduced in *Butterworths Trading and Consumer Law* (London: Butterworths, 1994, looseleaf); Council Directive of 3 Oct. 1989 on the co-ordination of certain provisions laid down by law or administrative action in Member States concerning the pursuit of television broadcasting activities, 89/552/EEC, Arts. 13 and 15; Council of Europe, European Convention on Transfrontier Television 1989, Art. 15.

hospital of the aged and infirm. The second is the issue of fluoridation of water, which raises significant questions about the manner in which individual autonomy should be balanced against the needs of the public health.

(i) Infectious Disease Control

Under section 13 of the Public Health (Control of Disease) Act 1984, the Secretary of State may make regulations 'with a view to the treatment of persons affected with any epidemic, endemic or infectious disease'. On the face of it this would seem to permit regulations to be made authorizing compulsory treatment. Kennedy and Grubb have argued that the words of the statute are ambiguous, and that a court would have to interpret them so that the common law right to refuse treatment was preserved (as such rights could only be compromised by the express wish of Parliament).[147] However, it would be open to a court to hold that the words were clearly broad enough to encompass regulations that permitted compulsory treatment.

The only such provision that has so far been made under the Act is ambiguous. It authorizes the issue of notices requiring the destruction of lice on a person's body and clothing where there is a suspected outbreak of typhus or relapsing fever.[148] However, it is not clear that the destruction can be done without the consent of the infected person. One clear example where there is no need for consent concerns the cleansing of people from vermin. This may be done compulsorily under a court order provided that the court is satisfied that it is 'necessary' to cleanse the person.[149] Women may only be cleansed by a registered medical practitioner, or a woman authorized by the local authority.

(ii) The National Assistance Acts

The power to remove a person to hospital under the National Assistance Act 1947 may be used where the person concerned is either suffering from 'grave chronic disease' or is 'aged, infirm or physically incapacitated' and living in 'insanitary conditions'.[150] In both cases it is also necessary that the person is unable to devote to him- or herself proper care and attention, and is not receiving it from others. The power can be exercised only by order of a court, including a magistrate, on the application of the relevant local authority.

---

[147] *Medical Law: Text with Materials* (2nd edn., London: Butterworths, 1994), 332–3.
[148] Public Health (Infectious Diseases) Regulations 1988, n. 24 above, Sch. 3.
[149] Public Health Act 1936, s. 85.
[150] There may be some overlap with powers under the Mental Health Act 1983, see P. Fennell, 'The *Beverley Lewis* Case: Was the Law to Blame ?' (1989) 139 *NLJ* 1557–8.

Seven days' notice of the application must be given to the person to be removed or that person's carer. The application must be supported by certificate from a medical officer designated by the authority for the purpose, most commonly the director of public health. This certificate must state that the doctor is satisfied that removal is necessary either to prevent an injury to the health of, or serious nuisance to, other people, or would be in the interests of the person to be removed. Before the court can make an order it must be satisfied that the designated medical officer's assessment is correct.

If the court accepts that an order should be made, it may order that the person be removed to a specified hospital or other suitable place, and detained there. Such an order does not give physicians any power to treat the patient without consent. The court may not specify a hospital whose manager has not been involved in the proceedings unless seven days' notice of the application has been given to it. Detention cannot be ordered for more than three months at a time, but can be renewed. It has been suggested that, once a court order has been made ordering people to be detained for a specified period, it is not within the discretion of the hospital to which they were committed to release them before that period expires.[151] Doing so would constitute the offence of wilful disobedience of an order under the Act.[152] There is no provision in the 1948 Act for medical discharge, and the Act envisages that an application for revocation of the order would be made to a court.[153] Such an application cannot be made until six weeks have elapsed since the order was made. This problem could be avoided if the court ordered that detention was to be until a specified date, or until the responsible medical practitioner certified that the order was no longer necessary, whichever event occurred sooner.

The Act as originally passed made no provision for emergency removal, but such powers were created in 1951.[154] They allow the local authority to authorize the director of public health to apply for a section 47 order directly. Where that doctor certifies that it is in the interests of a person to be removed without delay, a single magistrate may make the order without the requirement that the person be notified and without giving him or her a chance to participate in the hearing. The requirement that the hospital manager be given advance warning is also removed. An emergency order of this sort may only last for three weeks, but may be renewed under the standard section 47 procedure.

No centralized statistics are collected on the use of these powers.[155] Such evidence as exists on their use suggests that approximately 200 people are

[151] E. Counsell, 'Compulsory Removal and Medical Discretion' (1990) 140 *NLJ* 750–1.
[152] S. 47(11).   [153] S. 47(6).   [154] National Assistance (Amendment) Act 1951.
[155] A. Norman, *Rights and Risk* (London: National Corporation for the Care of Old People, 1980), 33.

taken from their homes each year, usually under the powers of immediate removal and almost always in respect of the elderly. A survey of community physicians revealed that there was no consistent pattern of use of the provisions; approximately a quarter of those responding made no use of them, and among those who did there was a wide variation in the number of times they had done so.[156] The provisions remain vague in scope, with inadequate safeguards, and the scope for abuse is substantial.[157]

(iii) Compulsory Health Promotion? The Case of Fluoridation

The areas of law considered so far illustrate the involvement of the law in the protection of health, through removal of some of the causes of ill-health. It may also have a role to play in health promotion, which aims to improve standards of health, not merely preserve them. The protection of health is relatively uncontroversial, but views differ on the proper scope of the law in promoting good health. Some argue that the law should not go further than health protection, leaving citizens to choose for themselves whether to aim to improve their health. This debate raises wide issues of political theory concerning the proper role of the state.[158] This section aims to describe a particular area, water fluoridation, where the law currently plays a role so that these wider matters can be explored in an informed manner.

The provision of wholesome water supplies ensures that water-borne diseases are reduced, but it is also possible to use water as a resource for health promotion. Some £800 million is spent on dental health care each year in England and Wales. Much of the damage is done during childhood, and one of the best means for preventing the deterioration of teeth is to provide children with fluoride. Probably, the most effective way to do this is to ensure that the water children drink contains the substance.[159] Fluoridation has, however, proved to be a controversial issue. To be effective the water supply to the whole community must be fluoridated. Fluoride may occur naturally in some supplies, in which case no addition is necessary, but often it needs to be added by the water suppliers. Controversy is fuelled by the fact that there are health dangers associated with high concentrations of fluoride, although not with the levels permitted by the Water Industry Act 1991.

---

[156] M. Gray, 'Section 47' (1981) 7 *JME* 146–9; M. Gray, 'The Ethics of Compulsory Removal' in M. Lockwood (ed.), *Moral Dilemmas in Modern Medicine* (Oxford: Oxford University Press, 1985).

[157] Norman, n. 155 above, 29–37.

[158] See J. Montgomery, 'Recognising a Right to Health' in R. Beddard and D. Hill (eds.), *Economic, Social and Cultural Rights: Progress and Achievement* (Basingstoke: Macmillan, 1992), 184–203; Montgomery, n. 16 above, 83–107.

[159] Smith and Jacobson, n. 1 above, 182–3.

In 1983 a Scottish case accepted that 'fluoride would involve an encroach-ment of individual rights to the extent that persons would be forced to drink water containing a substance, fluoride, which they did not wish to drink'.[160] In the light of this, the court felt obliged to interpret the powers of water sup-pliers restrictively, as they might involve overriding this right, and found that there was no power to add fluoride to the water. Given the impossibility of separating water supplies, the acceptance of such a right makes it very difficult to take steps to promote health through environmental means, rather than merely to prevent its breakdown. Lord Jauncey accepted that the phrase 'wholesome water' could be interpreted as embracing health promotion, a 'positive definition', but chose to adopt the negative version, which restricted its meaning to removing impurities and threats to health. This distinction raises a fundamental division in views as to the appropriate scope of health promotion through the law. The court's position assumes a narrow definition of health and a correspondingly narrow definition of health rights.[161]

Parliament intervened in 1985 to give water undertakers the right to fluo-ridate when asked to do so in writing by a health authority.[162] The statutory provisions specify the compounds of fluorine that may be used and limit the concentration, so far as is reasonably practicable, to one milligramme per litre.[163] There is no obligation to comply with health authorities' requests, and since the privatization of the water industry the financial disincentives to do so are significant. Consequently, the Secretary of State has the power to indemnify the water undertaker in respect of the costs of fluoridation and any liabilities that may arise from it.[164]

The balance between the rights of individuals and the public interest in health promotion is achieved through an element of democratic consulta-tion.[165] The relevant local authority must be informed three months before a health authority proposes to make or withdraw a request to the water under-taker to fluoridate. The health authority must also publish details of the pro-posals in a local newspaper twice, again three months in advance of any proposal for change. Consultation with the local authorities must be carried out and any representations that the publicity elicits must be considered. The health authority is not, however, bound to accept the views expressed.

[160] *McColl* v. *Strathclyde* [1984] JPL 351. The equivalent English legislation was in very similar terms.

[161] See Montgomery, 'Recognising a right to health', n. 158 above.

[162] Water (Fluoridation) Act 1985. The provisions are now to be found in the Water Industry Act 1991, ss. 87–91.

[163] Water Industry Act 1991, s. 87(4), (5). S. 88 permits the Secretary of State to vary the per-missible compounds.

[164] Water Industry Act 1991, s. 90.

[165] Water Industry Act 1991, s. 89. See also the Parliamentary discussion of this issue in 1985 at *Hansard*, HC, Vol. 73 col. 953 ff.

Although the statutory provisions were designed to facilitate fluoridation, it has proved far more difficult to implement schemes since they were introduced than it was previously.[166] This may be because the public consultation requirement has enabled a minority movement of objectors to influence decisions. It may also be that the privatization of the water industry has made it less responsive to public health concerns, and more worried about controversy. Companies that depend on consumer loyalty for success have a considerable incentive to avoid controversy because it may affect business. Further, they are accountable to shareholders, not as public bodies, and the shareholders may be more reluctant to run any commercial risk in the interests of public health.

I. Conclusion

Public health law has not really developed as a separate area of law since its origins in the Nineteenth Century. The focus of environmental law has moved away from immediate threats to health to longer-term protection of the natural heritage. The control of contagious diseases is still achieved under a legal framework designed to deal with the highly contagious disease that concerned the Nineteenth Century sanitary reformers. The needs of modern public health medicine may be rather different, and the requirements of human rights law need to be considered. The law's contribution to tackling the contemporary threats to health is incidental rather than planned. The Government's 'Health of the Nation' initiative raises legal issues only peripherally.

---

[166] P. Castle, 'The Future of the Water Industry and its Implications for Water Fluoridation' (1992) 9 *Community Dental Health* 323–7; J. Manson, 'Fluoride: Just Looking for Trouble ?' (1993) 97 *Water Services*, No 1169, 10–13.

3   Rights to National Health Service Care

It has already been noted that rights to health care are recognized in human rights law. Under the European Social Charter, the United Kingdom has undertaken to ensure that necessary care is provided for those who are sick and without adequate resources to secure such assistance for themselves.[1] This commitment does not require states to provide a comprehensive health service, as it covers only the treatment of illness, not health promotion, and extends only to those unable to purchase care privately. A second avenue is the European Convention on Human Rights. It might be argued that the right to life provided by Article 2 of that Convention includes a right to health care. Although the matter has not come before the Court, the Commission has accepted that the Convention requires states to take steps to preserve life.[2]

In Britain, the Government's obligations to honour the right to health care have been met through the establishment of the National Health Service. From a sociological perspective, it is difficult to identify a single purpose of the NHS, or even a range of definite objectives.[3] However, some guidance can be obtained from official statements and the framework of legal duties that underpins the NHS. The Royal Commission on the National Health Service, reporting in 1979, noted that there were no detailed publicly declared objectives for the NHS. It therefore proposed the following to fill the gap: encouragement and assistance of individuals to remain healthy, equality of entitlement and access to health services, a broad range of high quality services, services that are free at the time of use, satisfaction of the reasonable expectations of users, a national service responsive to local needs. The Commission recognized that some of these were controversial and some unattainable, but believed that a statement of the aspirations of the service would be helpful.[4] Some years later, the House of Commons Social Services Select Committee offered its own summary of principles behind establishment of NHS. This was that it should be comprehensive, that there should be

---

[1] Art. 13.

[2] *Association X* v. *United Kingdom* (1978) 14 D&R 31 (App. No 7154/75).

[3] D. Seedhouse, 'Does the National Health Service have a Purpose?' in A. Grubb (ed.), *Challenges in Medical Care* (Chichester: Wiley, 1992).

[4] *Report of the Royal Commission on the National Health Service* (1979, Cmnd 7615), ch. 2.

equality of access to health care when needed, that the Service should be equitable, offering equal service for equal need, and that it should be free at the point of delivery.[5]

These fundamental principles constitute the guarantee that British citizens are given that their right to health care will be honoured. This Chapter examines rights to health care. It considers the definition of those rights, and the scope for enforcement of them by citizens. It explains that individuals can rarely vindicate their rights by action through the courts. Instead, the managerial structure of the NHS is designed to ensure that the NHS achieves its tasks. The main components of the constitution of the NHS are set out in order to locate responsibility for planning and managing the ability of the Service to meet its objectives, and to explain the mechanisms for quality control. Analysis of the legal structure of the NHS market, the chosen mechanism for delivering high quality services where they are needed as economically as possible, is to be found in the next chapter. The NHS complaints machinery is described in Chapter 5.

A. Rights to Health Care

The legal framework of the NHS imposes upon the Secretary of State for Health a number of specific legal obligations to provide services. Identifying the scope of these obligations is therefore the first stage in considering how well the United Kingdom recognizes these rights. A full picture requires the examination of an additional area, that of enforceability. Some argue that, without direct enforceability by patients, there can be no proper right to health care.[6] However, the nature of health care makes such rights problematic. Resources are scarce and hard managerial decisions have to be made about their allocation. In addition, the need for health professionals to identify what care is appropriate makes unconditional rights inappropriate. It may be more satisfactory to provide indirect methods of enforcement, through complaints procedures, professional accountability, and litigation.[7]

The statute defining the scope of the NHS services is the National Health Service Act 1977. It obliges the Secretary of State to promote 'a comprehensive health service designed to secure improvement—(a) in the physical and

---

[5] 5th report, 'The Future of the National Health Service' (1987–88), HC Pap. 613, para. 12, ix.

[6] R. Plant, *Can There be a Right to Health Care?* (Southampton: Institute for Health Policy Studies, University of Southampton, 1989).

[7] J. Montgomery, 'Rights to Health and Health Care' in A. Coote, *The Welfare of Citizens: Developing New Social Rights* (London: Rivers Oram/Institute for Public Policy Research, 1992).

mental health of the people of [England and Wales], and (b) in the prevention, diagnosis and treatment of illness.'[8] Services must be provided free of charge unless the law expressly permits charges to be made.[9] Charges can be made in relation to treatment after road traffic accidents,[10] for the treatment of in-patients who leave hospital during the day to do paid work,[11] and for the supply of wigs, drugs, and optical and dental appliances.[12] The provision of NHS care in a hospital does not preclude the acceptance of paying private patients,[13] nor so-called 'amenity beds' which enable NHS patients to obtain single rooms by paying a small premium.[14] NHS trusts are able to provide extra facilities without relying on the provisions for amenity beds, from which they are actually excluded.[15] This enables them to make charges for other amenities, over and above accommodation in a single room or smaller ward, such as private television facilities.[16] Charges may also be made for those who are habitually resident abroad.[17]

(i) Hospital and Community Services

The 1977 Act further defines the general duty of the Secretary of State by imposing a number of more specific duties. These are phrased in a number of different ways, giving the Secretary of State a varying degree of discretion as to the services which must be provided. In addition, the Act empowers, but does not oblige, him to offer other services. The fact that there is a high degree of discretion on the part of the Secretary of State makes enforcement of the duties difficult. The range of legal techniques available for this purpose will be discussed below, but the prospects of success will vary according to the way in which the duties are defined.

The strictest duty is to provide for the medical examination and care of state school pupils at appropriate intervals.[18] The only discretion that the Secretary of State has is to determine what intervals are appropriate. However, most of the duties are limited by the proviso that the Secretary of State is bound to provide services only 'to such extent as he considers necessary to meet all reasonable requirements'. This phrase qualifies the duties to provide

---

[8] S. 1(1).

[9] NHS Act 1977, s. 1(2). See generally, J. Finch, *Speller's Law Relating to Hospitals* (7th edn., London: Chapman & Hall, 1994), ch. 22.

[10] Road Traffic Act 1988, ss. 157, 158; Road Traffic Accidents (Payments for Treatment) Order 1990, SI 1990 No 1364; Road Traffic Accidents (Payments for Treatment) Order 1995, SI 1995 No 889.

[11] NHS Act 1977, s. 64.   [12] *Ibid.*, ss. 77–82.   [13] *Ibid.*, ss. 65, 72.

[14] *Ibid.*, s. 63.   [15] *Ibid.*, s. 63(1C).

[16] See also NHS (Wheelchair Charges) Regulations 1996, SI 1996 No 1503.

[17] *Ibid.*, s. 121; NHS (Charges to Overseas Visitors) Regulations 1989, SI 1989 No 306.

[18] *Ibid.*, s. 3(1).

hospital accommodation (including 'special hospitals' for those suffering from mental disorders), medical, dental, nursing, and ambulance services, such other services as are required for the diagnosis and treatment of illness, family planning services, and school dental services.[19] Illness is not fully defined, but the Act provides that it includes mental disorder within the meaning of the Mental Health Act 1983 and any injury or disability that requires medical or dental treatment or nursing.[20] Under a further set of duties, subject to the same proviso as to the satisfaction of reasonable needs, the Secretary of State is bound to provide facilities for expectant and nursing mothers, young children, care of those who are or have been ill, and the prevention of illness. These obligations are additionally qualified by their limitation to such facilities as the Secretary of State considers appropriate.

In addition to this range of duties, the Act specifically empowers, but does not oblige, the Secretary of State to provide vehicles for the disabled, a microbiological service for the control of infectious diseases, and to support medical research.[21] It also provides a general power to provide any services which are considered appropriate in connection with the duties imposed by the Act.[22] In addition to providing services directly through the NHS and social services departments, the health minister and local authorities have the power to give financial support to voluntary organizations.[23]

The 1977 Act is drafted in terms of the provision of services. When it was passed, there was no division of responsibility between planning services and providing them. Under the current arrangements, which are discussed in the next chapter, the statutory responsibilities of the Secretary of State are delegated down two different channels. In general, Health Authorities carry a commissioning role and no longer provide services directly to the public (although the 'Special Health Authorities' are still mainly providers of services). Service providers are separate organizations, and are required by Health Authorities to supply services under a form of contract. The majority of these providers are NHS trusts, and are part of the NHS. Both arms of the NHS carry out the statutory duties of the Secretary of State, which have not been formally subdivided.

(ii) Primary Health Care

The availability of general medical practitioner (GP), dental, ophthalmic, and pharmaceutical services is guaranteed through a duty to secure these services

---

[19] Ss. 3(1)(a)–(c), and (f), 4, 5(1)(b), (1A).
[20] *Ibid.*, s. 128(1).   [21] *Ibid.*, s. 5(2).   [22] *Ibid.*, s. 2.
[23] Health Services and Public Health Act 1968, ss. 64, 65.

that lies directly on the Health Authorities rather than on the Secretary of State.[24] That duty is to arrange with practitioners in the locality for the provision of services for all persons in the geographical area for which they are responsible. Unlike contracting for hospital and community health services, the terms of the contracts for primary health care are fixed, and established by statutory instrument.[25] There is, therefore, no local negotiation over the terms of service for general practitioners. Health Authorities are responsible for regulating and managing primary care in their area. They must ensure that prospective patients can find a GP. They maintain lists of practitioners in their area, deciding whether to permit new practices to be established. They also administer the lists of patients and deal with complaints that cannot be resolved within practices (see Chapter 5).

Each of the professions has a separate contractual framework. Only that for general medical services is discussed here. It is important to recognize that GPs may have two discrete roles in the NHS. This section is concerned with the role of GPs as providers of services. However, some GPs have become 'fundholders'. This is not a 'provider' function, but a 'purchaser' function in the NHS market. This aspect of GPs' work is examined in the next chapter.

The services to be provided by general medical practitioners are described as 'personal medical services', but there is no definition of that term, either in the Act or in the regulations. Instead, doctors are obliged to give patients on their lists 'all necessary and appropriate personal medical services of the type usually provided by general medical practitioners'.[26] This self-referring definition is supplemented by a number of specific duties.[27] Thus, 'personal medical services' include the provision, where appropriate, of advice about general health and in particular about diet, exercise, smoking, drinking alcohol, and misusing drugs or solvents. General practitioners are required to offer examinations for identifying, and reducing the risk of, injury or disease, and vaccinations for a range of diseases.[28] They must refer patients for other services provided under the 1977 Act, and must also give appropriate advice to enable patients to use social services.

These duties are owed to the GP's 'patients'. These are primarily those who are on that GP's 'list'. This list is held by the relevant Health Authority.

[24] NHS Act 1977, ss. 29, 35, 38, 41.

[25] NHS (General Medical Services) Regulations 1992, SI 1992 No 635, r. 3(2), Sch. 2. For the other professions, see NHS (General Ophthalmic Services) Regulations 1986, SI 1986 No 975; NHS (General Dental Services) Regulations 1992, SI 1992 No 661; NHS (Pharmaceutical Services) Regulations 1992, SI 1992 No 662.

[26] NHS (General Medical Services) Regulations 1992, n. 25 above, Sch. 2, para. 12(1).

[27] *Ibid.*, Sch. 2, para. 12(2).

[28] These are measles, mumps, rubella, pertussis, poliomyelitis, diphtheria, and tetanus; n. 25 above, Sch. 2, para. 12(2)(c).

Potential patients apply to the GP, who then decides whether to accept them. Both patients and doctors therefore have a degree of choice. However, doctors are free to refuse to accept patients and to remove them from their lists without giving a reason. Health Authorities do have the power to require GPs to treat patients who cannot find a doctor who is willing to accept them, but only for a limited time.[29] In addition to those on their lists, GPs are obliged to provide immediately necessary treatment after accidents or other emergencies in their practice area.[30] They may also accept patients on a temporary basis while they are resident in the practice area.[31]

In principle, GPs are obliged to treat their patients personally.[32] However, they are absolved from this duty provided that they take 'reasonable steps' to secure continuity of treatment. This permits the uses of deputies. It also enables the doctor to delegate to people who are not medically qualified, provided that it is clinically reasonable to do so in the circumstances, and the doctor is satisfied that they are competent to carry out the treatment.[33] Services will usually be provided at the GP's practice premises, but shall be given at home, or elsewhere in the practice area, 'if the condition of the patient so requires'.[34]

The terms of service seek to encourage preventive measures. The contractual obligation to offer lifestyle advice is one aspect of this. So is the requirement that GPs offer new patients a consultation at which a medical history (including hereditary conditions, any previous tests for breast and cervical cancer, social factors, and lifestyle factors) should be taken. The new patient should also be invited to have a physical examination comprising height, weight, blood pressure, and tests for diabetes.[35] Similar consultations should be offered to patients between 16 and 74 (inclusive) who have not been to see their GP for three years.[36] Patients who are aged 75 or more should be offered an annual consultation, at home if they wish. These consultations should include, where appropriate, the patient's sensory functions, mobility, mental and physical condition (including continence), social environment, and use of medicines.[37]

Separate provision is made for child health surveillance, contraceptive services, minor surgery, and medical maternity (obstetric) services. These are not ordinarily part of 'personal medical services', and there is no obligation for all GPs to provide them.[38] There are specific lists for each of these services, on which GPs may apply to be included if they wish to provide those services. Health Authorities must be satisfied that they have the prescribed experience

[29] N. 25 above, r. 21. [30] *Ibid.*, Sch. 2, para. 4(1)(h). [31] *Ibid.*, Sch. 2, para. 4(1)(f).
[32] *Ibid.*, Sch. 2, para. 19(1). [33] *Ibid.*, Sch. 2, para. 19(2). [34] *Ibid.*, Sch. 2, para. 13.
[35] *Ibid.*, Sch. 2, para. 14. [36] *Ibid.*, Sch. 2, para. 15. [37] *Ibid.*, Sch. 2, para. 16.
[38] *Ibid.*, r. 12(3).

and training before a doctor is accepted on these lists. It is also possible for a doctor to provide only one or more of these specific services, without agreeing to provide general medical services.[39] Patients may go to a different GP from the one from whom they usually get care for contraceptive and obstetric services.[40]

(iii) Community Care

Under the NHS and Community Care Act 1990, local authorities are obliged to prepare and publish plans for community care services in their areas.[41] These services, sometimes known as social care, comprise a range of services provided by local authorities.[42] They are the provision of accommodation for adults who cannot look after themselves;[43] services for adults who are blind, deaf, dumb, or substantially and permanently handicapped by illness, injury, or congenital disability, including the adaptation of homes and provision of meals and special equipment;[44] and services promoting the welfare of elderly people.[45] Community care also includes non-residential services for pregnant women and mothers, home help and laundry facilities for households caring for a person who is ill, handicapped, or pregnant.[46] With the Secretary of State's approval, local authorities may also provide services for those who are ill, including after-care and preventive care.[47] Finally, community care services cover after-care for those discharged from mental health services.[48]

Under section 47 of the 1990 Act, local authorities must assess the needs of anyone who appears to them possibly to be in need of community care services, and decide whether such services should be provided in the light of that assessment. There is no formal requirement to respond to a request for an assessment, save in respect of those who are blind, deaf, dumb, or substantially and permanently handicapped by illness, injury, or congenital disability.[49] Those clients are entitled to be involved in the assessment process under the Disabled Persons (Services Consultation and Representation) Act 1986. They are also entitled to a written explanation of the assessment and the right to make representations about unsatisfactory aspects of the assessment.[50]

---

[39] *Ibid.*, r. 12(3).   [40] *Ibid.*, rr. 29(1), 31(2).

[41] S. 46. See also Chronically Sick and Disabled Persons Act 1970, s. 1.

[42] NHS and Community Care Act 1990, s. 46(3). See M. Mandelstram, with B. Schwehr, *Community Care Practice and the Law* (London: Jessica Kingsley, 1995).

[43] National Assistance Act 1948, s. 21.

[44] *Ibid.*, s. 29; Chronically Sick and Disabled Persons Act 1970, s. 2.

[45] Health Services and Public Health Act 1968, s. 45.   [46] NHS Act 1977, s. 21, Sch. 8.

[47] *Ibid.*, s. 21, Sch. 8.   [48] Mental Health Act 1983, s. 117.

[49] NHS and Community Care Act 1990, s. 47(2); Disabled Persons (Services Consultation and Representation) Act 1986, ss. 4, 16; National Assistance Act 1948, s. 29.

[50] Disabled Persons (Services Consultation and Representation) Act 1986, s. 3(2),(4).

Where a substantial amount of care is already being, or will be, provided (otherwise than for money) for the individual to be assessed special provisions apply. These require the abilities of carers to be taken into account.[51] If the care is being given by someone who is neither employed to do so, nor working for a voluntary organization, then the carer may require a local authority to carry out an assessment of his or her ability to continue to provide the care before deciding what services should be provided.[52]

The provisions of the 1990 Act confer on citizens a right to an assessment, but they do not guarantee them services. However, it may be difficult for local authorities to justify refusing people community care services when an assessment has identified that they are in need of them without acting irrationally. If a local authority does act unreasonably or irrationally, an action for judicial review may be available to challenge the decision. This may be easier if the reasons for an assessment have been revealed under the 1986 Act. Such actions are discussed below. The position of disabled clients, those who are blind, deaf, dumb, or substantially and permanently handicapped by illness, injury, or congenital disability, is stronger. Under section 2 of the Chronically Sick and Disabled Persons Act 1970, local authorities have a duty to provide services that are necessary to meet the client's needs.

One key difference between community care services provided by local authorities and those under the NHS is that the former are not free of charge. Local authorities may recover as much of the cost of providing or securing the services as it is reasonably practical for a client to pay.[53] In the case of residential services, there is a fixed rate, with means testing for those who cannot afford to pay it.[54] The transfer of responsibility for aspects of long-term care and community services from NHS responsibility to that of local authorities has therefore resulted in those services ceasing to meet one of the objectives for the NHS, that health care should be free at the point of delivery.

(iv) The Patient's Charter

In addition to these legal rights, the NHS has committed itself to attaining certain standards through its Patient's Charter.[55] This Charter does not create legally enforceable rights. If the rights it contains are enforceable, it is because they are already recognized by the law, not because they are set out in the Charter. Many of the 'rights' are considered in relation to the legal framework

---

[51] Disabled Persons (Services Consultation and Representation) Act 1986, s. 8.
[52] Carers (Recognition and Services) Act 1995.
[53] Health and Social Services and Social Security Adjudications Act 1983, s. 17.
[54] National Assistance Act 1948, s. 22.
[55] *The Patient's Charter and You* (London: DoH, 1995).

in the appropriate chapters. In general, it will be shown that they are only rights in a weak sense.[56] However, failure to meet the requirements of the Charter is a ground for complaint, under the procedures described in Chapter 5. This does not mean that the standards set out in the Patient's Charter are insignificant. The performance of NHS trusts against the Charter standards is monitored, and published in the form of league tables.[57]

The Charter states that NHS patients possess ten general rights. Six refer to access to health care; to receive it on the basis of clinical need rather than ability to pay, to be registered with a general practitioner (and therefore receive primary care), to receive emergency care, to be referred to a consultant or for a second opinion, to information on the quality of local services (according to measures chosen by the Government or NHS rather than the patient), to be admitted for inpatient treatment within two years of being placed on a waiting list by a consultant. Three refer to the position of patients once they are receiving care; to a clear explanation of proposed treatment (including alternatives and risks), to have access to records (which are guaranteed to be confidential), and to be permitted to choose whether or not to be involved in research or training. The final charter right is to have complaints investigated and receive a full and prompt written reply.

The general charter rights have been supplemented by specific targets (aspirations rather than rights) in relation to waiting times for hospital and community appointments. All patients must be admitted to hospital within eighteen months of a consultant deciding that treatment is necessary. 90 per cent of people referred should be seen as outpatients within thirteen weeks, and all within twenty-six weeks. Urgent cases should be seen more quickly, and by January 1995, nearly half of all NHS patients waiting for treatment were admitted within five weeks.[58] Outpatients should be given a specific appointment time, and be seen within thirty minutes of that time. Visits to a patient's own home should take place within a two-hour time band agreed with the patient. These targets have had a considerable influence on the behaviour of NHS trusts.

The Patient's Charter contains a number of other commitments. Patients have the right to know whether they will be on a mixed-sex ward. They can expect respect for their privacy, dignity, and religious and cultural beliefs. They should find that hospitals are clean and safe, well signposted, with enquiry points to help them find their way around. They should be given a

---

[56] For discussion, see J. Montgomery, 'Patients First: The Role of Rights' in K. W. M. Fulford, S. Ersser, and R. A. Hope, *Essential Practice in Patient-centred Care* (Oxford, Blackwell Science, 1996) 142–52.

[57] National Health Service Executive, *The NHS Performance Guide 1994–95* (London: DoH, 1995).

[58] N. 55 above, 11.

written explanation of catering services and standards. Local NHS bodies are expected to elaborate further on the Charter standards, and to set themselves more challenging targets where this is achievable. The Patient's Charter initiative therefore provides an important, although not legally enforceable, set of benchmarks for respecting the rights of patients in the NHS.

B. Enforcing Rights to Health Care

Although there is an explicit framework of legal duties to provide health services, attempts to use the law to enforce those duties have proved frustrating for litigants. While the courts have played a significant role in securing equitable access to health care in the United States, judges in the United Kingdom have declined to intervene in the same way.[59] A number of ways to argue that services should be provided have been placed before the courts, but the prospects of patients succeeding in using the law to force health service bodies and individual professionals to offer care are extremely limited. In one case Bridge LJ stated that he hoped the applicants had 'not been encouraged to think that [the] proceedings offered any real prospects that this court could enhance the standards of the National Health Service, because any such encouragement would be based upon manifest illusion'.[60]

Two basic strategies have been used to enlist the assistance of the courts. The first is to claim that the NHS has failed to perform its statutory duties. If this claim succeeds, the court will strike down decisions to refuse treatment. In exceptional cases judges might order treatment to be offered, but this is less likely. This strategy uses the procedure called judicial review,[61] and is a public law matter. The second approach appeals to the civil law obligations of the NHS to perform its functions properly. It alleges that decisions on the provision of services have been made negligently. If the case succeeds, it will result in the patient being compensated for the loss suffered as a result of his or her needs not being met. In practice, it will also ensure that a different approach to service provision is taken in the future in order to avoid further claims.

---

[59] D. Longley, 'Diagnostic Dilemmas: Accountability in the National Health Service' [1990] *PL* 527, 539–45. See also M. Brazier, 'Rights and Health Care' in R. Blackburn, *Rights of Citizenship* (London: Mansell, 1994), 56–74.

[60] *R.* v. *Secretary of State for Social Services, W. Midlands RHA & Birmingham AHA (Teaching), ex p. Hincks* (1980) 1 BMLR 93, 97.

[61] Under O. 53 of the Rules of the Supreme Court.

(i) Public Law Actions

Judicial review of failures to provide health services have been brought against decisions both on the allocation of resources and also on the clinical priority to be granted to particular patients. The legal actions have not been successful in the courts. However, it should not be assumed that they have therefore been worthless. They may well have achieved a wider purpose of highlighting inadequate services, and have encouraged more resources to be provided in the light of adverse publicity. It is also possible that, even though the courts have refused to order procedures to be carried out, the patients concerned have been given the treatment they wanted in order to defuse the situation. The discussion here is concerned with the legal principles, not the role of law as a tool in a wider campaign.

The general law of judicial review establishes that the grounds on which a challenge might succeed are limited.[62] The courts are not concerned with whether the best decision was made, but with whether the public body concerned had acted responsibly. Three categories of argument are available; first, that decisions were made illegally, secondly that they were made irrationally, and thirdly that there was a procedural impropriety.[63] The concept of 'irrationality' is in fact technical shorthand for a wide range of issues. It covers cases where the decision is one that no reasonable authority could have made, which have been made on the basis of considerations that should have been seen as irrelevant, or has ignored considerations that were in fact relevant. It is also an abuse of discretion to disregard 'legitimate expectations'; where it can legitimately be expected that a public authority will continue to act in a particular way, then it may be unfair to deny those expectations. A further heading of judicial review concerns the importance of public authorities exercising their discretion and not merely following rigid policies. These latter two doctrines may have important ramifications for the working of the NHS market, and are discussed in more detail in the next chapter.

Most of the NHS cases concern inadequate resources, and the first legal problem to be resolved concerns whether the statutory obligations of the NHS to provide services are defined by reference to the available resources. If they exclude resource considerations, then health authorities will be unable to rely on lack of money as a reason for failing to provide services because that would be an irrelevant consideration and make the decision 'irrational'. However, in

---

[62] See H. W. R. Wade, and C. F. Forsyth, *Administrative Law* (7th edn., Oxford: Oxford University Press, 1994), Pt IV, and P. Craig, P. *Administrative Law* (3rd edn., London: Sweet & Maxwell, 1994), Pt 2.

[63] *Council of Civil Service Unions* v. *Minister for the Civil Service* [1985] 1 AC 374, 410, *per* Lord Diplock.

*R. v. Secretary of State for Social Services, W. Midlands RHA and Birmingham
AHA (Teaching), ex p. Hincks* the Court of Appeal rejected the argument that
the duties of the Secretary of State under section 3 were absolute and overrode
the constraints provided by the limited resources available for the NHS.[64] The
case was brought by four patients waiting for orthopaedic surgery. The building of an extension to a hospital in their area, which would have enabled the
services that they needed to be provided, had been approved by the Secretary
of State in 1971. However, when tenders were sought, the costs were far
greater than had been an anticipated. As a result the work was not carried out.
The patients argued that their requirement of a hospital for treatment was
reasonable, and that there was therefore a legal duty to provide services that
met their needs under section 3 of the NHS Act 1977. They pointed out that
the statute did not provide that limited resources constituted an exception to
this duty.[65] However, the Court of Appeal held that the statute had to be read
as if it included such a limitation. Lord Denning said that the Secretary of
State's duties were to provide services 'to such extent as he considers necessary
to meet all reasonable requirements such as can be provided within the
resources available'.[66]

This leaves a considerable degree of latitude, and decisions will usually be
upheld by the courts unless they were taken in bad faith.[67] The Court of
Appeal has said that the courts could strike down a decision on the allocation
of resources,[68] but they have not actually done so. *R. v. Cambridge HA,
ex p. B*[69] concerned a 10-year-old girl with leukaemia. An earlier bone-mar-
row transplant had proved unsuccessful. The doctor treating the girl in
Cambridge believed that she had only six to eight weeks to live and that further treatment was inappropriate. Doctors from the Royal Marsden Hospital
in London agreed with that assessment. The father was unhappy with these
views and found doctors in the United States who would have treated the girl,
and also a professor from the Hammersmith Hospital in London who
believed that it would be appropriate to embark on a further course of
chemotherapy. His position was that such treatment would serve at least a
palliative purpose, and if successful might make it possible to consider a
second transplant. After discussion with officer from Cambridge HA, this
professor stated that this approach was experimental rather than standard

---

[64] N. 60 above.
[65] See G. P. Morris, 'Enforcing a Duty to Care: The Kidney Patient and the NHS' [1983] *Law
Society Gazette* 3150–65 for an elaboration of this argument.
[66] At 95. In *R. v. Sheffield HA, ex p. Seale*, 17 Oct. 1994, unreported (QBD), it was also held that
Health Authorities were entitled to have regard to resources.
[67] *Ross v. Secretary of State for Scotland* [1990] 1 Med. LR 235.
[68] *R. v. Secretary of State for Social Services, ex p. Walker* (1987) 3 BMLR 32.
[69] [1995] 2 All ER 129 (CA).

therapy. The Health Authority refused to support the treatment. This decision was explained in the judicial review proceedings as based first on the clinical advice that the further treatment was not in B's best interests, and secondly on guidance from the Department of Health in relation to the funding of unproven treatment. On this basis is was decided that 'the substantial expenditure on treatment with such a small prospect of success would not be an effective use of resources'. Thus, while it was not the only factor, there was a suggestion that the fact that resources were limited had influenced the Authority.

In the High Court, Laws J sought to limit the extent to which health authorities could rely on lack of resources in questions of life or death. He quashed the Health Authority's decision and required it to re-examine the matter. He suggested that the girl's fundamental right to life required that the health authority show compelling objective reasons for giving other patients priority over her. It could not merely state that resources were limited. It had to set out the other calls on its funds.[70] This requirement to explain the decision would have enabled the father to seek to show that the reasons given were unreasonable.

Although the father was successful in challenging the decision in the High Court, the Court of Appeal was robust in its rejection of the application. It considered that it was not the role of the courts to determine the merits of the dispute. The fact that life-saving treatment was in issue was an important factor, but it did not alter the criteria against which the Authority's decision was to be judged (as Laws J had suggested it did). The court should not become drawn into resource allocation decisions. It was wrong even to suggest that the Authority should have shown where the money that might have been spent on B was actually going to be used because that was not a practicable exercise. In effect, the Court of Appeal was content not to press the resources issue beyond the Authority's assertion that resources were limited. It must be emphasized, however, that the main reason given for Authority's decision was not that there was insufficient money to fund it, but that (on medical advice) it was not in the girl's best interests to undergo experimental treatment.

These decisions have concerned the relevance of scarce resources to the interpretation of the general duties under the section 3 of the NHS Act 1977. It is possible that the position might be slightly more favourable to patients where the statutory duties are more specific, such as in relation to medical examinations for school children.[71] This would be because the usual limitation of the obligations to what is 'reasonably' necessary is absent. In addition, the duties under section 3 are acknowledged to be highly discretionary by the

---

[70] *R. v. Cambridge DHA, ex p. B* [1995] 1 FLR 1055 (QBD).   [71] NHS Act 1977, s. 5(1).

reference to the Secretary of State's own assessment of what is required. Other provisions leave less scope to discretion.

The duties to provide services to disabled persons under section 2 of the Chronically Sick and Disabled Persons Act 1970 are an example of a much stronger type of duty, owed to individual clients. Local authorities are required to make arrangements where they are *necessary* to meet the needs of disabled people. There is no reference to what the authority considers necessary, nor to the reasonableness of the clients' needs. In a group of cases local authorities have been attacked for withdrawing services that they could no longer afford.[72] The clients sought judicial review, and contended that the lack of resources was no excuse for the authority's actions.

In the High Court McCowan J found that the statutory provisions envisaged a two-stage process. First, the local authority had to determine what was 'necessary' to meet the client's needs. McCowan J thought that at this stage the authority was entitled to take the available resources into account. What was 'necessary' in the circumstances and what constituted the client's 'needs' were both to be judged in the light of the size of the cake available to be distributed, and how it would be fairest to cut it. It was therefore necessary to consider the needs of others and the resources available, as well as the position of the individual being assessed. Thus, resources could be used as an excuse for declining to provide services on the basis that the client's needs were not sufficiently compelling when their priority relative to others and the resources available were considered. Only if the assessment was one that no reasonable authority could make would there be grounds for judicial review. McCowan J suggested that this might be the case where a client would be at severe physical risk if practical assistance was not provided. On this basis, he was able to decide that Mr Mcmillan's application failed because he had been assessed and it had been decided that it was not necessary to provide services to him, even though it left him without support when his carers were ill or away. The other applicants succeeded because Gloucestershire had failed to give specific consideration to their cases, and could not, therefore, have properly balanced their needs against those of others. The Authority had treated the resources available as the sole relevant factor, which was unlawful.

McCowan J went on to consider, briefly, the second stage of the process envisaged by section 2 of the 1970 Act. He indicated that once an assessment had been made, and it had been decided that it was 'necessary' to make arrangements for services to be provided, then the duty to do so was absolute. At this stage, there was no longer scope for using lack of resources as an

---

[72] *R. v. Gloucestershire CC, ex p. Mahfood, Barry, Grinham, Dartnell; R. v. Islington LBC, ex p. McMillan, The Times,* 21 June 1995 (QBD); *R. v. Gloucestershire CC, ex p. Barry; R. v. Lancashire CC, ex p. RADAR, The Times,* 12 July 1996 (CA).

excuse.[73] This approach distinguishes between the discretionary stage of identifying the services that are required, and the actual provision of services. The
first stage involves considering the situation of an individual client in relation
to other actual and potential clients. At the second stage, only the individual
client's situation is relevant, and the duties are quite specific, and enforceable.

The majority in the Court of Appeal approached the case differently. It held
that the question of need was a matter of assessment, not discretion.
Resources were thought not to be relevant to that assessment. A distinction
was drawn between what clients needed and what it was desirable for them to
receive. Where services were 'needed', the Court found that the wording of the
section left no scope for the local authority to use resources as a reason for not
providing them. This decision is very important for the provision of community care for those with disabilities.[74] However, it concerns only the 1970
Act. The Court of Appeal explicitly observed that the position under the NHS
and Community Care Act 1990 would be different. Under that statute it noted
that resources would be relevant.

Resource constraints have been a key aspect of judicial review actions in the
NHS context, but they have often been closely linked with clinical issues.
These are a highly significant factor in determining what treatment should be
offered to individuals. It has become clear that the courts are unlikely to question such clinical assessments in judicial review proceedings. Clinical factors
involve both what treatment is appropriate, as in the *Cambridge* case, and also
the relative priority of patients. In *R. v. Secretary of State for Social Services, ex
p. Walker*[75] the applicant was the mother of a child who needed an operation
to rectify a congenital heart defect. She sought an order from the court that
the operation be carried out. The evidence showed that the problems
stemmed from the lack of qualified nursing staff in the neonatal intensive care
unit, which severely limited the number of children on whom operations
could be performed. Every time an intensive care cot became free it was found
that a baby other than Mrs Walker's son needed the operation more urgently.
The Court of Appeal refused to overturn the decision of Macpherson J that
the health authority had acted properly in giving priority to more urgent
cases.

It was expressly noted in the *Walker* case that there was no immediate danger to the baby at the time of the hearing. It was accepted that if the operation
had become necessary, it would have been performed even if the after care
would have been inadequate on available staffing levels. It would be wrong,

---

[73] See also *R. v. Kent CC, ex p. Bruce*, *The Times*, 8 Feb. 1986.
[74] A. Bradley and S. Cragg, 'Needs of the Disabled—A Question of Resources?' (1996) 146 *NLJ*
1071–2. An appeal to the House of Lords is anticipated.
[75] N. 68 above.

however, to assume that to refuse to operate in those circumstances would have been amenable to legal challenge. For even then, it could be argued that it was reasonable to decide that the prospects of success did not justify attempting the procedure. The courts are reluctant to force doctors to offer care that in their honestly held clinical judgement is not in the patient's best interests.[76] In a slightly different context, the courts have gone so far as to say that to order doctors to treat against their clinical judgement would be an abuse of judicial power.[77] Provided decisions about resource allocation are taken on clinical advice they will be difficult to challenge.

These cases suggest that judicial review is unlikely to be successful if it is based on an attack on the substance of the decision. Applications will be stronger if they allege that the process by which the decision was taken was flawed. One such approach is to show that irrelevant considerations were taken into account or relevant ones ignored. Rational decisions must be based on the consideration of appropriate factors. If the irrelevant factors make the decision discriminatory, the chances of success may be higher still, because discrimination is irrational, and sometimes illegal. Such an argument was presented in *R. v. Ethical Committee of St Mary's Hospital (Manchester), ex p. Harriott*.[78] The applicant had been refused IVF treatment on the basis that she was unsuitable. The unit had a policy of using the same criteria as local adoption agencies in order to determine whether applicants would make satisfactory parents. The applicant had a criminal record of prostitution and brothel keeping. In addition, the adoption agencies to which she had applied had decided that she had a poor understanding of the role of a foster-parent. She had not been accepted as a prospective adopter. The IVF unit also rejected her request for treatment. She sought judicial review, claiming that the unit had acted improperly.

The judge refused to overturn the refusal to provide her with infertility services. He made it clear that, had the unit decided to 'refuse all such treatment to anyone who was a jew or coloured [sic]' the policy would have been struck down. These are categories where discrimination is illegal.[79] It can be presumed that sex and marital status would normally be improper considerations for the same reason.[80] It is possible that the enactment of the Disability Discrimination Act 1995 may have significant impact on this type of argument. That Act, when fully implemented, will make it illegal for service providers to discriminate on the basis of disability. Disability is defined as 'a physical or mental impairment which has a substantial and long-term adverse

---

[76] See *R. v. Ealing DA, ex p. Fox* [1993] 3 All ER 170, 183.
[77] *Re J* [1992] 4 All ER 614; see Ch. 18.
[78] [1988] 1 FLR 512.
[79] Race Relations Act 1976.
[80] Sex Discrimination Act 1975.

effect on [a person's] ability to carry out normal day-to-day activities'.[81] Some health problems will fall within this definition. The Act may make it more difficult for a health authority to justify refusing to fund services for people suffering from such conditions.

There are some cases other than those concerning sex and race discrimination where illegality may be an issue. It has been held that European law requires the NHS to provide dialysis to an EC national who comes to the United Kingdom in order to work, or to a member of such a person's family, providing that he or she was receiving it regularly in another Member State.[82] This is because to refuse treatment would contravene the principle that people should be able to move freely to work in another EC country. Without a guarantee that their treatment would continue, they would not be free to take up employment elsewhere. Patients who move in order to seek treatment cannot rely on this decision. Attempts to charge NHS patients for services when there is no specific legal power to do so would also be illegal.[83] Thus, an authority that sought to provide NHS services to those who could bear part of the cost would be acting unlawfully. Limiting the scope of services is not in itself illegal, despite the obligation of the Secretary of State to provide 'comprehensive' services.[84]

Whether discrimination that is not outlawed by statute, such as on the basis of religion, age, or sexual orientation, would be regarded as acceptable depends not on the issue of illegality, but on whether it is rational to take the characteristics into account. In the *Harriott* case the issue was therefore whether it was rational to use the criteria used by the adoption agencies.[85] The judge found that it was proper to use such a policy, providing that applicants who were excluded were given the chance to show why they were a special case. This opportunity was required to make the process fair. Ms Harriott had been given such an opportunity by the time the matter came to court (although not initially). She had therefore been treated fairly and had no grounds for complaint in law.

Procedural aspects of judicial review may come to the fore in relation to the process of purchasing services under the NHS market system. However, as a technique for enforcing citizens' rights, they may be important to the success of a legal action, but they will not guarantee the provision of services. A failure to follow the proper procedures will result in a health authority being told

---

[81] Disability Discrimination Act 1995, s. 1(1). See also Sch. 1, para. 4, and the Disability Discrimination (Meaning of Disability) Regulations 1996, SI 1996 No 1445.

[82] *Re Dialysis Treatment* [1984] 3 CMLR 242.   [83] NHS Act 1977, s. 1(2).

[84] R. v. *Sheffield HA, ex p. Seale*, n. 66 above.

[85] For discussion of this point see R. Singh, 'Infertility Treatment and the Courts' [1988] *Fam. Law* 299–303 at 301–2. Reference would now need to be made to the provisions of the Human Fertilization and Embryology Act 1990 (see Ch. 16).

to reconsider the case, but will not lead to it being ordered to provide the care. These issues relate to the proper conduct of responsibilities in the NHS market and are considered in the next chapter as constraints on the purchasing of services.

The cases considered here show that there is very limited scope for patients to enforce health care rights through public law. The courts have shown themselves reluctant to become embroiled in resource allocation, whether at the level of the Secretary of State's decision whether to fund the building of a new hospital or a health authority's decision about an individual patient's care. Nor will they look closely at clinical decisions about patients' best interests, or the priority of their needs in relation to others on the waiting list. It is therefore necessary to consider whether private law actions might provide more chance of success.

(ii) Private Law

Patients who feel that their rights to NHS care have not been honoured may also seek to bring a private law action alleging that they have wrongfully suffered harm. If they succeed, they may be awarded damages to compensate them for their loss. They may also be able to obtain an injunction preventing the relevant NHS body from acting in breach of their rights, or a declaration establishing what their legal rights are. These two latter remedies may be brought in order to ensure that care is actually provided. An action for damages would necessarily take place after there had been a failure of care, and may therefore be too late for many patients. However, it would be necessary to show that, in principle, an action for damages would lie before either an injunction or a declaration would be granted. There are two main routes to do this. The first is the action for breach of statutory duty. The second is to sue under the general principles of negligence. The application of those principles to clinical malpractice is discussed in detail in Chapter 7. Here, the question of liability of NHS organizations for failure properly to provide services is examined.

(a) Breach of Statutory Duty

In an action for the tort of breach of statutory duty, it is alleged that damage has been caused to the plaintiff due to the failure to perform a statutory duty which exists for the benefit of the aggrieved individual, and which Parliament intended to be enforceable, through the courts, by that individual.[86] Thus, patients denied services could argue that the NHS body responsible had failed

---

[86] *X* v. *Bedfordshire CC; M* v. *Newham LBC; E* v. *Dorset CC* [1995] 3 All ER 353, 364–5.

to perform its statutory obligations and had harmed them. The prospects for success of this form of action depend in part upon the particular statutory duty in question. However, the courts have shown themselves to be reluctant to permit actions for the breach of duties to provide welfare services, and it is unlikely that such an action could be brought under the NHS Act 1977.

The House of Lords has noted that there has been no case in which statutory social welfare schemes, established for the benefit of the public at large, have been held to give rise to a private-law action for damages.[87] In *Re HIV Hæmophiliac Litigation*, the Court of Appeal accepted (in a preliminary action) that the general duties to provide services under the 1977 Act did not provide a foundation for such a suit.[88] They also noted that Wein J had taken a similar view, obiter, in the High Court in *R. v. Secretary of State for Social Services, ex p. Hincks*.[89] However, the point was not considered in the Court of Appeal in that case.[90] Against this authority, there was a suggestion in *R. v. Ealing DHA, ex p. Fox* that a specific duty to provide services for discharged mental patients could be spelt out from the provisions of section 3(1) of the NHS Act 1977.[91] It was not necessary for the judge in this case to consider this point, as such a duty was explicitly set out in section 117 of the Mental Health Act 1983, and he was not concerned with the issue of compensation. Consequently, it would be dangerous to rely on his comment.

It is possible that the courts will prove themselves less reticent where the statutory duties are more specific, because it is easier to show that the individual was entitled to expect a service to be provided. Thus, a failure to provide after-care services under the Mental Health Act 1983, section 117, might more readily form the basis of an action for breach of statutory duty. There, it will be clear that the individual patient, who has now been discharged, should be receiving help. It is not a general duty owed to the public, but a specific one owed to an identified individual.[92] It may also be possible to use the action for breach of statutory duty where patients are promised specific services after an assessment of their needs, and are then not given them because the relevant authority failed to execute their decision.[93] However, this sort of failure may be more amenable to a claim in negligence.

(b) Negligence

Most negligence actions against NHS bodies will be in respect of clinical malpractice. There patients allege that they were improperly treated by NHS staff.

---

[87] *Ibid.*, 364.   [88] (1990) 140 *NLJ* 1349.   [89] [1980] JSWL 113.
[90] See n. 60 above.   [91] [1993] 3 All ER 170, 181–2.
[92] *R. v. Bexley LBC, ex p. B* [1995] *CLY* 3225. See *Holtom v. Barnet LBC, The Times*, 30 Sept. 1993 (QBD) for a similar argument in the education context.
[93] R. Gordon, *Community Care Assessments* (London: Longman, 1993), 70–2.

That area of law is discussed in Chapter 7. Here, the concern is with whether negligence suits can be used to enforce the rights to health care that have been set out above. Although, as has been seen, actions for breach of statutory duties are unlikely to succeed, that does not mean that public bodies are immune from allegations that they carried out their functions carelessly. The basis of a claim that a health authority or NHS trust has carried out its functions carelessly is not that those functions derive from a statute, but that they owe a duty of care, under general tort law principles, to act properly towards those they can reasonably foresee will be affected by their actions.

The courts will consider such allegations only if they are justiciable, and if it would be just and reasonable to impose a duty of care on the public authority in question. Justiciability concerns whether the courts are in a position to determine whether particular actions of the authorities that are to be challenged are acceptable. The House of Lords has suggested that the exercise of public powers can be analysed according to the extent to which it raises policy questions or merely operational issues.[94] The difference between these concepts can be seen in the case of *DHSS* v. *Kinnear*.[95] The plaintiffs claimed that they had suffered brain damage as a result of vaccination against whooping cough. The DHSS argued that the law would not allow such claims to be brought, and sought to have the actions struck out as misconceived. Stuart-Smith J held that there could be no negligence claim in relation to the policy decision to promote the vaccination programme. However, the allegation that misleading advice had been given about the manner and circumstances in which the vaccinations should be given was a justiciable matter. That aspect of the action could continue. Thus, while operational issues may be the subject of negligence claims, policy matters will usually raise issues of discretion that are not justiciable unless no reasonable authority could have reached the decision that was actually taken. This does not completely preclude the possibility that a decision on resource allocation could be the subject of a negligence claim,[96] but it makes it unlikely that it would succeed.

The position may be different if policy has been determined and the failure has been in the implementation of that policy. Then it is more likely that an action could be brought. This means that purchasing authorities may be liable for failing to secure the services that they have identified as necessary in their purchasing plans, for buying services from a provider they should have

---

[94] See n. 86 above.   [95] (1984) 134 *NLJ* 886.

[96] In a judicial review case on community care, *R.* v. *Gloucestershire CC, ex p. Mahfood, Barry, Grinham, Dartnell; R.* v. *Islington LBC, ex p. Mcmillan, The Times,* 21 June 1995 (QBD), it was suggested that there would be some circumstances where the need for care was so obvious that no reasonable authority could fail to purchase it (although that was not the case on the facts). This point does not seem to have been addressed in the Court of Appeal: *R* v. *Gloucestershire CC, ex p. Mahfood and others, R.* v. *Lancashire CC, ex p. RADAR,* both n. 72 above.

known was unsatisfactory, or for failing to draft contracts effectively. In such cases, plaintiffs would be able to argue that there is no dispute about the policy element of decisions (i.e. how resources should be allocated). The allegations of negligence would concern only the purchaser's failure to do what it set out to do properly and the courts would, correspondingly, be more likely to entertain them. There is no doubt that providers of health services can be liable in negligence for inadequate standards of care (see Chapter 7). It is possible that where the inadequacies of the NHS are the result of badly implemented policy decisions, health authorities that are purchasing services may also be liable.

Even if the issues are justiciable, the courts will not accept that a negligence action can be brought unless it would be just and reasonable for a duty of care to exist. Particular problems arise with this in the context of welfare services because of the impact that the potential for liability may have. The House of Lords has held that it would not be just and reasonable to superimpose a common law duty of care on local authorities carrying out their child-protection responsibilities, nor on education authorities considering whether special educational provision should be made for children.[97] Their Lordships reasoned that other remedies were available through complaints procedures, and that a flood of (largely unmeritorious) claims would disrupt the system and drain resources from it. These arguments would apply equally to the NHS.

Other factors that led the House of Lords to its conclusion may be less relevant to the NHS position. Their Lordships emphasized the fact that the statutory child protection framework explicitly acknowledged that local authorities had to balance potentially conflicting pressures: to protect children from harm, but also to keep them with their families. There is no such tension on the face of the NHS statutes, but the responsibilities of health authorities for planning services and allocating limited resources inevitably lead to a form of rationing. This could be seen to raise similar conflicts, and would probably lead to the judiciary taking a similar view of the imposition of common law liability for planning decisions.

The House of Lords also emphasized how delicate an operation this would be, and noted the potential for conflict between professionals and clients. It was worried that permitting litigation would divert local authorities from concentrating on their tasks. It might make them cautious, and encourage them to take decisions that would satisfy those likely to complain rather than the ones that they believe were the best use of their resources. There would probably be similar concern in relation to NHS purchasing. Already vulnerable groups, such as those with mental or physical disabilities, might be seen

---

[97] N. 86 above.

as less likely to complain. The consequence of permitting litigation might be that resources are devoted to higher profile services.

There is, therefore, reason to believe that the courts might be reluctant to impose a duty of care in relation to the planning aspects of the work of NHS bodies. However, one Court of Appeal decision, which predates the leading House of Lords case on the liability of public authorities, has suggested that a negligence action could be brought by patients in respect of the failure of NHS bodies to perform their statutory duties properly. The plaintiffs alleged that the NHS had negligently failed to ensure that blood products used for trans-fusions were free from infection with HIV. In a preliminary action, the Court of Appeal held that their claim for negligence in the performance of their stat-utory powers could not be struck out as doomed to failure.[98] This decision must be treated warily as the issue was at the operational end of the spectrum and the Court of Appeal was not asked to decide whether the action would succeed, merely whether it was arguable.

C. Quality Control

Given the problems confronting patients who seek to use the courts to enforce their rights, considerable reliance is placed on the ability of the NHS to iden-tify and remedy failures in the delivery of the care required by the statutory duties. A wide range of mechanisms exists to monitor the effectiveness of the NHS, to highlight problems, and canvass solutions. This section considers the ways in which the constitutional position of the Service seeks to ensure it identifies and deals with problems as they arise. The separate framework for responding to the complaints of individuals is examined in Chapter 5.

(i) The Health Select Committee

The Health Select Committee of the House of Commons is responsible for examining the work of the Department of Health. It consists of eleven elected Members of Parliament, with the main political parties represented according to the make up of the whole House. Its remit is to examine the expenditure, administration, and policies of the Department of Health.[99] It has the power to require people to appear before it, and to receive papers and records. It may also appoint specialist advisers to inform its work. The Health Committee has produced some important reports, including those concerning community

---

[98] N. 88 above.   [99] Standing Order No 130 of the House of Commons.

supervision orders for the mentally ill,[100] the funding of community care,[101] dental services in the light of the crisis produced by changes in contractual arrangements,[102] maternity services,[103] and the operation of NHS trusts.[104]

(ii) Community Health Councils

Community Health Councils (CHCs) were introduced in the reorganization of 1974. They exist in relation to every health authority.[105] The councils are intended to ensure that the interests of consumers are not overlooked, and they are obliged to 'keep under review the operation of the health service in its district and make recommendations for the improvement of that service' and to advise health authorities about the local operation of the NHS.[106] The position of CHCs has become problematic in the modern NHS. Their role in ensuring democratic accountability in the NHS has been described as 'symbolic rather than real'.[107] They are premised on the assumption that consumers should exercise influence indirectly through representatives, although no clear concept of representation has emerged.[108] This approach has been threatened by two aspects of new thinking on consumerism in the NHS.[109] The first is direct empowerment of patients, primarily through increased choice. The second is the focusing of health service management on improving patient satisfaction. This places the role of protecting consumer interests directly in the hands of the managers, and reduces the importance of the CHCs. A third factor in the reduction of the influence of CHCs is the introduction of the 'internal market' whereby health service bodies are placed in economic competition. First, it means that health authorities need to be able to keep some of their planning confidential in order not to prejudice their negotiating positions. CHCs have rights only to information which they may 'reasonably' require,[110] and it may well now be unreasonable to require commercially sensitive information. NHS trusts are not required to allow CHCs access to their meetings.

Beyond being a vehicle for consumer influence, CHCs have never had their functions precisely defined. One study summarized the work carried out by

---

[100] HC Pap. (1992–3), 667.
[101] HC Pap. (1992–3), 309.
[102] HC Pap. (1992–3), 264.
[103] HC Pap. (1991–2), 29.
[104] HC Pap. (1992–3), 321.
[105] NHS Act 1977, s. 20, Sch. 7; Community Health Councils Regulations 1996, SI 1996 No 640.
[106] SI 1996 No 640, n. 105 above, r. 17.
[107] L. Doyal, with I. Pennel, *The Political Economy of Health* (London: Pluto Press, 1979), 185.
[108] R. Klein, and J. Lewis, *The Politics of Consumer Representation* (London: Centre for Studies in Social Policy, 1976), 17–23.
[109] E. Scrivens, 'Consumers, Accountability and Quality of Service' in R. Maxwell (ed.), *Reshaping the National Health Service* (Oxford: Hermitage's Policy Journals, 1988).
[110] N. 105 above, r. 19(1).

CHCs under the headings of receiving information, visiting institutions, observing health authority meetings (with differing levels of participation), consultation on health authority plans (particularly on hospital closures), providing information about health promotion and services to the public, and assisting complainants.[111] It is likely, however, that particular councils may carry out only some of these activities, and the amount and nature of the work done under these headings varies enormously.[112]

CHCs are set up and funded by Secretary of State, through the NHS Executive under the Community Health Councils Regulations 1996. The Regulations do not provide precise requirements, but ensure that at least half the members are appointed by the relevant local authority and at least one third by local voluntary organizations.[113] It has been found that most CHCs consisted of about twenty people who are predominantly middle-aged and middle class, although there are patterns of regional variation.[114] Members are appointed for four years and may be reappointed.[115] A register of members and the basis of their appointment must be made available for public consultation at the Council's office.[116] Councils must meet at least once every three months,[117] and their meetings are open to the public,[118] although non-members may be excluded for matters involving the discussion of confidential information.[119] The public is also entitled to see agendas, minutes, and background papers.[120]

The Regulations provide councils with limited rights. Health authorities must consult the local CHC on proposals for 'substantial development' of their services including the establishment of an NHS trust.[121] There is no obligation to take notice of any representations a Council makes. Health authorities must meet for discussion with the CHC at least once a year.[122] Visiting rights exist in respect of health authority premises and those of NHS trusts in the area covered by the CHC.[123] These rights do not cover all places where patients from the district go for treatment, as health authorities may

---

[111] R. Levitt, *The People's Voice in the NHS* (London: King's Fund, 1980).

[112] Klein and Lewis, n. 108 above; R. Levitt, 'Community Health Councils' in C. Farrell and R. Levitt, *Consumers, Community Health Councils and the NHS* (London: King's Fund, 1980).

[113] N. 105 above, r. 2.   [114] Klein and Lewis, n. 108 above, ch. 2.

[115] Rr. 3, 6.

[116] Community Health Councils (Access to Information) Act 1988, s. 2.

[117] N. 105 above, Sch. para. 2.

[118] Community Health Councils (Access to Information) Act 1988, s. 1; Local Government Act 1972, s. 100A.

[119] Local Government Act 1972, s. 100A(2).

[120] Community Health Councils (Access to Information) Act 1988, s. 1; Local Government Act 1972, s. 100B–D.

[121] N. 105 above, r. 18; NHS Trusts (Consultation on Establishment and Dissolution) Regulations 1996, SI 1996 No 653.

[122] N. 105 above, r. 21.   [123] *Ibid.*, 20.

have contracts with providers outside their districts. An examination of the annual reports of three CHCs shows an annual range of visits from six to twenty-eight.[124]

While individual CHCs have strictly local responsibilities, the 1977 Act also provides for a national body to advise them on their work.[125] This body, the Association of Community Health Councils for England and Wales (ACHCEW), was set up in 1977.[126] Not all local CHCs affiliate to the national organization, but it represents the majority. In addition to supporting local work, ACHCEW acts as a national consumer pressure group. In 1986 it published a Patient's Charter outlining the standards and practices to which it believed patients were entitled. In 1992 it issued proposals for reform of NHS complaints procedures.

(iii) The Audit Commission

The Audit Commission has two main roles in relation to the NHS. The first is to provide external 'regularity' audit of the accounts of NHS bodies. As public bodies, health authorities and NHS trusts are not permitted to select their own auditors. The Audit Commission appoints the auditors of health authorities, NHS trusts, and GP fundholders (in respect of the purchasing functions only).[127] These auditors may be from a private firm of accountants, or may be from the Commission's in-house District Audit Service. The Commission has the power to undertake an extraordinary audit if it believes it is necessary, or the Secretary of State requests it.[128] However, members of the public cannot initiate an extraordinary audit as they may in relation to local authorities.[129]

The second main task of the Commission is to report on the economy, efficiency, and effectiveness of services.[130] It has defined those terms in its *Code of Audit Practice for Local Authorities and the NHS in England and Wales* (1990). 'Economy' relates to the terms on which resources are acquired, an economical organization being one that acquires them at the lowest cost. 'Efficiency' is concerned with the services provided in relation to the costs of provision, an efficient operation producing either the maximum services for a fixed level of resource, or providing a fixed level and quality of services for the minimum input. 'Effectiveness' is a measure of how well a service achieves

---

[124] Annual Reports of Basingstoke & North Hampshire CHC, Bath CHC and Southampton and South West Hampshire CHC for the years 1975–88.

[125] NHS Act 1977, Sch. 7 para. 5.

[126] NHS (Association of Community Health Councils) Regulations 1977, SI 1977 No 874; NHS (Association of Community Health Councils—Establishment Order 1977, SI 1977 No 1204.

[127] NHS ACT 1977, s. 98; Local Government Finance Act 1982, s. 12.

[128] Local Government Finance Act 1982, s. 22.

[129] *Ibid.*, s. 22(4A).

[130] *Ibid.*, s. 27(1).

its goals. This is to be measured against the statutory frameworks governing NHS bodies, and any relevant guidance issued by the Secretary of State. However, the Audit Commission is not permitted to question the merits of the Secretary of State's policies.[131]

Some of the Audit Commission's work has focused specifically on the process of management. It has looked at internal audit agendas for NHS trusts and examined the detection and elimination of fraud and corruption.[132] It has audited the monitoring systems which generated the data for the NHS performance tables. However, the Audit Commission does far more than just examine managerial efficiency, and is also concerned with promoting high quality services. It has reported on the effectiveness of mental health services on delivering appropriate care when and where it is needed. The Commission highlighted the need for inter-agency co-operation and proper planning, including a central lead from the Departments of Health and the Environment.[133] This can be seen as implying concerns over the fragmentation created by the devolution of planning in the NHS market. Other clinical areas studied include hospital services for children, pathology services, accident and emergency services, and medical record-keeping.[134] The Audit Commission has also analysed the roles of district health authorities and family health services authorities (now combined into unitary health authorities), issuing advice on how they can be carried out effectively.[135]

(iv) The Clinical Standards Advisory Group

The NHS and Community Care Act 1990 introduced a new body to inquire into the provision of services. The Clinical Standards Advisory Group (CSAG) was set up by section 62 to provide advice, investigate, and report on standards of clinical care, access to, and availability of services. This remit includes waiting times. Matters can be referred to the group by the Secretary

---

[131] Local Government Finance Act 1982, s. 27(6).

[132] Audit Commission, *Trusting in the Future: Towards an Audit Agenda for NHS Providers* (London: HMSO, 1994); Audit Commission, *Protecting the Public Purse 2: Probity in the NHS* (London: HMSO, 1994).

[133] Audit Commission, *Finding a Place: A Review of Mental Health Services for Adults* (London: HMSO, 1994).

[134] Audit Commission, *Children First: A Study of Hospital Services* (London: HMSO, 1993); Audit Commission, *Critical Paths: An Analysis of the Pathology Services* (London: HMSO, 1993); Audit Commission, *By Accident or Design: Improving A & E Services in England and Wales* (London: HMSO, 1996); Audit Commission, *Setting the Records Straight: A Study of Hospital Medical Records* (London: HMSO, 1995).

[135] Audit Commission, *Their Health, Your Business: The New Role of the District Health Authority* (London: HMSO, 1993); Audit Commission, *Practices make Perfect: The Role of the Family Health Services Authority* (London: HMSO, 1993).

of State, health authorities, and NHS trusts, but not by individuals.[136] It is expected mostly to respond to such requests, although the Government has accepted that it can initiate investigations.[137] The Group consists of a lay chair, nominees from the medical, dental, nursing, and midwifery royal colleges, and the Chairs of the Standing Medical Advisory Committee, the Standing Dental Advisory Committee, and the Standing Nursing and Midwifery Committee (*ex officio*).[138] Consumer views are not represented.

The first two reports to be published by the Group concerned access to specialist services and standards of care for people with diabetes.[139] It has also considered urgent and emergency referrals, maternity services, services for those with back pain, and schizophrenia (the last in collaboration with the Health Advisory Service). The report on diabetes services was published together with the Government's response. The latter is indicative of the difficulties faced by the Group in influencing NHS provision. While most of the Report's recommendations were accepted, the Government's principal comment was that responsibility for implementing them lay with purchasers and providers, not centrally. This would seem to confirm concerns that the CSAG lacks the resources and jurisdiction to constitute an avenue of public accountability.[140]

(v) Health Advisory Service

The Health Advisory Service (HAS) began life as the Hospitals Advisory Service in 1969.[141] The current name, introduced in 1976, indicates a wider remit. The functions of the HAS are to advise on the maintenance and improvement of standards of management, organization, and delivery of patient care services, mostly those for mentally ill and elderly people; to keep Government aware of the standards of service provision; to identify and disseminate good practice; to identify areas of difficulty in the provision of services; to publish guidance for health and local authorities.[142] These functions involve monitoring the purchasing performance of health authorities, but the Service will not investigate individual complaints or matters of clinical

---

[136] S. 61(1). [137] *Hansard*, HL, vol. 520, No 98, col. 246–8.

[138] Clinical Standards Advisory Group Regulations 1991, SI 1991 No 578.

[139] Clinical Standards Advisory Group, *Access to and Availability of Specialist Services* (London: HMSO, 1992); Clinical Standards Advisory Group, *Standards of Clinical Care for People with Diabetes* (London: HMSO, 1994).

[140] D. Longley, *Public Law and Health Service Accountability* (Buckingham: Open University Press, 1993), 113.

[141] The work of the HAS over its period of existence is reviewed in Health Advisory Service, *Making a Mark: The Annual Report of the Director for 1994–95* (London: HMSO, 1996).

[142] Health Advisory Service, *A Unique Window on Change: The Annual Report of the Director for 1992–1993* (London: HMSO, 1993), 7.

judgement. The HAS is independent of the NHS and Department of Health, and reports directly to the Secretary of State.

Some of the work of the HAS is concerned with specific problem areas. The Secretary of State may commission a review of services which are causing concern. This may result in a formal report, or merely constitute an informal advisory process. There are also a number of longer-term thematic reviews. Over the period 1992–5 these thematic reviews have covered the prevention of suicide, services for the homeless mentally ill, mental health services for children and adolescents, schizophrenia (in collaboration with the Clinical Standards Advisory Group), services for those with brain-injury, presenile dementia, and the pre-lingually deaf.[143] These thematic studies have replaced a programme of routine cyclical reviews, which gave the HAS a more inspectorial role. That change has been related to the responsibility of purchasers for monitoring the quality of the services they fund.[144]

(vi) The Social Services Inspectorate

The Social Services Inspectorate is a division of the Department of Health, and advises ministers on the formulation, implementation, and monitoring of social services and related health policies. It also inspects social services provision to improve the quality of services and to promote effectiveness and efficiency. In 1993–4 it examined all the community care plans of local authorities and gave feedback to the originating authorities. Amongst the studies it commissioned were those on care management, services for those with HIV/AIDS, hospital discharge, day care for people with learning difficulties, and residential care for older people.[145] It has also developed standards for the residential care of the elderly mentally ill,[146] and examined local authority complaints procedures.[147]

(vii) Inquiries

The structure of the NHS allows for the investigation of practice through managerial initiative via a number of avenues. Myriad informal processes may

---

[143] Health Advisory Service, *Guiding through Change: The Annual Report of the Director 1993–1994* (London: HMSO, 1994).

[144] N. 142 above, 14.

[145] Social Services Inspectorate, Department of Health, *Putting People First: The Third Annual Report of the Chief Inspector, Social Services Inspectorate* (London: HMSO, 1994).

[146] Social Services Inspectorate, Department of Health, *Standards for the Residential Care of Elderly People with Mental Disorders* (London: HMSO, 1993).

[147] Social Services Inspectorate, Department of Health, *The Inspection of Complaints Procedures in Local Authority Social Services Departments* (London: HMSO, 1993).

be used, but two more formal procedures should be particularly noted. These have been used sparingly, as they are primarily to deal with serious problems which cannot be resolved by the more usual complaints and disciplinary channels. The adverse effects of public inquiries on the reputation of hospitals and the morale of staff may be considerable, but experience has demonstrated that they do result in changes in practice.[148]

At a central level, section 84 of the National Health Service Act 1977 provides the Secretary of State with the power to set up formal independent inquiries. The scope of this power is very wide, covering 'any case where he deems it advisable to do so in connection with any matter arising under [the 1977] Act'. Its exercise is entirely discretionary and has not been delegated to health authorities. Once established a section 84 inquiry has the power to summons witnesses and require documents to be produced. Evidence may be taken on oath if the inquiry so chooses.[149] Failure to respond to a summons and concealing or altering evidence are punishable by fine or imprisonment.[150] Financial responsibility for the inquiry falls upon the Secretary of State and not upon the relevant local health authority.[151] The expenses of witnesses must be covered before they are obliged to attend or provide the inquiry with documents, and the Secretary of State may make an order requiring some parties to pay the costs of others.[152]

Inquiries may also be set up by health authorities under HM(66)15, 'Methods of Dealing with Complaints by Patients'. There is a range of approaches to the composition of such inquiries. Less serious matters may be investigated by a member of the relevant district or regional health authority. Where an inquiry needs to be independent of the authority the circular suggests that it should be carried out by 'an independent lawyer or other competent person' either acting alone or as chair of a small committee. The inquiry should have the benefit of expert advisers on professional or technical matters. Practice has varied as to whether reports are produced by the chair, with other members of the inquiry acting merely as assessors, or by the team collectively.[153] Complainants and those complained against should be permitted to be represented if they wish, legally or otherwise, and given the opportunity to cross-examine witnesses. Unlike those established by the Secretary of State co-operation with such investigations is voluntary.

---

[148] J. Martin, *Hospitals in Trouble* (Oxford: Blackwell, 1984); Department of Health and Social Security and the Welsh Office, *Annual Report of the Hospital Advisory Service for 1972* (London HMSO, 1973).

[149] S. 84(2).   [150] S. 84(4).   [151] S. 84(5).   [152] S. 84(3).

[153] Martin, n. 148 above, 74–5.

D. Conclusion

This Chapter has set out the legal, and quasi-legal, rights to health care within the NHS. It has shown how those rights mainly take the form of general statutory duties rather than individual entitlements. This character makes it difficult for patients to enforce their rights, and means that the quality control mechanisms of the Service are extremely important in ensuring that citizens' rights to health care under international law are honoured. The legal structure of rights to NHS care is still essentially in the same form as it has been since the inception of the unified NHS. That structure is more paternalistic than rights-based. Within that framework, however, a constitutional structure for planning, commissioning, and providing care has been established which seeks to be more responsive to the needs, rights, and views of patients. This is examined in the next chapter.

4 The NHS Market

The previous chapter set out the statutory duties that the National Health Service is required to perform, and the mechanisms for enforcing them, either through individual actions in the courts or on behalf of the community through a range of quality assurance mechanisms. This Chapter outlines the organizational structure that enables the NHS to honour those entitlements. It explains the legal basis of the mechanisms for policy-making and centralized planning. This is the responsibility of the Department of Health and, in particular, the NHS Executive. Under the current NHS regime, the role of the NHS Executive lies essentially in planning and monitoring the overall operation of the Service. The actual delivery of care is secured by a process of contracting. Health Authorities and GP fundholders are responsible for purchasing services for NHS patients from a range of providers. Most of those are also NHS bodies, usually NHS trusts, but others are independent organizations. The constitutions, powers, and regulation of these various bodies, and the operation of the NHS market are the subject of most of this Chapter.

During the history of the NHS, there have been a number of tiers of health authority. Under the initial structure, introduced in 1948, hospital services were administered by regional boards (responsible for planning and co-ordination) and by local management committees. In 1974 regional boards were replaced by regional health authorities, an intermediate tier was introduced (the area health authority), and each area was subdivided into district management teams. In 1982, the ninety area health authorities were abolished and replaced by approximately 200 district health authorities. Family health services were administered through a framework of, first, family practitioner committees (until 1991) and then family health services authorities. These bodies existed alongside the hospital authorities.

The Health Authorities Act 1995, which took effect in April 1996, simplified this system, and there is now only one level of health authority. Regional health authorities were abolished, and district health authorities were merged with family health services authorities in order to form an integrated purchasing authority, responsible for securing health services for their local populations. This Chapter examines the current system.

A. Central Planning and Control

Under the Ministry of Health Act 1919, the Secretary of State is bound to

> secure the preparation, effective carrying out and coordination of measures
> conducive to the health of the people . . . including measures for the preven-
> tion and cure of diseases . . . the treatment of physical and mental defects, the
> treatment and care of the blind, the initiation and direction of research, the
> collection, preparation, publication, and dissemination of information and
> statistics relating thereto, and the training of persons for health services.[1]

This has been interpreted as giving the Department of Health three main
responsibilities: public health, health care, and social care. While operational
responsibility for the public health and social care functions has been retained
within the Department, establishing the direction of the NHS is the task of the
NHS Executive.[2]

The core functions of the NHS Executive relate to strategic planning and
market regulation.[3] The Executive supports ministers in meeting the requirements of Parliamentary and public accountability, ensuring that purchasers
and providers within the NHS have a clear framework for accountability for
their use of public funds. It also establishes policy, priorities, and standards
for the NHS, and allocates the resources provided by Parliament to the
Service. This process of strategic planning includes human resource issues,
performance management, and research and development. Responsibility for
assessing local health needs and securing services for local populations,
within the strategic framework established by the NHS Executive, is delegated
to health authorities.[4]

At the core of the NHS planning process is the NHS Policy Board, which is
chaired by the Health Secretary. It is non-statutory and was set up to advise
the Secretary of State.[5] The Policy Board includes Ministers, senior officials
including the Chief Medical Officer and the Chief Nursing Officer, and eight
non-executive members representing each of the regions of England in which

[1] S. 2.

[2] Department of Health and NHS Executive, *Managing the New NHS: Functions and
Responsibilities in the New NHS* (London: DoH, 1994). See also *The Review of the Wider Department
of Health* (London: DoH, 1994), and *Public Health in England: Roles and Responsibilities of the
Department of Health and the NHS* (London: DoH, 1994).

[3] Many of the bodies and responsibilities discussed in the following paragraphs are non-
statutory, and therefore not allocated by law. The main document setting out the allocation of functions is the Department of Health's *Statement of Responsibilities and Accountabilities* (London: DoH,
1995).

[4] Department of Health & NHS Executive, n. 2 above.

[5] N. 3 above, para. 4.1–4.2. D. Longley, *Health Care Constitutions* (London: Cavendish
Publishing, 1996), 112–14.

the outposts of the NHSE are situated.[6] The Policy Board is concerned with the objectives and strategy of the NHS Executive in managing the service, and holds it to account for the delivery of those objectives.

There is also a NHS Executive Board, comprising the senior officers of the NHS. It is chaired by the Chief Executive of the NHS, and comprises the directors of the eight regional offices of the NHSE and the eight headquarters directors. These include those responsible for finance, human resources, health care (primary, secondary and community), research and development, nursing, and planning. The functions of the Executive Board are to provide a single corporate body to bring closer together policy making and implementation, to support the Chief Executive of the NHS in advising the Secretary of State on setting the strategic direction for the Service, and to support him in managing its overall performance.

The three main outcomes of this strategy setting are the establishment of priorities for improving the health of the nation,[7] the Patient's Charter (see Chapter 3) and related performance monitoring, and the management of the NHS market. The NHSE has a considerable influence in the operation of the NHS market. The discretion of local health authorities to choose their own priorities is limited by the NHSE's annual strategic guidance, which orientates the process of contracting towards the objectives set nationally for the Service. This covers both the priorities that purchasers should be following and the nature of the contracts that they should agree.[8]

Quality standards in contracts are dominated by the targets set by the Patient's Charter and the Performance League Tables.[9] These deal with minimum waiting times for the arrival of an emergency ambulance, for first appointments as outpatients, for admission for treatment, and for assessment in accident and emergency units. They also record the percentage of patients admitted as day cases for certain operations and the percentage of people seen at outpatients' clinics within thirty minutes of their appointment time. There is little freedom for health authorities to decide that in their area it would be better to let some waiting times rise in order to give higher priority to funding other services.

One of the Government's intentions in introducing a market system into the NHS was to keep costs low. This was originally anticipated to be the result

[6] Seven of these eight previously chaired the Regional Health Authorities before they were abolished by the Health Authorities Act 1995.

[7] See *The Health of the Nation* (London: HMSO, 1992, Cm 1986). This programme has now spawned a large number of initiatives and documents. These are beyond the scope of this book, although legal aspects of the public health are discussed in Ch. 2.

[8] National Health Service Executive, *Priorities and Planning Guidance for the NHS: 1996–7* EL(95)68 (1995); National Health Service Executive, '1995–96 Contracting Review: Handbook' EL(94)88.

[9] National Health Service Executive, *The NHS Performance Guide 1994–5* (London: DoH, 1995).

of competition between provider units, which would seek to raise standards and reduce costs in order to win contracts. In fact, outside the metropolitan areas, the scope for competition proved to be relatively small.[10] As a result, the NHSE has imposed targets for 'efficiency savings'. These have required health authorities to secure the same services at, typically, 3 per cent less cost each year. These savings are required from providers through the contracts made with them. Thus, central direction has driven cost containment more than competition. Separate targets have been set by the NHSE in relation to the reduction of management costs by 5 per cent in 1996–7.

It can be seen that the NHSE has not been prepared to risk the market reforms undermining national priorities.[11] The official position is that it will intervene to prevent abuses of position in the market, such as collusive behaviour between providers to establish cartels.[12] This implies that the objective is to enable market competition to have full effect. In fact, intervention by the NHSE has been used to manage the market quite closely. In the main, however, the purchasers and providers of NHS care are able to agree the terms on which care is to be provided within the guidance issued by the NHSE without the need for intervention in individual cases. The NHSE, through its regional outposts, monitors the performance of NHS purchasers and providers, supports community health councils, and co-ordinates public health initiatives. The regional outposts are also responsible for emergency planning, public consultation on the establishment of NHS trusts, the implementation of the NHS information strategy, medical workforce planning, and GP vocational training.[13]

B. Purchasers of Services

Since 1991, the principal functions of health authorities have been to operate the NHS market system, in which services are procured for patients through a system of contracting. Initially, this was done by both district and regional health authorities. However, the regional health authorities' role in purchasing was always moribund, and services for which RHAs were responsible were

---

[10] J. Appleby, P. Smith, W. Ranade, V. Little, and R. Robinson, 'Monitoring Managed Competition', 43–6, and J. Le Grand, 'Evaluating the NHS reforms', 253–7, both in R. Robinson, and J. Le Grand, *Evaluating the NHS Reforms* (London: King's Fund Institute, 1994).

[11] D. Hughes, 'Health policy: letting the market work?' (1993) 5 *Social Policy Review* 104–24.

[12] NHSE, *The Operation of the NHS Internal Market: Local Freedoms, National Responsibilities* (London: DoH, 1994).

[13] See the discussion on the Health Authorities Act 1995 in Standing Committee A, *Hansard*, 7 Feb. 1995, Col. 142.

quickly delegated to district level. The active function of the RHAs in the market system was monitoring the performance of purchasers. The abolition of the RHAs in 1996 was prefigured by a restructuring in 1994, in which the number of regions was reduced from fourteen to eight and administrative arrangements effectively combined their functions with those of the regional outposts of the NHS Executive. Since April 1996, the responsibility for monitoring the operation of the NHS market, both purchasing and providing, has lain with the NHS Executive. The main responsibilities of the new health authorities are to deal with the purchasing of services.

A further fundamental change was introduced in 1991 by the creation of GP fundholding. This fragmented the planning (through purchasing) of hospital and community services by creating a new set of purchasers whose task is to secure services for the patients on their lists, not the whole of the resident population of a geographical area. To some extent, this system creates competition between purchasers, but the purchasing functions of GPFH are not identical to those of health authorities. The picture is further complicated by the interaction with the social service purchasing of social care.

(i) Health Authorities

Health authorities are charged with the purpose of ensuring that the services provided meet the needs of those usually resident in their area, or those resident outside the United Kingdom but present in that area. Ambulance and accident and emergency services have to be secured for all those present in the area.[14] The Secretary of State has delegated to health authorities these powers in order to cover his obligations to provide services under the 1977 Act.[15] While there are significant legal limitations upon the powers of GPFH (and safety-net provisions in relation to expensive patients), health authorities exercise those delegated powers with little restriction. However, they are expected to collaborate with GPs, and with local people and organizations when exercising their functions.[16] They must also make arrangements for securing professional advice from health care professionals.[17] The way in which they do so is largely a matter for their discretion, although guidance has been issued.[18]

As the previous chapter explained, primary health services are secured by a statutory contract. The health authorities retain managerial functions in

[14] NHS Function (Functions of Health Authorities and Administrative Arrangements) Regulations 1996, SI 1996 No 708, r. 3.
[15] For the full list, see *ibid.* Sch. 1.
[16] Department of Health and NHSE, n. 1 above, paras. 3.9–3.13, Annex C.
[17] NHS Act 1977, s. 12(1), as inserted by Health Authorities Act 1955, Sch. 1, para. 3.
[18] *Ensuring the Effective Involvement of Professionals in Health Authority Work*, HSG(95)11.

relation to matters such as the transfer of patients between lists and are responsible for ensuring that the doctors and dentists do not breach their contracts. They must also operate the independent review stage of the complaints procedures.[19] Although it is the responsibility of the local health authority to secure services for its population, applications by doctors to practise in an area must be approved by the Medical Practices Committee.[20] That Committee has the power to reject applications where adequate services already exist.[21] This power provides only a partial solution to a problem that has bedeviled the NHS throughout its history, the need to ensure that general medical services are available to all, as there is no power to force medical practitioners to practise in any particular area.[22] Further control is provided by the power of the Secretary of State to establish the maximum total number of general practitioners for England and Wales.[23] Enforcement of the contracts with general practitioners is considered below.

Health authorities comprise five officers, up to seven non-officer members, and a non-executive chairman (or woman).[24] The officers must include the chief executive, director of finance, and director of public health. The remaining two officer posts on the authority are filled by appointment by the chairman and non-officer members. The chairman and non-officer members of the authority are appointed by the Secretary of State. Health authorities whose areas include medical schools will have a non-officer member from the relevant university.[25] The functions of health authorities are elaborated in the Code of Accountability, to which (along with the Code of Conduct) members are expected to subscribe on appointment. These Codes apply to both health authorities and NHS trusts and are discussed in the section on corporate governance later in this Chapter.

(ii) GP Fundholders

GP Fundholders provide an alternative purchaser. Money is removed from the health authority's budget and reallocated to be spent by the GPFH. The conditions for becoming a GPFH are that the practice must have at least 5,000 patients (originally this figure was set 11,000 but has dropped progressively

---

[19] NHS (Functions of Health Authorities) (Complaints) Regulations 1996, SI 1996 No 669; see Ch. 5.

[20] NHS Act 1977, s. 30.   [21] *Ibid.*, s. 33(1).

[22] Even the limited power that now exists to refuse to allow practitioners to practise in the area of their choice had to be dropped from the original proposals for the NHS: R. Klein, *The Politics of the NHS* (2nd edn., London: Longman, 1989), 10–16.

[23] NHS Act 1977, s. 33(1A).

[24] *Ibid.*, Sch. 1, as inserted by Health Authorities Act 1995, Sch. 1, para. 59; Health Authorities (Membership and Procedure) Regulations 1996, SI 1996 No 707.

[25] Health Authorities (Membership and Procedure) Regulations 1996, n. 24 above, Sch. 1.

since 1991). In April 1996 a new form of fundholding was introduced in England, known as 'community fundholding'. This is available to smaller practices, with 3,000 patients or more, and deals with a more limited range of purchasing decisions than full fundholding. Applicants for fundholding status must be capable of managing a purchasing budget (known as the 'allocated sum') effectively and efficiently. Practice members must be bound together either by a general partnership agreement, or by a partnership in relation to GPFH budget. GPFHs have dual responsibilities. As fund holders, they are purchasers of community and hospital services. However, they are also providers in respect of primary care, for which they contract on the usual statutory terms with the relevant health authority. There must be separate accounting for the purchasing budget.[26] A further innovation introduced on a non-statutory basis in April 1996 was 'total purchasing', which is being piloted in a number of areas. This involves constituting a group of GPs as a sub-committee of the relevant health authority and delegating purchasing decisions for their practice areas to them. This enables GPs to control a fuller range of purchasing decisions than fundholders.

GP fundholders are able to purchase services on behalf of patients on their list (not geographically defined populations as with health authorities). However, they only purchase a subset of the care for those patients, taken from a specified and limited range of services for which GPFHs can contract.[27] Further, there is a safeguard for GPFHs against expensive patients, in that the DHA must pay costs over £6,000 in relation to an individual patient in any one financial year.[28]

The regulations set out a number of legal restrictions on GPFH purchasing.[29] District nursing and health visiting services must be purchased from a health authority or NHS Trust, which must have been providing such services for the whole of the previous year. The level of such services must be at least that which was expected to be purchased when the budget of the GPFH was determined. To police these requirements, health authority approval of contracts for these services is required. There are also restrictions aimed at avoiding conflicts of interests. GPFHs cannot purchase from a body with which a member of the practice is connected without the written approval of the health authority. This excludes people who employ one of the doctors, or the doctors' close relatives, and also partnerships and companies whose directors are similarly connected. Close relative here means spouse, sibling, parent, or child. Exceptions to the requirement of consent exist where it is impracticable to obtain that consent because of a patient's condition, and where the other

---

[26] NHS (Fundholding Practices) Regulations 1996, SI 1996 No 706, Schs. 1, 2.
[27] *Ibid.*, r. 20. Different lists are provided for ordinary fundholders and community fundholders.
[28] *Ibid.*, r. 21.   [29] *Ibid.*, r. 20.

provider is a health service body other than a GPFH. The health authority may not give its consent if a member of the GP practice would receive payment from the purchasing budget more than half of which is attributable, even indirectly, to the treatment of patients of that practice. Such approval may be given to a general arrangement for the provision of services, rather than in relation to individual patients.[30]

Any savings made by a GPFH can be used for the benefit of patients within four years for purposes within the normal use of the budget allocation, and also to purchase material or equipment to treat patients, enhance the convenience of patients, or to improve practice management, health education, or premises.[31] There are clawback provisions for misapplied funds.[32] The Secretary of State may withdraw recognition from fundholding practices which refuse to accept their budget allocation or fail to comply with the conditions for recognition (including size of practice and accounting arrangements).[33] This can be done with immediate effect where it is necessary in the interests of patients, members of the practice, or to ensure proper management of the budget.[34] However, it would usually be after the practice has been given an opportunity to make representations.[35] It is also possible for the fundholding practice to renounce that status.[36]

(iii) Social Services Departments

Local authorities can either provide community care services themselves, or purchase them from other providers (including NHS trusts) on behalf of clients.[37] They have the power to inspect establishments in which community care services are provided, and to see non-medical records, unless the premises are registered under the Registered Homes Act 1984[38] (when inspections will take place under that Act). In practice, arrangements for the purchasing of social care vary. Progress towards a separation of purchasing and providing functions has been gradual, and many Social Services Departments purchase services from themselves. However, the Social Services Inspectorate has reported little evidence to substantiate complaints from independent providers that social services residential provision was being preferred to purchasing from the independent sector.[39]

Some authorities devolve budgets to individual care managers, a strategy that may make purchasing more sensitive to individual needs. In others,

[30] NHS (Fundholding Practices) Regulations 1996, SI 1996 No 706, Schs. 1, 2 rr. 20(8), 24.
[31] *Ibid.*, r. 25.   [32] *Ibid.*, r. 26.   [33] *Ibid.*, r. 13, Sch. 2.   [34] *Ibid.*, rr. 15, 16.
[35] *Ibid.*, r. 14.   [36] *Ibid.*, rr. 11, 12.   [37] National Assistance Act 1948, s. 26, as amended.
[38] NHS & Community Care Act 1990, s. 48.
[39] Social Services Inspectorate, Department of Health, *Putting People First: The Third Annual Report of the Chief Inspector, Social Services Inspectorate* (London: HMSO, 1994), 42.

purchasing budgets are controlled by team managers, who may have a clearer picture of the market, and be better able to counter the market power of providers.[40] There is considerable variation in the types of contracts being used to secure care by social services departments. Most have used 'spot-contracting' for the residential care of elderly people. This affords greater opportunity to provide client choice, being specific to each client, unlike most contracting in the NHS market. It also provides flexibility for social services purchasers when levels of need are uncertain. Block contracts, similar to those used in the NHS, have been used by many authorities in relation to specialist services.[41]

C. Providers of Services

It is still possible for health authorities and social services departments to provide services themselves. Where this happens, there will usually be agreements in the format of contracts to set out the services to be provided, budget allocation, and quality measures. However, these would be enforced through administrative steps rather than as proper contracts. Direct provision of services by health authorities, through what are generally known as directly managed units, is now rare. By April 1996 the market reforms had progressed to the stage at which fewer than 2 per cent of NHS services are now provided in this way. The main providers of NHS services are NHS trusts and a range of organizations independent of the NHS, some voluntary and some commercial (although not necessarily profit-making). These independent bodies are not regulated as providers of NHS services (save in so far as health authorities exercise indirect control through contract terms). However, they will be governed by law in their other capacities. Company and charity law may be applicable. This section first considers NHS trusts, and then examines the system of regulation specifically aimed at ensuring adequate standards of care in the independent sector (whether or not funded by the NHS).

(i) NHS trusts

The primary duties of NHS trusts are to assume responsibility for providing and managing services.[42] Each is established by statutory instrument, and under that instrument the obligations of the Secretary of State for Health to

---

[40] G. Wistow, M. Knapp, B. Hardy, J. Forder, R. Manning, and J. Kendall, *Social Care Markets: Progress and Prospects* (London: DoH, 1994), 8.

[41] *Ibid.*, 9.   [42] NHS and Community Care Act (NHSCCA) 1990, s. 5(1).

provide services under sections 3 and 5 of the NHS Act 1977 are delegated to the trust in general terms.Three statutory objectives are set for NHS trusts, and they are all financial. First, functions must be carried out 'effectively, efficiently and economically'.[43] This is widely interpreted in the NHS as requiring 'value for money'. Secondly, NHS trusts are duty bound to ensure that revenue covers outgoings taking one financial year with another.[44] Thirdly, 'it shall be the duty of every NHS Trust to achieve such financial objectives as may from time to time be set by the Secretary of State'.[45] Currently, this is to secure a fixed rate of return of 6 per cent on the Trust's assets.

NHS trusts are run by a chief executive, accountable to a board of directors and also to Parliament (as an 'accounting officer'). This board comprises a non-executive chair, and equal numbers of executive and non-executive directors. The functions of NHS trust boards are set out in the Code of Accountability, to which (along with the Code of Conduct) directors are expected to subscribe on appointment. These Codes apply to both NHS trusts and health authorities, and are discussed in the section on corporate governance later in this Chapter.

The configuration of these boards is defined by the NHS trusts (Membership and Procedure) Regulations.[46] Two of the four non-executive directors are appointed to represent the local community. All are appointed by the Secretary of State. The executive members must be the chief executive, chief finance office, the medical director, and the director of nursing (who may in fact be a nurse or a midwife). The chief executive is appointed by the chair and non-executive directors.[47] The other executive directors are appointed by chair, non-executives, and the chief executive.[48]

Variations to this model are provided for in two cases. Where a trust carries out a substantial teaching function, then an additional non-executive director will be appointed by the Secretary of State from the appropriate university.[49] The other variation applies where the trust does not provide services directly to patients, or where its principal function is to provide ambulance services. In these cases, there is no requirement for medical, nursing, or midwifery representation on the Board.[50]

NHS trusts are separate from health authorities, but still accountable to the Secretary of State through the NHS Executive. They are obliged to comply with directions from the Secretary of State on a range of issues, including various staffing issues, compliance with health service circulars, and disposal of

---

[43] NHSCCA 1990, Sch. 2, para. 6(1).   [44] NHSCCA 1990, s. 10(1).
[45] NHSCCA 1990, s. 10(2).   [46] SI 1990 No 2024.   [47] *Ibid.*, r. 17.
[48] *Ibid.*, r. 18.   [49] NHSCCA 1990, Sch. 2, para. 3(1)(d).
[50] SI 1990 No 2024, r. 4(2).

significant assets.[51] Subject to these control powers, NHS trusts have been given a number of freedoms beyond those permitted to the old directly managed units.[52]

They have the power to own and dispose of assets, including compulsory purchase with the consent of the Secretary of State.[53] This is intended to ensure that the most effective use is made of those assets. Trusts have to pay 'capital charges' on any assets they own, providing an incentive to hold only those assets that can be put to work. Where assets are sold, the proceeds can be used for other NHS purposes. NHS trusts also have the power to offer private health care or extra amenities for NHS patients who are prepared to pay for them[54] (although they may not charge for NHS care). These powers may not be exercised in any way that interferes with the ability of the trust to comply with directions from the Secretary of State, in any way which is *ultra vires* its establishment order or which significantly interferes with the performance of its obligations under any NHS contract.[55]

NHS trusts have the power to establish their own terms and conditions of employment. Previously, most NHS staff were employed on national terms and conditions, agreed through the Whitley Council machinery. Pay-bargaining was also carried out on a national basis. Now, the national pay settlements have incorporated an element of locally-negotiated pay (except in respect of medical staff). Further, staff on local NHS trusts' terms and conditions will have their pay determined by local negotiation. This 'trust freedom' has had less impact than was originally expected because staff transferring to NHS trusts had a statutory right to retain their previous terms of employment.[56] It has, therefore, been necessary for most trusts to provide improved pay and conditions before staff will voluntarily transfer to locally negotiated contracts. This has often not been affordable. In many trusts, only those staff appointed since trust status was conferred are actually on local terms and conditions. It should also be noted that the appointment of consultant medical and dental staff is regulated by statutory instrument and binding directions.[57]

NHS trusts also have the power to borrow money, within limits agreed annually with the relevant outpost of the NHSE (known as the 'external

[51] NHSCCA 1990, Sch. 2, para. 6(2).

[52] NHS Management Executive, *NHS Trusts: A Working Guide* (London: HMSO, 1990).

[53] NHSCCA 1990, Sch. 2 paras. 16(1), 26.

[54] NHSCCA 1990, Sch. 2 para. 14, 15. The latter provision gives NHS trusts the powers given to the Secretary of State by s. 7(2) of the Health and Medicines Act 1988.

[55] NHSCCA 1990, s. 5(9).   [56] *Ibid.*, s. 6.

[57] NHS (Appointment of Consultants) Regulations 1996, SI 1996 No 701; 'Direction— Appointment of Consultants to NHS Trusts', attached to HSG(96)24; NHSE, *NHS (Appointment of Consultants) Regulations 1996: Good Practice Guide* (London: DoH, 1996). See also B. Raymond, 'Employment Rights of the NHS Hospital Doctor' in C. Dyer (ed.), *Doctors, Patients and the Law* (Oxford: Blackwell Scientific, 1992).

financing limit'). They may also invest subject to Treasury approved guidelines.[58] This freedom has also produced less variation than might have been expected. The freedom to borrow money from private sources was initially curtailed by advice that government funding would almost always be cheaper. With the tightening of government expenditure in the Autumn of 1995, government funding for capital developments became severely reduced, with access to capital being barred until the possibility of funding through the Private Finance Initiative had been explored.

Despite these freedoms, NHS trusts may not, however, make 'profits' in any significant sense of that word. They may not spend money outside their statutory powers. There is no mechanism for distributing excess funds: no shareholders. Any profits that are made can be clawed back by the Secretary of State. Where a trust has built up reserves that are surplus to its foreseeable requirements, the Secretary of State may require that the funds are paid into the Consolidated Fund.[59]

NHS trusts cannot be created or dissolved without local consultation.[60] For the establishment of trusts, the consultation is to be with the local community health council. The Secretary of State may dissolve NHS trusts by statutory instrument on the application of the trust itself or if it is considered necessary in the interests of the health service.[61] Initially, the Secretary of State was given a discretion whether to transfer to himself or to another health service body the property, rights, and liabilities of a trust.[62] However, that concerned potential partners in private financial arrangements because it meant that they would have to bear the risk of a trust going bankrupt. Subsequently, legislation has made it obligatory for the liabilities of a dissolved NHS trust to be accepted by the NHS.[63] Where the Secretary of State plans to dissolve one NHS trust and transfer its property, rights, liabilities, and staff to another NHS trust, then staff representatives must be consulted in addition to the relevant community health council. Ordinarily, dissolution without such a transfer requires consultation only with the community health council. The statute also provides for dissolution without consultation where this is necessary as a matter of urgency.[64]

(ii) Independent Sector

There are no formal legal restrictions on the people and bodies with whom health and social care purchasers may contract. However, in relation to local

---

[58] NHSCCA 1990, Sch. 3.

[59] *Ibid.*, Sch. 3, para. 6.

[60] *Ibid.*, s. 5(2), Sch. 2 para. 29; NHS Trusts (Consultation on Establishment and Dissolution) Regulations 1996, SI 1996 No 653.

[61] *Ibid.*, Sch. 2, pt IV.

[62] *Ibid.*, Sch. 2, para. 30(1).

[63] NHS (Residual Liabilities) Act 1996.

[64] NHSCCA 1990, Sch. 2, para. 29(3).

authorities, funding has been earmarked for community care with the proviso that 85 per cent of it must be spent outside social services departments, and purchasers have been exhorted to encourage competition by stimulating the independent sector. European competition rules may also require purchasers to ensure that organizations across the Member States of the EC are able to compete for some contracts (see below). These rules relate to the contracting process, which itself provides the scope for some form of quality control. In addition, however, there is a licensing system to regulate independent health providers. This applies even when they are not using public funds.

Residential care homes and nursing homes must be registered under the Registered Homes Act 1984, and are subject to inspection by local authorities and health authorities respectively. Children's homes are governed by a similar system under the Children Act 1989. This section considers those regimes. Some independent providers of health and social care will also be charities, and as such fall within the jurisdiction of the Charity Commissioners. That area of law is not considered here.[65]

The Registered Homes Act 1984 draws a distinction between residential care homes, which fall within Part I of the Act, and nursing and mental nursing homes, which are regulated under Part II. A residential care home is an establishment which provides accommodation with board and personal care for people in need of the latter because of old age, disablement, dependence on alcohol or drugs, or mental disorder. It is not relevant whether that accommodation is provided for reward.[66] Personal care is defined in section 20(1) as including assistance with bodily functions, but also 'embraces care in many forms, emotional or psychiatric as well as physical'.[67] By implication, personal care requires less professional expertise than nursing care, which takes homes into a different category, where they are regulated by health authorities rather than local authorities.[68]

Nursing homes are defined by reference to activities that are carried out in the premises.[69] A general definition is provided that nursing homes are premises that provide 'nursing' (which is not further defined by the statute) for persons who are sick, infirm, or injured. A category of maternity home is also recognized for premises that receive women who are pregnant, or who have recently given birth. Premises that are used for the termination of pregnancy,[70]

---

[65] For discussion of particular issues in relation to voluntary hospitals, see J. Finch, *Speller's Law Relating to Hospitals* (7th edn., London: Chapman & Hall, 1994), ch. 3.

[66] Registered Homes Act 1984, s. 1(1).   [67] *Harrison* v. *Cornwall CC* (1991) 90 LGR 81, 97.

[68] NHS (Functions of Health Authorities and Administration Arrangements) Regulations 1996, SI 1996 No 708.

[69] S. 21.

[70] Such premises will need to be approved under the Abortion Act 1967, s. 1(3), as well as registered under the 1984 Act.

dialysis, surgery under anæsthetic, and endoscopy will also be nursing homes within the Act. There is provision for the Secretary of State to specify other types of treatment as bringing an establishment within the definition of a nursing home.[71] This has been done in respect of surgery, including cosmetic surgery, involving class 3B and 4 laser products.[72] Mental nursing homes do not fall within the general definition of nursing homes. They are places used for the nursing and medical treatment (including rehabilitation) of mentally disordered people.[73] In all three categories of home, NHS hospitals are excluded from the definitions.

Although the details differ between the categories of homes, the main features of the Registered Homes Act framework are common. Evading the registration system is prohibited. It is an offence to carry on a residential or nursing home without the appropriate registration.[74] In relation to nursing homes, mental nursing homes, and maternity homes, it is also an offence to hold out unregistered premises as being establishments of those types.[75] All residential care homes must be registered with the relevant local authority, although those with fewer than four clients need provide less detailed information.[76] All nursing and mental nursing homes must be registered with the local health authority. They will need dual registration unless they operate solely as nursing homes with no clients receiving merely personal care.[77]

The statute sets out the grounds on which registration may be refused. For residential homes, these are that the people concerned with carrying on the home are unfit to do so, the premises are not fit for the purpose (including matters relating to staffing and equipment), or that the services or facilities that would be provided are not reasonably required.[78] For nursing and mental nursing homes the list is longer. Registration may be refused if the applicant or proposed employees are unfit to carry on or work in a nursing home. It may also be refused if the home will not be in the charge of a registered nurse, doctor, or (in the case of maternity homes) midwife. The health authority may require specified numbers of qualified staff before registration will be granted. Registration may again be refused if the premises are not fit for the purpose (including matters relating to staffing and equipment), and they be may be made unfit by being put to improper or undesirable uses.[79] This enables homes adopting unsatisfactory treatment regimes to be refused registration.

The registration of a home may be subject to conditions as to the numbers of clients to be accommodated and their age, sex, or category.[80] It seems that

---

[71] S. 21(4).

[72] Nursing Homes and Mental Nursing Homes Regulations 1984, SI 1984 No 1578, r. 3. The classes of laser products are specified in BS4803:83.

[73] S. 22.   [74] Ss. 2, 23(1).   [75] S. 24.   [76] S. 1(4)–(4B).   [77] S. 23(2).

[78] S. 9.   [79] S. 25.   [80] Ss. 5, 29.

these are the only types of condition that may be imposed,[81] but there are no statutory criteria governing their use.[82] Registration may be cancelled by the relevant authority after an opportunity has been given for representations to be made.[83] If an urgent necessity arises, the authority may apply to a magistrate, who may cancel a registration forthwith if there would be a serious risk to the life, health, or well-being of the patients in the home if the order for immediate cancellation was not made.[84] The basis of a decision to cancel a registration, whether made on application to a magistrate or through the usual procedure, must be the factors that would justify refusal of an initial application.[85] An appeal can be made against a refusal of registration or the cancellation of a registration, including those by magistrates, to the Registered Homes Tribunal.[86]

The Registered Homes Act does not rely solely on the fact that a home is registered to ensure that standards are satisfactory. Regulations made under the Act set out the facilities and services that should be provided.[87] Two codes of practice have also been produced, giving guidance that is not binding, but which is used by inspectors and by the Registered Homes Tribunal as an indication of the standards to be expected.[88] The registration authorities can inspect at any time premises, and their records, that are, or are reasonably believed to be, being used as a residential or nursing.[89] They should do so at least twice a year, and for residential care homes at least one of the visits should be unannounced.[90]

A further regulatory system in relation to providers of care independent of the public sector exists in relation to children's homes under the Children Act 1989.[91] This system is not designed to deal with health care; rather it concerns more broadly the accommodation of children away from home. Where health care is provided, the home will need to be registered under the Registered Homes Act 1984, not the Children Act. However, the Children Act requires such homes to notify the local authority if they accommodate a person under

---

[81] *Warwickshire CC* v. *McSweeney*, unreported, 8 Dec. 1988.
[82] *Isle of Wight CC* v. *Humphreys* (1991) 90 LGR 168.   [83] Ss. 12–13, 31–32.
[84] Ss. 11, 30; *Hillingdon LBC* v. *McLean* (1989) 88 LGR 49.
[85] S. 9–10, 25, 28; *Lyons* v. *E. Sussex CC* (1988) 86 LGR 369.
[86] Ss. 15, 34 and Pt. III of the Act; Registered Homes Tribunals Rules 1984, SI 1984 No 1346.
[87] Nursing Homes and Mental Nursing Homes Regulations 1984, SI 1984 No 1578, r. 12; Residential Care Homes Regulations 1984, SI 1984, No 1345, r. 10.
[88] *Home Life: A Code of Practice for Residential Care* (1984), *Registration and Inspection of Nursing Homes* (1984, supp. 1988).
[89] Ss. 17, 35.
[90] Nursing Homes and Mental Nursing Homes Regulations 1984, SI 1984 No 1578, r. 11; Residential Care Homes Regulations 1984, SI 1984, No 1345, r. 18.
[91] Children Act 1989, Pts. VI–VIII and the regulations and guidance issued under it. See R. White, P. Carr, and N. Lowe, *Clarke Hall and Morrison on Children* (London: Butterworths, looseleaf), Div. 1, ch. 17.

the age of 18 for three months or more, of if they envisage doing so.[92] A similar provision applies in relation to NHS facilities.[93]

D. Corporate Governance in the NHS

It has been seen that the NHS is largely managed by NHS boards. The main responsibilities of these boards are set out in the Code of Accountability for NHS Boards. They are to set the strategic direction of the organization for which they are responsible, within the overall policies and priorities of the Government and NHS, by defining its objectives, agreeing plans to achieve them, and monitoring performance. Boards must also ensure effective financial stewardship through value for money, financial control, and planning. They must also ensure that high standards of corporate governance and personal behaviour are maintained. Finally, they must ensure that there is effective dialogue with the local community, so that the organization's plans and performance are responsive to that community's needs.

NHS boards thus play a pivotal role in the NHS market structure. Their members are largely appointed by the Secretary of State, concentrating a lot of power in his hands, and leading to accusations of political patronage.[94] Broader concern about the need to ensure high standards of probity in public life led to the establishment of the Nolan Committee on Standards in Public Life. In the NHS, concern had already been raised about the quality of financial control as a result of a number of well-publicized scandals arising under the pre-market system. The response was to establish a task force on corporate governance, whose report was circulated in January 1994.[95] The combination of internal NHS developments and the response to broader initiatives on open government and probity in public office has been the creation of new appointments procedures for non-executive members of NHS bodies and the publication of three Codes to establish standards of corporate governance.[96] The three codes are the Code of Conduct for NHS Boards, the Code of Accountability for NHS Boards, and the Code of Practice on Openness in

---

[92] Children Act 1989, s. 86(1).

[93] *Ibid.*, s. 85(1).

[94] See e.g. S. Weir and W. Hall, *Ego Trip: Extra-governmental Organisation in the United Kingdom and their Accountability* (London: Charter 88 Trust, 1994).

[95] *Public Enterprise Governance in the NHS: Report of the Corporate Governance Task Force* (1993).

[96] These developments are discussed in A. Belcher, 'Codes of Conduct and Accountability for NHS Boards' [1995] *Public Law* 288–97.

the NHS. The former two were published together in April 1994.[97] The latter was published in April 1995.[98]

All board members are required on appointment to subscribe to the Code of Conduct. It begins by setting out three public-sector values that are expected to underpin the workings of NHS boards. These are accountability, probity, and openness. Accountability requires actions to stand the tests of parliamentary scrutiny, of public opinion on propriety, and of professional codes of conduct. Probity implies an absolute standard of honesty in dealing with NHS assets, decisions affecting patients, staff, and suppliers and in the use of information acquired during NHS work. The commitment to openness means that the confidence of staff, patients, and the public should be promoted by transparency in the way activities are pursued. Although not mentioned as one of the three key principles, it can be suggested that achieving value for money is given as much (if not more) prominence in the body of the Code. High ethical standards are also mentioned, including the highest professional standards in relation to accounting, tendering, and employment practice. NHS board members are expected to lead by example.

One commentator has suggested that, unlike its private sector equivalent, corporate governance in the NHS relies on the attitudes of personnel rather than systems to identify and correct abuse.[99] However, the Code of Accountability does require a number of such systems to be established. NHS boards should establish audit and remuneration committees, which report to the full board. The latter committee, consisting of non-executives, should appoint, appraise, and determine the pay of the chief executive. For the other executive board members, the remuneration committee should sit with the chief executive.[100] The remit of audit committees is to review financial systems, the robustness of financial information within the organization, and compliance with the law, guidance, and codes of conduct.[101] NHS bodies are also subject to the jurisdiction of the Audit Commission (see Chapter 3). Detailed guidance is also issued by the NHSE on a range of areas of financial control.

A register of interests, available to the public, must also be maintained. Board members are required to declare any business interests, positions of authority in charities or voluntary bodies in the field of health and social care,

---

[97] See also NHSE, *Codes of Conduct and Accountability: Guidance* (Leeds: 1994), issued with EL(94)40.

[98] See also NHSE, *Guidance on Implementation of Code of Practice on Openness in the NHS* (Leeds: May 1995).

[99] N. 96 above.

[100] Strictly, the legal requirements extend only to NHS trusts, and deal only with appointment, not appraisal and remuneration: see NHS Trusts (Membership and Procedure) Regulations 1991, SI 1991 No 2024, rr. 16, 17. The Code of Accountability spells out the additional responsibilities.

[101] N. 97 above, Sect. A.

and any connection with a body contracting for NHS services. The law specifically renders certain potential conflicts of interest and unsatisfactory past connections bars on appointment. Health authority members may not hold paid appointments with other authorities, and may not be directors of an NHS Trust. They may not hold paid appointments with a health service trade union. They are disqualified if they have been bankrupt, been dismissed (other than for redundancy) by a health service employer, suspended or removed from the list of general practitioners, or been sentenced to three months' or more imprisonment within the previous five years.[102] Similar disqualifications exist in relation to non-executive directors of NHS trusts, where there is a complete bar on the appointment of chairmen, members, directors, and employees of health service bodies.[103] Board members are required to disclose any financial interests in matters being discussed and should usually take no part in the discussions. Exceptions to the bar on participating exist where the financial interest is insignificant or the Secretary of State removes the disability.[104]

Steps have also been taken to make the system for the appointment of non-executive members to health authorities and NHS trust boards more transparent.[105] The existence of such posts will normally be advertised. Candidates are 'sifted' by a panel of at least three existing chairmen or non-executives, sometimes including also an independent member, such as a magistrate, someone from the local community health council, a voluntary agency, or a local employer. A general 'person specification' has been drawn up, identifying the need for appointees to be 'good communicators with plenty of common sense' and being able to meet most, but not necessarily all, of a list of requirements. That list comprises keen interest in health care, commitment to the public-sector values set out in the Codes for NHS boards, understanding of top management in large commercial or public-sector organizations, specialist skills (such as finance, law, public relations), experience of work with voluntary organizations (especially if associated with the NHS), the confidence to question and challenge other directors without damaging team relationships, and an ability to analyse complex problems. Appointees should live and work in the area served by the NHS body, be available for about three days a month and usually would not be aged in their late 60s or more. Candidates over 70 would only be appointed in exceptional circumstances. The Secretary

---

[102] Health Authorities (Membership and Procedure) Regulations 1996, n. 24 above, r. 10.

[103] NHS Trusts (Membership and Procedure) Regulations 1991, n. 46 above, r. 11.

[104] Health Authorities (Membership and Procedure) Regulations 1996, n. 24 above, r. 16; NHS Trusts (Membership and Procedure) Regulations 1991, n. 46 above, r. 20.

[105] DoH/NHSE, *The Appointment of Chairmen and Non-executive Directors to NHS Authorities and Trusts* (Leeds: 1995).

of State may terminate appointments if it is thought that it is not in the interests of the health service that the person continue in post.[106]

Concerns have also been expressed about the accountability of NHS bodies to the public. Awareness of the decisions taken by health authorities is promoted by the fact their meetings are open to the public under the Public Bodies (Admission to Meetings) Act 1960. When the public is admitted, the press must also be permitted to observe the proceedings.[107] The Act applies to health authorities, including special health authorities if the order establishing the authority so specifies.[108] The Act also applies to committees of health authorities.[109] Where meetings are to be held in public under the Act, at least three days' public notice must be given of the time and venue (unless the meeting is convened at short notice, in which case the details must be made public when it is convened). Agendas must also be supplied on request, and supporting papers may (but need not) be made available if the authority thinks fit.[110] Where an auditor's report is being considered, it must be supplied to the press.[111] An authority can pass a resolution excluding the public where publicity would be prejudicial to the public interest because of the confidentiality, or other special nature, of the business.[112] This would cover personnel issues relating to individual staff, and matters relating to the breaches of terms of service by general practitioners are specifically excluded from being discussed in public session.[113] There is also a power to hold meetings in private, and expel the public or particular members of the public in order to maintain order.[114]

Unlike health authorities, NHS trusts are not obliged to hold board meetings in public. Nor do community health councils have rights to be present. NHS trusts need hold only one annual public meeting before the end of September, to present accounts, although many in fact hold more.[115] However, if they receive the report of an extraordinary audit under section 15(3) of the Local Government Finance Act 1982 they must hold a public meeting to present it.[116]

It has also been noted that the direct accountability of individual members of NHS boards is less stringent than that of local councillors. Unlike the

[106] Health Authorities (Membership and Procedure) Regulations 1996, n. 24 above, r. 8(4); NHS Trusts (Membership and Procedure) Regulations 1991, n. 46 above, r. 9(3).

[107] S. 1(4)(c), (7).   [108] Sched., para. 1(g) to the 1960 Act as amended.

[109] S. 1(6).   [110] S. 1(4).   [111] Local Government Act 1972, s. 160(2).

[112] S. 1(2), (3).

[113] Sched., para. 1(f) to the 1960 Act as amended.

[114] S. 1(8); *R. v. Brent HA, ex p. Francis* [1985] 1 All ER 74.

[115] NHSCCA 1990, Sch. 2 para. 7(2); NHS Trusts (Public Meetings) Regulations 1991, SI 1991 No 482, r. 2.

[116] NHSCCA 1990, Sch. 2, para. 7(3); NHS Trusts (Public Meetings) Regulations 1991, n. 115 above, r. 3.

latter, members of the NHS boards are protected from individual liability for their actions in that capacity provided that they were done in good faith.[117]

The Code of Practice on Openness in the NHS is aimed to go some way towards reducing this 'democratic deficit'. The Code identifies a range of information that must be made available by NHS bodies. It does not create any new obligations, but reinforces existing requirements. Information that must be made available to the public includes annual reports, audited accounts, five-year strategy documents, annual purchasing plans, annual business plans (for NHS trusts), registers of interests, contracts for the provision of services. The Code also identifies other information that it is good practice to provide to the public. It suggests that, as a general principle, the NHS should respond positively, quickly, and helpfully to requests for information. However, the Code notes that information may be withheld on a number of grounds. Confidentiality usually precludes disclosure of personal information. Information about internal discussion will not be revealed, because it would hinder frank debate. Matters that are commercially sensitive need not be made public (other than internal NHS contracts). NHS bodies may also refuse requests for information that 'are manifestly unreasonable, far too general or would require unreasonable resources to answer'.[118]

E. Contracting for Services

As yet, NHS contracting has not given rise to much litigation. That which has occurred has been primarily concerned with the allocation of resources in ways that leave some patients, or potential patients, with grievances. These actions have mostly been brought without reference to the contracting issues and were discussed in Chapter 3. This section reviews the extent to which the law provides limits on the powers of purchasers. It also explains the different legal categories of contract for NHS services, and examines issues relating to enforcement.

(i) Constraints on Purchasing

As public bodies exercising statutory powers, NHS purchasers are subject to a number of general public law constraints on purchasing policy.[119] The deci-

---

[117] NHS Act 1977, s. 125, applying the immunities set out in the Public Health Act 1875, s. 265.
[118] Para. 9.
[119] General studies of public bodies as contracting agents can be found in C. Turpin, *Government Procurement and Contracts* (2nd edn., Harlow: Longman, 1989) and S. Arrowsmith, *Civil Liability*

sions of public bodies must not be unreasonable. That is, they must be decisions that could be reached by a reasonable NHS purchaser, allowing for the possibility that there could be a divergence of reasonable views. The application of this doctrine in relation to resource allocation was explored in Chapter 3. There is also a legal prohibition on the adoption of rigid of policies, because they prevent the exercise of the discretion that is at the heart of the statutory duties. This may give rise to difficulties in respect of certain types of purchasing decision. If there is no scope for certain individuals to be treated at all, it might fall foul of the rule against fettering discretion. Publicly discussed examples of this would be access to bypass surgery for smokers and provision of infertility services. It is probably acceptable to restrict the use of certain types of treatment, but not to exclude completely whole categories of individuals or conditions from services.

It is also probably necessary to make provision for some flexibility in exceptional cases. In *R. v. Ethical Committee of St Mary's Hospital (Manchester), ex p. Harriott*,[120] the court highlighted the need to give patients a chance to explain why they should receive treatment, and to be told why they are being denied it. These are merely procedural requirements, and there is nothing to prevent the decision to refuse treatment being confirmed after patients have had their say. However, proper procedures are important, because it may often be possible to influence decisions if you are allowed to explain your case. This area was explored in *R. v. Cambridge DHA, ex p. B.*[121] It was alleged that the wishes of the patient, as represented by her parents (the girl herself had not been told how ill she was and had therefore no views to present), had been disregarded. The Court of Appeal accepted that this was a relevant factor. However, unlike the trial judge, the Court of Appeal accepted that the girl's position had been fully considered. It was not necessary for the girl's parents to be able to address the decision-makers directly, provided that their views were properly considered. They accepted that this had happened even though the Health Authority had a policy not to correspond directly with patients, preferring to deal with the clinicians responsible for their care.

The *Cambridge* case also illustrates the need for public bodies to take decisions on appropriate criteria. Decisions based on improper considerations, or which fail to take into account relevant considerations, will be regarded by the courts as improperly made.[122] Purchasing that was not based on appropriate professional advice, or was influenced by political factors rather than the need

---

and Public Authorities (Winteringham: Earlsgate Press, 1992). See also P. Vincent-Jones, 'The Limits of Contractual Order in Public Sector Transacting' (1994) 14 *Legal Studies* 364–92 and M. Freedland, 'Government by Contract and Public Law' [1994] *Public Law* 86–104.

120 [1988] 1 FLR 512.   121 [1995] 2 All ER 129.

122 See P. Craig, *Administrative Law* (3rd edn., London: Sweet & Maxwell, 1994), 407–9.

to secure the best services for patients, might be challenged on this basis. However, the efficacy of treatment is clearly a proper consideration.[123] National guidance on purchasing priorities would probably be a consideration that should not be ignored.[124] There is no indication whether age would be seen as an acceptable criterion for prioritization (in the absence of age-linked variation in effectiveness). Nor is it clear whether a purchasing body could properly take into account the extent to which a patient had already received services (for example to limit the number of specific procedures that would be performed on a single patient) or the cause of the medical condition. Discrimination on the basis of some factors, such as sex and race, is prohibited by law. These factors would need to be ignored in purchasing decisions.[125]

The prohibition on the fettering of discretion may provide an obstacle to long-term planning and investment, as it provides a limit to the extent to which purchasers can commit themselves to long-term contracts, or to place contracts with particular providers in the future. It is not open to public authorities to develop a policy that precludes them considering new situations on their own merits.[126] In some circumstances, long-term commitments may constitute a fetter on the future exercise of discretion if they prevent the purchaser considering changes in the needs of the local population. Contracting is the manner in which discretion is exercised, but it may also prevent future exercises of discretion. A contract which unlawfully fetters the discretion of a purchaser is *ultra vires* and invalid.

There are, however, examples of long-term contracts being accepted by the courts provided that they are made in the exercise of the statutory powers of the authority, not as part of a collateral arrangement.[127] Whether a long-term commitment constitutes an improper fetter on the purchaser's discretion will depend partly upon the interpretation of the statutory duties outlined in Chapter 3. If it is incompatible with exercising those duties in the future it will be void, but if the long-term arrangement was honestly and reasonably made in order to carry out those duties it will probably be valid.[128] A long-term arrangement for joint funding of a leisure complex has been accepted as valid

---

[123] *R.* v. *Sheffield HA, ex p. Seale,* unreported, 17 Oct. 1994.

[124] In *R.* v. *Cambridge DHA, ex p. B* [1995] 2 All ER 129 the health authority argued that it was following national guidance on the purchase of experimental treatment. However, it never produced that guidance and the court therefore disregarded the point.

[125] This is discussed in Ch. 3.

[126] *Stringer* v. *Ministry of Housing and Local Government* [1971] 1 All ER 65.

[127] See *Ayr Harbour Trustees* v. *Oswald* (1883) 8 App. Cas. 623, and *York Corporation* v. *Henry Leetham & Sons Ltd* [1924] 1 Ch. 557 as interpreted in *Dowty Boulton Paul Ltd* v. *Wolverhampton Corporation* [1971] 2 All ER 277.

[128] *R.* v. *Hammersmith and Fulham LBC, ex p. Beddowes* [1987] 1 All ER 369.

in a local authority case[129] (although the question whether it constituted an unlawful fetter on discretion was not faced directly). There is no relevant case law on the NHS duties.

This constraint on contracting is particularly significant in relation to the drive to secure private-sector finance, where some sort of assurance that there will be a secure stream of income is probably vital. In *Public Service, Private Finance—Putting Private Capital to Work for the NHS* the examples offered of successful joint financed projects include a ten-year contract.[130] However, if health authorities are not permitted to prevent themselves exercising their discretion in the future, it is not possible for them to guarantee that they will commit future years' revenue expenditure to services not yet in existence. They can offer an indication of their position, but cannot bind themselves to it.

Some force may be given to their promises, through the doctrine of 'legitimate expectations', which prevents public bodies unfairly altering their policies to the detriment of those who have relied upon the bodies, being consistent with their previous conduct.[131] This doctrine provides a constraint on at least the manner in which decisions to shift resources are made, and arguably may even generate substantive restraints.[132] Where providers have been given a legitimate expectation that they will receive revenue, then it may not be removed without the provision of an explanation (which could give rise to a challenge if it is unreasonable) and an opportunity to make representations to the authority. There are some indications that the doctrine might sometimes be used to prevent public authorities reneging on their promises, but this seems unlikely in the NHS context because of the need to preserve discretion.[133]

It is also important to note that there are sometimes specific procedural requirements placed on decision-making. Where substantial developments of services are proposed, the relevant Community Health Councils must be consulted.[134] Before an NHS Trust can be dissolved, the local Community Health Council and staff representatives must be consulted unless the case is urgent.[135] Where the statutory consultation procedures have not been followed, the courts can strike down the decision, forcing the Authority to act properly. However, this remedy may be of limited effect. In one case, the court

---

[129] *Islwyn BC and Gwent CC* v. *Newport BC* (1994) 158 LGR 501. [130] EL(93)101.

[131] See S. Arrowsmith, 'Protecting the Interests of Bidders for Public Contracts: The Role of the Common Law' (1994) 53 *CLJ* 104–39.

[132] R. Baldwin, and D. Horne, 'Expectations in a Joyless Landscape' (1986) 49 *MLR* 685–711.

[133] The principles are discussed in Craig, n. 122 above, 394–6, 672–5.

[134] Community Health Councils Regulations 1996, SI 1996 No 640, r. 18.

[135] National Health Service Trusts (Consultation on Establishment and Dissolution) Regulations 1996, n. 60 above.

declined to intervene because it though it would not bring any practical bene-fit. The unit in questions had already been relocated, and it was too late to require the proper consultation to be carried out.[136]

Under the European Community Services Directive,[137] public-service con-tracts are subject to procedural requirements designed to ensure proper com-petition for them. The Directive is implemented by the Public Service Contracts Regulations 1993.[138] Health service bodies are bound by these pro-visions. However, contracts for health services, like those for social services, are subject to the less onerous 'restricted procedure'. This requires that the European Commission be notified of contracts once awarded, but not before. Advertising of tenders is not necessary under the restricted procedure. Contracts offered by NHS bodies that do not come within this area, such as those for the construction of hospitals, will need to be offered for tender more widely.[139]

(ii) Types of Contract

The NHS market uses a variety of contractual mechanisms. Some are con-tracts in the usual sense, and enforceable in the courts. Others are unusual contracts, in that they are not freely negotiated by the parties, and incorporate special mechanisms for dealing with breaches of the terms. Others are not really contracts at all, but rather a newly created legal hybrid: the 'NHS contract'. It has been argued that there is more rhetoric than reality in this contractual analogy.[140] This section explains these different forms of arrange-ment; the following section considers the arrangements for enforcement of contracts between NHS bodies.

Primary care is secured by a statutory 'contract' between health authorities and general practitioners. Its terms are negotiated nationally with representa-tives of the profession and then enshrined in a statutory instrument (see Chapter 3 for discussion of those terms). Where agreement is not forthcom-ing, the government can use its legislative power to impose a contract. Many of the main terms of the current contract were imposed in this way in 1989, although amendments have been since made with a greater degree of consen-sus. General practitioners offer services under those terms as independent contractors. However, those contracts are not identical to contracts struck in private sector markets. Enforcement by health authorities takes place through

---

[136] *R. v. NW Thames RHA, ex p. Daniels* [1993] 4 Med. LR 364.
[137] 92/50/EEC [1992] OJ L209/1.   [138] SI 1993 No 3228.
[139] For an outline, see Craig, n. 122 above, 685–9.
[140] D. Hughes and R. Dingwall, 'Sir Henry Maine, Joseph Stalin and the reorganisation of the National Health Service' [1990] *JSWL* 296; D. Hughes, 'The Reorganisation of the National Health Service: The Rhetoric and Reality of the Internal Market' (1991) 54 *MLR* 88.

NHS Discipline Committees rather than the courts (see below). However, the GP contract also gives rise to private law rights, and doctors can bring actions for breach of contract if payment is wrongly withheld.[141]

The nature of contracts made by health authorities for hospital and community services will depend upon the nature of the contracting parties. Where a contract has been made between a health authority and a private sector body, the general law of contract will apply. The obligations of both sides to the arrangement will be fixed by its terms. Should there be a breach, then a legal action could be brought which, if successful, would usually result in damages being paid equivalent to the financial loss caused by the breach. In some circumstances, specific performance could be ordered, but this would only be where financial remedies were unable to compensate for the loss caused.

Arrangements between two health service bodies, including NHS trusts, will be governed by the new hybrid concept, the 'NHS contract' which was created by section 4 of the 1990 Act. NHS contracts are only contracts in a loose sense. Their terms are not created in the free manner in which most private contracts are supposed to be made. Their shape is largely determined by central planning, and the availability of a realistic choice between providers will often be limited. Most importantly, however, NHS bodies are not free to walk away from bargains that they do not find acceptable, because the Secretary of State has the power to impose terms upon them.

The Act provides for referrals to the Secretary of State for the determination of disputes, and that such referrals can be made where the terms of a proposed contract seem to one of the bodies to be unfair by reason of the other taking advantage of an unequal bargaining position.[142] The parties are bound to accept the directions of the Secretary of State as to the resolution of the dispute.[143] This makes the NHS contracting process radically different from a private-sector market because it ensures that the interests of the service as a whole can be protected, even when the market fails to respect them. In practice this degree of control is not exercised at the level of formal arbitration, but through non-statutory conciliation at a regional level. As this process is not governed by the regulations, there is considerable variation in its operation across England and Wales.[144]

---

[141] *Roy* v. *Kensington and Chelsea FPC* [1992] 1 All ER 705 (HL).   [142] S. 4(4).

[143] S. 4(6),(7).

[144] See I. Harden and D. Longley, 'NHS Contracts' in J. Birds, R. Bradgate, and C. Villiers, *Termination of Contracts* (Chichester: Chancery Law Publishing, 1995); D. Hughes, J. McHale, and L. Griffiths, 'Settling Contract Disputes in the NHS: Formal and Informal Pathways' in R. Flynn and G. Williams, *Contracting for Health: Quasi-markets and the NHS* (Oxford: Oxford University Press, 1996, forthcoming).

In fact, the significance of the contract form may be overplayed. The relationship between parties to an NHS contract will often be governed by considerations other than the words used in the contract. Studies of commercial practice where, as in health services, the parties hope to sustain their relationship over a long period suggest that the exact terms of contracts become less important than informal practices.[145] The nature of health services is such that precision in quality measures is difficult, and building up a relationship of trust between the parties may be as important as the drafting of terms.[146] In general, as we shall see below, there has been little use of arbitration in either the formation of contracts or their enforcement.

It also important to note two further types of arrangement under which care is provided by an NHS trust and payment sought from health purchasers. The first is really a variation of the position just described. It is known as the 'extra contractual referral' (ECR). This term is misleading, because there will in fact be a contract. However, it will be a contract agreed in relation to a particular patient, possibly at any time during the year. The more common form of contract is one negotiated for the provision of services over a period (usually a financial year) in relation to a group of patients, to be provided as and when they require them. Where an ECR is refused, the connection between the purchaser's decision and an individual who is affected by it is much more direct. In contrast to the dearth of material in relation to the main contracting process, there have been challenges to refusals to fund ECRs in the courts,[147] through non-statutory arbitration,[148] and with the Health Service Commissioner.[149]

Finally, the 1990 Act provides for reimbursement for NHS trusts which have cared for patients when no contract existed. This provision only applies where the patient needs the services and, having regard to her or his condition, it is not practicable to enter into a contract before providing the treatment. In those circumstances, the NHS trust can treat the patient and then claim remuneration from the health authority whose function it was to purchase care for the patient.[150]

---

[145] Hughes, n. 140 above, 299–304.

[146] P. Allen, 'Contracts in the NHS Internal Market' (1995) 58 *MLR* 321–42 found that the contracts she studied were imprecise on these points.

[147] *R. v. Cambridge HA, ex p. B*, n. 124 above.

[148] M. Forsythe, 'Arbitration and the Internal Market' (1994) 308 *BMJ* 151–2; E. Scott and R. Stokoe, 'Challenging Professional Opinion: The Use of Independent Arbitration' (1994) 308 *BMJ* 177–8.

[149] HSC, *Annual Report for 1993–4*, HC Paper 1993–4, 499, para. 3.3, 3.8, App. E.

[150] NHSCCA 1990, Sch. 2, para. 19.

(iii) Enforcement of 'NHS Contracts'

A further respect in which the contract terminology is misleading is in relation to enforcement. Section 4(3) of the 1990 Act provides that NHS contracts
'shall not be regarded for any purpose as giving rise to contractual rights or
liabilities'. This precludes the use of the courts to enforce them in the usual
way. Instead, the statute provides for a statutory arbitration procedure. This
has already been noted in relation to cases where contracts cannot be agreed.
It also applies where a breach of contract is alleged.[151] Arbitration is binding,
and the parties are bound to accept the directions of the Secretary of State as
to the resolution of the dispute.[152] Resolution may be by way of variation of
the terms or termination of the agreement.[153] The Secretary of State provides,
by regulations, for the appointment of persons to consider such disputes.[154]

In addition to this statutory arbitration, which was used only once in the
whole of England and Wales during the first five years of the market, there is
a non-statutory system for conciliation and arbitration through the Regional
Health Authorities.[155] Guidance from the NHSME advises that this should be
achieved by including in contracts terms agreeing informal arbitration.[156]
This could use private arbitrators, but the initial recommendation was to use
regional general managers. The terms of arbitration agreements are for the
parties to decide.[157]

The principles to be applied by arbitrators are not specified by the law.[158]
The guidance from the NHSME states that the presumption is that the aim is
to give effect to the agreement made, not to substitute a different contract that
the parties should have made.[159] However, the statute clearly establishes the
right of the arbitrator to impose new contract terms.[160] The scheme also
envisages that the Secretary of State may make representations to the arbitrator even though he is not a party.[161] This could be taken to suggest that general service issues may be relevant, as well as contract terms. Under the legal
arbitration scheme, the adjudicator is obliged to give written reasons for the
determination.[162] It was anticipated that this would lead to principles being

---

[151] S. 4(3).   [152] S. 4(6),(7).   [153] S. 4(8).

[154] S. 4(5); National Health Service Contracts (Dispute Resolution) Regulations 1996, SI 1996 No
623.

[155] Department of Health, *Contracts for Health Services: Operating Contracts* (London: HMSO,
1989), para. 4.33.

[156] 'NHS Contracts: Guidance on Resolving Disputes' EL(91)11.

[157] D. Longley, *Public Law and Health Service Accountability* (Buckingham: Open University
Press, 1993).

[158] See D. Hughes, J. McHale, and L. Griffiths, n. 144 above, for discussion of the range of understandings within the NHS of how the system should work.

[159] Para 9.   [160] NHSCCA 1990, s. 4(8).

[161] NHS Contracts (Dispute Resolution) Regulations 1996, SI 1996 No 623, r. 2.

[162] NHS Contracts (Dispute Resolution) Regulations 1996, SI 1996 No 623, r. 3.

established through the practice of arbitrators, which it would then become irrational and unfair to depart from,[163] but the limited use made of the system has so far prevented this happening.

The fact that NHS contracts do not give rise to liability under the law of contract does not necessarily mean that they are devoid of legal significance. It has been suggested that liability might arise under restitutionary principles.[164] Under this doctrine, services which are provided at the request of one party must be paid for, once rendered, even if no legally binding contract has been created.[165] However, it seems highly unlikely that the courts would permit the use of restitution to evade the statutory policy that the courts should be excluded.[166] However, the terms of NHS contracts may well be relevant in determining whether there is liability for failures to provide adequate services. The extent of duties in tort to provide services will be affected by the terms of the contract and failure to deliver them properly could be the subject of a negligence action. This is discussed in Chapter 7.

Contracting also falls within the jurisdiction of the Health Service Commissioner. Although commercial matters are generally excluded from his remit, matters arising from arrangements between NHS authorities and outside bodies for the provision of services are explicitly within the Commissioner's jurisdiction. Contracts between NHS bodies may be investigated provided that they are not deemed to be 'contractual or other commercial transactions'. As NHS contracts do not give rise to contractual liability, they do not fall within this exclusion. The Commissioner may be brought in by the relevant health bodies, or by patients who can show that they have suffered injustice or hardship as a result of maladministration in the negotiation or implementation of a contract. The Commissioner has a discretion to refuse to investigate matters referred to him (see Chapter 5), and it is probable that he will choose to steer clear of substantive disputes about arrangements for the provision of services.

(iv) Enforcement of Primary Care Contracts

The nature of the contract for services that general practitioners and dentists are required to provide was discussed in the previous chapter and earlier in this one. Here we are concerned with the process for ensuring that the services contracted for are actually provided. Once again, the statutory framework aims to keep disputes away from the courts. Failure to perform satisfactorily

---

163 I. Harden, *The Contracting State* (Buckingham: Open University Press, 1992), 48.
164 J. Jacob, 'Lawyers go to Hospital' [1991] *Public Law* 255–81.
165 P. Birks, *Introduction to the Law of Restitution* (Oxford: Oxford University Press, 1985).
166 K. Barker, 'NHS Contracts, Restitution and the Internal Market' (1993) 56 *MLR* 832–43.

on those contracts is taken up through discipline committees created solely for the purposes of policing them.[167] Each health authority is required to have separate committees to deal with the various services: medical, dental, ophthalmic, and pharmaceutical.[168] There will also be a joint services committee. The procedures of these committees are essentially common and are therefore discussed together. Usually disciplinary committees consist of up to three lay people appointed by the health authority, up to three professionals from a list nominated by the relevant local representative committee, and a legally qualified chairman or woman. However, joint disciplinary committees will comprise two lay people and two members of each of the professions, with a lawyer in the chair.[169]

If a health authority receives information that there may have been a breach of the terms of service, it may decide to take no action.[170] If it decides that the matter should go further, it may take one or more of a series of actions. The first is to invoke a disciplinary committee investigation. This is done by referring the matter to another health authority. The second is to inform the NHS Tribunal, which can suspend and disqualify practitioners.[171] This happens only rarely. The third is to inform the police or the relevant professional body (see Chapter 6). If the matter has arisen in the course of a complaint being made against the practitioner, the health authority should await the completion of the complaints procedure. In such circumstances, any referral must be made within twenty-eight days of the resolution of the complaints procedure. In other cases, referral must be within thirteen weeks of the incident (where doctors, opticians, or chemists are concerned). For dentists the period can be extended to up to six months after the completion of treatment.[172]

If a matter is referred to a discipline committee, the health authority must notify the practitioner concerned within two days and send a statement of case to the committee and practitioner within twenty-eight days.[173] The practitioner then has twenty-eight days to provide a response, which may be extended for a further twenty-eight days at the discretion of the chairman of the discipline committee. A hearing will then be convened by the health authority to whose discipline committee the matter was referred. That hearing will take place in private, and although the practitioner may be assisted by one person,

---

[167] The National Health Service (Service Committees and Tribunal) Regulations 1992, SI 1992 No 664, as amended. The old service committees also investigated complaints brought by patients. These are now dealt with under separate procedures, which are discussed in Ch. 5. Disciplinary committees follow essentially the same procedures as the old service committees, and were constituted by amending the old regulations rather than replacing them.

[168] SI 1992 No 664, r. 3.   [169] SI 1992 No 664, Sch. 2, paras. 1, 2 (as amended).

[170] SI 1992 No 664, r. 4(1) (as amended).

[171] NHS Act 1977, ss. 46–49E and Sch. 9; NHS (Service Committees and Tribunal) Regulations 1992, n. 168 above, as amended, Pt. III.

[172] SI 1992 No 664, r. 6 (as amended).   [173] *Ibid.*, Sch. 4, para. 1 (as amended).

legal representation is not permitted (in that if that person is a barrister or solicitor she or he may not address the committee or question witnesses).[174]

After the hearing, the discipline committee reports to the health authority which referred the case to it. That report will set out the evidence given to it, its findings on relevant questions of fact, the inferences that the committee believes might properly be drawn from those facts as to whether there has been a breach of the terms of service (with reasons for doing so), and its recommendations for action to be taken by the authority.[175] The authority must accept the findings of fact made by the discipline committee, and its inferences as to a breach of the terms of service. It must then consider whether to take further action, having regard to the recommendations of the discipline committee. It is not bound to accept those recommendations, but if it does not accept them it must record its reasons in writing.[176] The regulations specify the actions available to the authority. Where the authority, after consultation with the local medical committee, believes that the doctor has more patients than she or he is able to give adequate treatment to, it may limit the number of patients the doctor may take on.[177] It may also warn the practitioner about compliance with the terms of service, or impose a fine (possibly by deduction from the remuneration to be paid). In the case of dentists, there is also provision to require the practitioner to seek prior approval of some kinds of treatment as specified by the authority.[178] The authority may also refer the matter to the relevant professional body, so that it may consider disciplinary proceedings.[179]

The Regulations provide for appeal by practitioners to the Secretary of State against the findings of a disciplinary committee or the subsequent decisions of the health authority.[180] These appeals are handled by the Family Health Services Appeal Authority.[181] In order to exercise the right of appeal, written notice, including a concise statement of the grounds for appeal, must be sent to the Secretary of State within thirty days of the health authority notifying the practitioner of its decision.[182] An appeal may be dismissed without a hearing if the Secretary of State considers that there is no reasonable ground of appeal, or that it is otherwise vexatious or frivolous.[183] If not, the other parties will be notified of the particulars of the appeal and given the opportunity to make any comments within twenty-eight days.[184] Any such observations

---

[174] SI 1992 No 664, Sch. 4, para. 5 (as amended).
[175] *Ibid.*, Sch. 4, para. 7 (as amended).   [176] *Ibid.*, r. 8(2), as amended.
[177] *Ibid.*, r. 8(3), as amended.   [178] *Ibid.*, r. 8(5), as amended.
[179] *Ibid.*, r. 37, as amended.   [180] *Ibid.*, r. 9(1), as amended.
[181] Family Health Services Appeal Authority (Establishment and Constitution) Order 1995, SI 1995 No 621; Family Health Services Appeal Authority Regulations 1995, SI 1995 No 622.
[182] SI 1992 No 664, r. 9(2), as amended.
[183] *Ibid.*, r. 10(1), as amended.   [184] *Ibid.*, r. 10(2), as amended.

will be sent to the appellant, who must make any comments within twenty-one days.[185] There will then be an oral hearing unless the appellant does not want one.[186] It will take place before a panel of three persons. Two of these must be members of the same profession as the practitioner concerned. The third, who takes the chair, must be a lawyer.[187] New evidence of allegations will not be admitted without the agreement of the panel or the Secretary of State.[188] The panel will then report to the Secretary of State, who will consider it and decide whether the appeal should be allowed.[189] He must provide the parties with a written statement of his reasons.[190]

F. Conclusion

The previous chapter set out the services to which patients are entitled under the National Health Service, and the mechanisms for enforcing those rights. It showed how difficult it is for individuals to use the courts to make the NHS deliver the services they want. In practice, reliance has to be placed on the NHS authorities to make sure the service acts properly. This Chapter has set out the administrative structure of the service, and explored the legal issues that it raises. The current system of market provision is complex, and its legal implications have not yet been fully explored by the courts. Where that system fails to ensure that patients are properly treated, it provides its own mechanisms for redress through the NHS complaints systems. These are explored in the next chapter.

[185] *Ibid.*, r. 10(3), as amended.
[186] *Ibid.*, r. 10(4),(5) as amended.
[187] *Ibid.*, r. 10(6),(7),(8) as amended.
[188] *Ibid.*, r. 10(11), as amended.
[189] *Ibid.*, r. 10(12), as amended.
[190] *Ibid.*, r. 10(14), as amended.

Research indicates that there is a wide range of motives behind complaints.[1] Some complainants wish to do no more than express their grievance, and have it taken seriously. Others seek explanations and apologies. Some want compensation. Occasionally complainants may want steps taken against individuals who they believe should be punished.[2] Complaints procedures also serve management functions, providing information on the degree of satisfaction with services and indication of quality. Complaints procedures may also divert cases from litigation.

There is no doubt that complaints have increased during the existence of the NHS. Long-standing concern about the inadequacy of procedures eventually led to the Hospital Complaints Procedure Act 1985,[3] which obliged the Secretary of State to issue directions instructing hospital authorities to set up complaints procedures and specifying the nature of the arrangements to be made. After consultation with the health authorities these directions were issued in June 1988.[4] The Wilson Committee, reviewing the system in 1994, reported that the number of hospital complaints received in England increased from 16,218 in 1982 to 44,680 for the year 1991–2,[5] although NHSME figures put the latter figure at 51,130.[6] The rate of increase was steeper in the last year, possibly as a result of better public information about the right to complain consequent upon the Patient's Charter initiative. A significant proportion of the hospital cases for 1991–2 (40 per cent) related to

---

[1] L. Mulcahy, and S. Lloyd-Bostock, 'Complaining—What's the Use?' in R. Dingwall, and P. Fenn, *Quality and Regulation in Health Care: International Perspectives* (London: Routledge, 1992); S. Nettleton, and G. Harding, 'Protesting Patients: A Study of Complaints Submitted to a Family Health Service Authority' (1994) 16 *Sociology of Health and Illness* 38–61; L. Mulcahy, and S. Lloyd-Bostock, 'Patient-centred Health Care and Complaints' in K. Fulford, S. Ersser, and T. Hope (eds.), *Essential Practice in Patient-centred Care* (Oxford: Blackwell Science, 1996).

[2] *Being Heard: The Report of a Review Committee on NHS Complaints Procedures* (London: DoH, 1994), ch. III.

[3] The first important investigation into the defects of the system had been over ten years earlier: DHSS and Welsh Office, *Report of the Committee on Hospital Complaints Procedures* (London: HMSO, 1973).

[4] Annex A to the explanatory circular 'Hospital Complaints Procedure Act 1985' HC(88)37, HN(FP)(88)18.

[5] *Being Heard*, Annex E, para. 27.   [6] HC (1993–4) 33–II 275.

clinical matters, although this was so in only 22 per cent of the community complaints. This is a similar proportion to that reported for 1989–90.[7] These figures constitute a rise in the rate of complaints as well as in absolute numbers. The rate of complaints per 1,000 in-patients and day cases rose from 2.5 in 1982 to five in 1991–2. The rise in complaints for community services was even steeper, from 3.4 to 13.3 over the same period.[8] Complaints therefore cause major concern in the modern NHS.

There is a range of procedures by which health professionals may be called to account.[9] This Chapter considers the complaints procedures within the NHS, but there are a number of other important channels of accountability. Health professionals are subject to a regime of internal discipline which, although it can be initiated by concerned lay people, is primarily in the hands of the profession itself. As employees, they are responsible to the managers to whom they report, although the nature of the professional is such that this accountability is different from that of non-professional employees. Professional discipline is discussed in Chapter 6. Malpractice litigation is the subject of Chapter 7. Aspects of the disciplinary procedures of the NHS were examined in Chapter 4.

Professionals are also accountable to their clients. There are two main routes by which aggrieved patients may seek redress for unsatisfactory health care. One is through the courts. The other is through complaints procedures. Private patients may be restricted to recourse to litigation or to the professional bodies, as there is no legal requirement that they are offered a less formal route to complain. However, within the NHS complaints procedures are guaranteed by the *Patient's Charter*. They are mandatory and should be available to all patients. NHS purchasers should, by contract, require that similar procedures are available to NHS patients treated in the independent sector.[10] This chapter explains the NHS procedures. Technically, they fall into three categories. Grievances arising in hospital are covered by the Hospital Complaints Procedure Act 1985 and the directions given under it. Matters relating to general medical practitioners, and community pharmacists,

[7] NHSME figures reported at HC (1993–4) 33–II 275. The Wilson Committee put the proportion at 43%. In 1989–90 the figure was similar at 42%: Statistics and Management Information Division, Government Statistical Service, *Return of Written Complaints by or on Behalf of Patients: England—Financial Year 1989–90* (London: DoH, 1991).

[8] HC (1993–4) 33–II 285, figures for England. See also Mulcahy, and Lloyd-Bostock, 'Complaining—what's the use?', n. 1 above, 55.

[9] For overviews of the issues, which predate the current NHS complaints procedures, see M. Stacey, 'Medical Accountability: A Background Paper' in A. Grubb (ed.), *Challenges in Medical Care* (Chichester: Wiley, 1992) and R. Palmer, 'Accountability and Discipline' in C. Dyer (ed.), *Doctors, Patients and the Law* (Oxford: Blackwell Scientific Publications, 1992).

[10] 'Miscellaneous directions to health authorities for dealing with complaints' made on 15 Mar. 1996 and issued by the NHSE on 20 Mar. 1996. No EL reference was given.

opticians, and dentists fall within the jurisdiction of Health Authorities. Under the current system of complaints, these two categories are in fact governed by the same guidance. This provides for two levels of procedure; internal resolution and a process of semi-independent review for some circumstances where this does not satisfy the complainant. Finally, the Health Service Commissioner provides a further tier of investigation. For those detained under the Mental Health Act 1983, there is yet another avenue of complaint, to the Mental Health Act Commission, see Chapter 13.

This system has replaced an even more confusing system that was criticized both for its complexity and some of its substantive aspects. That system drew a categorical distinction between general complaints and those concerning medical and dental clinical judgement, which were governed by a procedure that retained extensive control of investigation and report within the medical profession. In 1994 the Department of Health published the report of a review committee into NHS complaints procedures, chaired by Professor Alan Wilson.[11] That Committee made proposals for improving and streamlining the procedures. It rejected the suggestion that clinical issues required a completely different system. The Government implemented the new procedures on 1 April 1996, issuing new statutory instruments, a series of binding directions to health authorities and NHS trusts, and an overarching document giving guidance on implementation. It will be seen that the new system remains quite complex, and one of the roles of Community Health Councils is to assist complainants in finding their way through the maze.

A. The Basic Structure of the Complaints System

The NHS complaints procedures are intended to achieve a number of key objectives. These are expressed as being ease of access, simplicity (with common features for complaints in all parts of the NHS), separation of complaints from disciplinary matters, fairness (for both complainants and staff), speed, openness, honesty, and thoroughness.[12] It is also intended that the new procedure should make it easier for lessons to be learnt from complaints in order to improve the system. It is hoped that most complaints will be resolved by an immediate informal response by front-line staff. Where this is not possible, there should be a procedure for resolving complaints internally. If that fails to satisfy the complainant, they may seek an independent review, although they

---

[11] N. 2 above.
[12] NHSE, *Guidance on Implementation of the NHS Complaints Procedure* (London: DoH, 1996).

are not absolutely entitled to have one held. The ultimate level of complaint is the Health Service Commissioner.

To put this system into place, health service bodies are required to adopt and publicize written complaints procedures which explain the arrangements for local resolution and independent review, how to initiate them, the role of the community health council, and the way to complain to the Health Service Commissioner.[13] Trusts and health authorities must identify a designated complaints manager, readily accessible to the public, to oversee the procedure.[14] They must also appoint at least one person to act as 'convenor' for the purposes of the independent review stage of the procedure. At least one such person must be a non-executive director of the body, and practising or retired clinicians, or recently retired NHS staff should only be appointed in exceptional circumstances.[15] General practices must nominate someone to administer the complaints procedure, and identify them to patients and clients.[16]

The guidance also explains the application of the NHS procedures in cases of mixed sector complaints.[17] Sometimes, there will be more than one avenue for complaint available. This will be the case where clients are detained under the Mental Health Act 1983. They may complain to the Mental Health Act Commission as well as the NHS trust providing their care (see Chapter 13). Where clients receive both NHS and social care, then both the NHS and local authority complaints procedures will be available. The coroner's jurisdiction does not supplant the responsibility of NHS bodies to investigate complaints. Where complaints are made that involve more than one NHS body, then they are expected to co-operate in resolving the complaint. Complaints must be referred immediately to the appropriate body if they are initially made to the wrong organization (providing the complainant agrees to the referral). If matters cannot be resolved internally, and an independent review is needed, then technically separate panels need to be convened from each of the bodies complained about. The guidance envisages that there should be as much common membership as possible, and that the same person might chair the panel. The panels might also try to meet at the same time and place. Separate reports would need to be produced, but they should be co-ordinated to ensure that everything is covered.

One area of concern for patients who may wish to complain is the possibility that they may be victimized. To seek to avoid this, the Guidance advises

---

[13] 'Directions to NHS trusts, health authorities and special health authorities for special hospitals on hospital complaints procedures' made on 7 Mar. 1996, issued with EL(96)19, para. 3; NHSE, *Guidance*, n. 12 above, paras. 1–4.4.

[14] 'Directions', n. 13 above, para. 4.16.

[15] 'Directions', n. 13 above, para. 14; NHSE, *Guidance*, n. 12 above, paras. 4.22–4.26.

[16] NHSE *Guidance*, n. 12 above, paras. 4.19–4.20.   [17] *Ibid.*, paras. 3.14–3.19.

that records of complaints should be kept separate from clinical records.[18] Sometimes, however, it is important to record in the clinical notes information discovered in the course of investigating a complaint because it relates directly to the patient's health needs. This is permitted by the Guidance.[19]

The Directions and Guidance on the complaints system identify 'complainants' (i.e. those who may use the system) as existing or former patients using the services of the body complained about, and those who complain on behalf of the patient, with the patient's consent.[20] Third parties may make oral complaints on behalf of a patient without that patient's consent. It is also recognized that third parties can complain on behalf of patients who are unable to complain themselves. Complaints managers may refuse to accept complaints in this last category if they believe that the person bringing the complaint is not a suitable person to pursue it on behalf of the patient. In such circumstances, they may either refuse to deal with the complaint or nominate another person to act on the patient's behalf. The unsuitability must relate to the identity of the person complaining. Issues about the substance of the complaint are not relevant. The Guidance indicates that complaints coming from visitors, contractors, and other users of a health service body's facilities should be accepted. However, this is a matter of good practice rather than legal obligation.

Like the courts in malpractice actions, the NHS system operates a time limit within which complaints are expected to be brought. This should normally be within six months of the incident, or of awareness that there is a problem, providing that it is still within a year of the incident.[21] There is a discretion to extend these time limits where the complaints manager thinks that it would have been unreasonable for the complainant to make a complaint within the normal period, and that it will still be possible to investigate the complaint properly. In those circumstances, the complaint shall be investigated. The only example given in the Guidance refers to cases where the complainant has suffered such distress or trauma as to prevent a complaint being made earlier.

According to the Guidance, this discretion should be used 'flexibly and sensitively', but the phrases used in the Directions are quite specific. On the wording, it is not enough that there are reasons for the complainant's delay, nor that it would be unreasonable to expect the complainant to have acted sooner. It seems that it must be thought that any complaint within the period would have been unreasonable. It is unfortunate that the Directions seem to

---

[18] NHSE *Guidance*, n. 12 above, paras. 3.9, 4.31.   [19] *Ibid.*, para. 3.9.
[20] 'Directions', n. 13 above, para. 11; NHSE, *Guidance*, n. 12 above, paras. 4.7–4.10.
[21] 'Directions', n. 13 above, para. 10; NHSE, *Guidance*, n. 12 above, paras. 4.11–4.15.

have precluded local organizations operating a more flexible policy of accepting all complaints that can be properly investigated.

Where the complaints manager refuses to extend the time limit, that decision may be the subject of a complaint. The complainant may request that an independent review be set up to consider whether the late complaint should be considered. If the convenor refuses that request, the complainant may refer the complaint to the Health Service Commissioner.

The NHS complaints procedures are not designed to deal with disciplinary matters, nor those that are so serious that a different mechanism is needed. The Directions and Guidance ensure that such complaints are processed appropriately.[22] Sometimes, there will be a need for investigation under the employer's or the professional disciplinary procedures. Occasionally, an inquiry under section 84 of the NHS Act 1977 will be needed. This is the power of the Secretary of State to establish a formal inquiry with the power to summon witnesses, require documents to be produced, and take evidence under oath (see Chapter 3). Where a criminal offence may have been committed, the matter should be referred to the police. Neither the complaints manager nor the convenor is to be responsible for deciding whether to initiate any of these steps. Instead, if the complaint indicates a *prima facie* need for referral because of any of these types of problem, then it must be referred to a suitable person. If this happens, then a full report of the investigation to that date should be made available to the complainant with an explanation of the referral. Those aspects of a complaint that are being dealt with through one of these other mechanisms are no longer to be investigated under the complaints procedure. The rest of the complaint should continue to be investigated. If the complaint remains wholly or partly unresolved by the other proceedings, then investigation of the complaint may resume. The decision whether this is the case is for the complaints manager, convenor, or chairperson of the independent review (whichever stage the complaint reached before it was referred for other consideration) not the complainant.

The other exclusion from the complaints procedure concerns cases where the complainant has explicitly stated that she or he intends to pursue a remedy in the courts.[23] There must be an oral or written statement of this intention, it is not enough that the complaints manager infers that litigation is planned. Nor is it enough that the complainant's initial communication is via a solicitor's letter. The Guidance points out that the exclusion of litigation cases from the complaints procedure should not prevent a full and thorough investigation as part of good risk and claims management. It also observes that complainants may be happy to drop their legal case if they receive an

---

[22] 'Directions', n. 13 above, para. 7; NHSE, *Guidance*, n. 12 above, paras. 4.32–4.36.

[23] 'Directions', n. 13 above, para. 7; NHSE, *Guidance*, n. 12 above, paras. 4.37–4.39.

explanation and, if appropriate, an apology (which is not an admission of liability).

B. Local Resolution in Health Authorities and NHS Trusts

The details of local resolution procedures are a matter for the bodies establishing them. The Directions require the complaints manager to accept and investigate eligible complaints. It seems to be assumed that all written complaints are sufficiently serious that they must be investigated. However, with oral complaints there should be a preliminary consideration of the complaint. If the complainant wishes to pursue the matter further, then the complaint must be turned into a written complaint (either by the complainant, or by the complaints manager and signed by the complainant). This seems to preclude the possibility that some people who complain in writing might not wish a full investigation, but would be happy with an immediate response.

The system also precludes front line staff from dealing with written complaints, even if they are the recipient. The chief executive of the organization must inform the complainant of the outcome of the investigation of *all written complaints* (emphasis supplied).[24] This may involve the chief executive signing the full response, but it may be only a covering letter that the chief executive signs. The Guidance, although not the Directions, seems to suggest that in matters of clinical judgement the professional concerned must agree the response before it goes to the complainant.[25] This would seem to give clinicians a veto on responses to which they object.

Beyond these requirements, the procedures must be designed by each health service body. The Guidance expects the local procedures to provide for a range of responses, avoiding rigid, bureaucratic, and legalistic approaches.[26] Oral complaints may be dealt with entirely orally, although it is recommended that there should still be a final written response.[27] The final response should indicate that the complainant may seek an independent review if still unsatisfied. The main mandatory requirements are in terms of the time taken to resolve complaints.[28] It is expected that most oral complaints should be resolved within two working days. Where this is not possible, health authorities and NHS trusts should aim to acknowledge the complaint within two

---

[24] 'Directions', n. 13 above, para. 13; NHSE, *Guidance*, n. 12 above, paras. 5.8–5.13.
[25] NHSE, *Guidance*, n. 12 above, para. 5.12.   [26] *Ibid.*, para. 5.2.   [27] *Ibid.*, para. 5.18.
[28] *Ibid.*, para. 5.21.

working days unless they are able to resolve the whole complaint within five working days. This acknowledgement should always be in writing where the complaint was made in writing, either originally or after initial consideration failed to resolve it. The target for full resolution of all complaints is twenty working days. Performance against these targets is monitored nationally as part of the Patient's Charter initiative.

C. Complaints in Family Health Services

Prior to 1 April 1996, complaints about family health services were dealt with as allegations of breach of contract by the practitioner. Monitoring of the performance of contracts is now a separate process (see Chapter 4). Disciplinary issues arising from complaints will now only be considered after the complaint has been dealt with unless action is necessary to protect patients, such as referral to professional bodies, the police, or the NHS Tribunal (which can suspend practitioners).[29] Practices are obliged by their terms of service to operate practice-based complaints procedures.[30]

Under this procedure, which must be the responsibility of a designated person, all complaints must be recorded in writing and properly investigated. No distinction is drawn between written and oral complaints.[31] They should be acknowledged either orally or in writing within three working days, beginning with the day on which the complaint was made. Family health service practitioners should aim to complete their internal process within ten working days,[32] although it is anticipated that period will be extended where the help of the health authority is sought, or conciliation is used.[33]

Some patients may feel reticent about complaining to the doctor who has continuing responsibility for their care. To counter this difficulty, the Guidance suggests that health authorities may act as 'honest broker' between general practitioners and complainants if the latter either does not wish to use the practice-based procedure or is having difficulty getting the complaint dealt with. This function includes the provision of lay conciliators, continuing the practice under the previous procedures.[34]

---

[29] *Ibid.*, para. 4.31.
[30] For doctors, see NHS (General Medical Services Regulations) 1992, SI 1992 No 635, Sch. 2, paras. 47A–47B. The terms of service of the other professions have been similarly amended.
[31] NHSE, *Guidance*, n. 12 above, para. 5.19.
[32] NHS (General Medical Services Regulations) 1992, SI 1992 No 635, Sch. 2, para. 47A(6)(c).
[33] NHSE, *Guidance*, n. 12 above, para. 5.22.   [34] *Ibid.*, paras. 5.15–5.16.

D. Independent Review

(i) The Role of the Convenor

Complainants who are not satisfied with the response given by the internal complaints process may seek an independent review of the matter. The first step in this process is to inform the 'convenor' appointed by the health authority or trust. Unresolved complaints about family health services are taken to the convenor of the health authority for the relevant district. The complainant must request such a review within twenty-eight calendar days from the completion of the local resolution process. Requests later than this may be accepted on the same grounds as late complaints (see above). Before the convenor considers whether an independent review should be held, she or he must obtain a signed statement setting out the unresolved grievances, and why the complainant is dissatisfied with the outcome of the local procedure.[35]

Dissatisfied complainants have no absolute right to an independent review; it is a matter for the convenor's discretion. The convenor must exercise that discretion in consultation with an independent lay chairman, taken from a regional list. The criteria are set down in the Guidance and Directions.[36] An independent review panel shall not be convened where the convenor believes that further action can be taken by the trust or authority without it. In these circumstances, the convenor should refer the matter back to the complaints manager or chief executive for further investigation. At the other extreme, a panel should not be set up where the convenor believes that all practical steps towards satisfying the complainant have been taken, and nothing would be achieved by convening it. Where the complaint raises a matter of clinical judgement, the convenor must take appropriate clinical advice. This will usually come from the local professional head, provided that they are not in any way associated with the complaint.[37] Convenors should not move to independent review where there is an explicit intention to initiate legal proceedings, or where they are already in progress. Nor should they do so where disciplinary issues have been identified.

Once the convenor has reached a decision, it must be communicated in writing to the complainant.[38] If a panel is to be appointed, then the terms of reference must be set out. If the decision is to refuse a panel, then the reasons must be set out and the complainant told of the right to complain to the Health Service Commissioner. A refusal may indicate that the convenor

---

[35] 'Directions', n. 13 above, para. 15; NHSE, *Guidance*, n. 12 above, paras. 6.1–6.5.
[36] 'Directions', n. 13 above, para. 16; NHSE, *Guidance*, n. 12 above, para. 6.12–6.14.
[37] 'Directions', n. 13 above, para. 17(1)(a); NHSE, *Guidance*, n. 12 above, paras. 6.15–6.19.
[38] 'Directions', n. 13 above, para. 18; NHSE, *Guidance*, n. 12 above, paras. 6.21–6.25.

believes that further actions could be taken internally. If the complainant is still dissatisfied after those steps are taken, then a further request for an independent review may be made.[39] The convenor's decision and the reasons for it must also be notified in writing to any person complained against, and to the chief executive of the health authority, NHS trust, or family practitioner. The decision should normally be made within twenty working days of the complainant's request for an independent review being received.[40]

(ii) The Review Panel

The independent review will be carried out by a panel of three members, formally constituted as a committee of the health authority or NHS trust.[41] The panel should be established within four weeks of the convenor's letter being sent to the complainant. Panels in respect of complaints about general practitioners will be panels of the health authority in whose district they practise. One of the members of the panel will be the convenor, who will be a non-executive director of the NHS trust or authority (or an associate member appointed by that body for the purpose). A second will be a representative of the relevant purchaser for trust panels. This may be a non-executive member of the health authority or a GP fundholder nominated by the purchasing practice. In relation to health authority panels, this person will be another independent person nominated by the Secretary of State. The panel will be chaired by a person nominated by the Secretary of State from a regional list of persons drawn up for the purpose. All members of the panel will be lay people. Only exceptionally will they be recently retired NHS staff or non-executives of other health service bodies.

The panel function is to investigate according to the terms of reference established by the convenor.[42] It will meet in private, with details of procedure determined by the panel (and fixed by the chairman in the case of disagreement). The complainant and persons complained against must be given a reasonable opportunity to express their views on the complaint. They may be accompanied by a person of their choosing, although legally qualified people acting as advocates are not permitted. The panel will have access to the relevant records. It has no executive authority and may not suggest disciplinary action or that a person be referred to the relevant professional body. The panel should aim to complete its work within twelve weeks.

If the complaint raises a question of clinical judgement, then the panel will sit with at least two assessors.[43] These assessors will be taken from the

---

[39] NHSE, *Guidance*, n. 12 above, para. 6.26.   [40] *Ibid.*, para. 6.29.
[41] 'Directions', n. 13 above, para. 22; NHSE, *Guidance*, n. 12 above, paras. 7.2–7.5, 7.51.
[42] 'Directions', n. 13 above, paras. 24, 27(3); NHSE, *Guidance*, n. 12 above, paras. 7.8–7.12, 7.51.
[43] 'Directions', n. 13 above, paras. 23, 25; NHSE, *Guidance*, n. 12 above, paras. 7.13–7.29.

appropriate professional discipline or disciplines and will be members of a national list of people identified by relevant professional bodies for the purpose. Assessors should not act independently to resolve the complaint, but advise the panel on clinical issues. At least one of the assessors must be present at interviews of the parties when matters of clinical judgement are under consideration. They must have access to the clinical records, and may interview or examine complainants. Assessors' reports are made in the first instance to the panel. The panel may decide to release the reports to the parties if this will aid the resolution of the dispute. In any event, the assessors' reports must be attached to the panel's final report.

The panel's report must include findings of fact, the opinion of the panel on the complaint, the reasons for that opinion, the report of any assessors, and, if the panel disagrees with an assessor, the reason for its disagreement.[44] The Guidance suggests that the panel may find it helpful to give the parties an opportunity to check the report, although not necessarily the conclusions reached, in draft form for factual accuracy. Once finalized, the report must be sent to the complainant, the patient (if not the complainant, but competent to receive the report), any person subject to complaint, the assessors, any person interviewed during the inquiry, the chairman and chief executive of the NHS trust or health authority, and the purchaser. The Guidance indicates that it should also be sent to the regional directors of public health and performance management.

(iii) Responses

The final stage in the procedure is a letter from the chief executive of the health authority or NHS trust advising the complainant of the outcome of the independent review and the right to complain to the Health Service Commissioner.[45] According to the Guidance, the chief executive should also seek to inform the complainant within twenty working days of the publication of the panel's report of any formal apology that is to be made, any *ex gratia* payment, and an indication of the timescale in which the board of the organization has agreed to consider the policy issues. Subsequent board decisions relating to the complaint should be notified to the complainant. The Directions merely require a response within a reasonable time. If it is decided that no action should be taken, the reasons for that decision must be given in the chief executive's letter. In relation to complaints against general practitioners, the chief executive of the relevant health authority will send the panel's report to the complainant.

---

[44] 'Directions', n. 13 above, para. 27; NHSE, *Guidance*, n. 12 above, paras. 7.30–7.34.
[45] 'Directions', n. 13 above, para. 28; NHSE, *Guidance*, n. 12 above, para. 7.38.

E. Complaints About Purchasing

One of the major gaps in the previous complaints procedure was the absence of a means of redress in relation to purchasing decisions. This has now been remedied. Under the current procedures, health authorities are required to appoint complaints managers to assist complainants and manage the complaints procedures.[46] Complaints may be made about health authority decisions or failures to act by any person affected or likely to be affected by the decision (or on behalf of such a person). The system is essentially the same as that for complaints against NHS trusts, and on most points the Directions for trusts are incorporated into those for health authorities. There is a slight difference in relation to the remit of independent review panels, which are to consider whether the health authority acted properly, rather than whether they reached the same decision as the panel would have reached. This concentrates on process rather than outcome. Thus, the panel should check that the health authority had regard to all the relevant matters and ignored those that were irrelevant. Complaints about purchasing decisions by GP fundholders should be processed within their practice-based procedures.

F. Complaints about NHS Services from Independent Providers

Health authorities are required to make arrangements to operate complaints procedures in respect of independent providers who are contracted to provide services to NHS patients.[47] Contracts should include terms requiring the independent providers to set up complaints procedures at least as good as the NHS local resolution stage. The independent review stage will be organized by the health authority. The final stage in the procedure is a letter from the chief executive of the health authority for the district. It should be noted that there may be an alternative avenue for complaint under the Registered Homes Act 1984, through the registration officer of the health authority.

---

[46] N. 10 above; NHSE, *Guidance*, n. 12 above, paras. 8.1–8.8.
[47] N. 10 above, Pt. IV; NHSE, *Guidance*, n. 12 above, paras. 8.9–8.15.

G. Health Service Commissioners

The final tier in the NHS complaints procedures is the jurisdiction of the Health Service Commissioner.[48] The position was originally established by the NHS Reorganization Act 1973 and is now governed by the Health Service Commissioners Act 1993, as amended in 1996. Technically there are three Commissioners, for England, Wales, and Scotland. In practice, however, these posts have so far been held by the same person, who has also held the position of Parliamentary Commissioner for Administration. There are no prescribed qualifications for the job, but to date the holders have all been male with backgrounds in the civil service or the law. Unlike the bodies concerned in the complaints procedures already discussed, the HSC is independent of both the NHS and the health professions. The Commissioner is assisted by deputy commissioners. The holders of these posts to date have had backgrounds in health service management. The office has a number of investigation units, staffed mostly by personnel on secondment from the NHS or Civil Service.

The Commissioner's powers of investigation are extensive.[49] He may require to see whatever documentation he believes to be relevant. Refusal to co-operate may be referred to a court and is punishable as contempt of court. It is the usual practice for the investigators to go to the health authority to examine the patient's records. The complainant will be interviewed, often at home. Health service bodies and the staff involved, who may number as many as fifty for a single complaint,[50] must be allowed to comment on the allegations. The parties may, if the Commissioner permits it, be represented by lawyers or others.

The reports which result are widely regarded as meticulous and fair,[51] but the detailed investigations necessarily mean that the resolution of complaints takes some time. Until 1989–90, the average time taken to complete investigations had risen steadily, peaking at 69.4 weeks.[52] This was regarded as too long by the Commissioner, the Parliamentary Select Committee which oversees his work, and the representatives of the medical profession.[53] By 1994 the

---

[48] For general discussion see, F. Stacey, *Ombudsmen Compared* (Oxford: OUP, 1978), ch. 8, M. M. Rosenthal, *Dealing with Medical Malpractice: The British and Swedish Experience* (London: Tavistock, 1987), 95–9; P. Giddings, 'Complaints, Remedies and the Health Service Commissioner' (1993) 71 *Public Administration* 377–94. However, these works predate the extension of the Commissioner's jurisdiction to clinical judgement and the work of family health services.

[49] Health Service Commissioners Act 1993, ss. 12, 13.

[50] Health Service Commissioner, *Annual Report for 1989* (1988–9) HC 457, ch. 1.

[51] *2nd Report from the Select Committee on the Parliamentary Commissioner for Administration* 1989–90 HC 441, xxv.

[52] *Second Report from the Select Committee on the PCA* (1989–90), HC 441, para. 5.

[53] *Ibid.*, paras. 5–8, Apps. I and II.

figure had come down to 48.6 weeks.[54] An additional factor reducing the practical significance of the Commissioner's work is the relatively small number of cases he investigates by comparison to other avenues of NHS complaints. The statistics published by the Commissioner show that the number of complaints gradually increased from around 400 in 1974–5, the first full year, to a peak of 807 in 1985–6. There was then a reduction and in 1988–9 the Commissioner received only 641 complaints, although more reports were published in that year than ever before.[55] Since then the number of complaints has increased again and 1384 new complaints were received in 1993–4. However, a high proportion were rejected as premature or outside the jurisdiction of the commissioner, and only 351 were actually investigated.[56]

(i) The Scope of the Commissioner's Powers

The Commissioner may investigate allegations of maladministration and failures in the provision of services by health authorities, NHS trusts, family health service providers (doctors, dentists, pharmacists, and opticians), independent providers of NHS services under contract, the Dental Practice Board, the Public Health Laboratory Service Board, the Mental Health Act Commission, the Disablement Services Authority, and the Health Education Authority.[57] Complaints about family health service providers and clinical matters in all contexts were excluded from the jurisdiction of the Commissioner until the implementation of the Health Service Commissioners (Amendment) Act 1996.

On the face of it this is a wide remit, but a number of types of complaint are specifically excluded from the jurisdiction of the HSC. First, the Commissioner may not investigate cases where there is a remedy before a tribunal or a court of law unless it is unreasonable in the circumstances to expect this remedy to be pursued.[58] This restricts the HSC's consideration of cases where a malpractice action might be brought before the courts. Secondly, the Commissioner may not investigate matters which have been or are being investigated by inquiries set up by the Secretary of State under section 84 of the NHS Act 1977.[59] Thirdly, personnel matters, including appointments,

---

[54] Health Service Commissioner *Annual Report for 1993–4*, HC Paper 1993–4 499, para. 5.8.
[55] N. 50 above, App. F.   [56] N. 54 above, fig. 3.
[57] Health Service Commissioners Act 1993, ss. 2, 2A, 2B; see also the orders made under the old provisions extending the Commissioner's jurisdiction: The Health Service Commissioner for England (Mental Health Act Commission) Order 1983 (SI 1983 No 1114); The Health Service Commissioner for England (Disablement Services Authority) Order 1987 (SI 1987 No 1272); The Health Service Commissioner for England (Health Education Authority) Order 1988 (SI 1988 No 589); The Health Service Commissioner for Wales (Welsh Health Promotion Authority) Order 1988 (SI 1988 No 597).
[58] Health Service Commissioners Act 1993, s. 4(1).   [59] *Ibid.*, s. 4(2).

pay, and discipline, may not be investigated by the Commissioner.[60] Fourthly, issues relating to commercial transactions, save those relating to the provision of health services for patients, are excluded.[61] Since the relationship between family practitioners and health authorities is a contractual one, this exclusion prevents the HSC investigating complaints by doctors about health authorities.[62] The Health Service Commissioner is, however, entitled to entertain complaints relating to 'NHS Contracts' under which NHS Trusts provide services, and also genuine legal contracts with independent providers which serve the same purpose: securing services for patients.

There are little data yet on the involvement of the Commissioner in purchasing matters. In 1993–4 he investigated five complaints concerning 'policy decisions', and extra-contractual referrals. Three of the complaints were upheld.[63] In one case, he found that the authority had been guilty of maladministration in refusing an extra-contractual referral without seeking clinical advice.[64] However, the Commissioner has been reluctant to become involved in the substance of policy decisions. In dealing with one complaint concerning the purchasing of IVF treatment, he restricted his investigation to establishing what had been intended by an ambiguous policy, and examining whether it had been implemented in the complainant's case without maladministration.[65]

The exclusions imposed on the Commissioner narrow his jurisdiction and, even when he is permitted to investigate a matter, he may choose not to.[66] The reasons for rejecting complaints are published in the Commissioner's annual reports. Most are because the Commissioner has no jurisdiction. In 1993–4 45.8 per cent of cases were rejected. Of these, the grounds for rejection were: complaint concerning clinical judgement, which was then excluded from his jurisdiction (30.2 per cent), out of time (9.2 per cent), personnel matters involved (3.6 per cent), terms of service for GPs etc. in issue (12.3 per cent), body complained against outside jurisdiction (7.3 per cent), no apparent maladministration (9.2 per cent), the availability of a legal remedy (5.7 per cent), exercise of discretion to refuse to investigate (13.6 per cent) and 'others' (8.9 per cent).[67] Whenever the Commissioner decides not to investigate, he is obliged to write to the complainant and the relevant health service body explaining his reasons.[68] The Commissioner may not investigate complaints unless the earlier stages in the NHS complaints procedure have been invoked

---

[60] Health Service Commissioners Act 1993, s. 7(1).   [61] *Ibid.*, s. 7.
[62] See Health Service Commissioner, *Annual Report for 1991–2* (HC Paper 1992–3, 82) para. 10, commenting on the effect of *Roy* v. *Kensington & Chelsea & Westminster FPC* [1992] 1 All ER 705.
[63] N. 54 above, App. E.   [64] *Ibid.*, para. 3.3.   [65] *Ibid.*, para. 3.8.
[66] Health Service Commissioners Act 1993, s. 3(2).   [67] N 54 above, para. 5.15, fig.7.
[68] Health Service Commissioners Act 1993, s. 14(2).

and exhausted unless it is not reasonable in the circumstances to expect the complainant to use them.[69]

(ii) Invoking an Investigation by the Commissioner

Complaints may reach the Commissioner by one of two routes. First, health service bodies may themselves refer written complaints for consideration by him provided they do so within a year of receiving them.[70] Secondly, allegations may be made by a person who has sustained injustice or hardship as a result of the failure in question.[71] Such applications must be written and should be lodged within a year of the grievance coming to the complainant's notice, although the Commissioner may accept late complaints if he believes it reasonable to do so.[72]

Complaints may be made through representatives when people are unable to act for themselves. However, pressure groups cannot refer general grievances, nor can they raise specific problems on behalf of unidentified persons. Thus the Commissioner had no jurisdiction to investigate a case where a man had masqueraded as a doctor because the health authority had not notified the patients he had treated. They therefore did not know they had a grievance and could not make a complaint. The Commissioner had to reject an attempt by the Patients' Association to involve him, even though he believed that it would have been in the public interest to investigate the matter.[73] The Select Committee has suggested that the Commissioner should have the power to initiate investigations, but this has yet to be acted upon.[74]

(iii) Outcomes

At the end of each investigation the Commissioner sends a report of his conclusions to the complainant, to the relevant health service body, and to any person who was the subject of the complaint. If an MP has been involved, then he or she too should receive a copy.[75] These reports can be candid and are given absolute privilege for the purposes of the law of defamation.[76] The Commissioner has no power to require the health service to do anything, but if he finds that the complaint was justified and that the injustice or hardship caused to the complainant has not been remedied, he may lay a special report before the Houses of Parliament.[77] Any health authority which declines to act on the Commissioner's findings therefore risks considerable adverse publicity.

---

[69] *Ibid.*, s. 4(5).   [70] *Ibid.*, s. 10.   [71] *Ibid.*, s. 3.   [72] *Ibid.*, s. 9(4).
[73] Health Service Commissioner, *Annual Report for 1979–80* (1979–80), HC 650, paras. 26–29.
[74] HC (1984–5) 597, xix.   [75] Health Service Commissioners Act 1993, s. 14.
[76] *Ibid.*, s. 14(5).   [77] *Ibid.*, s. 14(3).

In addition to providing redress for the aggrieved party, the Commissioner publishes reports of cases where there may be lessons to be learnt by health service personnel. These include both full reports of specific investigations and the highlighting of instructive cases in an annual report. The matter does not rest here, however. The Commissioner's reports are considered by the House of Commons Select Committee on the Parliamentary Commissioner for Administration. This is a committee of MPs whose remit embraces the review of the Commissioner's work. This covers consideration of the handling of particular cases, including the extent to which recommendations have been implemented and considering whether the limits of the jurisdiction are satisfactory. The Committee can summon witnesses, and it is an added incentive to compliance with the Commissioner's suggestions that failure to do so may result in a grilling before it.

In practice, the recommendations of the HSC are usually followed. In 1989 the Commissioner reported that every single one had been accepted by the relevant health authority by the end of the year.[78] Where the Commissioner is given an undertaking by a health authority he follows it up to see that it has been honoured. Defaulters are reported to the Select Committee.[79] If recommendations are not followed, it is the usual practice for the Select Committee to call the officers of the relevant health authority before them as witnesses when considering the HSC's annual report.[80] In 1984 the Permanent Secretary to the Department of Health told the Select Committee that the Commissioner had had a significant effect on the NHS. In addition to recommendations to specific authorities, summaries of reports were widely circulated in order to improve practice. He put the influence of the Commissioner down to the personal responsibility he took for investigations, the reinforcement of his position by the Select Committee, the high standard of objectivity achieved by reports, and the public nature of investigations.[81]

H. Conclusion

Prior to the introduction of the current system for resolving complaints there were persistent calls for reform of NHS complaints procedures from official bodies and consumer groups.[82] The criticisms were usually similar and gen-

---

[78] Health Service Commissioner, n. 50 above, para. 98.

[79] *Fifth Report from the Select Committee for the PCA* (1983–4) HC 620, para. 44.

[80] N. 52 above, para. 49.   [81] N. 79 above, Minutes of Evidence, para. 181.

[82] See e.g. Association of Community Health Councils for England and Wales and Action for Victims of Medical Accidents, *A Health Standards Inspectorate* (ACHCEW/AVMA 1992), K. Steele, *NHS Complaints Procedures: The Way Forward* (London: Consumers' Association, 1992);

erally covered the following. Parallel systems with different approaches led to unnecessary complexity. Lack of publicity about complaints procedures discouraged patients from complaining. The lack of independence of procedures from the NHS undermined confidence that complaints would be handled impartially. The procedures were generally thought to be weighted in favour of practitioners. There was excessive delay in resolving complaints. The procedures were unsuitable for dealing with the grievances of complainants. This was especially true of the old family health services system, which was not concerned with the complainants' worries at all, but with whether the terms of service had been broken. Most proposals for reform suggested that there was a need for a simplified single complaints procedure that was independent of the NHS body against which the complaint was made.

The current system is based on the Wilson Committee proposals, including the general principles on which complaints procedures within NHS provider units should be based: responsiveness, quality enhancement, cost effectiveness, accessibility, impartiality, simplicity, speed, confidentiality, and accountability.[83] It includes time limits designed to speed up the process. The extension of the remit of the Health Service Commissioner and the introduction of 'independent review' has increased the independence of the system. This is so despite the fact that the independent review is, in fact, only semi-independent, in that a non-executive director of the NHS trust or authority plays a crucial role. The relaxation of the medical stranglehold on clinical complaints procedures is a significant step towards independence. Further, it can be said that there is now a single NHS complaints system, with the Health Service Commissioner at its apex. That system is comprehensive, including purchasing decisions and independent organizations providing NHS services. It remains to be seen whether complainants are more fully satisfied by the new procedures.

J. Montgomery, 'Rights to Health and Health Care' in A. Coote, *The Welfare of Citizens: Developing New Social Rights* (London: Rivers Oram and Institute for Public Policy Research, 1992) 102–7.

[83] N. 2 above; J. Hanna, 'Internal Resolution of NHS Complaints' (1995) 3 *Med. L Rev.* 177–88 has criticized this adoption of private-sector models of complaints procedures.

Part II

Health Care Practice and the Law

6　Professional Regulation

The relationship between patients and health care professionals is based largely on trust that the latter are competent. Membership of the profession should indicate a level of training and expertise which enables the public to rely on the skill of the practitioner. This depends on the efficacy of the bodies which regulate the professions. There are a large number of such bodies in the health care context. They exist in relation to doctors,[1] nurses,[2] dentists,[3] opticians,[4] pharmacists,[5] osteopaths,[6] chiropractors,[7] and the suppliers of hearing aids.[8] Under the Professions Supplementary to Medicine Act 1960 professional boards and registers exist for chiropodists, dieticians, medical laboratory technicians, occupational therapists, orthoptists, physiotherapists, and radiographers.

The principal functions of the professional bodies are to maintain a register of qualified practitioners and to remove those who are unfit to practise because of ill-health or by reason of improper conduct, to oversee professional education, and to give guidance on matters of professional ethics. This Chapter will concentrate on two of these professional bodies, the General Medical Council and the United Kingdom Central Council for Nursing, Midwifery, and Health Visiting. These have been chosen because they govern the two most important professional groups. Nurses constitute by far the largest occupational group employed by the NHS, accounting for over 47 per cent of the total staff.[9] Doctors, although numerically less significant, have considerable impact on the operation of the NHS. These two professional

[1] The General Medical Council: see the Medical Act 1983.

[2] The United Kingdom Central Council for Nursing, Midwifery and Health Visiting: see the Nurses, Midwives and Health Visitors Act 1979.

[3] General Dental Council: see the Dentists Act 1984.

[4] General Optical Council: see Opticians Act 1989.

[5] The Council of the Pharmaceutical Society of Great Britain: see the Pharmacy Act 1954.

[6] General Osteopathic Council: see the Osteopaths Act 1993.

[7] General Chiropractic Council: see the Chiropractors Act 1994.

[8] The Hearing Aid Council: see the Hearing Aid Council Act 1968 and the Hearing Aid Council (Amendment) Act 1989.

[9] National Association of Health Authorities, *NHS Handbook* (10th edn., Tunbridge Wells: JMH Publishing 1995), 95.

bodies differ in a number of important respects, and between the two schemes, most aspects of professional regulation can be illustrated. In particular, differences in relation to disciplinary jurisdiction and composition should be noted.

The GMC can examine only 'serious professional misconduct' while the UKCC can consider allegations of 'professional misconduct' *simpliciter*. The meanings of these phrases are considered in detail below. The dentists, opticians, and hearing aid suppliers adopt the approach taken by the GMC.[10] The pharmacists have the same powers as the UKCC. The professions supplementary to medicine use the older phraseology, 'infamous conduct in a professional respect'.[11] This is not identical to 'serious professional misconduct' but it is nearer to the formulation used by the medical profession than that of the nurses. The phrase was used by the medical profession until the Medical Act 1969, and its meaning is discussed briefly in the section on medical discipline. The two latest schemes of professional regulation concern the complementary therapists, osteopaths, and chiropractors. Here, there is a departure from the traditional approach, and the disciplinary jurisdictions cover 'conduct which falls short of the standard required of a registered chiropractor' (or osteopath) and 'professional incompetence'.[12] This and a number of other unusual features of the regulatory regimes introduced by the Osteopaths Act 1993 and the Chiropractors Act 1994 merit brief consideration towards the end of the Chapter. It should also be noted that the GMC will be able to regulate the competence of doctors when the Medical (Professional Performance) Act 1995 is fully implemented.

The composition of the professional bodies also gives an indication of the degree of autonomy that they have established. This should be considered in relation to the position, first, of lay people and, secondly, of other health professions. One commentator has argued that the medical profession in Britain has been able to avoid lay intervention far more effectively than has been the case elsewhere.[13] The General Medical Council has succeeded in resisting pressure to include amongst its members representatives of other professions. Although it is possible for such persons to be appointed to the GMC by the Privy Council, they are not there to represent their own professions but for

---

[10] Dentists Act 1984, s. 27; Opticians Act 1989, s. 10; Hearing Aid Council Act 1968, s. 7. The latter is not expressly limited to 'professional' misconduct, but this is to be implied, see *R. v. Hearing Aid Disciplinary Committee, ex p. Douglas and Brown, The Times*, 30 Jan. 1989.

[11] Professions Supplementary to Medicine Act 1960, s. 9.

[12] Osteopaths Act 1993, s. 20(1); Chiropractors Act 1994, s. 20(1).

[13] M. Rosenthal, *Dealing with Medical Malpractice: The British and Swedish Experience* (London: Tavistock, 1987); M. Rosenthal, 'Medical Discipline in Cross-cultural Perspective: The United States, Britain and Sweden' in R. Dingwall, and P. Fenn (eds.), *Quality and Regulation in Health Care: International Perspectives* (London: Routledge, 1992), 26–50.

their individual qualities.[14] The UKCC has been even more successful in ensuring self-regulation; there is no legal requirement for lay people to be members at all.

A. Medicine

Doctors have long been organized into collective bodies to regulate competition, enforce standards, and promote good practice.[15] Initially a number of independent bodies grew up to represent specific areas of practice. Many of these, including the Royal Colleges and the British Medical Association, predate statutory regulation and continue to play an important role today. Self-regulation therefore has a long history and the modern statutory regime is the development of medical initiatives, not the imposition of outside control.

Medicine was first constituted as a single profession in 1858 with the creation of the General Medical Council.[16] The modern structure of the Council was shaped by the Merrison Report of 1975,[17] and is now set out in the Medical Act 1983 and the various instruments made under it. These reforms represented a development rather than a break with tradition. The terms of reference of the Merrison Committee did not contemplate any challenge to the assumption that the profession should regulate itself,[18] and the report was based almost entirely on the GMC's own proposals.[19] The Medical Act 1978, which followed the report, did, however, make important changes in response to internal professional controversies. It made the GMC more accountable to the profession itself, extended the Council's functions in relation to medical education and separated the disciplinary processes from the supervision of doctors whose capacity to practise was impaired by ill-health. It did nothing to increase the influence of non-medical professionals or the general public. The provisions of the 1978 Act were consolidated into the Medical Act 1983.[20]

[14] M. Stacey, *Regulating British Medicine: The General Medical Council* (Chichester: Wiley, 1992), 69–85.

[15] J. M. Jacob, *Doctors and Rules* (London: Routledge, 1988), 88–108; M. Rosenthal, *Dealing with Medical Malpractice*, 61–70.

[16] Medical Act 1858.

[17] *Report of the Committee of Inquiry into the Regulation of the Medical Profession* (London: HMSO, 1975), Cmnd. 6018.

[18] M. Stacey, 'The General Medical Council and Professional Accountability' (1989) 4 *Public Policy and Administration* 12–27.

[19] M. R. Draper, 'The General Medical Council from 1950–1982: A Registrar's Impression' in GMC, *Annual Report for 1982* (London: 1983), 11–16. Sir John Richardson (then President of the GMC), in *Minutes of the General Medical Council, Committee and Branch Councils for the Year 1975 with Reports of Committees etc.*, Vol. 112 (London: 1975), 12.

[20] For a discussion of the recent history of the GMC, see Stacey, n. 14 above.

(i) The Constitution of the GMC

The General Medical Council is made up almost entirely of doctors. There are 104 members. Of those, fifty-four are elected by those on the medical register, in four constituencies, one for each of the countries of the United Kingdom. Twenty-five members of the Council are appointed by the Royal Colleges and various universities, and only fully registered medical practitioners are eligible for appointment. The remaining twenty-five members of the GMC are nominated by the Queen on the advice of the Privy Council. There must be at least one nominated member for each of the four countries of the United Kingdom, and more than half of those nominated must not be medically qualified. [21]

There are four statutory committees of the GMC; the Education Committee, the Preliminary Proceedings Committee, the Professional Conduct Committee, and the Health Committee.[22] The constitutions of those committees are established by law. In addition, there are a number of other standing committees. These include one that deals with standards of professional practice. The work of the disciplinary committees is explored in some detail below. Only their constitutions are examined at this point. Both the constitutions and the work of the Education and Health Committees are discussed, briefly, here.

The Preliminary Proceedings Committee comprises the President of the Council, or his nominee, four elected members of the Council, one appointed member, and two lay members. The quorum is five, with the requirement that at least one lay member is present.[23] The Professional Conduct Committee consists of thirty members; the President or nominee (as chair of the Committee), two members of the Council appointed by the President as deputy chairs, altogether sixteen elected members, seven appointed members, and seven lay members. The quorum of the PCC is five, including at least one lay member.[24] The Health Committee has nine members; the President or nominee (as chair of the Committee), a member of the Council appointed by the President as deputy chair, making five elected members, two appointed members, and two lay members. There is a quorum of five.[25] The Council elects the membership of these Committees annually from within itself, and has to approve the President's nominations.[26] The rules prevent people being on

---

[21] Medical Act 1983, Sch. 1; General Medical Council (Constitution) Order 1979, SI 1979 No 112, as amended.

[22] Medical Act 1983, s. 1(3). An Assessment Referral Committee and Committee on Professional Performance will also exist from January 1997.

[23] GMC (Constitution of Fitness to Practise Committees) Rules 1996, SI 1996 No 2125, r. 3.

[24] *Ibid.*, as amended, r. 4.   [25] *Ibid.*, as amended, r. 5.   [26] *Ibid.*, r. 9.

more than one of these Committees, save that the President may be on both the PCC and the Health Committee. There is also a rule preventing members being involved in the full hearing of a case that they have already heard in its earlier stages.[27]

The interest of the GMC in the health of doctors concerns problems that affect their fitness to practise. Before the Medical Act 1978 doctors whose ill-health made them a threat to patients could only be dealt with through the disciplinary procedures. Now health matters are dealt with separately. As with misconduct allegations, there is a preliminary screening process, but the intention is that cases will be treated clinically rather than legalistically. Where there is a *prima facie* case that a doctor may be unfit to practise due to health issues, then she or he will be invited to undergo a medical examination. Where a doctor's fitness to practise may be seriously impaired by ill-health, physical or mental, the Health Committee has the power to suspend his or her registration or make it conditional upon compliance with directions imposed by the Committee in the interests of the doctor, or for the protection of the public.[28] Proceedings before the Committee are governed by formal rules, designed to ensure that the practitioner is able to challenge evidence.[29] However, the Committee also has to protect the public from unsafe doctors. If necessary, the Health Committee may hear a case without the doctor being present, provided that it is satisfied that all reasonable steps have been taken to serve notice of the referral on the practitioner.[30]

The constitution of the Education Committee is not prescribed by law.[31] In practice it is dominated by university professors.[32] The general functions of the Committee are to co-ordinate medical education and to promote high standards. It does this by determining the extent of knowledge and skill required for a medical qualification, determining the standard of proficiency to be required at qualifying examinations, and prescribing the pattern of experience needed to obtain full registration (see the next paragraph below).[33] The Education Committee has the power to require educational establishments to provide information about the courses that they run, and to appoint inspectors.[34] A list of approved institutions is found in the Medical Act 1983, and further universities may be added by the Privy Council on recommendation by the Education Committee.[35] The Committee may also

[27] *Ibid.*, rr. 11, 12.   [28] Medical Act 1983, s. 37(1).
[29] GMC Health Committee (Procedure) Rules 1987, SI 1987 No 2174.
[30] *Ibid.*, r. 17(3); *Crompton* v. *GMC*, unreported, 29 July 1986.
[31] Medical Act 1983, Sch. 1, para. 19.   [32] Stacey, n. 14 above, 103–6.
[33] Medical Act 1983, s. 5.   [34] Medical Act 1983, ss. 6, 7.
[35] Medical Act 1983, s. 8.

recommend that the Privy Council withdraw such recognition.[36] Maintaining recognized status is extremely important, as a qualification from an approved institution is the only route by which a United Kingdom-trained doctor can become qualified.

(ii) The Medical Register

There are two medical registers.[37] The first is the 'register of medical practitioners' and is sub-divided into four lists, the principal list, the overseas list, the visiting overseas doctor list, and the visiting EEA practitioner list. The second is 'the register of doctors with limited registration' and contains only overseas doctors (see below). The principal list of the main register contains both fully qualified practitioners and also those completing their training. Doctors training in the United Kingdom are entered onto the register on a provisional basis once they have acquired an approved qualification.[38] When they have also gained a year's practical experience, they receive full registration.[39] The principal list also contains doctors who are nationals of other Member States of the European Community. They are entitled to be admitted to the principal list as fully registered practitioners if they have a recognized EC qualification.[40] Such doctors may also practise temporarily in the United Kingdom without applying for full registration. Instead, they must inform the Registrar of the services that they intend to offer, if necessary retrospectively in urgent cases. The registrar will then enter them on the list of visiting EEC practitioners.[41]

Accreditation of specialists is not undertaken by the GMC, but by a non-statutory committee set up by the medical Royal Colleges, known as the Joint Committee on Higher Medical Training. The JCHMT has a discretion as to the basis for accreditation, but it must act fairly and follow its published criteria.[42] The GMC allows doctors to record specialist training in the register,[43] but they need not do so and there is no formal register of specialists. European law requires that equivalent specialist qualifications obtained in other EC countries be recognized,[44] but there is no formal registration process for this purpose under the Medical Act 1983. The GMC issues certificates of specialist training for the purposes of recognition in other EC countries on the

[36] Medical Act 1983, s. 9.   [37] Medical Act 1983, s. 2.
[38] Medical Act 1983, s. 15.
[39] Medical Act 1983, ss. 3, 10, 11, and Medical Act 1950 (Period of Employment as House Officers) Regulations Approval Order 1952, SI 1952 No 2050.
[40] Medical Act 1983 s. 3. Mutual recognition of qualifications is required by Council Directive 93/16/EEC [1993] OJ L165. The provisions are incorporated into the 1983 Act by the European Primary Medical Qualifications Regulations 1996, SI 1996 No 1591.
[41] Medical Act 1983, s. 18.   [42] R. v. JCHMT, ex p. Goldstein [1992] 3 Med. LR 278.
[43] Medical Act 1983, s. 16.   [44] Council Directive 75/362/EEC, n. 40 above, chs. III and IV.

recommendation of the JCHMT. The standards for United Kingdom accreditation and EC certification should be the same.[45]

Overseas doctors from non-EC countries are treated slightly differently.[46] The General Medical Council acts unlawfully if these differences amount to unjustifiable discrimination under the Race Relations Act 1976.[47] Full registration, on the overseas list, is accorded to those who have a qualification recognized by the GMC, have a satisfactory standard of English, are of good character, and have practical experience equivalent to that required of those qualifying in the United Kingdom.[48] Practitioners from EC countries need show only that they have the requisite qualifications. Language tests had to be abandoned as breaching EC law.[49] Non-EC overseas doctors with the qualifications, but not the necessary experience, may be accorded provisional registration on the overseas list.[50] Temporary registration for up to a year is also available to overseas doctors.[51] Where the treatment of non-EC practitioners differs is in relation to the limited registration.[52] Here, doctors are registered only for specified period and in respect of a particular post, and must work under supervision. Limited registration can be extended, but only for a maximum of five years. A doctor with limited registration may apply for full registration on the overseas list.

Being a registered medical practitioner confers a specific legal status which carries a number of privileges. There is no general legal monopoly on practising medicine, although professional monopolies are created for a number of areas of practice. Some are restricted solely to registered doctors; abortions,[53] tattooing children,[54] removal of human tissue for transplant,[55] treatment for venereal disease for reward,[56] female circumcision for medical purposes.[57] Others are shared with other health professionals; attending childbirth,[58] eye tests, fitting contact lenses, selling or supplying optical appliances,[59] dentistry.[60] Only doctors may prescribe certain medicines, although dentists, midwives, and some nurses are allowed to prescribe some 'prescription only'

---

[45] R. v. JCHMT, ex p. Goldstein, n. 42 above; Case 115/78; Knoors v. Secretary of State for Economic Affairs (Netherlands) [1979] 2 CMLR 357.

[46] See Stacey, n. 14 above, 125–38.   [47] GMC v. Goba [1988] IRLR 425.

[48] Medical Act 1983, ss. 19, 20; R. v. GMC, ex p. Virik, The Times, 31 Oct. 1995.

[49] Stacey, n. 14 above, 136–8.   [50] Medical Act 1983, s. 21.

[51] Ibid., s. 27.   [52] Ibid., s. 22.   [53] Abortion Act 1967.

[54] Tattooing of Minors Act 1969, extending also to persons under the direction of a doctor.

[55] Human Tissue Act 1961.   [56] Venereal Disease Act 1917.

[57] Prohibition of Female Circumcision Act 1985. There is a specific provision in relation to childbirth that also covers midwives.

[58] Nurses, Midwives and Health Visitors Act 1979, s. 17 (shared with registered midwives). See further Ch. 17.

[59] Opticians Act 1989, ss. 24, 25, 27 (shared with opticians).

[60] Dentists Act 1984, ss. 38, 41 (shared with dentists).

drugs. There are also various powers of certification (e.g. death, sick leave from work) which can only be exercised by doctors.[61]

However, economic reality creates an effective monopoly over most medical practice through two provisions. First, only registered practitioners may recover fees through the law courts for 'medical advice, attendance, or for the performance of any operation, or for any medicine which he has both prescribed and supplied'.[62] Special savings apply to protect chemists and dentists from this prohibition.[63] Secondly, only a registered doctor can hold an appointment as a physician, surgeon, or medical officer in a public institution.[64] It is also an offence to pretend to be registered.[65] However, there is no protection of medical titles as there is for dentists, opticians, osteopaths, and chiropractors.[66]

(iii) Discipline

The disciplinary function of the General Medical Council is perhaps the area of its work that has attracted the most criticism.[67] The Council is charged not only with ensuring that doctors may not be entered onto the register unless they are properly trained, but also that those who are subsequently proved to be unfit to practise are removed from it. The Medical Act 1983 gives the Council the power to administer disciplinary sanctions to doctors whom it finds guilty of serious professional misconduct. A separate procedure exists to consider the position of doctors who are unfit to practise for reasons of ill-health. There is no time limit on the bringing of a complaint, but the rules of natural justice may sometimes make it unfair to hold a disciplinary hearing long after the event complained about.[68]

(a) Procedure

The procedure for considering allegations of serious professional misconduct contains four stages. Some complaints are directed away from the GMC by its

[61] Medical Act 1983, s. 48, provides that where legislation requires certification by a doctor, then the doctor must be fully registered.

[62] Medical Act 1983, s. 46.   [63] *Ibid.*, s. 54.

[64] *Ibid.*, s. 47. Arguably this provisions covers all hospitals, save those which are not publicly funded and in which no charges are made.   [65] *Ibid.*, s. 49.

[66] Dentists Act 1984, s. 39; Opticians Act 1989, s. 28; Osteopaths Act 1993, s. 32; Chiropractors Act 1994, s. 32.

[67] R. G. Smith, *Medical Discipline: The Professional Conduct Jurisdiction of the General Medical Council, 1858–1990* (Oxford: Oxford University Press, 1994); R. Smith, 'Discipline I: The Hordes at the Gates; II: The Preliminary Screener—A Powerful Gatekeeper; III: The Final Stages' (1989) 289 *BMJ* 1502–5, 1569–71, 1632–4.

[68] *R.* v. *GMC, ex p. Shaikh*, unreported, 3 July 1990. In this case the court refused to quash a decision to proceed with a case involving a rape allegation over four and a half years after the alleged incident.

staff, acting under standing orders that require them to suggest that NHS complaints procedures are used before the Council gets involved. A significant proportion of cases never get beyond this stage, in 1983 it was as high as 27 per cent, but in 1993 it had fallen to 9.9 per cent.[69] There is no statutory basis for this administrative filtering process and it has attracted criticism.[70]

At the second stage, cases are considered by a preliminary screener.[71] The preliminary screener will be a doctor, either the President of the Council or another member appointed by him. Since 1990, the screener has been assisted by a lay member of the Council. A decision that an allegation should not proceed to the second stage can now only be made if that lay person agrees. In practice, a large number of cases get no further than the preliminary screener. In 1983 57 per cent were disposed of at this stage and during the 1980s the proportion rose, until in 1990 it was 66.5 per cent. When lay screeners become involved, the proportion of cases that did not proceed to the third stage dropped to 40 per cent, but it has risen again to 50.6 per cent in 1993.[72] The vast majority of cases are either rejected completely by the preliminary screener or referred on to the Preliminary Proceedings Committee (PPC), but where issues are raised about treatment it is quite common for the doctor to be sent a letter of advice.[73] Some types of case routinely pass the preliminary screening stage. In 1989–90, all the allegations of alcohol abuse and all criminal conviction cases were forwarded to the PPC.[74] Complainants will not know why their allegations have not reached the later stages and it would be very hard to challenge a refusal to pass a case on. In principle, the courts will allow a complainant to challenge the preliminary screener's decision to reject a complaint.[75] However, such attempts are unlikely to succeed unless the screener has made a mistake of law.

At the third stage of the disciplinary process, allegations are reviewed by the Preliminary Proceedings Committee of the Council. In 1993 10 per cent of complaints reached this stage.[76] The PPC will refer the case to the Professional Conduct Committee (PCC) if there are matters which it believes raise a question whether there has been serious professional misconduct, and will identify those matters for the PCC. This does not prevent new issues being raised at a later stage, after further investigations, which have not been considered by

---

[69] GMC, *Annual Reports* for 1983 and 1993.

[70] J. Robinson, *A Patient Voice at the GMC* (London: Health Rights, 1988).

[71] GMC Preliminary Proceedings Committee and Professional Conduct Committee (Procedure) Rules of Council 1988, SI 1988 No 2255, rr. 4–10.

[72] Figures from GMC, *Annual Reports* for 1983 to 1993.   [73] Smith, n. 67 above, 8–9.

[74] Conviction cases have, by law, to be forwarded, GMC (Preliminary Proceedings Committee and Professional Conduct Committee (Procedure) Rules, n. 71 above, r. 10.

[75] *R. v. The President of the General Medical Council, ex p. Petch* (CA), unreported, 9 Dec. 1988.

[76] GMC, *Annual Report* for 1993.

the PPC.[77] A case may also be referred to the Health Committee, but only after the doctor has been invited to submit to a medical examination.[78] Finally, the PPC may determine that the case should not be referred on. In 1993, this happened in approximately 52 per cent of the cases considered by the PPC.[79] If this happens, then the complainant and the practitioner will be informed, but there is no obligation to give reasons for a decision, and the Committee meets in private, so the basis for declining to refer a case will not be known to them.[80] This may not be the end of the matter, however, for if the practitioner comes before the GMC again having been convicted, or a further complaint about professional misconduct is made within two years, the President may refer the allegations that have been dismissed back to the Committee along with the new matters.[81] The PPC has the power to require further investigations into allegations before it decides what to do, and may make an order for interim suspension or interim conditional registration if necessary to protect the public, or, in the case of conditions only, in the interests of the doctor.[82]

The fourth and final stage is a full hearing before the Professional Conduct Committee. Over the period 1983–90 only 5 per cent of complaints to the GMC reached this point.[83] The proportion has been gradually dropping, and in 1993 it was only 3.6 per cent.[84] As already discussed, the majority of the members of this committee must be those elected to the Council by doctors on the register. This is designed to ensure that standards reflect the realities of daily practice.[85] There has been criticism of the small lay involvement,[86] although it has also been argued that lay people's inclusion in disciplinary matters is flawed because they cannot adjudicate on medical issues.[87]

Hearings before the Professional Conduct Committee can proceed without the doctor being present,[88] but usually the procedure is formal and not unlike that of a court of law.[89] However, it is important to note that the parties to the hearing are the GMC, a quasi-prosecutor, and the doctor. The complainant is not represented. The PCC has first to consider whether the facts have been proved, and whether such facts as have been proved constitute serious professional misconduct. At the end of the evidence presented by the GMC's

---

[77] GMC (Preliminary Proceedings Committee and Professional Conduct Committee (Procedure) Rules, n. 71 above, r. 11(2).

[78] *Ibid.*, r. 11(3).   [79] Calculated from GMC, *Annual Report* for 1993.

[80] GMC (Preliminary Proceedings Committee and Professional Conduct Committee (Procedure) Rules, n. 71 above, rr. 11(5), 15, 16.

[81] *Ibid.*, r. 14.   [82] *Ibid.*, rr. 12, 13.   [83] Smith, n. 67 above, 11–12.

[84] Calculated from GMC, *Annual Report* for 1993.

[85] M. Stacey, *Regulating British Medicine: The General Medical Council* (Chichester: Wiley, 1992), 59–60.

[86] Robinson, n. 70 above.   [87] Smith, n. 67 above, 80–2.   [88] N. 71 above, r. 23.

[89] For accounts of the flavour of proceedings, see Stacey, n. 85 above, 141–9; M. Rosenthal, *Dealing with Medical Malpractice*, n. 13 above, 59–61, A. Dally, *A Doctor's Story* (London: Macmillan, 1990).

solicitor, the doctor may submit that the facts have not been proved, or that they do not constitute serious professional misconduct. Only once the PCC has rejected those submissions does the doctor need to present a defence.[90] After the defence is heard, the PCC decides whether the facts alleged to constitute serious professional conduct have been proved. If it concludes that they have, then the circumstances of the offence and the character and previous history of the practitioner are considered in order to determine whether there has been serious professional misconduct.[91] The criteria for that decision, and the sanctions available if it is made are discussed in the following sections. In some cases, there is no need to undergo the fact-finding stage of the proceedings, either because the facts are admitted, or because they have already been established in criminal proceedings.[92]

(b) Criteria

The disciplinary jurisdiction of the General Medical Council enables it to censure doctors who have been found guilty of 'serious professional misconduct'. This phrase is not defined in the Medical Act 1983, and its meaning is left mainly up to the PPC itself to determine. In *Doughty* v. *General Dental Council* the Privy Council held that the words 'serious professional misconduct' indicated 'conduct connected with [the] profession in which the [practitioner] has fallen short, by omission or commission, of the standards of conduct expected among [members of the profession] and that such falling short . . . is serious'.[93] In its view, it was no longer appropriate to consider whether the practitioner's conduct had been 'infamous' or 'disgraceful' (the old phrase). Their Lordships also indicated that they thought that 'serious professional misconduct' was a broader category than that which was 'infamous and disgraceful'. They noted that a less serious sanction had been introduced when the phrase was substituted, indicating that less serious conduct might now be dealt with by the disciplinary procedures. In *McCandless* v. *GMC*[94] the Privy Council confirmed that the *Doughty* approach applied to doctors. It also held that serious negligence that fell 'deplorably short' of the standard patients are entitled to expect from their doctors could constitute serious professional misconduct. These comments imply that cases on the old law where a practitioner was found guilty would probably be treated similarly today, while conduct that was not regarded as sufficiently serious to come within the old definition could be covered by the new one.

Examples of conduct which has led to doctors being disciplined, where the

---

[90] N. 71 above, r. 27(1).   [91] *Ibid.*, r. 28.   [92] *Ibid.*, rr. 25, 27(1)(a).
[93] [1987] 3 All ER 843, 847. The quotation has been adapted, as indicated, to generalize the original references to dentists.
[94] [1996] 1 WLR 168.

Privy Council has upheld the decision, include failures to visit patients,[95] sexual relationships with patients,[96] falsely representing that an abortion had been performed,[97] improperly supplying drugs to a spouse,[98] disparaging medical colleagues,[99] offering patients money not to report conduct to the GMC.[100] However, it was not necessarily infamous professional conduct to be associated with a company, providing clinical services, from which financial benefit was to be gained.[101] Other behaviour that has been found to constitute serious professional misconduct includes breach of confidence, treatment without consent, false certification, and neglecting patients.[102] It has been expressly stated by the Privy Council that the categories of serious professional misconduct are never closed,[103] so that these precedents are in no sense exhaustive.

It has been observed that the GMC rarely concerns itself with the sorts of conduct that might constitute professional negligence and give rise to a malpractice suit.[104] However, in recent years there have been examples of individual cases of malpractice being treated as serious professional misconduct. In 1992, a consultant obstetrician was found guilty of such misconduct for failing to explain sufficiently the risks of vaginal delivery to a woman who had undergone two previous Caesarian sections. Despite her knowledge of the case, the consultant had failed to arrange to be present personally, or for another experienced doctor to be there instead, and had given an insufficiently detailed plan for the management of labour to the midwifery and nursing staff. The consultant was suspended from the register for six months.[105] In 1993, the name of an anæsthetist working as a locum consultant was erased from the register for failing to monitor properly a patient's condition and failing to initiate and direct resuscitation. Concerns had previously been expressed about the doctor's competence in a number of hospitals.[106] It is clear, therefore that a single incompetent act may sometimes constitute serious professional misconduct.[107]

---

[95] *Rodgers* v. *GMC*, unreported, 19 Nov. 1984; *Robindra Nath Datta* v. *GMC*, unreported, 26 Jan. 1986.

[96] *de Gregory* v. *GMC* [1961] AC 957; *McCoan* v. *GMC* [1964] 3 All ER 143; *Sivarajah* v. *GMC* [1964] 1 WLR 112; *Battacharya* v. *GMC* [1967] 2 AC 259; *Libman* v. *GMC* [1972] AC 217.

[97] *Sloan* v. *GMC* [1970] 2 All ER 686.   [98] *Finegan* v. *GMC* [1987] 1 WLR 121.

[99] *Allinson* v. *General Council of Medical Registration and Education* [1894] 1 QB 750 (CA).

[100] *Libman* v. *GMC*, n. 96 above.   [101] *Faridian* v. *GMC* [1971] AC 995.

[102] Smith, n. 67 above, 33–42, 101–11; J. Mitchell, 'A Fundamental Problem of Consent' (1995) 310 *BMJ* 43–6.

[103] *Sloan* v. *GMC*, n. 97 above.

[104] Rosenthal, *Dealing with Medical Malpractice*, n. 13 above, 61.

[105] GMC, *Annual report* (1992), 20.   [106] GMC, *Annual report* (1993), 20.

[107] *McCandless* v. *GMC* [1996] 1 WLR 168. See also *R* v. *Pharmaceutical Society, ex p. Sokoh*, *The Times*, 4 Dec. 1986.

(c) Sanctions

When the Professional Conduct Committee has decided that a practitioner has been guilty of serious professional misconduct, a range of sanctions is available. It can decide to take no further action, sometimes issuing an 'admonition' to the practitioner in respect of his or her conduct.[108] If the Committee feels that more serious action is necessary, it has three sanctions at its disposal: first, imposing conditions on the doctor's licence to practise; secondly, suspending the doctor's registration; thirdly, erasing the doctor's name from the Medical Register. The Committee is obliged to consider these options individually, beginning with the least serious and moving on only if it believes that the lesser sanction is inadequate.[109] If the Committee needs further evidence before taking a decision, it can postpone consideration of the sanction.[110] The effect of each of these sanctions is further defined by the legislation.

Conditions may be imposed both in order to protect the public and also for the benefit of the practitioner. Examples of conditions that have been imposed include that doctors should not prescribe or possess controlled drugs, that they must undertake further training, should refrain from providing certain types of care, should not work unsupervised, and should only practise in NHS facilities.[111] Conditions must be imposed for a fixed period, which cannot be longer than three years.[112] If it believes it appropriate, the Committee can declare that at some time before the end of the period of conditional registration it will reconsider the case to decide whether the period should be extended.[113] Extensions can only be for twelve months at a time,[114] and it is unclear whether the total period of conditional registration must be limited to three years. The Committee also has the power to revoke or vary the conditions. Should a doctor fail to comply with the conditions, then the Committee has the power to impose more onerous conditions, extend the period of conditional registration, suspend the practitioner for up to a year, or erase her or his name from the Register.[115] In some cases, something similar in effect is achieved by the less formal route of undertakings being given by the doctor, often in a plea in mitigation in order to avoid a more serious sanction.[116]

Suspension from the Register must also be for a fixed period, in this case for up to a year. The Committee has the same power to reserve the right to

---

[108] GMC Preliminary Proceedings Committee and Professional Conduct Committee (Procedure) Rules of Council 1988, n. 71 above, rr. 30, 34.

[109] *Ibid.*, r. 31.   [110] R. 30(1).   [111] Smith, n. 67 above, 160–8.

[112] GMC Preliminary Proceedings Committee and Professional Conduct Committee (Procedure) Rules of Council 1988, n. 71 above, r. 31(2).

[113] R. 31(4).   [114] R. 42 and Medical Act 1983, s. 36(4).   [115] R. 42(3).

[116] Smith, n. 67 above, 158–60.

consider extending suspension as it has with conditional registration. On such reconsideration, conditional registration, an extension of the suspension, and erasure are all available. It is clear that the total period of suspension imposed can be more than a year,[117] but the Committee cannot extend a suspension merely because it thinks that the initial decision was too lenient.[118] Suspension has a serious effect on an employed doctor's position. A person who has been suspended is to be treated as not being registered,[119] and only those entered on the Register can be employed as doctors in a public hospital.[120] Consequently, a suspension will effectively terminate a doctor's employment.

Erasure will clearly also have a serious effect on a doctor's employment and right to practise. However, it is perhaps not quite as drastic a sanction as at first appears. A doctor can apply to be restored to the register ten months after he was originally struck off.[121] Over the period 1858–1990 48.8 per cent of those struck off the register were reinstated.[122] However, restoration has become less common, with only just over 20 per cent of those struck off in 1980 being restored by 1990.[123] Factors that influence decisions on restoration are contrition, future intentions, educational standards, the availability of suitable employment, and the views of the original complainant.[124]

(d) Appeal and Review

A doctor whose registration is erased, suspended, or rendered conditional by the Professional Conduct Committee, the Health Committee, or by the GMC itself for fraudulently obtaining registration may appeal to the Privy Council. The Privy Council may dismiss the doctor's appeal, it may quash the original decision, or, in cases of fraudulent registration, it may remit the case to the GMC with a direction as to its disposal.[125] However, the court's task is not to substitute its own view for that of the Professional Conduct Committee, but to ascertain whether there was evidence on which the Committee could take the view that there had been professional misconduct of a serious nature.[126]

(e) Assessment

If the GMC's disciplinary jurisdiction is considered as a procedure for handling complaints, it is seriously defective.[127] Complainants are not able to

---

[117] This is implied by the ability to extend for not more than 12 months *at a time*.
[118] *Taylor* v. *GMC* [1990] 2 All ER 263.   [119] Medical Act 1983, s. 36(8).
[120] Medical Act 1983, s. 47.
[121] Medical Act 1983, s. 41; GMC Preliminary Proceedings Committee and Professional Conduct Committee (Procedure) Rules 1988, n. 71 above, r. 46.
[122] Smith, n. 67 above, 208.   [123] *Ibid.*, 206.
[124] *Ibid.*, 210–20.   [125] Medical Act 1983, s. 40.
[126] *McCandless* v. *GMC*, n. 107 above; *Doughty* v. *General Dental Council* [1987] 3 All ER 843, 847.
[127] Robinson, n. 70 above.

cross-examine the doctor and will not receive any compensation if the doctor is found guilty. While there was a dramatic increase in the number of complaints processed through the NHS procedures, the GMC handled a similar number of cases throughout the 1970s and 1980s. One commentator has suggested that this is a direct result of the limited resources at the Council's disposal.[128] Another argues that it is better explained as the consequence of the desire to avoid alienating the doctors who pay the costs of the Council. Enough doctors must be disciplined to encourage members of the profession to accept that standards must be maintained, but it does not seem to have been the Council's practice to aim to root out all incompetent doctors.[129]

One commentator, who compared the GMC with professional disciplinary bodies in Sweden and the United States, concluded that the GMC was more dominated by doctors, more concerned with internal professional matters (as opposed to malpractice), and more reluctant to impose severe penalties than its foreign counterparts.[130] The GMC has also been accused of being more concerned with the sexual conduct of its members than with the way in which patients are treated. This is probably no longer fair, as a trend towards increased scrutiny of professional competence can be detected.[131] Smith's study of the disciplinary jurisdiction of the GMC noted that in the 1980s the GMC considered far more cases of neglect than it had done previously. Over the period 1858–1990, sexual offences accounted for 12.12 per cent of complaints and neglect of patients only 7.79 per cent.[132] However, Stacey's analysis of the period 1983–9 showed that the PPC considered 259 cases of disregard of professional responsibility to patients and only sixty-five of misuse of professional power (only some of which were sexual misconduct). Over the same period, the PCC considered 121 cases of disregard of professional responsibility and only thirty relating to misuse of professional power.[133] In 1993, the PCC heard twenty-six cases of alleged neglect of patients, and eleven concerning sexual misbehaviour. However, only two of the latter concerned 'improper emotional/sexual relations with patients/colleagues'.[134]

It has also been argued that the GMC disciplinary system fails to do justice to the doctors brought before it. Smith has raised questions about the legality of some aspect of the proceedings, especially the fact that some hearings are in secret and the inadequate drafting of some charges. He has also suggested that the GMC does not deal fairly with disputes of principle over how medicine should be practised and that reasons should be given for decisions.

---

[128] Rosenthal, n. 13 above, 115, 119–20, 122.   [129] Stacey, n. 14 above, 220–1.

[130] Rosenthal, 'Medical Discipline in Cross-cultural Perspective', n. 13 above, 26–50. See also Rosenthal, n. 13 above.

[131] *Ibid.*, 117, 123.

[132] Smith, n. 67 above, 102–10, table 4.3, fig. 4.3 and fig. 4.11.

[133] Stacey, n. 14 above, 162–3.   [134] GMC, *Annual Report* for 1993, 18.

Linked with this are problems of partiality, due to the fact that there is potential for those sitting in judgment on their colleagues to have preconceived views. Smith has proposed a number of detailed reforms to deal with these issues.[135]

The most important changes under way concern the introduction of greater jurisdiction over the competence of doctors. The Medical (Professional Performance) Act 1995 will allow the GMC to examine more closely allegations of professional incompetence, which fall short of being serious professional misconduct under the present legislation. There will be scope for audit of a practitioner's work, and counselling and retraining if required. The machinery of professional discipline would only need to be brought into play if these less drastic measures failed.[136]

(iv) Medical Ethics

The GMC also has a statutory responsibility to issue guidance on medical ethics and the standards of conduct expected of practitioners.[137] Until 1995, the principal means by which this was done was the booklet *Professional Conduct and Discipline: Fitness to Practise*, known as the 'blue book'.[138] Revising that guidance is the task of the non-statutory standards committee. The guidance is divided into four parts. The first explains the disciplinary processes of the Council. The second illustrates the forms of professional misconduct that may give rise to disciplinary proceedings. The fourth outlines the procedures used when a doctor is alleged to be unfit to practise for health reasons. The third section offers advice on standards of conduct and medical ethics. It discusses a number of issues of professional etiquette, including referral to specialists and various aspects of the advertising of services. In relation to the former, the guidance seeks to preserve the principle that access to specialists should usually be via general practitioners. Patients should not be encouraged to seek specialist services directly. The Council's position on advertising has been relaxed in response to outside pressure.[139] It now allows for the publication of factual information about services, providing that superiority is not implied, nor other doctors disparaged. The only extensive discussion of an issue of medical ethics concerns confidentiality (see Chapter 11 for details). There is some guidance on the conduct of clinical trials, but it covers the need to resist financial inducements from pharmaceutical compa-

---

[135] Smith, n. 67 above, 221–32.
[136] The GMC's proposals are reviewed and appraised in *ibid.* 45–52.
[137] Medical Act 1983, s. 35.   [138] A new edn. was published in 1992.
[139] Stacey, n. 14 above, 190–4; Monopolies and Mergers Commission, *Services of Medical Practitioners* (London: HMSO, 1989, Cm 582).

nies rather than the principles that determine whether the design of a trial is ethical.

In the past, it could be said that the primary focus of the GMC's guidance was more concerned with professional conduct than medical ethics in the wider sense. Early moves towards more extensive discussion of the place of patients were primarily in response to outside pressures,[140] and the GMC tended to leave ethical matters to be explored by the non-statutory bodies. Thus, statements on medical ethics were more commonly issued by the Royal Colleges and the British Medical Association than by the GMC itself.

In 1995, in an important development, the GMC published a set of four booklets on standards of conduct expected of doctors which focus on the principles of medical ethics.[141] The booklets establish the following set of core principles designed to justify patients putting trust in their doctors. Doctors must make the care of the patients their first concern, treat every patient politely and considerately, respect their dignity and privacy, listen to and respect their views, inform them in a way they can understand, and respect their right to be fully involved in decisions about their care. Doctors must also keep their professional knowledge and skills up to date, recognize the limits of their competence, be honest and trustworthy, respect and protect confidential information, make sure their personal beliefs do not prejudice patients' care, act quickly to protect patients from risk due to their own or colleagues' unfitness to practise, avoid abusing medical colleagues, and work with colleagues in patients' interests. Doctors should not discriminate against patients or colleagues.

B. Nursing, Midwifery, and Health Visiting

As with medicine, the history of the nursing professions predates their statutory regulation. However, there is now a far greater concentration of power in the statutory bodies than is the case in medicine.[142] The Royal College of Nurses, the Royal College of Midwives, and the Health Visitors Association do not have the formal positions of power that are held by the medical Royal

---

[140] M. Stacey, 'The General Medical Council and Medical Ethics' in G. Weisz (ed.), *Social Science Perspectives on Medical Ethics* (London: Kluwer, 1990), 163–84.

[141] See GMC, *Good Medical Practice* (London: GMC, 1995), published with three booklets of specific guidance—GMC, *Confidentiality* (London: GMC, 1995); GMC, *HIV and AIDS: The Ethical Considerations* (London: GMC, 1995); and GMC, *Advertising* (London: GMC, 1995).

[142] For a succinct overview from the then Assistant Registrar (Standards and Ethics) of the UKCC, see R. Pyne, 'The Professional Dimension' in J. Tingle and A. Cribb (eds.), *Nursing Law and Ethics* (Oxford: Blackwell Science, 1995), 36–58.

Colleges. Prior to 1979, there were separate bodies administering the three professions. The first Midwives Act was passed in 1902, nurse registration dates back to 1919, and the Health Visiting and Social Work Training Act was passed in 1962 (although prior to this time health visiting had already been restricted to qualified nurses). The professions were brought together by the Nurses, Midwives and Health Visitors Act 1979 under the United Kingdom Central Council for Nursing, Midwifery and Health Visiting (UKCC). There remains considerable dissatisfaction amongst midwives at the perceived loss of status that the 1979 Act represented, and there is a campaign for a separate Midwifery Act.

(i) The Constitution of the UKCC

The UKCC consists of sixty members.[143] Of those members, forty are elected by the professions.[144] The electorate is subdivided according to profession and country of residence. The electoral scheme ensures that at least seven nurses, two midwives, and a health visitor are returned for each of the countries of the United Kingdom. Candidates are elected by the single transferable vote method.[145] The remaining twenty places on the Council are filled by appointment by the Secretary of State. There is no requirement that those appointees are from other health professions or lay. They must be taken either from amongst the ranks of registered nurses, midwives, and health visitors or from those with 'such qualifications and experience in education or other fields as . . . will be of value to the Council in the performance of its functions'.[146] In practice, the Secretary of State has appointed lay people (including two nominated by consumer organizations) and doctors to the UKCC.[147] Members of the UKCC are appointed for five years.[148]

The principal functions of the UKCC are set out in section 2 of the Nurses, Midwives and Health Visitors Act 1979. They are to establish and improve standards of training and professional conduct, including giving advice on standards of professional conduct. The Council must also maintain the pro-

[143] Nurses, Midwives and Health Visitors Act 1979, Sch. 1, para. 1, as substituted by the Nurses, Midwives and Health Visitors Act 1992, s. 1 and Sch. 1; UKCC for Nurses, Midwives and Health Visitors (Membership Proposal) Approval Order 1992, SI 1992 No 2160.

[144] Technically, these members are appointed by the Secretary of State, but only on being elected under the statutory electoral scheme, Nurses, Midwives and Health Visitors Act 1979, s. 1(3) as substituted by the Nurses, Midwives and Health Visitors Act 1992.

[145] UKCC Nurses, Midwives and Health Visitors (Electoral Scheme) Order 1992, SI 1992 No 2159, r. 4(1).

[146] Nurses, Midwives and Health Visitors Act 1979, s. 1(4)(b), as substituted by the Nurses, Midwives and Health Visitors Act 1992.

[147] Pyne, n. 142 above, 36–58, 38.

[148] The UKCC for Nursing, Midwifery and Health Visiting (Term of Office of Members) Order 1993, SI 1993 No 590.

fessional register.[149] Standing committees of the Council are required by the Act on midwifery and finance.[150] There are also two committees that deal with professional conduct (the Preliminary Proceedings Committee and the Professional Conduct Committee), and a Health Committee (which deals with cases where a practitioner may be unfit to practise for health reasons).[151]

Unlike the medical scheme, there are separate bodies to deal with educational matters. Since April 1993, the National Boards for Nursing Midwifery and Health Visiting (one for each country of the United Kingdom) have been executive bodies, whose principal function is to oversee the education of nurses, health visitors, and midwives. Previously, the National Boards actually provided courses, but their function is now restricted to accrediting institutions who provide such courses, and informing the public about careers in the professions.[152] Prior to April 1993, the National Boards also carried out preliminary investigations into allegations of professional misconduct. That function is now carried out by the UKCC. The members of the National Boards are appointed by the Secretary of State (previously they were elected by the profession). They each comprise a chair; the chief executive; six appointed members, of whom one must be from each of the three professions, and one with educational experience and qualifications; a finance officer; and a professional officer.[153] The responsibility for the actual provision of professional education was devolved to the regional health authorities after the implementation of the Nurses, Midwives and Health Visitors Act 1992. This was in direct conflict with the proposals of the independent review of the UKCC, which preceded the Act.[154] With the demise of regional health authorities, education is mostly provided by higher education institutions.

(ii) The Register

Since 1983, when the 1979 Act was implemented, there has been a single professional register.[155] It is divided into a number of categories according to the

[149] S. 10.   [150] Ss. 3 and 4.

[151] Nurses, Midwives and Health Visitors (Professional Conduct) Rules 1993 Approval Order, SI 1993 No 893.

[152] Nurses, Midwives and Health Visitors Act 1979, s. 6, as amended by the Nurses, Midwives and Health Visitors Act 1992, s. 5. See also the functions added by para. 12 of the National Board for Nursing, Midwifery and Health Visiting for England (Constitution and Administration) Order 1993, SI 1993 No 629, as amended by the National Board for Nursing, Midwifery and Health Visiting for England (Constitution and Administration) Amendment Order 1994, SI 1994 No 586.

[153] Nurses, Midwives and Health Visitors Act 1979, s. 5, as amended by the Nurses, Midwives and Health Visitors Act 1992, s. 4; National Board for Nursing, Midwifery and Health Visiting for England (Constitution and Administration) Order 1993, SI 1993 No 629.

[154] Peat Marwick McClintock, *Review of the United Kingdom Central Council and the Four National Boards for Nursing, Midwifery and Health Visiting* (London: DoH, 1989).

[155] Nurses, Midwives and Health Visitors Act 1979, s. 10; Nurses, Midwives and Health Visitors (Parts of the Register) Order 1983, SI 1983 No 667, as amended.

qualifications held. There are fifteen categories in all. They distinguish between the professions of midwifery, health visiting, and nursing. The latter is subdivided according to the specialties of general, mental illness, mental health, mental handicap, adult, and children's nursing.

Some of this complexity relates to the historical patterns of training, under which nurses obtained a range of different qualifications. The nursing categories differentiate between those with first and second-level qualifications. Second-level nurses are generally known as enrolled nurses and first-level nurses as registered nurses. Registration indicates a higher level of training than enrolment. There is no longer split-level training for nurses. The principal divisions that arise in the current system for professional education are related to areas of expertise. They are between midwifery, health visiting, adult nursing, mental health nursing, mental handicap nursing, and children's nursing.

To be entered upon the register, applicants must hold an appropriate professional qualification and satisfy the UKCC that they are of 'good character'. Qualifications gained in the United Kingdom are validated by the National Boards. European Community law requires the mutual recognition of qualifications, and this has been incorporated into the 1979 Act. Qualifications outside the EC must be recognized by the UKCC.[156] Practitioners pay a periodic fee to be kept on the register, which funds the activities of the UKCC. Their registration will cease to be effective if they do not pay. They must be notified by the Registrar at least forty-five days before the fee is due, and it is open to them to avoid the sanction for non-payment by showing that they did not receive such notification.[157] While being on the register brings few privileges, it is a criminal offence to falsely to represent that you have qualifications in nursing, midwifery, or health visiting, or that you are on the professional register.[158] Registered midwives share (with doctors) a monopoly on attendance at childbirth.[159]

(iii) Discipline

The disciplinary jurisdiction of the UKCC is ostensibly very similar to that of the GMC. However, there are a number of significant differences. The criterion applied to determine what conduct should come within the system is broader, being 'professional misconduct' without any requirement that it be serious. The UKCC has proved itself more concerned with standards of

---

[156] Nurses, Midwives, and Health Visitors Act 1979, s. 11.
[157] *R. v. UKCC, ex p. Bailey* [1991] 2 Med. LR 145.
[158] Nurses, Midwives and Health Visitors Act 1979, s. 14.
[159] *Ibid.*, s. 17. See further Ch. 17.

professional practice than its medical counterpart. Arguably, this has been at the expense of individual autonomy, and aimed at supporting the claims of the profession as a whole to higher status. There are also subtle differences in the sanctions available.

(a) Procedure

Disciplinary proceedings go through a number of stages. Allegations must initially be made to the UKCC. There is no time limit restricting them being brought. Once a complaint is received an officer of the council considers it to see whether it might, if substantiated, lead to removal from the register.[160] There may be an initial investigation at this stage, possibly by a solicitor, to see whether there is a case to answer.[161] If it is thought that the allegations might lead to the practitioner against whom they have been made being struck off, she or he will be notified in writing that the matter will come before the Preliminary Proceedings Committee, given a summary of the allegations, and invited to make a preliminary response.[162]

The Preliminary Proceedings Committee (PPC) then considers the matter and obtains whatever reports it believes necessary, including a sworn statement from the complainant if appropriate.[163] The practitioner will then be sent a Notice of Proceedings, copies of the allegations, and any statements, and will be asked to respond in writing.[164] The PPC serves as a filter to ensure that only cases which might succeed result in a full hearing. It is not its responsibility to decide whether the nurse is guilty of professional misconduct, but merely to consider whether there is a case to be answered.

The PPC may proceed in a number of ways. If a full hearing of the case is justified, then the matter is referred to the Professional Conduct Committee.[165] If it is not then the allegation will be dismissed and the practitioner and complainant will be informed of the decision. No reasons need be stated for that decision, and the papers relating to the case are not made available to the parties.[166] As an intermediate step, the PPC may direct the registrar to issue a caution, provided that the practitioner has admitted the facts on which the allegation was based.[167] The PPC may decide that the matter raises the question of the practitioner's fitness to practise on grounds of health, in which case it will refer it to a professional screener to see whether the matter should be considered by the Health Committee.[168] If the Health Committee decides that it is not a health issue it may be referred back to the PPC for further consideration.[169]

---

[160] Nurses, Midwives and Health Visitors (Professional Conduct) Rules 1993, SI 1993 No 893, rr. 6, 8(1).

[161] *Ibid.*, r. 8(2).   [162] *Ibid.*, r. 8(1).   [163] *Ibid.*, r. 8(3).   [164] *Ibid.*, r. 9(1).

[165] *Ibid.*, r. 8(3).   [166] *Ibid.*, r. 9(5).   [167] *Ibid.*, r. 9(3),(4).   [168] *Ibid.*, rr. 9(3), 30, 34.

[169] *Ibid.*, r. 44.

The UKCC has been responsible for these preliminary stages only since 1993. The task was previously carried out by the National Boards. Statistics published by the English National Board indicated that there was a consistent trend whereby approximately 30 per cent of cases were sent on for a full hearing and 30 per cent result in the sending of the Code of Conduct to the relevant practitioner.[170] In approximately one quarter of the cases, a proportion which has grown steadily from only 10 per cent in 1983–4, no action is taken. In 1989–90 the English National Board considered 496 cases, a increase of 15 per cent over the previous year. It forwarded 30.9 per cent to the UKCC's Professional Conduct Committee, and 3.4 per cent to its Health Committee. The Code of Conduct was sent to 29 per cent of the practitioners in question. Further enquiries were needed into 12.1 per cent of the issues. In 24.6 per cent of the cases no action was taken and the matter was closed.[171]

If the allegations are forwarded to the Professional Conduct Committee, there will be a full hearing. Although previously both the complainant and the practitioner had a right to appear, now the complainant is merely to be given notice of the hearing.[172] Practitioners may choose to be represented by a lawyer or an officer of their professional organization or trade union.[173] The Committee must consider three separate questions. First, it must establish what happened; secondly, it must decide whether what happened constituted 'professional misconduct'; and thirdly, it must determine what action should be taken. The practitioner's representative is permitted to make representations in relation to each of those stages separately.[174]

Practitioners may admit the facts on which the allegations are based. If they do not evidence must be called and witnesses may be cross-examined by practitioners or their representatives.[175] If the Professional Conduct Committee decides that the facts have not been proved or that they are insufficient to constitute professional misconduct they will declare that the respondent is not guilty. A significant proportion of matters investigated originate in criminal convictions against practitioners which have then been reported to the UKCC.[176] Special provisions apply in such cases. The facts have already been

---

[170] English National Board for Nursing, Midwifery and Health Visiting, *Annual Reports 1983–90* (London: 1984–90).

[171] *Ibid.*, 16.

[172] Compare the Nurses, Midwives and Health Visitors (Professional Conduct) Rules 1987, SI 1987 No 2156, r. 6, with the Nurses, Midwives and Health Visitors (Professional Conduct) Rules 1993, n. 160 above, r. 13.

[173] Nurses, Midwives and Health Visitors (Professional Conduct) Rules 1993, n. 160 above, r. 13(5).

[174] *Ibid.*, r. 17, 18.   [175] *Ibid.*, r. 17(3).

[176] Under the old system, for notifications received by the ENB, the figures range from 50% in 1983–5, to 33% in 1986–7. ENB, *Annual Report 1983–4*, App., ix; ENB, *Annual Report 1986–7*, App. 5.1.

established by a court, and the validity of the decision cannot be challenged before the Professional Conduct Committee.[177] The facts are therefore taken to be as the earlier court found them, and no further proof is necessary. This principle does not, however, apply to cases where the accused was sentenced only to probation, or received a conditional or unconditional discharge.[178]

If the Committee finds that the practitioner has been guilty of misconduct it will then decide whether to give judgment as to the appropriate penalty immediately or to postpone it.[179] Postponement allows consideration of whether the lesson has been learnt and practice improved. Where there is no postponement, or when a postponed case comes back for judgment, the Committee must decide whether the misconduct should lead to the practitioner being removed from the register. If it does not, then no further action will be taken.[180] On postponing judgment, the PCC may make recommendations to the practitioner.[181] This allows for what is in effect a warning combined with a probationary period.

(b) Criteria

If the facts are proved then the Committee must decide whether they constitute 'professional misconduct'. The meaning of 'professional misconduct' is defined by the professional conduct rules as 'conduct unworthy of a nurse, midwife or health visitor, as the case may be, and includes obtaining registration by fraud'.[182] Conviction for a criminal offence does not necessarily mean that the nurse was guilty of professional misconduct,[183] only that certain facts have been proved. The Committee must therefore consider whether those facts amount to misconduct in the relevant sense. The UKCC has identified a number of common reasons for removal from the register, including 'reckless and wilfully unskilled practice', concealing mishaps, failing to keep or falsifying records, patient abuse, and breach of confidentiality.[184] These are matters relating to professional work. In some older cases practitioners were struck off for general immorality, which it was argued made them unfit for their work.[185] It is unlikely that the modern UKCC would take this view, but it might be open to it to do so under the terms of the rules.

[177] Nurses, Midwives and Health Visitors (Professional Conduct) Rules 1993, n. 160 above, r. 16(5),(6). Subr. (6) reverses the decision in *R. v. The Professional Conduct Committee of the UKCC, ex p. UKCC*, unreported, 15 July 1985, which allowed decisions to be challenged.

[178] Nurses, Midwives and Health Visitors (Professional Conduct) Rules 1993, n. 160 above, r. 16(1); *Crabtree v. UKCC, The Times*, 22 Mar. 1990.

[179] Nurses, Midwives and Health Visitors (Professional Conduct) Rules 1993, n. 160 above, r. 18(4).

[180] *Ibid.*, r. 18(7).   [181] *Ibid.*, r. 18(8)(b).   [182] *Ibid.*, r. 1(2)(k).   [183] *Ibid.*, r. 16(7).

[184] UKCC, '. . . *with a view to removal from the register* . . .'? (London: UKCC, 1990) 8–10.

[185] e.g. *Stock v. Central Midwives Board* [1915] 3 KB 756—misconduct for a midwife to cohabit with a man who was not her husband.

One important matter which has been considered by the courts hearing appeals against decisions by the Committee is the relevance of employers' policies to misconduct proceedings. In *Singh* v. *UKCC*[186] a nurse had administered drugs without the certificate of competence that his employer's general instructions required. Such a certificate is not prescribed by the law. The Committee found that the nurse was guilty of professional misconduct and ordered that he be removed from the register. The court rejected his appeal. In *Hefferon* v. *UKCC*[187] the court held that a decision to strike a practitioner from the register for failing to report an incident to her superior could not be supported because there was no evidence of a system requiring her to do so. These decisions indicate that failure to abide by the guidelines for practice established by employers may give rise to professional misconduct proceedings as well as internal disciplinary procedures.

A second area which has been highlighted by appeals is the responsibilities of nurses for their colleagues. The UKCC has emphasized that failure to act 'knowing that a colleague or subordinate is improperly treating or abusing patients' is a ground for removal from the register.[188] Nurses may be guilty of professional misconduct in respect of managerial responsibilities. Such charges were found to be proved against a nurse who failed to provide trained support to a nursing sister who requested it and instructed a trainee nurse to administer drugs contrary to the hospital's policy.[189] A district nursing officer was struck off for putting patients at risk by failing to suspend one of his staff.[190] One interesting area of concern is the relevance of inadequate services. The Code of Professional Conduct expressly requires practitioners to challenge unsafe work practices.[191] However, the UKCC does not seem to have used the provisions to discipline nurses for working in substandard services. The UKCC's booklet '. . . with a view to removal from the register . . .?' does not include this type of case in its list of conduct likely to lead to removal. In practice, in cases where resource problems arise, nurses are not penalized for their managers' failures.[192]

(c) Sanctions

Once it has decided that there has been misconduct, the Committee hears further evidence about the practitioner's general record.[193] Once again the

---

[186] Unreported, 26 June 1985 (QBD).   [187] (1988) 10 BMLR 1.

[188] UKCC, n. 184 above, 8–10.   [189] *Singh* v. *UKCC*, unreported, 26 June 1985.

[190] *Haygarth* v. *Committee of the UKCC*, unreported, 26 Oct. 1988 (QBD).

[191] Cl. 11–13.

[192] See R. Pyne, *Professional Discipline in Nursing, Midwifery and Health Visiting* (2nd edn., Oxford: Blackwell Scientific, 1992), Case A13, 108–9 and 168–9, and Case A20, 117–20 and 171–2.

[193] Nurses, Midwives and Health Visitors (Professional Conduct) Rules 1993, n. 160 above, r. 18(3).

practitioner has the right to cross-examine any witnesses and to answer any new allegations which are made. A failure to permit this will enable the practitioner to challenge a decision to strike her or him off.[194] It does not automatically follow that every practitioner found guilty of misconduct should be removed from the register. There is a range of sanctions available. Since 1993, it has been possible to issue a formal caution.[195] It is also open to the PCC to suspend registration.[196] However, there is no power to make continued registration conditional upon compliance with directions from the Committee, as there is with doctors. Instead, the PCC may use its power to postpone decisions to encourage improvement pending a final decision.[197]

The Council has drawn attention to matters which have led to decisions not to strike practitioners off. Reasonable mistakes made in good conscience, cases where the failure was virtually inevitable in the circumstances, and isolated incidents which are out of character come into this category. Where the fault is thought to lie with managers who were aware of deficiencies in the work environment but have failed to act, the Professional Conduct Committee has decided that removal of the individual practitioner from the register is inappropriate.[198]

(d) Appeals

The 1979 Act gives practitioners a right to appeal to the High Court against an adverse decision to remove them from the register.[199] The court is entitled to hear fresh evidence on the appeal if it is necessary in order to do justice to the practitioner.[200] As far as determinations of the meaning of 'misconduct' are concerned, the courts are reluctant to challenge the Committee's decision as they regard the profession as the best judge in such matters.[201] The same applies to challenges to the penalty imposed.[202] They will, however, interfere where the committee was mistaken on a point of law, there was no admissible evidence to support the findings, or where procedural irregularities made the hearing unfair to the practitioner.[203]

---

[194] *Hefferon* v. *UKCC* (1988) 10 BMLR 1; *Smith* v. *UKCC*, unreported, 14 Apr. 1988.

[195] Nurses, Midwives and Health Visitors Act 1979, s. 12A, inserted by the Nurses, Midwives and Health Visitors Act 1992.

[196] Nurses, Midwives and Health Visitors Act 1979, s. 12(1).

[197] Nurses, Midwives and Health Visitors (Professional Conduct) Rules 1993, n. 160 above, r. 18(4).

[198] UKCC, n. 184 above, 8–10.   [199] Nurses, Midwives and Health Visitors Act 1979, s. 13.

[200] *Hefferon* v. *UKCC*, n. 194 above; *Stock* v. *Central Midwives Board*, n. 185 above, 762.

[201] *Slater* v. *UKCC*, unreported, 16 May 1988 (QBD); *Sinclair* v. *UKCC*, unreported, 28 June 1988 (CA).

[202] *Haygarth* v. *Committee of the UKCC*, n. 190 above.

[203] *Stock* v. *Central Midwives Board*, n. 185 above; *Hefferon* v. *UKCC*, n. 194 above; *Smith* v. *UKCC*, n. 194 above; *Sinclair* v. *UKCC*, n. 201 above.

(e) Assessment

The UKCC has been more concerned with questions of professional competence than has the GMC. This is partly due to the different statutory criterion for the exercise of the disciplinary powers; the lack of a threshold of seriousness. Nurses, midwives, and health visitors might feel that they are being disciplined for conduct that would not get them into trouble were they doctors. This might suggest that the public is more effectively protected by the UKCC than the GMC. However, it should also be noted that there is no statutory requirement for lay involvement in the UKCC's disciplinary machinery. As with the GMC, the procedure is not really a method of satisfying complainants' grievances, because they have very limited status in the proceedings.

(iv) Supervision of Midwives

One exceptional feature of the scheme of professional regulation under the 1979 Act is the supervision of midwives. In addition to coming under the jurisdiction of the UKCC, midwives are subject to an additional layer of regulation, local supervisors of midwives. These are experienced midwives with specific training for supervision,[204] who are appointed by the local supervising authority to oversee midwives who practise in their area.[205] Each year midwives must notify the supervisors of the areas in which they intend to practise.[206] Supervising authorities must publish at least bi-annually details of how supervision will be carried out, the means by which allegations of misconduct will be investigated and resolved, and all their policies that affect midwifery practice.[207]

Where there is cause for concern about a midwife's safety, the local supervising authority, through the supervisor of midwives, may suspend her or his right to practise. The supervisor must then notify the UKCC that this has been done. Suspension may be a result of possible misconduct, or because the midwife presents a risk of spreading infection.[208] If the latter, then midwives are obliged to submit to a medical examination.[209]

The system of supervision of midwives provides a unique mechanism for scrutinizing the day-to-day competence of professionals, and ensures that the

---

[204] Midwives Rules, r. 44, as amended by the Nurses, Midwives and Health Visitors (Midwives Amendment) Rules Approval Order 1993, SI 1993 No 2106.

[205] Nurses, Midwives and Health Visitors Act 1979, ss. 15, 16.

[206] Nurses, Midwives and Health Visitors Rules 1983, n. 160 above, r. 36 as amended.

[207] Midwives Rules, r. 45, as inserted by the Nurses, Midwives and Health Visitors (Midwives Amendment) Rules Approval Order 1993, SI 1993 No 2106.

[208] Nurses, Midwives and Health Visitors Rules 1983, n. 160 above, r. 38 as amended.

[209] *Ibid.*, r. 39, as amended.

regulation of midwifery is concerned with professional competence, and not merely extreme cases of unacceptable conduct. It has been criticized as undermining the professional status and autonomy of midwives.[210] However, the UKCC shows no signs of wishing to relax the system, and is considering extending clinical supervision to nurses and health visitors.[211]

(v) Professional Conduct and Ethics

Like the GMC, the UKCC has a statutory responsibility to provide advice on standards of professional conduct.[212] The principal vehicles for doing this are the *Code of Professional Conduct for the Nurse, Midwife and Health Visitor*[213] and the *Midwife's Code of Practice.*[214] However, the UKCC regularly issues further documents elaborating particular issues. These have included confidentiality, the extended role of practitioners, the administration of medicines, and record-keeping.[215] A particularly important document, *Exercising Accountability*, discussed raising problems with managers, aspects of informed consent, advocacy on behalf of patients, teamwork in health care, and conscientious objection to participation in care.[216] This document and that on confidentiality have now been revised and published as part of *Guidelines for Professional Practices.*[217] Ethical issues are monitored by the UKCC's Ethics Advisory Panel.

C. Complementary Therapists[218]

For a long period, there was considerable hostility to complementary therapists on the part of the medical profession. However, there is now an increased

---

[210] C. Flint, 'Big Sister is Watching You' (1993) 89(46) *Nursing Times,* 17 Nov. 66–7; R. Jenkins, *The Midwife and the Law* (Oxford: Blackwell Scientific, 1995), 50–66.

[211] 'Clinical Supervision for Nursing and Health Visiting Practice' (1994) *Register* No 15, 3. *Register* is the UKCC's newsletter.

[212] Nurses, Midwives and Health Visitors Act 1979, s. 2(5).

[213] (3rd edn., London: UKCC, 1992.)

[214] (2nd edn., London: UKCC, 1989, reprinted 1991.)

[215] *Confidentiality: An Elaboration of Clause 9 of the Second Edition of the UKCC's Code of Professional Conduct for the Nurse, Midwife and Health Visitor* (London: UKCC, 1987); *The Scope of Professional Practice* (London: UKCC, 1992); *Standards for the Administration of Medicines* (1992); *Standards for Records and Record Keeping* (London: UKCC, 1993).

[216] *Exercising Accountability: A Framework to Assist Nurses, Midwives and Health Visitors to Consider Ethical Aspects of Professional Practice* (London: UKCC, 1989).

[217] (London: UKCC, 1996).

[218] J. Stone and J. Matthews, *Complementary Therapies and the Law* (Oxford: Oxford University Press, 1996).

willingness to work with them in appropriate circumstances.[219] The Government has not been willing to introduce legislation to regulate such therapists, but has supported two private member's bills, which have become the Osteopaths Act 1993 and the Chiropractors Act 1994. The Government view is that statutory regulation is appropriate where the therapies can be shown to be based on a systematic body of knowledge, where a voluntary registration scheme already exists, where there is a code of professional conduct, the profession itself seeks a statutory regime, and where the medical profession is supportive of that project.[220]

For current purposes, the main interest of the two recent statutes lies in the points at which they depart from the approaches to professional regulation that already exist, as illustrated by medicine, nursing, midwifery, and health visiting. It is those points that are raised here. The Chiropractors Act 1994 is examined, but the Osteopaths Act 1993 is in essentially the same terms. The General Chiropractic Council will have twenty members, of whom six must not be chiropractors. At least one of those will be a registered medical practitioner.[221] Thus, in contrast to the other professions discussed, there is a significant membership external to the profession. As with all the health professions, the regulation of chiropractors is based around a register, with the right to use the term chiropractor as a title being restricted to registered chiropractors.[222] Entry on the register depends on possessing a recognized qualification (although there are transitional provisions for those already experienced), but also on being of good character (as with nursing) and in good physical and mental health (a requirement only of chiropractors, osteopaths, and dentists).

Like equivalent bodies, the General Chiropractic Council is to publish a code of practice. Unusually, however, it is bound to consult before issuing it or varying its terms.[223] The statute also spells out the Code's status in a way that has not previously been done. Departure from the Code does not in itself constitute 'unacceptable professional conduct', but it will be taken into account in disciplinary proceedings.[224] The criteria for disciplinary jurisdiction under the Act are 'conduct which falls short of the standard required of a registered chiropractor' (to be known as 'unacceptable professional conduct'), 'professional incompetence', conviction of a criminal offence, and serious impairment of health affecting the ability to work as a chiropractor.[225]

---

[219] BMA, *Complementary Medicine: New Approaches to Good Practice* (Oxford: Oxford University Press, 1993).

[220] *Hansard*, HC, Vol. 237, cols. 1204–5.

[221] Chiropractors Act 1994, Sch. 1, paras. 1, 11.   [222] *Ibid.*, s. 32.   [223] *Ibid.*, s. 19(3).

[224] *Ibid.*, s. 19(4).   [225] *Ibid.*, s. 20(1),(2).

These tests are different from the older formulations in at least two respects. First, there is specific reference to incompetence, ensuring that the General Chiropractic Council is able to deal with malpractice. Secondly, the change from 'professional misconduct' to that which 'falls short of the standard required' may reduce the relevance of the practitioner's culpability. Misconduct implies something more wilful than the more external and objective criterion used in the new statute. This change suggests a greater concern for protecting the public in difficult cases rather than protecting the chiropractor from an 'unfair' restriction on business. A further indication of the importance given to safeguarding the public is the fact that the Council will be able to require chiropractors to carry professional indemnity insurance.[226]

The sanctions available to the Professional Conduct Committee are also slightly different from those used by the other health professions. There is a power to admonish practitioners (as with medicine), and the usual powers of suspension and erasure of registration. However, there is also a new 'conditions of practice order', which only exists in relation to Chiropractic and Osteopathy.[227] Such an order imposes conditions on a practitioner's right to practise. It can be made initially for a specified period up to three years, but can be extended for a further period of up to three years on any number of subsequent occasions if this is necessary to protect the public.[228] A conditions of practice order may also specify a test of competence that must be passed by the practitioner in order to lift the conditions. This may be required either instead of or in addition to a period of conditional practice. This order will enable issues of incompetence to be more appropriately handled than the more traditional penalties.

D. Conclusion

Professional regulation in the United Kingdom remains built upon the principle of self-regulation rather than external accountability. The professional bodies hold considerable responsibilities for the future of the professions and their members. They address those duties in different ways. Professional discipline is not to be seen as a complaints procedure, as complainants play little part in the proceedings once the matter has been raised. Instead, it is characterized by a formality that is commensurate with the possibility that practitioners' right to a livelihood may be at risk if their right to practise is removed.

---

[226] *Ibid.*, s. 37.   [227] *Ibid.*, s. 22.   [228] *Ibid.*, s. 22(10),(13).

Yet, the professional bodies become involved with disciplinary proceedings according to different criteria, indicating different levels of concern with day-to-day competence. The variations between the professional regimes outlined in this Chapter are more than merely historical, and comparing them can illuminate an assessment of their merits.

7 Malpractice Litigation I: The Law

Malpractice litigation plays a number of functions. In general terms it can be seen as an avenue by which health care professionals can be held accountable for their actions. It can therefore be considered, along with the NHS complaints system and the professional disciplinary machinery, as a mechanism for investigating mishaps. It is often said by groups that support the victims of health care accidents that one of the most important factors that leads to legal actions being brought is the quest for an explanation of what went wrong.

A second function of malpractice law is to provide an incentive to practitioners to maintain a high standard of care. The fact that falling short of the proper standards of care may lead to being sued and paying out money is thought to deter poor practice. This function is somewhat different from the role of the professional bodies, which are concerned to maintain and raise standards of competence. While those bodies are interested in promoting higher standards, the law is concerned to guarantee that a minimal level of competence is achieved. Most malpractice cases concern the law of negligence. The standard of care in negligence does not represent the quality of care that professionals should aspire to provide. Rather, it establishes the basic standard of practice that patients are entitled to expect as a minimum.

Thirdly, bringing a malpractice action might be seen by injured patients as a way of gaining retribution against health professionals who they believe need to be punished for wronging them. Malpractice law is part of the civil law, governing the relationship between citizens. In this area of the law, victims can choose whether they wish to sue the person who caused the action. It is therefore their choice whether to pursue the matter. In contrast, the criminal law establishes standards on behalf of society, and when the rules are broken society punishes the wrongdoer irrespective of the victim's position. The wrong is committed against society as a whole.

Finally, malpractice law is concerned with compensation. If patients win their case, they receive compensation, designed to put them as far as possible in the position in which they would have been if nothing had happened to them. This is probably the major function of negligence actions. It also constitutes an important distinction between this form of legal redress and professional and health service mechanisms of accountability. If patients need compensation, then they will need to go the courts, rather than the NHS or professional bodies, to get it.

This Chapter provides an outline of the law of negligence, with particular concern for the problems that arise in relation to the work of health care professionals.[1] The next chapter examines the implications of malpractice litigation for the NHS; considering the way in which malpractice costs are met within the service, and the validity of claims that we are moving towards a 'malpractice crisis'.

A. The Basis of Liability

The overwhelming majority of malpractice cases are brought under the law of negligence. To win a negligence case it is necessary to prove three things. If the court is not satisfied that they have all been proved, then the case will fail. The first is whether the professionals sued were responsible for the victim's care at the time of the mishap (i.e. did they have a 'duty of care'?). The second issue concerns the standard of care given. The plaintiff has to show that the professionals failed to reach the standard of practice required by the law, essentially to act in a manner acceptable to their professional peers. Finally, victims have to show that the injuries that they suffered were caused by the failure to practise properly, and not by some independent accident. These tests are considered further below.

Outside the NHS actions may also be brought in contract law. This is not possible under the NHS, because NHS patients do not have a contract with those who treat them. In private medicine, where patients pay their professionals (even if the fees are later reimbursed under some form of insurance), there will be a contract. The patient would be able to sue in both negligence and contract. In theory it is possible for a health professional to contract to provide a standard of care that is higher than that required in negligence. However, the courts have shown themselves very reluctant to accept that they have done so. They have refused to accept that surgeons have agreed to exercise closer personal supervision than is normal[2] or to guarantee success.[3] These decisions were made on the particular facts of the cases, but they indi-

---

[1] The is a considerable literature on medical negligence. The most important texts are M. Jones, *Medical Negligence* (2nd edn., London: Sweet & Maxwell, 1996) and R. M. Jackson, and J. L. Powell, *Professional Negligence* (3rd edn., London: Sweet & Maxwell, 1992).

[2] *Morris* v. *Winsbury-White* [1937] 4 All ER 494.   [3] *Thake* v. *Maurice* [1986] 1 All ER 497.

cate the courts' general reluctance to allow the usual standard of care to be modified.

It has also been argued that the basis of liability in medical malpractice litigation is unique, resting upon the public nature of the professional calling and governed by its own particular principles.[4] There is considerable insight in this suggestion. Historically, the liability of surgeons was fixed by law, as one of the common callings, not by individual negotiation.[5] It also serves to explain why the courts have shown themselves to be extremely reluctant to interfere with the standards of medical practice, tending to rely on accepted professional practice far more than would usually be the case in relation to other professions. This problem is explored in some detail below. However, it is clear that legal actions are now pleaded in negligence. Even though it can be argued that the doctrines of negligence have not always been strictly applied,[6] it is clear that the courts use the language of negligence. The analysis that follows will therefore concentrate on that concept.

B. The Law of Negligence

(i) The Duty of Care

Establishing a duty of care is not usually a major problem in health care cases. Where patients are in hospital, the staff are clearly responsible for their care. In general practice, it is obvious that doctors have a duty of care to those on their lists. Sometimes, however, things are less straightforward. It is more difficult to ascertain when professionals are responsible for people who are not already their patients. Candidates might be the victims of accidents, people who are placed at risk of infection when a patient is discharged from hospital, a woman who goes into labour in a public place. The legal test for the extent of duties of care in negligence is designed to answer this sort of question.

The first step is to consider whether it is reasonably foreseeable that the victim could be affected by the defendant's actions. Where health professionals could have foreseen that what they did would affect other people, then they may have a duty of care towards them. However, that does not mean that they are always bound to do what is best for everyone that they know may be affected. That is an aspect of the 'standard of care' issue.

---

[4] See J. Jacob, 'Introduction' in J. Jacob, J. Montgomery, I. Persaud, and J. Davies (eds.), *Encyclopedia of Health Services and Medical Law* (London: Sweet & Maxwell, 1987–91), paras. 1–050–1–077 and J. Jacob, 'Lawyers go to Hospital' [1991] *Public Law* 255–81, 274–8.

[5] S. F. C. Milsom, *Historical Foundations of the Common Law* (London: Butterworths, 1981), 317–19.

[6] N. 4 above, paras. 1–050–1–077.

The first stage in answering the duty of care question is likely to result in a long list of people whose position might be altered by a practitioner's actions. This list can sometimes be shortened. The first way to do this is to consider the connection between the victim and the defendant. That may be too remote for the law to be interested in it. If the connection between the professionals and victims is very tenuous, then the courts might accept that it is inappropriate to hold the professional responsible for their well-being. Thus, doctors giving contraceptive advice do not have a duty of care to future sexual partners of their patients.[7]

The principal example of this type of limitation is the fact that there is no legal obligation to help the victims of an accident merely because they might benefit from assistance. In general, professionals who pass a road traffic accident have no legal obligation to stop and minister to anybody who has been injured,[8] although they may have a professional obligation to so.[9] The only circumstances in which they would have a legal duty of care towards that person, and would therefore be bound to help, are when they are already under such a duty because of their job. Thus, a district nurse or health visitor employed to give care to anybody who presents needing it in a geographical area might be obliged by her contract of employment to stop and care for an accident victim. A community midwife who became aware that a pregnant woman was in difficulties would need to offer assistance if her employment contract stipulated that she had a general obligation to provide necessary support to pregnant women in the area. General Practitioners are obliged by their contracts to provide services to those in their practice area who are in need of care as a result of an accident or other emergency.[10]

The second way to limit the scope of the duty of care is to appeal to arguments of public policy. A duty of care will only exist when it is 'just and reasonable'. Where widening the obligations of health professionals would adversely affect patient care, it is probable that the courts would shy away from such an extension. The law also sometimes holds that certain types of claim should be barred as contrary to public policy. Thus, the circumstances in which a duty of care is owed to an unborn child are severely limited by the Congenital Disabilities (Civil Liability) Act 1976 and the courts have set themselves against 'wrongful life' claims (where children claim they would have been better not being born).[11]

---

[7] *Goodwill* v. *British Pregnancy Advisory Service* [1996] 2 All ER 161.

[8] *F* v. *W. Berkshire HA* [1989] 2 All ER 545, 567.

[9] General Medical Council, *Good Medical Practice* (London: GMC, 1995), para. 4; UKCC, *Guidelines for Professional Practice* (London: UKCC, 1996), para. 14.

[10] NHS (General Medical Services) Regulations 1992, SI 1992 No 635, Sch. 2, para. 4(1)(h).

[11] For discussion of the 1976 Act, see Ch. 17. For the position on 'wrongful life', see *MacKay* v. *Essex AHA* [1982] QB 1168.

These principles do not prevent health professionals being responsible for the well-being of non-patients.[12] If patients are negligently discharged while they are still infectious, then there is a duty of care to those who might be infected. Thus, members of the patient's family who become infected may sue.[13] There may be liability for nervous shock caused to the partner of a woman in labour,[14] and psychological injury to the parent of a child patient wrongly diagnosed as having been sexually abused.[15] It has been accepted that a hospital might be liable to a person injured by a mental patient negligently released with inadequate supervision,[16] but there are some doubts as to whether that decision remains good law since the enactment of the Mental Health Act 1983.[17] Staff also have a duty of care to their colleagues, so that they may be liable for negligent practice that puts them at risk. These duties to third parties do not mean that their interests must be put above those of patients, merely that they should be taken into account. The crucial question is how health professionals should carry out their duties of care. Lawyers deal with that question as an issue about the standard of care required.

(ii) The Standard of Care

In most cases, the key question that arises is whether the professionals have acted properly. That is, whether they have reached the standard of care required of them by the law of negligence. That standard was established in a case in 1957 called *Bolam* v. *Friern HMC*. That case held that: 'A doctor is not guilty of negligence if he has acted in accordance with a practice accepted as proper by a responsible body of medical men skilled in that particular art.'[18] This test has been adopted by the House of Lords in a number of cases,[19] and it is now applied to all health professionals.

The essence of the *Bolam* test is that professionals are to be judged against the standards of their peers. They will win a negligence action if the experts from their profession who are called to give evidence are prepared to accept

[12] K. de Haan, 'My Patient's Keeper: Liability of Medical Practitioners for Negligent Injuries to Third Parties' (1986) 2 *Professional Negligence* 86–91.

[13] *Evans* v. *Liverpool Corp.* [1906] 1 KB 160. The case went to appeal on a point relating to vicarious liability, but the finding of negligent discharge by the doctor was not challenged.

[14] *Tredget & Tredget* v. *Bexley HA* [1994] 5 Med. LR 178, but see *Sion* v. *Hampstead HA* [1994] 5 Med. LR 170 for difficulties in sustaining such a claim on the facts.

[15] *G* v. *North Tees HA* [1989] FCR 53, but cf. *M.* v. *Newham LBC* [1995] 3 All ER 353.

[16] *Holgate* v. *Lancashire Mental Hospitals Board* [1937] 4 All ER 19.

[17] See Jones, n. 1 above, 73–8; B. Hoggett, *Mental Health Law* (London: Sweet & Maxwell, 1990), 247–9; D. Miers, 'Liability for Injuries Caused by Violent Patients' (1996) 36 *Med. Sci. Law* 15–24.

[18] [1957] 2 All ER 118, 121.

[19] *Maynard* v. *W. Midlands RHA* [1985] 1 All ER 635 (diagnosis); *Whitehouse* v. *Jordan* [1981] 1 All ER 267 (treatment); *Sidaway* v. *Bethlem RHG* [1985] 1 All ER 643 (disclosure of information).

that their actions were proper. That does not mean that the experts would have done the same, but they regard the defendant's actions as within the range of acceptable practice. This means the minimal level of acceptable practice, not what they would like to have seen happen. It is to be judged at the time of the incident, to protect professionals from being disadvantaged by hindsight.[20] This does not mean that innovative practice is negligent merely because it is unusual. Professionals will be called upon to justify novel therapies or procedures, but seeking to improve on normal standards is the opposite of negligence provided that it is done properly.[21]

In many cases there will be disagreements amongst professionals about how problems should be handled. In *Maynard* v. *W. Midlands RHA*[22] the House of Lords explicitly said that it will not choose between different bodies of competent medical opinion. Their Lordships went on to say that fitting in with one acceptable school of thought is a sufficient defence to a negligence claim, even though another body of professional opinion might be vehemently opposed to it. Further, the court may reach the conclusion that one approach is preferable to another, but should not base a finding of negligence on that opinion. This comes very close to being a rule that doctors themselves set the standard of care required of them and that all that negligence does is to reinforce existing professional standards. Thus, to have support from eminent expert witnesses is in itself a defence to a negligence allegation.[23] Even a small number of such experts will suffice, providing that they hold responsible positions in relation to the relevant specialty.[24] Such a rule would run against the normal principles of negligence, which require the judiciary to scrutinize standard practice to see whether it is reasonable. Usually where they find that professional practice is unacceptable, judges can hold defendants to be negligent even though their professional colleagues think they acted appropriately. The position in medical negligence cases seems to be rather more favourable to the doctors.

In order to understand this problem it is necessary to consider whether the unusual deference shown to medical expertise is a matter of law or practice. If the interpretation of the *Bolam* test in *Maynard* precludes judicial intervention to declare standard medical practice to be negligent, then doctors are treated differently as a matter of law. However, if the true situation is that the judges are entitled to intervene, but have chosen not to do so in practice, then the problem is rather different. The crux of the matter is whether negligence

---

[20] *Roe* v. *Minister of Health* [1954] 2 All ER 131.

[21] *Waters* v. *W. Sussex HA* [1995] 6 Med. LR 362, *Wilsher* v. *Essex AHA* [1986] 3 All ER 801, 812. See also *Sidaway* v. *Bethlem RHG*, n. 19 above, 657.

[22] N. 19 above.   [23] *Hughes* v. *Waltham Forest HA* [1991] 2 Med. LR 155.

[24] See *Defreitas* v. *O'Brien* [1995] 6 Med. LR 108 (CA), rejecting the suggestion that the body of opinion had to be 'substantial'.

is a normative doctrine, setting standards for the professions, or a descriptive doctrine, merely reflecting reality.[25]

The judiciary have at times explicitly rejected the suggestion that they are unable to declare that practice acceptable to doctors is nevertheless negligent.[26] One High Court judge has suggested that the *Bolam* test does not involve abdicating responsibility for setting the standard of care to the courts. He stated that the judges must satisfy themselves that the medical opinions offered are 'both respectable and responsible'.[27] In the Court of Appeal in *Sidaway* v. *Bethlem RHG* Lord Donaldson MR argued that the courts could override a unanimous medical view if satisfied that it was manifestly wrong. In his view the *Bolam* test had to be read as if the word 'rightly' was inserted, so that a defence to a negligence claim existed when a practitioner had complied with a practice 'rightly' accepted as proper by a responsible body of professionals.[28]

However, in the House of Lords in the same case, Lord Scarman attacked the *Bolam* test for 'leaving the determination of a legal duty to the judgment of doctors'. Thus he has interpreted it as permitting the medical experts to establish the standard of care, not the courts. He seemed happy to allow that to be the case in relation to diagnosis and treatment—indeed he delivered the leading speech in *Maynard*—but he found it unacceptable in relation to informed consent.[29] Writing extra-judicially Lord Scarman has commented:

> the law's standard is, in effect, set by the medical profession. If a doctor can show that his advice or his treatment, reached a standard of care which was accepted by a respectable and responsible body of medical opinion as adequate, he cannot be made liable in damages if anything goes wrong. It is a totally medical proposition erected into a working rule of law.[30]

Lord Scarman's view of the *Bolam* test was not, apparently, shared by Lord Bridge. He rejected the suggestion that applying *Bolam* handed the whole question of the scope of the duty of disclosure to the medical profession. Yet, the example that he gave of the potential for judicial intervention was that a judge would find that disclosure of a 10 per cent risk of a stroke was one that 'no reasonably prudent medical man would fail to make'. This indicates that

[25] J. L. Montrose, 'Is Negligence an Ethical or a Sociological Concept?' (1958) 21 *MLR* 259–64.

[26] For discussion see K. Norrie, 'Common Practice and the Standard of Care in Medical Negligence' [1985] *Juridical Review* 145–65; K. Norrie, 'Medical Negligence: Who Sets the Standard?' (1985) 11 *Journal of Med. Ethics* 135; A. Grubb, 'Causation and the *Bolam* Test' (1993) 1 *Med. L Rev.* 241, 245–6; M. Puxon, case commentaries at [1993] 4 *Med. LR* 298, [1993] 4 *Med. LR* 399, [1994] 5 *Med. LR* 249.

[27] *Hills* v. *Potter* [1983] 3 All ER 716, 728.   [28] [1984] 1 All ER 1018, 1028.

[29] [1985] 1 All ER 643, 649.

[30] L. Scarman, 'Law and Medical Practice' in P. Byrne (ed.), *Medicine in Contemporary Society* (London: King Edward's Hospital Fund for London, 1987), 131–9, 134.

he was not thinking of overriding the medical standards so much as taking a short-cut to identifying them. This becomes clear when Lord Bridge continued that even such an obvious risk could be withheld from a patient if there were a 'cogent clinical reason' for doing so.[31]

On close scrutiny, therefore, it is unclear how far Lord Bridge was prepared to challenge medical opinion. While some commentators have argued that the *Sidaway* case left the door open to judicial intervention to set disclosure standards,[32] the subsequent Court of Appeal cases suggest that the courts have not been prepared to seize the opportunity.[33] It is, in fact difficult to find cases where the courts have decided that health professionals have been negligent, even though they have conformed with medical practice. In *Clarke* v. *Adams* a physiotherapist failed to warn a patient of the danger of being burnt in the course of the treatment. He was found to be negligent even though an expert from the Chartered Society of Physiotherapists stated that he had given a proper warning.[34] However, this case predates the ascendance of the *Bolam* test, and cannot be relied upon today. Although the *Bolam* case was decided in 1957, it did not become the cardinal test for medical negligence until it was adopted by the House of Lords in *Whitehouse* v. *Jordan* in 1980.[35] Cases before that date need, therefore, to be treated carefully.

A few modern cases have implicitly assessed the reasonableness of medical practice as it appeared to the judge,[36] and even directly rejected expert opinion.[37] However, these High Court cases have not addressed the legal basis of the decisions, and do not provide binding precedents. The most important piece of evidence in the quest for the answer to the question whether English law permits judges to impose standards on the health professions is the case of *Hucks* v. *Cole*, decided in 1960.[38] Dr Cole failed to respond to a pathology report indicating that Mrs Hucks should have been treated with penicillin. The expert witnesses in support of Dr Cole gave evidence that they would have acted in the same way as he had. The Court of Appeal refused to regard that as the end of the matter. Two of the judges found that Dr Cole was negligent, without spelling out how this could be so when he had medical experts who supported him.

---

[31] At 663.

[32] e.g. Scarman, n. 30 above, 131–9, at 134–6; I. Kennedy, *Treat Me Right* (Oxford: OUP, 1991), 193–212.

[33] J. Montgomery, 'Power/Knowledge/Consent: Medical Decision-making' (1988) 51 *MLR* 245–51; see Ch. 9.

[34] (1950) 94 SJ 599.   [35] N. 19 above.

[36] *Judge* v. *Huntingdon HA* [1995] 6 Med. LR 223; *Lybert* v. *Warrington HA* [1996] 7 Med. LR 71.

[37] *Smith* v. *Tunbridge Wells AHA* [1994] 5 Med. LR 334; see also *Newell & Newell* v. *Goldenberg* [1995] 6 Med. LR 371, 374.

[38] Reported at [1994] 4 Med. LR 393.

Sachs LJ, however, examined the matter in some detail. He stated that if there was no proper basis for a failure to take precautions, and that it was 'definitely not reasonable' to take the risk involved in not taking them, then the court should find that the practice was negligent.[39] He went on to explain his intervention in the case by pointing out that the views of one of the defendant's witnesses might have stemmed 'from a residual adherence to out-of-date ideas' and a disrespect for laboratory results. This seems to be a reflection on the credibility of the witness' claim to represent a competent body of opinion, as much as a judicial intention to override medical knowledge. The judge's later comments also indicate that he was unimpressed by the defendant's witnesses. He noted that the admissions that they made showed that Dr Cole's failure to prescribe penicillin 'was not merely wrong but clearly unreasonable'.[40] Once again, the attack was principally on the credibility of the witnesses, exposing internal inconsistencies in their evidence, rather than indicating a willingness to challenge settled medical practice. Sachs LJ explicitly noted that it was not a case of conflict between two schools of thought, but a case 'of doctors who said in one form or another that they would have acted or might have acted in the same way as the defendant did, for reasons which on examination do not really stand up to analysis'.[41] *Hucks* v. *Cole* is therefore authority for the need to scrutinize the reasoning of medical expert witnesses, not merely to accept them at face value. However, it would be dangerous to assume that it encourages the courts to override the considered opinion of responsible medical experts that a practice is reasonable.

The case has recently been discussed by the Court of Appeal in *Bolitho* v. *Hackney HA*,[42] and some commentators have suggested that this case provides a indication that the judges are becoming less reluctant to set standards for doctors.[43] The test for negligence was only indirectly in issue, as the case turned on a point of causation. However, two of the three judgments considered the meaning of the *Bolam* test. Counsel for the patient invited the Court of Appeal to use the decision in *Hucks* v. *Cole* to declare the expert evidence in the doctor's support to provide no defence because it had been irresponsible to run a significant risk by not intubating the patient, when the risk of intubation itself was slight. Farquharson LJ declined the invitation. He found that there would have been no negligence because the defendant had been supported by experts, who constituted a responsible body of professional opinion. He accepted the trial judge's assessment that the evidence of one of the defence witnesses represented such a body of opinion. That assessment was based on the fact that he had a 'profound knowledge' of the relevant specialty, was impartial, and had presented his evidence clearly and moderately, so that

[39] *Ibid.*, 397.   [40] *Ibid.*, 398.   [41] *Ibid.*, 399.   [42] [1993] 4 Med. LR 381.
[43] See Grubb, n. 26 above, 245–6.

there was no doubt that his views were genuine.[44] Thus the basis of his acceptance of the evidence was the status and credibility of the witnesses, rather
than an assessment of the reasonableness of the content of their views.

The possibility of an accepted medical practice being held to be negligent
because it puts the patient unnecessarily at risk was noted by Farquharson LJ.
However, he did not regard that as even being in issue in *Bolitho* and gave no
examples of when it might arise. Dillon LJ also rejected any suggestion that
Hucks v. *Cole* might be applied in the case. Considering its scope, he noted that
it had to be reconciled with the decision in *Maynard*. He achieved this by
reformulating the grounds for overriding medical opinion in terms of the
public law concept of *Wednesbury* unreasonableness.[45] He suggested that a
court could only exercise the option of rejecting medical opinion about the
propriety of care if it, 'fully conscious of its own lack of medical knowledge
and clinical experience, was none the less clearly satisfied that the views of that
group of doctors were . . . such as no reasonable body of doctors could have
held'.[46] While it recognizes the authority of *Hucks* v. *Cole*, as a Court of Appeal
decision, *Bolitho* does not challenge the *Maynard* rule. Both Farqharson and
Dillon noted the need to interpret *Hucks* v. *Cole* in the light of the higher
authority *Maynard*. Farqharson LJ said that he saw no conflict between the
cases, although he did not elaborate on this point of view. The comments of
Dillon LJ on the rule in *Hucks* v. *Cole* would seem to place a restriction on its
use, in order to bring it into line with the position of the House of Lords in
Maynard and to justify rejecting the suggestion that it was relevant to the case
before him. Neither judge indicated that he was keen to avail himself of the
opportunity to override medical expertise.

The best interpretation of these cases would seem to be that the fundamental principle is that medical negligence is to be judged against the standards of the medical profession (the *Bolam* test). The evidence of medical
experts should be examined carefully to ensure that it is honest and objective,
and in *Hucks* v. *Cole* this was found not to be the case. While there have been
some suggestions in that and other cases that the courts might intervene to
override medical opinion about acceptable standards of care, these seem to be
incompatible with the clear ruling in *Maynard*. That case held that, where
there are two schools of thought, adherence to either provides a defence to
negligence. If there remains scope for intervention under the rule in *Hucks* v.
Cole, then it exists when the medical experts hold views that the judges believe

---

[44] N. 42 above, 386.

[45] This concept is explained in Ch. 3 in the context of seeking to force health service bodies to
provide treatment.

[46] N. 42 above, 392. A move towards recasting the *Bolam* test itself in similar terms can be seen in
Hughes v. *Waltham Forest HA* [1991] 2 Med. LR 155, 161.

no reasonable doctor could hold. This is tantamount to suggesting that they must be either dishonest or lacking in the necessary objectivity. In another recent case, in which *Hucks* v. *Cole* was cited, the judge examined the evidence very carefully, but ultimately his finding that there had been no negligence was based on the fact that the relevant specialist witnesses said that the doctor's actions had not been unreasonable. The fact that he had found that the doctor had falsified the records did not alter that fact. What mattered was that he was satisfied that the expert witnesses were from the appropriate specialty and had given their evidence with integrity.[47]

The position was summarized in *Ratty* v. *Haringey HA* in these terms: 'In my judgment it was important in the present case, once it was accepted that Mr Mann and Mr Addison represented a responsible and respectable body of colo-rectal opinion, to accept their formulation of the Marnham rule [a practice guideline] when evaluating the conduct of the second defendant.'[48] Thus, once the credibility of the witnesses was established, their evidence should be accepted without further questioning. Similarly, in *Tucker* v. *Tees HA* the judge rejected an expert's evidence because he did not believe that he did in fact support the defendant's decision as he appeared to do.[49] *Bowers* v. *Harrow HA* may be a similar case. The judge rejected the evidence given by the defendant's witnesses as to what reasonable professional practice was.[50] He seems to suggest that their belief that a responsible body of practitioners might have acted as the defendant had was inaccurate. This challenges their credibility on a matter of fact rather than their assessment of standards of practice.

It seems that the Court of Appeal may have adopted a slightly different stance in *Joyce* v. *Wandsworth HA*.[51] In the High Court,[52] the judge seemed to suggest that the issue might be reasonableness as assessed by the judge, but he actually considered what reasonable doctors might think. The Court of Appeal may have gone further in relation to the adequacy of a warning, but it is unclear what the medical evidence on the point was.[53] Importantly, however, the Court of Appeal considered that the judge's direction to himself on the meaning of the test for negligence would have been inadequate if it had merely referred to accepted clinical practice. It was accurate only because it had included the words 'Provided that clinical practice stood up to analysis and was not unreasonable in the light of the state of medical knowledge at the time.'[54] This seems a clear indication that the judges should consider the

---

[47] *Defreitas* v. *O'Brien* [1993] 4 Med. LR 281. This decision was upheld by the CA, see [1995] 6 Med. LR 108. The appeal itself concerned whether a small group of practitioners could constitute a 'body of responsible opinion.' It was held that it could.

[48] [1994] 5 Med. LR 413, 416.

[49] [1995] 6 Med. LR 54, 56.

[50] [1995] 6 Med. LR 16, 23.

[51] [1996] 7 Med. LR 1.

[52] [1995] 6 Med. LR 60. Compare 64 and 88.

[53] [1996] 7 Med. LR 1, 12.

[54] [1996] 7 Med. LR 1, 13.

reasonableness of medical opinion. However, the Court of Appeal did not consider the possibility that such an interpretation of the law might conflict with the *Maynard* rule, despite the fact that it was binding on it.[55]

Even if there is now some ground for believing that the courts may, as a matter of law, intervene by setting standards for the medical profession, it is clear that they are very reluctant to do so. If it is right to interpret *Hucks* v. *Cole* as a case in which the medical experts were not credible witnesses, then the only clear reported example of this happening is *Clarke* v. *Adams*. That case is inconsistent with the modern law relating to doctors. It may be relevant that it concerned a physiotherapist rather than a doctor. The law outlined above is unusually friendly to doctors. It is not clear whether the same lenience would be shown to the other health professions. The *Bolam* test certainly applies, but the *Maynard* rule may not. The courts are extremely reluctant to challenge medical clinical judgement, possibly because they feel unable to comprehend medical practice. They may feel that the expertise of other groups is less esoteric, and be less wary of judging it. However, other factors behind the reticence of the judiciary apply equally to other health professions. These include the characterization of their work as altruistic, the feeling that they are generally undeserving of liability, the need to provide a comfortable working environment to encourage them to continue to offer their services to society, the importance of permitting them to exercise clinical judgement without constantly worrying about litigation, and the cost implications of litigation for the NHS.[56]

(iii) Tailoring the Standard of Care to the Circumstances: Health Care Teams

The *Bolam* test emphasizes that the standard of care to be expected of professionals is that required of those skilled in the particular specialty in question.[57] Thus, a general medical practitioner is not to be judged against the standards of consultant specialists but against what it is reasonable to expect of a general practitioner.[58] A general practitioner may, therefore, fail correctly to diagnose a patient's condition without being negligent, even though a specialist's failure to make an accurate diagnosis in the same patient would be

---

[55] The summary of the law from *Joyce* was used alongside discussion of the *Maynard* case in *Waters* v. *W. Sussex HA* [1995] 6 Med. LR 362 (QBD) without any apparent concern that there was any conflict between the approaches.

[56] For a survey of the reasons for judicial non-intervention, see J. Montgomery, 'Medicine, Accountability and Professionalism' (1989) 16 *Journal of Law and Society* 319–39.

[57] *Sidaway* v. *Bethlem*, n. 19 above, 660; *Whitehouse* v. *Jordan* [1981] 1 All ER 267, 280.

[58] *Stockdale* v. *Nicholls* [1993] 4 Med. LR 190, 198; *Durrant* v. *Burke* [1993] 4 Med. LR 258, 267; *Thornton* v. *Nicol* [1992] 3 Med. LR 41, 44. See also *Gordon* v. *Wilson* [1992] 3 Med. LR 401, 425.

unacceptable. Conversely, embarking on an inherently difficult procedure might be negligent if done by a generalist, but quite acceptable if undertaken by an experienced specialist.[59]

The same principle, that the standard of care follows from the category of skills that the practitioner professes, also leads to it being tailored to the position held by the professional. It is well established that patients are entitled to receive competent care. Inexperience is no excuse,[60] and students are expected to attain the standard of qualified staff.[61] However, different standards of expertise may be expected of those in different posts. A member of a specialist unit will be expected to display greater skills that someone in an equivalent post (staff nurse, house officer, registrar) in a general ward.[62] Where, however, professionals attempt to do something that they are not qualified to do, the failure to refer the patient to someone properly skilled may well itself be negligent.[63]

In a number of cases, the courts have recognized the implications of the fact that health professionals work in teams, in which they have different responsibilities. The suggestion that each team member is expected to deliver the high standards of care that the team as a whole could offer has been rejected because it would require a student nurse to exercise the skill of a consultant.[64] Similarly, the English courts have rejected the approach known as the 'captain of the ship' doctrine, whereby professionals in charge of teams are responsible for the negligence of their members, even though they may not be personally at fault.[65] The nearest that they have come to it is the personal responsibility of a surgeon to check that no swabs have been left inside a patient's body, even though a nurse was responsible for counting them in and out.[66] However, this did not make the surgeon responsible for the nurse's error, but for his own failure to check. Where a nurse draws up an incorrect anæsthetic dose, this does not make the anæsthetist negligent merely because he bore overall responsibility for anæsthesia.[67]

This does not mean that those charged with ensuring the proper working of a team do not have special responsibilities. The consultant takes overall responsibility for the medical care, and the primary nurse will be accountable

---

[59] *Defreitas* v. *O'Brien*, n. 47 above, 296–7.

[60] *Jones* v. *Manchester Corporation* [1952] 2 All ER 125; *Wilsher* v. *Essex AHA*, n. 21 above, 813, 831, but see 833; *Djemal* v. *Bexley HA* [1995] 6 Med. LR 269, 271.

[61] This is a general principle, established in a non-medical case: *Nettleship* v. *Weston* [1971] 3 All ER 581.

[62] *Wilsher* v. *Essex AHA*, n. 21 above, 813. [63] *Ibid.*, 833. [64] *Ibid.*, 813.

[65] See J. Montgomery, 'Doctors' Handmaidens: The Legal Contribution' in S. McVeigh, and S. Wheeler (eds.), *Law, Health and Medical Regulation* (Aldershot: Dartmouth, 1992), 141, 150–3.

[66] *Mahon* v. *Osborne* [1939] 1 All ER 535, *Urry* v. *Biere*, *The Times*, 15 July 1955; *James* v. *Dunlop* (1931) 1 BMJ 730.

[67] *Fussel* v. *Beddard* (1942) 2 BMJ 411.

for co-ordinating the patient's nursing care. If they carry out these roles negligently, they will be liable for their mistakes. They need to ensure that care plans are properly recorded, that appropriate information is passed on to those who need it, and that junior staff are qualified to carry out the tasks delegated to them. Failures in communication have led to liability where instructions were illegible,[68] where a cottage hospital failed to write to the main hospital about a patient's case,[69] and where there was a failure to ensure that a doctor to whom the patient was referred was given full and accurate information.[70] The key point, however, is that professionals are responsible only for their own mistakes and not for those of the members of their team. This distinguishes the position of senior professional staff from that of employers, who are vicariously liable for their employees' negligence, even if they are themselves blameless (see Chapter 8).

At the lower echelons of the health care team, the courts have recognized that junior staff may meet the standards required of them by acknowledging their inexperience. Thus, a house officer who inserted a catheter into a vein and not an artery was not negligent because he called in his senior registrar to check what he had done. The registrar, who made the same mistake, was negligent, but the house officer was protected by his referral.[71] Inexperienced practitioners are entitled to rely upon the clinical judgement of their senior colleagues, even where they suspect they may be wrong. In *Junor* v. *McNicol*, a junior doctor had been told to treat a fracture, but not to administer penicillin. Even though she suspected that the failure to prescribe the antibiotic was 'unsuitable and improper', this did not outweigh her responsibility to carry out the instructions of her superior. She was protected from liability in negligence by her instructions.[72]

This principle also has implications for the relationships between professions. All members of the health care team have separate, if sometimes overlapping, specialist skills. In some circumstances, they are permitted to rely on the decisions of others, even where those decisions are actually negligent. Thus a dentist was found to have acted properly in relying on a doctor's opinion that a patient was responding satisfactorily to antibiotic treatment.[73] A nurse who failed to turn a patient regularly to avoid bedsores would usually be negligent, but not if she had so refrained on the express instructions of the surgeon who had recently operated on her.[74] A theatre nurse who relies on the

---

[68] *Prendergast* v. *Sam & Dee Ltd* [1989] 1 Med. LR 36.
[69] *Coles* v. *Reading District Hospital MC* (1963) 107 SJ 115.
[70] *Chapman* v. *Rix* [1994] 5 Med. LR 239, decided in 1960.
[71] *Wilsher* v. *Essex AHA* n. 21 above, 831, 834.   [72] *The Times*, 26 Mar. 1959.
[73] *Tanswell* v. *Nelson*, *The Times*, 11 Feb. 1959, CLY 2254.
[74] *Pickering* v. *Governors of United Leeds Hospital* [1954] Lancet 1075.

instructions of the surgeon is not negligent, even if they turn out to be improper.[75] Nurses who administer drugs according to the instructions of a doctor are not negligent if those instructions are for an excessive dose.[76]

There are, however, two limitations to the principle that health professionals are entitled to rely on their colleagues' expertise. The first is procedural. Professionals must challenge decisions that appear to them to be wrong. Where nurses believe that a drug dose is incorrect, it is negligent to administer it without obtaining confirmation.[77] A pharmacist who failed to seek confirmation of a patently erroneous prescription was for that reason negligent.[78] The second limitation is substantive. Professionals should not follow instructions, even if confirmed, that are 'manifestly wrong'.[79] In the case mentioned above, the dentist's right to rely on a doctor's assessment of the patient's recovery would have evaporated if it was clearly inconsistent with the observable facts.[80] Thus, where an error is grossly obvious, health professionals cannot rely merely on the fact that their colleagues told them to go ahead.

A final way in which the standard of care is tailored to the circumstances relates to the immediate situation in which an error occurs. The judges have recognized that in an emergency responsible professionals may be more prone to errors than when there is less pressure. Thus, where the circumstances force a practitioner to do too many things at once, the fact that a mistake is made should not lead lightly to a finding of negligence. This has been described as the recognition of 'battle conditions'.[81] It does not mean that the standard of care is lowered, but that it is necessary to ask what a responsible professional would have done in the circumstances that actually arose.

This leads to a difficult problem about the relevance of inadequate resources. Health professionals regularly feel that they are working with insufficient staffing levels. However, this would not justify the care that they offered falling below the basic standard required by the law of negligence. Nevertheless, this does not mean that it is entirely irrelevant whether failures of care are really due to levels of resourcing rather than individual error.

(iv) A Variable Standard of Care? Resource Issues

One potential difficulty facing the courts is how to deal with the suggestion that there has been negligence, even though services were provided to the

---

[75] *Gold* v. *Essex* [1942] 2 All ER 237.
[76] *Smith* v. *Brighton and Lewes HMC, The Times,* 2 May 1958.
[77] *Hillyer* v. *St Bartholemew's Hospital* [1909] 2 KB 820.
[78] *Dwyer* v. *Roderick* (1983) 127 SJ 806, 80 LSG 3003.
[79] *Junor* v. *McNicol, The Times,* 26 Mar. 1959.
[80] *Tanswell* v. *Nelson,* n. 73 above.   [81] *Wilsher* v. *Essex AHA,* n. 21 above, 812.

standard for which a provider has been resourced.[82] Where a policy decision has been taken that only a certain level of staffing is necessary, can it be argued that it remains negligent to provide care to that inadequate level of resources? This may become an increasingly important issue as NHS purchasers make decisions about the levels of resources that they are prepared to commit to particular services, restricting the ability of providers to choose the models of care that they wish to offer. The courts have shown themselves reluctant to get drawn into debates about resources in the context of rights to care (see Chapter 3), but it is possible that they will still provide a guarantee of minimum standards through the law of negligence.

This problem was touched upon in *Knight* v. *Home Office*, where it was alleged that the prison had been negligent in providing insufficient supervision to prevent a prisoner hanging himself.[83] The judge found that it was wrong to compare the staffing ratios in a prison hospital wing with those in a specialist psychiatric hospital. The fact that staffing levels were lower than they would have been in a psychiatric hospital did not prove that there was negligence. He also noted that it had been suggested in *Wilsher* v. *Essex AHA* that resource issues were a matter for Parliament, not the courts.[84] However, he held that this could not provide a 'complete defence'.[85] He pointed out that, where no funds were available to provide any medical care for prisoners, then there would have been a failure to provide an appropriate standard of care. Nevertheless, he accepted that the court would need to bear in mind that one factor in its decision was that public resources are limited and that the allocation of scarce resources was a political matter.

It seems from this approach that there are two ways in which a health provider might plead that limited resources lowered the standard of care. First, in relation to identifying the appropriate comparators, it could argue that the standard could be fixed by looking at a less prestigious hospital. Thus if the purchaser commissioned only generalist services, providing resources to cover them and no more, then a provider might be able to show that it would be wrong to expect them to meet the standard of care that could be expected of a specialist unit. This is equivalent to the Home Office persuading the judge to compare that care to that given in other prison hospital wings, and not on a specialist psychiatric unit. This approach could lead to the terms of the contracts between purchasers and providers having a limited but significant effect on fixing the standard of care. This may operate to raise the standard of care,

---

[82] Jones, n. 1 above, 217–25; C. Newdick, 'Rights to NHS Resources after the 1990 Act' (1993) 1 *Med. L Rev.* 53–82, 56–60; C. Newdick, *Who Should We Treat?* (Oxford: Oxford University Press, 1996), 106–18.

[83] [1990] 3 All ER 237.   [84] [1986] 3 All ER 801, 834.

[85] [1990] 3 All ER 237, 243. See also the comment of Mustill LJ in *Bull* v. *Devon HA* [1993] 4 Med. LR 117, 141.

as well as lower it, where contract standards create an expectation of better care.[86]

The second way in which resources may be relevant is in permitting a health provider to argue that the cost of improving services or taking precautions justified a lower standard of care than would normally be expected. This sort of argument would not be accepted outside the health care sector. There the standard of care in tort is precisely concerned with establishing whether unreasonable risks have been taken.[87] However, the public law cases suggest that the courts may be prepared to accept that additional considerations arise in the NHS context, which make it more likely that a plea of lack of resources might be heard.[88] *Knight* v. *Home Office* indicates that such a plea will not automatically be accepted, but the example cited for rejecting it is an extreme one. No case has yet had to confront this issue directly, because the cases have been decided on other grounds. Until the matter comes up before a court for final decision, it will be unclear how much weight the judges would place on resource levels. However, the reluctance of the courts to regard policy issues as justiciable must make it unlikely that they will entertain such litigation.[89]

One solution to the problem would be to fix liability for malpractice due to inadequate resources on the purchaser rather than the provider. Under the NHS market, decisions about resourcing are principally for purchasers. Where they make a negligent purchasing decision, it would be unjust to leave the providers liable for its effects. On the other hand, providers have a duty to refuse to provide unsafe services, and are obliged to voice their concerns in the contracting process. Balancing the responsibility of purchasers and providers could be done by holding both the purchaser and provider to be jointly liable for unacceptably resourced services. The patient would be able to sue either for the full damages, leaving them to sort out the apportionment between them.

A similar approach has been taken in the past to apportion liability between an individual member of staff and the hospital for which she worked. The Court of Appeal found that the cause of an anæsthetic accident was primarily the inadequacy of the support and supervision provided for a junior doctor. The hospital was held to be responsible for 80 per cent of the damages payable, and the doctor only 20 per cent.[90] The patient was entitled to expect the proper standard of care from both the hospital and the individual doctor,

---

[86] K. Barker, 'NHS Contracting: Shadows in the Law of Tort?' (1995) 3 Med. L Rev. 161–76.

[87] For an exploration of how medical negligence would operate if this approach were taken, see I. S. Goldrein, '*Bolam*—Problems Arising out of "Ancestor" Worship' (1994) 144 *NLJ* 1237.

[88] See Ch. 3.

[89] See *X* v. *Bedfordshire CC*; *M* v. *Newham LBC*; *E* v. *Dorset CC* [1995] 3 All ER 353, discussed in Ch. 3.

[90] *Jones* v. *Manchester Corporation*, n. 60 above.

but in determining how much of the damages should be paid by each, the court could consider the extent to which the doctor was able to take precautions against the mishap within the context of her working environment. The question of civil liability for negligent purchasing was discussed in Chapter 3. The issue of provider liability for inadequate services, independent of negligent actions by any individual member of their staff, has been considered in a number of cases. These will be examined in the next section.

(v) Direct Liability

One important development in the law of malpractice concerns the direct liability of provider units for failures in their services.[91] This should be distinguished from the principle of vicarious liability, under which the hospital or NHS trust is liable to pay damages arising from the negligence of its employees. Instead, the provider is itself negligent for failing to manage its services properly. In *Wilsher* v. *Essex AHA*, Browne-Wilkinson V-C suggested that a hospital that failed to provide staff of sufficient skill and experience to give the treatment offered by the hospital would be negligent, even if the staff had done their best in the circumstances.[92] A number of examples of the application of direct liability can be found in decided cases. Thus, a trust might be liable if the consent forms it uses are negligently drafted,[93] if up-to-date information on care is not communicated to staff when it should be,[94] if there is no proper system for checking equipment,[95] if staff are inadequately supervised,[96] or drug procedures are too lax.[97]

It may be that there is more scope for the judges to set standards for the health service under the head of direct liability, than for them to intervene in relation to professional standards. In the *Wilsher* case, Browne-Wilkinson V-C suggested that it might be difficult to show that a hospital that followed standard practices was negligent.[98] However, in *Jones* v. *Manchester Corporation*, the fact that a junior doctor had been left with little supervision in accordance with common practice was no defence.[99] In *Knight* v. *Home Office* Pill J said that, in principle, there could be negligence even if current practice in the prison medical service was followed in every respect.[100] Most

---

[91] See J. Bettle, 'Suing Hospitals Direct: Whose Tort was it Anyhow?' (1987) 137 *NLJ* 573; J. Montgomery, 'Suing Hospitals Direct: What Tort?' (1987) 137 *NLJ* 703; Jones, n. 1 above, 399–409.
[92] N. 21 above, 833. See also Glidewell LJ at 831.
[93] *Worster* v. *City & Hackney HA, The Times,* 22 June 1987.
[94] *Blyth* v. *Bloomsbury HA* [1993] 4 Med. LR 151.
[95] *Denton* v. *South West Thames RHA* (1981) 131 NLJ 240.
[96] *Jones* v. *Manchester Corporation,* n. 60 above.
[97] *Collins* v. *Hertfordshire CC* [1947] 1 All ER 633.
[98] N. 21 above, 833.
[99] [1952] 2 QB 852, 864.
[100] N. 83 above, 242.

importantly, in *Bull* v. *Devon AHA* the Court of Appeal examined a hospital's system for providing obstetric support for a woman in labour in some detail.[101] The authority's services were split between two sites, with a mile between the two hospitals. Medical staff would sometimes need to be called from one to the other. Mrs Bull was pregnant with twins and the problem arose because of an unacceptably long delay between the delivery of the first baby and that of the second. The court had to consider how far that delay was the result of an inadequate system for summoning assistance. Slade LJ noted that the system was such that there was 'a real inherent risk that, through the fault of no one and nothing but the system itself, the attendance of an obstetrician might not in practice be arranged within 20 minutes'.[102] On this basis Dillon LJ found that the health authority had been negligent in implementing a system that was 'unreliable and essentially unsatisfactory'.[103] While it was accepted that the overall staffing levels could not be challenged because they were in line with current professional practice, the administrative systems were judged against judicial conceptions of what was acceptable.

(vi) The Significance of Policies and Protocols

The development of hospital policies may also have a significant impact on the way in which the standard of care is defined. It will be very much easier to prove that health professionals have been negligent if they have failed to follow policies or protocols. Such protocols will usually have been designed in order to clarify what constitutes acceptable practice and guard against risks by incorporating suitable safeguards.[104] Departure from a protocol is not automatically negligent. The proper approach is probably to say that it raises a *prima facie* case of negligence and, unless the circumstances indicate that there were good reasons for departing from the usual practice, the professional will be found liable.[105] In one case, it was held that a nurse who failed to follow the prescribed procedure for referring a patient complaining of a lump in her breast was for that reason negligent.[106] In another, the judge found that there was a general practice amongst gynæcologists to delay performing an anterior colporrhaphy after childbirth for at least three months. The defendants had performed the procedure after only four weeks. It was held that departing from the standard practice was not necessarily negligent,

---

[101] [1993] 4 Med. LR 117. [102] *Ibid.*, 130.
[103] *Ibid.*, 138; see also 137.
[104] J. Grimshaw, M. Eccles, and I. Russell, 'Developing Clinically Valid Practice Guidelines' (1995) 1 *J Evaluation in Clinical Practice* 37–48. See also B. Hurwitz, 'Clinical Guidelines and the Law: Advice, Guidance or Regulation?' (1995) 1 *J Evaluation in Clinical Practice* 49–60.
[105] *Clark* v. *Maclennan* [1983] 1 All ER 416, as interpreted in *Wilsher* v. *Essex A.H.A.* n. 21 above.
[106] *Sutton* v. *Population Family Planning Programme Ltd*, unreported, 30 Oct. 1981.

but that the clinicians had to justify their failure to follow the usual approach. As they had failed to provide such a justification, they were negligent.[107]

(vii) Causation

The third step in proving a negligence claim is showing that the failure to provide a satisfactory standard of care was the cause of the injuries that the victim suffered. Unless this can be proved, the claim will fail, even if the defendants were clearly at fault. The basic rule enshrines what is known as the 'but for' test. Victims have to show that 'but for' the defendant's negligent conduct they would not have been injured. Where the injury is caused by the care a health professional gives, for example severing a nerve during the course of an operation, it is relatively easy to show that the professional's actions caused the injury. However, many health care cases are rather more difficult because patients very often suffer from their underlying complaint which they say should have been cured or alleviated but was not.

In one case, a patient was sent away from casualty, complaining of stomach pain, without a proper examination and told to see his GP if the symptoms persisted. Before he could do this he died. The doctor, who had refused to see the man, had clearly failed to act responsibly and in that sense was negligent. However, the evidence showed that even if the man had been examined and the problem correctly diagnosed he would still have died. He had been suffering from arsenic poisoning and it would have been too late to administer an antidote.[108] This meant that the unacceptable conduct of the doctor made no difference. Even if he had acted properly, the man would still have died. Consequently the claim against the doctor failed because it had not been proved that the injury to the man had been caused by the defendant's conduct.

In many cases, proving that injury has been caused by the defendant is very difficult. Any uncertainty will operate in favour of the defendant. A patient's legal action will fail unless it can be shown that it was more probable that the injuries were caused by professional negligence than by some other innocent cause. Often it cannot be proved that the patient's injuries were not the result of natural causes, such as the underlying medical problems or an unavoidable accident. In one case involving a prematurely born child it was possible that the blindness suffered by the child was a consequence of being born at an early stage of development rather than the result of his poor care, even though that had been negligent. Unless it could be proved that the poor care, and not the

---

[107] *Clark* v. *Maclennan*, n. 105 above.
[108] *Barnett* v. *Chelsea and Kensington HMC* [1968] 1 All ER 1068.

prematurity, probably caused the blindness, the child could not win the case.[109]

In *Howard* v. *Wessex RHA*,[110] the only explanation of the patient's injuries other than negligence was that it was an example of a natural accident that had been reported in only twenty-nine cases worldwide. However, the judge found that this remote possibility meant that the patient had failed to prove that her injuries had been caused by the health authority. Sometimes the courts will accept that the nature of the injury is such that it must have been caused by the negligent behaviour; this is described as the principle of *res ipsa loquitur* (the thing speaks for itself). In *Glass* v. *Cambridge HA*,[111] in similar circumstances to the *Howard* case, the health authority's claim that the cause might have been a natural accident was rejected because there was no evidence that the precise consequences suffered by the plaintiff had occurred before.

The patient has to establish on the balance of probabilities that the injuries were caused by the health professional, that is that it was more likely than not that this was the case. An important rule has been established in cases of misdiagnosis, that the courts will not recognize the loss of a chance of recovery as enough to prove that injury has been caused by a mistake. In *Hotson* v. *E. Berkshire AHA* a boy had fallen out of a tree.[112] He argued that, had his injuries been properly diagnosed and had he been given the appropriate treatment, he would have had a 25 per cent chance of recovery. The health authority admitted that the failure to diagnose the injury was negligent. However, the House of Lords held that it was not enough to show that if a proper diagnosis had been made, treatment could have been offered that would have given the patient a chance of recovery. It must be shown that the treatment would probably have worked. The trial judge's approach of awarding the boy 25 per cent of what he would have received if the health authority had been wholly to blame was rejected.

A final point about causation is that the courts will consider whether the link between negligence and the injuries suffered has been broken by some intervening event.[113] One example of this is seen in the case of *Rance* v. *Mid-Downs HA*.[114] It was alleged that when the plaintiff was about twenty-six weeks pregnant, staff working for the health authority negligently failed to diagnose that the foetus suffered from spina bifida. However, the judge found that even if there had been a negligent misdiagnosis, the chain of causation was broken by the intervention of the law, which would (as drafted at that

---

[109] *Wilsher* v. *Essex AHA* [1988] 1 All ER 871 (HL).   [110] [1994] 5 Med. LR 57.
[111] [1995] 6 Med. LR 91.   [112] [1987] 2 All ER 909.
[113] This principle is sometimes known by the Latin tag *novus actus interveniens*.
[114] [1991] 1 All ER 801.

time) have prevented the termination of the pregnancy. The fact that the plaintiff was left with a disabled child resulted from the rules of law, not the alleged negligence.

Sometimes, the victims of the negligence may themselves be responsible for breaking the chain of causation. If a patient unreasonably refuses to accept remedial treatment that would have effected a complete cure, then the injuries become attributable to the decision to refuse treatment, not to the original error. However, it will probably be rare for a patient's refusal to consent to care to constitute an intervening event breaking the chain of causation. It may often be reasonable for a patient who has suffered injury as a result of a professional's care to be wary about accepting his or her advice again. It will be more common for a patient's decision not to take steps to minimize his or his injuries to be taken into account when damages are calculated, under the principle of that patients must mitigate their injuries (discussed below).

It is also possible for a court to hold that patients' conduct contributed to the original injury, perhaps where they refuse to accept precautionary measures. Here too the link between the professional's mistake and the injuries will be weakened. The injuries would be attributable partly to the professional's mistake and partly to the choice made by the patient. In such circumstances, patients must bear their share of the responsibility for the accident. The amount of damages that they will receive will be reduced *pro rata*, according to the degree of responsibility that they must shoulder. This is known as the doctrine of contributory negligence.

C. Damages

If patients win their case, they are entitled to 'damages', an amount of money to compensate them for their injuries. No special rules exist for medical accident cases and the general principles for calculating damages are applied.[115] Under those rules, damages are made up of a number of categories. First, there is 'fair and reasonable' compensation for the injury suffered. This is inevitably somewhat arbitrary, as there can be no precise determination of the value of a limb or organ, and the courts have developed an approximate tariff in order to achieve consistency.[116] Damages will also include a figure for the pain and suffering and loss of amenity experienced by the victim.

---

[115] Jones, n. 1 above, 454–92.
[116] Details can be found in D. Kemp (ed.), *Kemp and Kemp on The Quantum of Damages* (London: Sweet & Maxwell, 1994, looseleaf).

While these first two categories of damages cannot be calculated precisely, other losses can be proved more reliably and can then be recovered by the plaintiff. Expenses incurred as a result of the injuries up to the court hearing can be claimed. So can loss of earnings up to that point. The court then needs to speculate as to future losses that will flow from the injuries. It has to estimate the difference between the money that the patient would have earned if the accident had not happened and that which will be earned in the light of any disability suffered. This involves both calculating the annual sum, and working out the patient's life expectancy so that the money lost over his or her lifetime can be recompensed. In essence, this suggests multiplying the estimated annual loss of earnings by the number of years the patient is expected to live. In practice, however, the courts will only multiply the figure by eighteen, even when the patient is expected to live longer.

The most important point to note about the process of calculating damages is that the courts are trying to assess what the patient has lost. Damages reflect real costs, not punishment for the defendant. Sometimes the sums awarded in damages are vast, over £1 million, but they will only be so large when the patients can show that they have really lost out to that extent as a result of the accident. The mere fact that the payment made is very big does not make it excessive if the injuries and resulting losses are also extensive. There are circumstances when awards can include an extra element to reflect the fact that a defendant's wrongdoing was particularly heinous, but it is hard to envisage them arising in the context of health care.[117]

Finally, there is the possibility that damages will be reduced because the patient is partly responsible for the extent of the injuries suffered. Contributory negligence, discussed above, covers situations where the patient was partly to blame for the original accident. In addition to this, there is an expectation that the victims of accidents take reasonable steps to mitigate the severity of their injuries. Thus, if a patient refuses physiotherapy to improve impaired mobility, then the amount of damages awarded will be reduced to reflect the degree of disability that would have been suffered if the physiotherapy had been given.

D. Criminal 'Negligence'

In most circumstances, malpractice is only the concern of the civil law. However, in extreme cases, there may also be criminal implications. Where a

---

[117] Jones, n. 1 above, 456–7.

mistake causes the death of a patient, it is possible that the health professional could be prosecuted for manslaughter.[118] For this to happen, there must have been not merely negligence, but gross negligence. The legal test has been settled by the House of Lords in a case which concerned a health professional.[119] The defendant was an anæsthetist who failed to notice for over four minutes that an endotracheal tube had become disconnected during an operation under general anæsthetic. An alarm was sounded, but the connection of the tube was not checked until the patient had suffered cardiac arrest. One expert prosecution witness stated that a competent anæsthetist should have spotted the problem within fifteen seconds. The defendant accepted that he had been negligent, but denied that he was 'grossly negligent' so as to be guilty of involuntary manslaughter.

The House of Lords held that the question whether the degree of culpability was such that the anæsthetist should be liable to criminal sanctions was essentially a matter for the jury. Lord Mackay accepted that this was essentially a circular proposition: that criminal negligence is when a jury thinks the negligence was criminal. However, the House of Lords declined to offer a more precise definition. It did approve tests from earlier cases, which adopted the suggestion that gross negligence describes cases where the defendant has shown such disregard for the life and safety of others as to deserve punishment.[120] While this remains a circular definition, it does focus attention on the recklessness of the professionals' behaviour, that is their failure to concentrate on the patient's interests.[121]

The House of Lords upheld the decision of the Court of Appeal, which had spelt out a number of situations where gross negligence might exist.[122] While these were not expressly approved by the House of Lords, they remain indicative of the sort of case which might constitute manslaughter due to criminal negligence. The first of these was where health professionals had shown an obvious indifference to risks to the patient. The second was where they were aware of the risk, but decided to run it. The third was where their attempts to avoid a known risk were so grossly negligent that the jury believed that they deserved to be punished. The fourth was where there was inattention or a failure to advert to a serious risk that went beyond mere inadvertence.

Further indications of where the line has been drawn can be seen in the out-

---

[118] For a consideration of the policy issues, and the law set out by the CA prior to the decision of the HL that is discussed below, see A. McCall Smith, 'Criminal Negligence and the Incompetent Doctor' (1993) 1 *Med. L Rev.* 336–49.

[119] *R. v. Adomako* [1994] 2 All ER 79.

[120] See *R. v. Bateman* (1925) 19 Cr. App. R 8 and *Andrews* v. *DPP* [1937] 2 All ER 552.

[121] The HL rejected the suggestion that the word 'reckless' should be given any technical meaning: *R. v. Adomako*, n. 119 above, 87–9.

[122] *R. v. Prentice; R. v. Adomako; R. v. Holloway* [1993] 4 All ER 935, 943–4.

comes of cases. However, it must be remembered that it is for a jury to decide whether an offence has been committed on the facts, and previous decisions do not constitute any sort of formal precedent. The anæsthetist in the above case was found guilty and his conviction was upheld in the House of Lords. In another case, doctors who prescribed a lethal cocktail of drugs in excessive doses were convicted of manslaughter after the death of a remand prisoner who had requested a tranquillizer.[123] In a case on the other side of the line, two junior doctors injected a drug into a patient's spine which should have been injected into a vein. The patient died. Neither doctor checked the label of the drug, which would have told them the appropriate method of administration. The Court of Appeal quashed their convictions because the jury had not been told to consider whether there were any mitigating circumstances that reduced the doctors' culpability. These might have included the lack of supervision from more experienced staff.[124] The fact that their convictions were quashed does not mean that they might not have been found guilty if the jury had been properly directed. However, it does indicate that the situation in which an error takes place may be crucial to determining criminal responsibility.

E. Conclusion

It can be seen that English malpractice law is not particularly well placed to fulfil the functions identified at the beginning of this Chapter. As it revolves around the *Bolam* test, it is not generally able to render the health professions accountable to their patients and clients. Usually tort law aims to establish objective standards that define where a reasonable balance is to be drawn between risks and benefits. In the health care context, that balance is drawn by the professions and merely policed by the courts. Consequently, the deterrent effect of the law is weak. It certainly cannot contribute to raising professional standards. It is further diluted by the fact that health professionals will rarely find themselves liable to pay any damages that are awarded out of their own pockets. Malpractice litigation has come to be seen as a collective problem, to be addressed by the NHS as an institution, not by individuals (see the next chapter).

From the perspective of patients, using litigation as a means of retribution may feel highly unsatisfactory. The most blatant cases of malpractice will be quickly settled, with the minimum embarrassment for the professional. Only

---

[123] D. Brahams, 'Death of a Remand Prisoner' (1992) 340 *Lancet* 1462.
[124] *R. v. Prentice; R. v. Adomako; R. v. Holloway,* n. 122 above, 944–9.

those where liability is arguable will be fought. Further, the way that the NHS handles claims means that the real defendant will almost always be an NHS trust or health authority, not the individual who made the mistake (see the next chapter). As far as compensation is concerned, the rules of negligence are to some extent a lottery. The difficulties of proving breach of the standard of care, and especially of showing a causal link between breach and injury, mean that many deserving cases go without financial relief. This has led many to question the way in which medical accidents are handled.   ·

8 Malpractice Litigation II: In practice

The previous chapter discussed the substantive law that governs malpractice cases. This one examines practical aspects of litigation, and considers the significance of litigation for the future of health care, particularly under the NHS. It begins with the initiation of claims, and the way that they are handled within the NHS. It then discusses the possibility that the United Kingdom is facing a malpractice crisis, such as is thought to bedevil American medicine.

A. Encouraging Claims: A Duty to Explain Mishaps?

One of the most unfortunate aspects of the adversarial system of English malpractice litigation is the way in which it encourages doctors and patients to see themselves in opposition to each other. One of the major complaints made against the way in which doctors handle medical accidents is that they fail to explain what happened.[1] One of the most common explanations offered for this practice is the fear that explanations might be seen as admissions of liability and lead to litigation.[2] This is said to be because the defence societies advise doctors to be careful, although the societies themselves deny this.[3] The Medical Defence Union has advised that 'the patient is entitled to a prompt, sympathetic and above all truthful account of what has occurred'.[4]

There have been some suggestions that the law may impose a duty to give a candid explanation when things go wrong. Patients remain in the professional's care even after accidents occur and Lord Donaldson MR has suggested that general principles indicate that failing to answer questions about their treatment might constitute malpractice.[5] Support for this duty is found in

---

[1] R. Vallance, 'Preliminary Legal Steps for the Patient' in M. Powers and N. Harris (eds), *Medical Negligence* (London: Butterworths, 1990), 102–3.

[2] A. Simanowitz, 'Medical Accidents: The Problem and the Challenge' in P. Byrne (ed.), *Medicine in Contemporary Society* (London: Kings Fund, 1987), 125–9.

[3] C. Hawkins, *Mishap or Malpractice* (Oxford: Blackwell, 1985), 161–3.

[4] Medical Defence Union (1986) 2 *Journal of the MDU* No 2, 2.

[5] *Lee* v. *S.W. Thames RHA* [1985] 2 All ER 385, 389–90; *Naylor* v. *Preston* [1987] 2 All ER 353, 360.

Gerber v. *Pines* where a needle broke in the course of an injection and the doctor failed initially to tell the patient what had happened.[6] The court accepted that the accident itself was not negligent; the needle had broken because of a muscle spasm, not because of any fault on the part of the doctor. Nevertheless, the failure to inform the patient on the day of the accident was negligent.[7] Whether the exact content of the duty to explain will be defined by the standard professional practice is unclear. This would be consistent with the courts' usual approach. If it is, the chances of bringing a successful legal action must be remote. If doctors do not usually give full explanations and the standard of care is determined by the profession's usual practice, then a failure to explain will not usually be negligent. This may be an area, however, where the courts might intervene to set standards for the profession.

Lord Donaldson has also argued that there is a duty to tell patients that they may have a right to sue, analogous to that imposed on lawyers to advise clients that they should seek independent advice when the lawyers have made mistakes.[8] The solicitors' duty to which he refers is imposed by their professional code of conduct rather than the law. Neither the GMC's 'Blue Book' nor the UKCC's *Code of Professional Conduct* makes any statement about the matter, and it is therefore unlikely that failing to advise patients that they may have a legal case would constitute professional misconduct.

B. Bringing a Case: The Law of Limitation

Health professionals are often concerned about the length of time that elapses between the event of alleged malpractice and the hearing of a case. The law does impose limits on the delay that can exist between an accident and beginning a malpractice action; these are found in the law of limitation.[9] Most health malpractice cases involve 'personal injury', a category which includes impairment of physical or mental health. For this type of case, the legal action must be commenced within three years of the date on which the negligence occurred, or the date on which the patient realized that an action could be brought.[10] This latter provision deals with cases where patients did not at first realize that they might have a case. Then the three-year period begins to run only when they appreciate that they have suffered a significant injury for which the defendants may be to blame.[11] Such delays in the patient becoming

---

[6] (1933) 79 SJ 13. [7] See also *Cooper* v. *Miron* [1927] 2 BMJ 40.

[8] J. Donaldson, 'The Court of Appeal' (1985) 53 *Medico-Legal Journal* 148, 157–8.

[9] See generally, M. Jones, *Medical Negligence* (2nd edn., London: Sweet & Maxwell, 1996), 493–544.

[10] Limitation Act 1980, s. 11.   [11] *Ibid.*, s. 14.

aware of the possibility of litigation may arise because the injuries did not manifest themselves immediately, or because she or he was unaware of any error that could have caused them, or because no link between a known error and the injuries was initially established. Where alleged malpractice causes the death of a patient within three years, then a new three year period will run from the date of the death, or the dependants' knowledge that a case could be brought.[12] This gives the dependants a chance to consider suing.

Although malpractice cases will generally be subject to a three year limitation period, there will be some exceptions. Some mistakes will result, not in personal injury, but financial loss. For example, the damage incurred after a failed sterilization procedure will primarily be the costs of bringing up the unexpected child. In non-personal injury cases, the limitation period is six years, not three.[13] The second important exception to the three-year period concerns injuries suffered by children and those of unsound mind. In such cases, the three-year period only begins to run when they become sane or adult.[14] This is why cases involving children may be brought so long after the alleged negligence. In relation to problems at the time of birth, children may sue at any time up to twenty-one years after the event, because the three-year period will only begin to run against them when they become an adult at 18.

Even though these time limits are set to ensure that professionals will not have potential malpractice claims hanging over them for ever, the court retains a discretion to extend the limitation period.[15] It must consider whether it is equitable to permit the plaintiff to begin an action out of time, taking into account the extent to which the parties would be prejudiced by the lateness. This includes examining the reasons for the delay and the conduct of the defendant.

The limitation period deals with delay between the event complained about and the issuing of the writ. This is the first formal stage in the litigation process, and there may be further delays before a matter comes to court. The courts retain a limited power to strike out applications that are unduly delayed. However, there may be a significant period between the issuing of the writ and any court hearing, even without the case being mishandled. This is partly because of the difficulties in proving a malpractice claim. Some of the reasons for this will appear from an examination of the substantive issues that arise in such cases.

---

[12] *Ibid.*, s. 11.   [13] *Ibid.*, s. 2.   [14] *Ibid.*, s. 28.   [15] *Ibid.*, s. 33.

C. Who Pays? Financial Aspects of Malpractice Litigation

Financial issues are a crucial aspect of understanding malpractice litigation. Cases are usually brought for financial reasons: to obtain compensation. Plaintiffs may sometimes be unable to bring cases because they cannot afford to do so. Legal aid is available to support some people in this situation. Financial questions are also important for defendants. While most malpractice cases will involve allegations against individual practitioners, in practice the primary responsibility for handling claims will fall upon NHS trusts and other employing authorities. In general terms, this is usually because they will be vicariously liable for the negligence of their staff. However, there are also specific arrangements within the NHS, known as NHS indemnity, which provide for the employing institution to deal with litigation. This section examines the way in which malpractice claims are managed and funded.

(i) Costs and Legal Aid

It is impossible to consider the impact of litigation on patients, professionals, and the health service without considering the role of costs. Litigation is expensive and cost represents a major disincentive to plaintiffs bringing malpractice actions. It also imposes an additional financial burden on defendants. A study of cases in the Oxford Region found that plaintiffs' costs constituted nearly 20 per cent of the total recovered and defendants' costs about 14 per cent.[16] Parliamentary data indicate that legal costs accounted for approximately 12 per cent of the total cost of English NHS cases in 1991–2 and approximately 10 per cent in 1992–3.[17] While US lawyers receive a higher proportion of damages in fees,[18] it is clear that a considerable amount of the money at stake in a malpractice action is eaten up by the costs of fighting it. This leaves less for the purpose of compensating victims.

For potential plaintiffs whose financial resources are very limited, legal aid may be available to cover their legal costs.[19] It has been suggested that the increase in litigation has in part been a product of easy access to legal aid

[16] P. Fenn and R. Dingwall, 'The Tort System and Information: Some Comparisons between the United Kingdom and the US' in R. Dingwall, and P. Fenn (eds), *Quality and Regulation in Health Care: International Experiences* (London: Routledge, 1992), 20–2.

[17] Calculated from written answers, *Hansard*, HC, Vol. 239, cols. 537–8; Vol. 243, cols. 85–6; and Vol. 246, col. 193.

[18] Fenn and Dingwall, n. 16 above, 20–2.

[19] Legal aid does not necessarily mean free legal services; a means-tested contribution is required from assisted parties.

funding even for meritless claims.[20] Two arguments are offered. First, that plaintiffs are more likely to start litigation and less likely to settle cases out of court when they are not paying their own costs. This is undoubtedly true, but if there is a strong case that a professional has been negligent it would be wrong to regard the deterrent effect of costs as a just way of diverting complaints from the legal system. It protects professionals at the expense of patients with legitimate grievances. The real issue is whether frivolous cases, which have no chance of success and waste scarce time and money, are being supported by the Legal Aid Board.

It has been alleged that the Legal Aid Board has granted legal aid too readily. In principle, legal aid is not granted unless the case has a reasonable prospect of success. Nevertheless, a high number of legally aided plaintiffs fail. One study of 100 cases found that seventy-three were withdrawn, one was lost in court, and twelve were settled out of court.[21] The authors examined the files and suggested that in only forty-five cases was there even a possibility of negligence. They argued that legal aid was being granted in cases that the plaintiffs had no chance of winning. Others have suggested that the large number of unsuccessful claims is more likely to be a result of general difficulties in assessing the strength of cases without the full evidence than profligacy on the part of the Legal Aid Board.[22]

Nevertheless, the existence of legal aid does push up the overall costs to the NHS of defending medical accident claims.[23] In the ordinary course of litigation the people who win may apply to the court for an order that the other side pays their legal expenses. Where the losing person is legally aided such an order cannot usually be made. Many victims of medical accidents are supported by the legal aid fund, and so the costs of unsuccessful claims will often fall upon the NHS trust or health authority defendant. In 1984 Jandoo and Harland illustrated how this can encourage health authorities to settle cases that they would have expected to win in court.[24] Imagine that a legally aided plaintiff makes a claim for damages that he or she is prepared to settle for £500. The health authority takes expert advice and is told that its staff acted properly and that the claim would fail if brought before a court. Nevertheless, the cost of fighting it in court may be of the region of £5,000 (1984 figures) and this will not be recoverable from the plaintiff. It would therefore be

---

[20] C. Hawkins and I. Paterson, 'Medico-legal Audit in the West Midlands Region: Analysis of 100 Cases' (1987) 295 *BMJ* 1533–6.

[21] *Ibid.*

[22] P. Fenn and C. Whelan, 'Medical Litigation: Trends, Causes, Consequences' in R. Dingwall (ed.), *Socio-legal Aspects of Medical Practice* (London: Royal College of Physicians, 1989), 15–17.

[23] W. A. Harland and R. S. Jandoo, 'The Medical Negligence Crisis' (1984) 24 *Med. Sci. Law* 123–9.

[24] R. S. Jandoo and W. A. Harland, 'Legally Aided Blackmail' (1984) 134 *NLJ* 402–4.

cheaper to agree to pay the £500, even though the authority is not legally liable to do so, than to defend the case.

It is possible for a court to order the Legal Aid Board to pay a health service body's costs only in exceptional circumstances. In relation to the initial court proceedings these are when it would suffer 'severe financial hardship' if an order for costs were not made.[25] If a case goes to appeal and the legally aided person loses, the costs of the appeal may be ordered to be paid by the Legal Aid Board if it is 'just and equitable' to do so.[26] Health authorities and defence organizations will rarely be able to show that they face 'severe financial hardship' if they do not recover their costs, because the sum in question will usually represent a small proportion of their budget. Nor is it likely that the less stringent test applied to appeals will benefit health authorities, because the Court of Appeal has indicated that where public bodies funded out of general taxation are concerned payment of costs out of legal aid funds is inappropriate.[27]

One area where the legal aid rules are undoubtedly a significant factor in encouraging litigation is the reform introduced in 1990 that provides that the financial position of children is separately assessed when eligibility for legal aid is considered.[28] The implication of this is that actions on behalf of children will almost always be eligible for legal aid. This may be the explanation for the steep rise in legal aid certificates issued for medical negligence from 6,140 in 1989–90 to 18,658 in 1991–2. The level reduced again for 1992–3 to 11,677, but this is still a significant increase. The long limitation period for actions by children means that there would have been a large number of potential claimants in a position to benefit from this relaxation of the legal aid rules, and it was to be expected that there would be a large bulge in the rate of legally aided malpractice cases brought by children. Once those who would have sued before, but were previously unable to fund the litigation, have explored their chances of obtaining legal aid, it will be possible to ascertain the longer-term impact of these legal aid changes. It is probable that actions in respect of injured infants, particularly for the mismanagement of labour, will be made substantially more common by the availability of legal aid.

Finally, the Courts and Legal Services Act 1990 introduced a new method of dealing with legal costs, the conditional fee.[29] This makes it possible for lawyers to take on a case on the basis that they will receive no fee if their client loses, but will be paid more than usual if they win. This new provision resem-

---

[25] Legal Aid Act 1988, s. 18.

[26] *R. v. Greenwich LBC, ex p. Lovelace (No 2)* [1991] 3 WLR 1015.   [27] *Ibid.*, 1023.

[28] The Civil Legal Aid (Assessment of Resources) (Amendment) Regulations 1990, SI 1990 No 484, removed r. 8 of the Civil Legal Aid (Assessment of Resources) Regulations 1989, SI 1989 No 338, which had enabled maintenance payments to be taken into account.

[29] Courts and Legal Services Act 1990, s. 58, brought into force on 5 July 1995.

bles the contingency fees which have been blamed for the alleged malpractice crisis in the United States. It is suggested that the contingency fee system first encourages more plaintiffs to sue and, secondly, pushes up the level of damages because juries take into account the fact that a percentage of the award will go to the lawyers. It is far from clear that these suggestions are well founded, but the latter seems more consistent with the data than the former.[30]

The British conditional fee differs from the US model of contingency fees because payment will not be a proportion of damages received but will be based on the actual costs, as calculated by the usual methods, uprated by an agreed percentage up to 100 per cent.[31] This may increase the number of legal actions against health authorities because potential plaintiffs who cannot afford to pay costs out of their own pockets and do not qualify for legal aid will now be able initiate litigation without having to pay for it. However, the impact of this will be partially offset by the fact that if they lose they may have to pay the costs of the defendants. In addition, it has been suggested that the introduction of contingency fees will actually make little difference because lawyers will have insufficient incentives to take on risky cases.[32] If this proves to be true, then it will encourage only claimants who have a good chance of success, but would otherwise be unable to fund litigation. There is less danger than in the United States that conditional fees will increase the level of damages because in Britain awards are made by judges rather than juries. Nor will defendants who lose be made to pay more because the plaintiff's lawyers are being paid extra under a conditional fee. The Act specifically prevents this being taken into account when making an order for costs.[33]

(ii) Vicarious Liability and the NHS Indemnity Scheme

While it is health professionals who feel the impact of allegations of malpractice most directly, they do not usually bear the cost of claims. Cases are fought principally in order to obtain compensation, and individuals can rarely be guaranteed to have the financial resources to pay damages. In practice, it is usually the professional's employer who is sued. The plaintiff can be confident that it will have the resources to meet a successful claim. This is possible because employers are liable for any negligent acts committed by their employees under the doctrine of 'vicarious liability'. This does not absolve the employee of liability, and patients could choose to sue an individual.

---

[30] Fenn and Dingwall, n. 16 above, 19–20.

[31] S. 58(2); Conditional Fee Agreements Order 1995, SI 1995 No 1674, r. 3.

[32] J. Peynser, 'Health Care Litigation: Examination, Diagnosis and Prognosis' [1995] *J Personal Injury Litigation* 91–106, 99–100.

[33] S. 58(8).

However, they may also elect to bring their legal action against the practice, hospital, NHS trust, or health authority for whom the professional worked. They will not receive damages twice over, but it does not matter whether they go to the employee or employer first. In theory, employers can seek reimbursement from negligent employees for anything they have had to pay out. However, in practice, this is rarely done. There is some concern that NHS trusts may be more willing to pursue their employees than health authorities were under the pre-market NHS, but there is no firm evidence that this is happening.

Within the NHS, an agreement has been reached with the medical profession that, since 1 January 1990, the costs of hospital litigation are borne by the NHS trusts.[34] This replaced the previous arrangement under which medical staff were required to carry professional indemnity insurance.[35] General practitioners remain responsible for meeting malpractice liabilities, and therefore need to continue to carry insurance. Malpractice claims against health professionals other than doctors and dentists have long been handled by their employers. Thus the position of hospital doctors and dentists has been brought into line with that of the other professions.

The current regime makes the NHS trusts responsible for minimizing their exposure. This has increased the extent to which managers are responsible for handling claims, and has led to a concentration on risk management, intended to reduce the risks of accidents.[36] One concern that this raises is that managers may choose to settle cases out of court for financial reasons, and fail to defend the reputation of the practitioner who is accused of negligence. The circular specifically draws the attention of NHS bodies to the need to consider the views of practitioners about the damaging effect of cases on their reputation. However, it envisages that those views will be weighed against other factors, including the costs involved.[37] The costs of dealing with claims are significant, even where many of those claims are ultimately unsuccessful. If the patient drops the case before the matter comes to court, the health authority or NHS trust defending the action will not be able to recover its costs. Even if it wins a case in court it will not be able to do so if the plaintiff was legally aided.[38]

[34] *Claims of Medical Negligence against NHS Hospital and Community Dentists*, HC(89)34. For commentary, see R. Bowles and P. Jones, 'Better Safe than Sorry' (1991) *HSJ* 21 Mar., 18–19; P. Reeves, 'National Health Service Indemnity' (1990) 87/18 *LSG* 24–5; P. Fenn and R. Dingwall, 'Medical Negligence and Crown Indemnity' in J. Gretton (ed.), *Health Care United Kingdom 1989* (Birmingham: Policy Journals, 1990), 39–46; R. Dingwall and P. Fenn, 'Is NHS Indemnity Working and is There a Better Way?' (1994) 73 *British J Anæsthesia* 69–77.

[35] HM(54)32.

[36] NHS Management Executive, *Risk Management in the NHS* (London: DoH, 1993), issued with EL(93)111.

[37] HC(87)34, para. 5.   [38] See text to nn. 25–7 above.

The introduction of NHS indemnity was a response to the increasing costs of medical accident litigation.[39] It was thought that it would be more cost effective than continuing to fund claims indirectly by meeting the costs of insurance through increased pay settlements for doctors. By combining legal representation for practitioners and health authorities, it was thought that there would be cost savings. Removing the need to negotiate the division of liability between authorities and defence societies was also expected to reduce costs by facilitating early settlements. However, there are also significant disadvantages of the NHS indemnity system.[40] It dilutes the expertise available to defend claims by decentralizing the legal work previously carried out by the defence organizations. It encourages patients to think of litigation in less personalized terms, possibly making it more likely that they will sue an impersonal trust than the doctor who was treating them. It is also unclear whether it will actually save the NHS money.

The principal problem that NHS indemnity raises is how to distribute risk amongst the provider units which are likely to be sued. The further such a loss can be spread, the less directly the impact will be felt.[41] NHS trusts are not permitted to take out insurance to cover malpractice costs, and must look to meet payments within their NHS funding. This will mean that larger settlements must be funded by a long-term loan, or through membership of the Clinical Negligence Scheme for Trusts.[42] In both cases, the costs, either of interest and repayments or subscriptions to the CNST, will have to be recouped through contract prices. This will clearly affect the competitiveness of trusts. Settlements may take the form of a single lump-sum payment directly to the patient. However, they can also be funded by the purchase of an annuity or on the basis of periodical payments from revenue. These will give the patient a regular income rather than a one-off sum. As yet, there is little understanding of the long-term implications of these options.[43]

When NHS indemnity was introduced, the Department of Health secured an agreement with the defence societies who had previously handled litigation that a proportion of their reserves would be made available to meet the costs of large settlements. Under the arrangements, the first £300,000 of any claim would be met locally. Above that threshold, health service bodies could draw upon the central fund to meet 80 per cent of the costs (including both

[39] Fenn and Dingwall, n. 34 above, 39–46.

[40] Bowles and Jones, n. 34 above, 18–19; M. Brazier, 'NHS Indemnity: The Implications for Medical Litigation' (1991) 6 *PN* 88–91; Fenn and Dingwall, n. 34 above, 39–46.

[41] See Bowles and Jones, n. 34 above, 18–19 for discussion of ways to spread the risk.

[42] NHS Management Executive, *Clinical Negligence: Proposed Creation of a Central Fund in England* (London: NHSME, 1994) para. 7; see also EL(90)195.

[43] See R. Lewis, 'Health Authorities and the Payment of Damages by Means of a Pension' (1993) 56 *MLR* 844–55.

damages and legal costs).[44] This arrangement was replaced on 1 April 1996 by what is known as the 'Existing Liabilities Scheme' administered by the NHS Litigation Authority.[45] This Scheme applies to claims in respect of incidents occurring before 1 April 1995. It gives NHS bodies access to the residue of the fund drawn from defence society reserves, provided that they operate in accordance with the terms of the scheme. These relate to standards of claims handling and securing approval from the Authority. Even when eligible for funding from the Scheme, the NHS bodies have to meet the first £10,000 of claims, and 20 per cent of the cost between £10,000 and £50,000. The rest of the costs of claims will be met from the Scheme's fund.

For claims arising from incidents after 1 April 1995, a central fund has been established under section 21 of the NHS and Community Care Act 1990, which enables NHS trusts to spread their clinical negligence costs.[46] As with the Existing Liabilities Scheme, access to funding is dependant upon operating appropriate risk management and claims handling procedures and approval from the NHS Litigation Authority. It would be open to the Secretary of State to make participation in the fund compulsory,[47] but this power has not been used, although NHS trusts are encouraged to join.[48] There are no plans to relax the restrictions on NHS trusts seeking commercial insurance.[49]

In addition to overseeing the availability of central funding for malpractice settlements, the NHS Litigation Authority will play an important co-ordinating role in relation to litigation. NHS trusts and health authorities have responsibility for handling claims. Prior to December 1995, Department of Health approval was required for all settlements above £5,000. This limit has been dramatically raised to £1 million, subject to the NHS bodies following the NHSE guidance on handling clinical negligence[50] (which identifies standards for claims handling and imposes reporting requirements). The guidance emphasizes that local settlement should not be made in relation to cases involving novel claims that might establish precedents that would be unfortunate for the NHS without referral to the NHSLA and the Treasury.[51] This may go some way towards overcoming the fragmentation of expertise introduced by NHS indemnity.

---

[44] HC(89)34, para. 11.

[45] NHS (Existing Liabilities Scheme) Regulations 1996, SI 1996 No 868; NHSE, 'Clinical Negligence Funding: New Arrangements for Claims Incurred Before 1 April 1995', FDL(95)56.

[46] The NHS (Clinical Negligence Scheme) Regulations 1996, SI 1996 No 251; see also NHS Management Executive, n. 42 above.

[47] S. 21(4)(a).

[48] NHS Management Executive, n. 42 above, para. 10 iii.   [49] *Ibid.*, para. 8.

[50] NHSE, 'Clinical Negligence and Personal Injury Litigation: Claims Handling', EL(96)11.

[51] Paras. 12.1, 12.2.

(iii) Apportionment between Defendants

Where there is more than one defendant, it is necessary to consider how much of the damages each of them should pay. The general principles governing the apportionment of liability are, first, that a successful plaintiff may obtain the whole of the damages from any one of the defendants to the case and, secondly, that that defendant may sue the others for reimbursement of their share of the money paid. The amount of the share depends on the degree of responsibility each party holds for the accident.[52] The operation of these principles in the health care context can be seen in two cases concerning pharmacists and doctors.

In *Dwyer* v. *Roderick*,[53] the doctor had made a gross mistake in making out a prescription. The pharmacist dispensed the drugs as instructed. The patient took them and suffered a fatal overdose. Negligence was admitted and the litigation concerned the apportionment of responsibility between the professionals. The doctor was held to be liable for 45 per cent of the damages and the pharmacist for the rest. He was more to blame than the doctor for failing to check the dosage when the drug was dispensed.

In a second case the pharmacist misread the doctor's handwriting and dispensed a drug that caused irreversible brain damage.[54] The doctor was found to be negligent for writing illegibly, but the court found that this amounted to only one quarter of the responsibility. The pharmacist was primarily responsible, as the dosage prescribed should have alerted him to the fact that there was a misunderstanding and he should have queried the instructions. His failure to do so was more significant than the poor handwriting.

The operation of NHS indemnity means that apportionment will rarely be an issue in hospital cases. However, it will continue to be significant in general practice (where the indemnity scheme does not apply) and where more than one provider is involved. This latter situation may well become far more common, as partnerships between NHS and independent providers increase, and as more services are provided on an outreach basis, particularly in primary care clinics.

D. Litigation Crisis?

From the perspective of the health professions any increase in malpractice litigation is threatening. It seems to represent an attack on their competence,

---

[52] Civil Liability (Contribution) Act 1978.　　　[53] (1983) 127 SJ 806 (1983) 80 LSG 3003.
[54] *Prendergast* v. *Sam & Dee Ltd* [1989] 1 Med. LR 36.

their position in society, and ultimately their financial security. Thus in December 1990 Sir Donald Acheson, then Chief Medical Officer, felt it necessary to discuss the impact of litigation under the title 'Are Obstetrics and Midwifery Doomed?' and to suggest that the answer was probably yes, unless significant reforms were introduced.[55] On the other hand, non-medical commentators have been highly sceptical of claims that there is some sort of malpractice crisis.[56] They point out that the data supporting claims of crisis are poor and that they are rarely analysed carefully. On this view, the supposed malpractice crisis is a powerful myth that serves largely to insulate the medical profession from close scrutiny.[57]

There is little doubt that there was a sharp increase in the amount of medical accident litigation initiated in the United Kingdom in the 1980s. However, it remains hotly debated whether this was properly described as a crisis, and it is unclear how far litigation has continued to escalate. Disagreements have surfaced over the factual basis for claims of crisis and also over whether the increase in litigation should be welcomed rather than bemoaned. The absence of hard evidence has not prevented commentators, particularly those from the medical profession, making extravagant claims about the impact of litigation on clinical practice. It is only recently that information about what is actually happening has begun to be available so that the merits of the arguments can be assessed. This Chapter examines what we know about the current level of malpractice litigation, looks at its causes and effects, and considers the claim that there is a crisis.

In order to assess the validity of the suggestion that there is some sort of crisis, it is first necessary to consider the level and nature of litigation. The rate of legal claims needs to be considered both in terms of frequency and severity. The former relates to the number of claims brought, the latter to their cost. An increase in litigation does not necessarily indicate that there is some form of crisis, but it is probably a necessary precondition. Once what is happening has been established, the implications of litigation need to be considered. Some consequences of legal actions may be seen as productive, while others are not.

---

[55] D. Acheson, 'Are Obstetrics and Midwifery Doomed?' (1991) *Midwives Chronicle & Nursing Notes* 158–66.

[56] e.g. C. Ham, R. Dingwall, P. Fenn, and D. Harris, *Medical Negligence: Compensation and Accountability* (London: King's Fund Institute, 1988); I. Kennedy, 'Malpractice Litigation Crisis? What Crisis?' in P. Byrne (ed.), *Medicine in Contemporary Society* (London: King's Fund, 1987), 52–63.

[57] A. Simanowitz, 'Defensive Medicine: Myth or Reality?' in P. Byrne (ed.), *Health, Rights and Resources* (Oxford: Oxford University Press, 1988), 166–76; M. Jones, 'The Rising Cost of Medical Malpractice' (1987) 3 *PN* 43–6.

(i) What is Actually Happening?

The Pearson Commission estimated that in 1973 there were only 700 medical accident claims (i.e. 1.6 per 100,000 population). Until the 1990s, data were poor, partly because the NHS did not record them and partly because the information was regarded as commercially sensitive by the medical defence societies, which then handled the claims on behalf of the medical profession.[58] The best evidence for the period comes from work at the Centre for Socio-legal Studies at Oxford. Surveying the rate of claims for six English regional health authorities for 1986–7 it found that there was considerable variation, but that the typical rate of claim was between six and nine per 100,000 population. Two of the regions experienced far more claims, with rates of 17.2 and 20.5 per 100,000 population. There is, thus, clear evidence of an increase in the number of claims. However, the rate of claims still fell considerably short of their incidence in the United States where, in 1984, the comparable rate was 29.4 per 100,000 population.

The Oxford study found that the pattern of increasing litigation during the decade to 1987 could be seen whether the region had a relatively high rate of claims or a low one.[59] There is some evidence that there was a peak of litigation in 1987, as the two regions that had data on 1987–8 showed that the rate of claims fell in that year. This may be partly explained by the changes in the delay between adverse occurrences and the bringing of claims resulting in a stabilization of the rate of claims.[60] This pattern of increasing litigation, together with a levelling off around 1986, is consistent with the study of a further health authority carried out by Bowles and Jones.[61]

The Oxford researchers followed up their general survey of the position, with a detailed study of the experience of the Oxford Regional Health Authority, which they found to have a rate of claims close to the United Kingdom median.[62] They identified 470 claims that had been resolved by 1988 and studied those in detail. Within this, relatively small, sample, the specialties that were most likely to be the subject of litigation were obstetrics and gynæcology (22 per cent), orthopædics (15.6 per cent), accident and emergency (10.8 per cent), general surgery (10.3 per cent) and anæsthesiology (6.8 per cent). Almost exactly a third of cases resulted in patients receiving

---

[58] Fenn and Whelan, n. 22 above, 6–7; Fenn and Dingwall, n. 16 above, 12–13. For a detailed analysis of claims settled by one of the defence societies, the Medical Defence Union, in 1989, see P. Hoyte, 'Unsound Practice: The Epidemiology of Medical Negligence' (1995) 3 *Med. L Rev.* 53–73.

[59] Fenn and Whelan, n. 22 above, 8.

[60] Fenn and Dingwall, n. 34 above, 39–46.

[61] R. Bowles and P. Jones, 'Medical Negligence: A Health Authority's Experience' (1989) 139 *NLJ* 119–23.

[62] Fenn and Dingwall, n. 16 above.

compensation. The likelihood of success was not related to the frequency with which a specialty gave rise to litigation. Although obstetrics and gynæcology attracted the most claims, it was the specialty in which patients were least likely to receive compensation (25 per cent). Conversely, plaintiffs in cases concerning anæsthetics were most likely to receive damages (51 per cent).

The full significance of the increasing rate of claims can only be appreciated when the value of those claims is also considered. Then the cost of malpractice litigation can begin to be assessed. In this area, too, it is possible to identify a significant increase in the pressure on the system. The highest sum awarded in a medical negligence case in 1977 was approximately £133,000. In 1987 it was £1.03 million.[63] Media attention has tended to focus on the biggest claims, which suggests an eightfold increase, but a better picture can be obtained by looking at the average level of settlement. The Oxford study showed that average payments (taking a five-year average to avoid random distortion) in 1982–6 were roughly three times as high as those in 1974–8 (after adjustment for inflation).[64] Taking the average costs of settlement, and the incidence of claims it is possible to assess the drain that litigation makes on the health care system.

In 1988, the Oxford group estimated that the total cost of medical negligence in the United Kingdom, including both damages paid out and the administrative and legal costs involved, was around £75 million. Official data are now becoming available for the 1990s because the Department of Health has collected statistical returns for clinical negligence litigation, and NHS trusts are required to include the costs of such cases in their annual accounts.

There has been some confusion about these figures. The total expenditure on clinical negligence for NHS bodies in England for the years 1990–3, as originally reported to Parliament, suggested that the cost of medical negligence (including damages awarded and legal costs) remained fairly static at a little over £50 million *per annum*.[65] These figures suggested that there had not been a continued escalation of the money eaten up by litigation.[66] However, revised figures indicate that there has been a renewed increase in money spent; being £80 million in 1992–3, £100 million in 1993–4, and an estimated £125 million in 1994–5.[67]

---

[63] Ham, Dingwall, Fenn, and Harris, n. 56 above, 11.

[64] Fenn and Whelan, n. 22 above, fig. 4.

[65] Written answers, *Hansard*, HC, Vol. 239, cols. 537–8 and Vol. 243, cols. 85–6. The data for 1991–2 and 1992–3 was said to be incomplete because not all returns were in when they were drawn up.

[66] The Oxford team speculated that this might be the case: see Fenn and Dingwall, n. 34 above, 39–46, 44. See also P. Fenn, D. Hermans, and R. Dingwall, 'Estimating the Cost of Compensating Victims of Medical Negligence' (1994) 309 *BMJ* 389–91.

[67] Written answer, *Hansard*, HC, Vol. 256, cols. 41–2. The figures for 1994–5 were expressed to be provisional.

Clearly, in times when the budget for health services is limited, there is concern for the amount of money diverted from patient care by litigation. However, before it is assumed that the interests of patients lie in restricting payouts it should be remembered that it is patients who are bringing the legal actions. The Pearson Commission discovered that only around 40 per cent of medical cases resulted in the claimants receiving compensation.[68] The equivalent figure for other types of personal injury claim was much higher. More recent data suggest that the current success rate in medical cases is even lower, at around 30 per cent.[69] This indicates that a significant proportion of people who need compensation are unable to obtain it through the tort system. It is also possible that increased public awareness of malpractice litigation has encouraged a rush of less meritorious claims and that the rise in the number of cases brought will not be reflected in an increase in the number of payments.[70] The figures reported above do not separate legal costs from damages paid out, so it is unclear how far the increase in expenditure is benefitting claimants or lawyers.

(ii) The Transatlantic Nightmare

It is often suggested that British malpractice litigation is following in the footsteps of the United States, and that this means that even if we are not yet in crisis, we soon will be.[71] This attitude may be over pessimistic for two main reasons. First, the position in the United States may not be so bleak as American doctors like to suggest. Secondly, there are important structural differences in both the health care and legal systems of the two countries that make it unlikely that the transatlantic experience will be repeated here.

It is clear that crude rates of claims in the United States are higher than they are in the United Kingdom. The figures discussed above showed that the US rate of claims was half as much again as the most litigation-prone regions surveyed by the Oxford researcher. The American rate was almost five times that of the region with the lowest experience of claims. It is also true that in the United States patients are more likely to receive damages; 42.3 per cent of American plaintiffs received damages, but only 33 per cent of those in the study of the Oxford Region.[72] This suggests that malpractice litigation is a more significant aspect of US medicine than its United Kingdom counterpart. More patients sue their doctors, and more of them win.

---

[68] *Report of the Royal Commission on Civil Liability and Compensation for Personal Injury* (London: HMSO, 1978, Cmnd. 7054–I), 284.

[69] Fenn and Whelan, n. 22 above, 8; Bowles and Jones, n. 61 above.

[70] Bowles and Jones, n. 61 above, 120.   [71] Acheson, n. 55 above, 159–60.

[72] Fenn and Dingwall, n. 16 above, 16–17.

The amounts awarded in damages are difficult to compare, partly because the figures are often calculated to include legal costs in the United States, and the underlying costs of medical care and living will tend to make US awards seem higher than they really are. It must also be remembered that the use of juries tends to foster inconsistency and occasionally leads to excessively large awards. When attention is diverted from these unrepresentative mega-awards, and adjustments are made to reflect the factors previously outlined, it can be suggested that levels of damages in the United States are not so very different from those in the United Kingdom.[73]

Two strands of the implications of the American pattern of litigation for doctors should be disentangled. The financial impact of the so-called malpractice crisis is less severe than it might seem. As long as insurance is available, the costs of litigation can be passed on to patients through increased fees. Only those who rely on reimbursement from the state, rather than private practice, suffer personally.[74] Even in the high risk specialty of obstetrics and gynæcology, insurance premiums constitute a relatively small proportion of practitioners' gross income.[75]

The psychological and social impact of litigation is more worrying. It is undoubtedly true that being sued is a traumatic experience. However, it is far from clear that the consequences that are attributed to malpractice litigation, such as defensive practices and decisions to give up professional careers, can really be linked to legal activity. The malpractice situation is only part of the environment in which doctors work. Defensive practices can perhaps be more closely correlated with the fee for service arrangement than with the risks of litigation.[76] Doctors' disillusionment with American law may be a symptom of resistance to broader trends towards a loss of independence and prestige rather than the concrete difficulties with the courts.[77]

Given this assessment of the position in the USA, it may be that moving towards that situation might not be such a disaster. However, there are good reasons to believe that it is unlikely that the United Kingdom will do so anyway. Quam *et al.* argue that the existence of the National Health Service

[73] B. S. Markesinis, 'Litigation-mania in England, Germany and the USA: Are We so Very Different?' (1990) 49 *CLJ* 233–76.

[74] L. Quam, R. Dingwall, and P. Fenn, 'Medical Malpractice in Perspective I The American Experience' (1987) 294 *BMJ* 1529–32.

[75] L. Quam, R. Dingwall, and P. Fenn, 'Medical Malpractice Claims in Obstetrics and Gynaecology: Comparisons between the United States and Britain' (1988) 95 *Brit. J Obstetrics & Gynaecology* 451–61, 455.

[76] Quam, Dingwall, and Fenn, n. 74 above.

[77] P. Hubbard, 'The Physician's Point of View Concerning Medical Malpractice: A Sociological Perspective on the Symbolic Importance of "Tort reform" ' (1989) 23 *Georgia LR* 295–358. See R. Dingwall, 'Litigation and the Threat to Medicine' in J. Gabe, D. Kelleher, and G. Williams, *Challenging Medicine* (London: Routledge, 1994), 46–64 for a comparable analysis of the United Kingdom position.

reduces the likelihood of litigation.[78] They point out that, while access to continued and free medical care is secure without litigation, there is less need for compensation. The absence of any direct financial relationship between doctor and patient also lessens the incentive to think of the failure to deal with health problems as something to be compensated. In respect of general practitioners, at least, the continuing relationship that NHS patients have with their doctors makes it psychologically less likely that they will sue them. They note, however, that if confidence in future NHS provision wanes, then their analysis would suggest that litigation might increase.

They also argue that differences in the legal system of the United States and United Kingdom also make it unlikely that the transatlantic experience will be transplanted. Access to justice is easier in the United States, which has more lawyers per head of population and probably a greater propensity to see the courts as an appropriate place to resolve grievances.[79] It is often argued that contingency fees play a role in fuelling US medical malpractice litigation, although this is probably true only in relation to large claims. This is less likely with the British version (see above). In various ways, malpractice law is more favourable to doctors in the United Kingdom, than it is in some US states. This situation seems likely to persist as long as the judges continue to accept that medicine is an esoteric calling that they cannot understand.[80]

Taken together, these various factors suggest that the spectre of the supposed US malpractice crisis taking root in the United Kingdom is largely a myth. If a crisis develops in Britain it is likely to be the product of domestic developments. It is therefore more important to consider the implications of litigation within the English legal system than to worry about the United States.

(iii) Clinical Effects of Claims: Defensive Practices

Although much has been made of the claim that malpractice litigation forces professionals to act defensively, there is little agreement about the meaning of this assertion and the evidence to support it is tenuous. While some doctors regard defensive medicine as commonplace,[81] others see it as 'wholly exceptional'.[82] It is generally assumed that 'defensive medicine' is bad medicine.

---

[78] L. Quam, R. Dingwall, and P. Fenn, 'Medical Malpractice in Perspective II The Implications for Britain' (1987) 294 *BMJ* 1597–1600.

[79] But see Markesinis, n. 73 above, for some scepticism on these points.

[80] J. Montgomery, 'Medicine, Accountability and Professionalism' (1989) 16 *J Law & Society* 319–39.

[81] M. A. Jones and A. E. Morris, 'Defensive Medicine: Myths and Facts' (1989) 5 *J Medical Defence Union* 40–3, 42.

[82] Quoted in H. Genn and S. Lloyd-Bostock, 'Medical Negligence—Major New Research in Progress' (1990) 6 *J Medical Defence Union* 42–4.

However, that is not necessarily the case. Improved record-keeping, fuller communication with patients, more careful assessments of the risks involved in certain treatments might all be encouraged by the fear of litigation. They might also arise from a concern to improve professional practice that is quite unrelated to the desire to avoid litigation. Thus, it could be that the main reason for a change in practice is the drive for improvement, not the law. This makes it difficult to determine what effect the law has. Where the law is implicated in alterations of practice, it could merely be that it has performed one of its functions effectively; that is, it has deterred poor practice. Consequently, abstract assessments of defensive medicine, without careful consideration of the context, may be unhelpful.

This can be illustrated by one of the areas often used as an example of the deleterious effects of the law and defensive medicine: the rise in Caesarean section rates. There is no doubt that the rate of such operations has increased significantly. However, despite the widespread beliefs of obstetricians,[83] it is very difficult to show that this is related to the incidence of litigation. Dingwall has pointed out that since 1970 an increase in Caesarean sections has been seen in countries such as the United States and England, where there is rising litigation, but also in others, such as Norway and Holland, where it is more rare for legal actions to be brought.[84] Data for the mid-1980s indicated that the rates in England were similar to those in New Zealand, where litigation has been effectively excluded by the introduction of no-fault compensation. The highest European section rate for the period was in Portugal, which had very little malpractice litigation.

Dingwall has also observed that it is possible to explain the increase in Caesarean section rates without reference to litigation. Changing clinical indications may have resulted in the change. Improved anæsthetics have reduced the risks of the procedure, making it more likely that the benefits outweigh the risks in individual cases. In the United States, at least, the fee for service system makes it more lucrative for doctors to deliver babies by Caesarean than vaginally. Worldwide, it can be argued that Caesareans are more attractive to doctors than 'natural' childbirth because they reduce the threat of midwifery taking over. Further, women who have previously delivered by Caesarean section are more likely to have the operation in subsequent pregnancies. This means that a small initial rise will tend to fuel a steeper one.

---

[83] In one survey, 47% of obstetricians believed that litigation contributed to the rise in British Caesarean section rates: see C. Francombe, W. Savage, H. Churchill, and H. Lewison, *Caesarean Birth in Britain* (London: Middlesex University Press, 1993), 126.

[84] R. Dingwall, 'Negligence Litigation Research and the Practice of Midwifery' in J. Alexander, V. Levy, and S. Roch, *Midwifery Practice: A Research-based Approach* (Basingstoke: Macmillan, 1993), 172–84.

Even if the most commonly cited example, Caesarean sections, may be less clear than it seems, there can be little doubt that doctors believe that they practise defensive medicine. Jones and Morris carried out a pilot study on attitudes to defensive medicine by postal questionnaire amongst the 'high-risk' specialities of anæsthetics, obstetrics, and gynaecology, surgery, and accident and emergency/orthopædics.[85] Respondents were asked whether they ever adopted procedures *simply* to avoid litigation. Half said that they did so occasionally, 27 per cent frequently, and 5 per cent always. Jones and Morris noted that they had not explored what the respondents understood by defensive medicine, but did discover that many doctors misunderstood the legal test for negligence. They argued that, as the *Bolam* test makes legal liability turn on professional standards, to alter practice in order to avoid litigation was legal nonsense. The only way to ensure that a claim could be defended is to meet professional standards, so that it is illogical to think that the law can require professional practice to be altered. They suggested that the root of the problem created by doctors' fear of litigation was not the legal doctrine at all. It possibly arose out of ignorance of the legal rules, and possibly from a desire to minimize the probability of patients wishing to complain.

A later survey of a random sample of 400 hospital doctors and general practitioners, carried out in Hertfordshire, found that over a third of hospital doctors reported 'often' making referrals for diagnostic tests in order to reduce the risk of litigation. It also showed that the respondents did not understand the nature of the legal test for negligence. A number of them stated that they believed inaccurate statements about the law to be true.[86] This tends to confirm the suggestion that defensive practices are engendered by ignorance of the law rather than a real threat of litigation.

Overall, consideration of the phenomenon of defensive medicine invites a careful response. It is important to recognize that there is a considerable amount of mythology that clouds rational discussion. There is a need for clarification over what is being referred to in the debates because some so-called defensive practices may be no more than improvements. However, where patients are being given care that the professionals caring for them believe is inappropriate merely because they fear legal intervention, there is cause for concern. The obvious response to this problem is better education for health professionals on what the law requires. Defensive practice is usually the result of ignorance of the law, not of the legal doctrine itself.

---

[85] M. Jones and A. Morris, 'Defensive Medicine: Myths and Facts' (1989) 5 *JMDU* 40–3.
[86] D. Tribe and G. Korganoar, 'The Impact of Litigation on Patient Care: An Enquiry into Defensive Medical Practice' (1991) 7 *PN* 2–6.

E. A Move to No-fault?

One response of the medical profession to the perceived malpractice crisis is to propose the introduction of a no-fault compensation scheme, such as exists in New Zealand and Sweden.[87] The Royal College of Physicians and the BMA have produced papers advocating such a scheme in general terms.[88] The new-found support of the doctors for no-fault compensation has not won over the Government. The furthest a proposal has got is the National Health Service (Compensation) Bill, introduced by Rosie Barnes MP in December 1990.[89] It proposed a rather different scheme from those established in New Zealand and Sweden. A Medical Injury Compensation Board was to be established, comprising lawyers, doctors, health service managers, non-medical health professionals, and lay people. The Board would have investigated claims that unreasonable or unforeseeable injuries had occurred during NHS care. A threshold would have excluded trivial claims, defined by reference the need for 'significant' harm or to the length of hospital stay or inability to engage in normal activities. Claims would have to have been brought within six months, and should have been resolved within three. Payments might have been made over a period of years when appropriate.

The most radical aspect of the Bill concerned the Board's role in quality control. The first clause stated that one of the Bill's purposes was 'to minimise mishaps and compensation payments from public funds by enabling other action to be taken so as to maintain standards of care and management within the National Health Service'. This was to be achieved by retaining the possibility of action against culpable practitioners, without making this a precondition for compensation. If they decided to accept payments under the scheme, claimants would have been obliged to transfer their rights to sue to the Board. This was intended to enable the Board to take action where they found that there had been 'reprehensible behaviour or repeated acts of negligence'.[90] In addition, the Board was to have been given the duty of preparing a code of practice indicating the factors it would take into account when

---

[87] For discussion of these schemes, see M. Brahams, 'The Swedish "No Fault" Compensation System for Medical Injuries' (1988) 138 *NLJ* 14 and 31; S. McLean, 'No Fault Liability and Medical Responsibility' in M. Freeman (ed.), *Medicine, Ethics and the Law* (London: Stevens, 1988); M. McGreor Vennell, 'Medical Injury Compensation under the New Zealand Accident Compensation Scheme: An Assessment compared with the Swedish Medical Compensation Scheme' (1989) 5 *PN* 141–57. See also M. Brahams, 'No Fault in Finland: Paying Patients and Victims' (1988) 138 *NLJ* 678–81.

[88] Royal College of Physicians, *Compensation for Adverse Consequences of Medical Intervention* (London: RCP, 1990); British Medical Association, *Report of the Working Party on No-fault Compensation for Medical Injury* (London: BMA, 1983).

[89] HC Bill 21.   [90] Mrs Rosie Barnes, *Hansard*, HC, Vol. 184, col. 1226.

deciding whether to bring such legal actions. This would have offered guidance to the professions on the practice found to be acceptable to the Board,
providing a new way of establishing standards.

The Government chose to resist the Bill, and as a result it was lost after failing to get a second reading in February 1991.[91] The main objections put forward in the debate are worth noting as an indication of the obstacles to be
overcome. First, it was argued that the compensation would remain a lottery
even if the no-fault scheme was introduced. It was said that the scheme would
introduce unjustifiable discrimination, not only between those injured in the
course of health care practice and the victims of other types of accident, but
also between NHS and private patients. In addition the need to define which
injuries qualified for compensation and the continuing need to prove causation would ensure that many accident victims remained uncompensated.
Secondly, it was argued that the cost would be prohibitive, although it was
accepted that no reliable figures existed on which to base an assessment.

Much of the debate concerned itself with the effect of introducing the
scheme on medical practice. It was observed that Action for Victims of
Medical Accidents objected that it would actually reduce the provision of
information and accountability about accidents. This despite the provisions
allowing for investigation and legal action by the Board. Others suggested that
the possibility of court actions would place doctors in an unfair dilemma, co-
operation with the Board would benefit their patients but leave them more
vulnerable to being sued. In addition, the fact that patients could choose to
sue instead of using the scheme was said to perpetuate the risks of defensive
medicine. This placed the proponents of no-fault in a difficult position, as an
earlier bill removing the right to sue had been criticized as failing to respect
the fundamental rights of citizens to go to court.

F. Conclusion

It can be seen from the above discussion that claims that there is a medical
malpractice crisis in the United Kingdom are overstated, although there has
been a significant increase in litigation. Individual practitioners have been
insulated from the financial implications of litigation by the introduction of
NHS indemnity, and insurance remains affordable for most of those not covered by that scheme. Legal doctrine makes defensive medicine nonsensical,
and that problem needs to be tackled by improved education rather than law

---

[91] HC, *Hansard*, Vol. 184, col. 1223–92.

reform. The major concern that is raised by the rising claim rate is the drain which it makes on NHS resources. Money paid out in damages by a health authority is money diverted from patient services. Thus, the large sums being paid in this way may represent a malpractice crisis from the perspective of patients even if the impact on the professions is less acute than is sometimes alleged. Fear of the cost implications has diverted the Government's attention from no-fault schemes,[92] which also have other disadvantages. The current focus is on risk management and reducing the costs of handling claims. One possibility is to use arbitration as a mechanism for disputes to be resolved without a full hearing,[93] and procedural changes such as this are under review. However, at present, radical reform seems unlikely.

[92] For discussion, see Fenn, Hermans, and Dingwall, n. 66 above.
[93] M. Jones, 'Arbitration for Medical Negligence Claims in the NHS' (1992) 8 *PN* 142–6.

9   Medicines and the Law

This Chapter provides an outline of the law relating to medicines. It is concerned primarily with those aspects of this large area of law that touch upon the position of health professionals giving care directly to patients. It will be insufficiently detailed for the needs of pharmacists.[1] However, it will enable most of those working in the health professions to understand the requirements placed upon them. It begins with the framework within which the development of new drugs takes place. This overlaps with the more general principles governing medical research (see Chapter 14). It explores some aspects of the regulation of the market in medicines. It looks at the various controls over the use of medicines which are feared to be harmful in the wrong hands. The Chapter ends with a consideration of the remedies for drug-induced injury.

This Chapter does not deal with the general law of negligence, which would be used in cases of careless prescription of administration of medicines, nor with the apportionment of liability between the different professions involved. These are examined in Chapters 7 and 8 respectively. That discussion includes consideration of the obligations of nurses and pharmacists to question the prescriptions of doctors.[2] It should also be remembered that patients will need to give their consent to the use of medicines. The law on consent is covered in Chapter 10. Medicines are the particular province of pharmacists, who come under the jurisdiction of their own professional body, the Royal Pharmaceutical Society of Great Britain.[3] Professional regulation is explored in Chapter 6, although the detailed consideration is given to doctors and nurses rather than pharmacists.

---

[1] G. See Appelbe and J. Wingfield, *Dale and Appelbe's Pharmacy Law and Ethics* (5th edn., London: Pharmaceutical Press, 1993) and J. Merrills and J. Fisher, *Pharmacy Law & Practice* (Oxford: Blackwell Science, 1995) for more detailed material.

[2] See Ch. 7, sect. B(iii).   [3] Pharmacy Act 1954.

A. The Development and Licensing of Medicines

The development, manufacturing, distribution, and importation of medicines are regulated under the Medicines Act 1968.[4] Responsibility for licensing drugs under the Act formally lies with the Secretary of State for Health. However, in practice, it is exercised by the Medicines Control Agency, which is part of the Department of Health. As part of the statutory framework, advice is available from the Medicines Commission, whose members are to have expertise in medicine, pharmacy, non-pharmaceutical chemistry, and the pharmaceutical industry. There are also a number of statutory committees, including the Committee on Safety of Medicines. Powers to enforce the provisions of the Medicines Act 1968 lie with the Secretary of State, who has delegated them concurrently to the Royal Pharmaceutical Society. This section outlines the licensing system that these bodies operate, from the early trials of drugs to their being given product licences.

Medicines are required to go through a rigorous testing process before they will be licensed for use in humans. The framework discussed in this section is specific to research into pharmaceutical products. In addition to the requirements set down in this area, research will need to be approved by the appropriate local research ethics committees, and properly informed consent will need to be given by the research subjects. Those issues are examined in Chapter 14. Here, it is only the statutory requirements for the development of medicines that are in issue. Without satisfying these, no research can go ahead, but even if these regulations are complied with, a local committee may still refuse to authorize research in their district.

Drug trials fall into a number of phases.[5] It will be usual to begin with animal studies, regulated under the Animals (Scientific Procedures) Act 1986.[6] The first step involving human subjects (phase I trials) will be to determine the levels at which the drug can be tolerated. These will be carried out on healthy volunteers rather than patients. They are not regulated by the Medicines Act 1968, because until a drug is used on patients it is not a medicinal product within the terms of the Act.[7] They are, however, subject to the controls provided by local research ethics committees (for research carried out in the NHS) and by the law of consent. It has been argued that the law

---

[4] See H. Teff, 'Regulation under the Medicines Act 1968: Continuing Prescription for Health' (1984) 47 *MLR* 303–23. For an overview, see Appelbe and Wingfield, n. 1 above, chs. 1, 2.

[5] G. Blackledge and F. Lawton, 'The Ethics and Practical Problems of Phase I and II Studies' and E. Holdener, G. Decoster, and C. Lim, 'Ethical Aspects of Phase I Studies in Cancer Patients' in C. Williams (ed.), *Introducing New Treatments for Cancer: Practical, Ethical and Legal Problems* (Chichester: Wiley, 1992).

[6] See Ch. 14.   [7] Medicines Act 1968, s. 130(4).

would make consent to a phase I trial ineffective because it is by definition a trial that intends to harm subjects (as it is designed to subject subjects to increasing doses until one is reached that they will not tolerate).[8] It has been suggested that it would therefore be contrary to public policy to regard the consent as valid.[9] This argument has never been tested in the courts. It is considered further in Chapter 14. In phase II trials, the drug is tested to see whether it has clinical effects at the dosage identified as tolerable in phase I. If the drug has potentially useful effects, then phase III trials are used to compare its benefits with existing treatments. At phases II and III, trials will be unlawful without the appropriate licence (or exemption) because the drug cannot lawfully be manufactured without it.

Trials that are sponsored by a drug company can only go ahead either under a clinical trial certificate (CTC) or under the exemption scheme (CTX).[10] To obtain a trial certificate, the manufacturer needs to apply to the Medicines Control Agency. Detailed toxicological and pharmacological data must be produced to show that the trial is not likely to involve risk to the research subjects.[11] The exemption scheme permits trials to go ahead for three years on the basis of much more limited information, provided that the drug company produces a certificate signed by a registered medical practitioner who is satisfied of the accuracy of the information and that it is reasonable for the trial to be undertaken.[12]

Where a trial is not arranged by a drug company, but is to be carried out independently by a doctor or dentist, then a further exemption exists, known as the DDX. This is available where the drug is used within an existing product licence, trial certificate, or exception, or is supplied by the manufacturer solely for the purpose of the trial, provided that the Medicines Control Agency has been notified of the product, use, and the details of the supplier.[13]

If trials indicate that the drug may be useful, the drug company will seek a product licence from the Medicines Control Agency. This is necessary because it is unlawful to import, market, sell, or supply a medicinal product without a licence. To acquire such a licence, applicants have to specify the use to which

---

[8] V. Tunkel, 'Legal Aspects of Clinical Trials in the UK' in Williams, n. 5 above, 13–16, developing the views of I. Kennedy and A. Grubb, *Medical Law: Text with Materials* (London: Butterworths, 1994), 1054–5.

[9] See Ch. 10, sect. A(ii), for discussion of the general principles.

[10] Medicines Act 1968, s. 31.

[11] Medicines Act 1968, s. 31; Medicines (Standard Provisions for Licences and Certificates) Regulations 1971, SI 1971 No 972, as amended, Pt. II.

[12] Medicines (Exemptions from Licences) (Clinical Trials) Order 1995, SI 1995 No 2808; Medicines (Exemptions from Licences and Certificates) (Clinical Trials) Order 1995, SI 1995 No 2809.

[13] Medicines (Exemption from Licences) (Special Cases and Miscellaneous Provisions) Order 1972, SI 1972 No 1200, art. 4.

the medicine is to be put, including proposed dosage, and methods and routes of administration. Details of experiments (laboratory and clinical) that the applicants believe to be relevant to the safety, quality, and efficacy of the product must be provided. So must details of the manufacturing process, including quality-control mechanisms. Specimens or mock-ups of containers, packaging, and leaflets must also be made available.[14]

The Agency has to decide whether to issue a licence on the criteria of safety, quality, and efficacy.[15] This includes consideration of whether it poses a threat to the health of the community if used without proper safeguards, and whether it might interfere with the treatment, prevention, or diagnosis of disease, or harm the person administering it.[16] However, the Agency is not entitled to have regard to the question whether any other product is more effective, or to matters relating to price.[17] Product licences cannot be refused without consulting the Committee of Safety of Medicines or the Medicines Commission.[18] A streamlined system for the parallel import of products licensed elsewhere in the EC reduces the need for medicines to go through the full rigour of obtaining in licences in all European countries.[19]

Obtaining a product licence does not mean that the regulatory system ceases to be concerned with the drug. It is a condition of all licences that the Medicines Control Agency is informed of any information suggesting that the data on which the licence was granted are inaccurate. They must also maintain a record of adverse effects from the use of the medicine, which must be open for inspection by the MCA.[20] It is also possible for drugs to remain the subject of trials after licensing. Such trials are known as phase IV trials. Provided the trial involves using the drug within its product licence, no further approval is required from the Medicines Control Agency so long as it is notified of the trial and proper arrangements exist for reporting adverse reactions.[21]

B. Marketing Medicines

Once drugs have reached the market, the law seeks to ensure that patients are adequately informed about the medicines they are taking.[22] Labels must iden-

[14] Medicines (Applications for Product Licences and Clinical Trial and Animal Test Certificates) Regulations 1971, SI 1971 No 973, as amended.

[15] Medicines Act 1968, s. 19.   [16] S. 132(2).   [17] Ss. 19(2), 20(2).   [18] S. 20(3).

[19] M. Weller, 'EC Drug Licensing' (1995) 145 *NLJ* 1106.

[20] Medicines (Standard Provisions for Licences and Certificates) Regulations 1971, n. 11 above, as amended.

[21] Exemptions From Licences(Clinical Trials) Order 1974, SI 1974 No 498.

[22] See Appelbe and Wingfield, n. 1 above, ch. 14; Merrills and Fisher, n. 1 above, ch. 19.

tify the product by name, active ingredients, and pharmaceutical form. Instructions for use, contra-indications, warnings, and precautions must be given. Products which are dispensed directly to specific patients must name that patient and specify directions for use.[23] The precise requirements for labelling and packaging, including safety aspects such as child-resistant containers, vary according to way in which the product is packaged.[24]

There are also legal requirements for information leaflets to go with medicines. These require the name of the product to be stated, including the common name for the active ingredient if the brand name has been invented. There must be a full statement of the active ingredients, and details of the pharmaceutical form. The therapeutic indications must be specified, together with contra-indications, precautions for use, and interaction with other substances (including alcohol, tobacco, and food). Any special warnings must be included. These should take into account the condition of users, and the effects on driving and operating machinery. Instructions on dosage and method and frequency of administration must be given. They should include, where appropriate, action to be taken in case of an overdose and the risks of withdrawal.[25]

The law is also concerned to protect consumers from inappropriate advertising. It is an offence under the Medicines Act 1968 to issue misleading advertisements.[26] This covers advertising that may mislead as to the purposes for which the product may safely be used, purposes for which it cannot safely be used, or as to the effects of the drug.[27] There is a ban on advertising prescription-only medicines directly to the public. These may only be marketed to health professionals, and the contents of advertisements are prescribed.[28] Advertisers may not make unsubstantiated claims that the product is superior to any other, suggest it is safe without qualification, nor use unfairly presented or irrelevant graphs.

There are certain areas that are thought to be so likely to spawn misleading adverts that advertising to the public is banned. These include treatments for venereal disease, cancer treatment, bone diseases, cardiovascular diseases, chronic insomnia, diabetes and other metabolic diseases, diseases of the liver, biliary system and pancreas, endocrine diseases, genetic disorders, psychiatric diseases, serious disorders of the eye and ear, serious gastrointestinal diseases, serious infections diseases, including HIV-related diseases and tuberculosis,

---

[23] Medicines (Labelling) Regulations 1976, SI 1976 No 1726, as amended.
[24] Appelbe and Wingfield, n. 1 above, ch. 14.
[25] Medicines (Leaflets) Regulations 1977, SI 1977 No 1055, as amended.
[26] S. 93; Medicines (Advertising) Regulations 1994, SI 1994 No 1932.   [27] S. 130(10).
[28] Medicines (Advertising) Regulations 1994, n. 26 above, r. 7 and Pt. IV.

serious neurological and muscular diseases, serious renal diseases, serious respiratory diseases, and serious skin diseases.[29]

C. Control of the Use of Medicines

The legislation introduces a number of provisions aimed to ensure that medicines are used safely and for licit purposes. The UKCC has usefully categorized four stages in the therapeutic use of medicines; prescription, dispensation, administration, and patient acceptance.[30] The last is primarily regulated by the law of consent (see Chapter 10). Administration is generally regulated by malpractice law. Certain controlled drugs may only be administered by or under the direction of medical and dental practitioners,[31] but the actual administration is not restricted to professionals. The dispensation stage covers the process by which drugs are released for use, ceasing to be subject to any storage requirements that applied (depending on the class of drug in question). This section explains the ways in which drugs are classified, and the significance of the different classifications.

Drugs are divided into a number of categories. Under the Medicines Act 1968, there is a threefold distinction into (a) prescription-only medicines, (b) medicines that can only be supplied by a pharmacist (but which can be dispensed without a prescription), and (c) general-list medicines (which need not be obtained through a pharmacist). The Misuse of Drugs Act 1971, which is primarily concerned with the control of illicit drug use, creates three categories of controlled drugs, known as classes A, B, and C. More importantly for the health context, controlled drugs are further classified by the Misuse of Drugs Regulations 1985, which places them into one of five schedules.[32] Schedule 1 drugs are not used for medicinal purposes. Schedule 2 drugs include opiates and major stimulants, such as amphetamines. Schedule 3 drugs include most barbiturates, and some minor stimulants. Schedule 4 contains benzodiazepine tranquillizers. Schedule 5 contains preparations of controlled drugs where there is minimal risk of abuse.[33]

Drugs from Schedules 2 and 3 can only be dispensed on prescription. To be valid, a prescription has to be written in ink, or some other indelible mater-

---

[29] Venereal Disease Act 1917, s. 2; Cancer Act 1939, s. 4; Health and Medicines Act 1988, s. 23, HIV Testing Kits and Services Regulations 1992, SI 1992 No 460; Medicines (Advertising) Regulations 1994, n. 26 above, sch. 1. See also the Medicines (Labelling and Advertising to the Public) Regulations 1978, SI 1978 No 41.

[30] United Kingdom Central Council for Nursing, Midwifery and Health Visiting, *Administration of Medicines* (London: UKCC, 1986).

[31] Misuse of Drugs Regulations 1985, SI 1985 No 2066, r. 7.   [32] *Ibid.*, as amended.

[33] This summary is taken from Appelbe and Wingfield, n. 1 above, 172–5.

ial, dated, and signed by the prescriber.[34] The name and address of the person for whom it is prescribed must be set out, together with the dosage to be taken. If the patient is under 12 years of age, his or her age must also be recorded. Where a controlled drug is prescribed, the prescription must be handwritten personally by the prescriber (otherwise it may be written by means of carbon paper). Where a drug from Schedules 1 to 3 of the Misuse of Drugs Regulations 1985 is prescribed, the dosage must be written in both figures and words to avoid errors.

There are also requirements as to the storage of controlled drugs and record-keeping. There must be a special register, in the form of a bound book (a card index will not suffice) for controlled drugs in Schedules 1 and 2 of the 1985 Regulations. An entry must be made every time such a drug is obtained or supplied, recording the person from whom it was obtained or to whom it was supplied, the quantity involved and the form in which the drug was transferred. Regulations on the safe custody of controlled drugs apply to those in Schedules 1, 2, and 3. Such drugs must be kept locked away.[35]

Regulation of the use of drugs centres on the legal power to prescribe. The use of those drugs which are not available only on prescription is not regulated beyond the licensing system. That deals with the availability of drugs on a general basis. Prescription-only medicines are restricted to those patients that a health professional has identified as an appropriate recipient. Such medicines may only be dispensed under a prescription, made usually only by a medical practitioner or dentist. Limited provision has also been made for prescription by and use under the direction of midwives, occupational health nurses, and practice nurses.[36] Midwives may possess and use specified controlled drugs under a 'midwives supply order', which must be signed by a doctor or by their supervisor of midwives.[37] Occupational health nurses may use prescription-only medicines without immediate directions provided that they do so only in circumstances specified in writing by a medical practitioner.[38] Certain district nurses and health visitors, whose registration with the UKCC is annotated to show that they are qualified to do so, may prescribe drugs under a limited formulary.[39] Ambulance paramedics are also able to use

[34] Medicines (Products other than Veterinary Drugs) (Prescription Only) Order 1983, SI 1983 No 1212, as amended.

[35] Misuse of Drugs (Safe Custody) Regulations 1973, SI 1973 No 798, as amended, Sch. 12. There is an exception for certain specified liquid preparations.

[36] Through regulations made under s. 58 of the Medicines Act 1968, as amended.

[37] Medicines (Products other than Veterinary Drugs) (Prescription Only) Order 1983, n. 34 above, Sch. 3, Pts. I and III; Misuse of Drugs Regulations 1985, n. 31 above, r. 11.

[38] Medicines (Products other than Veterinary Drugs) (Prescription Only) Order 1983, n. 34 above, art. 9 and Sch. 3, Pt. III, para. 5.

[39] *Ibid.*, art. 2, Sch. 1A; NHS (Pharmaceutical Services) Amendment Regulations 1996, SI 1996 No 698, r. 8.

certain prescription-only medicines.[40] Special restrictions exist on the prescription of medicines for drug addicts.[41]

Finally, mention needs to be made of the use of unlicensed products by doctors for individual patients.[42] Under section 9 of the Medicines Act the usual licensing requirement are waived where a doctor or dentist uses a drug specially prepared or imported for a particular patient. This is usually known as use on a 'named patient basis'. This enables doctors to use drugs that have not yet been licensed, or to use licensed drugs in a new way that is not within the scope of the product licence. This may mean use in a different form, dosage, or with a different mode of administration. It may mean using the drug for a patient who falls outside the group for which the drug is licensed (for example using the drug for children or pregnant women when the drug has only been licensed for use in non-pregnant adults).

D. Compensation for Drug-induced Injury

The use of medicines does not always go smoothly. This section considers the availability of compensation for drug-induced injury. Sometimes, the principles of malpractice law (see Chapter 7) may provide patients with a legal remedy. If a drug was negligently selected or administered, that will be as much malpractice as a negligent diagnosis or carelessly performed operation. The law of consent (see Chapter 10) may also play an important role in cases of drug-induced injury. Patients who would not have agreed to take medication if they had been more fully informed about its side effects may be able to sue on the basis that they were negligently counselled about the treatment. This section does not examine these areas of law. Instead, it looks at principles that are specifically important in cases where injuries result from the use of medicines. These come under the general heading of 'product liability'. This is not restricted to drugs. The same principles would apply to a medical device, such as a pacemaker, that was unsafe. However, drugs probably provide the most common situation in which product liability may be relevant.

The law of negligence may give rise to liability on the part of manufacturers where their products harm the person who uses them.[43] To succeed in

---

[40] Medicines (Products other than Veterinary Drugs) (Prescription Only) Amendment No 2 Order 1992, n. 34 above.

[41] Misuse of Drugs (Notification of and Supply to Addicts) Regulations 1973, SI 1973 No 799.

[42] Merrills and Fisher, n. 1 above, 128–9.

[43] *Donoghue* v. *Stevenson* [1932] AC 562. For discussion, see M. Jones, *Medical Negligence* (2nd edn., London: Sweet & Maxwell, 1996), 419–441 and C. Newdick, 'Strict Liability for Defective Drugs in the Pharmaceutical Industry' (1995) 101 *LQR* 405–31.

such a claim, the patient would need to show that the manufacturer had failed to take reasonable care to make sure the drug was safe, and that this failure had been the cause of the patient's injuries. Problems may arise in relation to the design of the drug, the manufacturing process, and its presentation to doctors and patients (covering the marketing and labelling of the medicine, information leaflets, and what was said to the patient when consent was obtained to using the drug). At each stage, it will be necessary to assess whether the drug company acted reasonably. This would be assessed by reference to both the technical ability to improve processes and the reasonable expectations of the industry. Standard industry practice would often, but not automatically, be sufficient to protect the manufacturer.

In the context of medicines, it may be particularly difficult to prove a causal link between a negligent mistake made by the company and the mishap that has occurred. Medicines are generally used to cure or alleviate medical problems, and it may be unclear whether the injuries resulted from the original medical condition or from the drug. In addition, medicines usually operate by changing the patient's body in some way. This almost always carries risks of side effects, some of which may not be predictable. Those side effects can occur without negligence, although it may be negligent to fail to warn the patient of them. A further practical difficulty may arise because it is difficult to obtain information about the research and production of drugs, which is often regarded as confidential to the manufacturer.[44] It is, therefore, quite possible for a patient to be adversely affected while using a medicine without there having been any negligence for which compensation would be available.

One response to these difficulties has been the introduction of the Consumer Protection Act 1987, which applies to goods marketed after 1 March 1988. This Act aimed to make it easier for consumers (in all areas, not just health care) to sue when defective products cause them harm. It enables patients to sue the producer of the drug they believe injured them. The meaning of 'producer' is extended to cover importers, and also the person who supplied the drug to the patient, unless that person can identify the person who supplied her or him.[45] This makes it important that health professionals are able to identify the source of drugs that they use. 'Product' covers any goods, and thus will embrace not merely medicines, but also medical devices. It is not clear whether substances such as blood, tissue, and organs would be considered products under the Act. The test is probably whether there has been a 'producer' who 'manufactured, won or abstracted' the 'product'.[46]

In order to succeed, the patient would have to show that the product was 'defective' within the meaning of the Act. This means that it was not as safe as

---

[44] M. Brazier, *Medicine, Patients and the Law* (2nd edn., London: Penguin, 1992), 173–5.
[45] Consumer Protection Act 1987, ss. 1, 2.   [46] See the definitions in s. 1(2).

people are generally entitled to expect, having regard to the manner in which the product was marketed (including warnings given) and the use to which it could reasonably be expected to be put.[47] Given the fact that drugs are generally accepted to have side effects, this may often present plaintiffs with difficulties. Even if it can be established that the drug was defective, the manufacturers may still have a defence if they can show that the state of scientific and technological knowledge was not such that the manufacturer could reasonably have been expected to discover the defect.[48] This combines a test of technical feasibility with one of reasonable industry standards, and may limit the effectiveness of the Act.[49] Compliance with the requirements of the licensing system may be all that could reasonably be expected of the manufacturer.

Three further avenues may be open to patients. The first is available to patients who buy their medicines themselves. They have a contract with the person who sold them the drugs. Under the Sale of Goods Act 1979, the goods sold must be of merchantable quality and fit for the purpose for which they are sold.[50] Similar requirements are made under the Supply of Goods and Services Act 1982.[51] Thus, the sale of a medicine that is unsuitable for its recommended use may constitute a breach of the contract of sale. This remedy cannot assist those whose medicines were received under an NHS prescription, for provision under the NHS does not constitute a sale for the purposes of the Act (despite prescription charges).[52]

A second, but remote, possibility is that the Medicines Control Agency could be sued for negligently licensing a drug.[53] The key question here would be one of public policy. It is probable that the courts would find that it was inappropriate to hold that the regulatory agency owed a duty of care to those who used a licensed drug.[54] They have already shown that they were not prepared to interfere with a policy decision to promote vaccination.[55] However, they have accepted that there was an arguable case that liability would arise for failing to supervise the supply of blood products properly.[56] The relevant principles were discussed in Chapter 3.[57]

Finally, there is one area where Parliament has intervened to provide genuine no-fault compensation. Under the Vaccine Damage Payments Act 1979,

[47] S. 3.   [48] S. 4(1)(e). S. 4 also provides other defences.
[49] C. Newdick, 'The Development Risk Defence of the Consumer Protection Act 1987' (1988) 47 *CLJ* 455–76.
[50] S. 14.
[51] Ss. 4, 9. See A. Bell, 'The Doctor and the Supply of Goods and Services Act 1982' [1984] *Legal Studies* 175–84.
[52] *Pfizer* v. *Ministry of Health* [1965] 1 All ER 450.   [53] See Jones, n. 43 above, 420–4.
[54] See *Yuen Kun-yeu* v. *AG of Hong Kong* [1987] 2 All ER 705.
[55] *DHSS* v. *Kinnear* (1984) 134 NLJ 886.
[56] *Re HIV Hæmophiliac Litigation* (1990) 140 NLJ 1349.   [57] See sect. B(ii).

a payment of £30,000 may be made to a person, or his or her personal representative, who was severely disabled as a result of vaccination against diphtheria, tetanus, whooping cough, poliomyelitis, measles, rubella, tuberculosis, smallpox, mumps, or Haemophilus type b infection (hib).[58] In order to come within the Act, applicants must show that they were vaccinated in the United Kingdom or Isle of Man on or after 5 July 1948. In the case of smallpox, they must also have been vaccinated before 1 August 1971. Save in respect of poliomyelitis and rubella, the vaccination must have been given while the patient was under 18, or to anyone during an outbreak of the disease in question.[59] For the purposes of the Act, 'severe disablement' means disablement to the extent of 80 per cent.[60] The applicant must satisfy the Secretary of State that the injuries were caused by the vaccination. Applicants are entitled to a review if the Secretary of State refuses to accept that this is the case. Proof has to be made out on the balance of probabilities.[61] Although the courts have rejected in civil litigation the suggestion that pertussis vaccine (against whooping cough) caused injuries, such a causal link has been accepted for compensation under the Act.[62]

E. Conclusion

Patients seeking to sue for drug-induced injuries face an up-hill struggle. Commentators have suggested that no drug company has yet lost a case in the British courts, although there have been some out-of-court settlements.[63] Part of the problem is the reluctance of English law to facilitate group actions.[64] This means that heavy reliance has to be placed on the regulatory system to prevent mishaps wherever possible. This Chapter has outlined that system, covering the development, marketing, and use of medicines. The earlier stages rely upon the drug companies producing reliable information for the licensing agencies to scrutinize. Controls specific to drug research were noted in this Chapter. The more general regulation of research, which covers drug research amongst other types, is discussed in Chapter 14. The

---

[58] Vaccine Damage Payments Act 1979, s. 1; Vaccine Damage Payments (Specified Disease) Order 1990, SI 1990 No 623; Vaccine Damage Payments (Specified Disease) Order 1995, SI 1995 No 1164.

[59] S. 2.   [60] S. 1(4).   [61] S. 3.

[62] *Loveday* v. *Renton & Wellcome Foundation* [1990] 1 Med LR 117; R. Goldberg, 'Vaccine Damage and Causation—Social and Legal Implications' (1996) 3 *J Social Security Law* 100–20.

[63] e.g. *Davies* v. *Eli Lilley Co—Terms of Proposed Settlement* (1987) 137 NLJ 1183.

[64] See e.g. *Davies* v. *Eli Lilley* [1987] 1 All ER 801, *Davies* (*Joseph Owen*) v. *Eli Lilley* [1987] 3 All ER 94.

immediate needs of individual patients are protected by the health professionals who prescribe, dispense, and administer their medicines. This Chapter has shown how that system seeks to ensure that only such experts can authorize the use of the more dangerous (prescription-only) drugs. In general, however, the law of malpractice will be as important as this framework in protecting patients (see Chapter 7).

Part III

The Position of the Patient

10   Consent to Treatment

The *Patient's Charter*[1] states that all citizens have an established National Health Service right 'to be given a clear explanation of any treatment proposed, including any risks and alternatives, before [they] decide whether [they] will agree to the treatment'. In fact, it is debatable whether the law does confer such a right. Although it demands that a consent be given in most cases before treatment is lawful, English law does not require that consent to be fully informed. Many commentators have suggested that it therefore fails to give proper respect to the rights of patients. This Chapter aims to outline the basic legal position for the treatment of adult patients. The special problems that arise in relation to children and young people are considered in Chapter 12. Consent to treatment for mental disorder is explored in Chapter 13. Chapter 14 discusses the law governing consent to research.

Lord Donaldson has pointed out that consent plays two quite different functions in the doctor–patient relationship.[2] One, which he called the legal, is to provide a legal justification for care. Without such a consent health professionals would commit a crime (battery) and a tort (trespass to the person) when they touched their patient. The other function, termed 'clinical' by Lord Donaldson, is to secure the patient's trust and co-operation. This aspect of consent may involve far more extensive counselling on the implications, risks, and side effects of treatment than the laws of trespass and battery require. Although the primary motivation for this is clinical, it is given limited legal effect through the law of negligence. If professionals fail to counsel patients in the way recognized by their peers as appropriate they may be negligent.[3] Thus, in English law, patients who allege that they have been given insufficient information must argue that the professionals have been negligent in carrying out their duty to advise them about the decision. This means that this important aspect of consent is governed by the same principle that applies to ordinary malpractice cases, although the application may be slightly different (see below).

---

[1] Department of Health (London: HMSO, 1991), 9.   [2] *Re W* [1992] 4 All ER 627, 633.
[3] *Sidaway* v. *Bethlem RHG* [1985] 1 All ER 643.

The English courts have been consistent in holding that actions for battery should play a very limited role in health care law.[4] Although this position has been criticized,[5] it seems highly unlikely that it will be altered.[6] Indeed, the courts have proved reluctant to encourage the use of battery even in the few situations in which it is still available.[7] The principal importance of battery lies in its role in emphasizing that patients are entitled to veto the care proposed by health professionals: a right to refuse treatment. It is not concerned with the ethical doctrine of informed consent. The criminal law has proved of even less practical significance. As the requirements of consent under the criminal law are almost certainly the same as under the civil law, they will not be considered separately here.[8]

The distinction between an action based on battery (trespass to the person) and one for negligence is important for a number of reasons.[9] Battery, a non-consensual touching, is itself a legal wrong, whether or not any specific damage can be shown to result. Thus a patient may bring a successful action for battery even when the procedure which was carried out without consent was clearly for his or her benefit. In contrast, careless behaviour itself is insufficient to support a valid negligence claim. In addition to showing that the professional fell below the required standard, the patient must prove that some damage resulted. This means that patients will lose their case when the procedure benefited them or where the carelessness of the professional did not cause the accident. The most common example of the latter situation in the consent context would be where, even if the patient had been told of the risk which was not mentioned, she or he would have been prepared to take it. The professional may have withheld information that should have been disclosed, but it would have made no difference had he or she acted properly. There are also advantages to patients in relation to the damages that they may be awarded if they win a battery case. All damage flowing from the operation performed without consent will be compensated, but in negligence unforeseeable damage will not be recoverable. In addition, in exceptional cases, punitive damages can be awarded for battery. These require a particularly

---

[4] *Chatterton* v. *Gerson* [1981] 1 All ER 257; *Hills* v. *Potter* [1983] 3 All ER 716; *Freeman* v. *Home Office* [1984] 1 All ER 1036; *Sidaway* v. *Bethlem RHG*, n. 3 above.

[5] Tan Keng Feng, 'Failure of Medical Advice: Trespass or Negligence?' (1987) 7 *LS* 149–68.

[6] M. Brazier, 'Patient Autonomy and Consent to Treatment: The Role of Law?' (1987) 7 *LS* 169, 179–80.

[7] e.g. *Blyth* v. *Bloomsbury AHA* [1993] 4 Med. LR 151 (concerning patients who ask questions); see for discussion J. Montgomery, 'Power/Knowledge/Consent: Medical Decision Making' (1988) 51 *MLR* 245–51.

[8] For discussion of the criminal aspects of consent, see P. Skegg, *Law, Ethics and Medicine* (Oxford: Clarendon Press, 1988), 29–46.

[9] H. Teff, 'Consent to Medical Procedures: Paternalism, Self-determination or Therapeutic Alliance'? (1985) 101 *LQR* 432, 438–40.

blameworthy defendant to pay more than the cost of compensation in order to reflect the unacceptability of their conduct. The decision of the English judiciary to use negligence rather than battery as the principal legal framework for consent can therefore be seen as advantageous to the health professions.

This Chapter begins by considering requirements for a valid consent, the precondition of treatment for the treatment of competent adults. It then explores the circumstances in which it may be permissible to give care despite the absence of a valid consent. Finally, it discusses the obligation on professionals to advise their patients and clients of risks, side effects, and alternatives when counselling them about possible care.

A. Real Consent

Consent must be obtained from the person who is to receive care. English law does not recognize rights of proxy consent on behalf of an adult. This means that relatives and spouses do not have the power to authorize treatment and any purported consent is invalid.[10] Only in relation to children can people, providing they have parental responsibility, consent on behalf of others.[11] Where adult patients are unable to give consent themselves, English law takes the matter outside the law of consent completely and permits treatment despite the absence of consent according to the principles discussed in the next section of this Chapter.

In theory it is possible for competent adults to appoint a proxy to act on their behalf by granting them a power of attorney. This practice does not seem to occur in England.[12] Any such appointment would lapse if the person making it became mentally incompetent.[13] The Enduring Powers of Attorney Act 1985 does permit powers of attorney to remain valid beyond this point in relation to the management of property. However it covers only a person's 'property and affairs'[14] and in *F* v. *W. Berkshire HA*[15] it was held that the same phrase in the Mental Health Act 1983 did not cover medical decisions.

---

[10] Although there is provision for samples to be taken from a mentally disordered person in order to establish paternity on the basis of consents given by carers and the doctor responsible for the patient, Family Law Reform Act 1969, s. 21(4).

[11] This is discussed in detail in Ch. 12.

[12] It has been adopted in some US jurisdictions as a mechanism for giving patients greater control over life and death decisions; for discussion see J. Montgomery, 'Power over Death: The Final Sting' in D. Morgan and R. Lee (eds.), *Death Rites: Law and Ethics at the Ending of Life* (London: Routledge, 1994). See also Law Commission, *Mental Incapacity* (Law Com No 231, 1995).

[13] *Drew* v. *Nunn* (1879) 4 QBD 661.   [14] S. 3(1).   [15] [1989] 2 All ER 545.

The validity of a patient's consent depends on a number of factors. In order to be valid, consent must be 'real'. For this to be the case, patients must be competent to give consent. They must know in broad terms what they are consenting to. They must give their consent freely and without being deliberately misled. These principles, and some common problems that they raise, are discussed below.

(i) Competence[16]

Many of the cases on the legal test for competence have concerned children and young people, and they are discussed in detail in Chapter 12. In essence they establish that patients are competent if they can understand the decision that is before them. The leading case on adults' competence is *F* v. *W. Berkshire HA*, where Lord Brandon indicated that the issue is whether patients are able to understand the nature and purpose of the care.[17] This probably involves appreciating what will be done to them if they accept treatment, the likely consequences of leaving their condition untreated, and understanding the risks and side-effects that the health professionals explain to them. The level of understanding that is required must be commensurate with the gravity of the decision to be taken, more serious decisions requiring greater capacity.[18]

The case of *Re C*[19] required the court to apply the test for competence to a paranoid schizophrenic who was a patient in Broadmoor. His doctors thought that he needed to have his leg amputated, as it had become gangrenous, and that he might die if the operation was not performed. He refused to consent to the procedure and sought a declaration from the court that the amputation could not proceed without his consent. The judge held that, in order to ascertain whether the patent understood the nature, purpose, and effects of the proposed treatment, the capacity to adopt three stages of decision-making should be examined: first, comprehension and retention of the information about the treatment; secondly, believing that information; thirdly, weighing up that information in the balance so as to arrive at a choice. The patient's general incapacity due to schizophrenia was irrelevant. His understanding of the operation proposed for his leg was all that mattered. The judge found that it had not been proved that the patient did not understand

---

[16] M. Brazier, 'Competence, Consent and Proxy Consents' in M. Brazier and M. Lobjoit, *Protecting the Vulnerable: Autonomy and Consent in Health Care* (London: Routledge, 1991), 34–51; S. Lee, 'Towards a Jurisprudence of Consent' in J. Eekelaar and J. Bell, *Oxford Essays in Jurisprudence* (3rd series, Oxford: Oxford University Press, 1987), 199–220; British Medical Association and Law Society, *Assessment of Mental Capacity: Guidance for Doctors and Lawyers* (London: British Medical Association, 1995).

[17] N. 15 above, 551.   [18] *Re T* [1992] 4 All ER 649, 661.

[19] [1994] 1 All ER 819 (FD).

the choice he was being asked to make, and consequently he was competent to withhold his consent. An order was made forbidding the amputation without the patient's written consent.

The low level of comprehension that the test for capacity entails means that most patients will be competent to consent. The basic rule is that health professionals should presume that their patients are able to consent to, or refuse, treatment.[20] An assertion that a patient could not understand would need to be supported by evidence. It is important to note that the fact that a patient does not appear to the professional to make a wise choice is not itself evidence of incapacity. 'The patient is entitled to reject [professional] advice for reasons which are rational, or irrational, or for no reason.'[21]

(ii) Limits to the Validity of Consent

Although the principle that patients can choose to accept the care that health professionals offer them is extensive, it is not absolute. In some areas a purported consent may be invalid because it is contrary to public policy.[22] At one time it was thought that this principle might prevent some types of surgery which were then the subject of controversy. The most famous example is the dictum of Lord Denning disapproving sterilizations 'done so as to enable a man to have the pleasure of sexual intercourse without shouldering the responsibilities attaching to it' as illegal.[23] This is no longer good law, if indeed it ever was.[24] The law has now tacitly accepted the legality of the following once controversial operations: sex change operations,[25] non-therapeutic sterilizations,[26] and organ transplantation.[27] It was suggested in *Re F* by Neill LJ that a consent to an irreversible operation for money might be invalid.[28] However, this is of doubtful authority. The House of Lords decided the case on different grounds. Further, the fact that it was thought necessary to pass the Human Organ Transplants Act 1989 in order to proscribe the sale of non-regenerative organs suggests that the common law did not already outlaw such operations.[29]

[20] *Re T*, n. 18 above, 661.
[21] *Sidaway* v. *Bethlem RHG*, n. 3 above, 666, *per* Lord Templeman.
[22] *Attorney General's Reference (No 6 of 1980)* [1981] 2 All ER 1057; *R.* v. *Brown* [1993] 2 All ER 75.
[23] *Bravery* v. *Bravery* [1954] 3 All ER 59, 68. The other judges in the CA expressly declined to accept this view.
[24] See K. M. Norrie, *Family Planning Practice and the Law* (Aldershot: Dartmouth, 1991), 11–13.
[25] *Corbett* v. *Corbett* [1971] P 83.
[26] *Gold* v. *Haringey HA* [1987] 2 All ER 888, *Re B* [1987] 2 All ER 206, *F* v. *W. Berkshire HA*, n. 15 above. See also the statutory provision for NHS vasectomy services in the now superseded NHS (Family Planning) Amendment Act 1972.
[27] Human Organ Transplants Act 1989. For discussion of the common law position see G. Dworkin, 'The Law Relating to Organ Transplantation in England' (1970) 33 *MLR* 353, 355–64.
[28] [1989] 2 FLR 376, 401–2.   [29] See Ch. 19.

Lord Lane CJ has stated that 'reasonable' surgical interventions are justified as being in the 'public interest'.[30] More recently, Lord Mustill has suggested that consent to 'proper medical treatment' is valid, even though the bodily invasion involved may be extreme.[31] It is therefore probable that surgical procedures accepted by the medical profession may legitimately be consented to unless there is an express statutory legal prohibition. Such provisions are rare. Even where operations are generally outlawed, there are usually exceptions for cases where they are carried out for medical reasons.[32] The main areas where a public policy argument against the legality of consent to treatment can be maintained are abortion and euthanasia. These are discussed in Chapters 15 and 20.

(iii) Coercion and Undue Influence

It is possible for an otherwise capable patient to be prevented from giving free consent because of coercion or undue influence. In such circumstances any apparent consent would be invalid because it is not the voluntary consent of the patient. It is rare for the law to find that this is the case. In one case it was held that it was not enough that the patient felt that he had no choice but to submit to the prison medical officer's decision. Only if he had proved that he had been forcibly restrained could he have said that his consent was invalidated.[33] The fact that patients are exhausted or in severe pain will not normally remove their capacity to give a valid consent.[34] Finally, a consent induced by economic necessity will remain valid.[35] Thus, people who only agree to an HIV test because they fear they will lose their jobs or be denied insurance or a mortgage if they do not take the test cannot claim that their consent is involuntary and therefore invalid.

The possibility that consent might be vitiated by undue influence was examined by the Court of Appeal in *Re T*.[36] The case concerned a young woman who had told hospital staff that she did not wish to have a blood transfusion when she was admitted to hospital after a car accident. She made that

---

[30] *Attorney General's Reference* (*No 6 of 1980*), n. 22 above, 1059. At one point in the speech of Lord Jauncey in *R*. v. *Brown*, n. 22 above, the more strict word of 'necessary' surgery is used, but taken as a whole it is clear that His Lordship adopted the reasonableness test: compare 88 and 90.

[31] *R*. v. *Brown*, n. 22 above, 109–10.

[32] e.g. Tattooing of Minors Act 1969, s. 1, Prohibition of Female Circumcision Act 1985, s. 2.

[33] *Freeman* v. *Home Office*, n. 4 above.

[34] *Wells* v. *Surrey AHA*, *The Times*, 29 July 1978, but see also the comments of Lord Donaldson in *Re T*, n. 18 above, 661. A claim of negligence might still succeed if the doctors acted improperly in forcing a decision on the patient.

[35] *Latter* v. *Braddell* (1881) 50 LJCP 166 (CP), 448 (CA).

[36] N. 18 above, 661, 666–8. Other aspects of this decision are explored in Chs. 17 and 20. Undue influence was discussed briefly in *Re S* [1994] 2 FLR 1065, but without clarifying the law.

decision after talking to her mother, a Jehovah's Witness. The Court of Appeal found that, while it was to be expected that patients seek advice before deciding whether to accept treatment, it was possible that their will might be overborne by pressure brought by others. If that happened the purported consent would be invalid. Health professionals therefore need to consider whether the choice expressed by their patients is an independent one. If it is not they should ignore the consent and ask the patient again in circumstances when they are free from the influence of other people. If this is not possible, for example where the patient is now unconscious, they should proceed on the basis that the patient is incompetent to make a choice (see below).

The need to bear in mind the possibility of undue influence places health professionals in a difficult position and there is little guidance on how to assess the situation. Staughton LJ suggested that the most precise test available was whether the external influences caused the patient 'to depart from her own wishes to such an extent that the law regards it as undue'.[37] This begs the very question on which guidance is sought. Lord Donaldson noted that when considering whether patients have been unduly influenced so as to negate the independence of their judgement, it would be necessary to consider their relationship with the person influencing them. The closer the relationship, the more difficult it will be to resist pressure. His lordship specifically mentioned spouses, parents, and religious advisers. It would be wrong, however, to assume that decisions made after discussing matters with such people are invalid. In the vast majority of cases they will remain the decision of the patient. Lord Donaldson also pointed out that patients who were tired, in pain, or depressed would be less able to resist being influenced.[38] In practice, problems are likely to arise only where a choice seems incompatible with the earlier views of a patient.

(iv) Information

For consent to be 'real' and provide a defence to an allegation of battery, the patient must be 'informed in broad terms of the nature of the procedure which is intended'.[39] The amount of information that this requires is not great. The courts have repeatedly stated that the law of battery is not appropriate to deal with disputes over how informed patients ought to be.[40] According to the judges, that issue should be tackled through the law of negligence (see below). As a result, lack of consent can normally be successfully

---

[37] N. 18 above, 669.   [38] *Ibid.*, 662.

[39] *Chatterton* v. *Gerson*, n. 4 above, 265. See also *Freeman* v. *Home Office*, n. 4 above, 1044.

[40] *Chatterton* v. *Gerson*, n. 4 above; *Hills* v. *Potter*, n. 4 above; *Freeman* v. *Home Office*, n. 4 above; *Sidaway* v. *Bethlem RHG*, n. 3 above.

alleged only where there was no consent to the procedure actually carried out. This is rarely a difficult issue. Such cases usually involve blatant errors by staff, for example performing a completely different procedure from the one intended or failing to ask the patient for consent at all,[41] and liability will be admitted.

(v) HIV Testing

One area where there has been much debate is the legality of testing for HIV without an explicit consent.[42] Some health professionals wish to test patients for their HIV status without informing them that they are doing so. This is usually done for one of three reasons; as part of the diagnostic process when it is possible that HIV is the cause of the patient's problems, in order to collate epidemiological information about the incidence of HIV infection, or in order to enable the professionals to protect themselves against infection. This issue is distinct from mandatory testing, overriding an explicit refusal to be tested, which may be ordered under the Public Health (Control of Disease) Act 1984, section 35. It concerns cases where patients know they are being tested for some things, but do not know that they include HIV status. The matter turns on the amount of information it is necessary to give them before their consent to blood tests will be valid.

Some lawyers have argued that it is not enough to obtain a general consent to diagnostic testing, but that it must be given specifically to testing for HIV. They argue that the requirement that the patient understands the nature of the procedure necessitates a specific authorization of HIV testing.[43] Others suggest that, provided the taking of blood has been consented to, then additional tests will be lawful unless contrary to an express prohibition by the patient.[44] The latter view is more in line with the general approach taken by the courts, but it is unclear whether the judiciary would regard the special problems that HIV raises as requiring a departure from the normal principles. It is conceivable that they would draw a distinction between cases where the tests were performed in order to assist diagnosis and those where they were to protect professionals or for the public benefit in collecting knowledge about

---

[41] *Devi* v. *W. Midlands RHA* (1981, unreported, CA). See also the unreported case cited by Bristow J in *Chatterton* v. *Gerson*, n. 4 above, 265, where a boy was admitted for a tonsillectomy but was in fact circumcized.

[42] For overviews, see J. Keown, 'The Ashes of AIDS and the Phoenix of Informed Consent' (1989) 52 *MLR* 790–800 and A. Grubb, and D. Pearl, *Blood Testing, AIDS and DNA Profiling* (Bristol: Family Law, 1990), ch. 1.

[43] e.g. M. Sherrard and I. Gatt, 'HIV Antibody Testing' (1987) 295 *BMJ* 911–12; I. Kennedy and A. Grubb, 'Testing for HIV Infection: The Legal Framework' (1989) 86/7 *LSG* 30–5, 86/9 *LSG* 30–1.

[44] Keown, n. 42 above; Medical Defence Union, *AIDS: Medico-legal Advice* (London: MDU, 1988); J. Montgomery, 'Victims or Threats?—The Framing of HIV' (1990) 12 *Liverpool LR* 25, 44–8.

the disease. In the former case the patient's consent to diagnostic testing would cover the HIV test because it is being done for the very diagnostic purposes that the patient has sought help. In the other cases there is a conflict of interests because the patient will get no benefit from the test. Here an explicit consent might be required. As the courts have not yet had the opportunity to consider the matter, the law cannot be regarded as settled.

(vi) General Consents

A further common but difficult case concerns patients who are asked to agree in advance to additional procedures which become necessary in the course of treatment. The validity of such a general consent is problematic. It is difficult to see how a blanket consent could be supported by information 'in broad terms' of the nature of the procedure because the procedure has not been identified. A purported general consent is therefore probably ineffective and professionals should obtain the necessary specific consents when it becomes clear that unexpected actions are needed. Some writers have suggested that general consents might be valid by drawing an analogy with those implied by taking part in sports.[45] However, the validity of such a consent depends on the ability to assess in advance what is likely to be involved. Sportswomen and men have the knowledge which enables them to do this. Patients do not. The ineffectiveness of general consents does not restrict the ability of health professionals to provide appropriate care. Where it is not possible to obtain consent, they may proceed in what they believe to be the best interests of the patient.[46] The model consent form produced by the Department of Health invites patients to tell their professionals about any procedures they definitely do not wish to be carried out. Such a prohibition would bind the professionals.[47] Only in the absence of available evidence as to patients' views of what is in their interests, is it probably legitimate to assume that they coincide with the professionals'. Even if a general consent is valid, it could be withdrawn at any time by the patient.

(vii) Absence of Fraud

Finally, an apparently valid consent may be vitiated if it is obtained by fraud, which includes cases where a professional deliberately withholds information in bad faith,[48] or by misrepresenting the nature of the proposed care.[49] Health

---

[45] Skegg, n. 8 above, 80. [46] F v. *W. Berkshire HA*, n. 15 above; see below.

[47] *Ibid.*, 566; *Re T*, n. 18 above. By implication the acceptance of a general consent despite an explicit refusal in *Beatty* v. *Cullingworth* [1896] 2 BMJ 1525 could not be sustained today.

[48] *Chatterton* v. *Gerson*, n. 4 above, 265. [49] *Freeman* v. *Home Office*, n. 4 above, 1044.

professionals should therefore be wary of failing to answer questions about treatment candidly in case they invalidate the patient's consent. The judiciary has given no clear indication of where the line is to be drawn, and the problem of how to respond to patients' questions is discussed at greater length below.

(viii) The Form of Consent

It is the reality of the consent that matters, not its form, and there is no legal distinction to be drawn between the efficacy of written, oral, and implied consents. Written consent provides the clearest proof that the patient did in fact consent, and for that reason is preferred by health service bodies, which may need to defend legal proceedings if anything goes wrong. The NHS executive has provided a series of model consent forms to assist health authorities and trusts to cover themselves in this way.[50] The signature of the patient on such a form makes it difficult for her or him to deny that consent was given. However, if patients have not in fact consented an operation will be unlawful even if they have signed a form.[51] The reality prevails over the writing.

The main importance of writing is therefore that it provides good evidence. The best evidence of consent is a signed consent form. However, a record in the patient's notes that an explanation was offered and consent given would be almost as good, especially if it was contemporaneous or nearly so. Without a written record, any court trying to discover what happened later would have to decide whose evidence was more reliable, that of the patient or the professionals. Patients will argue that they are more likely to remember what happened because it was their only contact with health professionals, while the professionals would have seen a large number of patients in similar positions and might confuse them.[52] While judges are generally sympathetic to the health professions, a written record of consent will prevent confusion.

Written and oral consents are expressly given by patients. It is not always necessary for consent to be expressed if it is clear from the circumstances that the patient accepted treatment. This is described as implied consent. Thus, if a patient has been asked to undress so that the doctor can perform an examination, the act of disrobing will itself indicate his or her agreement. When patients roll up their sleeves to receive an injection, this is evidence of their consent to it. This doctrine of implied consent should be distinguished from

---

[50] 'Patient Consent to Examination or Treatment', HC(90)22, introducing the booklet, *A Guide to Consent for Examination or Treatment* (London: DoH, 1990), which has the model consent forms in an appendix. Two of the consent forms were replaced by HSG(92)32.

[51] *Chatterton* v. *Gerson*, n. 4 above, 265.

[52] This is not to say that the courts will accept this claim: see e.g. *Whitehouse* v. *Jordan* [1981] 1 All ER 267.

the suggestion that patients should be taken to have consented because they would have done so if asked. That is better described as 'imputed' consent and is discussed below under the heading of care without consent. The idea of implied consent is used to describe situations where the patient did in fact agree to treatment, but did not express that agreement verbally. Implied consents are legally effective because there is an actual consent, not because of a fictional consent that the law creates.

B. Care without Consent

There are four areas where it is important to consider whether care can be justified without consent. The first concerns activities which do not need to be consented to because they are insignificantly intrusive. The second raises the possibility that care may be authorized by public policy even when patients do not want it, in which case consent or its refusal is irrelevant. The third covers situations where consent cannot be obtained because there is no one legally capable of giving it. The fourth involves treatment for mental disorder where the Mental Health Act 1983 provides for treatment without consent in specified circumstances. These are discussed in the chapter on mental health. The first three contexts in which consent may be unnecessary are discussed in this section. A further suggestion that consent was only needed to hostile acts and that medical treatment, being benign rather than hostile, could therefore be administered without consent was disapproved by Lord Goff in *F v. W. Berkshire HA*.[53]

(i) The Vicissitudes of Everyday Life

The first category comprises 'all physical contact which is generally acceptable in the ordinary conduct of daily life'. Suggestions that medical treatment might sometimes come into this category have been disapproved.[54] At most it could be said to cover nursing care dealing with personal hygiene, dressing, and feeding—the tasks that patients would routinely do for themselves if they were not ill. However, even this is probably better explained as covered by an implied consent so long as the patients do not object. If no consent is needed because such care falls within this exceptional category, then it could be

---

[53] [1989] 2 All ER 545, 563–4, disapproving the contention made in *Wilson* v. *Pringle* [1986] 2 All ER 440, 447.

[54] *F* v. *W. Berkshire HA*, n. 15 above, 564; *T* v. *T* [1988] 1 All ER 613, 624.

imposed on unwilling patients. If it is justified by an implicit consent, then if that consent is withdrawn further care would be unlawful.[55]

(ii) Public Policy

The second suggestion, that public policy considerations may outweigh a refusal of consent, is of extremely limited scope in English law if it is applicable at all.[56] The question whether a consent could be invalidated by public policy considerations was discussed earlier in the chapter. Cases where there is no consent, or where an apparent consent or refusal is invalid, are covered by the principles under the third heading. The issue here is whether there is any general rule that public policy can justify disregarding a competent refusal of consent. This is sometimes referred to as the doctrine of necessity. In the Court of Appeal in *Re F* Neill LJ suggested that this doctrine founded on the public interest and that the views of the individual patient were irrelevant.[57] The House of Lords decided the case on the basis that this doctrine only applied where the patient could not consent and that it did not justify treatment against the wishes of the patient.[58]

The two circumstances in which this issue is pressing concern refusals of life-saving treatment and cases where pregnant women resist care designed to benefit the foetuses that they are carrying. In relation to the former, the judiciary has emphasized that patients may refuse life-saving treatment providing that they have the capacity to make that choice.[59] In relation to the latter situation the normal rule is that the duty of health professionals to care for the mother prevails over their obligations to the foetus,[60] and that not even a court will force a woman to be treated if she competently refuses care.[61] However, in one English case a Caesarian section was forced upon a competent woman and it has been argued that the justification for this might have been the public interest.[62] These scenarios are discussed more fully in the chapters on terminal care and childbirth respectively.

It is also conceivable that public policy might be invoked to justify procedures on incompetent patients who cannot give consent for themselves. The principles to be discussed in the next section concern therapeutic procedures.

---

[55] It has been suggested that the basis of the exception itself is that it is presumed that people consent to physical contact that is an inevitable part of everyday life. However, this was described as 'artificial' by Lord Goff in *F* v. *W. Berkshire HA*, n. 15 above, 563.

[56] Skegg, n. 8 above, 110–16.   [57] N. 28 above, 401–2.

[58] *F* v. *W. Berkshire HA*, n. 15 above, 566, *per* Lord Goff.

[59] *Ibid.*, 566, *per* Lord Goff; *Re T*, n. 18 above; *Re C*, n. 19 above.

[60] Congenital Disabilities (Civil Liability) Act 1976, see Ch. 17.

[61] *Re F* [1988] 2 All ER 193.

[62] *Re S* [1992] 4 All 671; K. Stern, 'Court-ordered Caesarian Sections: In Whose Interests' (1993) 56 *MLR* 238–43.

However, they leave the matter open in relation to non-therapeutic contexts. The most important of these is research, where the public interest in carrying out research might be argued to justify proceeding even though no legally valid consent is available. This is discussed in the chapter on research. Public policy justifications could also be offered in relation to tissue donation when the only suitable donor is not competent to consent. There is no judicial discussion of this problem in England. Skegg argues that a minor intrusion made without consent, such as taking blood, might be treated leniently by a court if it was the only way to obtain compatible supply needed to save another's life. However, he believes that it would nevertheless constitute a crime.[63]

(iii) Incompetent Patients

The final category of cases where care can be given despite the absence of consent concerns situations where no valid consent can be obtained because the patient is incapable of giving it and there is no one able to do so on his or her behalf. Here, the House of Lords has held that law of battery can have no application, as it would bar incompetent patients from receiving care.[64] Instead, health professionals are obliged to treat their patients in accordance with their best interests. Providing that they do so there is no need for prior authorization from a court because the lawfulness of the treatment depends on it being in the interests of the patient. Should there be a challenge to any care offered, the professionals will be found to have acted properly providing that their judgement as to what would best serve the interests of the patient proves acceptable to a responsible body of professional opinion from the relevant specialty.[65] The same criterion governs procedures assisting in the diagnosis of the problems suffered by the mentally incapacitated, even though the health professionals cannot be sure that they will benefit the patient because they do not yet know what is wrong with them.[66]

Strictly speaking, there is no need for health professionals to go to court before they can treat incompetent patients. However, there are some categories of case when it has been suggested that it is good practice to seek court approval. One is the withdrawal of life sustaining care from patients in a persistent vegetative state.[67] The most fully explored such category is sterilization operations.[68] These should normally be brought to court unless they are to be performed for therapeutic rather than contraceptive purposes.[69] The

---

[63] N. 8 above, 117.   [64] *F* v. *W. Berkshire HA*, n. 15 above.
[65] *Ibid.*, applying the test set out in *Bolam* v. *Friern HMC* [1957] 2 All ER 118, 121.
[66] *Re H* [1993] 1 FLR 28.
[67] *Airedale NHS trust* v. *Bland* [1993] 1 All ER 821; see further Ch. 20.
[68] *F* v. *W. Berkshire HA*, n. 15 above.   [69] *Re E* [1991] 2 FLR 585.

judiciary has been reluctant to set out the principles that determine whether procedures should be authorized, holding that the only principle at stake is the best interests of the patient.[70] Some guidance is given in relation to sterilization operations by a practice note issued by the Official Solicitor.[71] This is discussed in detail in the chapter on law and fertility.

The law has not clearly established that there are any other types of case in which it is desirable that the guidance of a court should be obtained. Lord Brandon explained the reasons for advising this in relation to sterilization in terms of the following features of such procedures:[72] first, that they will usually be irreversible; secondly, they will deprive the patient of a fundamental human right, namely the right to reproduce; thirdly, depriving someone of that right raises moral and emotional considerations that are widely regarded as significant; fourthly, court involvement reduces the risk of errors; fifthly, the court provides a protection against the introduction of improper considerations; finally, judicial authorization serves to protect doctors against criticism and legal action. It is possible that these considerations will exist only in relation to sterilization. However, non-regenerative organ donation and abortion have been mooted as being in a similar category.[73] One judge has since held that abortions need not be considered by the courts in advance.[74] No court has had the chance to decide specifically whether health professionals should take organ donation to court. It is, however, clear that court authorization should not be sought for diagnostic procedures.[75]

Regular recourse to the courts would be expensive and time-consuming. One judicial proposal in relation to sterilization may be of general importance. In *Re GF* it was suggested that there is no need to seek authorization for sterilizations where two registered medical practitioners are satisfied that the procedure is necessary for therapeutic purposes, in the best interests of the patient, and that there is no practicable, less intrusive, means of treating the condition.[76] It is doubtful whether these conditions must be satisfied in every respect before the operation would be lawful. However, they give useful practical guidance on a procedure to protect doctors without actually going to court. It would be very unlikely that it could be shown that no responsible body of professional opinion would support the procedure if two doctors have considered it in good faith and found it to be appropriate. Thus in more straightforward cases, it may be possible to seek reassurance from colleagues rather than the court.

---

[70] *Re B*, n. 26 above.   [71] [1990] 2 FLR 530, see also *Re C (Note)* [1990] 2 FLR 527.
[72] F v. *W. Berkshire HA*, n. 15 above, 552.
[73] *Re F*, n. 28 above, 390–1 (Lord Donaldson, abortion and organ donation), 404 (Neill LJ, organ donation), 411, 413 (Butler-Sloss LJ, abortion, organ donation).
[74] *Re SG* [1991] 2 FLR 329.   [75] *Re H*, n. 66 above.   [76] *Re GF* [1992] 1 FLR 293.

C. Counselling and Informed Consent

Any discussion of the English law governing counselling and informed consent must concentrate on the decision of the House of Lords in *Sidaway* v. *Bethlem RHG*.[77] There is now a considerable body of academic literature exploring the implications of this case, but the precise terms of the principles it established remain controversial.[78] Some commentators have welcomed the decision as a step towards the introduction of the doctrine of informed consent.[79] However, subsequent judicial interpretation of the decision has tended to take a conservative view of the extent to which the case requires doctors to inform patients.[80] This has left the literature in a state of some confusion. This section concentrates on judicial pronouncements in the cases, aiming to explain the current state of the law and to avoid an over-optimistic assessment of its recognition of patient autonomy. It begins by summarizing and comparing the different speeches in the *Sidaway* case. It then considers the interpretation of that case in subsequent decisions. It ends by examining the state of the law in relation to particular issues that have proved problematic.

(i) The *Sidaway* Case

Mrs Sidaway had suffered injury to her spinal cord in the course of an operation to free a trapped nerve and was left partially paralyzed. No complaint was made against the way in which the neurosurgeon had performed the operation; there had been a genuine accident, not a negligent mistake. However, Mrs Sidaway brought an action alleging that the risks involved had not been properly explained to her. She accepted that she had given a real consent, and the legal basis of her claim was therefore negligence.

The evidence showed that there were two specific risks of injury to a patient undergoing the operation that was performed on Mrs Sidaway. The first was damage to the nerve and the second was damage to the spinal cord itself. If the nerve were damaged, the patient would be left in pain. However, if damage

---

[77] N. 3 above.

[78] e.g. Brazier, n. 6 above; M. Jones, *Medical Negligence* (2nd edn., London: Sweet & Maxwell, 1996), 337–43; C. Newdick, 'The Doctor's Duties of Care under *Sidaway*' (1985) 36 *NILQ* 243–50; Teff, n. 9 above; A. Whitfield, 'Informed Consent: Does the Doctrine Benefit Patients in the United Kingdom' in D. Brahams (ed.), *Medicine and the Law* (London: Royal College of Physicians, 1990). See also the works cited in the next note.

[79] e.g. I. Kennedy, 'The Patient on the Clapham Omnibus' in I. Kennedy, *Treat Me Right* (Oxford: OUP, 1991); Lee, n. 16 above; A. Grubb, 'Conceiving—A New Cause of Action' in M. Freeman (ed.), *Medicine, Ethics and the Law* (London: Stevens, 1988).

[80] Although see the comments of Lord Scarman in a public lecture: L. Scarman, 'Law and Medical Practice' in P. Byrne (ed.), *Medicine in Contemporary Society* (London: King's Fund, 1987).

occurred to the spinal cord it could lead to paralysis. The judge found that the surgeon, Mr Falconer, had warned Mrs Sidaway of the risk of danger to the nerve, but had said nothing about the possibility of paralysis.[81] The expert witnesses testified that (at the time of the operation) some neurosurgeons would have regarded it as acceptable to keep silent about the risk of paralysis. The issue before the courts was how the law should assess whether Mrs Sidaway was told enough about these risks.

The case was taken all the way to the House of Lords. Mrs Sidaway's claim was rejected at all levels. However, this consensus about the outcome of the case was not matched by agreement on the legal tests to be applied. Each of the four judges of the House of Lords who delivered speeches gave different reasons for his decision.[82] It is therefore necessary to consider what each had to say and then to try to distil a legal principle from the case.

Lord Scarman argued that patients had a right to decide what happens to them. He believed that this right was supported by a further right to be given all the information that is material to deciding whether to accept the treatment that they had been advised to have. If a material risk was not disclosed, then the doctor responsible for counselling the patient was negligent. In order to decide whether something was a material consideration, the court should ask whether a reasonable person in the patient's position would have regarded it as being significant. He described this as a 'prudent patient' test. To operate the test in clinical practice, doctors would therefore have to ask themselves what a reasonable person in their patient's position would want to know.

Of all the judges, Lord Scarman's approach would impose the most extensive duty of disclosure on the health professions. However, the obligation that he proposed was subject to an important limitation: the defence of 'therapeutic privilege'. This would enable doctors to withhold even material facts if they reasonably believed that disclosure would be detrimental to the health (including the mental health) of the patient. Although Lord Scarman does not lay down a precise test for the scope of this 'therapeutic privilege', he does indicate that there must be a serious threat of psychological detriment to the patient.

Lord Diplock approached the case in a very different way. He observed that the normal legal standard to which doctors were held was that of a reasonably competent practitioner.[83] He argued that they had a single professional duty, to exercise their skill and judgement in the improvement of the patient's health. In his view, this duty should not be fragmented into different compo-

---

[81] It is difficult to be confident that this was in fact what happened, because Mr Falconer had died by the time of the court hearing and Mrs Sidaway's evidence was found to be unreliable. However, the decision of the HL was made on the basis that this finding was correct.

[82] Lord Keith did not deliver a separate speech, but agreed with the views of Lord Bridge.

[83] *Bolam* v. *Friern HMC*, n. 65 above.

nents such as diagnosis, advice, and treatment. In particular, it would be wrong to apply different standards to the different aspects of the professionals' responsibility towards their patients. Consequently, doctors could only be negligent if their failure to disclose a piece of information was unacceptable to all responsible practitioners in the relevant specialty. Lord Diplock went on to observe that it would be enough for one such school of thought to support the doctor being sued. The courts should not presume to give effect to any preference they might have between responsible bodies of professional opinion.

Lord Bridge began his explanation of the case by rejecting Lord Scarman's approach. He thought that it was incoherent and too uncertain. He then turned to consider whether professional standards provided the appropriate test. He argued that what to disclose to a patient was primarily a matter of clinical judgement. This meant that Mrs Sidaway's claim had to be assessed by asking whether a responsible body of practitioners would have accepted (at that time) that it was legitimate not to discuss the risk of paralysis. As they did accept this, then her case had to fail.

Lord Bridge went on to argue that this did not mean that the law handed the entire question of the scope of disclosure over to the medical profession, leaving it to police itself. Unlike Lord Diplock, he suggested that where there was a conflict of evidence on whether responsible practice approved the withholding of information in a particular case, then the court should resolve the disagreement. This appears to envisage that the judge could prefer one school of thought to another, something that Lord Diplock expressly rejected. Lord Bridge was prepared to go further still and countenance the possibility that, even when doctors accepted that non-disclosure was proper, a judge might declare that it was negligent not to explain a serious risk. He suggested that a 10 per cent risk of a stroke was an example of such a case, although it would be dangerous to place too much reliance on statistical probability.

The final speech was delivered by Lord Templeman. In his view, once the nature of the operation had been explained to Mrs Sidaway it must have been obvious to her that there was some risk of injury to the spinal cord. There was no need for Mr Falconer to explain about the paralysis. He noted that patients did not always want to know all the details of their care, and that if she had wanted to know more she would have asked him. Her silence should be taken as an indication that she believed that if Mr Falconer was satisfied that the benefits of the operation outweighed the risks, then she would trust his judgement. Lord Templeman suggested that where risks were special in magnitude or kind to the patient then they should be volunteered.[84] Where a general

---

[84] All the judges accepted that there was a distinction between general and specific risks, although the meanings given to the terms varied slightly, n. 3 above, 647 and 654 (Lord Scarman), 656 (Lord Diplock), 661 (Lord Bridge).

explanation of the treatment proposed would alert patients to risks, then health professionals could wait for them to ask for further information. It would be for the court to decide whether an explanation was sufficient to alert patients in this way. Standards of professional practice were not relevant.

Lord Templeman also explained the purpose of disclosure requirements. He said that doctors were not entitled to decide everything, and that the final decision lay with patients, who were entitled to reject medical advice for rational or irrational reasons, or for no reason. However, patients were not entitled to all the information available, as to tell them everything might conflict with the doctors' more fundamental duty to promote their best interests. Instead they must be given enough information to make a balanced judgement. Too much information might prevent a balanced judgement just as might too little information. A court would find a doctor liable in negligence if the patient were deprived of the information necessary to achieve this purpose.

On the basis of these four approaches to the case, it is impossible to find a majority view. However, it can be observed that Lord Scarman's 'prudent patient' approach was not supported by any of his colleagues. It can also be suggested that only Lord Diplock was happy to see the *Bolam* test applied without modification. The other members of the House of Lords were concerned that to do so would make doctors the only judges of how much patients were entitled to know. Beyond that, there is too little common ground to distil a consensus.

The Court of Appeal has cut through the complexities of the *Sidaway* decision by treating Lord Diplock's speech as laying down the law. In *Gold* v. *Haringey HA* there was no discussion at all of the other Law Lords' speeches.[85] The Court of Appeal accepted Lord Diplock's argument that the duties of doctors could not be subdivided, and that it followed that the *Bolam* test applied to all aspects of their work. In *Blyth* v. *Bloomsbury HA* the Court of Appeal did consider the difficulties of determining which of the speeches from *Sidaway* were to be taken as containing the legal rules.[86] Lord Scarman's approach was rejected as being a dissenting speech. The majority conclusion was said to be that the *Bolam* test should be applied. However, Kerr LJ found that the House of Lords had suggested that there might be circumstances in which a court could hold that some risks were so obvious that no prudent doctor could have failed to give some warning about them.[87]

---

[85] [1987] 2 All ER 888.

[86] [1993] 4 Med. LR 151. The case was actually decided in 1987. In *Palmer* v. *Eadie* (unreported, 18 May 1987) the CA applied the *Sidaway* decision, but found it unnecessary to consider which speech established the legal principles.

[87] N. 86 above, 155.

This could be seen as a slight move away from the usual non-interventionist interpretation of the *Bolam* test.[88] However, it must be noted that all that is being suggested is that judges can tell what responsible medical practice would be without hearing detailed evidence. Even where a judge feels able to assert that a risk should be disclosed, the need to inform the patient may yield to a 'cogent clinical reason'.[89] Thus medical opinion can prevail over judicial assertiveness. The Scottish case of *Moyes* v. *Lothian HB* considered the comments on the disclosure of obvious risk and observed that there was 'nothing in the majority view in *Sidaway* which suggests that the extent and quality of a warning to be given by a doctor to his patient should not in the last resort be governed by medical criteria'.[90]

There is only one recent English example of a judge actually deciding that disclosure practices accepted by a health profession were nevertheless negligent because the judiciary believed that the risks were so obvious that they must be disclosed. In *Smith* v. *Tunbridge Wells HA* there was expert evidence that 'a body of experienced competent surgeons' would not have warned the patient of a risk of impotence in the operation that he agreed to. Nevertheless, the judge regarded that omission as 'neither reasonable nor responsible' and found the surgeon negligent for failing to disclose the risk.[91] It is possible that this indicates a move towards greater judicial intervention in the field of informed consent. However, it should be noted that this is a single decision. It was made by a High Court judge, and is not therefore binding on subsequent courts. It is also arguably inconsistent with the decision of the House of Lords in *Maynard* v. *W Midlands RHA*.[92] In one older case, *Clarke* v. *Adams*, decided in 1950, the court held that a physiotherapist was negligent in failing to explain a risk, even though the warning that had been given was in accordance with current professional practice.[93] However, in general, the courts have not taken the opportunity to intervene in this manner and have been reluctant to develop more precise standards for the disclosure of information, preferring to maintain a commitment to the *Bolam* test. This can be illustrated by the way in which patients who ask questions have been dealt with.

(ii) The Patient who Seeks Information

The *Sidaway* case was concerned with the obligations of doctors to volunteer information to their patients. A number of comments in the speeches in the House of Lords indicated that different considerations might apply where a

---

[88] This is discussed in detail in Ch. 7.
[89] *Sidaway* v. *Bethlem RHG*, n. 3 above, 663, *per* Lord Bridge.
[90] [1990] 1 Med. LR 463, 469.
[91] [1994] 5 Med. LR 334, 339.
[92] [1985] 1 All ER 635. This point is discussed in detail in Ch. 7.
[93] (1950) 94 SJ 599.

patient sought more detailed information. Lord Diplock suggested that where someone wished to be fully informed of any risks involved and manifested his desire by means of questioning 'no doubt . . . the doctor would tell him what he wished to know'.[94] He supposed that highly educated people of experience such as judges would be likely to pursue such concerns. Lord Bridge was more explicit, suggesting that it would be the doctor's legal duty in such circumstances 'to answer both truthfully and as fully as the questioner requires'.[95] However, he recognized that he could not decide the point because it was not in issue in the case.

The scope of a doctor's duty to answer questions was considered in 1987 by the Court of Appeal in *Blyth* v. *Bloomsbury HA*.[96] The comments of Lords Bridge and Diplock were discussed, but were not taken to exclude the application of the *Bolam* test. Kerr LJ argued that 'there will always be grey areas, with differences of opinion, as to what are the proper answers to be given to any enquiry, even a specific one'.[97] It followed that doctors had to exercise their clinical judgement in deciding how much information to give to their patients. The latitude permitted by the *Bolam* test was designed to recognize the legitimacy of differences of opinion. The other judge to give reasons in the *Blyth* case, Neill LJ, said that *Sidaway* did not create

> any rule of law to the effect that where questions are asked by a patient, or doubts are expressed, a doctor is under an obligation to put the patient in possession of all the information on the subject. . . . The amount of information to be given must depend on the circumstances, and as a general proposition it is governed by what is called the Bolam test.[98]

It seems clear that the judges were prepared to accept that it would be lawful to withhold information from a patient who asked questions, if a responsible body of professional opinion supported such an action. However, as the Court of Appeal decided that Ms Blyth had not in fact asked any questions, the comments on the duty to answer questions are not technically binding on subsequent courts.

This leaves the law in some uncertainty. To apply the *Bolam* test to cases where the patient has asked questions permits doctors to withhold information deliberately provided that some of their colleagues would regard it as acceptable to do so. Effectively, this means that patients can be lied to. This position is in line with one early case,[99] but arguably not with modern under-

---

[94] *Sidaway* v. *Bethlem RHG*, n. 3 above, 659.   [95] *Ibid.*, 661.   [96] N. 86 above.
[97] *Ibid.*, 157.   [98] *Ibid.*, 160.
[99] *Hatcher* v. *Black*, *The Times*, 2 July 1954. See also *Lee* v. *S.W. Thames RHA* [1985] 2 All ER 385, 389, envisaging that information requested by a patient might sometimes be withheld.

standings of patients' rights.[100] It should also be noted that, were information to be withheld for reasons other than the interests of the patient, then her or his consent might be rendered invalid by reason of the rules on fraudulently obtained consent (see above). Possibly, the judges might be expected to be more likely to intervene to override professional standards in this area than in relation to the volunteering of information.

(iii) Non-therapeutic Contexts

Sidaway was concerned with the volunteering of information in relation to treatment. In that context it can reasonably be assumed that the principal objective of both patient and doctor is to improve the health of the former. However, this assumption does not so obviously hold in all areas of health care. At first instance in *Gold* v. *Haringey HA* the judge sought to distinguish *Sidaway*, arguing that it should not be applied in non-therapeutic contexts.[101] He further argued that a sterilization operation should be characterized as non-therapeutic. The Court of Appeal firmly rejected this attempt to evade the medical disclosure standards adopted by the *Sidaway* decision.[102] It found the distinction between therapeutic and non-therapeutic procedures unwarranted and artificial. It also suggested that it would be a departure from the principle that doctors' duty of care for their patients should not be subdivided.

In general, therefore, the courts seem reluctant to distinguish between categories of care. However, there are some areas of health care where there is a clear distinction between therapeutic and non-therapeutic activities. The most obvious are research, and the donation of tissue or organs for transplantation. Here, the research subjects and donors are not seeking the assistance of the health professional for their mutual benefit. Instead, they are offering a service to that professional, whose principal purpose is not their welfare but that of a potential recipient or of advancing knowledge. In these circumstances, the suggestion that different rules should be applied, with greater commitment to informed consent, is compelling.

Consent to research is governed by the common law and is discussed in detail in Chapter 14. In relation to transplantation there has been limited statutory intervention. For some live donations, within the scope of the Human Organ Transplants Act 1989, regulations require the donor to receive a explanation not only of the nature of the procedure for removal of the organ, but also of the risks involved.[103] This could be said to go beyond the usual

---

[100] However, compare I. Kennedy, 'Consent to Treatment: The Capable Person' in C. Dyer (ed.), *Doctors, Patients and the Law* (Oxford: Blackwell Scientific Publications, 1992), 68–9 with Jones, n. 78 above, 358–62.

[101] [1987] 1 FLR 125.   [102] N. 26 above.

[103] Human Organ (Unrelated Persons) Regulations 1989, SI 1989 No 2480, r. 3(2)(a). See further Ch. 19.

requirement of an explanation of the nature and purpose of the treatment. However, there is no definition of which risks should be disclosed and, in the absence of case law, it is unclear whether the standards are higher than *Sidaway* imposed. It is probable that the regulations should be regarded as a codification of the common law requirements. There would be an obligation to disclose risks to donors under that common law, which would cover all donations, and not just those within the scope of the 1989 Act. However, the key, and unresolved, question remains whether that obligation is defined by professional standards or lay ones. The Human Organ Transplant Regulations also require doctors to check that the information they give to patients has been understood.[104] One High Court judge seems to have adopted the view that the common law imposes a similar requirement, but the point was not considered on appeal.[105]

D. Conclusion

This Chapter has shown that, while the law of consent provides an important symbolic statement of patients' rights to self-determination, the commitment of English law to informed consent is lukewarm. As long as the adoption of professional disclosure standards in *Sidaway* dominates the law, moves towards greater involvement of patients in decisions must be led by the profession and not legal doctrine.[106] *Sidaway* did leave some scope for judicial activism in establishing higher standards, but there is little indication that the courts wish to take advantage of it. There are a few Parliamentary initiatives that suggest greater interest in enhancing patients' rights than the common law displays.Opticians are now required to provide their patients with a written statement of their diagnosis.[107] Dentists must produce a written treatment plan for their patients.[108] However, these operate only in marginal areas and are more concerned with subjecting professionals to market forces than with the quality of consent to care.[109]

---

[104] Human Organ Transplants (Unrelated Persons) Regulations 1989, n. 103 above, r. 3(2)(b).

[105] *Lybert* v. *Warrington HA* [1996] 7 Med. LR 71.

[106] J. Montgomery, 'The Role of Law in Raising Standards of Consent' in P. Alderson (ed.), *Consent to Health Treatment and Research* (London: Institute of Education Social Sciences Research Unit, 1992).

[107] Opticians Act 1989, s. 26; Sight Testing (Examination and Prescription) (No 2) Regulations 1989, SI 1989 No 1230.

[108] NHS (General) Dental Services) Regulations 1973, SI 1973 No 1468 as amended, Sch. 1, paras. 4(1)(b), 5(1)(b).

[109] J. Montgomery, 'Patients First: The Role of Rights' in K. W. M. Fulford, S. Ersser, and T. Hope (eds.), *Essential Practice in Patient-centred Care* (Oxford: Blackwell Science, 1996), 142–52, 147.

11 Confidentiality and Access to Health Care Records

Uncertain foundation [handwritten]

Hippocratic oath [handwritten]

Respect for the confidences of patients has long been part of the ethical tradition of health care and is enshrined in the Hippocratic Oath. Few doubt that it is an important principle, but there is considerable disagreement as to the justifications for and functions of the obligation of confidence. Some argue that confidentiality serves the interests of health care practitioners more than those of patients and have seen its origins in a conspiracy of silence designed to maintain the monopoly of practitioners over medical knowledge. Others emphasize the benefits to patients of having their affairs kept secret. In practice, there is often no need to distinguish between different justifications, but it becomes important to be able to do so when the limits of obligation come into question. The strength of claims that the obligation no longer applies or that it is outweighed by other considerations can only be assessed when the underlying values which confidentiality promotes are identified.[1]

Benefit Dr or Benefit pt. [handwritten]

Modern discussions point to a number of different sources of the moral duty to keep confidences.[2] An argument from efficiency points out that professionals can only practise effectively if they are fully aware of the circumstances, and that, unless patients are sure that what they say will remain confidential, they will withhold sensitive, but possibly essential, information from the practitioner for fear of embarrassment. A second approach points out that patients convey information on the understanding that it will remain secret and that a failure to keep it so is a breach of the tacit agreement between professional and client. Another approach emphasizes the patient's right to privacy. Breaches of confidence expose personal matters to the public and this in itself infringes the rights of the patient. Others argue that the right which is at stake is the patient's right to autonomy. They point out that unless they can control who knows about their personal affairs patients will lose some of their ability to shape their lives as they choose.

(1) withhold info [handwritten]
(2) Breach of agreement [handwritten]
(3) Right to privacy [handwritten]
(4) Right to autonomy [handwritten]

---

[1] P. D. Finn, 'Confidentiality and the Public Interest' (1984) 58 *ALJ* 497.
[2] Editorial, 'Medical Confidentiality' (1984) 10 *Journal of Medical Ethics* 3–4.

A. Sources of the Legal Obligation of Confidence

Uncertain in law.

In addition to confusion as to the ethical basis of confidentiality, there is also uncertainty as to its legal foundation.[3] One commentator has identified seven different grounds on which a legal obligation might be founded.[4] The main contenders are contract, implied or express, the general duty of care in negligence, and a special equitable obligation. In addition to these legal obligations, professional disciplinary procedures apply because all the health professions recognize that confidentiality is an essential aspect of their work. Finally, there are a number of statutory provisions which require that information be kept confidential. The most comprehensive concerns computerized records, and is discussed in a separate section below. Others deal with specific areas of health care. Under the Human Fertilization and Embryology Act 1990 such strict confidentiality is required in relation to certain information that an amending statute was passed in 1992 to relax some of its provisions.[5]

In relation to sexually transmitted diseases, special regulations apply.[6] They require health authorities to take 'all necessary steps' to ensure that any information obtained by their officers capable of identifying patients with such diseases is disclosed only for the purpose of treating people with the disease or preventing its spread. Even in these circumstances, disclosure can only be made to a doctor, or someone working on a doctor's instructions in connection with such treatment or preventive work. The regulations do not prevent contact-tracing. These specific provisions relating to venereal disease are now probably of limited significance, even though they have been said to cover HIV,[7] as it would now seem that the same results can be reached under the common law.

At one time, it was suggested that the right to control who had access to confidential information went hand in hand with the legal ownership of medical records in which it was recorded. The understanding of the Department of Health is that medical records are the property of the health authority on whose behalf they were made.[8] It is probable that NHS trusts own the records that their staff make. In relation to records generated in general practice, the

---

[3] Law Commission, *Breach of Confidence* (Law Com. No 110, 1981, Cmnd. 8388).

[4] R. Wacks, 'Breach of Confidence and the Protection of Privacy' (1977) 127 *NLJ* 328.

[5] The provisions are discussed generally in Ch. 16, but see below for their implications for disclosure with the patient's consent.

[6] NHS (Venereal Diseases) Regulations 1974, SI 1974/No 29.

[7] *X* v. *Y* [1988] 2 All ER 649.

[8] Advice by the Department's solicitor, Sept. 1987, regarded as current in May 1989 when the position was reported to the *Select Committee on the PCA, Second Report of the Select Committee on the PCA 1988–9*, HC 433, App. I.

Department's view is that records are owned by the Family Health Services Authority (now Health Authority) because they are made on standard forms that the Authority supplies.[9] The fact that a practice is a fundholding one does not affect this position, as the terms of service still apply. One consequence of the ownership of records is that health records made within the NHS (including NHS trusts), other than those relating to private patients admitted under section 5 of the NHS Act 1977, are public records within the scope of the Public Records Act 1958.[10] They would therefore ordinarily be available for public inspection thirty years after they were made. However, under section 5(2), where allowing records to be inspected would involve 'a breach of good faith' on the part of the person who obtained the information they contain, access may be restricted. Personal health records would come within this category, thus preserving confidentiality.

For most purposes, the mere fact of ownership is no longer seen as significant. Owning the records is not the same as having the right to do what you wish with them.[11] Confidentiality binds an owner of records just as much as it does the professionals who made them. An examination of the obligation of confidence is therefore more important than the question of ownership. Unfortunately, there remain considerable uncertainties about the nature and scope of the legal obligation of confidentiality in health care. These arise largely from the lack of clarity over the basis of the obligation.

If the legal source of confidentiality lies in contract, the extent of the obligation will be determined by the agreement between the parties. This would enable a patient who wished to ensure an especially strict obligation of confidentiality to do so by agreement with the professional before the information was imparted. In default of a specific arrangement an implied term of confidentiality would arise. It is unlikely that an implied contract term would impose a stricter duty than that existing in negligence.[12] The usefulness of a contractual basis for the obligation of confidence is also reduced by the fact that there is no contract between an NHS patient and those caring for them. A specific contract dealing with confidentiality would have to be found to make the contractual approach viable.[13]

There is little doubt that the tort of negligence could be used to sustain the obligation of confidence. Keeping patients' affairs private has long been an accepted part of medical care. It would therefore be part of responsible

---

[9] *Ibid.*   [10] Public Records Act 1958, Sch. 1, as amended. See HC(89)20.

[11] *R.* v. *Mid-Glamorgan FHSA, ex p. Martin* [1995] 1 All ER 356 (CA).

[12] *Thake* v. *Maurice* [1986] 1 All ER 497.

[13] There is an argument to this effect based on the case of *Mechanical and General Inventions* v. *Austin Motor* [1935] AC 346, but the probability of a court accepting it is small: see A. Grubb, and D. Pearl, 'Medicine, Health, the Family and the Law' [1986] *Fam. L* 227 and J. Montgomery, 'Confidentiality and the Immature Minor' [1987] *Fam. L* 101.

professional practice. It is foreseeable that the revelation of details of people's health status might cause them loss. Indeed, the courts in New Zealand have held that to cause injury by carelessly revealing confidential medical information is negligent.[14] Founding the duty of confidence in negligence has some advantages. The duty is not just to avoid telling unauthorized persons things that are confidential. It also covers taking proper precautions to ensure that confidential information does not fall into the wrong hands.[15] However, negligence requires proof of 'damage' and very often breach of confidence causes embarrassment rather than legally recognized losses. In addition, the extent of the duty of care in negligence will depend on responsible professional practice. This probably makes its scope identical to that under the professional disciplinary jurisdiction.

It is now most likely that a court would approach confidentiality on the basis that there is a specific equitable obligation to keep patients' details secret.[16] This approach was originally developed in commercial contexts and applies where three conditions are satisfied.[17] First, the information must be of a confidential nature. It has been accepted that information of a personal and intimate nature qualifies.[18] Secondly, the information must have been imparted in circumstances importing an obligation of confidence. It is well established that the relationship between doctor and patient constitutes such a circumstance.[19] Finally, it is probably necessary that the subject would suffer from the revelation of the information. An invasion of personal privacy will suffice.[20] It has been suggested that, even where there is no specific detriment caused by the revelation of confidential information, there may still be a public interest that supports the enforcement of confidentiality.[21] It has been held that just such a public interest exists in maintaining medical confidences.[22] Consequently, even if detriment is necessary, it will routinely be made out in the health care context.

---

[14] *Furniss* v. *Fitchett* [1958] NZLR 396.

[15] *H* v. *Home Office*, *Guardian*, 6 May 1992 (damages for insufficient safeguards to prevent computer print-out falling into fellow prisoner's hands). The case is also reported in *The Times* for 7 May 1992, but the decision on this point is not recorded there.

[16] 'Equity' and 'equitable' are terms that are used to refer to a subdivision of judge made law, generally regarded as particularly flexible in doing justice between parties.

[17] *Coco* v. *A. N. Clark (Engineers) Ltd* [1969] RPC 41, 47 (*per* Megarry J); see also *A-G* v. *Guardian (No 2)* [1988] 3 All ER 545.

[18] *Stephens* v. *Avery* [1988] 2 All ER 477.

[19] See e.g. Lord Keith in *A-G* v. *Guardian (No 2)*, n. 17 above, 639.

[20] *Margaret, Duchess of Argyll* v. *Duke of Argyll* [1965] 1 All ER 611. The need for detriment was left open in *A-G* v. *Guardian (No 2)*, n. 17 above.

[21] See Lord Keith in *A-G* v. *Guardian (No 2)*, n. 17 above, 639–40.

[22] *W* v. *Egdell* [1990] 1 All ER 835, although there was in fact a contractual source for the obligation in the case.

The formulation of the obligation in terms of these three tests tends to obscure a key problem. It is unclear from it whether the foundation of the equitable obligation lies in the private interests of the individual imparting the confidential information or in the broader public interest in ensuring that confidentiality is maintained. In the most important health confidentiality case, *W* v. *Egdell*, it was suggested that it was the latter, and that it was wrong to refer to W's private interest in confidentiality.[23] Bingham LJ thought that

> it is important to insist on the public interest in preserving W's right to confi-
> dence because the judge in his judgment concluded that while W had a strong
> private interest in barring disclosure of Dr Egdell's report he could not rest his
> case on any broader public interest. Here, I think the judge fell into error. W
> of course had a strong personal interest . . . in restricting the report's circula-
> tion. But these private considerations should not be allowed to obscure the
> public interest in maintaining professional confidences.[24]

This approach is in line with the majority reasoning in two key earlier non-health decisions,[25] and with the other main health case, *X* v. *Y*.[26] However, confidentiality is an aspect of the right to privacy recognized in human rights law,[27] and it could be suggested that patients' rights are insufficiently protected without recognition of their private interests in confidentiality. One commentator has argued that characterizing the obligation of confidence as a public interest matter makes it easier for judges to reach the conclusion that it is outweighed by other factors.[28] The judges have suggested that it would make little difference.[29] The problem is examined below.

---

[23] *Ibid.*, 847–8.   [24] *Ibid.*, 849.

[25] *A-G* v. *Guardian* (*No 2*), n. 17 above (although see Lord Griffiths at 650) and *Lion Laboratories* v. *Evans* [1984] 2 All ER 417.

[26] N. 7 above.

[27] Art. 8 of the European Convention on Human Rights, *Van Oosterwijck* v. *Belgium* (1981) 3 EHRR 557, *X* v. *Norway* (1978) 14 D&R 228.

[28] R. Lee, 'Deathly Silence: Doctors' Duty to Disclose Dangers of Death' in R. Lee and D. Morgan (eds.), *Death Rites: Law and Ethics at the End of Life* (London: Routledge, 1994), 291–2. See also J. Montgomery, 'Victims or Threats? The Framing of HIV' (1990) 12 *Liverpool LR* 25, 48–51. Kennedy and Grubb argue the opposite, that private interests more readily give way to wider public interests than would the public interest in confidentiality, *Medical Law: Text with Materials* (London: Butterworths, 1994), 649.

[29] *W* v. *Egdell*, n. 22 above, 853, *per* Bingham LJ. See also the discussion of the European Convention in *R* v. *Central TV* [1994] 3 WLR 20 by Hoffman LJ.

B. The Limits of the Legal Obligation of Confidentiality

While the legal source of confidentiality is unclear, the small body of case law has not sought to distinguish different sets of exceptions according to the basis of the obligation. In *X* v. *Y*[30] the original obligation arose from the contract of employment of the person leaking the information and from the NHS (Venereal Disease) Regulations 1974.[31] However, the court held that equity could be invoked to restrain publication by the press and the public interest arguments in favour of disclosure were discussed without distinction between the employees and the press. In *W* v. *Edgell*[32] the source of the obligation was contractual, but the discussion of the public interest drew on cases on employees' confidentiality (contractual in origin) and from the equitable jurisdiction without distinction between them. It would seem, therefore, that as a general rule the limits of the obligation of confidence have been regarded as uniform. This may account for the court's reluctance to spell out the basis for the legal duty, as it rarely matters what it is. This makes sense if the basis of the obligation is the public interest or the duty of care in tort, but it is more difficult to explain on the other grounds.

(i) The Patient's Consent

The first, and most straightforward, exception to the obligation of confidence is where patients agree to confidential information being disclosed. Doctors do not breach confidence when they disclose information at the request of the patient.[33] It is this exception that permits the sharing of what would otherwise be secret with relatives, and which allows some of the information obtained in occupational health services to be passed to employers. The fact that the patient's consent is the crucial factor means that the practice of informing relatives of a patient's diagnosis without first seeking consent to do so is of doubtful legality. It also means that where a patient refuses consent to disclosure, then relatives cannot be told (unless one of the other exceptions is made out). It is therefore important to ascertain the patient's wishes at an early stage so that the implications of confidentiality are understood. Once information is made public, it ceases to be confidential, because it has lost the confidential nature that is a precondition of the equitable obligation.

It is not always clear whether the patient's consent can override a statutory obligation of secrecy. Under the original confidentiality provisions of the

---

[30] N. 7 above.   [31] N. 6 above.   [32] N. 22 above.   [33] *C* v. *C* [1946] 1 All ER 562.

Human Fertilization and Embryology Act 1990 it was thought by some that patients were unable to authorize their general practitioners to be told that they were in receipt of infertility treatment.[34] The first annual report of the Human Fertilization and Embryology Authority drew attention to the problems and called for legislation to resolve them. This was forthcoming in the Human Fertilization and Embryology (Disclosure of Information) Act 1992. The content of the new confidentiality rules is explained in Chapter 16. The point here is that it is possible that a statutory regime may preclude even patients consenting to the disclosure of information. This was disputed in relation to the 1990 Act,[35] but was accepted by the Embryology Authority and the Government. It might therefore arise in other areas.

(ii) The 'Need to Know'

The second general exception to the obligation of confidence is where other professionals need to know the information to carry out the patient's care. This is vital to the operation of modern health care because it relies on a team of workers who need to share information about their patients in order to give them appropriate care. It is possible that this exception is based on the first, in that it is assumed that the patient consents to such sharing.[36] If so, then patients would be entitled to withdraw their consent and prevent the sharing of information with other members of the health care team.

However, there are also indications that the 'need to know' principle can justify disclosure against the express prohibition of the patient. In *W* v. *Egdell* (see below), Sir Stephen Brown P accepted that the principle might apply despite such an objection.[37] As the case was decided on other grounds this cannot be taken as an definitive statement. Another member of the Court of Appeal thought that the 'need to know' exception was not in issue in the case at all.[38]

Guidance on confidentiality from the Department of Health seems reluctantly to accept implied consent as the basis for the 'need to know' exception to confidentiality. However, it then catalogues a wide range of reasons why confidential personal information can be shared within the NHS. They

[34] Brahams, 'IVF Legislation: Error Causes Confidentiality Trap' (1991) 338 *Lancet* 1449–50; Medical Defence Union, 'Warning to Infertility Specialists' (1991) 7 *J Medical Defence Union* 94.

[35] D. Morgan, and R. Lee, 'Disclosure is Possible under HUFEA' (1992) *Bulletin of Medical Ethics* No 75, 25–8; cf the response by M. A. M. S. Leigh, and I. S. P. Barker, *Bulletin of Medical Ethics*, No 77, 10–11.

[36] In *Tournier* v. *National Provincial and Union Bank of England* [1924] 1 KB 461, 486, Atkin LJ stated that if it was permissible for bankers to share confidential information with each other this could only be justified on the basis of the implied consent of the customer.

[37] N. 22 above, 846. See also Scott J at first instance: [1989] 1 All ER 1089, 1104.

[38] See Bingham LJ at n. 22 above, 850.

include clinical audit, monitoring and maintaining public health, research (but only within the NHS), service planning, public accountability, investigation of complaints.[39] To suggest that patients give an implicit consent implies that they are actually aware of the possibility of this information-sharing. This is highly improbable. The guidance provides a model information sheet explaining the ways in which information may be used.[40] However, it does not suggest that patients will be taken to consent to these disclosures. Nor does it inform patients that they may be able to object to some of the uses. Nevertheless, the guidance advises that the wishes of patients who do not wish information to be shared should be respected, unless one of the other justifications for disclosure is available.[41] It may be more realistic to suggest that the justification for disclosure in these categories is the public interest, but there is no clear legal authority for such a view.

Even if the basis of the 'need to know' exception is the public interest, it should not be assumed that all sharing with other professionals is permitted. There must be a genuine need to know, not merely curiosity.[42] The Health Service Commissioner, supported by the Select Committee to which he reports, has stated that it is improper for a patient's previous doctor to be allowed to see records made after she or he ceased to care for the patient in question.[43] The Department of Health has accepted this view and advised FPCs (now Health Authorities) that GPs who wish to refresh their memories of incidents in relation to which a complaint has been made may see only the relevant part of records, not all of them.[44]

However, it should also be noted that it is not only health professionals who may need to know confidential information in order to provide patients with their care. Within health services, clerical staff will need to be able to process records. There will often also be a need for liaison with social services, particularly where a patient is receiving care in the community.[45] It may even be possible that relatives will need to know confidential information in order to play their part in a patient's care.

---

[39] *The Protection and the Use of Patient Information* (London: DoH, 1996), para. 1.2.

[40] Annex A. There is some discussion of the problem in Data Protection Registrar, *Tenth Report*, HC Pap. (1993–4) 453, 12.

[41] Para. 4.4, although the drafting of para. 4.15 is a little less clear on this point. The GMC is clearer: 'if a patient does not wish you to share particular information with other members of the team you must respect those wishes'. See *Confidentiality* (London: GMC, 1995), para. 7.

[42] *Birmingham CC* v. *O* [1983] 1 All ER 497.

[43] Select Committee on the PCA, n. 8 above, paras. 57–60.

[44] DHSS, *Confidentiality of Medical Records* (FPCL 80/88).

[45] The NHS and the agencies usually have statutory duties to co-operate: see e.g. Children Act 1989 (s. 27), Education Act 1996 (s. 322), Mental Health Act 1983 (s. 117).

(iii) The Public Interest I: Threats of Serious Harm to Other

The final general exception to confidentiality arises where the pub_ in disclosure outweighs the public interest in ensuring confidentiality. This does not oblige health professionals to breach confidence, but permits them to do so if they judge it necessary. It is hard to define the precise scope of the exception. There have been few decided cases on its application in the context of health care. Further, the exact scope of the exception may depend on the legal basis on which confidentiality rests.[46]

One strand of the public interest exception emphasizes the position of the people claiming confidentiality. Where they themselves present a threat to the public interest, they cannot rely on the protection of the law. In relation to the equitable jurisdiction, this is a consequence of the fact that equitable remedies are discretionary and will not be available to those who have behaved improperly. In a non-medical context, it has been said that courts will not allow confidentiality to 'restrain the exposure of fraud, criminal conduct, iniquity'.[47] This suggests that health professionals may reveal confidential information when they believe that it is necessary to expose their patients' wrongdoing.

This would justify informing the social services or police when evidence comes to light in confidential consultations to suggest that a patient may be abusing a child. There can be no doubt that breaching confidence would be lawful in such circumstances.[48] Some would go further and argue that there is an obligation to disclose information relating to child protection. The General Medical Council has adopted this position.[49] However, it is difficult to show that a legal obligation exists. Some find support for such a duty in the obligation of health authorities to co-operate with local authorities when requested to do so in order to assist them in carrying out their functions under the Children Act 1989.[50] However, the duty to assist relates only to functions under Part III of the Children Act 1989, which does not contain the child protection functions such as the duty to investigate information indicating that intervention may be necessary. Further, the duty to assist does not prevail if it would 'unduly prejudice' the discharge of a health authority's

---

[46] Y. Cripps, 'The Public Interest Defence to the Action for Breach of Confidence and the Law Commission's Proposals on Disclosure in the Public Interest' (1984) 4 *OJLS* 361–92.

[47] *Lion Laboratories* v. *Evans*, n. 25 above, 431.

[48] *Re M* [1990] 1 All ER 205, 213; Department of Health, *Working Together* (London: HMSO, 1988), para. 3.11.

[49] General Medical Council, *Annual Report for 1987* (London: GMC, 1987), para. 3.12; see also GMC, *Confidentiality*, n. 40 above, para. 11.

[50] Children Act 1989, s. 27.

functions.[51] It might be argued that a duty to breach confidentiality would prejudice the provision of health services by discouraging people from seeking help.

While the Children Act 1989 may not provide an obligation to disclose confidential information in order to protect children, there are some indications that the courts may be moving towards that result. In 1989 the Court of Appeal suggested that courts hearing domestic cases in which it became apparent that a child might be at risk should consider alerting the relevant social service department.[52] More recently, judges have said that where solicitors have information relating to the welfare of a child, they should disclose it to the court.[53] This suggests that the courts may be moving towards a duty to disclose. However, there has been no binding ruling on the point; indeed the House of Lords had the opportunity to decide the matter and declined to exercise it.[54] The cases have been concerned with the disclosure of information to parties during legal proceedings. The situation may well be different when there is no immediate prospect of a court hearing. The Law Society has taken the view that the cases are limited to the disclosure of experts' reports in care proceedings, and that the normal rules of confidentiality and legal professional privilege are otherwise unaffected.[55] The more general advice previously issued by the Law Society emphasizes that solicitors have a *discretion* to disclose information about child abuse.[56] They do not consider it a professional duty to do so. Even if the judiciary is developing a legal duty to disclose information relating to child abuse, it cannot be said that it is yet established.

The approach based on culpability of the patient can be extended to cases where the activities of patients present a threat to other people. Whether or not the patient is blameworthy has perhaps become less important than the degree of risk presented to others. The GMC guidance is that disclosure would be permitted to prevent a risk of death or serious harm.[57] The most illuminating case is that of *W v. Egdell*.[58] W had been convicted of manslaughter after multiple killings in circumstances of extreme violence. He was detained under the Mental Health Act 1983 as a patient in a secure hospital. Dr Egdell was instructed by solicitors acting on behalf of W to prepare a psychiatric

[51] S. 27(2), see *R. v. Northavon, ex p. Smith* [1994] 3 All ER 313.

[52] *G v. G* [1990] 1 FLR 395, 399.

[53] *Re DH* [1994] 1 FLR 679 (FD), *Re R* [1993] 4 All ER 702 (FD). See also *Oxfordshire CC v. M* [1994] 2 All ER 269 (CA) which probably implicitly adopted this approach. *Barking & Dagenham LBC v. O* [1993] 4 All ER 59 (FD) goes the other way.

[54] *Re L* [1996] 2 All ER 78.

[55] Law Society, 'Disclosure or Reports in Children's Cases' [1994] *Fam. L.* 540.

[56] Law Society, 'Confidentiality and Privilege—Child Abuse and Abduction' [1991] *Fam. L* 461].

[57] GMC, *Confidentiality*, n. 40 above, para. 18.

[58] N. 22 above. *R. v. Crozier* (1991) 8 BMLR 128, [1991] Crim. LR 138, was a similar case with the same result.

report for use before a mental health review tribunal. The doctor's opinion was that W remained highly dangerous and showed a persistent interest in explosives that was being disregarded by those caring for him. On receipt of his report, the application by W to the mental health review tribunal was dropped.

Dr Egdell believed that the contents of his report should be made available both to the medical director of the hospital caring for W and also to the Home Office. The former was responsible for the patient's care, the latter for ensuring that the public was not endangered by his early release. W applied to the court for an injunction preventing the disclosure of the report. The Court of Appeal refused to prevent the disclosure of the report. Their Lordships found that the public interest justified disclosure to the medical director and also to the Home Office. The report contained information as to W's dangerousness that was not known to these parties. To suppress it would have prevented material relevant to public safety from reaching the authorities responsible for protecting it. It was in the public interest to ensure that they took decisions on the need for such protection on the basis of the best available information. Consequently, in these circumstances, the public interest in protecting the public from violence took precedence over the general public interest in ensuring the confidentiality of medical consultations.

The *Egdell* case establishes that professionals may disclose confidences in order to protect members of the public. The exact scope of this licence is not clear, but three general guidelines emerge from the case law taken as a whole. First, it is probable that a real and serious risk of danger to the public must be shown before the public interest exception is made out. The public interest exception can only justify disclosure so long as the threat persists. Thus, where a drug created a risk to the public this would justify exposing it while it was on the market, but not once it was withdrawn.[59]

Secondly, disclosure must be to a person with a legitimate interest in receiving the information.[60] In *W* v. *Egdell* the Court of Appeal talked of disclosure to 'the responsible authorities'.[61] Thus criminal matters should usually be reported only to the police, although in some circumstances wider publicity through the press may be justifiable provided that it serves the public interest better.[62] Dr Egdell's case indicated that while it was legitimate to release information to the doctors treating the patient and to the Home Secretary, it would

[59] *Schering Chemicals* v. *Falkman Ltd* [1981] 2 All ER 321, 337, *per* Shaw LJ. See also *Distillers Co.* (*Biochemicals*) *Ltd* v. *Times Newspapers Ltd* [1975] 1 All ER 41.

[60] For cases from a non-health care context, see *Initial Services* v. *Putterill* [1968] 1 QB 396, 406; *Francombe* v. *Mirror Group Newspapers* [1984] 2 All ER 408, 413; *Lion Laboratories* v. *Evans*, n. 25 above, 423.

[61] N. 22 above, 853, *per* Bingham LJ.

[62] Department of Health, *Guidance for Staff on Relations with the Public and the Media*, EL(93)51.

have been a breach of confidence to sell it to a newspaper or to publish details that could have identified the patient in a professional journal.[63]

Thirdly, even where the public interest requires disclosure, it is necessary to confine it to the extent strictly necessary.[64] The fact that it is in the public interest to reveal some aspects of a patient's situation does not justify disclosing all his or her details. This does not prevent revealing further information that helps to explain the situation.[65] If breach of confidence is justified, it must be of a nature that permits a proper assessment of the position.

The application of the public interest exception to notification of HIV status has been the subject of much debate.[66] Disclosure of a patient's HIV status has been considered principally in relation, first, to those caring for them, and, secondly, to their sexual partners. Concern has also been raised about the rights of patients to know if the professionals caring for them are HIV positive. The legal principles discussed above suggest that the consequences of HIV infection are sufficiently serious to justify disclosure, providing that two conditions are satisfied: first, that there is a real risk to the people to be informed; secondly, that disclosure is the only practical way to protect them. Although there has been some discussion of a duty, and not merely a discretion, to warn those at risk, there is no indication that English law would adopt such a duty.[67]

In relation to health professionals caring for HIV positive patients, the degree of risk may not be that high, either of transmission by health workers to patients or vice versa. It will perhaps therefore be rare for disclosure to be justified. Sexual partners will be more vulnerable if they practise 'unsafe' sex than if their activities are low risk. It is likely that disclosure would be justified in law if the professional believes the risk to be real. It is important to recognize, however, that it would need to be shown that it would have been unreasonable to seek to manage the risk of transmission without disclosure. Thus, with disclosure to health professionals, consideration should be given to whether proper precautions would minimize the risk without HIV status being known. The general principles of confidentiality would also indicate

---

[63] N. 22 above, 848. See also Scott J at first instance, n. 37 above, 1102.

[64] X v. Y, n. 7 above, 656–7.   [65] N. 22 above, 853, *per* Bingham LJ.

[66] There are no relevant legal authorities, but see Department of Health, *AIDS—HIV Infected Health Care Workers: Practical Guidance on Notifying Patients* (London: DoH, 1993) and Department of Health, *Guidance on Partner Notification for HIV Infection,* PLICO (92)5; BMA, *Medical Ethics Today* (London: BMJ Publishing Group, 1993), 59–60; GMC, *HIV Notification and AIDS: The Ethical Considerations* (London: GMC, 1993), reprinted at BME No 90 8–11; GMC, *HIV and AIDS: The Ethical Consideration* (London: GMC, 1995), paras. 15–19; R. Gillon, 'AIDS and Medical Confidentiality' (1987) 294 *BMJ* 1675; K. M. Boyd, 'HIV Infection and AIDS: The Ethics of Medical Confidentiality' (1992) 18 *JME* 173.

[67] The best reviews are probably M. Jones, *Medical Negligence* (2nd edn., London: Sweet & Maxwell, 1996), paras. 2.77–2.86 and A. Grubb, and D. Pearl, *Blood Testing, AIDS and DNA Profiling* (Bristol: Family Law, 1990), 48–57.

that disclosure of the HIV status of health workers should be restricted to that necessary to protect patients. It may, therefore, be quite proper to restrict disclosure to NHS managers in order to ensure that the health worker does not undertake high risk tasks.

(iv) Public Interest II: Public Debate and Press Freedom

A second category where confidentiality is in conflict with other aspects of the public interest concerns the desirability of debate on matters of medical ethics. Here the dominant public interest is press freedom, protected by Article 10 of the European Convention on Human Rights. Free speech will be restricted only where the requirements of confidentiality are particularly strong.[68] In *X* v. *Y*[69] a newspaper had discovered that two doctors were being treated for AIDS. The hospital where they were being treated sought an injunction to prevent the information being made public. It was clear that it had been obtained in breach of confidence, but the newspaper argued that it was in the public interest that there should be a full debate on the implications of health professionals being HIV positive. It further argued that highlighting the case that had come to light was a contribution to that debate. The judge accepted that there was a public interest in the ethical debate. However, he noted that not all matters in which the public was interested came into this category, and he made it clear that it was for the court to judge whether it was in the public interest that a debate should occur in the press.

In the circumstances of the case, that public interest had to be weighed against three competing principles:[70] first, the principle that hospital records should remain confidential; secondly, the public interest in ensuring that employees did not disclose confidential information obtained in the course of their employment—this arose because the source of the newspaper's information had been a hospital employee; thirdly, the particular need to guarantee that AIDS sufferers could use hospitals without this fact being revealed. Considering these factors the judge ordered the newspaper to keep the information secret. He noted that there was already a wide-ranging public debate about AIDS. In his view, depriving the public of the information that was the subject of the case was of minimal significance in the wider context of that debate.

The courts have been called upon to make similar judgments in a number of cases concerning children. Where a child is a ward of court no publicity is permitted without the permission of the court. Consequently, if the press wishes to report a case, the judge must consider whether the public interest in

---

[68] See Hoffman LJ in *R.* v. *Central TV* [1994] 3 All ER 641, 651 ff.
[69] N. 7 above.   [70] *Ibid.*, 660.

debate outweighs the child's need for privacy. The case law yields a number of useful indications of the way in which press freedom and confidentiality should be balanced. Where a public debate is required, only the information necessary to inform that debate should be disclosed.[71] In particular, consideration will be given to whether the identities of the people involved need to be disclosed to allow debate.[72] The degree of harm that would be suffered by the child if information were disclosed must be considered. Where it is minimal, then it is likely that the interests of press freedom will prevail.[73] Where restrictions of press debate are needed, they must be no wider than necessary.[74] Once information is in the public domain, further restrictions in the name of confidentiality become otiose.[75] It should be noted, however, that the Court of Appeal has hinted that this line of cases may go too far in restricting the freedom of the press.[76]

(v) Public Interest III: Residual Problems

There are a number of areas where difficulties arise in relation to the limits of confidentiality, and where, if disclosure is justifiable, it can only be on the basis of the public-interest exception. The Department of Health guidance on confidentiality suggests that there are such public interest justifications for disclosing confidential information for the NHS purposes of public accountability, monitoring (e.g. statistical analysis of services and reporting of adverse drug reactions), and research and development.[77] There is no clear legal authority for such disclosures without patient consent. However, an analogy might be drawn with banking, where it has long been established that confidential customer information may be disclosed where the 'interests of the bank require' it.[78] This might be taken to justify the use of confidential information to ensure the proper workings of the bank. The main examples given, however, concern the bank's ability to protect itself against actions by the customer or third parties. Nevertheless, one judge suggested that it would be legitimate to disclose information to protect the public against fraud or crime,[79] and this might be taken to justify the Department of Health's public accountability ground.

---

[71] *Re C (No 2)* [1989] 2 All ER 791. This conclusion was reached on the basis of the medical obligation of confidentiality as well as the particular law concerning children.

[72] *Re W* [1992] 1 All ER 794, 797.

[73] *Re X* [1992] 2 All ER 595. Compare *Re T, The Times*, 4 Oct. 1989 with *Re C (No 2)*, n. 71 above.

[74] *Re W*, n. 72 above, 797; *Re M*, n. 48 above, 211, 215.

[75] *Cumbria County School* v. *X, The Times*, 25 June 1990.   [76] *R.* v. *Central TV*, n. 68 above.

[77] Para. 1.2. This is different from the 'need to know' justification in that it is not the patient's immediate care that the information assists, but the proper working of the system.

[78] *Tournier* v. *National Provincial & Union Bank of England*, n. 36 above, 473.

[79] *Per* Lord Atkin at 486.

Another difficult area concerns the rights of those unable to give consent to disclosure due to mental incapacity. It is clear that competent adults would often wish to allow details of their conditions and care to be discussed with friends and relatives. It is probable that the courts would regard such disclosure in relation to incompetent patients as permissible where professionals judge that it would be in the patients' interests. In *F* v. *W. Berkshire HA* Lords Bridge and Brandon observed that it would be bad law which prevented incompetent patients being cared for properly merely because they could not consent.[80] The solution was to permit professionals to act in their patients' best interests, subject to the safeguard that their assessment of those interests must not be negligent. The same approach could be taken to disclosing confidential information in the best interests of an incompetent patient, but the matter has not been specifically addressed by a court.

An emerging area of difficulty concerns genetic information.[81] Traditionally the relationship between patient and doctor has been seen as essentially personal. However, where diagnosis and counselling of patients is based on genetic inheritance, it is not always possible to proceed without information about other members of the family. Patients may therefore want their doctors to obtain confidential information about their relatives' genetic make-up in order to discover the magnitude of the risk that they, or their children, might carry genetic disease. In turn, doctors may realize that a relative of their patient should be offered counselling, but would need to reveal something of their patient's position in order to offer it.

The difficulty here is that the relatives are not threatened by maintaining the confidentiality of the patient's information (which might come within the well-established public interest exception). Rather, they are denied an opportunity to benefit. English law is generally reluctant to force people to assist others, and this distinction between protection from harm and conferring a benefit may be the key factor. If it is, then it would allow patients to refuse to permit their relatives to know information about their genetic status. On the other hand, it could be argued that relatives have a legitimate interest in receiving the information in order to make better informed choices about, for example, having children. If the law of confidentiality aims to identify where the balance of public interest lies, then it might be easier to suggest that genetic medicine is a special case where a less individualistic approach to confidentiality is appropriate. However, if the foundation of confidentiality is the

[80] [1989] 2 All ER 545, 548–9, 551.

[81] P. Boddington, 'Confidentiality in Genetic Counselling' in A. Clarke (ed.), *Genetic Counselling* (London: Routledge, 1994); I. Pullen, 'Patients, Families and Genetic Information' in E. Sutherland and A. McCall Smith (eds.), *Family Rights: Family Law and Medical Advance* (Edinburgh: Edinburgh University Press, 1990); Nuffield Council on Bioethics, *Genetic Screening: Ethical Issues* (London: Nuffield Council of Bioethics, 1993), ch. 5.

rights of the patient, and these must be shown to be outweighed by other factors, then disclosure will be more difficult to justify.

Many problems relating to confidentiality are addressed more quickly by the professions than the courts. The final problem to be discussed under the heading of the public-interest exception concerns the significance of the conclusions reached by professional bodies in the reasoning of the courts. Such guidelines are often made under statutory powers, but that does not mean that their content has any statutory authority.[82] In *W* v. *Egdell* the Court of Appeal considered two of the exceptions recognized by the GMC's guidance on confidentiality, 'need to know', and the public interest, and found that they are compatible with the law. In principle the validity of those exceptions is derived from the law, not from the guidelines. The relevant law has been discussed above. However, it is of interest that, in *W* v. *Egdell*, Sir Stephen Brown seems to regard Dr Egdell as acting legally because he falls within the terms of the GMC's guidance without needing to consider the law directly.[83] In the same case, Bingham LJ discusses the intention of the draftsman of one paragraph of the guidance as if it were a statute to be construed.[84] In *Re C*[85] the fact that the GMC believed that the obligation of confidence endured after the death of the patient was regarded as significant in interpreting the law.

The judges have, therefore, shown willingness to use the professional guidance as an influential guide to legal interpretation. Despite its uncertain legal status. It might be suggested that untested exceptions that are accepted by the professions are likely to be looked upon favourably by the courts. This is entirely consistent with legal principle if the basis of confidentiality is to be found in the tort of negligence, because that relies on professional standards. However, the equitable obligation of confidence is based upon public policy, and should not follow the professional lead slavishly. It remains to be seen how the law will develop in this respect.

(vi) Specific Statutory Provisions

It is also necessary to consider the increasing range of cases where specific statutory regimes apply, some of which go so far as to require disclosure. The notification of births and deaths is discussed in Chapters 17 and 20. Provisions relating to information on infertility treatment and children born as a result are discussed in Chapter 16. Many of the statutory provisions are designed to facilitate centralized planning and the collation of statistics or to assist in monitoring the operation of the law. The legislation covering notifiable diseases is discussed in Chapter 2. Notice of terminations of pregnancy

---

[82] *W* v. *Egdell*, n. 22 above, 843. See also *Re C* [1991] 2 FLR 478.   [83] N. 22 above, 846.
[84] *Ibid.*, 850.   [85] [1996] 1 FCR 605, 608.

under the Abortion Act 1967, including the name and address of the woman concerned, must be given to the relevant Chief Medical Officer.[86] Doctors who treat drug addicts are required to inform the Home Office of their names, addresses, sex, dates of birth, NHS numbers, and drugs to which they are addicted.[87] This must be done within seven days. Notification is not required if the doctor believes that it is necessary to continue administering the drug to treat an organic disease or injury. Nor is it necessary if the particulars have been notified in the previous twelve months. Poisonings and serious work accidents must also be reported.[88]

Other provisions cover doctors who remove certain organs for transplant or who implant donated organs of these types. They are required to report the details, including the names and hospital numbers of the donor and recipient, to the relevant health authority and to the United Kingdom Transplant Support Service Authority.[89] The organs in question are defined as the kidney, heart, lung, pancreas, and liver. Under the AIDS (Control) Act 1987 health authorities must provide anonymized information on patients with AIDS. The Act does not oblige individual practitioners to report cases and the notification provisions of the Public Health Act 1984 do not apply to AIDS.

The Children Act 1989 requires health authorities, residential care homes, nursing and mental nursing homes to inform local authorities when a child is accommodated with them for a consecutive period of more than three months or when they intend to look after a child for this long.[90] They are also obliged to inform the local authority in whose area the child intends to live when a child over the age of 16, whom they have looked after for more than three months, leaves them.[91] Inspectors of premises accommodating children, appointed under section 80 of the Act, have the right to information about any children living there as well as the condition of the premises.[92]

One difficult area concerns the status of the police. There is no general obligation on health professionals to disclose confidential information in order to assist the police with the investigation of crimes.[93] However, a number of specific statutory obligations to do so exist. Like any other citizen, health professionals are bound by law to provide the police, on request, with any information that might identify a driver who is alleged to have

---

[86] Abortion Regulations 1991, SI 1991 No 499. R. 5 restricts the disclosure of this information by the Chief Medical Officer to specified circumstances.

[87] Misuse of Drugs (Notification of Supply to Addicts Regulations 1973, SI 1973 No 799.

[88] Health and Safety at Work Act 1974; Reporting of Injuries, Diseases, and Dangerous Occurrences Regulations 1985, SI 1985 No 2023 as amended.

[89] Human Organ Transplants Act 1989, s. 3; Human Organ Transplants (Supply of Information) Regulations 1989, SI 1989 No 2108 (as amended by SI 1991 No 408).

[90] Children Act 1989, ss. 85, 86.   [91] *Ibid.*, s. 24.   [92] *Ibid.*, s. 80.

[93] *Sykes* v. *DPP* [1962] AC 528, 564, *per* Lord Denning.

committed a traffic offence.[94] They are also bound to disclose to the police as soon as possible any information that they have that may help prevent an act of terrorism connected with Northern Ireland or assist in apprehending or prosecuting such terrorists.[95] The lack of a general duty to assist the police does not permit obstructing police investigations, but refusing to answer their questions with a 'lawful excuse' does not constitute obstruction.[96] The obligation of confidence would probably constitute such an excuse. However, concealing information for gain is a crime in its own right.[97]

It may be that the general public interest exception applies to permit disclosure even in the absence of such statutory provisions. But this leaves the choice in the hands of the health professional. The British Medical Association has issued advice on the disclosure of confidential information to the police.[98] It suggests that doctors should consider informing the police only where the offence is grave, the prevention or detection of the crime will be seriously delayed or prejudiced if they do not do so, and the only use to which the information will be put is the detection and prosecution of the alleged criminal. It also advises that doctors should satisfy themselves that any material that they release will be destroyed after it has been used. The Department of Health gives essentially the same advice, but also includes examples of what it regards as sufficiently serious crimes; treason, murder, manslaughter, rape, kidnapping, some sexual offences, causing an explosion, some firearms offences, hostage-taking, hijacking, causing death by reckless driving.[99]

Special recognition is given to the need to preserve medical confidentiality in the Police and Criminal Evidence Act 1984. While most types of evidence can be obtained by the police under a magistrate's warrant, health records are 'excluded material' within section 9 of the Act. This means that an order for their seizure, with a right to enter premises and search for them if necessary, can only be made, in limited circumstances, by a circuit judge.[100] Excluded material includes personal records relating to physical and mental health as well as diagnostic samples.[101] In R. v. *Cardiff Crown Court, ex p. Kellam* it was held that this category is not restricted to the nursing and medical notes, and includes hospital administrative records that can identify patients.[102] The limitations imposed by section 11 do not prevent the voluntary disclosure of documents.[103]

---

[94] Road Traffic Act 1988, s. 172; *Hunter* v. *Mann* [1974] QB 767.
[95] Prevention of Terrorism (Temporary Provisions) Act 1989, s. 18.
[96] *Rice* v. *Connolly* [1966] 2 All ER 649.   [97] Criminal Law Act 1967, s. 5(1).
[98] BMA, *Philosophy and Practice of Medical Ethics* (London: BMA, 1988), 23–4.
[99] DoH, *The Protection and Use of Patient Information*, n. 39 above, paras. 5.8, 5.9, and Annex D.
[100] Police and Criminal Evidence Act 1984, s. 9 and Sch. 1.
[101] *Ibid.*, ss. 11,(1), 12(a).   [102] (1993) 16 BMLR 76.
[103] *R.* v. *Singleton, The Times,* 22 June 1994.

(vii) Confidentiality and Court Proceedings

Finally, if matters get to court, then it is clear that the public interest in the efficient conduct of justice overrides the obligation of confidentiality. The confidentiality of health information must be distinguished from legal privilege. Privilege is used to describe cases where the need for secrecy prevents even a court receiving the information. However, this applies only to communications between lawyers and their clients, and health care is not one of the circumstances in which privilege can be claimed. Accordingly, health professionals have no right to withhold confidential information from a court when called as witness. It is legitimate to ask permission from the judge to decline to answer a question because it would involve breaching confidence, but if the judge requires it the information must be revealed.[104] Failure to do so would leave the health professional in contempt of court, an offence punishable by imprisonment. In children's cases the obligation of medical confidentiality is also said to be outweighed by the need to put all information relating to the child's welfare before the court.[105] Kinder to the health professions, it should also be observed that the public interest in justice being performed permits hospitals to reveal confidential information in order to defend themselves in legal proceedings. This also would cover revealing the details of treatment sufficiently to sue for fees in private practice.[106]

C. Accountability for Unwarranted Breach of Confidence

One reason for the comparative dearth of legal cases on confidentiality in the context of health care, despite its wide acceptance, is the limited nature of the remedies. The law provides two remedies: an action for damages, and injunctions prohibiting the disclosure of confidential information. The former will only be available where the breach of confidence has caused financial loss to the patient. This will rarely be the case because breach of medical confidence mostly leads to embarrassment rather than pecuniary damage. Injunctions are of use only where the possibility of a breach is known in advance. In practice, this is not usually the case and where it is patients can usually confront

---

[104] *AG* v. *Mulholland* [1962] 2 QB 477, 489; *Hunter* v. *Mann* [1974] QB 767; *D* v. *NSPCC* [1978] AC 171, 244–6.

[105] *Re C*, n. 82 above (confidential medical information about mother to be disclosed to court in adoption proceedings).

[106] *Tournier* v. *National Provincial and Union Bank of England*, n. 36 above.

the health professionals and persuade them to respect their privacy without recourse to the courts.

Alternative remedies for breach of confidence lie with employers and the professional bodies. In extreme cases, the latter can revoke practitioners' registration. However, where this professional misconduct must be 'serious' before they have jurisdiction, as in medicine, such action is unlikely. These disciplinary procedures can be brought into play even where a patient has not suffered because of the breach of confidence. Employers can discipline and ultimately dismiss employees who fail to preserve patients' confidentiality. In practice, the disciplinary procedures operated by employers are most likely to be used to vindicate patients' rights.

In reality, the most solid foundation of confidentiality is the fact that it is accepted by the professions. The availability of sanctions cannot explain this acceptance because the likelihood of their being applied is too remote. The strength of the obligation depends on the moral and practical arguments that underpin the codes of professional ethics rather than its formal recognition in those codes and in law. We have seen that in many areas the law is uncertain. The professional codes are often much clearer. The easier availability of sanctions means that they are more likely to be called upon in practice. They therefore need to be discussed in their own right.

D. Professionally Recognized Limits to Confidentiality

All the health professions require their members to respect the confidences of their clients and each one defines the exceptions in its own terms. The principles governing nurses and doctors are discussed below. Breach of the professional obligation may lead to an accusation of professional misconduct and, if proved, may result in serious cases in removal from the relevant register. This can occur even if the patient concerned does not suffer any damage as a result of the disclosure, and for this reason will often provide a sanction when court action cannot be taken.

Nurses, midwives, and health visitors are obliged to keep their patients' confidences in all save three categories of circumstance. These are where the patient consents, where a court order requires it, and where disclosure is justified in the wider public interest.[107] The previous edition of the *Code of Professional Conduct* also included an exception where disclosure is required

---

[107] UKCC, *Code of Professional Conduct* (3rd edn., London: UKCC, 1992), cl. 10.

by law.[108] It is unclear whether the UKCC intends to penalize nurses who disclose information when required by law to do so. If this were to happen it is likely that an action for judicial review could be brought to vindicate the nurses' actions. It has been clearly stated that professional confidences based on contract are overridden by the obligation to obey the law.[109] It would be an improper exercise of the UKCC's statutory powers to contradict that position. Probably, the 'public interest' exception should be interpreted as embracing areas where disclosure is required by statute.

The UKCC has published an elaboration of the confidentiality clause contained in the *Code*, which remains an important source of guidance.[110] It emphasizes that disclosure should be regarded as exceptional, that nurses should consider the circumstances carefully before concluding that it is justified, and recommends consultation with other professionals. It gives as examples of cases where Council recognizes that the public interest might outweigh the normal principle of confidentiality those involving serious crime, child abuse, and drug trafficking. The UKCC's guidance also advises that a failure to take steps to prevent the accidental disclosure of information can constitute professional misconduct. The Royal College of Nursing has advised nurses that they should therefore avoid giving information over the telephone whenever possible as 'it is difficult, if not impossible, to identify callers, and . . . conversations can be overheard'.[111] Nurses must also be careful to protect confidentiality in circumstances when access by non-professionals might be feared, such as employee's records in occupational health settings.[112]

In many respects, the guidance offered by the General Medical Council is similar.[113] It, too, emphasizes the responsibility of doctors to ensure that confidential information remains confidential, not merely to avoid revealing it personally. It emphasizes that the main exception to the principle of secrecy is provided by the patient's authorization. In some circumstances, such as examinations for employment or insurance purposes, doctors are advised to ensure that patients have given their consent in writing before they are examined. Like the UKCC, the GMC advises that disclosure without consent must take place only in exceptional circumstances, preferably only after consultation with an experienced colleague. However, the GMC's list of recognized

[108] *UKCC Code of Professional Conduct* (2nd edn., London: UKCC, 1984) cl. 9.

[109] *Parry-Jones* v. *Law Society* [1969] 1 Ch. 1, 9, *per* Diplock LJ.

[110] UKCC, *Guidelines for Professional Practice* (London: UKCC, 1996), 26–30, superseding *UKCC Confidentiality: An Elaboration of Clause 9 of the Second Edition of the UKCC's Code of Professional Conduct for the Nurse, Midwife and Health Visitor* (London: UKCC, 1987).

[111] RCN, *Guidelines on confidentiality in nursing* (London RCN 1980).

[112] RCN, *Practical Aspects of Confidentiality Relating to the Health of Employees* (London: RCN, 1986).

[113] GMC, *Confidentiality* (London: GMC, 1995). See also 'Filming Patients for Television Programmes' (1995) Issue 7, *GMC News Review* 2.

exceptions is longer than that of its nursing equivalent. It accepts disclosure by court order or statutory authority. It includes a public-interest exception where secrecy would risk death or serious harm to the patient or another person. More controversially it suggests that there may be circumstances when doctors may decide that medical reasons prevent them obtaining the patient's consent. Disclosure to relatives or others is accepted in those cases. It is not clear what 'medical reasons' these might be. There is no clear authority for an exception to the legal obligation of confidence in these circumstances, although one early case involving a banker can be read as suggesting that it was legitimate to breach confidence when the intention was to assist the client and there was a reasonable hope of doing so.[114]

The GMC's guidance also covers three other situations that the nurses' professional body did not discuss. The first concerns research, teaching, and audit. It recognizes that where patients could be identified from the information, then they should be made aware that the information might be used for these purposes and their consent should be obtained. Refusal of consent must be respected. If patients could not be identified, no problem of confidentiality arises. The British Medical Association advises that doctors may permit confidential information relating to their patients to be used in research that has been approved by an ethics committee.[115] This will usually be subject to guarantees that the researchers will ensure that patients cannot be identified from published results and that data will be destroyed when the research is completed. A code of practice has been produced by the Institute of Medical and Biological Illustration to assist in relation to the use of clinical illustrations.[116]

The second situation discussed by the GMC is the responsibilities of doctors to pass information to the Driver and Vehicle Licensing Authority. Appendix 1 to the guidance on confidentiality indicates that doctors who cannot persuade patients who are unfit to drive to inform the authority or stop driving should immediately disclose the relevant medical information to the medical adviser at the DVLA in confidence. This should be a last resort, and the guidance indicates the alternative steps that the doctor should explore before informing the DVLA.

The remaining situation concerns patients who are unable to consent to treatment, because of immaturity, illness, or mental incapacity. In such circumstances, the GMC advises that doctors should try to persuade patients to

---

[114] *Hardy* v. *Veasey* (1868) LR 3 Ex. 107, 112, *per* Kelly CB.

[115] BMA, *Medical Ethics Today*, n. 67 above, para. 2:4.5.

[116] Institute of Medical and Biological Illustration, *Code of Practice on Confidentiality of Illustrative Clinical Records* (London: IMBI, 1988). A summary of this document is to be found in the *Institute of Medical Ethics Bulletin*, No 44, Nov. 1988, 8–9.

permit an appropriate person to be involved in the consultation. If this fails, then doctors may breach confidence, providing that it is essential to the patient's best medical interests. This denies such patients the protection normally accorded to adults. This may be at variance with the legal position in relation to children's rights to confidentiality (see Chapter 12). In one old case the GMC supported a doctor who informed the parents of a 16-year-old girl that she had sought contraceptive advice.[117] This provides an unreliable guide for current practice. It would almost certainly not be followed in respect of a young person of that age today. It is, however, possible that a similar conclusion would be reached where the patient was below the age of 16.

E. Computerized Records

The general legal obligation of confidence is supplemented by the Data Protection Act 1984 where confidential information is stored on computer. Personal information cannot be stored on computer unless the person holding the records is registered under the Act.[118] The entry on the register must include a description of the records and the purpose for which they are held, the sources from which data will be drawn, and the persons to whom data will be disclosed.[119] The Act enshrines a number of basic data-protection principles.[120] These include the need to ensure that information is fairly obtained, accurate, and no more or less detailed than required by the specified purposes. Information may not be stored for purposes other than those specified in the entry on the register. There is also a principle of confidentiality, and information may not be disclosed except to people within the categories described on the register. The Act permits the Secretary of State to supplement these data-protection principles with further safeguards in relation to certain types of personal information, including that relating to physical or mental health.[121]

The Act confers a number of rights on data-subjects (people about whom data is held). They are entitled to have access to their entries, although their rights are restricted by regulations made under the Act (see below).[122] If they suffer damage because information has been disclosed to people other than those specified on the register, then data subjects are entitled to compensation.[123] Compensation is also available in respect of inaccuracies.[124]

The operation of the Act is overseen by the Data Protection Registrar, who

---

[117] *Dr Browne* [1971] *BMJ Supp.* 79–80.   [118] S. 5.   [119] S. 4(3).   [120] Sch. 1.
[121] S. 2(3).
[122] S. 21, 29; Data Protection (Subject Access Modification) Order 1987, SI 1987 No 1903.
[123] S. 23.   [124] S. 22.

has various powers to enforce its provisions. He makes an annual report to Parliament,[125] and has considered health issues in most of these reports. He has suggested that special guidance to supplement the general data-protection principles may be necessary in relation to genetic information.[126] In the *Seventh Report of the Data Protection Registrar* concern was expressed at the implications of the NHS market for data protection,[127] although it also recorded that a survey had found that approximately 90 per cent of those questioned were satisfied that doctors and the NHS could be trusted to keep and use information responsibly.[128] The Registrar's staff have investigated the implications of the 'contract minimum data set' in order to ensure that practice complies with the data-protection principles set out in Schedule 1. Particular concern was expressed that NHS bodies failed to check that patients were aware of the uses to which confidential information about them might be put. Also that they failed to ensure that data were deleted when it was no longer necessary to hold them.[129] The Registrar has suggested that an order under section 2(3) of the Act to supplement those principles may be appropriate and that the basis for it might be a draft code produced by the British Medical Association. The results of consultation with the Department of Health on the drafting of non-statutory guidance were to be considered before any action was taken. That guidance was published in March 1996.

The *Seventh Report* also drew attention to the use of 'smart cards' to carry computerized patient data in machine-readable form. These can enable patients to carry detailed medical records with them, albeit in a form that can be read only by those with the appropriate machinery. Preliminary monitoring of a trial in their use has suggested that they do not give rise to major data-protection problems. However, it can be observed that they make it very difficult to guarantee that confidential information is accessed only when it is necessary. All the information will be available to a 'reader'. Thus if such data cards were to carry all the patient's records, then much wider access would be facilitated than would be usual in medical consultations.[130]

The Data Protection Act 1984 also creates rights of access for those on whom data are held. Within the scheme of the Act, this was primarily to enable data-subjects to check the accuracy of information held about them. On payment of a statutory fee, data subjects are entitled to be supplied with a

---

[125] S. 36(5).

[126] *Tenth Report of the Data Protection Registrar*, HC Pap. 453 (1993–4), 13–14.

[127] (London: HMSO, 1991), 2–3.   [128] At 79.

[129] A summary of the findings is to be found as App. 3 of the *Ninth Report of the Data Protection Registrar*, HC 1992–3, 736.

[130] A discussion of this nascent area, including the EC aspects, can be found in Y. Poullet and M. H. Boulanger, 'Legal Aspects of the Medical Data Card' [1990–1] *Computer Law and Security Report* 3/8–11, 4/25–28, 5/18–23.

copy of any data held on them.[131] These must be supplied within forty days, and the applicant can apply to court for an order forcing the data-holder to comply with the request for access.[132] In the context of health care these provisions introduced a completely new possibility—granting patients a general right of access to their records. Previously this had been possible only in the course of litigation. Since 1984 three new statutes have provided rights of access, and these are discussed later in this Chapter. All the Acts recognize the difficulties of open access to medical records. In relation to computerized records, provision was made for exemptions from the general principle of access to be created by statutory instrument.[133] This power has been exercised and the grounds on which access can be refused can be found in the Data Protection (Subject Access Modification) (Health) Order 1987.[134]

The Order applies to all data consisting of information about a person's physical or mental health either held by, or originally recorded by, a health professional. The definition of health professional includes registered doctors, dentists, opticians, pharmaceutical chemists or druggists, nurses, midwives, health visitors, chiropodists, dieticians, occupational therapists, orthoptists, physiotherapists, osteopaths, and chiropractors.[135] Therapists of various types employed by health authorities are also brought within the definition. If the data-users (persons who hold the computer records) are health professionals, then they can decide whether to permit or refuse access under the principles set out in the next paragraph. It does not matter if they did not record the data themselves. Where the records were made by a health professional, but are not held by one, then the record holder must consult the person who seems to be the appropriate health professional.[136] This person will be the doctor or dentist most recently responsible for the clinical care of the data-subject in relation to the information sought. If more than one person qualifies under this test, then the practitioner who is most suitable to advise in relation to the information sought will be the appropriate professional for the purposes of the Order. If there is no professional with clinical responsibility for the applicant, then any professional with the necessary experience and qualifications may be consulted.[137]

The Order recognizes two grounds on which access may be refused. The first is where it would be likely to cause serious harm to the physical or mental health of the data-subject.[138] The second concerns cases where access would breach the confidences of third parties.[139] Access can be prevented where it would lead to the identification of another individual to whom the

[131] S. 21(1).   [132] S. 21(6), (8).   [133] Data Protection Act 1984, s. 29.
[134] SI 1987 No 1903 as amended.   [135] Art. 2 and Sch.
[136] Art. 4(5).   [137] Art. 4(6).   [138] Art. 4(2)(a).
[139] Art. 4(2)(b).

information relates, or to the identification of the source of data. This justification for refusing access extends to cases where the information on the computer would reveal identities when combined with other information that the data-subject already has or is likely to get. This confidentiality can be waived. Thus, if the third parties consent to the release of the information, access cannot be denied. Nor does the confidentiality extend to cases where the only people identifiable are health professionals involved in the care of the data subject and the information relates to them only in their professional capacity.[140] Where there is a justification for refusing access under these provisions, it covers only that information that comes into the above categories. Other parts of the records must be disclosed.[141]

F. Access to Health Care Information by Patients

Patients have no general common law right to see their health records,[142] but there are now a number of statutory routes by which they may get to see them. The Data Protection Act 1984 introduced specific rights of access only in relation to computerized records. It was some years before the principle of patient access was more widely accepted. Some health professionals argued that patients wanted access and that it would improve the accuracy of records, relieve anxiety, improve communication, and increase trust.[143] Others doubted that patients wanted access, and suggested that they found records difficult to understand, leading to the need to spend considerable amounts of time dispelling misconceptions.[144] The arguments in favour of access have now prevailed, although the process was a gradual one, and there are now four statutes that give rise to rights of access (in addition to the Data Protection Act 1984, discussed above). The first governs the disclosure of records in the course of litigation and is part of the general law rather than specific to the health care context.[145] The second, the Access to Personal Files Act 1987, deals with social work files rather than health care records. However, these files may contain confidential information provided by health professionals. In 1988 a third statute, the Access to Medical Reports Act, conferred rights to see medical reports made for employment and insurance purposes. Finally, a general

---

[140] Art. 3(a).   [141] Art. 4(3)(b).

[142] *R. v. Mid-Glamorgan FHSA, ex p. Martin* [1995] 1 All ER 356 (CA).

[143] M. L. M. Gilhooley and S. M. McGhee, 'Medical Records: Practicalities and Principles of Patient Possession' (1991) 17 *JME* 138–43 provides an introduction to the literature.

[144] A. P. Ross, 'The Case against Showing Patients their Records' (1986) 292 *BMJ* 578.

[145] Supreme Court Act 1981, ss. 33–5.

right of access to health records was created in 1990. Each of these statutory regimes is discussed in turn.

(i) Supreme Court Act 1981

The Supreme Court Act 1981 provides litigants with the means to gain 'discovery' of evidence that they need to make their claim. They need not have actually commenced legal action, because one of the functions of discovery is to provide the information on which the strength of the possible claim can be assessed. However, the court must be satisfied that it is likely that an action will ensue.[146] There must be some prospect of success. Patients will not be granted discovery where their claims are 'ill-founded, irresponsible and speculative allegations based merely on hope'.[147] The chances need not be good, but the actions must not be doomed to failure.[148] The true chances will not be clear until the evidence is made available and any assessment will necessarily be uncertain. Once an action has commenced, discovery from the other parties is possible under the rules of court.[149] Further, once proceedings are under way, the Supreme Court Act 1981 provides the court with power to order discovery in relation to documents held by third parties.[150]

The courts will not allow these powers to be used for general 'fishing expeditions' when the applicants do not know what they are looking for and hope that a trawl will bring something useful to light. Sometimes, professionals may be worried that it will be detrimental to their patients' health to know what is in their records. Where appropriate the court can order that discovery is made to the patients' advisers, not the patients themselves.[151] At one stage it was suggested that records should be disclosed only to a doctor nominated by the patient.[152] However, under the 1981 Act, the court cannot prevent the patients' lawyers receiving the documents.

In practice, records will normally be released without recourse to the court where the defendants are satisfied that there is a genuine basis for the request to see them. The courts have indicated that it is good practice to make disclosure at an early stage.[153] In relation to records made after November 1991, this practice will be reinforced by the fact that patients will be entitled to see their records under the Access to Health Records Act 1990. However, in some circumstances, documents may have legal privilege, and if this is the case

---

[146] S. 33(2).

[147] *Dunning* v. *Board of Governors of the United Liverpool Hospitals* [1973] 2 All ER 454, 460.

[148] *Harris* v. *Newcastle HA* [1989] 2 All ER 273, 277.   [149] RSC O. 24.

[150] S. 34.   [151] S. 33(2).

[152] e.g. *Dunning* v. *Board of Governors of the United Liverpool Hospitals*, n. 147 above, 460. See *McIvor* v. *Southern Health and Social Services Board* [1978] 2 All ER 625 for the rejection of this view.

[153] *Naylor* v. *Preston AHA* [1987] 2 All ER 353.

discovery cannot be ordered.[154] This is the case where the document was produced in order to assist the fighting of the action. Litigants are thus entitled to collect evidence to support their case and seek legal advice knowing that they will not be forced to reveal what they say to their opponents. This will not protect incident reports that are made partly with a view to possible legal proceedings, but primarily to allow steps to be taken to prevent recurrence.[155]

(ii) Access to Personal Files Act 1987

The Access to Personal Files Act 1987 applies to files held by housing and local authorities that contain personal information. It is relevant for health care law because some of those files, particularly those held by social services departments will contain confidential health information. Regulations made under the Act require the authorities to permit people to have access to their files. However, they contain specific safeguards where information originated from a health professional.[156] Health professional is widely defined, and covers registered doctors, dentists, opticians, pharmaceutical chemists, nurses, midwives, health visitors, chiropodists, dieticians, occupational therapists, orthoptists, physiotherapists, osteopaths, chiropractors, and other therapists employed by NHS trusts.[157] Where a health professional is the source of the information, then access will not be permitted before the appropriate professional has informed the local authority whether there is a health ground for withholding the information. Those grounds are that disclosure would be likely to cause serious harm to the health either of the person seeking access or any other. There is also an exemption for information that would identify the informants.[158] The appropriate professional will be the doctor or dentist most recently responsible for the person's care. In the absence of such a person, an appropriately qualified health professional can take the decision.[159]

(iii) Access to Medical Reports Act 1988

The Access to Medical Reports Act 1988 applies to reports supplied by a medical practitioner for employment or insurance purposes.[160] It obliges those commissioning reports to seek the permission of the subject. It also gives the

[154] *Lee* v. *S.W. Thames* RHA [1985] 2 All ER 385.

[155] *Lask* v. *Gloucester HA* [1991] 2 Med. LR 379.

[156] Access to Personal Files (Social Services) Regulations 1989, SI 1989 No 206, as amended, r. 8. Access to Personal Files (Housing) Regulations 1989, SI 1989 No 503, as amended. The Social Services regulations are discussed in the text, but the provisions are essentially the same.

[157] Sch.   [158] R. 8(4).   [159] R. 8(2).

[160] G. Howard, 'Access to Medical Reports Act 1988: Implications for Practitioners' (1989) 86/13 *LSG* 22–4; J. Montgomery, 'Access to Medical Reports Act 1988' [1989] *JSWL* 129–33.

subjects of such reports a right to see them before they are sent to employers and insurers, to veto their release, and to append comments on matters that they feel are inaccurate. A right of access is also created to reports that were supplied without the subject exercising the right to see them. This right can be exercised within six months of the supply of the report. The Act came into force on 1 January 1989 and applies to all reports made after that date.[161] There are two ways in which doctors may satisfy the rights of access. They may allow the subject to inspect a copy of the report or they may supply a copy of it. A fee may be charged for making a copy.[162]

The Act clearly covers reports issued by a patient's general practitioner, but there is controversy as to whether it covers reports specially commissioned from an independent doctor. The Parliamentary sponsors of the original bill were advised that only those made by GPs would be included. The Act covers all reports supplied by 'a medical practitioner who is or has been responsible for the clinical care of the individual'.[163] If this means overall responsibility then the argument that only GPs' reports are covered is a strong one. However, the definition of 'care' is very wide and implies that it should not be limited to general practitioners. Under that definition ' "care" includes examination, investigation or diagnosis for the purposes of, or in connection with, any form of medical treatment'.[164] It might appear that a doctor who examines a patient purely for the purposes of an insurance report does not give such care. Yet, all doctors have an ethical obligation to recommend those they examine to have any treatment that seems necessary.[165] In the context of occupational health it has been held that there is a legal duty to protect the health of all those in the workplace, even those who have never consulted the doctor.[166] There is therefore a sense in which all consultations are potentially in connection with treatment and may therefore come within the Act.

The two substantive provisions of the Act concern the granting of permission for reports to be sought and the right to see them. The subject of the report must be notified in writing that a report is to be sought and must give a written consent to the application.[167] The notification must specifically inform individuals of their rights under the Act.[168] If they indicate that they wish to exercise their right to see the report before it is supplied, the person applying for the report must tell the doctor that this is the case and notify the subject of the report when he or she approaches the doctor. The notification sent to both doctor and subject must explain the way in which the right to see the report operates.[169] People who initially decided that they did not want to

---

[161] S. 10.   [162] S. 4(4).   [163] S. 2(1).   [164] *Ibid.*
[165] BMA, *Handbook of Medical Ethics* (London: BMA, 1984), para. 3.15.
[166] *Stokes* v. *Guest Keen* [1968] 1 WLR 1776.   [167] S. 3(1), read with s. 9.
[168] S. 3(2).   [169] S. 4(1).

see the report before it was sent off may change their minds by writing to the doctor concerned.[170]

Where the subjects of reports indicate that they wish to see them, doctors must wait for at least twenty-one days before sending the reports to the employer or insurer.[171] If, after this time, they have heard nothing from the subject in relation to arranging access, they may then supply the reports. Where subjects have seen reports, then they may not be sent off without the written permission of the subject.[172] Before giving this permission, subjects may ask doctors, in writing, to amend parts of reports that they believe to be incorrect or misleading. Doctors may then amend the reports, and if they decline to do so they must attach to the reports a statement of the patient's views on the disputed matters.[173] Even where reports were not seen before they were sent off, subjects may ask to see them later. Doctors are obliged to retain copies of reports for at least six months.[174] During that period a person may ask to see any report that has been supplied that relates to him or her.[175]

The right to see medical reports under the 1988 Act is not absolute. Doctors may refuse access to information that they believe would be likely to cause serious harm to the physical or mental health of the individual seeking it, or to others. They may also refuse to let a person see information that would indicate the practitioner's intentions towards a patient.[176] Access may also be refused in order to maintain the confidentiality of the doctor's informants. In addition, where permitting access to the report would disclose information about a third party, then it need not be permitted. In both these cases, the exception to the right to see the reports does not apply if the other person was a health professional involved with the person's care, or he or she has consented to the information being revealed.[177] All these exceptions to the general principle of access can be applied to parts of a report, as well as the report as a whole. Where doctors decline to allow access, they must inform the subject that they are doing so,[178] otherwise it might not be apparent that some of the report is missing.

(iv) Access to Health Records Act 1990

The Access to Health Records Act 1990 covers manual health records made since 1 November 1991. It creates rights of access for patients or their representatives to their health records. 'Health record' is defined as a record which consists of information relating to the physical or mental health of an individual, and was made by or on behalf of a health professional in connection

---

[170] S. 4(3).   [171] S. 4(2)(b), (3)(b).   [172] S. 5(1).   [173] S. 5(2).
[174] S. 6(1).   [175] S. 6(2).   [176] S. 7(1).   [177] S. 7(2).
[178] S. 7(3), (4).

with that person's care, other than a record already covered by the Data Protection Act 1984.[179] Health professional is widely defined, covering registered doctors, dentists, opticians, pharmaceutical chemists, nurses, midwives, health visitors, chiropodists, dieticians, occupational therapists, orthoptists, physiotherapists, clinical psychologists, child psychotherapists, speech therapists, osteopaths, chiropractors and art and music therapists employed by the NHS.[180]

Applications for access should be made to the health authority or NHS trust which holds the record, or in the case of primary care, to the general practitioner (or health authority if the patient has no GP). Applications can be made by the patient (including a child who can understand the nature of the application[181]), a person with written authorization from the patient, a person with parental responsibility for a child patient, a person appointed by the court to manage the affairs of an incompetent patient, the personal representative of a deceased patient, and anyone who may have a claim arising out of the patient's death.[182] When an application is received, the record-holder must permit access unless there is a specific ground for withholding information under the Act. For records made within forty days of the application, access must be given within twenty-one days. For records made earlier, or partly earlier, then the period within which access must be given is forty days.[183] Access means permitting applicants to inspect the records, and to have a copy if they wish.[184] Explanations must be given of unintelligible terms.[185] Patients may be charged for the cost of making copies, and a fixed fee for access to records that are older than forty days.[186]

Access to all or part of a record may be withheld for a number of reasons, and there is no obligation to tell the patients that they have not been given all their records.[187] Record-holders must consult the appropriate professionals in order to discover whether a reason to bar access exists. The appropriate professional will be the doctor or dentist currently or previously responsible for the person's care or, in the absence of such a person, any appropriately qualified health professional.[188] The grounds for withholding access are as follows: first, where the information would be likely to cause serious harm to the physical or mental health of the patient; secondly, where such harm would be likely to be caused to another person; thirdly, where the information would identify an informant, unless that informant consents to the application for access or is a health professional who has been involved with the patient; fourthly, because it was made before 1 November 1991, when the Act came into force: fifthly, where the record would show that an individual might have been born

---

[179] S. 1(1).   [180] See s. 2.   [181] S. 4(1).   [182] S. 3(1).   [183] S. 3(5).
[184] S. 3(2).   [185] S. 3(3).   [186] S. 3(4).   [187] S. 5.   [188] S. 7.

as a result of infertility treatment.[189] Special rules apply where the patient is incompetent or has died.[190] Access will not be permitted to information that the patient disclosed or consented to be ascertained in the expectation that the applicant would not know about it. Thus, the patient has a veto that restricts post-mortem disclosure. Where an application is made by someone who may have a legal claim, access is restricted to information relevant to that claim.

When the patient is a child, difficult issues arise about the position of his or her parents. The Act provides that parents should not be given access unless either the child consents to the application or is incapable of understanding what is going on. In the latter situation, access can still be denied to parents if the record-holder thinks it would not be in the child's best interests.[191] This would enable parts of the record that contained suspicions of non-accidental injury to be withheld from parents. Parents cannot be given access to information that the children disclosed in the expectation that their parents would not be told about it, nor to information generated by examinations or tests that were consented to on the basis of secrecy from parents.[192] Thus, family planning clinics are precluded from permitting parents to see their children's records if the children came to the clinic on the understanding that confidentiality would be maintained as against the parents. It is not necessary for the child to be able to understand the nature of any treatment, or of access to health records, for this restriction on disclosure to apply.

When they see their records, patients may believe that the information contained in them is inaccurate. This may be because it is incorrect, misleading, or incomplete. Under section 6 of the Act they can ask the record-holder to correct the mistake. After consulting the appropriate professional, the correction should be made if the record-holder is satisfied that it is inaccurate. If not, a note of the patient's view on the inaccuracy must be included on the record.[193] Failure to comply with this part of the Act, as with the others, can be remedied by an application to a court.[194]

G. Conclusion

There would be considerable benefits in consolidating the law of confidentiality and access to records into a single statutory code. There is too much uncertainty about the exceptions to the obligation of confidence and insuffi-

---

[189] Access to Health Records (Control of Access) Regulations 1993, SI 1993 No 746.
[190] S. 5(3),(4).   [191] S. 4, 5(3).   [192] S. 5(3).   [193] S. 6(2).
[194] S. 8(1). No regulations have yet been made, as envisaged by subs. (2) requiring complaints to be made before going to the court.

cient protection for confidentiality within the NHS bureaucracy. The British Medical Association has called for such legislation and has produced a draft bill.[195] It has criticized the Government's reluctance to legislate. In relation to access to health records, the problem is that there are too many statutory provisions. Apart from the Data Protection Act 1984, they all originated as private members' bills. The Government had expressed the wish to move to its own legislation, but had been unable to persuade the medical profession to support it. There may be a need to amend the law in order to implement the EC Directive on Data Protection adopted in October 1995. The deadline for implementation is 24 October 1998.

---

[195] BMA, n. 67 above, para. 2:5; extracts from the draft bill can be found in (1994) BME No 100, 13–17. It was introduced to Parliament in the 1995–6 session, but did not progress to legislation.

12 Care for Children

The care of children is governed by the general principles governing professional standards, as described in the preceding chapters, but it also raise a number of complexities. The law of consent is premised on the assumption that patients will normally be able to take decisions for themselves, but this will often not be the case with children. The first section of this Chapter therefore considers the capacity of children to authorize care by consenting in the usual way. In cases where children cannot consent a parent may usually give consent on their behalf, and the second section of the Chapter examines parental consent and its limits. In some circumstances a need arises for an independent review of a child's health care, and the procedures by which a court can be called upon to determine such matters are described. One advantage of one of these jurisdictions, wardship, is that it sometimes enables the court to make orders protecting the child from the adverse effects of publicity. This feature provides a significant advantage for children over the general law on confidentiality. The application of the obligation of confidence raises particular problems for paediatric care in relation to the position of parents, and this issue merits consideration in the penultimate section of the Chapter. It concludes with a brief outline of child care law.

A number of aspects of the law relating to children are dealt with in other chapters. Childbirth itself is the subject of Chapter 16, which also covers the registration of children's births. The compensation scheme for children injured by vaccines was described in Chapter 9. Access to health records of children was considered in Chapter 11. Research with children is included in Chapter 14. Legal aspects of the problems of selecting the appropriate management for neonates, particularly those with very low birth weights or handicaps, are discussed in Chapter 18.

A. Child Consent

Under the general law a child, or 'minor', is a person who has been born but is under the age of 18.[1] This principle is modified in respect of consent to treatment by section 8 of the Family Law Reform Act 1969 which provides that at 16 a child's consent is as effective as if he or she were an adult. 'Treatment' includes diagnosis, and procedures such as the administration of anæsthetics which are ancillary to treatment.[2] Beyond this 'treatment' is presumably to be defined according to its ordinary usage. It probably includes preventive measures intended to benefit the child's health, but is unlikely to extend to tissue donation, cosmetic surgery, or research.[3] In practice, however, the need to ascertain the exact extent of the statutory provision can be avoided by application of the common law principles which permit children to give valid consent even when the Act does not.[4] This will cover both cases where the child is under 16 and also where consent is sought for non-therapeutic procedures.

This area of law was examined by the House of Lords in the *Gillick* case.[5] Mrs Gillick challenged the validity of the advice given by the Department of Health and Social Security that in exceptional circumstances doctors could provide girls under the age of 16 with contraceptive advice and treatment without parental involvement.[6] She argued that the girl's consent would be legally ineffective and consequently no treatment could be carried out unless parental consent had been given. Although her approach was accepted by the Court of Appeal, it was rejected by the majority of the House of Lords. They argued that the test to be applied was whether the child had 'sufficient understanding and intelligence to enable him or her to understand fully what is proposed'.[7] They did not make it clear exactly what is meant by 'understand fully'. Lord Fraser required only understanding of the doctor's advice; Lord Scarman also included 'moral and family questions' and emotional implications.[8] It would be most consistent with the basis of their Lordships' decision and the general law governing capacity to consent to take the former approach and concentrate solely on understanding of the physical aspects of care.[9] This

---

[1] Family Law Reform Act 1969, s. 1.   [2] *Ibid.*, s. 8(2).

[3] D. Foulkes, 'Consent to Medical Treatment' (1970) 120 *NLJ* 194–5; P. D. G. Skegg, *Law, Ethics, and Medicine* (Oxford: Clarendon Press, 1984), 50–1.

[4] These rules are preserved by Family Law Reform Act 1969, s. 8(3).

[5] *Gillick* v. *W. Norfolk AHA* [1985] 3 All ER 402; J. Montgomery, 'Children as Property?' (1988) 51 *MLR* 323–42; S. P. de Cruz, 'Parents, Doctors and Children: The Gillick Case and Beyond' [1987] *JSWL* 93–108; H. Bevan, *Child Law* (London: Butterworths, 1989), 3–13, 18–30.

[6] HN(80)46.   [7] N. 5 above, 423, *per* Lord Scarman.

[8] *Ibid.*, 413, *per* Lord Fraser, 424, *per* Lord Scarman.

[9] Montgomery, n. 5 above, 337–9; I. Kennedy, *Treat Me Right* (Oxford: OUP, 1988), 102–6.

requires an appreciation of the consequences of treatment, including possible side-effects, and also the anticipated consequences of a failure to treat.[10] It does not, however, introduce the need for 'moral' maturity. The DHSS has taken a more cautious view in its revised advice, which recommends doctors to look for 'sufficient maturity to understand what [is] involved in terms of the moral, social and emotional implications'.[11] The law is established by the House of Lords rather than the Department; but although it has been suggested that the Department is wrong, it cannot be said that this is certain. In practice, save in the controversial area of reproductive freedom, the difference will usually be immaterial. \

The test of maturity established by the House of Lords must be assessed in respect of each individual child and each separate procedure.[12] A child will be able to consent to some procedures before others. Lord Fraser described it as absurd to suggest that a child of 15 could not consent to the examination of a trivial injury or the setting of a broken arm.[13] Lord Templeman thought that the consent of an intelligent child of the same age could permit tonsillectomies and appendectomies. Both considered whether this was true also of contraception; Lord Templeman suggested that a 15-year-old would never be mature enough to understand it; Lord Fraser and the majority of the court disagreed. Professionals must therefore assess the particular child in relation to the specific care in question. Previous experience of the treatment may indicate sufficient understanding. Thus before the tattooing of minors was made illegal,[14] the courts accepted that a valid consent could be given by a boy of 13 with twenty-two previous tattoos while consent to a first tattoo by children of similar age was unlawful because they were 'unable to appreciate the nature of [the] act'.[15]

The *Gillick* case was concerned with the legal principles rather than the capacity of a particular child. There have since been a number of cases in which the courts have had to consider whether children qualified as competent or not.[16] In *Re E*[17] a Jehovah's Witness boy of 15 was dying of leukaemia. He expressed his opposition to receiving a blood transfusion. The judge held that he did not appreciate the extent of the fear and distress he would suffer,

---

[10] *Re R*. [1991] 4 All ER 177, *per* Lord Donaldson.   [11] HC(86)1.

[12] *Re R*, n. 10 above, *per* Lord Donaldson MR, Farquharson LJ.   [13] N. 5 above, 409.

[14] Tattooing of Minors Act 1969. Medical practitioners, and those working under their direction, are exempt from the prohibition providing the tattoo is performed for medical reasons.

[15] *R.* v. *Dilks* (1964) 4 Med. Sci. Law 209; *Burrell* v. *Harmer* (1966) 116 NLJ 1658, [1967] Crim. LR 169.

[16] For discussion, see M. Brazier, and C. Bridge, 'Coercion or Caring: Analysing Adolescent Autonomy' (1996) 16 *Legal Studies* 84–109.

[17] [1993] 1 FLR 386. The boy continued to reject treatment, and when he was an adult he exercised his right to refuse it and died: see [1994] 2 FLR 1065, 1075.

and consequently did not really understand what he was demanding. He was therefore not *Gillick* competent. *Re S*[18] concerned a Jehovah's Witness girl of 15, who had suffered from thalassaemia virtually since her birth. The treatment involved regular blood transfusions. The judge held that she was not '*Gillick* competent' as she had only a very general understanding of some vital matters relating to her treatment, and the consequences of withdrawing from it. She did not want to die, and did not understand the way in which she would die if her treatment ended. She believed that the diagnosis might have been wrong, and that she might not die at all. Although she stated that God did not want her to receive someone else's blood, she seemed uncertain why this was, referring to the risk of HIV infection.

The greatest difficulties have arisen in respect of children suffering mental illness. This was discussed by the Court of Appeal in *Re R*.[19] The girl in question was lucid at some points, but not at others. In her lucid phases she refused to consent to the drug therapy through which her mental state had been stabilized. The Court decided that in these circumstances she was not *Gillick* competent, and that consent to the treatment could therefore be given on her behalf. The court was unclear whether this was because she did not fully understand the implications of the treatment even when she was lucid, or because her temporary competence was vitiated by her mental illness. The most satisfactory interpretation of the decision is that she did not really appreciate what would happen if she did not take her medication.[20]

In *Re W*[21] Lord Donaldson suggested that an anorexic girl of 16 was legally incompetent in respect of in-patient treatment for her condition. The girl had rejected the treatment, but Lord Donaldson decided that it was a feature of her condition that it destroyed the capacity to make an informed choice. However, the trial judge and the two other members of the Court of Appeal proceeded on the basis that she was *Gillick* competent. In *South Glamorgan CC* v. *B and W*[22] the psychiatrists were clear that it was necessary to admit their 15-year-old female patient for assessment as an in-patient. One gave evidence that she might not be capable of making a wise decision. However, Douglas Brown J found that this was insufficient to support a finding that she was *Gillick* incompetent.[23] The proper test is not whether a *wise* decision would be made, but whether the patient is capable of making a choice.

There is no reason to suppose that the *Gillick* principle is restricted to the context of treatment as is section 8 of the Family Law Reform Act 1969. Lord Scarman described it as an 'underlying principle' suggesting that it is of

---

[18] [1994] 2 FLR 1065.   [19] N. 10 above.
[20] J. Montgomery, 'Parents and Children in Dispute: Who has the Final Word?' (1992) 4 *JCL* 85–9.
[21] [1992] 4 All ER 627.   [22] [1993] 1 FLR 574.   [23] *Ibid.*, 582.   [24] N. 5 above, 421.

general application.[24] The only doubt on this point has been shed by the suggestion of one judge that the principle was not relevant to consent to a psychiatric assessment for the purpose of court proceedings.[25] This was probably because the courts' power to gather evidence should not generally be ousted by individual objections, rather than because the consent would be invalid. The Children Act 1989 has specifically overturned the decision by laying down that a child may refuse to submit to a medical or psychiatric assessment if 'of sufficient understanding to make an informed decision'.[26] If *Gillick* competence extends beyond the context of treatment, then mature children may be able to consent to becoming research subjects. They may also agree to donate tissue and organs for transplantation.[27]

The combined effect of the provisions of the Family Law Reform Act 1969 and the *Gillick* decision is as follows. Where the child has reached 16 the health professionals may assume that his or her consent will be valid for treatment as defined in the Act. However, this presumption will be overturned if the patient is not in fact competent to consent. Below the age of 16, or where non-treatment is in issue, they must assess the particular child's capacity to consent in relation to each proposed intervention. This is not an easy task and the criteria used to establish adult rationality may not be appropriate.[28] The general guidance produced by the British Medical Association and Law Society on assessing competence suggests that regard should be had to the young patient's ability to understand that there is a choice and that choices have consequences, willingness and ability to make a choice, understanding of the nature and purpose of the proposed procedure, and the available alternatives (including risks and side effects).[29] It has also been suggested that the past experience of the child is a vitally important factor.[30] It is probable that, were there any dispute, professional judgements as to capacity would be accepted as proper by the courts providing that they were made in good faith.[31] In Scotland this has been made explicit.[32] Where children are capable

---

[25] *R.* v. *Waltham Forest LB, ex p. G* [1989] 2 FLR 138, 143.

[26] Children Act 1989, ss. 38(6), 43(8), 44(7). Such a refusal may be overridden by the court: see *South Glamorgan CC* v. *B and W* [1993] 1 FLR 574.

[27] *Re W* [1992] 4 All ER 627, 639.

[28] P. Alderson, 'Consent to Children's Surgery and Intensive Medical Treatment' (1990) 17 *JLS* 52–65; P. Alderson, 'In the Genes or in the Stars? Children's Competence to Consent' (1992) 18 *JME* 119–24. For discussion of ways to determine capacity, see D. Carson, 'The Sexuality of People with Learning Difficulties' [1989] *JSWL* 355, 364–71, and Law Commission, *Mentally Incapacitated Adults and Decision-making: Medical Rreatment and Research* (1993) Consultation Paper No 129, 11–23.

[29] *Assessment of Mental Capacity: Guidance for Doctors and Lawyers* (London: BMA, 1996), 73.

[30] P. Alderson and J. Montgomery, *Health Care Choices: Making Decisions with Children* (London: Institute for Public Policy Research, 1996), 76. This report also offers a checklist for assisting practitioners to involve children in decisions and judge their competence, 69–71.

[31] Kennedy, n. 9 above, 107–11.   [32] Age of Legal Capacity (Scotland) Act 1991, s. 2(4).

of understanding the decision, then their consent will make treatment lawful. If they cannot understand the issue, then it will usually be necessary to get parental consent.

B. No Consent Needed

It should be remembered that no consent, from parent or child, will be needed when a case falls within the general exceptions to consent law of conduct acceptable in the course of everyday life and necessity.[33] In such circumstances parental consent need not be sought because the care would already be lawful. The former category includes 'all physical contact which is generally acceptable in the ordinary conduct of daily life'. Suggestions that medical treatment might sometimes come into this category have been disapproved,[34] although it might cover some aspects of nursing care.

The doctrine of 'necessity' is of uncertain scope. In the *Gillick* case, Lord Templeman considered three scenarios where he felt that a doctor might legitimately proceed without parental involvement:[35] first, emergencies, where children may be given care as a temporary measure; secondly, where the child had been abandoned by the parents. In both these cases children can be treated pending the parents being informed. The third scenario was where the child had been abused by the parent. In this case the proper course of action is to involve social services. However, it is probable that treatment without consent would be justified pending this action being taken. It is also generally assumed that life-saving treatment can be administered even against the wishes of parents.[36] However, two cases concerning the administration of blood transfusions to Jehovah's Witness children against the wishes of their parents have suggested that the approval of a court should be sought before such treatment is administered.[37] The better view would seem to be that health professionals should proceed with the transfusion in an emergency, but allow the parents an opportunity to involve the court in less urgent cases.

Lavery has argued that there is a further exception to the need for parental consent when the treatment is routine.[38] She argues that, where it would be

[33] See Ch. 10.
[34] *F* v. *W. Berkshire HA* [1989] 2 All ER 545, 564; *T* v. *T* [1988] 1 All ER 613, 624.
[35] *Gillick* v. *W. Norfolk AHA*, n. 5 above, 435; see also Lord Scarman at 424.
[36] This was accepted obiter in *Re S* [1994] 2 FLR 416, 420. See also Skegg, n. 3 above, 107–10; G. Williams, 'Necessity' [1978] *Crim. LR* 128, 132–4; NHS Circular HSC(GEN)81, 1975, see BMA, *Rights and Responsibilities of Doctors* (London: BMA, 1988), 6–7.
[37] *Re O* [1993] 2 FLR 149; *Re S* [1993] 1 FLR 376.
[38] R. Lavery, 'Routine Medical Treatment of Children' [1990] *JSWL* 375–384.

considered unreasonable in the opinion of most relevant experts to withhold the care in question, and it does not raise social or moral considerations, then it is permissible to proceed without parental consent and even in the face of parental objection. The basis of her argument is an analogy with the principles governing persons unable to consent by reason of mental incapacity.[39] Those principles allow care to be given when it is in the interests of a person who cannot consent and permit the health care professionals to judge where those interests lie.

The difficulty with Lavery's position is that the rationale behind giving parents the right to consent derives from the belief that they are best placed to judge the welfare of their child.[40] It must be presumed that where they refuse to consent this is because they believe it to be in the child's interest to do so. The issue is therefore whether their view or the doctor's should prevail. It is no different from the case of an adult refusing consent which a doctor believes is appropriate. It is true that, in *Gillick*, Lord Fraser does suggest that 'any *important* medical treatment of a child under 16 would normally only be carried out with the parents' approval' (emphasis added).[41] This might be taken to suggest that less important care does not need parental consent. However, the context makes it clear that he is talking about the involvement, as a matter of good practice, of parents even when the child gives consent.

Lavery's proposal that parental evaluation is unnecessary when the issue is a 'purely medical decision' would undermine the need for consent to routine treatment in relation to adults as well as children. It is unlikely that the courts would adopt such a radical view. An earlier case explicitly held that the principles permitting the treatment of those unable to consent only applied when no one could give a legally effective consent on their behalf.[42] The same view seems to be adopted by Lord Goff in *F* v. *W. Berkshire HA*, although less explicitly.[43] The best view is that parental consent must always be obtained if consent would be required were the patient an adult.

C. Parental Consent

Although the Family Law Reform Act 1969 provides that children of 16 can consent as if they were of full age, the Act specifically preserves the common law powers of parental consent.[44] At common law parents may consent on behalf of their children until they reach the age of 18. It follows that where a

---

[39] See *F* v. *W. Berkshire*, n. 34 above, discussed in Ch. 10.
[40] *Gillick* v. *W. Norfolk AHA*, n. 5 above, 412. [41] *Ibid.* [42] *T* v. *T* n. 34 above.
[43] N. 34 above, 566. [44] Family Law Reform Act 1969, s. 8(3).

16 or 17-year-old child is incapable of consenting by reason of mental incapacity parental consent will be valid. Where a consent is needed, but it cannot
be obtained from the child, the consent of one of the parents must be sought.
This apparently simple requirement gives rise to three particular difficulties.
The first concerns cases where the parents are in disagreement. The second
problem emerges when the parents are in conflict with an older child. The
third is created by the possibility that some types of care are beyond the scope
of parental consent and cannot be authorized by parental consent alone.

(i)   Who is a 'Parent'?

Before those issues are examined it is necessary to consider who a 'parent' is
for these purposes. The fundamental legal principle is that any person with
'parental responsibility' has the power to give a valid consent to health care.
The rules are set out in the Children Act 1989. Where the child's parents are
married they will both have parental responsibility for their child.[45] If they are
not married, then the mother will automatically have parental responsibility
but the father will not. This may present difficulties, particularly in the context of neonatal care, where the mother may be unconscious after a Caesarian
section or in a poor mental state. The father may be intending to play a full
role in the child's upbringing, but unless he is married to the mother, he will
not have parental responsibility at the time of birth. The father can acquire
parental responsibility by three methods, but they all take time: first, he may
make parental responsibility agreement with the mother. To be effective, this
must be done on a standard form and registered with the Family Division of
the High Court in London.[46] Secondly, he may apply to a court for a parental
responsibility order.[47] Thirdly, he may apply to court for an order that the
child reside with him. If such an order is made the court will automatically
also make a parental responsibility order.[48] It can be seen that there will always
be a document that shows that a father has parental responsibility: a marriage
certificate, a parental responsibility agreement endorsed by the High Court,
or a parental responsibility order. In cases of doubt, therefore, health professionals may ask to see the relevant documentation.

There are other important provisions in the Children Act 1989 concerning
the power to consent to care for children. Section 3(5) states that where a person has care of a child, but does not have parental responsibility, he or she may
do 'what is reasonable in all the circumstances of the case for the purpose of
safeguarding or promoting the child's welfare'. This will include the power

---

[45] Children Act 1989, s. 2(1).
[46] *Ibid.*, s. 4; Parental Responsibility Agreement Regulations 1991, SI 1991 No 1478 (as amended).
[47] Children Act 1989, s. 4.   [48] *Ibid.*, s. 12(1).   [49] *B* v. *B* [1992] 2 FLR 327.

to consent to medical treatment.[49] Where the court makes an order under section 8 of the Act settling the residence of the child, the person with whom he or she is to reside will acquire parental responsibility for the duration of the order.[50] Local authorities acquire parental responsibility for children under a care order, including the power to consent to admission to a mental hospital for assessment.[51] Child assessment and emergency protection orders may authorize medical assessments, although not against the wishes of the child.[52]

(ii) Where Parents Disagree

It is now clear that parents may act independently and the approval of one will be sufficient, even if there is a disagreement, unless a court order has been made restricting his or her right to consent.[53] However, the fact that an unilateral consent is valid does not mean that a doctor should always carry out the treatment. As Lord Donaldson has put it:

> Consent itself creates no obligation to treat. It is merely a key which unlocks a door. Furthermore, whilst in the case of an adult of full capacity there will usually only be one keyholder . . . in the ordinary family unit there will be two keyholders, namely the parents, with a several [ie independent] as well as a joint right to turn the key and unlock the door. If the parents disagree, one consenting and the other refusing, the doctor will be presented with a professional and ethical, but not with a legal problem because, if he has the consent of one authorised person, treatment will not without more constitute a trespass or a criminal assault.[54]

Thus while health professionals may proceed on the basis of consent from one parent, even though he or she is in dispute with the other, it may not be wise to do so. They might still be held accountable for their decision before their professional disciplinary body if the objecting parent alleged that it constituted professional misconduct. It is also possible that it might amount to negligence if no responsible body of professional opinion would support proceeding without the consent of both parents.

(iii) Where Parents and Children Disagree

The second area of difficulty arises when a competent child refuses to consent to care, but one at least of the parents is in favour of it proceeding. If the parents retain their right to consent even once the child is competent to autho-

---

[50] Children Act 1989, s. 12(2).   [51] R. v. *Kirklees MC, ex p. C* [1993] 2 FLR 187.
[52] Children Act 1989, ss. 43 and 44. However, see *South Glamorgan CC* v. *B and W*, n. 26 above, 583–4, for a possible way of overriding children's objections.
[53] Children Act 1989, s. 2(7); *Re R*, n. 10 above.   [54] *Re R*, n. 10 above, 184.

rize treatment, then the health professionals may proceed on the basis of the parental approval. If the parental power to consent is superseded as children become able to give a valid consent, then a competent child's refusal is conclusive. Most commentators initially interpreted the *Gillick* decision as adopting the latter solution, whereby parents cannot override their children's decisions.[55] Lord Scarman stated that

> as a matter of law the parental right to determine whether or not their minor child below the age of 16 will have medical treatment terminates if and when the child achieves a sufficient understanding and intelligence to understand fully what is proposed.[56]

Further evidence that Lord Scarman believed that the right to consent to treatment was lost by parents once the child became '*Gillick* competent' is to be found in his earlier comment that the 'parental right yields to the child's right to make his own decisions when he reaches a sufficient understanding and intelligence to be able to make up his own mind on the matter requiring decision'.[57] He clearly envisaged that the child's wishes should prevail over those of the parents.

However, this interpretation of the law was challenged by Lord Donaldson in *Re R*.[58] He argued that in the first passage just quoted Lord Scarman was talking not of the right to consent to treatment, but the right to control the child. He pointed out that there was no right to prevent the child receiving treatment once they were competent, because the child's consent would authorize it, but suggested that there was still the power to approve treatment in the face of the child's refusal. He did not regard this as in conflict with Scarman's position, although Staughton LJ did, and he did not explain how the second passage quoted here from Lord Scarman's speech was compatible with his interpretation.

Although there is some logic in the arguments he presents, Lord Donaldson's position is difficult to reconcile with that taken by Lord Scarman in the *Gillick* decision.[59] The House of Lords decided in that case that there was no right to control the child, so Lord Scarman cannot have had such a right in mind. The principle on which the decision rests is that parental responsibility exists in order to further the child's interests, and that once the

[55] e.g. D. Brahams, 'The *Gillick* Case: A Pragmatic Compromise' (1986) 136 *NLJ* 75–7, 75; S. P. de Cruz, 'Parents, Doctors and Children: The *Gillick* Case and Beyond' [1987] *JSWL* 93–108, 98; J. Eekelaar, 'The Emergence of Children's Rights' (1986) 6 *Oxford Journal of Legal Studies* 161–82, 181; Montgomery, n. 5 above, 337; P. N. Parkinson, 'The *Gillick* Case—Just What Has It Decided' [1986] *Fam. L* 11–14, 13. A. Bainham, 'The Balance of Power in Family Decisions' (1986) 45 *CLJ* 262–84, 278, accepts this interpretation of Lord Scarman's position, but argues that it is undesirable: see also J. Eekelaar, 'The Eclipse of Parental Rights' (1986) 102 *LQR* 4–9.

[56] *Gillick* v. *W. Norfolk AHA*, n. 5 above, 423. [57] *Ibid.*, 422.

[58] *Re R*, n. 10 above. [59] Montgomery, n. 20 above.

child is competent to judge where those interests lie, then the justification for parental responsibility evaporates. The *Gillick* decision confers on children the right to make mistakes.[60] As *Re R.* makes clear, there are court procedures whereby a child's decision can be overridden if it is dangerously unwise,[61] but this is not within the rights of parents.

Strictly speaking neither the comments of Lord Donaldson in *Re R*, nor those of Lord Scarman in *Gillick*, were binding on subsequent courts as it was not necessary to decide the point in either case. However, in a second decision, *Re W*,[62] these arguments were neutralized. Lord Donaldson reviewed the position, rejected the criticisms levelled at his earlier decision, and reasserted the view that parents do not lose the power to consent when their children become competent. This time he ensured that the ruling was central to the decision, and so binding in future cases. Balcombe LJ also expressed his agreement with Lord Donaldson's approach. The law must now be regarded as settled unless it is reviewed by the House of Lords.[63] The Court of Appeal has held that the position is so clear that costs were awarded against a health authority which took a case where the child refused to consent to court, even though a parental consent was forthcoming.[64] This is a departure from the usual reluctance to award costs in children cases and indicates that the court thought that the health authority's insistence on obtaining a court order was improper.

The result of this law is that doctors who wish to proceed with treatment may do so on the basis of any valid consent, from one of the parents or, if competent, the child. Any one consent will provide the necessary legal authorization. Whether it is ethically acceptable to ignore the refusal of one of these parties is a matter for the doctor's conscience. It would only become a legal matter if a doctor disregarded a refusal in circumstances when no responsible practitioner, as judged by expert witnesses from the medical profession, would have done so. If this were the case, then the doctor would be liable in negligence.[65]

(iv) The Limits of Parental Consent

The third problem to be discussed concerns the scope of the parental right to consent to treatment. There is surprisingly little authority on this point. It is universally assumed that parental consent to treatment expected directly to

---

[60] Eekelaar, n. 55 above, 182.
[61] See sect. D below.
[62] N. 27 above.
[63] *Re K, W and H* [1993] 1 FLR 854.
[64] *Northamptonshire HA* v. *Official Solicitor and Governors of St Andrew's Hospital* [1994] 1 FLR 162.
[65] *Bolam* v. *Friern HMC* [1957] 2 All ER 118; see Ch. 7.

benefit the child is valid. It has been established that parents may authorize blood tests for forensic as well as therapeutic and diagnostic purposes.[66] Further, the English courts have been reluctant to place too much weight on the distinction between therapeutic and non-therapeutic medical procedures.[67] It seems, therefore, that parental consent is unlikely to be limited to therapeutic circumstances. However, the *Gillick* decision made it clear that the purpose of parental rights is to benefit the child, not to further the interests of the parents.[68] Parental powers to take decisions which do not benefit the child may therefore be suspect.

In *Re B* (sometimes know as the *Jeanette* case) Lord Templeman suggested that sterilization of a girl was beyond the scope of valid parental consent.[69] The other members of the House of Lords in that case did not consider the point. However, they approved in general terms the judgments delivered in the Court of Appeal, all of which took the same position as that of Lord Templeman. It has been argued that the point is *obiter* and that it is wrong in principle.[70] This argument is based on the premise that the court in wardship is to act as a prudent parent would do and that if the court can permit a ward to be sterilized then it follows that a parent must also be able to do so. However, it is clear that the wardship jurisdiction allows orders to be made which go beyond the scope of parental power.[71] There is nothing inconsistent in holding that permitting certain types of medical treatment is one example of this aspect of the jurisdiction.

Since the *Jeanette* case, Lord Templeman's view has been approved at first instance,[72] and tacitly assumed to be correct in the House of Lords.[73] Against this, their Lordships could be taken to have argued that, as a matter of good practice, the court should be involved with the decision to sterilize a minor, but that lack of court approval would not render the operation unlawful. This was the interpretation offered by Lord Donaldson in the *F* v. *W. Berkshire* case in the Court of Appeal.[74] Until further clarification emerges, it would be safest to regard the sterilization of minors without court approval as unlawful. However, it has been held that the rule applies only to non-therapeutic sterilizations. Where an operation is needed to treat health problems other than

---

[66] *Re L* [1968] P 119, 132.

[67] *Re B* [1987] 2 All ER 206; *Gold* v. *Haringey HA* [1987] 2 All ER 888. However, the distinction was adopted in *Re E* [1991] 2 FLR 585.

[68] Montgomery, n. 5 above.   [69] [1987] 2 All ER 206, 214. The case is discussed in Ch. 16.

[70] A. Grubb, and D. Pearl, 'Sterilisation and the Courts' (1987) 46 *CLJ* 439–64, 452.

[71] e.g. *Re X* [1975] 1 All ER 697.

[72] *Re P* [1989] 1 FLR 182; *Re HG* [1993] 1 FLR 588.

[73] *F* v. *W. Berkshire HA*, n. 34 above, *per* Lord Brandon at 551, *per* Lord Griffiths at 561, *per* Lord Goff at 568.

[74] *Sub nom. Re F* [1989] 2 FLR 376, 391, but see the opposite view of Butler-Sloss LJ at 413 that the leave of a High Court judge was a 'requirement'.

the risk of pregnancy, but sterilization would be a necessary incidental effect, court approval is not needed.[75] Although the English cases have concerned female sterilization, presumably male sterilization would be treated in the same way.[76] It remains unclear, however, whether this is a single and exceptional case, or an example of a wider principle.

Lord Templeman's approach would encourage the development of a category of treatments which should be submitted to the courts for approval because of the seriousness of the issues which they raise. It has been suggested that this category would include, in addition to sterilization, refusal of life-saving treatment,[77] abortion, and donation for transplant of non-regenerative tissue.[78] In *Re W*, Lord Donaldson MR suggested that involving a court might not be mandatory in transplantation cases, although doctors might be well advised to do so.[79] Lord Bridge has pointed, in a slightly different context, to the fact that 'such treatment cannot be considered either curative or prophylactic' as the factor giving cause for concern.[80] It should also be noted that the treatments suggested to require the sanction of the court are irreversible.

The only case where a court has had the opportunity to consider whether any of these circumstances requires the intervention of the court concerned permitting a severely handicapped newborn child to die. There the court expressed the view that had the child not already been a ward of court the decision would 'have been solely a matter for her parents'.[81] This might be taken to indicate that only sterilization could come within the category of decisions which only a court can take. If the right to life is not protected by reference to a court, what is? However, refusal to authorize treatment is not the exercise of an invalid power, but a failure to exercise a valid one. That failure will be penalized by the criminal law of (at the least culpable level of) child neglect. This example does not therefore illuminate the problem of what powers parents have to give consent. A refusal of treatment can sometimes be overridden by reference to the principle of necessity (where applicable) or by seeking independent review of the decision.

In the absence of clear guidance as to the exact limits of the parental right to consent to treatment beyond the case of sterilization, recourse must be had to arguments from general principle. Three approaches might be taken.[82]

---

[75] *Re E*, n. 67 above.

[76] *AL* v. *GRH*, (1975) 325 NE 2d 501, vasectomy beyond parental power of consent.

[77] Bevan, n. 5 above, 25–6, but see *Re C* [1989] 2 All ER 737, below.

[78] *Re F*, n. 79 above, *per* Lord Donaldson MR at 390, *per* Neill LJ at 404 including only organ transplantation. See also Lord Bridge, only sterilization and organ donation, *F* v. *W. Berkshire HA*, n. 34 above, 549.

[79] [1992] 4 All ER 627, 635.   [80] *F* v. *W. Berkshire HA*, n. 34 above, 549.

[81] *Re C* [1989] 2 All ER 737, 784.

[82] P. D. G. Skegg, 'Consent to Medical Procedures on Minors (1973) 36 *MLR* 370–81, 380–1.

First, it might be possible for parents to consent only to treatment thought to be in the child's best interests. Secondly, the limits of valid consent might be set by the limits of consents which a 'reasonable parent' could give. Thirdly, parental consents might be valid providing that they did not go against the child's interests. Skegg argues that the best approach is the second, although the distinction between the second and third may be a very fine one.[83] This conclusion is based on the decision of the House of Lords in *S* v. *McC*; *W* v. *W*.[84] Their Lordships argued that parents had a power to authorize blood tests because a they have a right to control their child even against that child's wishes (sometimes described as a right of chastisement) provided that they act reasonably.[85] Lord Reid suggested that this can be assessed by asking whether the procedure is *against* the child's interests.[86]

This approach has much to commend it. It follows the *Gillick* philosophy in seeking to relate the law of parental rights to its purpose. It is in accordance with the provisions of the Children Act 1989, section 3(5), which permit any-one who has care of a child to 'do what is reasonable in all the circumstances of the case for the purpose of safeguarding or promoting the child's welfare'. It is, however, different in kind from the course taken by Lord Templeman in *Re B*. Instead of limiting the scope of the power by saying that some proced-ures may never be consented to it limits the *exercise* of the power. Whether a reasonable parent would consent to a particular procedure cannot be deter-mined without assessing the particular circumstances in which the decision is to be taken. Thus, it is not automatically unreasonable for a homosexual parent who wishes to care for the child himself to object to an adoption. His sexual orientation does not of itself prevent him caring properly for the child. In specific circumstances, however, such a decision may well be unreason-able.[87] Similarly, cosmetic surgery may be appropriate for children who suf-fer severe distress or peer abuse because of they way they look. But it would probably not be reasonable merely to satisfy the parent's desire for a pretty child.

The implications of this approach to the limits of the power to consent to medical treatment would seem to be as follows. Where treatment is expected to benefit the child patient, parents may consent to all treatments other than sterilization. Where health professionals believe that the proposed course of action will not benefit the child, they can, and perhaps should, seek the advice of the court using the wardship procedure, the inherent jurisdiction, or a spe-cific issue order under section 8 of the Children Act 1989 (see below). In the absence of court involvement, however, parental consent may be valid because

---

[83] Skegg, n. 3 above, 59–68. [84] [1972] AC 24.
[85] See *R*. v. *Rahman* (1985) 81 Cr. App.R for a recent consideration of the limits of this power.
[86] *S* v. *McC*; *W* v. *W* [1972] AC 24, 45. [87] *Re D* [1977] AC 602.

even where care is not expected to benefit the child the parents have the power to consent if it is reasonable to do so. If they act unreasonably they may be punished after the event for failing to live up to their duties, and may be restrained before the event through the wardship jurisdiction. However, until such intervention the consents offered would appear valid. Health professionals have a similar duty to act responsibly towards those in their care. Embarking on a course of treatment which was not in the interests of a patient might well be negligent. It would not, however, be unlawful by reason of absence of consent when the parents had given one.

A number of controversial areas call for the application of these principles, including consent to organ donation, cosmetic surgery, testing for genetic disorders that may not affect the child until he or she is adult, and research.[88] In such cases, the primary purpose of professional intervention may not be to benefit the child. In the first example it is to benefit the recipient of the organ. In the last it is to benefit children, or perhaps all humans, generally. There is no clear guidance on how the reasonableness of a parent's decision to consent on behalf of a child should be assessed. The most basic aspect of reasonableness would probably be consideration of the balance between the risks faced by the child and the benefits that she or he can hope to obtain. This would include an assessment of the likelihood of the risks and benefits being realized. The urgency of the decision should be considered. However, there is no reason why assessments of benefit should be restricted to health benefits; familial, social, and financial benefits are equally important to the child's well-being. Another major factor would be the wishes of the child, even when not yet able to take the actual decision. In cases where the decision can be postponed until the child can make it, then it would be reasonable to wait. Ultimately, however, the reasonableness of a decision can only be assessed in the particular circumstances that arise. In cases of difficulty health professionals would be best advised to seek the guidance of a court.

D. Independent Review

The need for independent review of child health problems may arise in a number of ways. The care proposed may be beyond the scope of the parental right to consent, the parents or the child may refuse to consent to treatment which the health care professionals believe is in the child's best interests, the professionals may be uncertain of their legal position and wish to have prior

---

[88] Consent to research with children is discussed in Ch. 13. Organ donation is discussed in Ch. 18.

authorization from the court before proceeding. In addition, if the child in question is already a ward of court it will be necessary to obtain leave before any major step is taken. In the past, such review took place under the wardship jurisdiction, but the Children Act 1989 has made new orders available, resolving specific issues or prohibiting parents from taking certain steps.[89] That Act has also placed restrictions on the uses of the wardship jurisdiction which may encourage the use of the Children Act orders in certain cases, although it has been held that the inherent jurisdiction of the court can be used despite the restrictions on wardship. All these jurisdictions must therefore be discussed.

Under the wardship procedure,[90] an interested party may make the child a ward merely by issuing a summons.[91] This would include concerned professionals. Originally there were no further restrictions, but the Children Act 1989 introduced restrictions on the use of wardship. It can never be used when a care order is in force in respect of a child.[92] It cannot be used to place a child in care or to give a local authority the power to determine matters within the scope of parental responsibility.[93] Even when wardship can be used, applications cannot be made by local authorities without the leave of a court, and leave cannot be given if another procedure is available.[94] It has been suggested that this could prevent the use of wardship to review health care matters.[95] However, health authorities are not within the definition of local authorities[96] and the problems could be overcome by a change in practice, whereby health authorities make applications for wardship rather than referring the matter to the social services department of the local authority. Alternatively, the inherent jurisdiction of the court can be used to deal with specific matters.[97] Unlike wardship, this will not involve continuing court supervision.

Once a wardship summons has been issued, the child is in the care of the court and no important step may be taken without the court's permission. Major treatment decisions and psychiatric examinations are considered to come into this category, but purely physical examinations would not normally do so.[98] Although the wardship takes automatic effect, it will lapse unless an application is made to the court for a hearing within twenty-one days of the

---

[89] Children Act 1989, s. 8.

[90] N. V. Lowe and R. A. H. White, *Wards of Court* (2nd edn. London: Butterworths, 1986).

[91] Supreme Court Act 1981, s. 41.   [92] Children Act 1989, s. 100(2)(c).

[93] *Ibid.*, s. 100(2)(a), (d).   [94] *Ibid.*, s. 100(3), (4).

[95] M. D. A. Freeman, 'Care After 1991' in D. Freestone (ed.), *Children and the Law* (Hull: Hull University Press, 1990), 130–71, 168–70.

[96] Children Act 1989, s. 105(1).   [97] *Re W*, n. 21 above.

[98] *Practice Direction* [1985] 1 All ER 832; *Practice Direction* [1985] 3 All ER 576.

[99] Supreme Court Act 1981, s. 41(2); Rules of the Supreme Court O. 90 r. 4(1) (SI 1965 No 1776 as amended by SI 1971 No 1269).

summons being issued.[99] The court must decide whether to continue the wardship, retaining its supervisory role, and whether it should make any order.

These decisions are taken according to what the court sees as the interests of the child, and the child will normally be represented by the Official Solicitor. The wardship procedure has been used to review decisions on sterilization,[100] termination of pregnancy,[101] the withholding of life-saving treatment,[102] the giving of life-saving treatment against parental wishes,[103] and surrogacy.[104] Each case is decided according to its particular facts and the courts have refused to allow rules to develop as to what should happen. However, a pattern has emerged of the courts listening to the health professionals' plans and, providing there is no serious disagreement between the professionals, authorizing them to carry out their proposed care. This support for professional opinion is in no way automatic. It is not a legal rule. However, it is in practice highly likely that it will be the outcome of applications to court.[105]

The range of orders which the court can make in wardship is very wide and embraces things which parents would not be entitled to do. Thus, the court can order third parties, including health professionals, to act in a particular way. In principle, the court should have jurisdiction to order health professionals to carry out a specified course of care. However, it has been held that it would be an abuse of the power of the court to require doctors to treat a child.[106] The usual approach is either to authorize or forbid, but not order, the professionals to carry out the care that they have proposed to the court.[107] The wardship jurisdiction provides a forum for disagreements between professionals to be aired, and to protect them by ensuring that care carried out has the support of the court.

The most important example of the power to make orders against third parties in the context of health care is the ability to restrain media publicity in relation to a ward's treatment. Orders have been made preventing newspapers from revealing the identity of wards of court who are receiving care, and in some circumstances protecting also the identities of the carers.[108] The latter will only be permitted if it is necessary to safeguard the child's welfare,[109] and

---

[100] *Re D* [1976] Fam. 185; *Re B* [1988] AC 199; *Re M* [1988] 2 FLR 497; *Re P* [1989] 1 FLR 182.
[101] *Re G-U* [1984] FLR 811; *Re P* (1981) 80 LGR 305; *Re B* [1991] 2 FLR 426.
[102] *Re B* [1981] 1 WLR 1421; *Re C* [1989] 2 All ER 782; *Re J* [1990] 3 All ER 930.
[103] *Re O* [1993] 2 FLR 149; *Re E* [1993] 1 FLR 386; *Re S* [1993] 1 FLR 376.
[104] *Re C* [1985] FLR 846; *Re P* [1987] 2 FLR 421.   [105] See the cases discussed in Ch. 18.
[106] *Re J* [1992] 4 All ER 614.
[107] See especially the wardship cases on the treatment of neonates, discussed in Ch. 18.
[108] *Re C (No 2)* [1989] 2 All ER 791.   [109] *Re T, The Times*, 4 Oct. 1989.
[110] *Re M and N* [1990] 1 All ER 205.

that welfare is not necessarily an overriding consideration.[110] The courts will not allow public debate on medical ethics to be stifled, but have pointed out that there is a distinction to be drawn between what interests the public and what is in the public interest.[111] It will rarely be the case that the identification of the people involved is necessary to permit the issues to be discussed. If an order restricting publicity is made it has serious consequences for press freedom and for those who breach it because they will be in contempt of court. Such orders must therefore be as narrow as possible while still protecting the ward.[112] The Court of Appeal has emphasized that the purpose of preventing publicity is to protect the court's ability to carry out its responsibility to oversee the child's welfare. It is not to give a child a right of privacy, which is denied to adults by English law.[113] Once information has reached the public domain, its future restriction will not usually be permissible, even if secrecy would have been justified had there been no prior publicity.[114] The courts have also permitted publicity in order to raise funds to pay for a ward's private treatment.[115]

Section 8 of the Children Act 1989 provides an alternative route whereby a review of a child's health care can be carried out. Under this section the court has the power to make 'prohibited steps' and 'specific issue' orders. These are designed to resolve disputes over the way in which parental responsibility, including health care decisions, should be exercised. These orders may be used to forbid a particular course of treatment, or to resolve a dispute by ordering that consent to it be given. It has been suggested that they might not be appropriate to deal with emergency cases, where there is no time for an *inter partes* hearing.[116] However, in *Re R*, Booth J held that specific issue orders could be used to authorize treatment and indicated that this could be done *ex parte* if necessary.[117] She added that applications should be heard in the High Court.

Section 8 orders are used to deal with problems arising from family breakdown, and can determine where children will live and with whom they should have contact, as well as the type of specific problems already discussed. If necessary the court may elaborate the effect of orders by issuing directions as to how an order should be carried into effect or by attaching conditions to it.[118]

---

[111] *Re C (No 2)*, n. 108 above; see also *Lion Laboratories* v. *Evans* [1984] 2 All ER 417 and *X* v. *Y* [1988] 2 All ER 649.

[112] *Re M and N* [1990] 1 All ER 205; *Re W* [1992] 1 FLR 99.

[113] *Mrs R.* v. *Central TV* [1994] 2 FLR 151. See the discussion in *Re Z* [1995] 4 All ER 961 for a full analysis of the principles.

[114] *Cumbria County School* v. *X, The Times*, 25 June 1990 [1990] Fam. Law 282 (news report).

[115] *R.* v. *Cambridge & Huntingdon HA, ex p. B (No 2)* [1996] 1 FLR 375.

[116] *Re O* [1993] 2 FLR 149.   [117] [1993] 2 FLR 757. See also *Re HG* [1993] 1 FLR 587.

[118] Children Act 1989, s. 11(7).

Thus it would be possible to specify that a Jehovah's Witness parent should consult with the other before refusing consent to a blood transfusion. It might be thought that such a parent could be instructed to give a consent, under a specific issue order. However, it has recently been suggested that it is inappropriate to require Jehovah's Witnesses to undertake to consent to transfusions contrary to their beliefs.[119] Exercising a similar power to issue directions in care proceedings, magistrates required that children be tested for HIV infection because their HIV status was thought to be relevant to assessing their needs.[120] The use of the power to issue directions to require health testing has not been challenged. However, it is now clear that an issue such as HIV testing should only be dealt with by the High Court, because it raises serious emotional, psychological, and practical problems.[121] The terms of any order or direction are important because they restrict the general right of parents to act unilaterally, including their right to consent to treatment.

Unless a person already has a close relationship with the child, the leave of the court must be obtained before an application for a section 8 order can be made.[122] In most cases, therefore, a health authority which wishes to invoke these powers will need to seek the courts' assistance through a two-stage process; first obtaining leave by showing why there is an issue to be examined, and secondly in the full hearing. Children may themselves apply for a section 8 order, if they are of sufficient understanding to do so. A two-stage procedure also applies to them, requiring the leave of the court before they can proceed to a full application. Leave will not be granted unless there is a reasonable prospect of the main application succeeding.[123] It is therefore possible for children to apply to the court for an order preventing a parent consenting to treatment on their behalf.

Once an application for a section 8 order reaches the court, it will be governed by the child's interests.[124] If there is a dispute, in assessing where the child's interests lie the court is directed to consider a checklist of factors.[125] This includes the wishes of the child, but does not make them prevail over other aspects of the circumstances.[126] As with the wardship jurisdiction, therefore, it will be possible to use the section 8 procedure to override a child's views.[127] However, a section 8 order can only be made in respect of a child who is over 16 if the circumstances are exceptional.[128]

---

[119] *Re S* [1994] 2 FLR 416.

[120] *Re O* [1993] 1 FLR 860. See also *Berkshire CC* v. *C* [1993] 1 FLR 569.

[121] *Re HIV tests* [1994] 2 FLR 116. See also *Re W* [1995] 2 FCR 184.

[122] Children Act 1989, s. 10.

[123] *Re SC* [1994] 1 FLR 96, although see the less satisfactory decision in *Re C* [1994] 1 FLR 26 in which the test was said to be whether it was in the child's interests to be allowed to apply.

[124] Children Act 1989, s. 1(1).   [125] *Ibid.*, s. 1(3).

[126] *Ibid.*, s. 1(3)(a).   [127] *Re W*, n. 21 above, 638; *Re E* [1993] 1 FLR 386, 393.

[128] Children Act 1989, s. 9(7).

E. Confidentiality

The general scope of the obligation of confidence has already been discussed. The general position in relation to young children is that they are entitled to confidentiality in health matters and that parents can determine when to consent to the disclosure of information. If they seek to do so against the interests of their children, then the courts can prevent them doing so by a prohibited steps order under the Children Act 1989, section 8.[129] However, further questions have to be considered in relation to older children who may wish information to be confidential as against their parents. The first of these questions concerns the circumstances in which an obligation of confidence arises. The second concerns any special justification for breaching confidence which may exist in relation to children which would not exist where adult patients were involved.

Most commentators agree that the implication of the decision of the House of Lords in *Gillick* is that a child who is competent to consent to a course of treatment is entitled to the same obligation of confidence as any adult patient.[130] Consequently, once professionals have found that a child has the legal capacity to consent to the treatment then they have also established the existence of an obligation of confidence. This would be to the same confidentiality as an adult, so that relatives could not normally be given information.

There has been dispute, however, over the position of children who are incapable of giving a valid consent to treatment, but maintain that their parents should not be informed that they have sought professional advice. Kennedy has argued that incompetent minors are not entitled to confidentiality, and that a professional has the right to discuss matters with the parents of such a child. He goes further and argues that there is a duty to pass on information which is not trivial and which has a bearing on the child's welfare.[131] In contrast, however, it has also been argued that the reasoning in the *Gillick* decision implies that children who can understand the obligation of confidence, even if they cannot understand the treatment in question, can impose such an obligation on a health professional.[132] The latter view is based on the fact that the preconditions of the legal obligation of confidence are made out

---

[129]   *Re Z* [1995] 4 All ER 961, 978–84.

[130]   e.g. de Cruz, n. 5 above, 105–7; Kennedy, n. 9 above, 115.

[131]   Kennedy, n. 9 above, 111–17.

[132]   J. Montgomery, 'Confidentiality and the Immature Minor' [1987] Fam. L 101–4; Lord Scarman, 'Law and Medical Practice' in P. Byrne (ed.), *Medicine in Contemporary Society* (Oxford: King's Fund, 1987), 131–9, 138; BMA, *Medical Ethics Today* (London: BMJ Publishing Group, 1993), 47, 80, 100.

in relation to children who claim the right of secrecy on exactly the same basis as in relation to adults.[133]

In order to sustain Kennedy's position it must be shown that there is some special reason to treat children differently. He offers two such arguments. First, he suggests that the basis of the obligation of confidence is the need to preserve an area of autonomous decision-making. Where children cannot make valid decisions about treatment he argues that the matter is outside their claims to autonomy. There are two problems with this approach. The first is that it fails if the basis of confidentiality is not the preservation of autonomy. As a matter of ethics, privacy rights also have a strong claim as the root of the obligation. As a matter of English law, however, it seems that the interest which gives rise to the obligation of confidence in the health care context is a public interest.[134] The arguments for confidentiality, even for an immature minor, are that unless children feel able to trust the professional to keep information secret they will not be candid about revealing it (this is one of the justifications for confidentiality for adult patients). In relation to children there is an even stronger public policy reason for enforcing confidentiality, in that without the guarantee of secrecy many problems will never come to light. Once the professional knows of the circumstances he or she can seek to persuade the child to allow the parents to be informed, but without the promise of confidentiality the professional will never be trusted with the information at all. Further, Kennedy's argument assumes that there is only one autonomous decision to be made, about accepting or refusing treatment offered. It is clear from the *Gillick* decision, however, that children can take decisions which they are competent to make as they reach that stage of competence and not at a single radical rite of passage whereby they become adults for all purposes. There is no reason of principle why the obligation of confidence cannot be created independently of any later treatment decision.

Kennedy's second argument is that the parents have a right to know information which is needed to enable them to carry out their common law duties to care for the child. If the child cannot give a valid consent, then he argues that the matter must fall within the responsibility of a parent to decide on the child's behalf. This is in line with the statement of Lord Templeman who said, in the *Gillick* decision, that 'confidentiality owed to an infant is not breached by disclosure to a parent responsible for that infant if the doctor considers that such disclosure is necessary in the interests of an infant'. The difficulty with such an approach is that it reaches too far. As children are mature for some purposes and not others it would seem that it would negate any right of confidentiality which existed in mature minors. It could always be argued that

---

[133] Montgomery, n. 132 above.   [134] *W* v. *Egdell* [1990] 1 All ER 835, see Ch. 11.

parents would need to know that a mature minor was having a sexual relationship in order to carry out their common law duties of care, yet this would be incompatible with the decision in *Gillick*. Further difficulties for Kennedy's view arise from the fact that parents retain their right to consent even when young people are mature enough to do so themselves. If it were true that parents are entitled to sufficient information to carry out their duties, and the latter include consenting on behalf of older children, then they would always be entitled to know of their children's health affairs. Thus, no patients under the age of 18 would be entitled to confidentiality against their parents.

Such a position is incompatible with the terms of the Access to Health Records Act 1990. Parents can normally demand information that the professionals do not wish to reveal through an application under that Act. However, it specifically provides that competent children may prevent their records being disclosed. Where they are able to appreciate the nature of the application for access and refuse to consent to their parents seeing the records, then the parents may not be given access.[135] Even when a child cannot appreciate the nature of the application, the health professional is not bound to allow the parents access if it would be against the child's interest.[136] Further, access cannot be given to any part of the record that would disclose information provided by a child in the expectation that it would not be disclosed to the applicant.[137] Thus, if children confide in health professionals on the basis that their parents will not find out, then parents must be refused access to the records of that consultation. The policy of the Act seems clearly to be one of confidentiality for children who seek it.

Kennedy is, of course, correct to say that it cannot be the case that there is an absolute obligation of confidentiality in relation to immature children. However, no obligation of confidence is absolute. The established exceptions will apply to children just as they would apply to an adult. But the first issue, when the obligation of confidence arises, is to be governed by general principles. Consequently, provided that the information is imparted to health professionals in the expectation that it will not be revealed, that information should be regarded as confidential. Any child who refuses to allow his or her parents to be informed indicates that this expectation exists.

So far as the exceptions to confidentiality are concerned, clearly children can consent to the sharing of information with their parents. As a matter of professional ethics it is undoubtedly acceptable to seek to persuade them to allow this to happen. It is pertinent to ask, however, whether the public

---

[135] S. 4(2)(a).
[136] S. 4(2)(b) for exclusion from all the records and s. 5(1)(a) for exclusion from part of the records.
[137] S. 5(3).

interest exception can be used to justify informing parents of their child's attendance for health care. The implication of the *Gillick* decision must be that there can be no general argument that parents have the right to know merely because they are parents. That case was premised on the recognition that the views of parents and children as to what is in the latter's interests may diverge and that where they do so the child's decision can be legally effective. This public policy is reinforced by the provisions of the Access to Health Records Act 1990. These not only permit the health professionals to prevent parents having access to the records of consultations that their children entered into on an understanding of confidentiality, they actually oblige the health professionals to prevent access being given under the Act.

The British Medical Association has now come to the view that children are entitled to expect confidentiality, quite independently of their capacity to consent to treatment.[138] This would seem to be in accordance with the law. However, as the law of confidentiality is essentially founded on public policy,[139] and there has been no definitive statement of where that policy lies, there is still scope for uncertainty.

F. Child Care Law

The final area to be considered in this Chapter is that of child care law. A brief outline of the orders that permit compulsory intervention into families in the interests of children who may be at risk is important because of the role that may be played by health professionals in that process. This section describes the basic philosophy of the Children Act 1989, the main orders introduced, and discusses the role of expert medical evidence in proceedings.

The two most fundamental principles on which the Children Act 1989 is built are, first, that the welfare of children is paramount, and, secondly, that the best way to protect that welfare is to support the care of children within their families.[140] The first principle is enshrined in the rule that governs all decisions made by courts that concern the upbringing of a child; that 'the child's welfare shall be the court's paramount consideration'.[141] This means that the courts should base their decisions on the needs of children, rather than legal technicalities. The presumption that family care should be supported, unless proved to be against the child's interests, runs through many of

---

[138] BMA, n. 132 above, 47, 57, 87–8.   [139] See Ch. 10.

[140] For an introduction to the philosophy and origins of the Act, see J. Eekelaar and R. Dingwall, *The Reform of Child Care Law* (London: Routledge, 1990).

[141] Children Act 1989, s. 1(1).

the provisions of the Act. The primary duties of local authorities are to safe-guard and promote the welfare of children within their areas who are in need, and to provide services to that end, so far as possible doing so by promoting the upbringing of such children by their families.[142] The responsibility of parents can only be restricted under a court order, providing a safeguard against over-zealous intervention by local authorities.

(i) Care and Supervision Orders

The main orders that will be used in child care cases are care and supervision orders. The grounds for those orders are identical, the difference between them lying in the powers given to the local authority.[143] Under a care order, the local authority shares parental responsibility with the parents. However, it can place restrictions on exercise of parental responsibility by the parents, and can remove the child from their care if it chooses. The fact that a care order does not remove the parental responsibility of the parents means that parents usually retain the right to consent to health care for the children. Only if the local authority had specifically decided to prevent them making such choices would they be unable to do so. One common problem is the extent to which parents are permitted to keep in contact with their children, including visiting them in hospital. Under the Children Act 1989, a local authority must permit children to have reasonable contact with their families unless a court has directed that it should not take place.[144] The only exception to this arises where there is an urgent need to prevent contact in order to protect the child's interests. Then the local authority may refuse to allow contact for up to seven days. If there is a need to bar contact for a longer period, then the local authority must seek a court order.

A supervision order does not give the local authority as much power as a care order. The local authority is obliged to 'advise, assist and befriend' the child, and has the power to require the person looking after the child to live in a specified place, or attend at such a place with the child. Supervision orders may also include directions for the child to undergo medical or psychiatric examination and treatment, but these must normally be made by the court, in the order itself. Supervisors can sometimes require that examinations take place, but only if the court specifically gives them the power to do so when it makes the order.[145] Such examinations and treatment cannot be ordered in

---

[142] *Ibid.*, s. 17(1).

[143] The Children Act 1989 permits 'authorized persons' to carry out many of the functions of local authorities in child protection cases. The only such body at present is the National Society for the Prevention of Cruelty to Children.

[144] Children Act 1989, s. 34.   [145] *Ibid.*, s. 35, Sch. 3.

respect of a child with 'sufficient understanding to make an informed decision' unless the child consents.[146] This phrase has been held to import the common law test for '*Gillick* competence'.[147] It has also been held that the inherent jurisdiction can be used to override the child's statutory rights to refuse examinations and treatment.[148] There is no sanction for failing to comply with a supervision order other than returning to court for a care order.

There are three steps in the decision that a court makes when determining whether to make a care or supervision order. First, it must consider the condition of the child. No care order can be made unless the child 'is suffering, or is likely to suffer, significant harm'.[149]

Harm is broadly defined so as to embrace damage to physical and mental health, and also the impairment of physical, intellectual, emotional, social, and behavioural development.[150] Clearly, the evidence of health professionals may be essential in establishing whether this part of the test for a care order is made out. The relevant time for assessing the situation is when the local authority first intervened to protect the child.[151]

The second step in showing that a care or supervision order should be made examines the causes of the harm, or risk of harm, suffered by the child. A care order cannot be made unless it is attributable to the care available to the child 'not being what it would be reasonable to expect a parent to give', or, alternatively, attributable to the child being beyond parental control.[152] Once again the evidence of health professionals may be important in determining what parenting skills could reasonably be expected. It is only the care offered by the child's parents that is relevant, not that from other members of the family[153] (although their care may be relevant to the third step in the decision making process).

The third stage in the process is to consider whether an order is necessary in order to promote the child's interests.[154] The courts are instructed not to make an order unless they consider that doing so will be better for the child than making no order at all.[155] Thus there is a 'no-order' presumption and it must be shown that, in addition to the threshold requirements described in the previous two paragraphs, the child will benefit from the order. The principle is that courts should not make orders merely because they have the legal power to do so; they must consider whether they will do any good.

---

[146] Children Act 1989, Sch. 3, para. 4(4), 5(5).   [147] *Re S* [1993] 3 All ER 36.

[148] *South Glamorgan CC* v. *B and W*, n. 26 above; see 583–4.

[149] Children Act 1989, s. 31(1)(2)(a).   [150] *Ibid.*, s. 31(9).

[151] *Re M* [1994] 3 All ER 298.   [152] Children Act 1989, s. 31(1)(2)(b).

[153] *Re M*, n. 151 above, implicitly overruling *Oldham MBC* v. *E* [1994] 1 FLR 568.

[154] Children Act 1989, s. 1(1).   [155] *Ibid.*, s. 1(5).

(ii) Child Protection

Care orders are used where the local authority, and the court, can be fairly clear that the child's needs require intervention. Should the need arise for local authorities to act urgently, then an emergency protection order can be obtained from a magistrate, if necessary out of hours without notice to the family. The local authority must satisfy the magistrate of four things.[156] First, that there is reasonable cause to believe that the child will suffer significant harm if not removed (with the same broad definition of harm discussed above). Secondly, that enquiries to ascertain whether intervention is necessary are being frustrated by an unreasonable refusal of access to the child. Thirdly, that there are reasons to believe that such access is urgently required. Fourthly, that it is in the child's interests to make the order. An emergency protection order gives the local authority parental responsibility, and permits it to remove the child from the parents, but not to prevent contact unless specifically directed in the order.[157] It lasts for eight days, or less if specified by the order itself, and can be renewed once for up to a further seven days. The court may add directions for medical or psychiatric examinations of the child.[158] It may also direct that the officers of the local authority may choose to be accompanied by a doctor, nurse, or health visitor when they exercise their powers under an emergency protection order.[159]

The child assessment order is designed to deal with a slightly different problem. Sometimes, there is cause to be concerned about a child, but no concrete evidence that he or she is at risk. Without such evidence, it may be difficult to prove the grounds for an emergency protection order. Instead, there is a need to examine the child in order to confirm or dispel suspicions. The child assessment order is designed to facilitate such investigation. It can be made where the court is satisfied that the local authority has reasonable cause to suspect that the child may be suffering or likely to suffer significant harm, but that an assessment of the child's health or development is necessary to determine whether this is in fact the case, and that such an assessment is unlikely to be made without a child assessment order.[160] As usual the court will also have to be satisfied that it would be in the child's interests to make the order.[161] If a child assessment order is made it will specify a date on which assessment should begin, and make any necessary directions about the manner of the assessment. The people looking after the child will be obliged to produce the child and comply with the directions. A child may only be kept away from home if that is specifically directed in the order.[162]

---

[156] *Ibid.*, s. 44(1). [157] *Ibid.*, s. 44(4),(6),(13). [158] *Ibid.*, s. 44(6).
[159] *Ibid.*, s. 45(12). [160] *Ibid.*, s. 43(1). [161] *Ibid.*, s. 1(1).
[162] *Ibid.*, s. 43(9).

A child assessment order also authorizes any person, quite probably a health professional, to carry out the assessment itself. However, children have a statutory right to refuse to be medically examined under a child assessment order or emergency protection order if they have 'sufficient understanding'. This imports the common law test for '*Gillick* competence',[163] although the inherent jurisdiction can be used to override the child's statutory rights to refuse examinations and treatment.[164]

(iii) Expert Evidence and Reports

Expert medical and psychiatric evidence often plays a crucial role in child care cases. The courts have now had to consider the responsibilities of expert witnesses, and the way in which their reports will be used in a number of cases. When directions are made for the appointment of experts, they should specify precisely the expertise required. Joint instructions, whereby one report is produced to be used by all parties, should also be considered.[165] In *Re AB* Wall J pointed out that judges would not normally become involved in medical controversies, and were therefore dependent upon the skill and integrity of expert witnesses.[166] Those experts are consequently expected to be objective, not partisan.[167] When producing their reports, experts should make use of any information already in their case notes, ask for more information if necessary, and confer with any other experts involved so that they can all be objective. They should also be updated by the lawyers if there are any developments in the case, to ensure that their evidence takes everything into account.[168] In *Re AB* it was reiterated that expert witnesses should make all their material available to the other experts in the case.

It is important to note that the need for the court to have all the relevant information to assess the child's position has important implications for the confidentiality of reports. While there are strict rules preventing publicity or dissemination beyond the confidential context of the proceedings,[169] medical experts cannot normally prevent their views being known to the parties. It is only in exceptional circumstances that evidence can be withheld from the parties in care proceedings.[170] This means that it is not possible for experts who interview children in relation to child care cases to guarantee that their parents will not find out what they say.[171] The courts have also advised that any experts' reports that are relevant to the case need to be disclosed, even if they

---

[163] *Re S*, n. 147 above.   [164] *South Glamorgan CC* v. *B and W*, n. 26 above; see 583–4.
[165] *Re G* [1994] 2 FLR 291.   [166] [1995] 1 FLR 181.
[167] *Re R* [1991] 1 FLR 291.   [168] *Re M* [1994] 1 FLR 479.
[169] Family Proceedings Courts (Children Act 1989) Rules 1991, SI 1991 No 1395, r. 23.
[170] *Re M* [1994] 1 FLR 760; *Re C* [1996] 1 FLR 797.   [171] *Re G* [1993] 2 FLR 293.

would be adverse to the client commissioning the report, and it is not intended to use them.[172] Thus medical experts can insist that their reports be put before the courts if they think that the party commissioning them might be reluctant to do so.[173]

G. Conclusion

It can be seen that, in general, the law is protective of health care professionals getting on with the task of caring for children. The judges believe that the legal role of consent is primarily to provide a defence to actions against health professionals.[174] Where there is difficulty, the courts can be involved as an independent body to review what care is appropriate. The judges are usually content to support the plans of health professionals, and they will certainly never force them to act against their clinical judgement. Provided the rules are understood and the proper consents sought, it is unlikely that the law will obstruct children's health care.

Sometimes, however, this tendency to support professional practice exists at the expense of the rights of young people to autonomy. The possibility of parents consenting for their competent children breaks the link between consent and refusal, and denies young people the right to control their treatment. Adults will have an effective legal veto on care that they do not want because no one is entitled to consent on behalf of a competent adult.[175] This means that there is only one source of a valid consent and, if that is not forthcoming, then no treatment is possible. In the same position, no matter how mature they are, young people who have decided to withhold consent do not have a right of veto. A valid consent may be provided by their parent(s), the local authority (if they are in care), or the courts.

The fact that the law puts the protection of health professionals above the autonomy of young people is no accident. Lord Donaldson argued that the fact that his approach supported doctors as evidence that he must have been right:

> If the position in law is that upon the achievement of 'Gillick competence' there is a transfer of the right of consent from parents to child and there can never be a concurrent right in both, doctors would be faced with an

---

[172] *Re L* [1996] 2 All ER 78; *Oxfordshire CC* v. *M* [1994] 2 All ER 269; *Re DH* [1994] 1 FLR 679; *Essex CC* v. *R.* [1993] 2 FLR 826.

[173] See also *W* v. *Egdell*, n. 134 above, which implies that a doctor could send a copy of the report to the other parties.

[174] See the introduction to Ch. 10.   [175] *Re T* [1992] 4 All ER 649, 653.

intolerable dilemma, particularly when the child was nearing the age of 16, if the parents consented but the child did not. On pain, if they got it wrong, of being sued for trespass to the person or possibly being charged with criminal assault, they would have to determine as a matter of law in whom the right of consent resided at a particular time in relation to the particular treatment.[176]

The law of consent has thus been carefully shaped in order to facilitate children's health care. It exposes young people to paternalistic judgments.[177]

The extent to which young people will actually be denied the chance to decide what health care they receive is in the hands of the health professionals who care for them. The law permits them to disregard young people's wishes. It does not force them to do so. That is a matter for their consciences. The United Nations Convention on the Rights of the Child gives all children who are capable of forming their own views the right to express those views in matters affecting them, and to have those views given due weight in the accordance with their age and maturity.[178] Professionals who wish to operate in the spirit of that Convention can do so by ensuring the maximum involvement of young patients in decisions. However, wide-ranging reforms are needed to enshrine such an approach in the law.[179]

In relation to confidentiality, the law seems more committed to the rights of young people. However, this may well be because in that context their interests in privacy coincide with the smooth running of the health care system. On the other hand, child care law is undoubtedly aimed at protecting the interests of children, with less concern for the position of adults. When health professionals become involved in legal cases, they need to remember that that objective partly displaces some aspects of confidentiality in order to ensure that the courts have the best information available to them.

---

[176] *Re R*, n. 10 above, 185.

[177] J. Murphy, 'W(h)ither Adolescent Autonomy?' [1992] *JSWFL* 529–44.

[178] Art. 12.

[179] P. Alderson and J. Montgomery, *Health Care Choices: Making Decisions with Children* (London: Institute for Public Policy Research, 1996).

13   Mental Health

This Chapter considers the law relating to mental health services. This is often assumed to be concerned only with the Mental Health Act 1983, which is the latest in a series of statutes dealing specifically with the mentally ill.[1] However, that Act deals primarily with compulsory detention in hospital. Mental health services cover much more than this. They aim to care for most patients in the community rather than in hospital. This means that most of the work of mental health professionals is governed by the general principles of health care law, rather than special rules for mental health. Even where patients are admitted to hospital, the majority are not compulsorily detained, but are there voluntarily (although the threat of detention may be sufficient to make them 'volunteer'). Such patients are often known as 'informal' patients because they do not come under the formal provisions of the Mental Health Act. It should also be remembered that services are provided to those who have learning difficulties as well as those suffering from mental disorder. For such patients, compulsory detention will often not be necessary, but they may spend long periods in the care of the NHS.

The Chapter begins by looking at aspects of care in the community. This includes the rights of clients to receive services (see also Chapter 3). Most of the Mental Health Act 1983 is drafted to deal with patients who need to be admitted to hospital. Only guardianship exists for patients who have never been liable to be detained compulsorily in hospital. However, the use of leave under section 17 of the Act and supervised after-care are examined as examples of laws that may help underpin community mental health care. There are also a number of protective powers that may be available outside the Mental Health Act. The law governing compulsory admission to hospital and the treatment of detained patients is then explored. The Chapter ends by explaining the ways in which patients may be discharged from hospital.

The focus of this Chapter on law that is specifically concerned with those with mental health problems should not obscure the fact that the general principles of health care law will be remain important for the work of

---

[1] C. Unsworth, *The Politics of Mental Health Legislation* (Oxford: Oxford University Press, 1987) explores the legislative history of psychiatry.

professionals who specialize in the area. Malpractice issues are common to all areas of practice (see Chapters 7 and 8). Issues of confidentiality and consent will be governed by the principles discussed in Chapters 10 and 11, save where the special provisions of the 1983 Act apply (see section E below). While patients detained under the Mental Health Act may make complaints to the Mental Health Act Commission, the NHS complaints procedures described in Chapter 5 are also available. Issues relating to family planning for those with learning difficulties are examined in Chapter 16.

One interesting feature of the Mental Health Act 1983 is the Code of Practice issued under it.[2] This Code gives guidance to practitioners. It explains and sometimes elaborates the law, and also encourages good practice beyond what is strictly required by law. Although it does not strictly have legal force, it is laid before Parliament, and cannot be issued if either House passes a resolution requiring it to be withdrawn or altered. The Code of Practice is mentioned at various points in this Chapter where it illuminates the law or explains how it should be implemented. Departure from the Code is not in itself illegal, but it might suggest that professionals have acted negligently.

A. Legal Aspects of Care in the Community

(i) Rights to Services

As with many areas of health care, the emphasis of much of the work of mental health professionals is on enabling clients to live in their own homes. The provision of appropriate services is crucial to achieving this. Rights to community care services have already been discussed in Chapter 3. People with learning difficulties and mental health problems would qualify for assessment for such services, and would be entitled to have their needs met under the Chronically Sick and Disabled Act 1970. However, it has been seen that it may be difficult to enforce these rights.

Those leaving hospital after detention under the Mental Health Act 1983 may be better off. They have a specific entitlement to after-care under section 117 of that Act. This requires the health authority for the area in which the patient will live on discharge to provide after-care services until it is satisfied that the patient no longer needs them. In *R. v. Ealing DHA, ex p. Fox*[3] a patient was conditionally discharged by a Mental Health Review Tribunal, one of the conditions being that he was supervised in the community. The health

---

[2] S. 118. For discussion, see P. Fennell, 'The Mental Health Act Code of Practice' (1990) 53 *MLR* 499–507 and M. Cavadino, 'Commissions and Codes: A Case Study in Law and Public Administration' [1993] *Public Law* 333–45.   [3] [1993] 3 All ER 129 (QBD).

authority's consultant psychiatrists assessed the patient and concluded that he was not appropriate for such services. The judge held that this did not enable the authority to evade its duty to provide services. While he refused to issue mandamus to force the authority actually to provide the services, on the basis that it would be to force a doctor to treat a patient against his clinical judgement, he did quash the decision not to provide services. He held that the authority was bound to explore other means of providing the services, either from its own resources or from other health authorities. If that failed, then it should refer the matter to the Secretary of State so that he could consider referring the matter back to the Mental Health Review Tribunal for further consideration.

It is not clear how the court would have dealt with the impasse that would have arisen if the matter had been referred back to the tribunal, but the tribunal had remained convinced that the patient should be discharged despite there being no consultant prepared to take responsibility for him. It seems that, while the statutory obligation is phrased in terms of providing services, the reality is that the authority is obliged to use its best endeavours to secure services. This is probably clearer now that the purchasing and provision of services have been separated under the NHS and Community Care Act 1990. Health authorities will now not ordinarily be providers of services and must fulfil their statutory obligations by contracting for them (see Chapter 4). This may open up the way to a remedy in damages where they fail to arrange for after-care services. In the *Fox* case, the judge held that the obligation to provide such services was a specific duty owed to the individual patient. Thus, a negligent failure to meet that duty will be easier to pursue in an action for compensation than a failure in the general obligations to provide mental health services under section 3 of the NHS Act 1977.[4]

(ii) Supervision in the Community

Sometimes, it will be appropriate for patients to be subject to some form of support and supervision if they are to be cared for properly in the community. Two non-statutory initiatives are aimed to ensure that patients get the care that they need. The first is known as the 'Care Programme Approach' (CPA), which was required to be implemented in 1991.[5] This is a system for co-

---

[4] See Ch. 3 for discussion of this possibility.

[5] See 'Care Programme Approach (CPA) for People with a Mental Illness referred to the Specialist Psychiatric Services' (HC(90)23); Department of Health, *Building Bridges—A Guide to Arrangements for Inter-agency Working for the Care and Protection of Severe Mentally Ill People* (London: DoH, 1995); and the non-mandatory form issued by the Department of Health on 6 Feb. 1996, 'After Care Form for the Discharge of Psychiatric Patients (Including Those Subject to the Mental Health Act 1983, s. 117)' under the signature of Ian Jewesbury.

operation between health and social services to ensure that an assessment is made of patients' needs and of any risks that they present to themselves or others. A programme of care should be agreed, and a key worker identified to be responsible for co-ordinating the implementation of that care programme. There should also be regular review of the care programme.

Such care programmes can be used for any patient in contact with specialist psychiatric services, but they should always be used when patients are discharged from psychiatric hospitals. Greater clarification of the content of care programmes should make it less likely that failures of communication lead to patients' interests being neglected. It will also make it easier to identify whether mental health professionals have failed to implement the care that they identified as appropriate.

In 1994 the Government introduced a political and administrative, but not legal, imperative to establish 'supervision registers' for those patients who are 'potentially at significant risk of committing serious violence or suicide or of serious self neglect as a result of severe and enduring mental illness'.[6] Risk assessments should be made of all patients who may need to be entered on the register. They may be patients who are in hospital and considered for discharge, or patients who are in the community (whether or not they have previously been in-patients). No new resources have been made available for the implementation of supervision registers, so that their effect is to target existing services more closely to those in the severest need, at the expense of the less severely ill. The legality and effectiveness of supervision registers has been questioned,[7] but health authorities have been instructed to ensure that they are in place through their contracts for services. Patients who are on the supervision register should be reviewed by the responsible medical officer at least once a month.

The care-programme approach and supervision registers are administrative mechanisms for ensuring that patients receive the care they need in the community. Neither initiative provides any legal powers to facilitate the delivery of that care. However, the Mental Health Act does provide three options that may do so. The first is guardianship.[8] A patient who is subject to guardianship may be required to reside in a specified place, and to attend specified places for the purpose of medical treatment, occupation or training. The guardian may also require that access to the patient be given to a doctor,

---

[6] NHS Executive, 'Introduction of Supervision Registers for Mentally Ill People' HSG(94)5. See also NHS Executive, 'Guidance on the Discharge of Mentally Disordered People and their Continuing Care in the Community' (HSG(94)27).

[7] T. Thomas, 'Supervision Registers for Mentally Disordered People' (1995) 145 *NLJ* 565–6.

[8] See M. Gunn, 'Mental Health Act Guardianship: Where Now?' [1986] *JSWL* 144–52; M. Fisher, 'Guardianship under the Mental Health Legislation: A Review' [1988] *JSWL* 316–27.

approved social worker, or other specified person at the patient's residence.[9] Guardianship does not provide a power of compulsory treatment.[10] Nor is there any sanction for the patient's non-compliance with conditions. However, some protection is given against abuse of the patient by others. It is an offence to refuse access to patients under guardianship, or to ill-treat or wilfully neglect them.[11]

An application for guardianship may be made if it is necessary in the interests of the patient, or for the protection of other persons, that the patient be received into guardianship. It can only be made if the patient is suffering from mental disorder of a nature and degree which warrants the use of guardianship.[12] Mental disorder here is defined as mental illness, severe mental impairment, psychopathic disorder, or mental impairment. The meaning of these terms is discussed further in relation to compulsory admission (see below). Applications for guardianship can be made by the patient's 'nearest relative' (see below for discussion of the meaning of this phrase) or by an approved social worker.[13] They must be supported by written recommendations from two doctors explaining why the conditions are made out.[14] One of them must be approved for the purpose of applications under the Mental Health Act 1983 and one must have had previous acquaintance with the patient.[15]

Guardianship applications are accepted by social services. Often the social services department will be the guardian, but it is possible for a private person to be the guardian. A private guardian is obliged to nominate a doctor to look after the patient, give the local authority such information with regard to the patient that it requires, and comply with directions given by the authority.[16] Patients received into guardianship should be visited at least every three months, and seen by a doctor approved to make recommendations under the Act at least once a year.[17]

Guardianship is available to patients irrespective of whether or not they have been hospital in-patients. Similar powers are available in relation to patients who have been detained under the Mental Health Act and who are to be discharged, if they need supervision to ensure that they receive after-care. The relevant provisions are to be found in sections 25A to 25J, inserted by the Mental Health (Patients in the Community) Act 1995.[18] As with guardian-

---

[9] Mental Health Act 1983, s. 8(1).
[10] *R.* v. *Hallstrom, ex p. W (No 2)* [1986] 2 All ER 306, 313. [11] Ss. 129(1), 127(2).
[12] S. 7(1). [13] S. 11(1).
[14] S. 7(3); Mental Health (Hospital, Guardianship and Consent to Treatment) Regulations 1983, SI 1983 No 893, r. 5, Sch., Form 19.
[15] S. 12(2). [16] N. 14 above, r. 12. [17] *Ibid.*, r. 13.
[18] See Department of Health, *Guidance on Supervised Discharge (After-care under Supervision) and Related Provisions* (DoH , London, 1996). For discussion, see A. Parkin, 'Caring for Patients in the Community' (1996) 59 *MLR* 414–26.

ship, the patient may be required to reside in a specified place and to attend specified places for the purpose of medical treatment, occupation, education, or training. The supervisor may also require that access to the patient be given to the supervisor, a doctor, approved social worker, or other specified person at the patient's residence.[19]

There are three main differences between being subject to supervised after-care and being under guardianship. The first is that the supervising authority is the health authority (although responsibility for supervision may be delegated to NHS trusts through the contract process) rather than the social services department of the local authority. The second is that supervised discharge offers a legal power to 'take and convey' patients to the places where they are required to be as a condition of the supervision. This provides slightly more authority for the supervisor than is offered by guardianship. However, it does not give any authority to treat the patient, nor does it enable the patient to be detained once he or she has been conveyed to the specified place.[20] If supervised discharge proves inadequate to meet the patient's needs, then the possibility of admission to hospital will have to be explored. The third difference between guardianship and supervised after-care is that patients subject to the latter will have a specific right to services under section 117 (see above). This is because they have been discharged from detention under the Act, not because they have been placed under supervision.

It seems unclear how much supervised discharge will be used. Interpreted strictly, the criteria for its use will exclude many patients.[21] There are three stages in identifying eligible patients. First, their mental condition: they must be suffering from mental disorder (including mental illness, severe mental impairment, psychopathic disorder, and mental impairment). Secondly, there must be a substantial risk of serious harm to the health or safety of the patient, serious harm to the safety of others, or serious exploitation of the patient. The risk is only sufficient to justify supervision if it is anticipated that it will exist *if the patient does not receive after-care services under section 117*. Thus, where the risk is present even with after-care, then it seems that supervised discharge is not available. Thirdly, being subject to supervision must be likely to help secure that the patient does receive those services. Further, if the patient will not co-operate, supervision will not actually help secure the services and the criteria will not be satisfied.

An elaborate process has been laid down for applications for supervised

---

[19] S. 25D(3).
[20] See *R. v. Hallstrom, ex p. W (No 2)*, n. 10 above, 313–14 for these points on the analogous provisions of guardianship.
[21] S. 25A.

after-care.[22] The applicant must be the responsible medical officer, but that doctor must consult with a range of people and take their views into account. These are the patient, one or more persons professionally concerned with the patient's medical treatment in hospital, one or more persons who will be professionally concerned with the after-care under section 117, any other person the doctor thinks will play a substantial role in the patient's care after leaving hospital, and the nearest relative. The patient may request that the nearest relative not be consulted, but that request will not be effective where the patient has a propensity for violent or dangerous behaviour and the responsible medical officer thinks that it is appropriate to consult the nearest relative. In addition to the consultation, a series of written recommendations are required, from the doctor to be responsible for the after-care, an approved social worker, and the supervisor. Details of the proposed after-care and any requirements to be imposed as conditions of the supervision must also be provided. Once in place, supervised after-care must be kept under review and, specifically, consideration must be given to either discharging the supervision or applying to admit the patient to hospital if there is refusal of after-care or non-compliance with the specified conditions.[23]

There is one provision in the Act that does effectively permit patients to be treated in the community. That is the power to permit patients to leave hospital on section 17 leave, without discharging them from their 'section.' They therefore remain 'liable to be detained in hospital'. This means that they come within Part IV of the Act,[24] which permits treatment without consent (see section E below). Patients on section 17 leave can be recalled to hospital, and if necessary a magistrate's warrant may authorize entry to private premises to enable the patient to be removed.[25] Leave can also be granted subject to conditions. These could be similar to those available with guardianship and supervised after-care if the responsible medical officer so chooses. Patients can remain on section 17 leave for the whole period of detention authorized by their section.[26] This permits the use of leave to oversee the care of patients in the community for up to twelve months.

B. Powers of Protection

In some cases, the concern of professionals will be less with powers of compulsion over clients than with the need to protect them. Many people with

---

[22] Ss. 25A–25B; The Mental Health (After-care under Supervision) Regulations 1996, SI 1996 No 294.

[23] S. 25E.   [24] *R.* v. *Hallstrom, ex p. W (No 2)*, n. 10 above, 312.

[25] S. 135(2).   [26] S. 17(5), as amended.

learning difficulties and mental health problems will be vulnerable to abuse. The courts have gone a little way to dealing with these problems through an imaginative use of the jurisdiction to issue declarations as to the best interests of incompetent persons. Such an order may be sought by those closely connected to the client, including carers.[27] Most of the case law has concerned decisions about sterilization, and the procedural aspects of seeking declarations are discussed in Chapter 16.[28] However, a few cases have concerned issues that are of importance to mental health care in the community. Here, the courts have used their power to declare what the rights of people are in order to determine important questions about their care. Thus, a physically handicapped young man obtained a declaration that he was entitled to choose where he wished to live, and evade the restrictions of his over-protective mother.[29] In *Re S* the court prevented an incapacitated patient being moved out of hospital in England, declaring that the move was unlawful pending a full assessment of his interests.[30] It was in breach of his right 'not to have his bodily integrity invaded without his consent or some other lawful justification'.

One important issue for those who are mentally incapacitated in some way will be to maintain contact with people who are of importance to them. It has been held that people have fundamental rights under common law and the European Convention on Human Rights which can be used to support this. In *Re C*[31] the judge held that if a carer were to prevent an incapacitated woman from having contact with her mother, that would be an infringement of her right to freedom of association, and the court could issue a declaration to that effect. Such a declaration will usually be sufficient to establish that contact should take place. However, if there continues to be no contact, then other actions could be used, such as a writ of habeas corpus (requiring the imprisoned person to be released) or an action for damages for the tort of wrongful imprisonment.

The use of declarations in this way is limited by the fact that it is necessary to show that a right recognized at common law is in issue. Thus, in *Cambridgeshire CC* v. *R*[32] it was held that no declaration could be made that

[27] *Re S* [1995] 3 All ER 290. See also *Re S* (*No 2*) [1995] 4 All ER 30, holding that this jurisdiction was available for incapacitated patients present in England and Wales.

[28] The application is brought under Ord. 15, r. 16 of the Rules of the Supreme Court.

[29] *Re V* [1995] 2 FLR 1003.

[30] [1995] 2 WLR 38; upheld by the CA in *Re S* [1995] 3 All ER 290, which was primarily concerned with whether the applicant had sufficient standing to bring the proceedings.

[31] [1993] 1 FLR 940 (FD). It should be noted that the case concerned the jurisdiction of the court. It did not consider whether the father, who was caring for his daughter, was in fact preventing her from having contact with her mother, or whether, if he was so doing, that was against the woman's interests.

[32] [1995] 1 FLR 50 (FD).

it would be against a client's interests if her family did have contact with her because the only right recognized by law was to associate with people. There was no right *not* to associate with them. Thus the social workers could not seek the court's help in protecting a client that they regarded as vulnerable to abuse from her family (she had been sexually abused by her father when she was a child). Protective powers are available for those under the age of 18 (see Chapter 12), but not for adults.

In the *Cambridgeshire* case, the client was expressing an interest in seeing her family. Where a client does not wish to see a person, it may be possible to obtain an order excluding that person from the client's home on the basis of his or her right to quiet enjoyment of the home. The courts will issue injunctions to prevent people disrupting the use of property. This can clearly be used where clients own, or are tenants of, a property and their rights to exclude other people from it are being ignored. It has also been accepted that people who live in a house with the permission of the owner, but with no formal legal rights to stay there, can be protected in the same way.[33] Protection may also be available under the Family Law Act 1996, when implemented, as those with mental health problems may be 'associated' with abusive persons within the meaning of the Act[34] (which is designed to deal with domestic violence).

The legal position will be stronger if a client is being physically, including for this purposes sexually, abused. All people have a right to bodily integrity, protected by the criminal law and the action for trespass to the person (discussed in the context of consent). If a client is being abused, criminal proceedings may be appropriate. However, the right to bodily integrity will be in issue if there is a dispute about how an incapacitated person is being cared for, whether at home or in hospital. As a right is at stake, it will be possible to secure a declaration that the 'care' being given is, or is not, in the best interests of the client.

Specific protection is given by the criminal law in relation to sexual abuse of those who are mentally incapacitated. It is an offence for a man to have unlawful sexual intercourse with a woman in a state of arrested or incomplete development of mind, including severe impairment of intelligence and social functioning.[35] It is also an offence for a male member of staff in a hospital or nursing home to have unlawful sexual intercourse with a patient or client. Under the same provision, it is also an offence for a guardian to have unlawful sexual intercourse with a woman in his care.[36] These provisions serve to protect women with learning difficulties, but they may also limit their rights

---

[33] *Khorasandjian* v. *Bush* [1993] 3 All ER 669 (CA).
[34] See Family Law Act 1996, Pt. III.   [35] Sexual Offences Act 1956, s. 7.
[36] Mental Health Act 1959, s. 128. 'Unlawful' has usually been taken to mean outside marriage, but it may be merely a superfluous word, see *R.* v. *R* [1991] 4 All ER 481.

to sexual expression.[37] Particular problems have arisen in relation to the use of sterilization to control the fertility of people with learning difficulties (see Chapter 16).

A final set of protective powers concerns the administration of the property of clients who are unable to manage it for themselves. Under the Enduring Powers of Attorney Act 1985, it is possible for people to appoint someone to manage their property on their behalf. Usually, such an appointment is automatically revoked when the patient becomes unable to deal with his or her property. However, under the Act proxies can be appointed to take control after the patient becomes incompetent. Such proxies can be removed by the Court of Protection if they abuse their powers. If the patient has not made an appointment under the Enduring Powers of Attorney Act, then it is possible to apply to the Court of Protection for it to oversee the patient's financial affairs. It may do this by appointing a receiver.[38]

C. Admission to Hospital

Most patients will agree to hospital admission. If this happens, there are no special legal implications. However, patients may be compulsorily detained under a number of sections of the Mental Health Act. Some of these relate to patients who are referred to mental health services in the course of criminal proceedings.[39] These are not described here. This section is concerned with the powers of compulsory admission available to health professionals.

Section 2 of the Mental Health Act provides doctors with the power to admit patients compulsorily for assessment over a twenty-eight day period. It can be used where two doctors recommend that the patient should be admitted in the interests of his own health or safety or with a view to the protection of other persons. They must also certify that they believe that the patient is suffering from a mental disorder of a nature or degree that warrants detention in hospital for a period of assessment.[40] This should probably be interpreted as meaning a disorder that, if shown to be present when the assessment is carried out, would warrant detention for treatment under section 3. Mental disorder is defined in section 1 of the Act and means mental illness, arrested or incomplete development of mind, psychopathic disorder, and any other disorder or disability of mind. A psychopathic disorder, for these purposes, is a

---

[37] See for discussion, D. Carson, 'The Sexuality of People with Learning Difficulties' [1989] *JSWL* 355–72.
[38] Mental Health Act 1983, Pt. VII.
[39] See Pt. III of the Act.
[40] N. 14 above, Sch., Forms 3–5, as amended.

persistent disorder or disability of the mind which results in abnormally aggressive or seriously irresponsible conduct. The Act specifically states that promiscuity or other immoral conduct, sexual deviancy or dependency on alcohol or drugs cannot be the sole basis for treating someone as suffering from a mental disorder.[41]

The power to detain a patient under section 2 expires after twenty-eight days. There is no provision for extension of that period.[42] Patients may be discharged before the end of this period, and may also be reclassified to one of the other sections of the Act (with the effect that further detention is authorized). Patients who are detained for assessment may also be treated without their consent because Part IV of the Act applies (see section E below).[43]

Where the doctors are reasonably certain of their diagnosis, admission for assessment will not usually be appropriate.[44] Usually, section 3 will be used. That section is available where two doctors certify that they believe the patient is suffering from mental illness, severe mental impairment, psychopathic disorder, or mental impairment.[45] Mental illness is not defined by the Act. The definition of psychopathic disorder was noted above. Severe mental impairment means a state of arrested or incomplete development of mind which includes severe impairment of intelligence and social function. It must be associated with abnormally aggressive or seriously irresponsible conduct to fall within the definition used by the Act. Mental impairment lacks this severity, but covers patients with significant impairment of intelligence and social functioning. Again, it must be associated with abnormally aggressive or seriously irresponsible conduct. The doctors must believe that the patient's condition makes it appropriate for hospital treatment.

In addition to the diagnosis of the patient's condition, to fall with section 3 treatment must be necessary for the health and safety of the patient or for the protection of others. It must also be thought that treatment cannot be provided without detention under the section. The purpose of the section is to secure treatment, and if it is not anticipated that treatment will be effective, then it is difficult to see how it can be 'necessary'. This is a particular problem with psychopathic disorders and mental impairment, which are often incurable. The statute deals with these two categories by requiring that treatment is likely to alleviate, or prevent deterioration of, the patient's condition. It does not matter that this may not happen immediately, or that there may be some deterioration before the patient's condition improves.[46]

[41] S. 1(3).   [42] R. v. *Wilson, ex p. Williamson, Independent*, 19 Apr. 1995 (QBD).
[43] S. 56(1).   [44] Code of practice, sect. 5.
[45] N. 14 above, Sch., Forms 10 and 11, as amended.
[46] R. v. *Cannons Park MHRT, ex p. A* [1994] 2 All ER 659.

Once the application is made, authority for detention under section 3 lasts for six months. It can be renewed, initially for a further six-month period and then annually.[47] There is no limit on the total period of detention (although there will be reviews by a Mental Health Review Tribunal: see section F below). Renewal takes place when the responsible medical officer furnishes a report indicating that three criteria are met:[48] first, that the patient suffers from one of the conditions required for section 3; secondly, that treatment is likely to alleviate or prevent deterioration of that condition (this is not limited to psychopathic disorders and mental impairment as under section 3 itself). In cases of mental illness and severe mental impairment there is an alternative second condition; that the patient, if discharged, is unlikely to be able to care for himself, to obtain the care needed, or to guard himself against serious exploitation. The third criterion is that continued treatment is necessary for the health and safety of the patient or for the protection of other persons, and can only be provided if detention continues.

Applications for compulsory admission under sections 2 and 3 are made by the patient's nearest relative or by an approved social worker[49] (approved for the purposes of the Act). The 'nearest relative' is a technical term. The Act provides a list of relatives, beginning with those that are 'nearer' for the purposes of the definition.[50] They are spouse (including unmarried persons living together as husband and wife), child, parent, sibling, grandparent, grandchild, uncle or aunt, nephew or niece. Within these categories, relatives of full blood have priority over those of half blood, and older relatives take priority over their juniors. However, where the patient lives with or is cared for by a relative, then that relative is regarded as the nearest relative.

As applications are not made by the health professionals and it may take time to secure the necessary recommendations, it is necessary to provide for powers to deal with immediate problems. Section 4 provides for emergency admissions for seventy-two hours on the basis of a single medical recommendation. There are also 'holding powers' that enable a mental nurse or doctor to prevent a patient leaving hospital pending an assessment for detention.[51] 'Holding powers' are also provided for the police, enabling them to detain those suspected of being mentally disordered so that they can be assessed for care. Constables may remove to a place of safety a person who appears to them to be suffering from mental disorder and in immediate need of care and control if they think it is in that person's interests to do so, or if they think it is necessary to do so to protect others.[52]

In some circumstances, it may become apparent that a person may be in need of care due to mental illness, but also that he or she needs to be removed

[47] S. 20.   [48] N. 14 above, Sch., Form 30, as amended.   [49] S. 11.
[50] S. 26.   [51] S. 5.   [52] S. 136.

to a safe place while arrangements for further care are made. Under section 135(1) of the Mental Health Act 1983, an approved social worker can apply to a magistrate for a warrant enabling a police officer to enter premises and remove a person to a place of safety. Such an order can be made where the magistrate is satisfied that there is reasonable cause to believe that the person is suffering from mental disorder, and that one of two conditions is met. The first is that the person has been (or is being) ill-treated, neglected, or not kept under proper control. The second, as an alternative, is that the person is living alone and are unable to care for him- or herself. This power may overlap with the power to remove people to hospital under the National Assistance Acts. Those Acts were discussed in Chapter 2, section H(ii).

D. Patients' Rights in Hospital

The Mental Health Act seeks to ensure that patients are given certain rights. Some of these have already been considered, for example after care services and reviews of detention. Others such as the right to apply for discharge and safeguards in respect of consent to treatment, will be considered in later sections. This section identifies other aspects of the rights of mentally ill patients.

One of these is the role of the Mental Health Act Commission in visiting hospitals where patients are detained and responding to complaints that they make.[53] The Commission takes a proactive role in ensuring that patients are properly treated, making visits so that patients have the opportunity to raise causes for concern. Visits may also involve scrutiny of records to ensure that the proper authority for detention is present. Conditions in hospitals will also be examined and commented upon. Following visits, the Commission will write to the hospitals detailing its findings and will expect defects to be remedied.

Under section 132 of the Act, the managers of hospitals in which patients are detained are obliged to take such steps as are practicable to ensure that patients understand their rights under the Act. The Code of Practice elaborates this obligation.[54] It advises that patients should be given as much information as possible about their care and treatment in a manner that they can understand. Information should be available on displays and notice boards and in admission leaflets, including details of complaints procedures. Particular needs for information to be given arise in relation to consent to treatment, renewal of detention, transfer of status (for example to informal

---

[53] The Commission is established under s. 121 of the Mental Health Act.   [54] In s. 14.

rather than detained under the Act), applications to Mental Health Review Tribunals, and visits by the Mental Health Act Commission. Patients have a statutory right to know under which provisions of the Act they are detained, the effect of those provisions and their rights to apply to a Mental Health Review Tribunal.[55]

In general, patients detained under the Mental Health Act will retain their general rights as citizens.[56] There are restrictions on those of 'unsound mind' standing or voting in public elections and serving on juries. Usually, however, people's capacity to understand what they are doing, rather than their status as a detained patient, will determine their ability to exercise their rights. This will apply, for example, to the management of property and to getting married or divorced. There is one specific limitation on the exercise of general rights that should be mentioned. It is that civil actions cannot be brought against individuals in respect of steps taken under the Mental Health Act without the leave of the court.[57] This means that mental patients are denied immediate access to the courts to vindicate their rights. The restriction is principally one of procedure rather than substance. However, the Act also protects defendants from liability for steps taken under the Act, providing they were not taken in bad faith or without reasonable care. This would not seem to preclude negligence actions (see Chapter 7) because the essence of such a claim is that reasonable care was not exercised.

E. Treatment

For those patients who are 'informal', the legality of treatment will depend on the general rules relating to consent (see Chapter 10). In summary, the law establishes that treatment can only be given to those who are competent to decide whether to accept it if they consent. In addition, safeguards are provided under the Mental Health Act even for informal patients in relation to surgical procedures that destroy brain tissue or its function and also hormone implants designed to reduce the male sex drive. These treatments may not be administered without both consent and a second opinion.[58] Generally, if the patient is unable to make a decision, then the professionals must act in the patient's best interests. Treatment will be lawful in such circumstances pro-

---

[55] S. 132(1).

[56] See B. Hoggett, *Mental Health Law* (3rd edn., London: Sweet & Maxwell, 1990), ch. 10, for discussion.

[57] MHA 1983, s. 139.

[58] S. 56(2) extends the provisions of s. 57 to informal patients. See below for detailed discussion.

viding that a responsible body of professional opinion would accept that it was in the patient's best interests.[59]

The position is different for patients who are liable to be detained under the Act. For them, Part IV of the Act provides a special legal regime for treatment for their mental disorder. These provisions do not apply to those detained under section 4 (emergency applications) unless a second medical opinion has been given. Nor do they apply to those detained under the holding powers in sections 5, 135, and 136.[60] Certain patients dealt with through the criminal justice process are also excluded from the application of Part IV. They are those liable to be detained on remand for report on their mental condition or who have been conditionally discharged.[61]

Part IV of the Act is concerned only with treatment for mental disorder, which includes nursing, and also care, habilitation, and rehabilitation under medical supervision.[62] Other aspects of the care of detained patients are governed by the general law of consent. The implications of this can be seen in *Re C*[63] where a schizophrenic Broadmoor patient was held to be entitled to refuse to have his leg amputated. Treatment could not be administered under the Mental Health Act without his consent because it would not have been treatment for his mental disorder. The issue therefore depended on whether he was competent to refuse treatment. The court found that, even though his illness caused him to have delusions that he was a world famous surgeon, he understood the nature and purpose of the treatment and realized that he might die if he refused treatment. As he was therefore competent, he was entitled to veto the treatment, and the court issued a declaration that his leg could not be amputated without his written consent. In fact, the amputation proved to be unnecessary, as the infection was successfully treated with antibiotics.

Where treatment for mental disorder is concerned, detained patients' rights to refuse treatment are considerably reduced. Under section 63 consent is not required for treatment for mental disorder given by or under the direction of the responsible medical officer unless it comes within the special provisions of section 57 or 58. Under the Code of Practice, staff should still seek to secure the patient's agreement,[64] but there is no legal right to refuse treatment as there is for informal patients. It has also been held that it is lawful to use restraint, so far as reasonably required and clinically necessary, to administer treatment under section 63.[65]

It is therefore important to identify what will constitute treatment for mental disorder within the terms of the Act. In *Re C* the treatment of the patient's

---

[59] *F* v. *W. Berkshire HA* [1989] 2 All ER 545.   [60] S. 56(1).
[61] See ss. 35, 37(4), 42(4), 73, 74.   [62] S. 145(1).
[63] [1994] 1 All ER 819.   [64] Para. 16.16.
[65] *Tameside & Glossop Acute Services Trust* v. *CH* [1996] 1 FCR 753, 766.

gangrene was seen as unconnected with his mental condition. However, in a number of cases, the courts have been prepared to regard treatment that is indirectly, rather than directly, related to the patient's condition as being treatment within section 63.

In *SW Hertfordshire HA* v. *KB*[66] the patient was detained under section 3, having anorexia nervosa. The doctors had initially used section 58 to 'treat' her by naso-gastric feeding even though she was withholding her consent. The Mental Health Act Commission took the view that this was food, not medicine, and told the second-opinion doctor to stop signing the necessary forms. The court took a different view. It held that consent was not required because feeding via a naso-gastric tube came within section 63. The judge reasoned that it had been established that such feeding was treatment,[67] and that this treatment was an integral part of the treatment for anorexia nervosa. The patient's refusal to eat was related to her mental illness, and was not unrelated, as was the infection in *Re C.*

This approach to the scope of section 63 was taken further by the Court of Appeal in *B* v. *Croydon HA.*[68] In that case, the patient suffered from a borderline personality disorder coupled with post-traumatic stress disorder. Her symptoms included depression and compulsion to self-harm resulting from poor self-esteem. When she was detained under the Mental Health Act, she refused to eat as a means of self-harm. The Court of Appeal held that she could be fed through a tube without her consent because such feeding was ancillary to treatment calculated to alleviate her disorder. This encompassed care designed to deal with the consequences of her compulsion to self-harm and would extend to treating the consequence of suicide attempts.[69] It was not necessary to show that each individual action was treatment for the mental disorder, provided that it was part of a plan of care was designed for that purpose. In the Croydon case, it was proposed to use psychotherapy, but it had to be discontinued pending B regaining weight.

Tameside & Glossop Acute Services Trust v. *CH*[70] has extended the scope of treatment under section 63 further still. In that case a patient suffering from schizophrenia was thirty-eight weeks pregnant. The obstetrician treating her was concerned that she might refuse to agree to a caesarean section. The evidence before the court was that she was incapable of understanding the situation, and was therefore unable to give or withhold consent to the operation. This would have made it lawful to perform the caesarean section without her consent because it was in her interests to have a live baby. However, the medical staff anticipated that the patient might resist the procedure. The court found that if it were treatment under section 63, then it would be possible to

---

[66] [1994] 2 FCR 1051 (FD).   [67] *Airedale NHS trust* v. *Bland* [1993] 1 All ER 821.
[68] [1995] 1 All ER 683.   [69] *Ibid.,* 687–8; see also 689.   [70] N. 65 above.

restrain her in order to carry it out. The judge found that it was indeed treatment for mental disorder within that section. The judge thought that this was because an ancillary aim of the caesarean section was to prevent deterioration of the mother's mental health. He argued that, unlike the treatment of the gangrene in *Re C*, the manner of the child's delivery would have a direct effect on the mother's mental state. In fact, the judge found, the psychiatrist had suggested that future treatment for her schizophrenia would be ineffective if she were to lose the baby.

Taken together, these three cases have extended the concept of treatment for mental disorder to such a degree that it would appear that non-psychiatric medical care can be given under section 63 without consent in a wide range of circumstances. Provided that the physical problems are related to the mental disorder, either in their origins or their effects, consent will be strictly unnecessary. The *Croydon* case showed that where self-harm is the product of compulsion brought on by mental illness, then its consequences can be treated. This is important in the management of those who attempt suicide. The *Tameside & Glossop* case suggests that, provided a psychiatrist is prepared to say that the lack of satisfactory medical care will have an adverse effect on the mental health of the patient, medical care can be given as if it were treating the mental disorder itself.

The Mental Health Act provides that some categories of treatment can only be used with special safeguards. The first such category covers surgical procedures that destroy brain tissue or its function and hormone implants designed to reduce the male sex drive.[71] Such treatment can only be given when the patient consents, and in addition a second opinion supports it. The second opinion must be provided by a panel of three people appointed by the Secretary of State.[72] One of them must be a doctor, who is obliged to consult two other people professionally concerned with the patient's medical treatment before giving the second opinion. One of those people to be consulted must be a nurse, the other must be neither a nurse nor a doctor. The second-opinion doctor must certify that the treatment should be given, having regard to the likelihood that it will alleviate the patient's condition or prevent it from deteriorating.[73] This involves considering whether the benefits of treatment would outweigh its disadvantages.[74] The panel collectively must certify that the patient is capable of understanding the nature, purpose, and likely effects of the treatment and has consented to it.[75] The issue is capacity to understand rather than actual understanding, and concerns the likely effects of the treatment, not its possible side-effects.[76]

---

[71] S. 57(1); n. 14 above, r. 16. [72] S. 57(2); n. 14 above, r. 16, Sch., Form 37. [73] S. 57(2)(b).
[74] *R. v. Mental Health Act Commission, ex p. X* (1988) 9 BMLR 77, 89. [75] S. 57(2)(a).
[76] *R. v. Mental Health Act Commission, ex p. X*, n. 74 above, 85.

Electro-convulsive therapy (ECT) is subject to the less strict procedure under section 58.[77] Here, unlike treatment within section 57, patients' refusal of treatment may be overridden. Treatment under this section may be given on the basis of either the patient's consent or a second medical opinion. The second opinion is therefore an alternative to the patient's consent, not an additional safeguard. Where ECT is given on the basis of the patient's consent, a doctor must certify on Form 38 that the patient is capable of understanding the nature, purpose, and likely effects of the treatment and has consented to it.[78] That doctor may be either the responsible medical officer or a doctor appointed by the Mental Health Act Commission to give second opinions under the Act. If consent is not forthcoming, then a second opinion from a doctor appointed for the purpose must certify that the treatment should be given, having regard to the likelihood that it will alleviate or prevent the deterioration of the patient's condition.[79] As with section 57, the doctor must consult two other people professionally concerned with the patient's medical treatment before giving the second opinion. Once again, one of them must be a nurse, the other must be neither a nurse nor a doctor.[80]

Section 58 also applies to the use of medicines after three months.[81] This gives psychiatrists time to establish whether the drug they plan to use is effective, but requires that they have long-term plans reviewed by a second-opinion doctor if the patient is unhappy with them. The three-month period runs from the first use of medication for patients to whom Part IV of the Act applies (see page 325 above). Thus, medication given to informal patients does not start the clock running. Although feeding patients is treatment under section 63, the food that is provided is not 'medicine' within section 58.[82] Consequently, there is no need to obtain a second opinion in relation to artificial feeding that is to be administered once the three-month period has expired. Where medicines are approved by a second opinion, it is not necessary for the doctor to specify a particular drug.

Consents for treatment under sections 57 and 58, and the certificates that are required, do not necessarily have to be obtained on every occasion on which care is given. So long as the treatment is part of a plan of care, consents and certificates may relate to the plan as a whole.[83] However, this does not prevent patients withdrawing their consent at any time.[84] In any event, treatment within the two sections must be regularly reviewed and reported to the Mental Health Act Commission when the authority for detention is renewed.[85]

---

[77] N. 14 above, r. 16(2). [78] S. 58(3)(a); n. 14 above, r. 16, Sch., Form 38.
[79] S. 58(3)(b); n. 14 above, r. 16, Sch., Form 39. [80] S. 58(4).
[81] S. 58(1)(b). [82] B v. Croydon HA [1995] 1 All ER 683.
[83] S. 59. [84] S. 60. [85] S. 62; see Form MHAC 1, produced by the Commission.

The procedures required under sections 57 and 58 are waived in certain circumstances.[86] These are, first, where the treatment is immediately necessary to save the patient's life. In addition care may be given despite the usual restrictions where (providing it is not irreversible) it is immediately necessary to prevent serious deterioration of the patient's condition. Similarly, treatment may be given that is neither irreversible nor hazardous but is immediately necessary to alleviate serious suffering by the patient. Treatment usually within the sections may also be given without the safeguards where it is immediately necessary to prevent the patient from being violent or a danger to himself (or herself) or others, providing that it is the minimum interference necessary and that it is neither irreversible nor hazardous.

F. Discharge

There are a number of ways in which mental health patients may be discharged from hospital. Informal patients are entitled to discharge themselves, although the 'holding powers' described above are available if it is thought that such patients should be detained compulsorily. Detained patients can be discharged whenever the responsible medical officer believes that it is no longer necessary to detain them, unless they are subject to a 'restriction order', when Home Office approval is required.[87] The nearest relative may also discharge the patient, giving seventy-two hours' notice.[88] This power will be rendered ineffective if the responsible medical officer certifies to the hospital managers that the patient would be likely to act in a dangerous manner, either to himself or others, if discharged.[89] The rights to after-care of patients who are discharged from detention under the Mental Health Act 1983 have already been discussed.

Where patients believe that they are being improperly detained they have a number of options for challenging the legality of their detention. If the hospital has detained the patient without the legal power to do so, for example because the application for detention was procedurally flawed, then an action for *habeas corpus* can be brought.[90] If patients show in such an action that their detention was unlawful, then the court will order their release. Such an action will not be appropriate to challenge the exercise of discretion. It will only be available where there is no power to detain, not where the allegation

---

[86] S. 62.

[87] MHA 1983, s. 41. These apply to certain patients who have been detained through the criminal justice system.

[88] Ss. 23(2), 25(1).   [89] S. 25(1).   [90] *Re S-C* [1996] 1 All ER 532.

is that the power was exercised inappropriately. Actions for judicial review may be used for this purpose,[91] although they will only succeed where the decision was irrational.[92]

Patients may also challenge their detention through an administrative mechanism internal to the hospital in which they are detained. This informal procedure is independent of the formal processes of the Mental Health Review Tribunal. Power to discharge a patient is conferred on the 'managers' of the relevant NHS trust by section 23 of the Mental Health Act 1983. For these purposes 'managers' has a special meaning. It refers to the non-executive directors of the NHS trust, and any associate members appointed for this purpose to a committee of the Board.[93] They are thus lay people, not health professionals.

Under the Code of Practice managers may initiate reviews at their discretion, but they should hold reviews in three circumstances;[94] first, at the patient's request unless a review has recently taken place and it is clear that the circumstances have not changed—these are sometimes known as 'managers' appeals'. Secondly, when the authority to detain a patient is renewed by the responsible medical officer under section 20 the 'managers' must hold a review of the case and decide whether to order the release of the patient. The power to renew detention is exercised by the doctor and remains effective unless and until the 'managers' order the patient's release. Thirdly, a 'managers' review' should be held when the responsible medical officer exercises the power under section 25 to bar the discharge of a detained patient by the nearest relative.

The Code of Practice also indicates the form that managers' reviews should take, although it does not prescribe specific procedures.[95] Informality should be balanced against the gravity of the task (reviewing the continuation of compulsory detention). Patients should be helped to explain why they wish to be discharged, with the assistance of a member of staff, friend, or representative if they wish. They must always be given the opportunity of speaking to the managers alone. The responsible medical officer and other relevant professionals should be actively and positively questioned about the need for detention. The nearest and most concerned relatives must be offered the opportunity to give their point of view (possibly though a social worker's

---

[91] *R. v. Hallstrom, ex p. W* [1985] 3 All ER 775.

[92] The bases on which judicial review can succeed were considered in Ch. 3, sect. B(i).

[93] Ss. 23(4) and 145(1), as amended by the Mental Health (Amendment) Act 1994.

[94] Department of Health and Welsh Office, *Code of Practice: Mental Health Act 1983* (London: HMSO, 1993), sect. 22.2. This provision is not strictly binding in law.

[95] *Ibid.*, sect. 22.5. See C. Williamson, *Hearing Patients' Appeals Against Continued Compulsory Detention* (Birmingham: National Association of Health Authorities and Trusts, 1991). See also Hazel Rumsey, 'Hot Seat' (1996) *HSJ*, 22 Feb., 32–3 for a discussion of how one NHS trust has approached the conduct of hearings.

report). This degree of formal process would seem more appropriate for appeals than for regular renewals of detention. It is open to 'managers' to adopt an abbreviated system of review for such cases, as the Code of Practice does not give rise to legal obligations.

No guidance is given on the criteria by which Mental Health Act 'managers' should exercise the power to discharge. It is widely accepted that, where it is thought that the statutory criteria for detention are not satisfied, the the patient should be discharged.[96] However, this does not appear in the statute. The grounds for detention need to be made out when patients are 'sectioned' and when 'sections' are renewed. Provided that this is the case, then the authority to detain continues to be effective until it expires for want of renewal or is revoked. There is no clarity about whether the 'managers' are entitled to discharge patients on the basis that they believe they should not be detained further, or whether their task is to review whether the responsible medical officer has reached a reasonable decision (even though it may be one with which they personally disagree). If 'managers' substitute their own views, they may effectively be overriding professional clinical judgement.

In addition to the internal review provided by Mental Health Act 'managers' there is a more formal process for review and appeal through the Mental Health Review Tribunals. Patients have the right to apply to a Tribunal once in each period for which their detention is authorized.[97] This means once in the first and once in the second six months of detention for treatment under section 3, and thereafter once each year. For detention for assessment and treatment under section 2, an application needs to be made within the first fourteen days of the 'section'. If a patient has been detained for three years since his case was last before a Tribunal, then the hospital 'managers' must refer the matter to a Tribunal on the patient's behalf.[98] Patients subject to supervised after-care may also apply to a Tribunal once in each of the first two periods of six months and thereafter annually.

There are eight regional Mental Health Review Tribunals.[99] Each maintains a panel of members subdivided into three categories, legal, medical, and lay. The panel for each Tribunal hearing will comprise at least one member from each of the three categories.[100] Procedural questions are largely within the remit of the tribunal itself, which is encouraged to act informally, subject to the need to meet the requirements of natural justice and to respect the interests of the patient.[101] However, the Tribunal will interview patients who ask to

---

[96] See R. Jones, *Mental Health Act Manual* (4th edn., London: Sweet & Maxwell, 1994), 73.

[97] Ss. 66, 77(2), as amended.   [98] S. 68(2).

[99] Mental Health Review Tribunals (Regions) Order 1996, SI 1996 No 510.

[100] MHA 1983, Sch. 2, para. 4.

[101] See generally L. Gostin and P. Fennell, *Mental Health: Tribunal Procedure* (2nd edn., London: Longman, 1992).

be seen.[102] Further, the Rules establish that patients are entitled to be represented,[103] and that there should be an opportunity to put evidence before the
Tribunal and cross-examine witnesses.[104]

The function of the Tribunal is to consider whether the patient should be
discharged.[105] It is obliged to discharge patients who satisfy it that they are not
suffering from the necessary mental disorder or illness or that detention is not
justified in their own health or safety or to protect others. Strictly, it is for the
patient to satisfy the Tribunal of the criteria for mandatory release;[106] however, as there is a discretion to release patients even when the minimum legal
criteria for detention are present it may not always matter that the burden of
proof is not met. The Tribunal has the power to defer the discharge of the
patient if it thinks fit.[107] The Tribunal must give full reasons for its decision
and communicate them to the patient within seven days.[108]

Finally, it is necessary to consider the scope for allegations that discharge
has been carried out negligently. Such challenges may be brought by the
patient or by someone injured by the patient. Civil actions cannot be brought
against individuals in respect of steps taken under the Mental Health Act
without the leave of the court.[109] However, this is a procedural hurdle rather
than a substantive objection. It does not, therefore, preclude the possibility of
an action, which would usually be brought in negligence.[110] In the case of
patients, the allegation is likely to be that they suffered harm because they
were discharged too early. Most such cases will turn on whether a responsible
body of psychiatric opinion would support the decision to discharge.[111]

The issue in relation to third parties who allege that they were injured as a
result of negligent discharge is more complex. Examples of such cases are
where a discharged patient attacked them. Here, an additional hurdle has to
be overcome, as the court will have to be persuaded that it should impose a
legal duty on the psychiatrist to exercise due care to protect the interest of the
third party. Although there are cases in which this seems to have been
accepted, they are doubtful authority because the points were not argued
through.[112] The court will have to be convinced that the relationship between
the decision to discharge the patient and the ultimate victim was foreseeable
and sufficiently close to require the psychiatrist to consider the risks. Even if
this test is satisfied, the courts may still decide that it would be contrary to

---

[102] Mental Health Review Tribunal Rules 1983, SI 1983 No 942, r. 22(2).   [103] R. 10.
[104] R. 22(4).   [105] MHA 1983, s. 72.   [106] *Perkins* v. *Bath HA* (1989) 4 BMLR 145.
[107] S. 72(3).   [108] N. 102 above, rr. 23, 24; *Bone* v. *MHRT* [1985] 3 All ER 330.
[109] MHA 1983, s. 139.   [110] See Ch. 7 for a full review of the law.
[111] *Bolam* v. *Friern HMC* [1957] 2 All ER 118.
[112] *Holgate* v. *Lancashire MHB* [1937] 4 All ER 19 and *Partington* v. *Wandsworth LBC*,
Independent, 8 Nov. 1989. The former was regarded with some suspicion in *Home Office* v. *Dorset
Yacht Co.* [1970] 2 All ER 294.

public policy to expose doctors to the risk of such litigation. The approach likely to be taken by the courts is at present unclear.[113]

G. Conclusion

This Chapter has sought to emphasize the fact that mental health law is not merely about the Mental Health Act 1983. That Act emphasizes compulsion and hospitalization. It is inevitable that compulsory detention is a central concern of the law, because of the civil rights that it infringes. Such infringements are legitimate under the European Convention on Human Rights, Article 5, providing that they are properly regulated. The Mental Health Act provides the framework to ensure due process and respect for the rights of patients. However, its focus on in-patient care makes it unsuitable for dealing with the care of patients in the community. The government and Mental Health Act Commission have suggested that a radical overhaul may be needed.[114]

[113] Compare D. Miers, 'Liability for Injuries Caused by Violent Patients' (1996) 36 *Med. Sci. Law* 15–24 with M. Jones, *Medical Negligence* (2nd edn., London: Sweet & Maxwell, 1996), 73–8.

[114] Mental Health Act Commission, *Fifth Biennial Report 1991–1993* (London: HMSO, 1993), App. 16.

14 Research

There are many forms of medical research. Some is laboratory science that does not involve research subjects as such. This form of research will not be regulated by law unless it involves human subjects, human gametes or embryos, or certain non-human animals. Where humans are involved, either as volunteers or as patients, there will be a number of legal implications. Consent will be needed for any invasive research. A failure to take due care in carrying out the research may give rise to litigation if research subjects are injured. Non-human research subjects will not have the ability to sue, so agencies may have to act to protect them. Even with human subjects, independent ethical review is also recommended, although it is usually on a non-statutory basis. This Chapter discusses the legal frameworks that govern these activities. The Chapter is divided into two main sections. The first, and most substantial, deals with research on human subjects. The second outlines the law dealing with animal research.

A. Research on Human Subjects

The modern concern about medical research on human subjects was stimulated by the revelation at the Nuremburg war crime trials that Nazi doctors had performed atrocities in the name of medical science. The Nuremburg Code of 1947 drew up ten principles which were to be satisfied before experimentation on human beings was acceptable. They included the need for consent, and the rights of subjects to withdraw, the principle that knowledge should be sought from human experimentation only when other sources had been exhausted, and the need for proportionality between the benefits expected from the research and the risks run by research subjects.

These principles were adopted and developed by the World Medical Association in the Declaration of Helsinki (originally agreed in 1964, with revisions in 1975, 1983, and 1989). The Helsinki Declaration introduced a distinction between clinical and non-clinical research, stating (in relation to the former) that: 'The physician can combine medical research with professional care . . . only to the extent that medical research is justified by its potential diagnostic or therapeutic value for the patient.'[1]

When treating patients, even with a novel therapy, the doctor's primary responsibility is to promote their well-being. Doctors should not be prevented from offering the care they believe would be most effective merely because the benefits are uncertain, although the chances of benefit and harm must still be carefully assessed. Greater safeguards are needed in relation to non-clinical research because the physician will no longer have the interests of the patient as the primary consideration. In particular, the Declaration affirms that the subjects of non-clinical research should be volunteers and their interests must always prevail over the interests of science and society, even if this means ending a trial.

These international standards form the basis of the English regulatory system governing research on humans. However, there is no single, planned, legal framework designed to ensure that they are followed. Instead, there is a combination of specific and general legal provisions and a pattern of established good practice. The piecemeal and often voluntary nature of the system has been criticised. As yet, however, it is all that exists to ensure that medical research on humans is carried out in an ethical manner. The analysis begins with a discussion of the nature of medical research. The various licensing regimes are set out. The process of ethical review of projects by research ethics committees is described. The application of the law of consent and confidentiality is considered, with particular reference to the problems that arise with children and adults who are unable to consent. Finally, compensation for those injured while research subjects is examined.

(i) Types of Research

Research involving human subjects can be categorized in a number of ways. First, according to the status of the research subjects. They may be healthy volunteers. They may be patients, but patients who are not expected to benefit directly from the research. They may be patients who it is hoped will derive therapeutic benefits from the trial. Research in the latter category is sometimes called 'therapeutic' or 'clinical' and that in the former two known as 'non-therapeutic' or 'non-clinical'. This terminology reflects the fact that non-clinical research must be regarded as being an activity in which the interests of the research subject are not the motivation for trying the experiment.

---

[1] Pt. II, para. 6. The Declaration of Helsinki (as amended) is reproduced as App. C of Department of Health, *Local Research Ethics Committees* (London: DoH, 1991) (HSG(91)5).

A second categorization may be made according to the nature of the research. It may be based on observation of patients or use of their records without any direct intrusion into their privacy or effect on their minds or bodies. This will raise issues relating to privacy and the confidentiality of information. Research may, however, involve direct interference with the subject through psychological or physical tests. This sort of research will usually be unlawful unless consented to by the subject (see section A(iv) below). Research may also be population-based, sometimes called epidemiological research, rather than concerned with individual patients.[2] Such research aims to chart the prevalence and effects of diseases in society. The legal implications of such research will depend on the manner in which it is carried out. In many cases, it will raise no more than issues of privacy. If, however, it involves taking samples, then further issues may arise.

A third type of division can be made according to the research methodology. Studies may be quantitative, designed to produce statistically valid results, or qualitative, intended to draw out subjective aspects of experiences. They may involve control groups, which will receive different treatment from that being tested or possibly no active treatment at all. Placebo-controlled trials enable comparison between treatment and non-treatment by giving patients a dummy product, made up to look like the product being tested, so that research subjects do not know whether they are receiving therapy or not. It is generally believed that subjects should usually be told that they may receive a placebo, otherwise they are being deceived about the nature of the trial. Allocation to the various trial groups may be random to avoid bias, but need not always be. Randomized controlled trials are widely regarded as the most powerful type of study design for many areas of research, but are not without controversy.[3] Researchers and subjects may not be aware of which group they are in. This is known as a 'blind' trial if only the subjects are unaware of this and a 'double blind' trial if the researchers do not know either.

Fourthly, research studies may be classified according to the stage that they represent in an overall project. They may be pilot studies preliminary to a fuller examination of the issues. New drugs usually go through four phases of trial. In phase I the toxicity and dosage of a drug are established, a process that it is envisaged may well actually harm the research subject. In phase II the drug is used on patients who have not responded to conventional treatments

---

[2] Council for International Organizations of Medical Sciences, *International Guidelines of Ethical Review of Epidemiological Studies* (Geneva: CIOMS, 1991); R. Benster and A. Pollock, 'Guidelines for Local Research Ethics Committees: Distinguishing between Patient and Population Research in the Multicentre Research Project' 107 *Public Health* 3–7.

[3] See e.g. A. Oakley, 'Who's Afraid of the Randomised Controlled Trial? Some Dilemmas of the Scientific Method and "Good" Research Practice' in H. Roberts (ed.), *Women's Health Counts* (London: Routledge, 1990).

to get an indication of its active effects. In phase III larger-scale trials are con-ducted to establish safety and efficacy on a scientifically valid basis. Phase IV trials involve the monitoring of the drug in use. They are usually large scale and carried out once the drug is on the market. These are sometimes know as 'post-marketing surveillance' (PMS).[4]

Research can also be classified according to the area that is being studied, possibly category of disease, or class of patients. Thus, special issues may arise in relation to research with the dying, AIDS, or genetic research.[5] Sometimes these problems are reflected in the legal rules or official guidance. Research on human embryos must be licensed by the Human Fertilization and Embryology Authority. Research with those who cannot consent for them-selves raises special legal and ethical problems. Research involving foetal tissue and gene therapy has been the subject of official reports. These prob-lems are considered below. Where difficulties emerge, groups of researchers often take the initiative in developing guidance on good practice, and this has happened in a number of areas that are not discussed further here.[6]

The assessment of the legality and morality of a research project may depend on how it fits into the systems of classification. The legal requirements for consent will depend on whether the research involves physical contact or breach of confidentiality. If it does not, there will be no legal need for a con-sent. The distinction between therapeutic and non-therapeutic research may be important for lawyers, because it is possible that the law may require a less detailed explanation of risks and side-effects for the former than is necessary for the latter. Licensing requirements are different for the various stages of drug trials.

[4] Joint Committee of the Association of the British Pharmaceutical Industry, British Medical Association, Committee on Safety of Medicines, Royal College of General Practitioners, 'Guidelines on Postmarketing Surveillance' (1988) 296 *BMJ* 399.

[5] G. Thorpe, 'Experiments on the Dying' in C. Williams (ed.), *Introducing New Treatments for Cancer: Practical, Ethical and Legal Problems* (Chichester: Wiley, 1992), 217–24; United Kingdom Central Council for Nursing, Midwifery and Health Visiting, *Anonymous Testing for the Prevalence of the Human Immunodeficiency Virus* (London: UKCC, 1989) (PC/89/01); Medical Research Council, *The Ethical Conduct of AIDS Vaccine Trials* (London: MRC, 1991); P. Harper, 'Research Samples from Families with Genetic Diseases: A Proposed Code of Conduct' (1993) 306 *BMJ* 1391–4.

[6] e.g. Medical Research Council, *Responsibility in Investigations on Human Participants and Material and on Personal Information* (London: MRC, 1992); British Psychological Society, 'Ethical Principles for Conducting Research with Human Participants' (1990) 3(6) *The Psychologist* 269–72; British Sociological Association, *Statement of Ethical Practice* (London: BSA, 1992); Royal College of Psychiatrists, 'Guidelines for Research Ethics Committees on Psychiatric Research involving Human Subjects' (1990) 14 *Psychiatric Bulletin* 48–61; Royal College of General Practitioners, *Guidelines for Payments to GPs Participating in Clinical Research* (London: RCGP); Royal College of Physicians, Faculty of Occupational Medicine, *Guidance on Ethics for Occupational Physicians* (3rd edn., London: RCP, 1986), 9–10; P. Alderson, *Listening to Children: Social Research and Ethics* (Basildon: Barnado's, 1995), see also P. Alderson, 'Ethics and Social Research: Principles plus Personal, Practical and Political Concerns' (1996) *BME* No 115, 13–14.

(ii) Research Ethics Committees

It is generally agreed that research on humans should not be carried out unless some form of independent ethical review body has scrutinized the proposals. It has been official policy within the NHS since 1968 that local research ethics committees (LRECs) should be set up to oversee medical research.[7] These committees now exist in nearly all NHS districts, but they have never been placed on a statutory footing, and there is wide variation in their practice.[8] The latest guidance from the Department of Health was issued in 1990 and recommended that district health authorities (now known simply as health authorities: see Chapter 4) establish LRECs by February 1992.[9] There is, however, no legal obligation to do so. Some independent organizations, including pharmaceutical companies, have their own ethics committees, which are outside the NHS structure.

The function of ethics committees, as described by the Department of Health, is to advise health service bodies whether a research proposal is acceptable on ethical grounds.[10] They should be consulted whenever research on NHS patients is proposed, including the use of their records, or on those recently dead on NHS premises, or which involves the use of NHS premises or resources. The ultimate responsibility for approving research in the NHS lies with managers, but in most places LREC decisions are probably routinely accepted without further question on the ethical aspects of trials. Ethics committees are expected to consider at least the following factors: (i) the scientific merits of the proposal, (ii) the effects on the health of the research subjects, (iii) possible hazards and whether they will be dealt with adequately, (iv) the degree of discomfort and distress that subjects will suffer, (v) the arrangements for supervision of the project by people with the appropriate qualifications and experience, (vi) any financial inducements involved, (vii) procedures for obtaining consent, and (viii) information sheets prepared for the research subjects. The Department of Health has issued further guidance to research ethics committees on how to ensure that they operate properly in scrutinizing proposals.[11]

---

[7] C. Foster, 'Research Ethics Committees in Britain' in Williams, n. 5 above.

[8] C. Gilbert, K. Fulford, and C. Parker, 'Diversity in the Practice of District Ethics Committees' (1989) 299 *BMJ* 1437–9; R. Nicholson (ed.), *Medical Research with Children* (Oxford: Oxford University Press, 1988), ch. 8; J. Neuberger, *Ethics and Health Care: The Role of Research Ethics Committees in the United Kingdom* (London: King's Fund Institute, 1992).

[9] Department of Health, *Local Research Ethics Committees* (London DoH, 1990) issued by the NHS Management Executive with HSG(91)5.

[10] *Ibid.*

[11] Department of Health, *Standards for Local Research Ethics Committees: A Framework for Ethical Review* (London: DoH, 1994).

Further important material on the responsibilities of research ethics committees has been produced by various bodies, including the Royal College of Physicians, the Medical Research Council, the British Paediatric Association, and the Royal College of Psychiatrists.[12] These highlight additional responsibilities of ethics committees to consider: (i) that the advance in knowledge sought is consonant with the public interest, (ii) that the risks and inconvenience involved are balanced by the anticipated benefits, (iii) that adequate literature review and experimental studies have been undertaken before research on human subjects, and (iv) that proper steps will be taken to preserve confidentiality. The guidance from the British Paediatric Association points out the need to recognize that the research subject's own estimates of risk and degree of pain should be considered, as well as objective statistical assessments.[13] This would seem important for adults as well as children. European guidance adds the importance of examining the methods for recruitment to the study.[14]

The guidance from the Department of Health recommends that LRECs should comprise between eight and twelve members. A study of the actual membership of LRECs in 1990 indicated that there was considerable variation, and that guidelines were not necessarily followed.[15] The suggested range of numbers was breached by 43 per cent of the committees surveyed. Approximately one-third of them had fewer than the two lay persons recommended. There was no GP on 15 per cent of the committees and no nurse in 12 per cent of cases. Women and those from ethnic minorities were poorly represented. In half of the LRECs surveyed women constituted only a quarter or less of the membership, and 4 per cent had no female members. Almost all the members were white. There was, however, evidence of a move towards a greater number of committees appointing lay chairmen or vice-chairmen (or women) as recommended by the Department. The study also observed that over half the LRECs examined lacked the assistance of either a pharmacist or a clinical pharmacologist, whose knowledge would have been useful in assessing research involving drugs.

LRECs differ in their workloads and methods of working. However, in

[12] Royal College of Physicians, *Research involving Patients* (London: RCP, 1990); Royal College of Physicians, *Guidelines on the Practice of Ethics Committees in Medical Research involving Human Subjects* (2nd edn., London: RCP, 1990); Royal College of Psychiatrists, n. 6 above. The MRC and BPA guidelines are discussed below in relation to research with children and the mentally incapacitated.

[13] British Paediatric Association, *Guidelines for the Ethical Conduct of Medical Research involving Children* (London: BPA, 1992), 8.

[14] Committee for Proprietary Medicinal Products Working Party on Efficacy of Medicinal Products, *Good Clinical Practice for Trials on Medicinal Products in the EC* (Brussels: EC Commission, 1990), para. 1.6.

[15] Neuberger, n. 8 above, ch. 2.

general they are thought to be insufficiently resourced to police research effectively.[16] Most are unable to follow through projects that they have approved, and committees have no powers to investigate possible breaches of the conditions on which they approve projects. Committees usually need to refer cases of suspected misconduct in carrying out research to the employer of the researcher for action to be taken. Even the requirement to seek ethical approval is administrative rather than legal, although it is unlikely that journal editors will publish the results of trials unless ethics committee approval has been given. Professional bodies would probably also regard carrying out unapproved research as misconduct.

Neuberger's study found that most ethics committees saw one of their key tasks as ensuring the research subjects were properly informed about the studies before they gave their consent.[17] The ethics committees explored the problems of consent to randomized controlled trials, where the subjects cannot be told exactly what will happen to them because it is not known which 'arm' of the trial they will go into. They paid particular attention to consent forms and information sheets. She found that they discussed ethical problems relating to research on children and on adults unable to consent for themselves, and judged the debate on children to be of a higher level. Neuberger found that committees were rather less likely to explore the financial aspects of trials, even though the guidelines suggested they should. She also found that some committees were reluctant to accept qualitative research methodologies, regarding them as unscientific.

Particular problems have arisen with multi-centre trials.[18] If the research protocol has, as at present, to be approved by all the LRECs for areas in which patients may be recruited, then the delays involved may prevent the study being carried out at all. A number of researchers have reported difficulties in varying requirements being made by different committees which have either held up studies, or prevented the studies being carried out because the required amendments were incompatible.[19] Some of the criticisms made of requests for amendments reflect differing views on ethical matters, which are precisely why ethical committees exist to scrutinize research. However, there are clearly also genuine difficulties. This has led to calls for national co-

[16] Nicholson, n. 8 above, ch. 8; Neuberger, n. 8 above; C. Gilbert Foster, T. Marshall, and P. Moodie, 'The Annual Reports of Research Ethics Committees' (1995) 21 *JME* 214–19.

[17] Neuberger, n. 8 above.

[18] Foster, n. 7 above, 91–102; P. Alderson, M. Madden, A. Oakley, and R. Wilkins, 'Access and Multi-centre Research' (1995) *BME* No 105, 13–16.

[19] T. Meade, 'The Trouble with Ethics Committees' (1994) 28 *J Royal College of Physicians of London* 102–4; U. Harries, P. Fentem, W. Tuxworth, and G. Hoinviolle, 'Local Research Ethics Committees: Widely Differing Responses to a National Survey Protocol' (1994) 28 *J Royal College of Physicians of London* 150–4; Benster and Pollock, n. 2 above, 3–7.

ordination of research ethics committees, and possibly a national committee.[20]

The Department of Health regarded the problem as sufficiently serious to warrant commissioning a report from the Centre for Philosophy and Health Care at University College, Swansea. That report was received in 1992, proposing a three-tier system of national, regional, and local committees.[21] Commentators have questioned how effective the model adopted in that report would be, and whether a national committee can actually solve the problems.[22] In April 1996, the Department of Health issued a consultation paper on the review of multi-centre research.[23] This proposed that each NHS region should set up a multi-centre research ethics committee (MREC), comprising a range of professionals with at least one third lay members. Those committees should develop a common application form and operate in accordance with the principles governing local research ethics committees. It would not supersede the responsibilities of local committees, which would still have to approve (and could therefore veto) multi-centre studies before they could be carried out in their area. However, local committees would not be permitted to amend the protocol. Their choice would be either to approve or reject the study in the form accepted by the MREC.

(iii) Specific Licensing Requirements

A number of areas of research come within specific licensing requirements, which will be additional to the usual requirement of approval by a local research ethics committee. The most elaborate are probably those relating to pharmaceutical research (see Chapter 9) and human embryology research (which is considered immediately below). Another relates to gene therapy, which is still regarded as experimental therapy and must be approved by the non-statutory Gene Therapy Advisory Committee.[24] That Committee will be concerned to assess the justification for the proposed research and its scientific validity, the relative weights of the risks of harm and potential benefits,

---

[20] M. Gelder, 'A National Committee for the Ethics of Research' (1990) 16 *JME* 146–7; J. Moran, 'Local Research Ethics Committees: Report of 2nd National Conference' (1994) 26 *J Royal College of Physicians of London* 423–31.

[21] D. Evans, *Report to the Department of Health on the Conduct of Ethical Review of Multi-location Research involving Human Subjects* (Swansea: Centre for Philosophy and Health Care, 1992).

[22] J. Montgomery, 'Improving Review of Multi-centre Trials' (1994) *BME* No 95, 19–22; P. Alderson, 'A National Research Ethics Committee?' (1995) BME No 107, 13–16.

[23] Department of Health, *Ethics Committee Review of Multi-centre Research: Consultation Paper* (London: Department of Health, 1996).

[24] Gene Therapy Advisory Committee, *Guidance on Making Proposals to Conduct Gene Therapy Research on Human Subjects* (London: GTAC, 1994), extracted in (1995) *BME* No 105, 8–11. See also *Report of the Committee on the Ethics of Gene Therapy* (London: HMSO, 1992, Cm 1788).

and the means of informing subjects and seeking appropriate consent.[25] It also acknowledges that particular problems will arise in relation to involving children as research subjects.

A further example is the special certificate that is required by anyone administering a radioactive medicinal product.[26] Such a certificate must be obtained for all clinical trials of medicines licensed under section 31 of the Medicines Act 1968 (see Chapter 9), for all volunteer (i.e. non-therapeutic) trials, and for all studies requiring local research ethics committee authorization (see section A(ii) above). Researchers will be expected to minimize exposure of subjects and to avoid involving children or pregnant women unless problems specific to those groups are being investigated. Even when a certificate is issued, trials can be carried out only with the approval of the relevant local research ethics committee.

European Community initiatives have led to the licensing of medical devices. Two directives cover powered implantable devices, such as pacemakers, and other medical devices respectively.[27] Clinical investigations of such devices must be licensed by the Secretary of State for Health, acting through the Medical Devices Directorate of the Department of Health. Specified information must be submitted to the Secretary of State, including the opinion of the local research ethics committee. If no objection on the basis of public health or public safety has been communicated to the researchers within sixty days, then the trial will go ahead. The Department of Health has indicated that it will never permit a trial to go ahead where the local research ethics committee has issued an unfavourable opinion.[28]

In vitro research on human embryos, and the storage of embryos and gametes, is illegal without a licence from the Human Fertilization and Embryology Authority.[29] Both the project and the premises on which it is carried out must be licensed.[30] The constitution and workings of that Authority, which also licences certain types of fertility treatment, are discussed in Chapter 16. Licences for research may only be issued for projects 'necessary or desirable' for specified purposes, but these are broadly defined and include 'promoting advances in the treatment of infertility' as well as increasing

[25] *Report of the Committee on the Ethics of Gene Therapy*, para. 3.

[26] Medicines (Administration or Radioactive Substances) Regulations 1978, SI 1978 No 1006; Medicines (Radioactive Substances) Order 1978, SI 1978 No 1004; Medicines (Committee on Radiation from Radioactive Medicinal Products) Order 1978, SI 1978 No 1005. See also 'Administration of radioactive substances to persons' (HN(84)5).

[27] Active Implantable Medical Devices Directive 90/385/EEC [1990] OJ L189/17; Medical Devices Directive 93/42/EEC [1993] OJ L199; Medical Devices Regulations 1994, SI 1994 No 3017. A third directive, the In Vitro Diagnostic Devices Directive, is in preparation: COM(91)287.

[28] 'Implementation of the Medical Devices Directives: Guidance to Local Research Ethics Committee', Annex B to a letter to LREC chairmen dated 23 Dec. 1993.

[29] Human Fertilization and Embryology Act 1990, ss. 3, 4.   [30] Sch. 2, para. 4.

knowledge about the causes of miscarriages and congenital disease.[31] These purposes are, however, narrower than the text of the bill as originally printed, which would have allowed research to be licensed 'for the purpose of increasing knowledge about the creation and development of embryos and enabling such knowledge to be applied'. Licences should not be granted unless it is necessary to use embryos for the research.[32] Further guidance on the exercise of the licensing powers may be given in regulations, but no such regulations have been issued at present. The practice of the Authority is to use academic referees to assess proposals, and to expect applicants to have already submitted them to a properly constituted research ethics committee.[33]

Certain statutory restrictions are placed on the research that can be licensed. It is not possible to authorize research on embryos older than fourteen days after fertilization, nor that involving placing a human embryo in a non-human animal or replacing the nucleus of a cell of an embryo.[34] Other genetic alterations are currently also prohibited, but the Secretary of State may lay regulations before Parliament permitting specified activities of this sort.[35] Staff are given a statutory right of conscientious objection to participation in research licensed under the Act.[36]

In addition to the need for a licence, the Act specifies that the donors must give their consent to the embryo being used for the purposes of any project of research.[37] This consent can be made subject to conditions and can be varied or withdrawn at any time before the embryo has been used in research. Consent should not be sought without providing an opportunity for counselling. Donors should also be given 'such information as is proper'.[38] This is not defined further in the statute.

(iv) Consent to Research by Competent Adults

Research that involves physical contact with its subjects will require them to give their consent before it can lawfully proceed. Without such a consent, the touching involved would be battery (see Chapter 10). Other types of research are unlikely to require consent in this way. However, as professional ethics generally recognize that consent is essential, it is likely that proceeding without consent is negligent. While any physical contact with research subjects without their consent would be unlawful even if no other harm is done,

---

[31] S. 11(3), Sch. 2, para. 3.   [32] Sch. 2, para. 3(6).
[33] Human Fertilization and Embryology Authority, *Code of Practice* (London: HFEA, 1995), pt. 10.
[34] S. 3(3)(d),(4).   [35] Sch. 2, para. 3(4).
[36] S. 38. The terms are essentially similar to those in the Abortion Act 1967, and would presumably be interpreted in the same way: see Ch. 15.
[37] S. 12(c), Sch. 3.   [38] Sch. 3, para. 3(1)(b).

actions for negligence must prove that the research subject would not have been harmed if a proper consent had been sought.

The English courts have not yet had the opportunity to consider how much information research subjects should be given, but it is generally accepted that the need for fully informed consent is greater in the context of research than it is in treatment. A consent will only be valid if the subject has been informed in broad terms of the nature of the procedure.[39] It is arguable that this requires researchers to tell subjects that they are involved in research, and possibly give them details of research design, but this has never been tested in court and would seem unlikely, in the light of the courts' reluctance to permit consent issues to be raise outside the law of negligence.[40] The nearest authority is the suggestion that a patient who had received treatment under the Mental Health Act 1983 would not have given a valid consent if he had not appreciated that the treatment was novel, and that it had not previously been tried on young men such as himself. However, as he did in fact know this, the court was not required to rule whether lack of such information would have invalidated his apparent consent.[41]

Commentators often cite a Canadian case, *Halushka* v. *University of Saskatchewan* as indicative of the approach the courts might take.[42] In that decision, the court held that for consent to research to be valid, it would have to be given after a 'full and frank' disclosure of the facts. The patient had been wrongly reassured that the experimental drug was safe and had been used many times before, and his consent was therefore invalid. While it is often dangerous to rely on overseas decisions, there are reasons to believe that the English courts might adopt this approach. At the time of the decision, the general law of consent to treatment in Canada was based on professional disclosure practices, not the doctrine of informed consent. Thus, it cannot be suggested that the court was building on legal doctrine that was more sympathetic to the idea of informed consent than the English courts have accepted.

The Canadian court also relied on English case law on the fiduciary duties of professional advisers. This analogy is important because it emphasizes the crucial difference between research and treatment, that in the former the interests of the subject and the researcher may be in conflict. In *Sidaway* v. *Bethlem RHG*, Lord Templeman explained the decision partly by reference to

---

[39] *Chatterton* v. *Gerson* [1981] 1 All ER 257, 265.

[40] M. Jones, *Medical Negligence* (2nd edn., London: Sweet & Maxwell, 1996), 374–5.

[41] *R.* v. *Mental Health Act Commission, ex p. X* (1988) 9 BMLR 77, 85–6.

[42] (1965) 53 DLR 436. See e.g. I. Kennedy and A. Grubb, *Medical Law: Text with Materials* (2nd edn., London: Butterworths, 1994), 1046–8, 1057; J. McHale, 'Guidelines for Medical Research' (1993) 2 *Med. L Rev.* 160–85, especially 168–70. See also D. Giesen, 'Civil Liability of Physicians for New Methods of Treatment and Experimentation: A Comparative Examination' (1995) 3 *Med. L Rev.* 22–52.

the fact that patients and doctors share the same objective: to make the patient well.[43] That was one reason strict disclosure obligations were not required. However, it must also be noted that the fiduciary analogy was expressly rejected by Lord Scarman in his minority speech.[44]

If the *Halushka* case is followed, then for non-therapeutic research it seems that research subjects need to have the risks of entering the study fully and honestly explained to them. The position is probably different where the experiment is hoped to benefit the individual patient.[45] Here, it seems likely that English law would apply the usual legal requirements for consent and counselling (see Chapter 10) because in such circumstances the health professional's main objective is still the welfare of the patient.

A final issue in relation to consent by competent adults to being involved in research concerns the possibility that the law may not permit them to consent to certain types of experiment. This is a matter of public policy. The law some-times regards it as unacceptable for people to expose themselves to high degrees of risk.[46] There is no relevant case law applying this principle to research, but some commentators have suggested that it would make consent to a Phase I trial invalid.[47] Phase I trials are where the study is designed to expose subjects to intolerable doses of drugs so that the limits of the drug's safe use can be established. However, the argument that public policy should preclude research subjects agreeing to expose themselves to such harm ignores the fact that consent is recognized as valid in relation to dangerous sporting activities such as boxing.[48] The crucial question is one of public acceptability. In the context of medical treatment, the test is whether 'proper medical treatment' is being carried out.[49] It seems highly unlikely that the courts would ban a standard research methodology, supervised by research ethics committees, on the basis that it was contrary to public policy for a competent adult to agree to be involved.

(v) Research with Children

Research involving children raises particular problems because of their vulnerability to being used to further adult interests. Nevertheless, it is important for the health of children that the effectiveness of treatment for them is properly assessed. Data based on studies in adults are not necessarily accurate

---

[43] [1985] 1 All ER 643, 665.
[44] [1985] 1 All ER 643, 651. The speeches are fully analysed in Ch. 10.
[45] This has been the position taken by the Canadian courts, see Jones, n. 40 above, 377–8.
[46] See Ch. 10, sect. A(ii), for discussion.
[47] V. Tunkel, 'Legal Aspects of Clinical Trials in the United Kingdom' in Williams, n. 5 above, 13–16, developing the views of Kennedy and Grubb, n. 42 above, 1054–5.
[48] *R. v. Brown* [1993] 2 All ER 75, 106–9.   [49] *Ibid.*, 109–10.

for the same treatment in children, and children may need types of care that are rarely appropriate for adults. The British Paediatric Association has therefore issued guidance to help ethics committees properly to consider research involving children.[50]

Those guidelines are based on the following six principles. Research involving children is important and should be supported, encouraged, and conducted in an ethical manner. Children have unique interests, and are not merely small adults. Research should only be done on children if comparable research on adults could not answer the same question. A research procedure that is not intended directly to benefit the child is not necessarily either unethical or illegal. The contrary had been asserted by some commentators in the past.[51] All proposals should be submitted to the local research ethics committee, which should be advised by people with close knowledge of babies and children (such as a children's ward nurse). Ethics committees should be particularly concerned in research involving children to satisfy themselves that the research is worth doing; that it sets out to answer useful questions, with the best possible methodology to answer them, and is likely to generate useful data in practice. Valid consent should be obtained from parents, children, or guardians, as appropriate. In addition, the agreement of school-age children taking part in research should be requested.

The issue of consent is the most significant legal matter. Chapter 12 set out the legal rules for consent to treatment, which may be given by a *Gillick*-competent child and anyone with parental responsibility. It also discussed the current position, whereby the consent of an adult with parental responsibility will be valid even when the child is able to give a valid consent but refuses to do so. No English court has yet had to decide whether the same principles would be applied in the context of research. There is no reason to think that the test for the validity of child's consent is any different, although the results of its application may be. Children are competent to consent if they understand the nature and purpose of the research.[52] They need to appreciate what will happen to them if they agree to enter the trial, and that the purpose of the trial is research, and that the trial will probably give them no direct benefit (unless it is a therapeutic trial). It is probable that children will have this degree of understanding less often in relation to research than well-established treatment, but there is no reason to suppose that no children will have that capacity.

---

[50] British Paediatric Association, n. 13 above.
[51] See for discussion G. Dworkin, 'Legality of Consent to Non-therapeutic Medical Research on Infants and Young Children' (1978) 51 *Archives of Diseases in Childhood* 443–6.
[52] See Ch. 12, sect. A.

The British Paediatric Association stressed the importance of securing the child's agreement to being involved, even though he or she is not able to give a valid consent. The doctrines used by English law are poorly adapted to secure this sort of participation.[53] It is probable that the only way of using the courts to ensure that researchers secure children's assent to being involved even where they cannot give a legally valid consent would be to argue that it is negligent to conduct a trial on any other basis. This is likely to be difficult, although the fact that the BPA guidelines suggest obtaining children's agreement from the age of five onwards may give rise to the researchers being required to explain why it was acceptable not to do so.[54]

In most cases, researchers will probably rely on the child's parents to give consent. The lawfulness of parental consent to research will depend, first, on whether there is any direct benefit to the child concerned. If the research can be said to be part of treatment or care then no problem would arise. Research which is trying a new procedure in the hope that it will be of therapeutic benefit to the patient would seem to be in the same category as ordinary treatment for the purposes of consent law. Researchers will therefore be able to rely on the validity of parental consent and will act lawfully provided they are not negligent. If the risks involved are sufficiently small that the research would not prejudice the child's interests then parental consent is also probably valid even though there is no direct benefit. It all depends on how far the parental power to consent extends.

The principles that determine the limits of the power of parents to consent were explored in Chapter 12.[55] It was suggested that the main issue is whether reasonable parents would consent to research on their children and, if so, in what circumstances. There is no single answer to this question and therefore there is a range of positions which can reasonably be taken. Only where no reasonable parent would consent would an apparent consent to enter a child into a trial be invalid.

Where children could reasonably be hoped to benefit personally from the research, either in the short or long term, it might be reasonable to allow them to take quite significant risks. For example, where children suffer from a serious disability and the research is aimed to alleviate or cure the condition, it may not be unreasonable for a parent to consent to their becoming a research subject even where there might be considerable discomfort and a risk of detrimental effects. The prognosis for benefit to the child can reasonably be weighed against the severity of the current state of health and the risks of the research project itself.

---

[53] P. Alderson and J. Montgomery, *Health Care Choices: Making Decisions with Children* (London: Institute for Public Policy Research, 1996).

[54] See Ch. 7 for the relevant law.   [55] See sect. C(iv).

Where the risks to the child are minimal, it is probable that a reasonable parent could agree to allow his or her child to be used as the subject of research even where no personal benefit to the child at all was anticipated. Cases in the context of adoption have established that a reasonable parent must take into account the child's interest, but is entitled to consider other factors.[56] Examples of research to which a reasonable parent could give consent even though his or her child would receive no benefit might include observational studies, single urine samples (other than by aspiration), and the taking of a little extra blood in the course of routine tests or the weighing of a baby as part of a study. The BPA guidelines suggest that in non-therapeutic research it is inappropriate to subject children to more than these minimal risks. They suggest that it is unethical to subject children to 'low' risk procedures (such as those which cause brief pain, tenderness, or scars) or 'high' risk procedures (such as lung or liver biopsy, arterial puncture, or cardiac catherization) unless there are hoped to be direct benefits for the child.[57] The BPA points out that some children may be unusually upset by the use of needles, and that for these children the taking of blood samples should be classified as low, rather than minimal, risk because of the distress it would cause.

In order to understand what it would be reasonable of parents to accept, it may be useful to consider further the concept of the interests of a child as understood by the courts.[58] It is a concept which pervades the whole of child law and examples of its application elsewhere may provide helpful analogies. It certainly ranges more widely than physical benefit. The blood-test cases hold that ascertaining the truth about a child's paternity is usually in the interests of that child, even though there may also be a significant risk that it will leave the child in a worse position than if it were unknown.[59] They also suggest that financial benefits may well be an appropriate consideration. The preservation of family relationships, with both parents and siblings, has been accepted as an important part of a child's welfare in divorce cases.[60] This may be relevant where research into conditions which are passed down familial lines is proposed. Educational benefits are also relevant, both formal[61] and informal.[62] It is possible to argue that taking part in research is part of the education of children, as it initiates them into the altruistic aspects of mem-

---

[56] e.g. *Re E* [1989] 1 FLR 126, reasonable to consider effect on other children of the family.

[57] For further discussion of the assessment of risk, see Nicholson, n. 8 above, ch. 5.

[58] Most of the cases cited were decided prior to the Children Act 1989, which has reduced the degree to which these factors are explicitly discussed by introducing a statutory checklist to which the judges now refer. That checklist was intended to codify rather than change the concept of welfare, so the older cases remain useful in the present context.

[59] *S* v. *S; W* v. *Official Solicitor* [1970] 3 All ER 107.

[60] *Re KD* [1988] 1 All ER 577; *Adams* v. *Adams* [1984] FLR 768.

[61] *Re S* [1967] 1 All ER 202.   [62] *May* v. *May* [1986] 1 FLR 325.

bership of society. However, it is unlikely that this argument can be taken too far in cases where there is any significant risk to the child.

In summary, it is possible to suggest that the principles governing the validity of parental consent to research are as follows. First, where there is expected to be personal benefit to the health of the child, whether immediately in the course of the treatment, or in the future once the results of the research become available, then parental consent is probably valid. Secondly, where there is indirect benefit to children, through benefit to a member of their family or as an educational exercise, then parental consent may also be legitimate, but the parent has to balance the degree of risk against the expected benefits. Even where no personal benefit at all is anticipated then minimal risks may be accepted by parents on behalf of their children. In all cases the crucial question is whether the parent has acted reasonably in balancing the risks to the child against the personal and public gains in issue.

(vi) Research with the Mentally Incapacitated

Even greater legal difficulties arise in relation to adults who are unable to give a valid consent by reason of mental incapacity. There may be a number of causes of such incapacity. There may be a mental handicap, a long-term condition. The incapacity may be rooted in a psychiatric disorder. There may be a sudden temporary loss of capacity, such as unconsciousness after an accident. Some have argued that research should not be carried out on these groups.[63] However, an outright ban on research is not necessarily in the interests of those unable to consent. Without research, advances in understanding of the causes and care of those with mental handicaps or psychiatric conditions may be undermined. Improvements in some techniques of intensive care may depend on research that can only be carried out on those who are unconscious and likely to need care after an unpredictable trauma. An ethical case can therefore be made for some research to be carried out even where the adult patient's consent cannot be obtained.

Some assistance on establishing an ethical framework for research on the mentally incapacitated can be obtained from general professional and European guidelines on research.[64] However, the Medical Research Council has now published guidance specifically on the subject.[65] It recommends that such research should only be carried out if it relates to the condition of the incapacitated person, and the relevant knowledge could not be obtained

---

[63] See e.g. D. Giesen, *International Malpractice Law* (London, Martinus Nijhoff, 1988), 569–73.

[64] Medical Research Council Working Party on Research on the Mentally Incapacitated, *The Ethical Conduct of Research on the Mentally Incapacitated* (London: MRC, 1991), paras. 5.1–5.9.

[65] *Ibid.*

through research on those able to consent. It must be approved by the appropriate LREC(s). An independent person should assess whether the interests and welfare of the research subject have been properly safeguarded. Non-therapeutic research should not be carried out if it involves risks greater than those encountered in everyday life or during routine physical or psychological tests. The guidelines cite observation of behaviour, non-invasive physiological monitoring, physical examinations, changes in diet, and taking blood and urine specimens as examples of acceptable non-therapeutic research methods. They also advise that no research should be carried out in the face of an apparent objection in words or action.

The legal justification for such work is less clear. Research that does not involve the performance of physical procedures on the subjects would be lawful because it would not require consent. Where consent is necessary there are problems. In contrast with the position in relation to children, there is no provision in English law for proxy consent on behalf of a mentally incapacitated adult.[66] Instead, the duty of health professionals is to act in what they perceive to be the interests of their patients.[67] In cases of therapeutic research, where it is hoped that the patient may benefit, this duty may be consistent with research on incapacitated patients. However, it is unlikely that non-therapeutic research could be justified under this principle. The working party convened by the Medical Research Council has suggested that a public-policy argument might be available to justify the participation of those unable to consent in non-therapeutic research that is intended to benefit the class of incapacitated persons to which they belong, provided that the risks involved are minimal.[68] However, it recognizes that there is no certainty that such an argument would prevail and recommends that the researchers seek a declaration from the court that the proposed procedures are lawful. Until such a case is brought it is impossible to be confident how the courts would respond.

(vii) Other Special Groups

Concern has been expressed about the conduct of research in a number of areas where particular problems arise. It is common to involve students in medical research, and they may sometimes feel pressurized into taking part by fear that their teachers will disapprove if they exercise their right not to do so. The National Union of Students has advised that it is inappropriate for students to be asked to take part in research being carried out by anyone who

---

[66] *Re T* [1992] 4 All ER 649, 653.   [67] *F* v. *W. Berkshire HA* [1989] 2 All ER 545.
[68] Medical Research Council Working Party on Research on the Mentally Incapacitated, n. 64 above, para. 7.3.4.

teaches them or is involved in assessing them.[69] Similar fears arise in relation to prisoners or members of the armed forces, who may be reluctant to refuse to participate for fear of reprisal by those in authority over them. The law prevents a consent procured by coercion being regarded as valid, but it is unlikely that social pressure would suffice.[70]

The Polkinghorne Committee has examined the difficulties that arise when foetal material is to be used in research.[71] It proposed a code of practice, which has been adopted by the Department of Health in its guidance to research ethics committees.[72] Under that code of practice, research may be carried out on the foetus or foetal tissue (material taken from the placenta is not included) with the written consent of the mother. However, the decision to terminate the pregnancy must have been taken by her before any reference was made to the possibility of research. Where abortion was spontaneous, consent should be sought only after the foetus has died. The mother's consent should be sought before screening the foetus for transmissible disease, or before other steps are taken which have consequences for the clinical management of the mother. The code suggests that the consent of the father might be sought where tests on the foetal tissue may have significance for him, and because he may have knowledge of a transmissible or hereditary disease. However, the code also states that the father's consent is not mandatory, and that he has no right to veto the use of the material. The code requires research ethics committees to satisfy themselves that the research is valid, that the objectives of the research cannot be achieved without the use of foetal material, and that the researchers have the necessary facilities and skill to carry out the research. Any conscientious objections of staff should be respected.

(viii) Problems of Confidentiality in Health Care Research

The general principles of confidentiality apply to those involved in research in the same way as they do to patients.[73] Professionals may often be asked to provide information about their patients to researchers. The General Medical Council recognizes that this is acceptable professional practice, provided that the patient has consented or cannot be identified from the data released.[74] The legal position would be the same.

---

[69] National Union of Students, *Guidelines for Students Participating in Medical Experiments*, reproduced at (1989) *BME* No 54, 10–11.

[70] *Freeman* v. *Home Office* [1984] 1 All ER 1036. See Ch. 10, sect. A(iii).

[71] *Review of the Guidance on the Research Use of Fetuses and Fetal Material* (London: HMSO, 1989, Cm 762).

[72] Department of Health, n. 9 above.   [73] See Ch. 11.

[74] General Medical Council, *Confidentiality* (London: GMC, 1995).

Research subjects may also have rights of access to the data held on them. Under the Data Protection Act 1984, if researchers hold on a computer data from which a subject could be identified, then the subject could apply for access. The Access to Health Records Act 1990 applies to manual records made in connection to an individual's care. It therefore confers rights of access to those taking part in therapeutic research, but not normally those involved in non-therapeutic studies. These statutes are discussed in Chapter 11.

The publication of research data may also raise problems of confidentiality. Publishing confidential information needs to be justified under the recognized exceptions to that principle. The most obvious of these is the consent of the research subject. Good practice indicates that this consent should be obtained in advance of the data being collected, although consent prior to publication is all that the law requires. In practice, only matters published in a way that enables the subject to be identified will give rise to difficulty. First, because no damage will be caused by anonymous information, so that no action could be brought. Secondly, because the research subjects will not know that it is their details that are being made public.

(ix) Compensation

It is widely accepted that those who take part in research have a stronger moral claim to receive compensation if something goes wrong than patients who are the victims of medical accidents.[75] Research subjects run risks not for their own benefit, but in the interests of others and the public good of scientific advance. If they are harmed in the course of the research it seems particularly unfair that they should bear that loss themselves. The guidelines for research ethics committees require them to consider the provision for compensation for research subjects in case of adverse events, and the need to inform subjects of these arrangements.[76] It is recommended that compensation should be available without proof of negligence.[77] The pharmaceutical industry accepts that this is good practice, and will normally offer *ex gratia* payments.[78] Universities and NHS bodies may sometimes do the same. However, there is at present no legal entitlement to compensation unless the injured research subject can show that the researcher had acted negligently. The rules of negligence are discussed in Chapter 7.

[75] *Report of the Royal Commission on Civil Liability and Compensation for Personal Injury* (London: HMSO, 1978, Cmnd. 7054), para. 1341; Royal College of Physicians, *Research Involving Patients* (London: RCP, 1990), 39–41.

[76] Department of Health, n. 9 above, 14; Committee for Proprietary Medicinal Products Working Party on Efficacy of Medicinal Products, n. 14 above, para. 1.6.

[77] Royal College of Physicians, n. 12 above, 35–9.

[78] Association of the British Pharmaceutical Industry, *Clinical Trial Compensation Guidelines* (London: ABPI, 1991).

It has been argued that individual members of research ethics committees could be held liable for failing to protect a subject who was injured during research.[79] In principle, this could be the case. The allegation would be that they had negligently failed to exercise due care in scrutinizing the design of the trial. However, such a failure would give rise to a legal claim only if it could be established that the members of the ethics committee owed a 'duty of care' in negligence to individual research subjects.[80] This is partly a question of public policy, and it is unlikely that the courts would find that it was just and reasonable to impose such a duty.[81] In any event, in practice the NHS trust, educational institution, or health authority that carried out the research is likely to be sued because it is more likely to be in a financial position to pay any damages awarded.[82] It should also be noted that, under the guidance from the Department of Health, responsibility for deciding whether the research should go ahead lies with the relevant NHS managers. This might make it difficult to establish a causal link between the careless acts by the ethics committee and the injury caused to the subject.

B. Animal Research

Much medical research is supported by experiments carried out on animals.[83] Although the precise moral status of animals is a matter for controversy, it is generally accepted that it is necessary to protect them from unjustifiable suffering and that there are limits to the acceptability of animal experimentation.[84] The Animals (Scientific Procedures) Act 1986 establishes a licensing system that seeks to control the use of animal experimentation, and ensures that animals are protected from inappropriate suffering.

The Act applies to experimental or other scientific procedures that may cause a protected animal pain, suffering, distress, or lasting harm.[85] A series of procedures that will cumulatively have such an effect is also covered.[86] Any steps taken to reduce the feeling of animals during procedures are to be disregarded for the purposes of assessing whether they may cause the animal pain,

---

[79] Kennedy and Grubb, n. 42 above, 1037–8.

[80] The relevant principles are discussed in Ch. 7, sect. B(i), and Ch. 3, sect. B(ii)(b).

[81] See *Yuen Kun-yeu* v. *AG of Hong Kong* [1987] 2 All ER 705.

[82] M. Brazier, 'Liability of Ethics Committees' (1990) 6 *PN* 186–90.

[83] D. Morton, 'The Animals (Scientific Procedures) Act 1986' in D. Blackman, P. Humphreys, and P. Todd (eds.), *Animal Welfare and the Law* (Cambridge: CUP, 1989).

[84] See e.g. P. Byrne, 'The Ethics of Medical Research' in P. Byrne (ed.), *Medicine in Contemporary Society* (London: King Edward's Hospital Fund for London, 1987); P. Singer, *Practical Ethics* (2nd edn., Cambridge: CUP, 1993), ch. 2, especially 65–8.

[85] S. 2(1).   [86] S. 2(2).

suffering, distress, or lasting harm.[87] Using anaesthetics, analgesics, or decerebration for the purposes of experiments or scientific procedures itself brings the procedure within the regulatory framework.[88]

The animals protected in this way are any living vertebrates (other than Man) and octopuses.[89] Animals at foetal, larval, or embryonic stages are also protected, provided that they are capable of independent feeding, or if they are mammals, birds, or reptiles who have reached half their species' gestation or incubation period.[90] Animals are regarded as living, for the purposes of the Act, until the permanent cessation of circulation or the destruction of their brain.[91]

The Act requires three forms of licence before animal research can go ahead. Unless all three are obtained, it will be unlawful to carry out the research.[92] The first relates to the premises on which it is to be carried out. The Secretary of State must issue a certificate designating the premises as a scientific procedures establishment and specifying the person responsible for the day-to-day care of the animals and the veterinary surgeon (or otherwise suitably qualified person) who should give advice on their health and welfare.[93]

The second type of licence relates to the project to be carried out.[94] Project licences may be given only for purposes specified in the statute.[95] The first is the prevention (including by testing products) or diagnosis or treatment of disease, ill-health, or abnormality in Man, animals, or plants. The second is the assessment, detection, regulation, or modification of physiological conditions in Man, animals, or plants. The third is the protection of the natural environment in the interests of the health or welfare of Man or animals. The fourth is the advancement of knowledge in biological or behavioural sciences. The fifth is education or training (other than in primary or secondary schools). The sixth is forensic enquiries. The seventh is breeding of animals for experimental or other scientific uses. If it falls within one of these legitimate purposes, a project must then be assessed to weigh the likely benefits against the likely adverse effects on the animals.[96] The Secretary of State must also be satisfied that adequate consideration has been given to achieving the purpose of the project without using animals.[97] If it is proposed to use cats, dogs, primates, or equidae (e.g. horses, zebras, asses), the Secretary of State must be satisfied that it is not practicable to use other species.[98] Project licences remain effective for up to five years, unless revoked.[99]

The third licence that is required relates to the individual who proposes to carry out the procedures. This permits the holder to carry out specified

[87] S. 2(4).   [88] S. 2(4).
[89] S. 1(1); Animals (Scientific Procedures) Act (Amendment) Order 1993, SI 1993 No 2103.
[90] S. 1(2).   [91] S. 1(5).   [92] S. 3.   [93] S. 6.   [94] S. 5.   [95] S. 5(3).
[96] S. 5(4).   [97] S. 5(5).   [98] S. 5(6).   [99] S. 5(7).

regulated procedures, in a specified place (or places), on animals of a specified description.[100] Such licences continue in force until revoked, but must be reviewed by the Secretary of State at least every five years. Personal licences will contain a condition that the holder will take precautions to ensure that only the minimum levels of pain, discomfort, or distress are suffered by the animals consistent with the purposes for which the authorized procedures are carried out. There will also be a condition specifying circumstances in which euthanasia should immediately be performed on the animal.[101]

The licensing scheme is supported and policed by inspectors appointed under the Act.[102] They visit places where procedures regulated under the Act are carried out to ensure that the appropriate licences are held and that conditions are being complied with. They also advise the Secretary of State, who may not grant a licence without consulting an inspector. The Secretary of State may also consult more widely, with an independent assessor or the Animal Procedures Committee.[103] Guidance on looking after animals is provided by the *Code of Practice for the Housing and Care of Animals Used in Scientific Procedures*.[104]

The Animal Procedures Committee consists of at least thirteen members, of whom at least one must be a barrister, solicitor, or advocate, and at least two-thirds are doctors, veterinary surgeons, or hold other qualifications or have experience approved by the Secretary of State as relevant.[105] This constitution means that wholly lay people will be in a minority on the Committee. However, it should not be assumed that all the professional members are involved in animal research, and the statute ensures that at least half the members do not hold licences under the Act and have not done so within the past six years. It also requires the Secretary of State to ensure that the interests of animal welfare are adequately represented.[106] The Committee advises the Secretary of State on matters relating to the Act. It may identify issues that need consideration in addition to the business referred to it.

C. Conclusion

It can be suggested that animal research is better regulated than that on human subjects. Under the Animals (Scientific Procedures) Act 1986, powers of inspection and enforcement exist that are not available to local research ethics committees. Only human embryos are given such protection. Human research subjects are protected mainly by non-statutory committees without

---

[100] S. 4.   [101] S. 10(2), Sch. 1.   [102] S. 18.   [103] S. 9(1).   [104] (London: HMSO, 1989).
[105] S. 19(2),(3).   [106] S. 19(3).

legal authority. The reason for this apparently less rigorous regulation is probably the assumption that human subjects can choose whether to take part in research. They can thus protect themselves. However, it has been seen that the law may not guarantee that sufficient information is given to such subjects. They must rely on the proper operation of research ethics committees, which should require that appropriately informed consent is obtained. Relying on informed consent as a safeguard raises particular problems in respect of those whose capacity to consent freely may be impaired. Special consideration has therefore to be given to such groups. Once again the legal position is unclear. The lack of clearly established legal protection through regulation is even more concerning when it is noted that the mechanisms for providing compensation are also weak. The proposed regional committees will do little to enhance the protection of research subjects because they are designed to make it easier for researchers to apply for approval. The same non-legal framework of principles will be used.

Part IV

Health Care Law and Ethics

15 Abortion

Abortion must be one of the most controversial areas of health care law. There is a fundamental, and highly charged, division between those who support 'a woman's right to choose' to terminate her pregnancy, and those who adopt a 'pro-life' stance that abortion is tantamount to murder. As these positions are adopted as issues of principle, it is difficult for the two groups to compromise without abandoning their beliefs. In consequence, any legal regime is likely to prove unsatisfactory to one or other side of the debate, and any search for a consensus is likely to be in vain.[1] Despite Ronald Dworkin's attempts to promote the possibility of progress by arguing that there is more common ground between the two fundamentalist positions,[2] it is probable that the historical pattern of regular attempts to reform the law will continue.[3] The focus in this Chapter is on the current state of the law, which has come to see the termination of pregnancy as essentially a medical procedure, albeit one that requires special regulation.[4]

The focus of that special regime has altered. It has probably never been the case that the law of homicide has covered foetuses.[5] That can only be used to punish killings which occur before or during the birth of the child, provided death does not occur until after delivery.[6] Early statutory interventions were aimed to protect the foetus. However, concern then turned to the protection of the mother from backstreet abortions.[7] The Abortion Act 1967, which was amended in 1990, was intended to satisfy these protective demands and has largely succeeded in removing the problems created by unqualified abortionists. This has permitted public debate to focus on the debate about the moral status of the foetus.

In general, English law facilitates therapeutic abortions and has chosen not to treat human embryos and foetuses as full legal persons. Nevertheless, it is

---

[1] S. McLean, 'Abortion Law: Is Consensual Reform Possible?' (1990) 17 *JLS* 106.

[2] R. Dworkin, *Life's Dominion* (London: HarperCollins, 1993).

[3] See J. Keown, *Abortion, Doctors and the Law* (Cambridge: Cambridge University Press, 1988).

[4] A. Grubb, 'Abortion Law in England: The Medicalisation of a Crime' (1990) 18 *Law, Medicine & Health Care* 146–61.

[5] *Ibid.*   [6] See P. Skegg, *Law, Ethics and Medicine* (Oxford: Clarendon Press, 1988), 19–26.

[7] G. Williams, *The Sanctity of Life and the Criminal Law* (London, Faber & Faber, 1958), 144–7.

misleading to go quite so far as to say that: 'The foetus cannot, in English law, in my view, have any right of its own at least until it is born and has a separate existence from the mother.'[8] If that were true, then you would expect that the abortion decision would be governed only by the law of consent. In reality, foetuses are protected by the law, even though they are not treated in the same way as they would be once born. Their destruction is restricted by the criminal law relating to abortion. Their pre-natal existence is recognized in various provisions of the civil law. Although rights to bring actions remain inchoate until after birth, they do extend to events prior to birth. Chapter 17 discusses the implications of these rules for maternity care. Here the concern is with the legal rules governing the abortion decision.

These principles developed when the only place where human embryos could be expected to exist was in a woman's womb. Advances in reproductive science have raised a new set of problems which the law is poorly equipped to solve. It is therefore necessary also to consider the status of the human embryo *in vitro*, an area regulated by the Human Fertilization and Embryology Act 1990. Chapter 16 looks at this problem in the context of fertility services, and Chapter 14 looked at the regulation of research on human embryos.

A. The Scheme of Abortion Law

The fundamental legal rules relating to abortion in English law are still to be found in the Offences Against the Person Act 1861 sections 58 and 59. Section 58 makes it an offence for a pregnant woman to administer noxious substances to herself or to use any instrument in order to procure her own miscarriage. It also creates a similar offence where persons other than the woman herself do these things. Such other persons will be guilty of an offence even if it turns out that the woman was not in fact pregnant, although it must be proved that they believed that she was.[9] A woman who seeks to terminate her own pregnancy cannot commit an offence unless she is actually pregnant.[10] In both cases the crime is to seek to terminate a pregnancy rather than to succeed. Section 59 criminalizes the supply and procuring of abortifacients or instruments for use in unlawful abortions. The Infant Life Preservation Act 1929 provides a separate regime to deal with pregnancies where the foetus has reached the stage of being 'capable of being born alive'.

---

[8] *Paton* v. *BPAS* [1978] 2 All ER 987, 989, *per* Baker P.   [9] *R.* v. *Price* [1968] 2 All ER 282.
[10] Although it is possible that the law of attempt would result in a woman who thought that she was pregnant being liable for trying to commit the crime on herself, see Grubb, n. 4 above, 149.

The basic prohibition on terminations has been mitigated by the Abortion Act 1967. That Act provides a set of defences to the crimes established by the 1861 and 1929 Acts. These constitute the grounds for lawful terminations. The Abortion Act was amended by the Human Fertilization and Embryology Act 1990, and the current legal regime took effect in 1991.[11] Some of those defences are only available in the first twenty-four weeks of pregnancy. It should also be noted that it is generally held that no offence is committed under the Offences Against the Person Act 1861 in the early stages of a pregnancy. As a result of these provisions, it can be said that English law divides human pregnancy into three stages for the purposes of abortion law; pre-implantation, between implantation and twenty-four weeks, and after twenty-four weeks. Each of these three stages is governed by a separate set of legal restrictions on termination. Sometimes it is necessary to reduce the number of foetuses carried in a multiple pregnancy. It is necessary to show that the grounds for abortion are made out in relation to such a 'selective reduction' even though the woman will remain pregnant.[12]

(i) From Conception to Implantation

A number of modern methods of contraception, including the 'morning after pill' and the intra-uterine device (IUD or 'coil'), might be classified as causing abortion rather than preventing conception as they take effect after fertilization. It is therefore important to determine whether they can only be used when the specific statutory defences are available. If this is so, then it will be necessary for doctors wishing to use them to get second opinions as to the existence of the statutory grounds (see section A(iii) below). There is still scope for controversy over this matter, as no court has ruled on it,[13] but the general consensus is that contraceptive techniques should not be classified as abortifacients unless they operate after implantation. Thus, it is argued that pregnancy only comes within 'the law relating to abortion' upon the implantation of the *conceptus* in the womb, not at the point of fertilization. This means that contraceptive methods taking effect prior to implantation may be offered by doctors as ordinary treatment.[14]

This interpretation of the law is based on the fact that the 1861 Act uses the term 'miscarriage'. This has led some to argue that a woman is not carrying a child until the point of implantation because there is no physical link between

---

[11] The amendments were made by s. 37 of the 1990 Act.　　[12] Abortion Act 1967, s. 5(2).

[13] Although in *R. v. Price*, n. 9 above, it was assumed that inserting an intra-uterine device when the woman was not pregnant would not be an offence.

[14] K. M. Norrie, *Family Planning Practice and the Law* (Aldershot: Dartmouth, 1991), 48–59.

mother and child prior to that point.[15] As a matter of strict legal analysis this argument is weak; it appears that both medical and legal usages in the nineteenth century would have assumed that pregnancy began at fertilization and that the term 'miscarriage' was applicable from that point.[16] Nevertheless, the view that implantation was the crucial point was adopted in 1983 by the then Attorney-General, Sir Michael Havers, in answer to a Parliamentary question.[17] This does not, of course, alter the law, but it has had the effect of rendering it extremely unlikely that prosecutions would occur. It should also be noted that Parliament has defined 'carrying a child' as referring to the stage of pregnancy after the embryo has been implanted for the purposes of the Human Fertilization and Embryology Act 1990.[18] This is of no direct assistance in construing the 1861 Act, but the general expectation that the law uses terms consistently gives weight to the accepted interpretation. Current advice from the Department of Health holds that post-coital contraception should be used only within seventy-two hours of conception, despite the fact that implantation is unlikely to occur for some eight to ten days.[19]

In the case of some techniques, it may not be clear whether in the particular case they act to prevent implantation or to dislodge an embryo. Fitting an IUD will displace an implanted foetus, and if this is done when it is known that the woman is pregnant then it will be defined by the law as an abortion.[20] Drugs designed to prevent implantation may in fact cause the expulsion of an embryo which is already implanted. This would also constitute an abortion in law. Nevertheless, if the doctor administers the drug soon after the act of unprotected intercourse, before it can be known whether conception has occurred, it is hard to see how knowledge of a pregnancy could be proved.[21]

(ii) Termination under the Abortion Act 1967

There is no doubt that it is *prima facie* an offence to terminate a pregnancy after implantation. However, the Abortion Act 1967 provides quite broadly defined defences. Under that Act, there is a period when all the grounds for termination under the Act are available. This runs up until the twenty-fifth week. After then, the most commonly used ground, sometimes known as the social ground, ceases to be available. The various grounds will be discussed

---

[15] D. Brahams, 'The Morning-after Pill: Contraception or Abortion?' (1983) 133 *NLJ* 417; I. Kennedy, *Treat Me Right* (Oxford: OUP, 1988), 32–41; J. K. Mason, 'Abortion and the Law' in S. A. M. McLean (ed.), *Legal Issues in Human Reproduction* (Aldershot: Gower, 1989), 45–79, 68–70; Norrie, n. 14 above, 29.

[16] I. J. Keown, ' "Miscarriage": A Medico-Legal Analysis' [1984] *Crim. LR* 604.

[17] 10 May 1983, *Hansard,* HC vol. 42, col. 238–9.   [18] S. 2(3).

[19] Mason, n. 15 above, 45–79, 69.   [20] *R. v. Price,* n. 9 above.

[21] Norrie, n. 14 above, 55.

individually, but it should be noted that there is no direct authority on the meaning of any of the specified grounds. This is probably not accidental, as the courts have expressed their reluctance to call into question the judgement of doctors on the existence of grounds for abortion:

> not only would it be a bold and brave judge . . . who would seek to interfere with the discretion of doctors under the [Abortion Act 1967], but I think it would really be a foolish judge who would try to do any such thing, unless possibly there is clear bad faith and an obvious attempt to perpetrate a criminal offence.[22]

In effect the courts have accepted that in this difficult area the interpretation of the law should be left mainly for the medical profession.

This is reinforced by the fact that the Abortion Act makes the legality of a termination depend, not on whether the grounds are actually made out, but whether two doctors believe that they are in good faith.[23] Any prosecution would have to show that the doctors had used the justification in bad faith, and this would be extremely difficult to prove.[24] The margin of medical discretion is further increased by the fact that the Act specifically provides in section 1(2) that reasonably foreseeable environmental factors may be taken into account when determining the risks of injury to health under section 1(1)(a).

There has been only one reported case concerning a prosecution under the Act, *R. v. Smith.*[25] It involved an abortion that was carried out privately and incompletely. The essence of the case against the doctor was that he had not formed an opinion in good faith as required by the Act. The evidence indicated that he had made no internal examination of the patient and had taken no steps to inquire into her personal history or situation. The only entry in the doctor's notes relating to the grounds on which the Act permits terminations was that the patient was 'depressed'. There was a conflict of evidence on whether the doctor who had given the second opinion had ever examined the patient. In his summing-up, the trial judge invited the jury to consider whether 'there was any balancing of the risks involved in allowing the pregnancy to continue and allowing the pregnancy to be terminated, or was this a mere routine abortion for cash?'[26] The jury convicted and the Court of Appeal refused to quash the conviction. In most cases, however, the doctor will be able to show that he or she did consider the balance of risks and will therefore be innocent of the criminal offence.

---

[22] Baker P in *Paton v. Trustees of BPAS*, n. 8 above, 992; approved *C v. S* [1987] 1 All ER 1230.
[23] Abortion Act 1967, s. 1(1).   [24] Mason, n. 15 above, 47–8.
[25] [1974] 1 All ER 376.   [26] *Ibid.*, 383.

(iii) Safeguards

Before examining the grounds in detail, it is appropriate to consider the range of regulatory safeguards that exist to ensure that the Act is operated properly. The first safeguard introduced by the 1967 Act, is that there is a medical monopoly on abortions. These may only be carried out by a registered medical practitioner.[27] However, the requirement that a doctor carry out the termination does not prevent other health professionals, such as nurses, carrying out the active steps which induce the abortion. All that the Act requires is that the decision to terminate the pregnancy and the choice of the method to be used are made by a doctor who remains on call and responsible for the woman's treatment throughout the procedure.[28]

A second safeguard is that abortions may only be carried out in an NHS hospital or other approved place.[29] Usually, this requires private clinics to be individually approved. However, under a provision introduced in 1990, the Secretary of State may approve a class of places, such as GPs' surgeries, for the purpose of terminations.[30] This would facilitate the use of drugs that will terminate pregnancies but do not require hospitalization. A third safeguard is the need for a second opinion. A termination will usually only be lawful if two doctors believe, in good faith, that one of the grounds under the Act is made out.[31]

It is possible that on some occasions these safeguards may actually obstruct the provision of care. Section 1(4) dispenses with the restrictions in respect of the place of termination and the need for a second opinion in cases where the abortion is 'immediately necessary' to save the mother's life or to prevent 'grave permanent injury' to her physical or mental health. The meaning of that phrase is discussed in relation to the second ground for termination below.

The final regulatory safeguard is provided by the notification provisions of the Act and the regulations made under it.[32] Prescribed certificates are set out for doctors to sign, certifying their opinion that grounds for lawfully terminating the pregnancy exist.[33] The doctor who performs the abortion has to fill in a specified form of notification.[34] This includes questions about the method of dating the pregnancy, the grounds on which the termination was certified as lawful, the method of diagnosis if the foetal-handicap ground was used, selective terminations, the method of termination, and any complications that resulted.

---

[27] S. 1(1).   [28] *RCN* v. *DHSS* [1981] 1 All ER 545.   [29] S. 1(3).
[30] S. 1(3A).   [31] S. 1(1).   [32] S. 2; Abortion Regulations 1991, SI 1991 No 499.
[33] Abortion Regulations 1991, n. 32 above, Sch. 1.   [34] *Ibid.*, Sch. 2.

(iv) The 'Social' Ground

The first ground for termination is only available up to the twenty-fifth week. It applies where the two doctors have formed the opinion, in good faith:

> that the pregnancy has not exceeded its twenty-fourth week and that the continuance of the pregnancy would involve risk, greater than if the pregnancy were terminated, of injury to the physical or mental health of the pregnant woman or any existing children of her family.[35]

While this ground clearly refers to health matters, it has been described as a 'social' ground, because doctors may take account of the woman's actual or foreseeable environment when they assess the risks involved.[36] This means that the inconvenience of having a child may provide a basis for an abortion. It has been argued that this makes it lawful to terminate a pregnancy on the basis of the sex of the foetus where the social and cultural pressures upon a woman to produce a child of a particular sex are strong.[37]

The majority of induced abortions are performed under section 1(1)(a). In 1993 there were 157,846 abortions to women resident in England and Wales. Approximately 1.2 per cent of these were performed on the basis of foetal abnormality. Just over 96 per cent were recorded as justified on the 'social grounds'.[38] This overwhelming pattern of 'social' abortions has led to the 1967 Act being criticized for allowing abortion on demand.[39] This assertion is based on the practice of some doctors who argue that there is statistical evidence that carrying a foetus to term is more dangerous to the woman than terminating the pregnancy in its early stages. This enables them to hold that section 1(1)(a) is made out whenever a woman is pregnant. This argument has never been tested in the courts, but it appears that doctors have given 'pregnancy' as the sole reason for believing that termination is less risky than continuing without being prosecuted.[40]

However, it does not follow from the fact that doctors are in practice usually immune from prosecution that the Abortion Act 1967 provides for abortion on demand. The Act does not provide women with rights to terminate their pregnancy.[41] Instead, it leaves them dependent upon finding a doctor who will co-operate with their wishes. This means that women who can afford to go to private clinics will usually have little difficulty obtaining a legal abortion. Those reliant on NHS provision, however, are faced with

---

[35] S. 1(1)(a).   [36] S. 1(2).

[37] D. Morgan, 'Foetal Sex Identification, Abortion and the Law' [1988] *Fam Law* 355–9.

[38] OCPS, *Abortion Statistics 1993* (London: HMSO, 1996), Table 13.

[39] e.g. by Denning MR in *RCN* v. *DHSS*, n. 28 above, 554.   [40] Keown, n. 3 above, 128–34.

[41] L. Clarke, 'Abortion: A Rights Issue?' in R. Lee and D. Morgan (eds.), *Birthrights: Law and Ethics at the Beginning of Life* (London: Routledge, 1989).

considerable variation between the practice of different doctors. Consequently, there is considerable disparity in the degree to which abortions are readily available both between and within different areas of the country. Official statistics showed that in 1973 only 10 per cent of those seeking an abortion in Walsall were able to get one through the NHS, while in Oxford the figure was 79 per cent.[42]

It is therefore doctors who control access to abortions.[43] Women's access to abortions is dependent on the ethical position of individual doctors and is vulnerable to prejudices of an essentially white middle-class profession. Norrie has pointed out that terminations sought because the child is the 'wrong' sex are as justifiable under the Act as those because the pregnancy is inconvenient for economic or career reasons. However, the former is far less likely to be accepted by the medical profession.[44] The Abortion Act 1967 may allow doctors to offer abortion on demand in the early stages of pregnancy, but it does not secure it for women.

(v) Dating the Pregnancy

The so-called 'social' ground for termination is only available during the first twenty-four weeks of pregnancy. Unfortunately, there is some confusion over the basis on which a pregnancy should be dated. The Act itself merely states that certain grounds for termination are only available if 'the pregnancy has not exceeded its twenty fourth week'.[45] This establishes that terminations are permissible *during* (but not after) the twenty-fourth week. It does not indicate when the period begins to run.

Commentators on the Act have canvassed a number of possible interpretations. Murphy argues that the dates should be calculated from the date of fertilization, because foetuses were thought to be viable from twenty-four weeks after this date.[46] As this was the basis for fixing the time limit at twenty-four weeks this can be said to be consistent with the intention of Parliament. Grubb holds that the best interpretation would be to begin the clock at the time when the embryo implants in the uterus. This is on the basis that the law relating to abortion does not apply until then, and that consistency should be maintained.[47]

---

[42] OCPS, *Registrar General's Supplement on Abortion, 1973* (London: HMSO, 1974).

[43] L. Doyal, *The Political Economy of Health* (London, Pluto Press, 1979), 228–34.

[44] Norrie, n. 15 above, 33–4.   [45] Abortion Act 1967, s. 1(1)(a).

[46] J. Murphy, 'Cosmetics, Eugenics and Ambivalence' [1991] *JSWFL* 375–93, 387–8. See also G. Douglas, *Law, Fertility and Reproduction* (London: Sweet & Maxwell, 1991), 98.

[47] A. Grubb, 'The New Law of Abortion: Clarification or Ambiguity?' [1991] *Crim. LR* 659–70, 663–6.

However, the twenty-four week period is the duration of the pregnancy; and the stage of pregnancy from which the term 'miscarriage' is used to describe its failure is not necessarily the beginning.[48] This undermines Grubb's interpretation. Similarly, the section refers to the dating of pregnancy rather than the age of the foetus. This points against Murphy's view, as the usual medical and midwifery practice is to date pregnancies from the first day of the woman's last menstrual period, not from conception (usually some two weeks later). In accordance with the canon of statutory interpretation that words should be interpreted according to their ordinary usage, and in their technical usage if appropriate, it would seem best to follow professional terminology. This means that the twenty-four weeks should be calculated from the last menstrual period (LMP). This seems to be the interpretation assumed by the Abortion Regulations 1991, which ask doctors notifying abortions to confirm the method of estimating the date in terms of LMP, ultrasound (from which results are usually dated in terms of LMP), or 'other'.[49]

(vi) Maternal Health Grounds

The Abortion Act includes two grounds for terminations that relate to the health of the mother. These are set out in section 1(1)(b) and (c). They apply where the doctors believe

> (b) that the termination is necessary to prevent grave permanent injury to the physical or mental health of the pregnant woman; or
>
> (c) that the continuance of the pregnancy would involve risk to the life of the pregnant woman, greater than if the pregnancy were terminated.

There has been no judicial interpretation of these phrases, although in the House of Lords debate on the 1991 amendments, Lord Mackay offered an example that he thought might be covered. This concerned severe hypertension, leading to a risk of permanent damage to the kidney, brain, or heart.[50] A leading case from the 1930s had extended the meaning of acts done to preserve the mother's life to embrace cases where 'the probable consequence of the continuance of the pregnancy will be to make the woman a physical or mental wreck'.[51] However, it is probable that this case law has been superseded by the introduction of the explicit ground relating to 'grave permanent injury'. Murphy has pointed out that this implies enduring and irreparable harm, and that it may be narrower than the judicial elaborations on the old law.[52] Where

---

[48] See Murphy, n. 46 above, 388–90. [49] SI 1991 No 499, Sch. 2, question 12.
[50] *Hansard*, Vol. 522, col. 1039.
[51] *R.* v. *Bourne* [1939] 1 KB 687, 694. See also *R.* v. *Bergmann and Ferguson* (1948) 1 BMJ 1008 and *R.* v. *Newton and Sturgo* [1958] Crim LR 469.
[52] Murphy, n. 46 above, 380–1.

termination on one of these two grounds is 'immediately necessary' then an abortion may proceed anywhere, and on the basis of a single doctor's opinion.[53]

(vii) The Foetal Handicap Ground

There has been some judicial discussion of the wording of section 1(1)(d), which permits terminations where two doctors believe, in good faith, 'that there is a substantial risk that if the child were born it would suffer from such physical or mental abnormalities as to be seriously handicapped'. In *Mackay* v. *Essex AHA*, Stephenson LJ suggested that the main purpose of that provision was to benefit the foetus in question. He suggested that it represented a recognition that 'it would be better for a child, born to suffer from such abnormalities as to be seriously handicapped, not to have been born at all'.[54] If this comment, which is only *obiter* and therefore not binding on subsequent courts, is correct it would seem that the foetal handicap ground should not be used to protect prospective parents from the difficulties which they will experience bringing up a disabled child.

Stephenson LJ also indicated that there might be a connection between the provisions and the law relating to the treatment of severely handicapped newborns. He suggested that such principles which can be discerned in this area might also be relevant to construing the Abortion Act. At present, however this seems to offer no detailed guidance. While it is possible to seek to draw guidance on the type of disability that may be relevant from the earlier cases, this approach has now been rejected in favour of restricting judicial scrutiny to the process of decision-making.[55]

Consideration of the statutory provision itself provides little help. It may be that 'substantial' refers to the probability of a handicap existing, and that the risk should be quantified without reference to the degree of handicap in question. There is no indication whether the 'seriousness' of a handicap should be considered in the abstract, or in relation to the circumstances in which the child would live. The specific statutory reference to the doctor's right to consider the foreseeable environment applies to only the first two grounds for termination.[56]

One problem that has been identified concerns genetic disorders, some of which will not afflict children for many years or may only affect their own children. If the child has to suffer from a handicap from the time of birth, such

---

[53] Abortion Act 1967, s. 1(4).   [54] [1982] QB 1168, 1180.   [55] See Ch. 18.
[56] See s. 1(2).

genetic disease might not come within the grounds for termination.[57] However, there is nothing in the Act to limit the grounds in this way. In practice, many abortions that follow pre-natal testing for genetic disorders may be performed in the first twenty-four weeks, and be justified on the social grounds (when the effects on the mother and any other children may be taken into account). Where this is not possible because of late diagnosis it is probable that doctors can hold, in good faith, the view that carrying a genetic disorder is a handicap, because it would impair the choices available to the child. Whether it is serious needs to be judged on the circumstances of the case, and it will be very difficult to challenge a clinician's decision.

B. Rights of Conscience

In the light of the highly charged moral context of terminations of pregnancy, the Abortion Act 1967 provides a right of conscientious objection to those who would otherwise be bound to 'participate' in treatment authorized by the Act.[58] This prevents people being under any legal obligation to participate in terminations, although the right does not extend to cases where the termination is 'necessary to save the life or to prevent grave permanent injury to the physical or mental health of a pregnant woman'.[59] This drafting would appear to mean that a professional cannot opt out of terminations on the first of the two maternal health grounds. However, it is probably better to regard it as preventing health professionals from refusing to terminate pregnancies in emergencies. This would have been clearer if the word 'immediately' had been inserted before necessary.[60] However, health professionals who argue that, in their view, the abortion was not 'necessary' because the threat was not pressing should be able to bring themselves within the conscience clause. The burden of proving the existence of a conscientious objection falls upon the person claiming it.

The word 'participate' is to be defined in accordance with its natural meaning. It is clear that this section does not entitle a medical secretary to refuse to type a letter of referral arranging for a patient to see another doctor with a view to ascertaining whether she or he agrees that an abortion is justified.[61] It may, however, be that initiating the arrangements intended to lead to an

[57] D. Morgan, 'Abortion: The Unexamined Ground' [1990] *Crim. LR* 687–94, 689–90. Similar problems may arise in relation to infections, such as HIV, contracted *in utero*, but which may not immediately impair the child's health: see Grubb, n. 47 above, 662–3.
[58] S. 4.   [59] S. 4(2).   [60] As in s. 1(4).
[61] *Janaway* v. *Salford HA* [1988] 3 All ER 1079 (HL).

abortion is to be seen as 'participating' in them. This would mean that a doctor can decline to refer a patient. This seemed to be the view of two members of the Court of Appeal in *Janaway* v. *Salford HA*.[62] In the House of Lords, Lord Keith believed that the conscience clause did not extend to permitting a doctor to refuse to sign the necessary forms to certify that an abortion would be lawful.[63] However, this conclusion was premised on the assumption that there was no duty to sign the form anyway, so no conscience clause was necessary to justify refusing to do so. Kennedy and Grubb point out that general practitioners are contractually obliged to arrange for patients to be referred for NHS services, which must include abortion services.[64] It is unclear how Lord Keith would have responded to that point.

It is also unclear whether a doctor is obliged to inform a patient that grounds for an abortion may be present even though he or she has a conscientious objection to participating in it. In *Mackay* v. *Essex AHA* Stephenson LJ seemed implicitly to approve the concession made by counsel that there was such a duty.[65] However, as any complainant would have to show that the doctor had failed to meet the required standard of care, set by the profession, it seems unlikely that an action would succeed.

In 1990, the operation of the conscience clause was examined by the House of Commons Social Services Committee. Some witnesses suggested that it effectively prevented abortion services being provided under the NHS in some areas of the country because staff refused to participate in them. Others gave evidence that staff felt unable to claim the right to refuse to be involved in abortions because of social pressures from colleagues and managers. The Select Committee supported the existence of the conscience clause, and recommended extending it to cover some ancillary staff, and that the burden of proving a conscientious objection should no longer fall upon the person claiming it.[66] However, the Government rejected the proposals for reform.[67]

---

[62] *R. v. Salford AHA, ex p. Janaway* [1988] 2 FLR 370, 379 (Slade LJ), 384–5 (Stocker LJ). Balcombe LJ disagreed, see 381.

[63] *Janaway* v. *Salford HA*, n. 61 above, 1083. All the other members of the House of Lords expressed their agreement with his speech.

[64] I. Kennedy and A. Grubb, *Medical Law: Text with Materials* (2nd edn., London: Butterworths, 1994) 896, referring to the NHS (General Medical Services) Regulations 1992, SI 1992 No 635, Sch. 2, para. 12.

[65] [1982] QB 1168, 1180.

[66] Social Services Committee, *Abortion Act 1967 'Conscience Clause'*, HC Paper (1989–90) 123.

[67] *Abortion Act 1967 Conscience Clause: Government Response to the Tenth Report from the Social Services Committee Session 1989–90* (London: HMSO, 1990, Cm 1538).

C. The Residual Importance of the Infant Life Preservation Act 1929

Once the foetus is capable of being born alive the Infant Life Preservation Act 1929 is applicable in addition to the Offences Against the Person Act 1861. The Infant Life Preservation Act has rarely been used. In 1988 Fortin reported that there had been only four prosecutions since 1957.[68] Its current importance is marginal. Where a doctor has a defence under the Abortion Act, it will also be a defence to a prosecution under the Infant Life Preservation Act.[69]

However, there may be some circumstances in which a prosecution could still be brought under the 1929 Act. It is unclear whether a non-medical health professional can rely on that provision. A termination will be lawful under the 1861 Act even when carried out by a nurse, provided that a doctor remains responsible.[70] Yet the defence created to the 1929 Act seems to relate to the doctor personally, not to the termination. Nurses may therefore be vulnerable to prosecution under the 1929 Act even when the doctor would not. They would therefore be well advised to require a doctor to deal with late terminations, where the 1929 Act might apply.

Section 1 of the Act creates the offence of 'child destruction' when a foetus that is 'capable of being born alive' is killed *in utero*. A defence is available where it is proved that the act which caused the death of the child was done 'in good faith for the purpose only of preserving the life of the mother'. The Act creates a presumption that a foetus of twenty-eight weeks' gestation is capable of being born alive.[71] This can be rebutted by evidence that an older foetus is not in fact capable of being born alive or that a younger foetus is in fact so capable. The Act does not further define the phrase 'capable of being born alive'.[72] The matter reached the Court of Appeal in *C* v. *S* where it was said that a foetus of between eighteen and twenty-one weeks which was incapable of breathing was not 'capable of being born alive' within the meaning of the Act.[73] A test based on 'real and discernible signs of life' was rejected. The exact meaning of the decision remains unclear. The best view seems to be that the Court required some capacity in the foetus to survive, thus making the test one of viability.[74] In *Rance* v. *Mid-Downs HA* the court said that a foetus had to be 'breathing and living by its breathing through its own lungs alone, without deriving any of its living or power of living by or through the connection

---

[68] J. Fortin, 'Legal Protection for the Unborn Child' (1988) 51 *MLR* 54, 64.
[69] Abortion Act 1967, s. 5(1).   [70] *RCN* v. *DHSS*, n. 28 above.   [71] S. 1(2).
[72] For discussions of the interpretation see Skegg, n. 6 above, 7–12 and I. J. Keown, 'The Scope of the Offence of Child Destruction' (1988) 104 *LQR* 120.
[73] [1987] 1 All ER 1230.
[74] A. Grubb and D. Pearl, 'Protecting the Life of the Unborn Child' (1987) 103 *LQR* 340.

to its mother'. A foetus which would have breathed unaided for at least two or three hours was 'capable of being born alive' within the meaning of the Act.[75] Despite the imprecision of the test, it is usually assumed that foetuses of twenty-four weeks are capable of being born alive and some would say that twenty-two weeks is the appropriate rule of thumb.

A second difficulty of interpretation raised by the Act concerns the phrase 'preserving the life of the mother'. The prosecution is required to prove that the act causing the abortion was not done in good faith only for this purpose. In *R. v. Bourne* it was suggested that abortions are carried out to preserve the life of the mother when 'the probable consequence of the continuance of the pregnancy will be to make the woman a physical or mental wreck'.[76] This guidance is not binding, as the 1929 Act was not in issue in the case. There are a number of difficulties with adopting it, but it remains the only relevant reported authority and is likely to be followed.[77]

D. Paternal Rights

The final matter which needs to be raised in respect of the law relating to induced abortions concerns the position of the father of a foetus. It is now clear that the Abortion Act 1967 does not provide any right of veto for the father, and that it is irrelevant whether the father is the husband of the woman.[78] Under the Abortion Regulations 1991, neither husband nor father is entitled to information about a proposed termination of pregnancy.[79] In the High Court in *C v. S* Heilbron J found that an unborn child could not bring an action and that it followed that the father could not litigate as the child's next friend.[80] The point was not decided in the Court of Appeal. The European Court of Human Rights has upheld English law's refusal to give a married father any say in the decision.[81] Consequently, the matter now seems to be beyond legal argument, although it will no doubt remain controversial.[82]

It is arguable that these decisions deal only with cases where the abortion would be lawful, and that where the relevant statutory grounds are not satisfied it may be open to a father to seek an injunction from the courts. However,

---

[75] [1991] 1 All ER 801.
[76] N. 51 above, 694. See also *R. v. Bergmann and Ferguson*, n. 51 above, and *R. v. Newton and Sturgo*, n. 51 above.
[77] Skegg, n. 6 above, 12–19.   [78] *Paton* v. *BPAS*, n. 8 above; *C* v. *S*, n. 22 above.
[79] *C* v. *S*, n. 22 above.   [80] *Ibid.*   [81] *Paton* v. *UK* (1980) 3 EHHR 408.
[82] P. T. O'Neill and I. Watson, 'The Father and the Unborn Child' (1975) 38 *MLR* 174; D. C. Bradley, 'A Woman's Right to Choose' (1978) 41 *MLR* 365; Kennedy, n. 15 above, 42–51.

the courts have indicated, without deciding the point, that they would be reluctant to entertain such an action.[83] They thought that if a prosecution were to be brought, it should be by the Director of Public Prosecutions and not by a private individual. This would prevent the law being used to harass women and doctors, as the DPP would prosecute only in extreme cases.

E. Conclusion

When English law is compared to the practice in other countries it can be seen that it is not particularly permissive.[84] There are still some countries, such as Belgium, which maintain a prohibition on abortions mitigated only by a defence of necessity to protect the health of the woman in extreme cases. In a survey of abortion laws in twenty 'western' countries, Glendon found that the majority allowed abortions only for specified causes (as in England), but that six countries respected women's right to choose for themselves in the early stages of pregnancy.[85] She also observed that a number of those in the majority group come closer than English law to allowing elective abortions. Thus English law seems to take a middle way between heavily restricting abortion services and leaving them largely unregulated.

What stands out about English law is its reluctance to become directly involved in the clinical decisions. The grounds for termination are filtered through the requirement that medical opinions be in good faith. The court is only indirectly concerned with whether the doctors were right. It is primarily interested in their honesty. Further, by restricting the father's right to intervene, the probability of cases coming to court is greatly reduced. The main safeguards against unlawful abortions are provided by administrative regulation. The medicalization of abortion is also reinforced by the existence of the conscience clause, which ensures that doctors rather than women control access to abortion.

[83] *Paton* v. *BPAS*, n. 8 above; *C* v. *S*, n. 22 above.
[84] M. Freeman, 'Abortion—What Do Other Countries Do?' (1988) 138 *NLJ* 233.
[85] M. A. Glendon, *Abortion and Divorce in Western Law* (Cambridge, Mass.: Harvard University Press, 1987), 13–39.

16 Fertility

Fertility is a highly personal and sensitive area of human life. Popular prejudice stigmatizes men who are sterile as unmanly. Women who are unable to conceive may be encouraged to feel that they unable to fulfil their 'proper' role. Since the end of the 1970s, the focus of popular debate has been on the plight of the infertile, and considerable effort has been concentrated on improving techniques to overcome their difficulties. Proclamations of the 'right' to have a child are now a familiar part of the campaign for more resources to be devoted to this cause. This has not always been the case, however. Earlier in the twentieth century, the main battles were concerned with giving women and men the opportunity to control their fertility.[1] The movements for information about family planning had to fight hard to overcome opposition, reinforced by an unsympathetic legal system. In one context, that of young people, this battle continues. The Government is promoting the reduction of unwanted teenage pregnancy by 50 per cent by the year 2000 as one of its targets for improving the nation's health. However, this is against the opposition of those (some of them within the Government itself) who believe that information about sexuality corrupts the young.[2]

This Chapter considers the law relating to the control of fertility. It considers the extent to which the 'right to reproduce' is recognized by English law. The European Convention on Human Rights recognizes a right to have children, although it may not be quite the individualistic privilege that some would support. Article 12 provides that: 'Men and women of marriageable age have the right to marry and to found a family, according to the national laws governing the exercise of this right.'

It is important to realize that the concept of fertility rights is a complex one.[3] At one extreme, it could mean only the negative right to be protected

[1] A. Leathard, *The Fight for Family Planning* (London: Macmillan, 1980).
[2] Compare the position of the Department of Health, *The Health of the Nation* (London: HMSO, 1992, Cm 1986) with the more moralistic Department for Education's circular 5/94, 'Education Act 1993: Sex Education in Schools'.
[3] See e.g. M. Freeman, 'Sterilising the Mentally Handicapped' in M. Freeman (ed.), *Medicine, Ethics and the Law* (London: Stevens, 1988) and S. McLean, 'The Right to Reproduce' in T. Campbell (ed.), *Human Rights* (Oxford: Blackwell, 1986).

from sterilization. In one case in the 1970s the judge explained her decision to refuse to authorize the sterilization of a girl with learning difficulties by saying that the procedure would have 'involved the deprivation of a basic human right, namely the right of a woman to reproduce, and therefore it would, if performed on a woman for non-therapeutic reasons and without her consent, be a violation of that right'.[4]

The right to reproduce could also mean a more positive claim: that the state should provide people with the assistance that they need to overcome their infertility. In English law, the provision of infertility services is governed by a licensing system, which does not confer on individuals the right to infertility services on demand, but creates a system that restricts them to those thought to be suitable. Attempts to force the NHS to provide services would almost certainly fail under the law discussed in Chapter 3.

In between these conceptions of the right to reproduce lies one in which the law is expected to facilitate attempts to overcome infertility by ensuring that no barriers are placed in the way of adults wishing to bring up children who were born as a result of assisted conception. This involves a consideration of the law determining the status of such children. If the law fails to define those born after assisted conceptions as the children of the people who are going to bring them up, then it obstructs rather than facilitates attempts to overcome infertility.

The problems faced by those who suffer unwanted infertility have received considerable attention from lawyers and ethicists. It is also important to recognize the importance of ensuring that those who are able to conceive can control their fertility. One aspect of this, the law relating to abortion, was discussed in the previous chapter. Here the law governing contraception will be examined, particularly in relation to young people under the age of 16.

A. Family Planning

Much of the law governing family planning has already been described. Rights to the existence of services are only enforceable through the mechanisms described in Chapter 3. Consent was discussed in Chapter 10. The principles that determine how much information family planning clients should be given were set out there. A few specific points are worth noting here. At one stage, it was argued by some that family planning was contrary to public policy. This enabled them to suggest that family planning would be unlawful

---

[4] *Re D* [1976] 1 All ER 326, 332.

because clients were not legally permitted to consent to it. However, no such public policy argument can now be advanced because contraception expressly comes within section 5 of the National Health Service Act 1977.[5] Nor can it be argued that male sterilization is contrary to public policy because the National Health Service (Family Planning) Amendment Act 1972 (now superseded by the 1977 Act) made provision for it.

Further, it is now clear that the only consent that is necessary is that of the client seeking family planning services. There is no need to consult the client's partner, even when the couple are married. The minority opinion of Lord Denning in *Bravery* v. *Bravery*,[6] that the sterilization of a married person should not be carried out without the consent of the spouse, is no longer good law (even if it was then).[7] Spouses may be able to petition for divorce on the basis that their partner behaved unreasonably in failing to consult them, but that does not alter the lawfulness of the health care. One judge has explicitly stated that no court would ever grant an injunction to stop a vasectomy or sterilization going ahead.[8] Informing a spouse that his or her partner has sought family planning services would normally constitute a breach of confidence.[9]

More difficult problems arise where those who seek family planning services are under the age of 16. The Government's commitment to reducing the number of unwanted pregnancies in this age group has created an uneasy relationship with the criminal law, as teenage pregnancies are usually the product of criminal activity. This does not directly affect the health professionals. However, there might be an indirect effect if the law were to regard the provision of family planning as inciting young people to commit criminal offences. This remote possibility can create a climate of fear in which professionals are unnecessarily deterred from doing their work. The implications of the criminal nature of sexual activity under the age of 16 will be discussed after the offences have been described.

The main offence is that of unlawful sexual intercourse.[10] This is committed by a boy or man who has sex with a girl under 16. The girl herself is not guilty of the offence. A boy over the age of 10 can be criminally responsible,[11] and the traditional presumption that a boy is incapable of sexual intercourse below the age of 14 has been abolished.[12] Thus, there can be no doubt that a

---

[5] *Gillick* v. *W. Norfolk AHA* [1985] 3 All ER 402, 425, *per* Lord Scarman.

[6] [1954] 3 All ER 59.

[7] The other judges in the Court of Appeal expressly declined to adopt Denning's position. See also K. Norrie, *Family Planning Practice and the Law* (Aldershot: Dartmouth, 1991), 11–13.

[8] *Paton* v. *BPAS* [1978] 2 All ER 987, 990.   [9] See Ch. 11.

[10] Sexual Offences Act 1956, s. 6.

[11] Children and Young Persons Act 1933, s. 50. Between the ages of 10 and 14 children must be shown to know that their actions were seriously wrong: *C* v. *DPP* [1995] 3 All ER 43.

[12] Sexual Offences Act 1993.

teenage boy could be prosecuted for the offence of unlawful sexual inter-course. The impact of this law is softened for young men under the age of 24, as they have a defence provided that they have not been charged with a sim-ilar offence before, and that they reasonably believed that the girl was over 16.

A more serious offence is committed if a man or boy has sex with a girl under 13, and there is no special defence for young males.[13] Intercourse with-out consent is rape, but for the purposes of that crime, a young woman may give consent under the age of 16. Sexual activity will also constitute an inde-cent assault. Here, the sex of the child is immaterial. This is the only way that sex between a boy under 16 and a woman over the age of 16 would be unlaw-ful. The absence of consent is an essential part of this offence, but, by statute, the consent of people under 16 does not count.[14]

It follows from this that even consensual sexual activity between 15-year-olds will be criminal in the eyes of the law. However, it is very rare for prose-cutions to be brought. This does not make the law irrelevant. Where clients are involved in criminal activity, it has sometimes been argued that assisting them to cope with the consequences of their actions may encourage them to commit the crime. Thus, such assistance might constitute inciting, aiding, or abetting a crime and, in the context of family planning for those under 16, it might constitute the specific offence of 'encouraging unlawful sexual inter-course'.[15]

This was one of the arguments put forward in *Gillick* v. *W. Norfolk & Wisbech HA*.[16] It was firmly rejected by the House of Lords, which held that there would be no encouraging of sexual intercourse within the legal prohibi-tion provided that the family planning advice was offered because the health professional believed it would be in the best interests of the girl's health (rather than intended to facilitate the sexual activity). This creates an import-ant, if sometimes unclear, line between advice and encouragement.[17] Those counselling young people should not feel constrained by the criminal law. However, they would be wise to ensure that their advice and literature cannot be interpreted as suggesting that young people ought to be sexually active. That might overstep the mark. It is unlikely that the acceptance that young people are, in practice, sexually active would cause any difficulties.

A further, and in practice pressing, problem concerns the rights of those under 16 to keep confidential the fact that they have sought family planning advice. Without the promise of confidentiality, young people may often pre-fer to go without advice, regarding the risk of pregnancy as less serious than the risk of their parents finding out that they are sexually active. The rules relating to confidentiality for young people were discussed in Chapter 12. It

---

[13] Sexual Offences Act 1956, s. 5.   [14] *Ibid.*, s. 14(2), 15(2).   [15] *Ibid.*, s. 28.
[16] N. 5 above.   [17] A similar line has been drawn in relation to assisting suicide: see Ch. 20.

was argued that, while the point has not been authoritatively established by the courts, young people are entitled to confidentiality as against their parents. There may be a justification for breaching that confidentiality in some circumstances. However, health professionals are not obliged to do so, and can properly guarantee confidentiality to their clients under 16 in the same way as they would to adults.

B. Non-consensual Sterilization

In most cases, the normal law of consent and malpractice provides the governing regime for sterilization procedures. As noted above, there an no longer be any suggestion that sterilization cannot be consented to as being contrary to public policy. However, there has been considerable legal scrutiny of the problems raised when sterilization operations are proposed for those who are unable to consent for themselves. The courts have been sufficiently concerned about the potential for such procedures to be used inappropriately that they have sought to prevent them going ahead without the prior sanction of a judge. This section considers how that requirement has been created, and whether it is sustainable as a matter of legal doctrine. It also examines how the courts have approached the task of deciding whether people unable to consent should undergo sterilization.

In relation to those under the age of 18, the necessity of coming to court has been created by declaring that non-therapeutic sterilization decisions are beyond the scope of parental consent.[18] This means that a court order is needed to supply the necessary consent before the operation can proceed. The court may authorize treatment by making an order under the inherent jurisdiction or under section 8 of the Children Act 1989. Whether or not such an order is made will depend on whether the court is persuaded that it is in the best interests of the child to be sterilized. These orders are discussed in Chapter 12.

Where it is proposed to sterilize an adult who is unable to consent, the position is more difficult. The court no longer has any supervisory jurisdiction to enable it to authorize treatment.[19] All it can do is to make what is known as a 'declaration'. This declares the legal position. Unlike the position in relation to children the court issuing a declaration cannot make something legal which

---

[18] *Re B* [1987] 2 All ER 206, 214; *Re P* [1989] 1 FLR 182; *Re HG* [1993] 1 FLR 588; *Re E* [1991] 2 FLR 585. The reasoning in these cases, and criticism of it, was examined in Ch. 12.

[19] *F* v. *W. Berkshire HA* [1989] 2 All ER 545; B. Hoggett, 'The Royal Prerogative in Relation to the Mentally Disordered: Resurrection, Resuscitation or Rejection' in Freeman, n. 3 above.

was not already lawful. Thus the court can only declare that the sterilization would have been lawful even without the order of the court. This has not prevented the judiciary urging doctors to take to court all cases where the sterilization of someone unable to consent is sought. This was the position taken by all the members of the House of Lords in *F* v. *W. Berkshire HA*.[20] They also recognized, however, that if a sterilization were to be performed on an incompetent adult without court involvement, it would still be lawful if it was in the best interests of the patient, as judged against responsible professional opinion.[21] The exhortation to come to court does not apply to abortions for those unable to consent for themselves,[22] nor to sterilizations that are incidental to a therapeutic purpose, such as to deal with excessive menstruation.[23]

The procedure for seeking such a declaration was discussed in the *Berkshire* case, and has now been summarized in a Practice Note produced by the Official Solicitor, whose general task it is to represent the interests of those unable to consent.[24] This procedure can only be used to provide a final resolution to a clinical problem. The courts have no power to make interim declarations of the lawfulness of treatment pending further inquiry.[25] Thus, it is important to seek the court's decision as soon as it is possible to anticipate that it will be needed. Applications should be made to the Family Division of the High Court either by those caring for the patient or by those planning to carry out the operation. The patient will be represented. This will usually be by the Official Solicitor and, even if it is not, the Official Solicitor will be an independent party. The Official Solicitor will meet the patient in private to discover her or his views, however limited the ability to form and express them. There will be an initial hearing at which directions will be given on how the matter should be resolved. In straightforward cases, decision can be taken at such hearings without hearing full oral evidence.[26] More usually, however, there will be full hearing at which all parties can call, examine, and cross-examine expert witnesses.

Once the matter is before the court, the judge will determine the case according to the best interests of the patient. The Official Solicitor's Practice Note advises that evidence will normally be required on the following issues in order to assess what the welfare of the patient requires: first, the capacity of the patient now and in the foreseeable future to take the decision; secondly, the probability of conception occurring (if contraception is the purpose of the operation); thirdly, the risks of pregnancy causing substantial trauma or psychological damage to the patient (if a woman); fourthly, the availability of

---

[20] N. 19 above.   [21] The rules were discussed in detail in Ch. 10.
[22] *Re SG* (1990) 6 BMLR 95.   [23] *F* v. *F* (1991) 7 BMLR 135.
[24] *Practice Note: Official Solicitor: Sterilization* [1996] 2 FLR 111.
[25] *Riverside Mental Health NHS trust* v. *Fox* [1994] 1 FLR 614.   [26] *Re C* [1990] 2 FLR 527.

practicable less intrusive alternatives to immediate sterilization (including whether a reversible method would be viable).

The reported cases in which support from the courts for sterilization has been sought suggest that the judiciary is reluctant to prevent the operation going ahead when the health professionals recommend it. In one early case, *Re D*,[27] the court refused to authorize the sterilization of an 11-year-old girl who had sufficient mental ability to marry. The professionals caring for her, and the expert witnesses, did not all agree that sterilization was appropriate, and Heilbron J found that the case for it had not been made out. The later reported cases, however, have all resulted in the operation going ahead.

In *Re B*,[28] the *Jeanette* case, the House of Lords emphasized that the only consideration of the court was the welfare of the client. Eugenic issues were said to be irrelevant. So, too, the judges said that the convenience of the carers should not influence the decision. The law lords also indicated that sterilization should only be used if it was the 'last resort'.[29] They would expect that the patient's welfare would only point towards sterilization where there was no practical alternative. This implies that the courts should not sanction sterilization unless the alternative means to protect the client against pregnancy are unsatisfactory. It also suggests that sterilizations should not be performed in response to a merely speculative risk of pregnancy. These comments provide rules of thumb which may serve to constrain welfare decision-making by limiting the justifications that can be used in support of sterilization.

However, since the *Jeanette* decision, a number of cases have demonstrated the weaknesses of these presumptions.[30] Eugenic arguments have been introduced through the back door. In *Re M*[31] the judge found that there was a 50 per cent chance that the woman to be sterilized would conceive a mentally handicapped child. This was said to justify the sterilization, because Bush J held that the woman would have to have an abortion if she were found to be carrying a handicapped child. He argued that this was not an eugenic argument because it focused on the interests of the woman, not of her potential child. However, it provides a routine means of bypassing the restriction on eugenic considerations. The woman's risk of carrying a child with learning difficulties was a result of her own disability, and the reasoning used could not apply to a woman with full mental faculties.

---

[27] N. 4 above.

[28] N. 18 above.

[29] This phrase was used by Lord Oliver at 218, and by Dillon and Stephen Brown LJJ in the Court of Appeal, at 210 and 211.

[30] I have argued that they even proved weak in the *Jeanette* case itself, see J. Montgomery, 'Rhetoric and "welfare" ' (1989) 9 *OJLS* 395–402. See also Freeman, n. 3 above, 55, 60–6 and R. Lee and D. Morgan, 'Sterilisation and Mental Handicap: Sapping the Strength of the State' (1988) 15 *JLS* 229.

[31] [1988] 2 FLR 497.

The last-resort principle has also been given short-thrift. It already looked weak in the light of its interpretation in *Re B*, where it was found that a 30–40 per cent chance of successful oral contraception was not a practicable alternative. In *Re P*[32] drug-based contraception was rejected on the basis that the woman might not take the drugs regularly in the future. Yet she was taking the oral contraceptive pill successfully at the time. The court still authorized her sterilization. The need for a real risk of pregnancy has also proved a flimsy safeguard. In *Re W*[33] the risk of pregnancy was found to be slight, but as there was a responsible body of medical opinion in favour of sterilization, Hollis J declared that the operation could lawfully be performed. In *Re HG*[34] the court went even further and permitted a girl to be sterilized when there was no evidence that she was even sexually active, let alone likely to become pregnant. This decision is even more disturbing because the judge took into account the 'legitimate aspirations and anxieties of the parents and other carers'. This means that the decision was influenced by the interests of those around the girl, not just her own rights.

It can be seen that the courts have proved ineffective in protecting the 'right' not to have one's fertility removed without consent. While they have instructed doctors to bring cases to court, they have not been able to develop any robust principles of law to recognize that sterilization is different from other treatments. Indeed, in *Re B*, Lord Hailsham even rejected the suggestion that there was a fundamental right at stake. He said that the right to reproduce only existed where reproduction would be the result of informed choice.[35]

C. The Surrogacy Arrangements Act 1985

Surrogate motherhood, where a woman carries a child on behalf of another, proved to be one of the most contentious issues discussed by the Warnock Committee set up by the Government to examine the legal, ethical, and policy issues in assisted human reproduction.[36] It was also the first area of that Committee's remit to be covered by legislation, in the form of the Surrogacy Arrangements Act 1985.[37] That statute is primarily concerned to outlaw

---

[32] N. 18 above.

[33] [1993] 1 FLR 381. This case concerned a woman over the age of 18. Consequently, strictly speaking, the court was not itself deciding what was in her best interests, but asking whether a responsible body of doctors could reasonably believe that it was in her best interests to be sterilized.

[34] N. 18 above.　　　　　　　　　　　　　　　　　　　　　[35] N. 18 above, 213.

[36] *Report of the Committee of Inquiry into Human Fertilisation and Embryology* (London: HMSO, 1984, Cmnd, 9314).

[37] See D. Morgan, 'Who to Be or Not to Be: The Surrogacy Story' (1986) 49 *MLR* 358–68 for discussion of the background to the Act.

commercial surrogacy. It applies to arrangements that are made before a woman becomes pregnant with a view to the child being handed over to be brought up by someone else.[38] The Act does not apply to agreements made after a woman has become pregnant. Where the process of reproduction has been assisted, the relevant time is when the embryos or gametes were placed in the woman's body. Section 1A of the Act makes it clear that surrogacy contracts are not enforceable. This means that disputes over the upbringing of children must be resolved according to the general rules relating to status. These are discussed later in this Chapter. It also means that it is not possible to force the commissioning parents to pay the money promised.

The main purpose of the 1985 Act is to ensure that commercial surrogacy is illegal. It makes it an offence to negotiate a surrogate arrangement 'on a commercial basis' or to compile information with a view to doing so.[39] The Act excludes cases where the only payment is to, or for the benefit of, the surrogate mother.[40] It also provides that the surrogate mother and the commissioning parents, that is those who are hoping to bring the child up, cannot be guilty of the offence.[41] This avoids tainting the child's upbringing with illegality, but there may still be difficulties in relation to adoption because of the ban on money changing hands in that area of law. This is considered below. It is also an offence to advertise the fact that a person is willing to be a surrogate mother, negotiate a surrogacy agreement, or is looking for someone to act as one. Both the advertiser and the publisher of the newspaper or other medium will be guilty of the offence.[42] Here, there is no exception for the surrogate mother or commissioning parents. The negotiating offences are punishable by up to three months' imprisonment or a £5,000 fine. The advertising offences carry only the fine.[43] Prosecutions cannot be brought without the permission of the Director of Public Prosecutions.[44]

D. The Human Fertilization and Embryology Act 1990

The Human Fertilization and Embryology Act 1990 provides a nearly comprehensive scheme for regulating assisted reproduction and research on

---

[38] Surrogacy Arrangements Act 1985, s. 1(2). The Act refers to where a woman carries a child. Presumably, if it became necessary to establish the precise point at which she began to 'carry' the child, the courts might have regard to the interpretation of that concept in the law relating to abortion: see Ch. 15.

[39] S. 2(1).   [40] S. 2(3).   [41] S. 2(2).   [42] S. 3.

[43] S. 4(1) fixes the fine at level 5 on the standard scale, and it will be increased as the standard scale fines are raised. The standard scale is set out in s. 37 of the Criminal Justice Act 1982, as amended, and was last increased in 1992.

[44] S. 4(2).

human embryos outside the human body. It also includes a conscience clause, ensuring that professionals may not be forced to participate in any of the activities governed by the Act.[45] The rules relating to research are discussed in Chapter 14. This section considers the provision of infertility services. The Act works by outlawing certain activities unless they are carried out under the auspices of a licence from the Authority. Section 3 sets out a wide ranging prohibition on creating, keeping, or using human embryos. Section 3A prohibits the use in fertility services of eggs taken from embryos or foetuses. Section 4 prohibits the storage and use of human gametes.[46] However, a special exemption has been granted in relation to the storage of gametes only for the purpose of research, including developing pharmaceutical and contraceptive products, and teaching.[47]

Although the 1990 Act covers most types of infertility treatment, some techniques do not come within it. There is no prohibition on artificial insemination where the sperm is provided by the woman's partner.[48] Thus this can be offered without a licence. The technique of gamete intra-fallopian transfer (GIFT) is not regulated by the Act because it does not involve an embryo being created outside the woman's body.[49] Instead, sperm and egg are inserted so that fertilization takes place in the fallopian tube. However, some GIFT treatments will fall within the Act because they involve using or stored or donated sperm (which come within the scope of the prohibitions). Self-insemination is not covered, provided that sperm are not stored, because it is only services offered to the public that fall within the definition of treatment services.[50]

In general, the offences under the Act are punishable by up to two years' imprisonment and an unlimited fine.[51] However, some breaches of these provisions carry much heavier sentences. Those who place non-human embryos or gametes into a woman, place a human embryo in a non-human animal, use female germ cells from an embryo or foetus, or mix human gametes with

[45] S. 38. The meaning of participation is discussed in relation to the similar provision in s. 4 of the Abortion Act: see ch. 15.

[46] The word 'gamete' is not defined in the Act, and some definitions may exclude certain controversial practices involving eggs taken from aborted foetuses. See A. Plomer and N. Martin-Clement, 'The Limits of Beneficence: Egg Donation under the Human Fertilisation and Embryology Act 1990' (1995) 15 *Legal Studies* 434–54, 442–3.

[47] Human Fertilisation and Embryology (Special Exemptions) Regulations 1991, SI 1991 No 1588.

[48] S. 4(1)(b).

[49] S. 1(2). For discussion of GIFT and the Act, see D. Morgan and R. Lee, *Blackstone's Guide to the Human Fertilisation and Embryology Act 1990: Abortion, Embryo Research, the New Law* (London: Blackstone Press, 1991), 124–30.

[50] S. 2(1).

[51] S. 41(4). Some offences may be tried in the magistrates' courts, in which case lower penalties are applied.

non-human ones are liable to a sentence of imprisonment of up to ten years and an unlimited fine or both.[52] Prosecutions cannot be brought without the consent of the Director of Public Prosecutions.[53]

The power to relax these prohibitions on dealings with human embryos and gametes lies with the Human Fertilization Authority. This statutory body can license specified people to store or use human embryos or gametes in treatment services on defined premises.[54] Only activities on those premises are covered, and only when carried out under the supervision of the persons named.[55] The power of the Authority to issue licences is limited by the Act. Licences may not authorize keeping an embryo beyond the appearance of the primitive streak,[56] placing a human embryo in an animal, or replacing the nucleus of an embryo[57] (intended to prevent cloning). In addition to these provisions specifying what may not be authorized, the Act also sets out the types of activities which can be licensed.[58] These are, however, broadly phrased, and include in relation to treatment 'using gametes' and 'placing an embryo in a woman'. Further guidance on the exercise of the licensing powers may be given in regulations, but no such regulations have been issued at present. The emerging science of genetic manipulation raises the possibility of overcoming a genetic defect by removing or inserting genes.[59] The Human Fertilization and Embryology Act 1990 prohibits the licensing of this sort of therapy on human embryos,[60] although the Act allows for regulations permitting it in the future.[61]

Licences are granted on a number of statutory conditions. No use may be made of gametes and embryos without the donors' consent.[62] Such consent must be specifically given and may be restricted, for example, to their use in treatment services but not research, or be given conditionally. The length of time for which storage is agreed to must be specified. The maximum period for which a consent may be given to the storage of gametes is normally ten years.[63] The maximum for embryos is normally five years.[64] However, regulations have extended these periods in a number of circumstances. Where people consent to storage only for the purpose of assisting themselves and their partner, and their fertility has or is likely to become significantly impaired since the donation, then the statutory storage period for gametes is

---

[52] S. 41(1).   [53] S. 42.   [54] S. 11, 12. Research licences are discussed in Ch. 14.
[55] Sch. 2, para. 4.
[56] This is 'to be taken' as appearing not later than 14 days after gametes are mixed, s. 4(3). This is a strange wording and may allow the prosecution to show that it had in fact appeared earlier, but not permit the defence to show that it had not in fact appeared by a later stage.
[57] These restrictions appear in s. 3(3).   [58] Sch. 2.
[59] See generally the *Report of the Committee on the Ethics of Gene Therapy* (the Clothier Committee) (London: HMSO, 1992, Cm 1788).
[60] Sch. 2, para. 1(4).   [61] Sch. 2, para. 3(4).   [62] Sch. 3.
[63] S. 14(3).   [64] S. 14(4).

extended until the donor reaches the age of 55.[65] Similar provision is made for the extended storage of embryos, even for donations to others, where two doctors certify that the donor, or woman to be treated, has or is likely to become prematurely and completely infertile.[66] Where a doctor certifies that such persons have developed or are likely to develop significantly impaired fertility, or carry a genetic defect, then the statutory storage period for embryos is extended to ten years, or until the donor reaches the age of 55 (whichever is earlier).[67]

A further condition relates to commercial dealings. No payment may be made in relation to the supply of gametes or embryos except under directions from the Authority.[68] Directions have permitted payments of up to £15 for donation of sperm, but nothing for egg donation.[69] It has been argued that the prohibition on the sale of organs introduced by the Human Organ Transplants Act 1989 applies,[70] so that payment would be illegal. However, it is doubtful that gametes or embryos are 'organs' within the meaning of the Act.[71] Even if they are, it is probable that the specific, and later, statutory provision in relation to embryology prevails over the general prohibition on payment. The 1990 Act also makes it a general requirement that proper records must be kept.[72]

Directions from the Authority can impose additional general conditions, including specifying what constitutes proper record-keeping, and also conditions specific to individual licences.[73] These directions are mandatory.[74] Failure to comply with them will sometimes constitute an offence,[75] but the main consequence is to empower the Authority to revoke a licence.[76] The Authority also gives guidance to practitioners through its Code of Practice. This is less coercive than the power to give directions, in that disobedience will not in itself constitute an offence, but it may be taken into account by the Authority when considering revocation.[77] The Authority is able to monitor compliance with the law and directions by inspecting licensed premises.[78]

Opportunities to challenge the decisions of the Authority are limited. Appeal against refusal of a licence by the Authority's licence committee lies to the Authority and takes the form of a full rehearing.[79] However, appeal

---

[65] Human Fertilisation and Embryology (Statutory Storage Period) Regulations 1991, SI 1991 No 1540.

[66] Human Fertilisation and Embryology (Statutory Storage Period for Embryos) Regulations 1996, SI 1996 No 375, r. 2(2)(a),(b).

[67] *Ibid.*, r. 2(2)(c),(d).   [68] S. 12(e).

[69] Issued in Aug. 1991, and under review according to Human Fertilization and Embryology Authority, *Third Annual Report* (London: HFEA, 1994), 33.

[70] D. Price and R. Mackay, 'The Trade in Human Organs' (1991) 141 *NLJ* 1272–3 and 1307–9, at 1273.

[71] S. 7(2).   [72] S. 12(d).   [73] Ss. 23, 24.   [74] Ss. 23(2).   [75] S. 41(2).
[76] S. 18(1)(c).   [77] S. 25.   [78] S. 12(b).   [79] S. 20.

beyond the Authority is available only on a point of law.[80] Consequently, the Authority's discretion on issues of ethical principle is difficult to challenge. The lack of independence of the appeal system has been criticized by the Council on Tribunals.[81]

(i) The Authority

Members of the Authority are appointed by the Secretary of State.[82] The statute requires that between one third and half of them will be drawn from the medical profession and interested researchers, and that the views of both men and women influence proceedings. Proposals to ensure formally that other disciplines were represented were rejected in Parliament, although in practice such members have been appointed to the Authority. The chair of the Authority must be lay, and must not have any involvement (even in the past) with activities that must now be licensed under the Act, or with the commissioning or funding of such work. The Authority is required to make annual reports to the Secretary of State, detailing both past activities and those projected for the following twelve months, which are to be laid before Parliament.[83]

The initial membership left the non-medical health professions poorly represented, with only Margaret Auld, a leading nurse and midwife, being included. A lawyer, Colin Campbell, took the chair (now succeeded by another academic lawyer, Ruth Deech). In addition to another lawyer, Brenda Hoggett (now Hale J), there are a number of non-medical members. Senior religious figures, Rabbi Julia Neuberger and Rt. Rev. Richard Holloway (the Anglican Bishop of Edinburgh), are members. An eminent sociologist, Robert Snowden, is included. There is also a senior social worker. Amongst the 'non-professionals' on the Authority are a television producer, a well-known actress, and a senior bank official. There is a nearly exactly equal representation of the sexes.

The Authority has set up a number of committees to perform its tasks. They deal with the Code of Practice, information issues, financial matters. There is also a Committee on Social and Ethical Issues. The core membership of that Committee is almost entirely lay. It is responsible for advising the Authority on ethical and social issues, identifying such issues, and considering the relevant arguments and sentiments.[84] The Authority has formally

---

[80] S. 21.
[81] Council on Tribunals, *Annual Report 1990* (London: HMSO, HC 1990–91, 64), paras. 2.25–30.
[82] Sch. 1 para. 4.
[83] S. 7.
[84] Human Fertilization and Embryology Authority, *First Annual Report* (London: HFEA, 1992), 26.

considered issues relating to sex selection and the use of donated ovarian tissue.[85]

(ii) Treatment Services and the Welfare of Children

In relation to treatment services, the statute makes it a condition of any licence that they will not be provided unless account has been taken of the welfare of any child who may be affected by the birth.[86] This covers not merely the child to be born, but also other children who will be affected. This 'welfare' provision also specifically requires note to be taken, in relation to the child to be born as a result of the services, of 'the need of that child for a father'. Some clinicians seem to have interpreted this as preventing services being offered to single women. However, this is not the case. Consideration must be given to the fact that there may be no father bringing the child up, but that is merely one component of the child's welfare.

The Code of Practice gives advice on the assessment of the welfare issues.[87] First, the treatment centre should ascertain who the legal parents of the children would be (applying the rules on status, discussed below), and who would actually bring them up. The clinicians should consider the commitment of those hoping to bring up the children, their medical history, their ability to meet the needs of the children (including the possibility of a multiple pregnancy). Where donated gametes are to be used, consideration also needs to be given to the prospective parents' attitude to informing the children about their origins if they ask questions as they grow up, the attitude of the wider family, particularly where the donor is a relative or friend, and the possibility that there may be a legal dispute over parentage. Assessment of these issues should be made on a multidisciplinary basis.

(iii) Information

The Human Fertilization and Embryology Act 1990 requires specified information to be recorded, and provides strict rules about its use. The Authority keeps a register recording the provision of infertility services under the Act to any identified individual, or showing that an individual was, or may have been

---

[85] Human Fertilization and Embryology Authority, *Sex Selection: Public Consultation* (London: HFEA, 1993); Human Fertilization and Embryology Authority, *Donated Ovarian Tissue in Embryo Research and Assisted Conception: A Public Consultation* (London: HFEA, 1994); Human Fertilization and Embryology Authority, *Donated Ovarian Tissue in Embryo Research and Assisted Conception* (London: HFEA, 1994).

[86] S. 13(5).

[87] Human Fertilization and Embryology Authority, *Code of Practice* (London: HFEA, 1995), pt. 3.

born as a result of treatment under the Act.[88] Individuals may seek disclosure of information about them on that register, provided that they are over the age of 18 and have been given an opportunity to receive proper counselling about the implications of receiving it.[89] However, they are only entitled to find out whether the register shows that their parents may not in fact be their natural parents, or whether they may be related to a person they propose to marry. No other information may be disclosed.[90] Although regulations may be passed identifying other information that may be disclosed, they cannot provide for the identity of the genetic parents to be revealed.[91] If people propose to marry under the age of 18, they may check to see whether they may be related to their intended spouse.[92]

Apart from these provisions for access by individuals, there are strict rules on the confidentiality of information, with criminal sanctions for their breach.[93] Exceptions to the principle of confidentiality exist in relation to disclosure within the authority, to a licensee, where necessary in relation to court proceedings or formal complaints procedures, or to the patient or other person able to access the patient's records under the Access to Health Records Act 1990.[94] There is also an exemption in relation to information disclosed with the permission of the patient or patients. Such consent must usually be given to disclosure to a specific person. However a general consent may be given where disclosure is necessary in connection with the person's treatment (covering all treatment, not just infertility treatment), or clinical or financial auditing.[95] Disclosure is permitted in an emergency when it is necessary to avert imminent danger to the patient, and it is not reasonably practicable to obtain his or her consent.[96] The confidentiality of gamete donors is nevertheless strictly protected.[97]

E. Status Provisions

English law on parental status has not developed to deal with the problems of assisted reproduction. Historically it was preoccupied with the implications

---

[88] S. 31(2).   [89] S. 31(3).   [90] S. 31(4).

[91] S. 31(5). No regulations have been made under this provision.   [92] S. 31(6),(7).

[93] S. 33, 41(1).

[94] S. 33(6) as amended by the Human Fertilization and Embryology (Disclosure of Information) Act 1992.

[95] S. 33(6B)–(6D), inserted by the Human Fertilization and Embryology (Disclosure of Information) Act 1992.

[96] S. 33(6E), inserted by the Human Fertilisation and Embryology (Disclosure of Information) Act 1992.

[97] S. 33(6A), inserted by the Human Fertilisation and Embryology (Disclosure of Information) Act 1992.

of birth outside marriage and, in particular, its impact on the law of inheritance. More recently, attention has turned to identifying who should be responsible for the upbringing of children. The basic legal rules on who has 'parental responsibility' for a child sometimes facilitate attempts to overcome infertility, by making the infertile couple the parents of the child. However, this is not always the case and, when it is not, the infertile couple will need to take legal action to have parental responsibility conferred upon them.[98]

Under the rules which allocate parental responsibility, the woman who gives birth to a child is in law the mother of that child.[99] If the child's mother is married, the law will presume that her husband is the child's legal father. However, that presumption may be overridden by proving that he is not the genetic father.[100] Under the common law principles of legitimacy and the provisions of the Family Law Reform Act 1987 the legal relationship between father and child is built on the existence of a blood tie between them. However, the blood tie alone is not enough. If the woman is not married, then only she will automatically have parental responsibility.[101] The unmarried genetic father can obtain parental responsibility by a formal registered agreement with the mother, or through the courts, but he will not otherwise have it.[102] This will not take away the legal status of the woman giving birth.

These rules create anomalies when applied to cases of assisted reproduction. Where a child is born as a result of embryo transfer into an infertile woman, she will be the mother even though she has contributed no genetic material. The rules also facilitate attempts to overcome infertility by artificial insemination where the parties are married. The husband will be presumed to be the child's father. Yet where a surrogate mother is commissioned to carry the child on behalf of the infertile couple, she will be the legal mother. This will be true even though it was always intended that she would hand the child over to the commissioning parents and even if, in the case of embryo transfer, the commissioning parents are the genetic parents.

Thus, in some cases at least, the general family law frustrates attempts to overcome infertility by defining many children born following assisted reproduction as attached in law to people other than those who propose to bring them up. The fact that the status of a child born after assistance varies

---

[98] See for discussion, G. Douglas and N. Lowe, 'Becoming a Parent in English Law' (1992) 108 *LQR* 414–32.

[99] *Ampthill Peerage Case* [1977] AC 545, 577. In theory there may be some doubt whether the claims of the birth mother prevail over the genetic mother, see J. Montgomery, 'Assisted Reproduction after the Family Law Reform Act 1987' [1988] *Fam. Law* 23–5. However, there will only be such a conflict where conception has been assisted, in which case the birth mother will be the legal mother under s. 27 of the Human Fertilization and Embryology Act 1990.

[100] See e.g. *Re G* [1994] 1 FLR 495.   [101] Children Act 1989, s. 2(2).

[102] Children Act 1989, s. 4.

according to the technique used cannot be regarded as a satisfactory position.[103] Further, the 'right' to overcome infertility is impaired in that attempts to do so are obstructed by the requirement to go to court, either through the adoption process or for lesser orders in relation to parental responsibility or the residence of the child to confirm parental status.

The Human Fertilization and Embryology Act 1990 sought to overcome these problems by introducing a new framework of status provisions for cases of assisted conception. It applies where conception has resulted from the placing in the woman of an embryo, eggs, sperm, or her artificial insemination.[104] Most of the new rules allocate parental status without the need to litigate the issue. However, there is an important new possibility, the 'parental order', which allows the court to supersede the usual allocation of parental responsibility.

The rule that the birth mother is the legal mother was confirmed by the 1990 Act.[105] So far as paternity is concerned, the husband of a woman assisted to carry a child will be treated in law as the father unless he did not consent to the assistance.[106] It is irrelevant that he consented only on the basis that another person would care for the child. The man will be placed in the same position as a 'natural' father, even when his relationship with the mother breaks down. In *Re CH* the court rejected the suggestion that a man who was the child's 'father' by reason of section 28 was to be treated differently from a 'natural father' in a dispute over contact with the child.[107] This should be contrasted to the fact that a man who donates sperm can be excused from parenthood by virtue of section 28(6).[108] If the woman giving birth after an assisted conception is not married, but she and her male partner have been treated under the 1990 Act, then her partner will be the child's legal father notwithstanding the lack of a blood tie or marriage to the birth mother.[109] There is no need to register an agreement or get a court order. It is technically possible that where a surrogate mother has conceived using the commissioning father's sperm, he may be the father by virtue of the fact that he and the surrogate mother have received treatment 'together'.[110] However, one court has already rejected the suggestion that this was the case on the facts before it.[111] If these rules on paternity lead to the identification of a legal father, then any other claimant will be excluded.[112]

In addition to these rules, which apply automatically, certain couples may

---

[103] For discussion of these issues see Montgomery, n. 99 above, and J. Montgomery, 'Constructing a Family—After a Surrogate Birth' (1986) 49 *MLR* 635–40.

[104] Ss. 28(1), 30(1).   [105] S. 27.   [106] S. 28(2).   [107] [1996] 1 FLR 569 (FD).

[108] This subs. also declares that where sperm are used after the donor's death the donor will not be the father of the child in law. This will avoid a number of difficulties in relation to inheritance.

[109] S. 28(3).   [110] S. 28(3).   [111] *Re Q* [1996] 1 FLR 369 (FD).

[112] Ss. 28(4) and 29.

use section 30 of the 1990 Act to apply for a parental order. This has been available since 1 November 1994.[113] This order was created at a late stage in the House of Commons proceedings on the Bill in response to a well publicized individual case.[114] Under section 30 qualified people may apply to the court within six months of the child's birth for an order that they shall be treated as a child's parents despite the application of sections 27, 28, and 29. In order to qualify it is necessary for applicants to show that they are over 18 and married to each other, that at least one is a genetic parent of the child (although another woman gave birth), that the child is resident with them, that those who are otherwise treated by the law as the parents have unconditionally agreed to the making of the order (if they can be found), and that no money has changed hands other than in respect of reasonable expenses unless authorized by the court. By analogy with the similar adoption provisions prohibiting payment (see below), the first reported case on the provision held that retrospective authorization can be given to expenses payments. No criterion is laid down in the Act to govern when authorization should be granted, but in the same case Johnson J authorized payments of £8,280 on the basis that they were reasonable. Those payments included £5,000 as compensation for loss of earnings (approximately one third of the surrogate mother's earning capacity at the time).[115] A parental order places the child in the same position as a child who has been adopted, including having an amended birth certificate.[116]

There will be circumstances in which the provisions of section 30 are not available: because the child is not living with the applicants, the applicants are not married, or the six-month period within which an order can be sought has expired. In such cases, the parties will need to apply to the courts for the more general family law orders. While these are not designed specifically for use in cases of assisted conception, they can go some way to regularizing the position of couples who have overcome their infertility with medical assistance. Residence orders under the Children Act 1989 may determine that the child will live with them.[117] That will give them parental responsibility during

[113] Human Fertilization and Embryology Act 1990 (Commencement No 5) Order 1994, SI 1994 No 1776. For the regulations which adapt the adoption procedures, see the Parental Orders (Human Fertilization and Embryology) Regulations 1994, SI 1994 No 2767.

[114] See [1990] Fam. Law 118 and 282; a letter to *The Times* from D. Forrest, the solicitor representing the parents, on 28 Feb. 1990; and the two cases *Cumbria CC* v. *X*, *The Times*, 25 June 1990, and *Re W*, *Guardian*, 30 Oct. 1990.

[115] *Re Q*, n. 111 above. It is possible that this decision is based on the misunderstanding of the law, and that the judge believed that expenses had to be authorized and could only be so authorized if they were reasonable.

[116] Adoption Act 1976, s. 39, as applied by the Parental Orders (Human Fertilization and Embryology) Regulations 1994, SI 1994 No 2767; Forms of Entry for Parental Orders Regulations 1994, SI 1994 No 2981.

[117] S. 8.

the life of the order, usually until the child is 16, but it will not remove the rights of the legal parents. Most couples will need to seek adoption, because this is the only way in which the parental responsibility of the people who are the legal parents can be terminated. It is not possible for parents to divest themselves of parental responsibility by agreement.[118]

Adoption requires a court order and elaborate procedures including the involvement of the local authority to report on the interests of the child. Two problems are likely to arise. Both are the result of rules constraining the adoption process in order to guard against the child's interests being overridden by the desire of the adults to arrange an adoption. The first of these restrictions is a ban on private placements for adoption unless the adopters are related to the child.[119] This will present a problem unless both of the social parents are also genetic parents.[120] The second restriction concerns the payment of money. The Adoption Act 1976 prevents adoption orders being made where any payment has been made in connection with the adoption.[121]

However, the court may authorize both private placements and payment. It is clear that the power to authorize payment can be exercised retrospectively, and this power has been used to enable a child to be adopted after commercial surrogacy arrangements.[122] There is conflicting case law on whether a private placement can be given retrospective authorization.[123] However, it appears that an adoption can go ahead after a private placement if the court believes that it is in the child's interests. The courts have held that the fact that criminal proceedings might be brought for an illegal placement does not prevent the adoption order being made.[124]

Where a case comes to court in all of these applications, the judge must make the order that best serves the interests of the child. Where arrangements have gone smoothly, this will normally result in the court supporting them. There is only one home in which the child is wanted, and the alternative would be to place the child in local authority care. Thus in *Re C*[125] commissioning parents were permitted to care for the child of a surrogate mother who was also the genetic mother. In *Re W*[126] a woman had carried and given birth to twins on behalf of their genetic mother. The court agreed that it would be in the children's interests to live with their genetic mother. Where the court is concerned about the quality of the home being offered by the commissioning

---

[118] Children Act 1989, s. 2(9).   [119] Adoption Act 1976, s. 11.

[120] See e.g. *Re MW* [1995] 2 FLR 759 (FD).   [121] S. 57.

[122] *Re Adoption Application* [1987] 2 All ER 826; *Re MW*, n. 120 above.

[123] Compare *Re AW* [1993] 1 FLR 62 and *Re A* [1988] 2 FLR 133 with *Re Adoption Application* [1993] 1 FLR 947 and *Re C* [1993] 1 FLR 87.

[124] *Re Adoption Application* [1993] 1 FLR 947, *Re ZHH* [1993] 1 FLR 83, *Re Adoption Application* [1992] 1 FLR 341, *Re MW*, n. 120 above. But see *Re AW*, n. 123 above, to the opposite effect.

[125] [1985] FLR 846.   [126] [1991] 1 FLR 385.

parents, it can ensure that the local authority investigate to see whether a care or supervision order is needed. However, unless and until the local authority decides to apply for such an order there is little choice but to permit the child to live with the commissioning parents.[127]

Where a birth mother wishes to keep the child, despite the prior agreement, she is likely to succeed. She is defined as the mother by section 27 of the 1990 Act. The commissioning parents cannot enforce any surrogacy contract.[128] The court's decision is governed solely by the best interests of the child, and the judges have adopted a theory of immediate and intense maternal bonding that will inevitably lead to the conclusion that it is important to maintain the birth mother's relationship with the child.[129] This is only likely to be displaced in cases where the child was removed from the woman at birth. Once a birth mother has given up a child, she will be unlikely to be able to object to the new family being regularized through adoption. In *Re MW* the court found that it was unreasonable of a mother in that position to withhold her consent to the adoption, and therefore dispensed with the need for that consent.[130]

F. Conclusion

It can be seen that the problems that fertility and infertility throw up have led to the application of special legal rules. However, in general, English law has not approached the control of fertility as a matter of individual entitlement. The Human Fertilization and Embryology Act 1990 provides an interesting example of an attempt to provide a coherent, sensitive, and flexible approach to resolving difficult issues of medical ethics. In many ways this system is of general importance because it pioneers an approach to the regulation of medical ethics that neither outlaws technological advance nor abdicates responsibility for guarding against abuse. Instead, it seeks to develop a more sophisticated regulatory stance that aims to facilitate medical care while maintaining a degree of democratic accountability.[131]

---

[127] *Re H* [1993] 2 FLR 541.   [128] Surrogacy Arrangements Act 1985, s. 1A.

[129] See *A* v. *C* [1985] FLR 445, especially 457, and *Re P* [1987] 2 FLR 421.

[130] N. 120 above.

[131] J. Montgomery, 'Rights, Restraints and Pragmatism: The Human Fertilisation and Embryology Act 1990' (1991) 54 *MLR* 524–34.

17 Maternity Care

Much of the law governing maternity care has already been considered elsewhere in this book. It is an area that gives rise to considerable concern in respect of malpractice litigation, particularly as the sums of money at stake if a baby is severely injured in a birth accident will be immense. It is said that obstetrics is a high risk specialty which is especially adversely affected by the shadow of litigation. These issues were explored in Chapters 7 and 8. Those caring for women during pregnancy, labour, and the neonatal period may also need to understand the law relating to abortion (Chapter 15) and selective treatment of the newborn (Chapter 18). Legal problems concerning fertility, both preventing unwanted conceptions and assisting people to conceive, were examined in Chapter 16. Obtaining consent and proper counselling of women about their options is an important part of the care of pregnant women. The legal rules were explained in Chapter 10.

This Chapter explores the law specifically relevant to maternity services. It looks at the rules that establish their structure; the division of responsibility between midwives and doctors, and access to maternity care, with particular reference to the role of general practitioners. It considers the extent and nature of women's rights to choose where and how they deliver their babies. It examines the legal problems that are created by the fact that health professionals caring for pregnant women may see themselves as having two clients, mother and baby, whose interests may not necessarily coincide. Finally, it provides an outline of the requirements for notification and registration of births.

A. The Legal Structure of Maternity Services

Unusually, attendance at the birth is restricted by law to two professional groups. Under section 17 of the Nurses, Midwives and Health Visitors Act 1979 it is a criminal offence to attend a woman in childbirth unless you are a registered doctor or midwife, or training to be one. Thus, a man who decided to deliver his wife's baby at home because they were unhappy with the care offered by the local maternity hospital was convicted of an offence under this section.[1] Some have argued that section 17 only prohibits attendance professionally, or for financial gain, but this cannot explain this conviction.[2] Technically, it seems that only midwives and doctors should be present when a woman gives birth, although this restriction is lifted where the attention is given in a case of sudden or urgent necessity.[3] This is out of step with practice, under which women would expect to choose whether to have their partner or other friend present.[4] It may be that the true analysis is that this right is conferred administratively by the professions and the NHS despite the legal position, and that doctors and midwives could require others to leave the woman if they thought it necessary.

Most women give birth with the assistance of midwives, the specialists in normal deliveries. A midwife may be responsible for the whole of a woman's care during pregnancy and labour. Sometimes, women will be under the care of an obstetrician, even though they will probably be delivered by a midwife unless a complication arises. Midwives are obliged by law to 'call to their assistance' a doctor if they discover 'a deviation from the norm' in the health of mother or baby.[5] However, this does not require the doctor to take over responsibility. The midwife may still be the appropriate person to provide care, albeit with the assistance of a doctor.

There is considerable emphasis on the importance of offering women choice over the way and place in which they give birth.[6] Where this choice is to have their babies away from the 'high-tech' environment of a big maternity unit, possibly at home, women will usually wish to have support from their GPs as well as from midwives. Maternity services are not part of the usual range of services available from general medical practitioners, although all GPs would have to attend women needing emergency care.[7] However, GPs may join the 'obstetric list' and, if they are on that list, may offer one or more of four stages of maternity cover.[8] The first covers the antenatal period; the second labour itself (intrapartum care); and the third is the provision of

---

[1] See J. Finch, 'Paternalism and Professionalism in Childbirth' (1982) 132 *NLJ* 995, 1011; B. Beech, 'The Politics of Maternity: Childbirth Freedom v. Obstetric Control' in S. Edwards (ed.), *Gender, Sex and the Law* (London: Croom Helm, 1985).

[2] See Finch, n. 1 above, 1011–12; J. Eekelaar and R. Dingwall, 'Some Legal Issues in Obstetric Practice' [1984] *JSWL* 258–70.

[3] S. 17(3).

[4] This is recognized by the *NHS Maternity Services Charter* (Department of Health, London, 1994), 3.

[5] Midwives Rules, r. 40; see Nurses, Midwives and Health Visitors Rules Approval Order 1983, SI 1983 No 873. It may be negligent to fail to refer a women to a doctor; see *Murphy* v. *Wirral HA* [1996] 7 Med. LR 99.

[6] Department of Health, *Changing Childbirth* (London: HMSO, 1993).

[7] NHS (General Medical Services) Regulations 1992, SI 1992 No 635, Sch. 2, para. 4(h).

[8] *Ibid.*, reg. 31(1).

personal medical services to the mother and baby during the post-natal period. The fourth aspect of maternity care is a full post-natal examination.

If GPs provide maternity cover, they do not undertake to provide services themselves, but to take all reasonable steps to secure that the woman receives personal medical services connected to her pregnancy.[9] Those steps will often be to ensure that a midwife provides the care. This is permissible where it is clinically reasonable to do so (for example, because the midwife is more experienced in dealing with normal pregnancies) and provided that the doctor is satisfied that the midwife is competent.[10] In the absence of specific causes for concern, the fact that a midwife is registered with the UKCC is probably sufficient to satisfy the latter requirement. It should also be noted that GPs are absolved of their responsibilities when the care is 'taken over' by a hospital.[11]

Concern has been expressed by the British Medical Association that GPs who take on responsibility for maternity care may be judged against unrealistic standards in malpractice litigation.[12] However, this seems unduly pessimistic. The standard of care required by the law is fixed by reference by what is accepted as proper by a responsible body of professional opinion from the relevant specialty.[13] What constitutes the relevant 'specialty', so that appropriate comparisons can be made, is fixed by considering the post that the practitioner holds, not his or her individual experience.[14] The standard will be refined to reflect sub-specialty within a larger area, such as GPs who are on the obstetric list. Thus, expert witnesses should be selected to give evidence as to what could be expected from that sub-group of GPs.[15]

The standard of care to be expected of a GP who is on the obstetric list is thus different from one who is not. However, that standard would reflect the limited obligations which are taken on by GPs, in particular the fact that they undertake to secure services, rather than to provide them. Thus, they need the skills to assess whether the woman's care should be given by them, a midwife, or a hospital-based obstetrician. They do not need to possess the skills of those other two professional groups.

The required standard of care would also reflect the degree of expertise indicated by inclusion on the obstetric list. This does not suggest a particularly high standard of experience or practice in obstetrics. General practitioners may be admitted to the obstetric list provided that they have spent six months working in a maternity hospital (with at least half that time spent on

---

[9] NHS (General Medical Services) Regulations 1992, SI 1992 No 635, Sch. 5, Pt. II.

[10] *Ibid.*, Sch. 2, para. 19.   [11] *Ibid.*, Sch. 5, Pt. II, para. 6.

[12] General Medical Services Committee, *Maternity Medical Services: Legal Advice* (London: BMA, 1995).

[13] *Bolam* v. *Friern HMC* [1957] 2 All ER 118. See Ch. 7 for a full discussion.

[14] *Wilsher* v. *Essex AHA* [1986] 3 All ER 801.

[15] *Defreitas* v. *O'Brien* [1995] 6 Med. LR 108.

obstetrics) within the previous ten years. If they have less recent experience, a week-long refresher course or a two-week stint as an obstetrics officer in a maternity unit is expected. Alternatively, it will suffice for a doctor to have attended at least 100 maternity cases involving responsibility for ante-natal care, and fifty cases involving the supervision of labour and responsibility for the post-natal period.[16]

B. Antenatal Care

Most antenatal care is concerned with informing women about their pregnancy and the choices available to them, and ensuring that it takes its normal course. It seeks to identify problems early so that they can be tackled. Occasionally, the problems may be serious for either mother or baby, or both. If they are harmed by a failure in antenatal care, and the mishap can be attributed to the negligence of staff, then an action for malpractice may be brought (see Chapter 7).

Some antenatal care is specifically directed at monitoring the development of the baby. It is now possible to test during pregnancy for a number of significantly disabling conditions.[17] Such tests enable women to decide whether to seek to terminate their pregnancy if the foetus they are carrying is affected.[18] There is no 'right' to prenatal testing, any more than there is a right to any treatment. Patients cannot force doctors who do not believe that a test is appropriate to carry one out. Only where to refuse a test would be negligent would there be any sanction against a refusal to test.[19] Some antenatal screening may come within the remit of the Human Fertilization and Embryology Authority (see Chapters 14 and 16). This will be the case where the tests are carried out on embryos (or gametes) *in vitro*, because it is unlawful to store human embryos without a licence from the authority. Here, it will be the Authority which determines the legitimacy of testing.

Antenatal testing may go wrong. Sometimes, women may be incorrectly told that the baby they are carrying is free from the genetic abnormality for

[16] N. 7 above, Sch. 5, Pt. I.

[17] M. Reid, 'Pre-natal Diagnosis and Screening: A Review' in J. Garcia, R., Kilpatrick, and M. Richards (eds.), *The Politics of Maternity Care: Services for Childbearing Women in Twentieth Century Britain* (Oxford: OUP, 1990), 300–24; G. Douglas, *Law, Fertility and Reproduction* (London, Sweet & Maxwell, 1991), 171–8; L. Abramsky and F. Chapple, *Prenatal Diagnosis: The Human Side* (London: Chapman & Hall, 1994).

[18] See Ch. 15 for the grounds on which this could legally be done.

[19] See J. Montgomery, 'Legal Aspects of Prenatal Diagnosis' in Abramsky and Chapple, n. 17 above (London: Chapman Hall, 1994), 23–36, 25–7.

which it was screened. If this happens, and it can be shown that the test was carried out negligently, then the woman, and possibly her partner, can sue for the distress caused to them by discovering that their baby was disabled. They may also claim compensation for the financial consequences of looking after the child, provided they can show that they would have terminated the pregnancy if they had been given accurate information.[20] However, English law will not permit the baby to sue, alleging that she or he should not have been born.[21] Public policy dictates that such a claim is rejected because it implies that it is unacceptable to be disabled. This does not prevent both the mother and baby being able to sue in respect of injuries caused in the process of testing. That sort of claim does not suggest that the baby's life is not worth living. Thus, an action could be brought if the baby was born disabled as a result of a negligently performed amniocentesis. A third possibility is that the antenatal test wrongly suggested that the baby was disabled. If the parents decided to terminate the pregnancy, it might later be discovered that the baby was in fact perfectly healthy. If the test had been negligently performed, then they could sue for their distress. These actions would have to show that there had been negligence. It is not enough to show that the test was inaccurate. The law of negligence was explained in Chapter 7.

C. The Place and Manner of Birth

There has been considerable controversy over the causes for the wholesale movement of childbirth into the hospitals, but it is clear that hospital deliveries have become by far the most common. Before the First World War, around 1 per cent of births took place in institutions. In 1946 the figure was 54 per cent. By 1990, 98 per cent of births took place in hospitals, the vast majority in consultant obstetric units.[22] In 1992, the Health Committee of the House of Commons reviewed the issues and concluded that the concentration on hospital care should be replaced by a system that was more responsive to the needs of women.[23] The Committee thought that such a service would be predominantly community-based, would provide greater continuity of care for women from people known to them throughout pregnancy and labour. They also expected midwives to be given a greater role in carrying their own caseloads.

---

[20] *Rance* v. *Mid-Downs HA* [1991] 1 All ER 801.
[21] *McKay* v. *Essex AHA* [1982] 1 QB 1166.
[22] *Maternity Services*, HC Pap. (1991–2) 29, paras. 15, 25.   [23] *Ibid.*, 29.

Following this report, the Department of Health established an expert working group, which produced the report *Changing Childbirth*.[24] That report emphasized the need to give women informed choices about their pregnancies and labour. It suggested that women should be able to choose to have a midwife as the lead professional responsible for their care. Every effort should be made to accommodate the wishes of women and their partners. This was to include ensuring that home birth was realistically available as a choice. These recommendations have been accepted as principles for restructuring maternity services, although it remains unclear how much progress is actually being made. The *Maternity Services* charter falls short of promising women the right to home births, instead giving women the right to information about 'where [they] can give birth (including at home)'.[25] The 1994 edition of the *Midwives Code of Practice* actually seems less encouraging of home births than the 1991 edition.[26]

There are no legal rules which relate specifically to women's rights to choose whether to give birth in places or manners which the professionals advise against. However, general principles create a stalemate in which it appears that women both do and do not have a right to choose how to have their babies, depending on how you define the meaning of such a right. In the context of private care, it is entirely a matter of the choice of women and professionals, none of whose decisions can be forced. Independent (i.e. non-NHS) midwives are free to refuse to accept women as clients if they are not prepared to offer the type of care requested.

Within the NHS, the position is more complicated.[27] Women are entitled to NHS care, and if they were completely abandoned by NHS maternity services they could both challenge the decision to deny them services and sue if something went wrong. However, they are not entitled to specific types of care, and it seems unlikely that the courts would support an attempt to make a health authority or NHS trust provide a midwife to deliver a woman at home. This suggests that there is no legal right to a home birth, if what is meant by such a right is that the courts will ensure that the necessary support is given. On the other hand, there is no legal power to force women to attend hospital. If a woman simply refused to leave home, then the maternity staff could not justify abandoning her and it would almost certainly be negligent

---

[24] Department of Health, *Changing Childbirth*, n. 6 above.

[25] Department of Health, *Maternity Services* (London: DoH, 1994).

[26] Compare United Kingdom Central Council for Nursing, Midwifery and Health Visiting, *A Midwives' Code of Practice* (London: UKCC, 1994), para. 55 with United Kingdom Central Council for Nursing, Midwifery and Health Visiting, *A Midwives' Code of Practice* (London: UKCC, 1991), sect. 4.

[27] Ch. 3 explains the relevant law in detail, this para. summarizes the position.

to do so.[28] General practitioners would be specifically obliged to attend if called in an emergency, even if they had previously refused to offer cover for a home delivery.[29] In one sense, therefore, women do have a legal right to a home birth. They may refuse to co-operate with the professionals' wish that they go into hospital. The professionals must then continue to care within the limitations of that refusal.

The position is similar in relation to decisions about the manner of birth. Sometimes women wish to deliver their babies in a particular position which they find comfortable, or to reject certain interventions. The legal position here again creates a stalemate. Women cannot force midwives or doctors to give them the sort of care they want, but they have the right to veto the care proposed for them. This latter right is the consequence of the law of consent to treatment.[30] Thus, a woman cannot demand to be allowed to give birth under water. Yet if she is in a birthing pool it would be unlawful forcibly to remove her against her wishes and the midwife would have no choice but to deliver her in the pool. Nor could a midwife impose pain relief or an episiotomy (cutting of the perineum to ease the passage of the baby) on a woman against her consent. Some health authorities and NHS trusts have developed disclaimer forms which they ask women who reject their advice to sign. These are almost certainly of no legal effect, and have been criticized by the Court of Appeal.[31]

A final question that commonly arises concerns the validity of birth plans drawn up in advance of labour, which purport to instruct midwives and obstetricians on how they should support the woman in labour. The law on such documents is not clear, but the principles are the same as those discussed in Chapter 20 in relation to 'living wills'. In summary, a birth plan will be binding on health professionals, providing that its meaning is clear and (when she drew it up) the woman had sufficient legal capacity to make the decisions recorded in it. Making a birth plan would not prevent a woman changing her mind, and the general rules of consent make it clear that it is only her consent that matters. Her partner cannot take decisions for her, and cannot force professionals to adhere to a birth plan when the woman has decided to reject it. However, choices recorded in a birth plan are only as effective as a currently expressed consent would be. Women can, therefore, veto treatment but not require particular types of care.

[28] This was recognized in United Kingdom Central Council for Nursing, Midwifery and Health Visiting, *A Midwives' Code of Practice* (1991), n. 26 above, sect. 4, although the current edition of the Code is less explicit (see United Kingdom Central Council for Nursing, Midwifery and Health Visiting, *A Midwives' Code of Practice* (1994), n. 26 above, para. 55).

[29] N. 7 above, Sch. 2, para. 4(h).

[30] See Ch. 10. For a full explanation of why the general rule of consent is not overridden by the claims of the foetus, see the next sect. of this Ch.

[31] *Re T* [1992] 4 All ER 649.

D. Maternal–Foetal Conflicts

One of the peculiar features of maternity care is that midwives and obstetricians have to deal with two patients, whose interests do not necessarily coincide. English law has rarely had to disentangle this conflict of interests directly. However, a number of areas of law impinge upon the problem, giving a confused picture. There is, first, the possibility that a mother who disregards the interests of her foetus may be punished for doing so. This could be directly, through a criminal prosecution, or indirectly through the threat of having her child removed into care. The second set of legal rules covers civil liability for injuries to the foetus. One hypothetical possibility is that a baby damaged by its mother's behaviour during pregnancy could sue her. If so, it could justify preventing her committing the tort in the first place. In addition, there is the risk that the health professionals might be sued for failing to protect the foetus from harm. In fact, English law avoids these problems (see section D(ii) below). The third area of law that deals with the relative status of mothers and foetuses is the law relating to wardship. If that jurisdiction were available it would make the interests of the foetus the paramount consideration and would enable a court to order a mother to accept care that she did not want in order to benefit her baby. The fourth legal possibility is that the law enables a mother's refusal of care to be overridden by the professionals or the courts. This would mean that treatment would be permitted despite the absence of consent.

(i) Deterring 'Foetal Abuse' through Punishment

The general principle of English law is that, until born alive, a foetus is not a legal person. Offences such as assault and homicide are not, therefore, available in relation to deaths *in utero*. However, if an unlawful act causes the death, after birth, of a baby who is born alive, then it can give rise to a prosecution for homicide.[32] This is possible even though the direct cause of death is premature birth, rather than any specific injury. Part of the reasoning behind this rule is that the law treats the foetus as a part of the mother, and thus injury to the foetus is unlawful in the same way that injury to the mother's body would be. This step in the argument is important, because it is not usually unlawful for the mother to harm herself, so that the rule cannot be used to criminalize women who damage their babies by actions such as taking drugs.

---

[32] *Re Attorney General's Reference (No 3 of 1944)* [1996] 2 All ER 10.

There are two exceptions to this general principle that pregnant women cannot be prosecuted for harming their unborn children. The first arises where they deliberately cause themselves to miscarry, or do something knowing that it is virtually certain that miscarriage will be the result.[33] The requirement of 'virtual certainty' means that it is unlikely that prosecutions will be brought. Although smoking, consuming alcohol, and taking some illicit drugs are known to increase the risk of harm to foetuses, it is highly improbable that they will be virtually certain to do so on any specific occasion. The second exception concerns the offence of child destruction under the Infant Life Preservation Act 1929. That may be available where a woman deliberately causes a child who is 'capable of being born alive' to die. Again this offence could also extend to doing something knowing that it is virtually certain that the child's death would be caused. Foetuses are 'capable of being born alive' when they can breath unaided for a few hours.[34] By statute, they are presumed to have attained this capacity by the twenty-eighth week of gestation, but are in fact likely to do so about a month earlier.[35]

In practice, the risk of criminal prosecution is not likely to arise. However, it seems that the law would be prepared to countenance the possibility that a mother whose lifestyle put the development of her foetus at risk might find that her child was taken into local authority care as a result. In *D* v. *Berkshire CC*[36] a child born to a registered drug addict was taken into care on the basis that her health was being avoidably impaired as a result of the drugs taken by her mother during pregnancy. After the birth, the baby girl suffered withdrawal symptoms and spent several weeks in intensive care. The basis of the decision was that the mother's behaviour during pregnancy had a continuing effect on the baby. Concern has been expressed that this approach risks women being threatened with the loss of their children in subsequent child-protection proceedings if they do not follow professional advice about diet and smoking.[37] However, the decision (which predates the Children Act) has been tacitly approved by the House of Lords in analysing the meaning of the Children Act 1989.[38]

---

[33] Offences Against the Person Act 1861, s. 58. This offence is discussed in detail in Ch. 15.

[34] *Rance* v. *Mid-Downs HA*, n. 20 above; cf. *C* v. *S* [1987] 1 All ER 1230. See Ch. 15 for further discussion of the 1929 Act.

[35] Infant Life Preservation Act 1929, s. 1(2). This should not be confused with the limitation of the 'social grounds' for abortion, which is imposed at 24 weeks (see Ch. 15), nor with the definition of still-birth, which makes babies born after 24 weeks still-births rather than miscarriages (see sect. F below).

[36] [1987] 1 All ER 20 (HL).

[37] J. Montgomery, 'Mothers and Unborn Children' [1987] *Fam. Law* 227.

[38] *Re M* [1994] 3 All ER 298.

(ii) Civil Liability for Injuries to the Foetus

In 1976, Parliament passed the Congenital Disabilities (Civil Liability) Act. The Act applies to all births taking place on or after 22 July 1976. It provides that, once born, a child may sue for injuries caused before the birth, even for those caused pre-conceptually (by reason of harm to the parents' ability to have normal children). This confirms that the interests of the foetus are protected by law. However, in relation to the problem of maternal–foetal conflict, the position is different. It is not possible to sue your own mother, save in respect of injuries caused while she was driving a motor car (when she should have been insured, so that there would be less direct conflict within the family).[39]

Even more importantly, other people are liable to the child only if they are in breach of their duties to the mother.[40] If the reason a professional failed to intervene to protect the interests of an unborn child was that the mother refused to consent to the intervention, then they are not liable to the mother. Consequently, they are not liable to the child either. Thus, professionals must advise women on their options, and may be liable to the child if they negligently fail to warn of a risk to the foetus. However, the law supports the right of women to choose to disregard such warnings.

In relation to births before 22 July 1976, the issue is governed by the common law. The position here is different, as it has now been established that there can be a direct common law duty to the unborn child.[41] In contrast to the position under the Act, this duty can be owed to the child by the mother. As the limitation period for birth injuries is twenty-one years,[42] there may still be some litigation in preparation under the common law. However, these common law developments are not significant for the care of women who are currently pregnant or delivering babies.

(iii) Wardship and the Foetus

Wardship is a protective jurisdiction which enables the court to ensure that the best interests of a child are followed. If foetuses were to be made wards of court, then the court would be obliged to take decisions in their interests even though the mothers' freedom would be curtailed. Although there has been considerable academic debate about the possibility of warding a foetus, the position has now been clarified by the Court of Appeal. In *Re F*[43] The Court of Appeal firmly rejected the suggestion that it should make the unborn child in question a ward. The mother suffered from severe mental illness, abused

[39] Ss. 1(1), 2. [40] S. 1(2). [41] *Burton* v. *Islington HA* [1992] 3 All ER 833 (CA).
[42] See Ch. 8. [43] [1988] 2 All ER 193.

drugs, and had a nomadic lifestyle. All of these factors caused the local authority to be concerned for the welfare of the child. It sought orders to search and find the mother (whose whereabouts were then unknown), that she should reside in a specified place and attend hospital, and in relation to the care of the child once born. May LJ indicated that he would have made the child a ward if he had the power to do so. However, the Court found that there was no such power because it was inherently incompatible with the rights of the mother. It was undesirable to create such a conflict of rights, and it would be impossible to enforce any order against the mother. Thus, the principle applied in the wardship jurisdiction is that, unless and until born, the rights of a foetus are subordinated to those of the mother.

(iv) Care without Consent

In 1992, for the first time, an English court authorized doctors to perform a caesarian section on a woman against her wishes.[44] The operation was the only way in which the baby could be born alive, and was also necessary to preserve the life of the mother. The matter came before the court as a matter of urgency. The hearing lasted only twenty minutes and the woman concerned was not represented. Although the decision was made by the President of the Family Division, an exceptionally experienced judge, its hurried nature means that it must be treated warily. The basis of the court's jurisdiction to make the order was barely discussed, nor was any clear explanation given of the reasons for the decision.

It was accepted that the wardship jurisdiction could not be used because it is not possible to make an unborn child a ward of court.[45] Instead a declaration was made that the operation would not be unlawful, notwithstanding the absence of the woman's consent. It is unclear why this was the case, but it is important to try to understand the reasons because a declaration does not alter the legal position. It merely sets out what the law is. This means that, if the decision is sound, it would have been permissible for the doctors to operate even without taking the matter to court.

Two points were emphasized in the course of the legal argument that give an indication of why the judge made the decision he did. First, it was stressed that the case concerned a baby at full term (not early in the pregnancy). Secondly, it was argued that there was no conflict between the interests of the child and those of the mother, and that the court would have approached the

---

[44] *Re S* [1992] 4 All ER 671. There have been two further unreported cases of court-ordered caesarian sections since *Re S*; see B. Hewson, 'Women's rights and legal wrongs' (1996) 146 *NLJ* 1385–6.

[45] Following *Re F*, n. 43 above.

case differently 'where treating the child in the way desired may adversely affect the mother'. These two features of the case could be taken as preconditions for any future decision. Nevertheless, the statement that there was no conflict of interest between the mother and the baby was surprising, given the fact that the mother was adamant that she did not want the operation performed.

It is possible that the court took the view that she was not competent to decide where her interests lay. She was a fundamentalist Christian who trusted in God to look after her. She and her husband rejected both medication and surgery. The evidence, however, indicated that she would die if the operation were not performed. The court may have thought that she was not in fact choosing to die but to live. If so, the fact that she failed to appreciate that she needed the operation to live indicated that she did not understand the position clearly enough to be competent. It could also be argued that, to the extent that it was a competent one, her decision did not apply to the circumstances before the court.[46] However, there is no indication in the judgment that the issue of competence was considered.

It is more probable that the court regarded the fact that the woman was pregnant as altering the usual position that patients have the right to refuse life saving treatment. The court was told that this possibility had been left open by Lord Donaldson in a previous case.[47] The two factors that were emphasized in argument were peculiar to pregnancy, and there was no discussion of the woman's competence. In view of this it seems that after *Re S* women may sometimes be given maternity care that they do not want. Two explanations may be offered of the limits of this almost unique power to treat someone against her wishes. The first is that women may be given care that doctors and midwives believe is necessary in the final stages of pregnancy and labour, provided that the mother's health is not placed at risk. The second is that treatment may be imposed when it is necessary to save both mother and baby. The latter position is easier to reconcile with the general principles of English law than the former, although neither fits comfortably.[48] While the basis of the decision remains unclear, it is probably unwise for health professionals to rely on it, and the Royal College of Obstetricians and Gynaecologists has advised that it would never be ethical to impose a Caesarean section on a competent woman who refused it.[49]

The decision in *Re S* was not relied upon in the second English court-authorized caesarean section. In *Tameside and Glossop Acute Services Trust* v.

[46] See *Re T*, n. 31 above, for a similar approach.   [47] *Ibid.*, 307.
[48] See M. Thomson, 'After *Re S*' (1994) 2 *Med. L Rev.* 127–48.
[49] Royal College of Obstetricians and Gynaecologists, *A Consideration of the Law and Ethics in Relation to Court-authorised Obstetric Intervention* (London: RCOG, 1994).

CH[50] the woman suffered mental disorder and was liable to be detained for treatment under the Mental Health Act 1983. Her medication had been stopped during her pregnancy, and it was thought that the consequent deterioration in her mental state might lead her to resist treatment. The Trust sought a declaration that it would be lawful to use reasonable restraint should it be deemed clinically necessary. The High Court found that the woman was not able to appreciate the need for the operation in order to ensure her baby's survival. It was clear that she wanted the baby. Although she was currently consenting to the operation, the doctors feared that she might withdraw that consent. The Court issued a declaration that the operation would be in the woman's best interests, accepting evidence that to lose the child would have a devastating effect on her mental health. This was not, therefore, a question of overriding a competent woman's choice, but of applying the rules used to determine when those unable to give or withhold consent should receive treatment.[51]

The remaining problem concerned the legality of restraint to ensure the treatment was actually given. The High Court thought that such force would be easier to justify if the treatment were given under the Mental Health Act 1983. The judge held that the caesarean section would be 'treatment' for her mental disorder under the broad definition of that term established in *B* v. *Croydon HA*.[52] That case suggests that if treatment alleviates the symptoms of the disorder, or prevents the patient's condition deteriorating, then it is treatment within the Act. In the court's view, preventing deterioration of her mental health by avoiding the stress of a still-birth was sufficient to bring a caesarean section within this definition. This may suggest that compulsory maternity care can be administered to all pregnant women who are 'sectioned' under the 1983 Act. However, it should be observed that the court heard specific evidence from the woman's psychiatrist that this would be a danger in her case. It did not merely assume that losing the child would be distressing.

E. Post-natal Care

For a period after the baby is born, meeting the health needs of mother and baby is seen as still part of maternity care. Thus GPs may accept women for care during the post-natal period under the provisions for maternity care, which may be separate from the woman's normal registration as a GP's patient (see the first section of this Chapter). For these purposes, post-natal care

---

[50] [1996] 1 FCR 753.   [51] These are discussed fully in Ch. 10.   [52] [1995] 1 All ER 683.

means personal medical services for both the mother and baby during the fourteen days following the birth.[53] For the mother, it is such services related to pregnancy and labour. For the baby, it is all such care unless another GP has accepted the child as a patient. In both cases, the GP's responsibility ends if the mother or baby becomes a hospital in-patient. A GP may also, as an independent matter, accept responsibility for doing a full post-natal examination of the woman, between six and twelve weeks after the delivery, and advising her of any treatment she may require.[54]

The responsibilities of midwives are determined by the Midwives Rules.[55] Midwives are responsible for providing midwifery care to mother and baby for at least the first ten days following delivery, and, if circumstances indicate, up to twenty-eight days thereafter.[56] This means that they will provide care unless matters 'deviate from the norm' when they are obliged to seek the assistance of a doctor.[57] After this stage, the care of mother and baby will become the responsibility of the primary health services, general medical practitioners and health visitors, rather than maternity services.

F. Administrative Aspects of Birth

After the birth of a child, it is the legal duty of the parents to register the details with the local registrar within forty-two days.[58] If they do not do so, that duty falls upon other 'qualified informants', which includes anyone present at the birth or having charge of the child.[59] The required details cover the child's date and place of birth, name, and sex. The parents' names (including the mother's maiden name if they are married and it has changed), places of birth, address, and the occupation of the father must also be recorded.[60] A special form is included for use by unmarried parents, which includes a solemn declaration that the partner is the father.[61]

In addition to these provisions relating to registration, there is also an obligation to notify the district medical officer of the birth. This falls upon the father of the child where the child is born at his home, and in all cases any person in attendance at the time of birth or within six hours of it. Notification will usually be given by the doctor or midwife, and if there is reasonable cause

---

[53] N. 7 above, r. 31(7), Sch. 5, Pt. II.   [54] *Ibid.*, Sch. 5 Pt II.

[55] Nurses, Midwives, and Health Visitors Rules 1983, n. 5 above, as amended, Pt. V.

[56] *Ibid.*, r. 27.   [57] *Ibid.*, r. 40.   [58] Births and Deaths Registration Act 1953, s. 2.

[59] *Ibid.*, ss. 1(2), 2.

[60] Registration of Births and Deaths Regulations 1987, SI 1987 No 2088, as amended, r. 7, Sch. 2, Form 1.

[61] *Ibid.*, r. 8, Sch. 2, Form 2.

to believe that another person has given the notification, others under the obligation to do so have a defence to any prosecution.[62]

These provisions are particularly sensitive in respect of still-births. For legal purposes, a baby born dead is classified as a still-birth if born after the twenty-fourth week of pregnancy.[63] Such a baby's birth must be registered. The details required are essentially the same as with a live birth, save that the cause of death is entered and it is not necessary to give the child a name.[64] A special certificate is required before a still-born child may be buried. It may not be possible to issue such a certificate without reference to the coroner. The coroner must be informed if there is reason to believe that the child was in fact born alive.[65] Although younger children who are born dead are technically classified as 'miscarriages' it is still possible for the parents to arrange a funeral. In such circumstances, funeral directors will require a letter or certificate from the midwife or doctor who attended the birth.[66] Should a baby be born alive, at any stage of pregnancy, and subsequently die, then both the birth and the death will need to be registered.

G. Conclusion

This Chapter has examined the law relating to maternity services. It has shown how the specific rules are more concerned with the demarcation of professional responsibilities than women's rights. However, it is possible to analyse the rules which structure women's choices so as to set out the way in which their rights are indirectly recognized. The law determining whether the interests of the mother or foetus should be given priority indicates that it is usually the former that should prevail. This may cause some distress to professional staff, forcing them to accept choices that they may feel jeopardize the interests of babies. Once babies are born, they are entitled to consideration as separate people, patients in their own right. The legal rules are, then, those relating to care for children, discussed in Chapter 12. Sometimes, however, difficult decisions have to be taken about the best way to care for newborn babies whose chances of survival, or survival without severe disabilities, are slim. The law governing this area is the subject of the next chapter.

[62] NHS Act 1977, s. 124; NHS (Notification of Births and Deaths) Regulations 1982, SI 1982 No 286.

[63] Births and Deaths Registration Act 1926, s. 12, and Births and Deaths Registration Act 1953, s. 41, as amended by the Still-Birth (Definition) Act 1992.

[64] N. 60 above, Pt. VIII, Sch. 2, Form 9.

[65] *Ibid.*, r. 33. For discussion of the role of the coroner, see Ch. 20.

[66] United Kingdom Central Council for Nursing, Midwifery and Health Visiting, *A Midwives' Code of Practice* (1994), n. 26 above, para. 76.

18 Selective Treatment of the Newborn

Considerable controversy has surrounded the suggestion that health professionals must be selective in their treatment of newborn children.[1] Two rather different strands of the problem deserve to be highlighted: resource-allocation and quality of life. On the one hand, the difficulties have arisen because of technological advances that make it possible to keep alive babies whose birth-weight is exceptionally low (usually after premature birth).[2] In the past these children would not have survived at all. Now it is sometimes possible to sustain them, although the lower their birth-weight the more likely it is that they will be left with permanent disabilities. In any event, they will survive only with the aid of intensive and intrusive life support. This is expensive, so that neonatal care provides a significant drain on scarce resources. It is therefore necessary to decide when this expense should be borne and when the chances of success are too small to justify diverting money from other areas of need.

Intensive neonatal care can also be distressing for the children themselves, and there may be circumstances when the limited prospects of saving the child's life are thought to be outweighed by the distress of being put through the treatment. Concern for the impact on the children is linked to the second major theme of debate. This is the question of the relevance of any disability that the child may suffer to the decision to treat. In a few cases, the courts have discussed the withholding of treatment from handicapped children and have been accused of regarding their lives as of less worth than those of the able-bodied and normally intelligent.[3] This raises important and wide-ranging

---

[1] For introductions to the issues see C. Wells, ' "Otherwise Kill Me": Marginal Children and Ethics at the Edges of Existence' in R. Lee and D. Morgan, *Birthrights: Law and Ethics at the Beginnings of Life* (London: Routledge, 1989); H. Kuhse and P. Singer, *Should the Baby Live: The Problem of Handicapped Infants* (Oxford: OUP, 1985); I. Kennedy, *Treat Me Right* (Oxford: OUP, 1991), 140–74.

[2] D. Meyers, *The Human Body and the Law* (2nd edn., Edinburgh: Edinburgh University Press, 1990), 83–8; D. J. Henderson-Smart, 'Low Birth-weight Babies: Where to Draw the Line?' in H. Caton (ed.), *Trends in Biomedical Regulation* (Sydney: Butterworths, 1990), 145–52.

[3] M. J. Gunn and J. C. Smith, '*Arthur's* Case and the Right to Life of Down's Syndrome Child' [1985] *Crim. LR* 705–15.

questions about the significance of assessments of a patient's quality of life in deciding whether to treat.

These issues involve difficult and emotive ethical problems. The doctrine of the sanctity of life is sometimes invoked to suggest that treatment should always be given to sustain life, whatever the cost. Others argue that this position is both unkind to the individual parents and children and an irresponsible use of scarce resources. Disputes also exist as to who should take decisions on the management of these children's care. Some argue that the parents should be dominant; others that their views are only one of the considerations. If the parents do not have the last word, the proper role of doctors and others needs to be specified. The concern here is with the legal framework within which these decisions on the appropriate form of care need to be taken.

In order to explain the legal rules, it is necessary to consider a number of areas of law. First, the criminal law places limits on the actions of health professionals and the parents of the child. Secondly, the respective positions of those two groups must be examined to identify the role that each should play in decisions. This demands an examination of the implications of a number of the general principles of health care law explored earlier in this book. Thirdly, consideration must be given to the practice of the courts, when called in to resolve disagreements, in scrutinizing the care given to the babies and recommending the course of care to be given.

A. Criminal Law and the Limits of Choice

Whatever the ethical merits of parental or professional decisions to withhold care, the criminal law limits their scope. If non-treatment constitutes a criminal offence then even a consensus of all those involved cannot justify failing to sustain life. The first step in setting out the legal framework governing decisions on neonatal care is therefore to identify these constraints.

First of all, parents are bound by law to take steps to provide medical care for their children, and a failure to do so risks prosecution for child neglect under the Children and Young Persons Act 1933.[4] For this type of criminal neglect, the culpable behaviour consists of failing to seek medical attention rather than refusing to consent to treatment, and if the child is under professional care in hospital the parents will not be guilty.[5] Assessing the need for medical care is not always easy, and parents will be not guilty of neglect if they

---

[4] S. 1(2).

[5] A. Bainham, *Children, Parents and the State* (London: Sweet & Maxwell, 1988), 135.

did not appreciate that it was needed.[6] However, they cannot escape responsibility by claiming that they did not think it was appropriate to seek assistance if they were aware that a reasonable parent would have done so.[7] A strong conviction that continued care was inappropriate will not therefore absolve parents from involving doctors. Nor will the fact that no treatment could in fact have been given by doctors be a sufficient reason for failing to call for assistance.[8]

The offence of child neglect can also be committed by a parent who refuses to consent to treatment, but only where that treatment is not dangerous and the objection to it is unreasonable.[9] The difficult nature of selective non-treatment decisions is such that it is probable that parents who refuse consent because they believe it to be in their child's interests to do so would be held to be acting reasonably and would therefore be innocent of any charge of neglect.

In addition to the specific offence of child neglect, there is the possibility of prosecution for homicide. Like anyone else, doctors and parents will be guilty of murder if they intentionally take steps to end the life of the child.[10] The position in relation to withholding life-saving treatment is less clear. A failure by parents to summon medical assistance may amount to manslaughter, or murder if the required degree of culpability is present, as well as neglect.[11] The courts have made much of the distinction between acts and omissions,[12] but its application in this legal context is limited.[13] The law does hold people responsible for failing to act if they are under a legal obligation to do so. There is no doubt that parents have a duty to care for their children, and that health professionals are bound to look after their patients. Neglecting to feed an elderly relative within your care who then starves to death is as much a crime as poisoning him or her.[14] So, too, negligently failing to treat a patient is as culpable as doing so in a negligent manner, and if death results a manslaughter charge could be brought.[15]

Consequently, the parties involved in deciding what care a newborn child should receive may be bound to take active steps to care for the child and can be held responsible for failing to act, as well as for taking positive steps to kill.

---

[6] *R. v. Sheppard* [1981] AC 394.   [7] *R. v. Senior* [1899] 1 QB 823.
[8] *R. v. S & M* [1995] Crim. LR 486.   [9] *Oakley* v. *Jackson* [1914] 1 KB 216.
[10] A mother who kills her child in the first year of its life may be prosecuted for the lesser offence of infanticide, Infanticide Act 1938.
[11] *R. v. Gibbins & Proctor* (1918) 13 Cr.App.R 134, see also *R. v. Lowe* [1973] QB 702.
[12] See *R. v. Arthur* (1981) 12 BMLR 1; *R. v. Lowe*, n. 11 above.
[13] See *Airedale NHS trust* v. *Bland* [1993] 1 All ER 821, discussed in Ch. 20. For discussion of the distinction between killing and letting die from the philosophical perspective, see Kuhse and Singer, n. 1 above, 74–97.
[14] *R. v. Instan* [1893] 1 QB 450; *R. v. Stone* [1977] 2 All ER 341.
[15] *R. v. Bourne* [1938] 3 All ER 615, 618; *R. v. Adomako* [1994] 3 All ER 79.

Liability turns on the extent of the duty to take active steps.[16] If the limits of this duty have been reached there can be no criminal liability for failing to act. But if there is still an obligation to treat patients actively, then a failure to do so that results in death may be murder. There is no obligation on health professionals to offer all the care that it is possible to give. The reports of *R. v. Arthur* conflict as to whether the court accepted that it might be legitimate to withhold food, although possibly not water, from a child.[17] However, in *Airedale NHS trust* v. *Bland* the House of Lords accepted that artificial nutrition and hydration could be ended in the extreme circumstances of that case.[18] There is therefore no categorical legal distinction between therapy and feeding.

In relation to parents, the duty to act is probably limited to seeing that the child is properly fed and looked after, and has medical attention when necessary.[19] It is unlikely that this extends any further than the duties under the Children and Young Persons Act 1933.[20] The duties of professionals to act are established by their obligations in contract and tort, which in practice both result in the requirement that doctors act in a way acceptable to their peers.[21] This means that there will be a duty to keep a child alive only where no responsible body of professional opinion would accept that allowing the child to die was an appropriate decision.

The only reported English criminal case on the responsibility of health professionals in this area is *R. v. Arthur*.[22] Dr Arthur, an eminent pædiatrician, was prosecuted for the attempted murder of a child with Down's syndrome. The initial charge of murder was dropped when it became clear from the post-mortem that the child would have died, whatever Dr Arthur had done to save it. The parents did not wish the child to survive and Dr Arthur instructed that there should be nursing care only, no food except water and that a drug (DF118), which was said to suppress the child's appetite, should be administered at the discretion of the nursing staff. The court found that this was

---

[16] *Airedale NHS trust* v. *Bland*, n. 13 above, 881–3. See further Ch. 20.

[17] Compare (1981) 78 LSG 1341 with the extract in I. Kennedy and A. Grubb, *Medical Law: Text with Materials* (London: Butterworths, 1994), 931. For discussion of the point see Kennedy, n. 1 above, 168–9; Gunn and Smith, 'Arthur's Case' n. 3 above, 710–11; D. Poole, 'Arthur's Case: A Comment' [1986] *Crim. LR* 383–7; D. Brahams, 'Putting *Arthur's* Case in Perspective' [1986] *Crim. LR* 387–9.

[18] N. 13 above.   [19] *R. v. Gibbins & Proctor*, n. 11 above, 139.

[20] G. Williams, 'Down's Syndrome and the Duty to Preserve Life' (1981) 131 *NLJ* 1020–1.

[21] *Airedale NHS trust* v. *Bland*, n. 13 above. *Bolam* v. *Friern HMC* [1957] 2 All ER 118 establishes the duty in tort. H. Benyon, 'Doctors as Murderers' [1982] *Crim. LR* 17–28, 27–8, discusses the contractual position. Her conclusion that doctors are employed to exercise their clinical freedom is reinforced by the reluctance of the Court of Appeal in *Thake* v. *Maurice* [1986] 1 All ER 497 to imply that doctors' contractual duties differ from those under the law of negligence.

[22] N. 12 above. The decision has been much discussed. See especially Gunn and Smith, n. 3 above; Kennedy, n. 1 above, 154–74; and Benyon, n. 21 above.

within the accepted limits of medical practice at the time.[23] Consequently, there was no issue in the *Arthur* case as to any duty to act that might have allowed the prosecution to claim that the failure to do so constituted an offence. Instead, the case turned on whether Dr Arthur could be said to have tried to kill the child or whether he had merely declined to intervene to prolong its life. If the latter was the correct categorization, then Dr Arthur was innocent.

The jury was directed that if they accepted that Dr Arthur ordered no more than a 'holding operation, in the nature of setting conditions where the child could . . . if it contracted pneumonia . . . or if it revealed any other organic defect die peacefully' then they should acquit him. The judge also instructed them that if 'it was a positive act on the part of Dr Arthur which was likely to kill the child . . . accompanied by an intent on his part that it should as a result of the treatment that he prescribed die' then they should find him guilty of the charge.[24] It was also pointed out that, in law, motive and intention are distinct concepts. Dr Arthur intended to kill the child if he knew that the child would die as a result of his actions, even if he did so because he believed it was in the child's interests to die. After receiving this direction the jury acquitted Dr Arthur of the charges against him.

As a matter of law, the direction given by the judge is the most important aspect of the *Arthur* case. It is that direction which can be used to guide future cases. The jury's decision turned on the particular facts of the case; the judge's direction was in general terms. It is therefore worth considering examples of practice that Farquharson J regarded as clearly legal or illegal when instructing the jury on the law.[25] He suggested that it would be murder to administer an excessive dose of a drug that caused the death of a baby who would not otherwise be about to die. On the other hand, he doubted that it would be murder for a doctor to decline to take a course that would save a child's life. This latter statement should be understood as limited to cases where non-treatment is accepted as proper medical practice, otherwise the doctor would be in breach of a duty to act and could therefore be guilty of murder by omission.

The final aspect of the criminal law meriting consideration concerns the sharpness of the line between killing and letting die. The courts have recognized in the context of terminal care that palliative measures may also have the effect of shortening a patient's life. It has been held that this would not constitute homicide providing that the patient was already dying, that the care given was proper medical treatment, and that the purpose was to

---

[23] There is some evidence to suggest that in fact few paediatricians would have acted as Dr Arthur did: see I. Kennedy, 'Reflections on the *Arthur* Trial', *New Society*, Jan. 1982, 13–15.

[24] N. 12 above, 6.

[25] *Ibid.*, 5–6.

relieve suffering not to end life.[26] This principle would also apply to neonatal care.

The criminal law thus prevents the taking of active steps to end the life of a child, but there are no precise principles governing non-treatment decisions. Parents must act reasonably and professionals must practise properly. Within these boundaries, responsibility for deciding what care is appropriate falls upon the parents of the children concerned and the health professionals who care for them.

B. Professionals and Parents

Lord Donaldson has described the relationship between the parental and professional roles in decisions over neonatal care as a system of checks and balances:

> No one can *dictate* the treatment to be given to any child, neither court, parents nor doctors. . . . The doctors can recommend treatment A in preference to treatment B. They can also refuse to adopt treatment C on the grounds that it is medically contra-indicated or for some other reason is a treatment which they could not conscientiously administer. The court or parents for their part can refuse to consent to treatment A or B or both, but cannot insist on treatment C. The inevitable and desirable result is that choice of treatment is in some measure a joint decision of the doctors and the court or parents.[27]

While this is an admirable summary of the general position, it is necessary to examine the legal principles to be applied to determine whether there are special circumstances that sometimes permit a unilateral decision. It is also necessary to consider whether the balance of power between parents and professionals is as even as Lord Donaldson suggests. Where an impasse is created because no agreement can be reached and no party is entitled to act without the co-operation of the other, it will be necessary to apply to the court to resolve the dispute. Ultimately, therefore, much depends on what the courts do when they are called upon to resolve disputes.[28]

As a general principle no care can be given to newborn children without the consent of one of their parents.[29] Thus, health professionals will be unable to proceed with the care they wish to offer unless the parents agree. In the context of life-saving treatment, however, this general position may be

---

[26] *R. v. Adams* [1957] Crim. LR 365. See Ch. 20 for further discussion.

[27] *Re J* [1991] 3 All ER 930, 934. The authority of these remarks was confirmed in *Re J* [1992] 4 All ER 614.

[28] The procedures for involving the courts are discussed in Ch. 12.   [29] See Ch. 12.

superseded. It is usually accepted that life-saving treatment may be offered even without parental consent under the doctrine of necessity.[30] This doctrine would provide a defence against any action that the parents might bring in the name of their child,[31] and it is difficult to envisage a court holding a doctor to be acting unlawfully in saving a child's life. If this is true, where parents are refusing to consent to life-sustaining treatment the health professionals could probably proceed even in the face of parental opposition.

It may be that the doctrine of necessity will be available only where an emergency requires speedy resolution of the conflict between the parents and professionals. Lord Templeman's recognition, in the *Gillick* decision, that the doctrine of necessity justified proceeding in the light of parental opposition was premised on the assumption that there was no time to involve the court.[32] It appears therefore that where immediate treatment is required to save the child's life, doctors may override the parent's refusal to consent. Where time is less pressing and it is possible to do so, the matter should probably be taken to court. Certainly, the courts have suggested that, where blood transfusions are proposed against the wishes of Jehovah's Witness children or parents, a court should be involved.[33]

Subject to the uncertain scope of the doctrine of necessity, the parents have a veto on care because they can refuse to consent to it. But this does not mean that health professionals are always obliged to treat when the parents wish them to do so. This would only be the case if the parents could bring an action either ordering that the care go ahead or suing for damages for a failure to carry out the treatment. As we shall see shortly, the courts have said that they will not order the doctors to carry out specific procedures, even when charged with the responsibility for resolving disagreements. The chances of a parent obtaining an order against a doctor are therefore slim.

The general principles governing legal actions to force NHS hospitals to treat particular patients were discussed in Chapter 3. It should be noted that two of the cases in which the courts have refused to order care concerned young babies.[34] In both it was accepted that, where the matter was a question of priorities determining which patients should be treated first, the courts could not override the decisions of the doctors. In both, however, the issue

---

[30] P. Skegg, *Law, Ethics and Medicine* (Oxford: Clarendon Press, 1984), 107–10; G. Williams, 'Necessity' [1978] *Crim. LR* 128, 132–4; NHS Circular HSC(GEN)81, 1975; see British Medical Association, *Rights and Responsibilities of Doctors* (London: BMA, 1988), 6–7. See also Ch. 12.

[31] There is no action that the parent could bring based on their own rights: *F* v. *Wirral MBC* [1991] 2 All ER 648.

[32] *Gillick* v. *W. Norfolk AHA* [1985] 3 All ER 402, 432. This point is fully discussed in Ch. 12.

[33] *Re E* [1993] 1 FLR 386; *Re S* [1993] 1 FLR 376; *Re O* [1993] 2 FLR 149.

[34] *R.* v. *Central Birmingham HA, ex p. Walker* (1987) 3 BMLR 32; *R,* v. *Central Birmingham HA, ex p. Collier,* 6 Jan. 1988, CA, unreported.

was the postponement of operations, not an outright refusal to carry them out. Further, it was accepted that there was no immediate threat to the children's lives and that the operations would be performed were an emergency to develop.[35] The parents and health professionals were agreed that the operations should eventually go ahead. These decisions are of little assistance where the dispute concerns whether the treatment is appropriate at all. However, R. v. *Cambridge DHA, ex p. B* shows that unless the decision not to treat is unreasonable the doctors cannot be forced to act.[36] It will be hard to show that a health professional who, after careful consideration of the case and discussion with the parents, believes that treatment is inappropriate is acting unreasonably. Even under the wardship jurisdiction where the courts have to decide what is best for the child, the judges have said that they will not order doctors to treat against their clinical judgement.[37]

To obtain damages against the professionals when their child has been allowed to die because further life-sustaining treatment was thought inappropriate, the parents must bring a negligence action. The chances of success will be small unless they can show that no responsible paediatric team accepts that withholding treatment was legitimate in the circumstances.[38] It will not be possible to argue that public policy always requires life-saving treatment to be administered, as the case law discussed below establishes that it can sometimes be in the interests of children to be permitted to die. Consequently, where the health professionals come to the considered conclusion that they cannot ethically continue prolonging a child's life it will be lawful for them to act on that opinion even when the parents wish them to carry on. Only if they could not persuade their professional colleagues that they acted responsibly would they be at risk.

The picture painted by Donaldson MR in the passage quoted at the beginning of this section is therefore slightly misleading. Parents are unable to proceed alone with a decision to treat unless they find themselves agreeing with the plans of the professionals. Nor can they guarantee non-treatment in emergencies if the professionals choose to rely on the doctrine of necessity. Depending on which interpretation of that doctrine prevails, either doctors may always save the child's life (and it is for the parents to involve the courts if they wish to prevent this happening), or doctors are constrained by the law from imposing treatment in cases when there is time to seek the view of a court. However, it is clear that where parents wish to withhold treatment, they are free to do so unless a court is involved. Thus the balance of power between parents and professionals is uneven and tilted in favour of the clinical freedom

---

[35] R. v. *Central Birmingham HA, ex p. Walker*, n. 34 above.
[37] *Re J* [1992] 4 All ER 614.
[36] [1995] 2 All ER 129.
[38] See Ch. 7.

of the latter.[39] A similar inequality can be seen when it comes to the practice of the courts when called upon to decide what treatment should be given to a neonate.

C. The Court Decisions

The first case in which a court was required to consider whether it was appropriate to withhold life-sustaining treatment from a disabled child arose in 1981 in what became known as the Baby Alexandra case.[40] The child in question was suffering from Down's syndrome, and in addition was born with an intestinal blockage that required surgery. There was no doubt that the surgical procedure would have been performed on a child without the handicap. The parents felt that, in the light of her condition, it would be kinder to allow their daughter to die and refused to consent to the operation. The health authority made the child a ward of court and the case eventually reached the Court of Appeal. The view of that court was that it could not be argued that it was in the interests of the girl to withhold treatment. She was expected to live for at least twenty years and, while she was said to be 'severely mentally and physically handicapped', there was no evidence that her life would be 'intolerable'. Templeman LJ suggested that it was necessary to show that the prognosis was of a life full of pain and suffering before it could be said that it was 'so awful that in effect the child must be condemned to die'. He implied that unless this was certain the court could not authorize the medical profession to withhold treatment.

Although it is very unlikely that a different decision would be taken on these facts today, especially since Down's syndrome would probably be no longer regarded as so severe a condition, the approach taken by the Court of Appeal in the Baby Alexandra case has been criticized in the subsequent decisions. In *Re J*[41] the Official Solicitor (representing the child) sought to persuade the Court of Appeal to establish objective principles for non-treatment decisions. He first suggested that the court should always choose life over death, in effect that the law should lay down that the sanctity of life outweighed any considerations of the quality of the child's life. This would enable the court to authorize the withholding of treatment only when it was impossible to save the child's life and all that could be done would be to prolong it for a short period. This was precisely what was done in *Re C*[42] where the child was suffering from particularly severe hydrocephalus and was terminally ill.

---

[39] For a similar conclusion on other grounds, see Wells, n. 1 above, 209–10.
[40] *Re B* [1990] 3 All ER 927.   [41] [1990] 3 All ER 930.   [42] [1989] 2 All ER 782.

However, that proposal would have prevented courts ever deciding that a life was not worth living. Such an absolutist approach was rejected by the Court of Appeal because it would introduce a public policy argument that could conflict with the welfare of the child.

When this sanctity-of-life approach was rejected the Official Solicitor sought to rely upon the Baby Alexandra decision as authority for the weaker proposition that 'a court is only justified in withholding consent to such treatment if it is certain that the quality of the child's subsequent life would be "intolerable" to the child, "bound to be so full of pain and suffering" and "demonstrably so awful that in effect the child must be condemned to die" '. In effect, the Court of Appeal was being asked to hold that the comments in *Re B* should be regarded as setting out legal rules to define when non-treatment was appropriate. This approach has been criticized as implying that handicapped children have a weaker right to life than the able-bodied.[43] In fact, the Court of Appeal refused to adopt it. It held that the only principle of law was that the court should act in the best interests of the child. This could not be reduced to a quasi-statutory yardstick as the Official Solicitor proposed. The facts of each individual case had to be examined on their own merits.

This judicial reticence leaves health professionals with little assistance in deciding what course of action they should take. However, *Re J* does provide guidance on the way in which the parents and professionals should approach their responsibilities.[44] The former should decide what to do in the best interests of the child, without regard to their own interests. The latter should care for the child in accordance with good medical practice, which undoubtedly places the child's welfare at its centre. It is appropriate to consult widely with all members of the health care team, the carers, and possibly with the social services department.[45] The Court of Appeal also suggested that decisions as to where the child's interests lie should be taken from the assumed point of view of the patient, recognizing that 'even severely handicapped people find a quality of life rewarding which to the unhandicapped may seem manifestly intolerable'.[46] It is difficult to see how this approach can be precise in relation to babies. With adults who have become incompetent it is possible to look back at choices they have made in the past to deduce how they would approach a decision. Babies have never made such choices, and the range of responses to life with a disability are such that it is impossible to say with certainty whether or not a particular neonate would choose to live such a life if able to do so.

When the judges turned to the position of J, the child in question, they illustrated how the problem should be approached. He was not on the point

[43] Gunn and Smith, n. 3 above.   [44] N. 41 above, 934.   [45] See *Re C* [1989] 2 All ER 782.
[46] N. 41 above, 938.

of death, nor even in the process of dying. However, he had previously needed artificial ventilation and the doctors caring for him suggested that, if such intervention were necessary again, it would be inappropriate to administer it. The Court of Appeal agreed, emphasizing that it was necessary to consider the quality of the life that the child would live and the intrusive nature of the treatment that would be needed to keep him alive. The evidence showed that the anticipated quality of life was very poor. The boy had suffered very severe and permanent brain damage around the time of his birth. He was epileptic. He was expected to be blind, deaf, dumb, and quadriplegic. It was thought that he could feel pain but that it was unlikely that he would develop even limited intellectual abilities. Artificial ventilation was itself invasive and would also involve a naso-gastric tube, drips, and constant blood sampling. This would cause the boy considerable distress and the Court of Appeal found that it was not justified by the limited benefits that it could secure for him.

It is important to note that this approach involves a balancing exercise. It does not decide that the boy's life was not worth living. The Court recognized that less intrusive treatment, such as short-term manual ventilation, might be in the child's interests. So, too, that antibiotics should probably be used to treat an infection. It would therefore be wrong to put too much weight on the degree of handicap alone. The decision in *Re J* illustrates the process that should be followed. It does not lay down any rules about the outcome.

It is also important to recognize that the Court of Appeal has consistently declined to order that the children should be left to die. In *Re J* the Court authorized the doctors to refrain from mechanically ventilating him, but permitted them to do so if they thought it appropriate when his condition reached the critical point. Similarly in *Re C*, the Court authorized the hospital to care for the girl in question in accordance with the recommendations of an eminent pædiatrician who had acted as an expert witness in the proceedings at the invitation of the Official Solicitor. These recommendations included non-treatment in certain circumstances, but the court order in no way prevented treatment if the doctors subsequently decided it was appropriate.[47] In essence, therefore, the modern approach to non-treatment cases has been to facilitate the exercise of clinical judgement, not to transfer the decision to the courts. Nor have the courts been prepared to go further than the professionals could have done without court intervention. The judges have emphasized that the court, like doctors, cannot decide that death should be caused, only that it is permissible to fail to avert it.[48] The courts have decided that their function is not to lay down standards for the professionals, but to provide them with a means of reassurance that they will be acting legally.

[47] See also *Re J*, n. 37 above.
[48] N. 41 above, 936 (*per* Lord Donaldson MR), 944 (*per* Taylor LJ).

It has also become clear that the courts will respect the clinical freedom of doctors and refuse to force them to act against their clinical judgement. In a second case called *Re J*[49] the Court of Appeal had to consider the position of a boy who was severely microcephalic following an accidental injury. He had been left with a severe form of cerebral palsy, epilepsy, and cortical blindness. The prognosis was poor, there was little prospect of improvement, and his condition might well have deteriorated. His life expectancy was uncertain but short. The doctors caring for the boy believed that it would be inappropriate to use mechanical methods of ventilation, should they be needed. The child's parents wanted him to be kept alive. The Court of Appeal held that doctors could not be ordered to go against *bona fide* clinical judgements of what was in their patient's best interests. This was despite the fact that another consultant pædiatrician had been found who would have been prepared to give the care that the parents wanted. Thus it seems that a court will defer to the professionals even where it believes that care should be given. Sir Stephen Brown P has suggested that the role of the court is to assist by taking responsibility for decisions and relieving the parents of some of the burden, but not to instruct doctors how they should perform their clinical and professional duties.[50]

D. Conclusion

It is difficult to draw firm guidance from the current state of English law on the selective treatment of neonates. Active steps causing the death of a child are outlawed, but non-treatment will usually be legitimate if the professionals believe it is appropriate. Parents must obtain professional advice, but are not usually obliged to agree to treatment. The courts have not been prepared to interfere with clinical freedom in this area. Some find this flexibility unsatisfactory, arguing that society should offer clearer guidance.[51] Others argue that the issues are so difficult that the law is too blunt an instrument with which to solve them.[52] As the law stands Parliament and the judiciary seem to have accepted the latter view.

---

[49] *Re J*, n. 37 above.   [50] *Re C* [1996] 2 FLR 43, 44.

[51] e.g. D. Brahams and M. Brahams, '*R* v. *Arthur*—is Legislation Appropriate?' (1981) 78 *LSG* 1342–3; J. K. Mason and R. A. McCall Smith, *Law and Medical Ethics* (4th edn., London: Butterworths, 1994), 159–62.

[52] e.g. J. Harvard, 'Legislation is Likely to Create More Difficulties than It Resolves' (1983) 9 *JME* 18.

19 Transplantation

The transplantation of organs is now an established part of medical practice. The figures for kidney transplantation can illustrate this. In 1993, nearly 4,000 patients were awaiting such transplants. In the same year, 1,799 kidneys were donated after death, of which 94 per cent were transplanted. Live donation is less common, accounting for only 140 transplants in 1993. However, that represents a increase of 49 per cent over the previous year, and there may be a trend towards more use of live donation.[1] In other areas, such as blood and bone marrow donation, living donors are the norm. A special health authority has been established to co-ordinate transplantation services: the United Kingdom Transplant Support Service Authority. This Authority holds information on possible donors and recipients of organs, provides organ matching and tissue typing services, and can arrange for safe transport of organs for transplantation.[2]

Some of the law governing transplantation is no more than the application of general principles. Thus, health professionals must exercise due care when carrying out the procedures involved and they must obtain the consent of the donor and recipient.[3] However, there is also a body of law specifically relating to transplantation. That is the subject of this Chapter. In relation to organs taken from corpses, transplantation has long been recognized by English law. The Corneal Grafting Act was passed in 1952. It was superseded by the Human Tissue Act 1961, which sets out the conditions on which cadaver donations are legal. It is an interesting statute for a number of reasons. Despite much-discussed ambiguities its main provisions have remained unamended.[4] It also displays a trust in the medical profession that later Parliamentary for-

[1] Figures from United Kingdom Transplant Support Services Authority, *Annual Report for 1993–4* (Bristol: UKTSSA, 1994), 26, 32, 35.

[2] The United Kingdom Transplant Support Service Authority (Establishment and Constitution) Order 1991, SI 1991 No 407; The United Kingdom Transplant Support Service Authority Regulations 1991, SI 1991 No 408.

[3] For an illustration of the application of these general principles in the context of transplantation see K. Norrie, 'Human Tissue Transplants: Legal Liability in Different Jurisdictions' (1985) 34 *ICLQ* 442, 443–50.

[4] The Act was amended by the Corneal Tissue Act 1986 and the Anatomy Act 1984, but the basic framework remains intact.

ays into the regulation of medicine have been reluctant to confide. Unlike the Human Fertilization and Embryology Act 1990, which is built around a fundamental criminal prohibition of unlicensed work, the 1961 Act fails to provide for any sanctions for its breach. It rests upon the assumption that, once it is clear how the law expects it to behave, then the medical profession can be expected to follow the rules.

Live donations failed to attract the attention of Parliament until a public scandal over the sale of organs for transplant in a private hospital in London led to the hurried passing of the Human Organ Transplants Act 1989. This statute proscribes commercial dealings in human organs. It goes further, however, and also requires live donations to be authorized by a special authority charged with overseeing live transplants, the Unrelated Live Transplant Regulatory Authority (ULTRA). Individual medical practitioners were no longer trusted to follow the rules. Breach of the 1989 Act is a criminal offence that can result in a fine or imprisonment. The Human Organ Transplants Act contains only part of the law governing live donations. It was passed to tackle one particular perceived abuse. The legality of live donations depends primarily on the basic common law principles that govern medical practice.

This Chapter begins by examining the prohibition on the sale of organs, which applies whether the donor is alive or dead. It then sets out the law on live donation. It continues by discussing the principles that govern the legality of cadaver donations, including the approach of the law to problem of determining whether a donor is alive or dead.

A. Sale of Organs

Section 1 of the Human Organ Transplants Act 1989 creates a number of offences related to commercial dealings in human organs. These offences only apply to parts of the body that fall within the statute's definition of 'human organ'. For the purposes of the Act, a human organ is 'any part of a human body consisting of a structured arrangement of tissues which, if wholly removed cannot be replicated by the body'.[5] This clearly covers the heart, kidney, liver, lung, and pancreas. It is not certain that the definition includes parts of these organs, but it is probable that the reference to 'if wholly removed' implies that partial removal falls within the scope of the definition.[6] This is important because liver transplants can be performed using only a portion of the donor's liver.

---

[5] S. 7(2).
[6] D. Price and R. Mackay, 'The Trade in Human Organs' (1991) 141 *NLJ* 1272–3 and 1307–9, at 1307.

Dealings in regenerative tissue, such as hair, skin, blood, and bone marrow are not prohibited by the 1989 Act. This does not resolve the matter but raises wider issues. It is arguable that such parts of the human body cannot be owned under English law and therefore cannot be sold.[7] However, there is no clear legal authority on the point.[8] In practice the need to resolve this legal technicality is avoided by paying donors for their inconvenience and services rather than for the things they donate. The sale of sperm or eggs is covered by the Human Fertilization and Embryology Act 1990 and was discussed in Chapter 16.[9]

The offences that the Act creates penalize all of those involved in commercial transactions. There is no exemption for the patients as there is under the Surrogacy Arrangements Act 1985 (see Chapter 16). The basic offence is committed by any person who pays or accepts payment for the supply of an organ intended for transplantation.[10] It does not matter whether the money changes hands before or after the organ is removed. It is no excuse that the transplantation will take place out of Great Britain. It makes no difference to the offence whether the organ will be removed from a dead person or from a living donor. Both are illegal. The Act also proscribes payment for an offer to supply. This prevents people receiving money for agreeing to donate organs when they die. It also means that prosecutions are possible even when completion of the arrangement is prevented.

In addition to the basic offence, committed by the purchaser and seller of organs, the Act criminalizes those who act as brokers of organs. Anyone who seeks out donors or potential purchasers is guilty of an offence.[11] Initiating or negotiating a deal for supplying an organ is illegal if payment is involved.[12] Managing an organization that is involved in initiating or negotiating the sale of organs is also an offence.[13] In relation to this second category of offence, there is no need for the brokers to receive any payment themselves. The maximum penalties for these two categories of offences are the same: three months' imprisonment and a £5,000 fine.[14] A further offence, carrying only the fine and no risk of imprisonment, is committed by a person who knowingly publishes or distributes advertisements for commercial dealings in human organs.[15]

---

[7] P. Matthews, 'Whose Body? People as Property' [1983] *CLP* 193–239; P. Skegg, 'Human Corpses, Medical Specimens and the Law of Property' (1975) 4 *AALR* 412–25.

[8] G. Dworkin and I. Kennedy, 'Human Tissue: Rights in the Body and its Parts' (1993) 1 *Med. L Rev.* 291–319. See also *Dobson* v. *North Tyneside HA, The Times,* 15 July 1996.

[9] See Price and Mackay, n. 6 above, 1273, for the suggestion that gamete donation also comes under the 1989 Act.

[10] S. 1(1)(a). [11] S. 1(1)(b). [12] S. 1(1)(c). [13] S. 1(1)(d); see also s. 4.

[14] Both may be imposed for a single offence. The Act fixes the fine at level 5 on the standard scale, and it will be increased as the standard-scale fines are raised. The standard scale is set out in s. 37 of the Criminal Justice Act 1982, as amended, and was last increased in 1992. [15] S. 1(2).

On the face of it, the Act is therefore very wide-ranging. However, not all cases where money changes hands will fall foul of it. Payments that cover only the cost of removing, transporting, and preserving the organ are not included. Nor are payments to the donor for the reimbursement of expenses and compensation for loss of earnings, if they are reasonably and directly attributable to the organ donation.[16] It should also be noted that, if the arrangement for the supply of organs is not illegal, then the related offences of broking and advertising will not be committed either. Finally, no prosecution may be brought unless approved by the Director of Public Prosecutions.[17]

B. Live Donors

(i) Consent

The general principle that surgery cannot be carried out without the consent of the person to be operated on is as applicable to organ transplantation as to any other procedure. The operation to remove the organ from the donor must therefore have the donor's consent and that to place it in the recipient must have the consent of the recipient. The latter raises no special legal problems. However, at one stage it was arguable that the donor's consent would be invalid because the operation was not expected to provide the donor with any benefit.[18] These worries were exacerbated in respect of the transplantation of non-regenerative tissue, where there is also a known and irreversible detriment to the donor. It now appears that this will not invalidate a consent, provided that the operation is acceptable on public-policy grounds and it is reasonable to perform it in the circumstances.[19] The fact that the Human Organ Transplants Act 1989 established the requirement of prior consent for some types of live transplants, but permits others without reference to ULTRA, implies that public policy supports transplantation. There can no longer be any doubt, if there ever was a real problem, that donors can consent to the necessary surgical procedures.

The regulations made under the 1989 Act codify the need for consent in cases that must be referred to ULTRA (see below). The donor must receive an explanation of the nature of the medical procedure involved in donation and of the risks involved. It is unlikely that this involves different standards from

---

[16] S. 1(3).   [17] S. 5.

[18] G. Dworkin, 'The Law Relating to Organ Transplantation in England' (1970) 33 *MLR* 353, 355–9. See also P. D. G. Skegg, 'Medical Procedures and the Crime of Battery' [1974] *Crim. LR* 693–70 and P. Skegg, *Law, Ethics and Medicine* (Oxford: Clarendon Press, 1988) 36.

[19] *Re Attorney General's Reference (No 6 of 1980)* [1981] 1 All ER 1057.

those the common law already imposes, although it is arguable that a fuller explanation of risks is required because the donor cannot be expected to benefit from the procedure. The only alteration to the requirements for consent is that it is also necessary to check that donors actually understand the explanations they are given. This is legally required in cases involving non-regenerative organs[20] from unrelated donors[21] that are not performed primarily for the donor's therapeutic purposes.[22] It would presumably be good practice in other cases.

More difficult problems arise in respect of donations from those unable to consent for themselves. In general, the validity of such consents turns on the common law. In relation to transplants within the scope of the Human Organ Transplants Act 1989 (see section A above) the common law principles have been partly displaced by the regulations made under the Act. The common law is discussed first, the provisions on consent in the regulations second.

Where children are involved, it may be that the potential child donor is sufficiently mature to decide whether to go ahead with the operation.[23] If this is not the case, then parents can consent on the child's behalf if it is reasonable to do so.[24] The test of reasonableness will demand a balancing of the risks and benefits involved. Clearly donation of non-regenerative organs involves higher risks than that of tissues which can be replaced. The risks inherent in recovering the tissue to transplant are also relevant; invasive surgery will be more dangerous than venepuncture. Thus donations of blood will be comparatively easy to justify, but giving a kidney would be more problematic. Benefit to the child of a number of kinds can be suggested. Where the proposed recipient is a member of the same family the contribution he or she make to the child's well-being will be relevant.[25] It may be suggested that there is an educational benefit in teaching the child altruism, but this argument must be difficult to sustain for irreversible procedures. Financial considerations will be usually irrelevant, given the prohibition of the sale of organs introduced by the Human Organ Transplants Act 1989.

In general, it will be difficult for parents to justify consenting to donations of non-regenerative organs when major surgery is needed to remove them. The risks involved would be high. Exceptional benefits need to be established. Possibly this could be shown when the child was dependent upon the recipient whose life was at risk without the transplant. In the USA the courts have permitted children to donate kidneys to their siblings, arguing that they

---

[20] The Act only applies to these: s. 7(2).

[21] Related donations do not need to be referred to the ULTRA: see sect. B(ii) below.

[22] In therapeutic cases, the ULTRA needs to be satisfied only that no payment is involved: see sect. B(ii) below.

[23] See Ch. 12 for discussion.   [24] See Ch. 12 for discussion.

[25] For US examples on this point see Skegg, n. 18 above, 60–3.

benefit from the siblings' prolonged life.[26] However, there is no guarantee that the English judiciary would accept this line of reasoning.

Where the incompetent potential donor is an adult, the legal principles are more restrictive. In such cases, the House of Lords has held that the duty of the health professionals is to act in their patients' best interests.[27] It would therefore be necessary to show that the patients will benefit from becoming donors, not merely that it is reasonable to expose them to the risk (as with children). This will be difficult to demonstrate, and some judges have suggested that it would be good practice to seek the approval of a court before permitting a adult who is unable to consent to become a donor.[28] It is possible that the public policy in favour of saving life would justify some donations that are not in the interests of the donor even without consent. However, there are no judicial pronouncements to indicate whether such an argument would be accepted. The matter has become more pressing with the development of 'elective ventilation', whereby patients are temporarily resuscitated solely in order to enable their organs to be transplanted.[29]

These general principles are partly superseded, in relation to the transplantation of non-regenerative organs, by the regulations made under the 1989 Act.[30] These specify that where the donor is not closely related to the recipient (see below for the required degree of relationship) and the primary purpose of the removal of the organ is to donate it to another person, then approval can only be given if the donor understands what is happening and gives consent. In order to permit donations by incompetent persons, it is necessary to construe 'donor' as including a person able to consent on the donor's behalf. However, the definition provided by the regulations does not extend its meaning in this way.[31] The regulations therefore preclude donations, save between close relatives or where the organ is 'spare', in the sense that it has been removed for therapeutic reasons.

(ii) Licensing

The Human Organ Transplants Act 1989 introduced restrictions on live transplantations, probably designed primarily to reinforce the prohibition on

[26] e.g. *Hart* v. *Brown* (1972) 289 A. 2d 386 (Conn.); see W. J. Curran, 'A Problem of Consent: Kidney Donation in Minors' (1959) 34 *NY Univ. LR* 891.

[27] *F* v. *W. Berkshire HA* [1989] 2 All ER 545. See Ch. 10 for discussion of treatment without consent.

[28] *Re F* [1989] 2 FLR 376, 390–1 (Lord Donaldson), 404 (Neill LJ), 411, 413 (Butler-Sloss LJ).

[29] See J. V. McHale, 'Elective Ventilation—Pragmatic Solution or Ethical Minefield' (1995) 11 *PN* 23–6; S. A. M. McLean, 'Transplantation and the "Nearly Dead": The Case of Elective Ventilation' in S. A. M. McLean (ed.), *Contemporary Issues in Law, Medicine and Ethics* (Aldershot: Gower, 1996).

[30] Human Organ Transplants (Unrelated Persons) Regulations 1989, SI 1989 No 2480.

[31] *Ibid.*, r. 1(3).

the sale of organs. They apply only to human organs within the definition of the Act (see section A above). In essence, they prevent transplants unless either the donor is a close blood relation of the recipient, or the transplantation has been licensed by the Unrelated Live Transplant Regulatory Authority (ULTRA). Outside these circumstances, the removal of an organ from a live donor and the placement of such an organ in another are both offences under section 2(1) of the Act. The offences carry the same penalty as those under section 1, and can also be prosecuted only with the permission of the DPP (see section A above). Transplants between natural parents and children, brothers and sisters (including those of half blood), uncles and aunts, nephews and nieces, and first cousins are not caught by this prohibition.[32] Doctors must actually test for these relationships in accordance with the regulations.[33] They may not rely on the evidence of the donor and recipient.

In all other cases, the doctor who is clinically responsible for the donor must obtain permission from ULTRA before the transplant can be legally performed.[34] Approval can be granted only where the Authority is satisfied that no payment is involved.[35] Where the primary purpose of the removal is the medical treatment of the donor, that is all that needs to be shown. In other cases, the Authority must also be satisfied of a number of other things:[36] first, that the donor has been given an explanation of the nature of the medical procedure for the removal of the organ and the risks involved; secondly, that the donor understands this explanation and consents to the procedure; thirdly, that there was no coercion or inducement; fourthly, that the donor understands that she or he is entitled to withdraw consent, but has not done so. In order to establish these things, the donor and recipient must have been interviewed by a suitably qualified person, who then reports to the Authority.[37]

C. Cadaver Donations

Cadaver donations are governed by the Human Tissue Act 1961, as amended by the Corneal Tissue Act 1986.[38] This Act applies to the removal of all human tissue and is not restricted to 'organs' like the 1989 Act. It permits the removal

---

[32] S. 2(2). The status provisions of the Human Fertilization and Embryology Act 1990 are to be disregarded when establishing a relationship for this purpose: Sch. 4 to the 1990 Act.

[33] S. 2(2); Human Organ Transplants (Establishment of Relationship) Regulations 1989, SI 1989 No 2107. The tester must be approved by the Secretary of State for these purposes.

[34] N. 30 above.   [35] Human Organ Transplants Act 1989, s. 2(3); n. 30 above, r. 3(1)(a).

[36] N. 30 above, r. 3(2).   [37] *Ibid.,* r. 3(2)(e).

[38] A number of provisions from the original Act were repealed by the Anatomy Act 1984 and the Statute Law (Repeals) Act 1974.

of tissue from corpses in specified circumstances. First, the donor must be dead.[39] Secondly, the removal must have been duly authorized.[40] Authorization can be given for all or any of the following purposes: medical treatment, medical education, or research. Thirdly, the removal must be effected by a registered medical practitioner.[41] In the case of an eye or part of an eye the Act also allows for removal by an NHS employee who is not a doctor, provided that it is carried out on the instructions of a registered medical practitioner.[42] Fourthly, no tissue can be removed where it may be necessary to hold an inquest or the coroner may require a post-mortem to be carried out unless the coroner has authorized the removal.[43] The meaning of the third condition is clear, but others require further discussion.

Although the statute sets out these requirements, it is silent on the consequences of disregarding them. Academic commentators have discussed various possibilities for legal actions, both of a criminal and civil nature.[44] Their tentative conclusion is that there is no legal sanction for breach of the statutory provisions. There has been one reported prosecution, *R. v. Lennox Wright*, brought against person who was not a registered medical practitioner.[45] The charge was disobedience of a statute, a common law offence that, if it exists, carries unlimited powers of imprisonment. However, doubt has since been thrown on this decision and it is unlikely to be followed in a subsequent case.[46] It is, nevertheless, probable that the professional bodies would consider any failure to abide by the legal requirements as professional misconduct.

(i) Authorization

Before tissue can be removed, authorization must be given by the person 'lawfully in possession of the body', although that person is not free to give consent merely because she or he thinks it appropriate. The meaning of this phrase has been the subject of much academic debate. However, it is now generally accepted that, for the purposes of the Human Tissue Act, the hospital management is lawfully in possession of a body on its premises unless the corpse is only there because the hospital has refused to allow someone with a right to possession to remove it for burial or cremation.[47] Hospital authori-

---

[39] S. 1(4), (4A).   [40] S. 1(1), (2).   [41] S. 1(4), (4A).   [42] S. 1(4A).

[43] S. 1(5). See Ch. 20 for discussion of the jurisdiction of the coroner.

[44] P. D. G. Skegg, 'Liability for the Unauthorised Removal of Cadaveric Transplant Material' (1974) 14 *Med. Sci. Law* 53–7; I. Kennedy, *Treat Me Right* (Oxford: OUP, 1991), ch. 11; P. D. G. Skegg, 'Liability for the Unauthorised Removal of Cadaveric Transplant Material: Some Further Comments' (1977) 17 *Med. Sci. Law* 123–6.

[45] [1973] Crim. LR 529.   [46] *R. v. Horseferry Road Magistrates' Court* [1986] 2 All ER 666.

[47] Skegg, *Law, Ethics & Medicine*, n. 18 above, 232–40; D. Lanham, 'Transplants and the Human Tissues Act 1961' (1971) 11 *Med. Sci. Law* 16–24, 18–20; Dworkin, n. 18 above, 366–8.

ties will normally be in a position to authorize the removal of tissue for transplantation, education, or research, providing that the other requirements of the Act are satisfied. The Act provides that hospital managers may nominate other people to exercise the power to give such authorizations on their behalf.[48]

The person in lawful possession of the body may authorize the removal of tissue only if the requirements of either section 1(1) or section 1(2) are satisfied. Section 1(1) permits the removal of tissue where the deceased person has requested it. To fall within the Act it is necessary for the deceased person's consent to have been expressed in one of two forms. The first is in writing, and can be made at any time. If an oral request is made, it will only come within the Act if it is expressed during her or his last illness in the presence of two witnesses. Provided that a request was made, then removal can take place, but only in accordance with the terms of the request. The deceased is entitled to revoke the consent at any time, but doctors will be protected by an earlier consent so long as they had no reason to believe that it had been withdrawn. The Act does not specify that a written request need be withdrawn in writing, nor that a revocation need be witnessed. It is probable that any indication that the person had changed his or her mind would serve to withdraw consent.

Where the deceased made no request within the scope of the statute, it is still possible for the removal of tissue for transplantation to be authorized under section 1(2) of the Act. Authorization cannot be granted under this provision if the person lawfully in possession of the body has reason to believe that the deceased expressed an objection to his body being used for treatment, education, or research. Nor can authorization be given if the surviving spouse or any surviving relative objects. The Act requires that such reasonable enquiries as are practicable must be made into these matters. This can be described as an 'opting out' provision, allowing hospitals to presume that tissue may be removed for transplant unless they know that the deceased or a relative objects. However, it differs from 'opting out' schemes as usually discussed, in that it permits relatives as well as the donor to opt out.

The provisions of section 1(2) have proved highly ambiguous.[49] On the face of it, the objection of any surviving relative, however remote, bars any transplant. The hospital is absolved from any responsibility for an unknown objection from a distant relative providing that it has taken reasonable steps to investigate the possibility that objections exist. It needs inquire only so far as is reasonably practicable, which has been take to mean that rudimentary inquiries will suffice because the tissue must be removed soon after death for

---

[48] S. 1(7).
[49] See Skegg, *Law, Ethics & Medicine*, n. 18 above, 243–52; Dworkin, n. 18 above, 366–8; Lanham, n. 47 above, 17–18.

it to be usable for transplantation. In practice this means that probably only those relatives already known to the hospital authorities need be consulted.

Section 1(1) allows people to choose to be donors before their deaths and, strictly speaking makes any objections by relatives irrelevant. However, even if people 'opt in' in this manner it does not guarantee that their wishes will be respected. The person lawfully in possession of the body is only permitted to authorize removal for transplant; there is no obligation to do so. It is generally thought that doctors are reluctant to rely on requests by deceased persons, and that they often prefer to respect the wishes of relatives even when they need not do so. This means that the practical effect of the law set out in the 1961 Act depends heavily on how health professionals choose to operate it.

(ii) Dead or Alive?

The Human Tissue Act 1961 provides no definition of death; it merely requires that the doctor removing the parts of the body must 'have satisfied himself by personal examination of the body that life is extinct'.[50] In essence, therefore, the law leaves it to the medical practitioner to decide what death means for these purposes. Unfortunately, the medical concept of death is now a complex one and there is no certainty as to what tests should be applied.[51] Many legal jurisdictions have sought to resolve the confusion through statutory definitions, but in England this approach has not been adopted.[52] The judiciary has been similarly reluctant to offer a legal definition of death. The issue has now been raised in three reported cases.[53] Two give little guidance on the tests that doctors should apply;[54] the third indicates that the courts will accept that a person is dead when death is diagnosed according to the unofficial guidelines that doctors have themselves produced (see immediately below for details). In Re A[55] the judge was asked to decide whether a child on life support was dead. He found that where the accepted tests established brainstem death, the child was dead for legal purposes and that it would not be

---

[50] S. 1(4), (4A).

[51] Skegg, *Law, Ethics and Medicine*, n. 18 above, ch. 9; J. K. Mason and R. A. McCall Smith, *Law and Medical Ethics* (4th edn., London: Butterworths, 1994) ch. 13; I. Kennedy, 'Alive or Dead' (1969) 22 *CLP* 102–28; A. Van Till-d'Aulnis de Bourouill, 'How Dead Can You Be?' (1975) *Med. Sci. Law* 133–47; F. Bennion, 'Legal Death of Brain Damaged Persons', evidence to the House of Lords Select Committee on Medical Ethics, reproduced in HL Paper (1993–4), 28–III, 8–12.

[52] It was rejected by the Criminal Law Reform Committee, *Offences Against the Person* (London: HMSO, 1980, Cmnd. 7844), para. 37.

[53] See also *R. v. Potter*, reported as a news item in *The Times*, 26 July 1963, and discussed in P. J. Pace, 'Defining Human Death' (1976) 126 NLJ 1232–4.

[54] *R. v. Malcherek, R. v. Steel* [1981] 2 All ER 422; *Mail Newspapers plc* v. *Express Newspapers plc* [1987] FSR 90.

[55] [1992] 3 Med. LR 303.

unlawful to turn off the life support. However, he did not expressly decide that the legal test for death was the same as the medical one.

It could be argued that doctors who believe that they should decide whether a person is dead by other means would be acting within the Human Tissue Act 1961, because that Act seems to impose a subjective requirement. However, if they were shown to have failed to follow the guidelines agreed by the profession a *prima facie* case of negligence would probably be made out. In practice, therefore, doctors who wish to ensure that they remain within the law should follow the guidelines.

Brain-stem death is the agreed criterion.[56] It should be diagnosed by two doctors, at least one of whom should be of consultant rank. Both should be independent of the transplant team. The first step is to ensure that the patient's condition cannot be explained by reversible factors. Any possibility that the apparent symptoms of death may be the result of drugs, hypothermia, or metabolic or endocrine disturbances must be excluded by considering the patient's medical history. A series of tests is recommended to check for reflex actions. Brain-stem death can be diagnosed when no reaction is found from the pupils to sharp changes in light intensity, there is no corneal reflex, no eye movement occurs when ice-cold water is injected into the patient's ear, no motor reflexes can be elicited from the cranial nerve,[57] and a catheter can be passed down the trachea without provoking a gag reflex. To avoid risk of error, these tests should normally be performed on two occasions, although this is not thought necessary where the patient has suffered a severe head injury that makes it obvious that his or her condition is irremediable. The guidance does not set a specific interval that should elapse between tests, but notes that the second series could be carried out as long as twenty-four hours after the first if there is any room for uncertainty. The results of tests should be recorded in the case notes.

(iii) The Role of the Coroner

The Act gives a complete discretion to coroners on whether they will give permission for organs to be used for transplantation. However, the Home Office has issued advice on the matter that indicates that there are only three cases where it would be proper to refuse permission. The first is when the tissue

---

[56] Conference of Medical Royal Colleges, 'Diagnosis of Brain Death' (1976) 2 *BMJ* 1187–8, and 'Diagnosis of Death' (1979) 1 *BMJ* 332. The status of these guidelines was reinforced by their acceptance in the code of practice published by the Medical Royal Colleges, *Cadaveric Organs for Transplantation* (London: DHSS, 1983); see Home Office Circular No 44 of 1983. See also British Paediatric Association, 'Diagnosis of Brain-stem Death in Infants and Children' excerpted in (1992) BME No 76 10.

[57] Spinal reflexes may still be present even after brain-stem death.

would be evidence in criminal proceedings that are likely to be brought. The second is where a malfunction in the organ in question may have been the cause of the donor's death. The third is where the removal would obstruct the coroner's enquiries. Coroners are not obliged to follow this guidance, but if they fail to do so a judicial review action might be available.[58]

D. Liability for Diseased Organs or Tissue

Transplant teams must exercise due professional care in the same way as in any other specialty. The general law of malpractice therefore provides important background principles. However, because transplantation involves implanting human tissue supplied by another person, there is additionally the possibility that product liability laws could be applied. Should it transpire that tissue transplanted harmed the recipients, for example by infecting them with the HIV virus, it might be alleged that either the health professionals or the donor were liable for supplying a defective product.[59] This area of law is explained in Chapter 9.

A number of legal uncertainties would need to be resolved before the chances of such cases succeeding could be assessed. First, it must be determined whether the courts would accept that human tissue was a 'product' for the purposes of the Consumer Protection Act 1987. If it is not, then the Act would be inapplicable. Section 1 of the Act defines products as 'goods'. This probably implies commercial activity that is usually absent in this field. The Act also assumes that there is a 'producer' and it is not obvious that it is appropriate to describe human tissue as having been 'manufactured' by the person whose body it is, or 'abstracted' from that body by the surgeon.

If the Act does apply, then cases can be brought against the immediate 'supplier' of the tissue or organ. This is particularly important because it makes the transplant surgeon, Transplant Support Services Authority, or National Blood Authority liable. It can avoid this by identifying the person who gave the product to it. Sometimes this will not be possible. For example, blood donors will usually be anonymous. An attempt to force the identity of a blood donor to be released failed in *AB* v. *Scottish National Blood Transfusion Service*, indicating judicial support for the continued anonymity of donors in order to avoid deterring them from donating.[60]

[58] Home Office Circular 65/1977; see also *Jervis on Coroners* (10th edn., London: Sweet & Maxwell, 1986), paras. 8.46–8.48.

[59] A. Grubb and D. Pearl, *Blood Testing, AIDS and DNA Profiling: Law and Policy* (Bristol: Family Law, 1990), 133–54.

[60] (1990) SCLR 263.

Even if the statute does apply, it may be that the courts would not accept that organs were 'defective' if they infect a recipient. The relevant standards depend on what recipients are entitled to expect, a controversial matter. Further, the Act provides a defence where the state of scientific knowledge was not such that the supplier could be expected to discover the defect. There are, therefore, a number of issues where public-policy considerations may be highly influential in determining whether there might be liability for the passing of infection during a transplant.

E. Conclusion

It can be seen from this discussion that there is considerable uncertainty about the precise meaning of a number of aspects of the law governing transplantation. Calls for reform have fallen into three broad categories.[61] The first comprises technical reform. Here the primary objective is to clarify the ambiguity of the Human Tissue Act 1961.[62] This would provide health professionals with proper guidance, enabling them to be confident that they are acting lawfully. The second concerns the need to secure more organs for transplantation in order to ensure that all those who require this treatment get it before it is too late.[63] There are two main proposals. First, replacing the current system with a proper opting-out system, whereby organs would be removed from corpses unless the deceased had registered an objection.[64] Others suggest imposing a duty on health professionals to seek permission from relatives for organs to be removed for transplantation (sometimes called 'required request' laws). The third category of criticisms of the existing law focuses on moral issues. The main focus of this category is the 1989 Act. Not all commentators accept that the sale of organs, which would increase the number available for transplant, is unethical.[65] The restrictive regulation of live donations has been criticized as going beyond the scope of the Government's objectives and unfounded on any sound moral principle.[66]

---

[61] For a general review, see Nuffield Council on Bioethics, *Human Tissue: Ethical and Legal Issues* (London: Nuffield Council on Bioethics, 1995), and the special issue of the *Medical Law Review* dedicated to discussing the report: (1993) vol. 3, pt. 3.

[62] Dworkin, n. 18 above, Price and Mackay, n. 6 above.　　[63] Kennedy, n. 44 above, ch. 12.

[64] R. Redmond-Cooper, 'Transplants Opting Out or In: The Implications' (1984) 134 *NLJ* 648–9.

[65] See e.g. R. Plant, 'Gifts, Exchanges and the Political Economy of Health Care' (1977) 3 *JME* 166–73 (1978) 4 JME 5–11; L. Andrews, 'My Body, My Property' (1986) 16 *Hastings Center Report* 28–38.

[66] M. Evans, 'Organ Donations Should Not be Restricted to Relatives' (1989) 15 *JME* 17–20; Price and Mackay, n. 6 above, 1309.

New developments in animal-to-human transplants may also require legislation.[67]

Further impetus for reform may be expected from Europe. A resolution was adopted by the Committee of Ministers of the Council of Europe in 1978 on the harmonization of the laws of the Member States in this area.[68] This resolution proposes a number of principles that are absent or at variance with current English law. A distinction is drawn between regenerative and non-regenerative organs. Transplantation of the latter from those who cannot consent for themselves should not be permitted (save where the removal is therapeutically indicated for the donor). The resolution also proposes no-fault compensation for donors who sustain damage as a result of the procedure. Anonymity between donor and recipient is also suggested, save where there is a close personal or family relationship. The sale of organs is disapproved, although it is acceptable to permit the refunding of loss of earnings and expenses.

Despite this resolution, European influences have not, so far, been significant in reform of the law, and the passing of the 1989 Act cannot be attributed to the resolution. However, there has been renewed European interest. In 1993 the European Parliament passed a further resolution on transplantation.[69] That calls for a code of conduct, a prohibition on commercial transplantation, a ban on donation by children and incapacitated adults, and agreed criteria for managing waiting lists. English law already bans commercial activity, but would need to be reformed in other respects.

[67] Nuffield Council on Bioethics, *Animal-to-human Transplants: The Ethics of Xenotransplantation* (Nuffield Council on Bioethics, London, 1996).

[68] Council of Europe Resolution (78) 29, 'On harmonisation of legislations of Member States relating to removal, grafting and transplantation of human substances'.

[69] 'Resolution on prohibiting trade in transplant organs' 14 Sept. 1993 (abstracted at (1994) 45 Int. Digest Health Legislation 111–13).

20 Terminal Care and Euthanasia

Terminal care presents health professionals with problems of a particularly difficult kind. Death is disconcerting for medical science because it is often seen as a type of failure. Care must often be palliative, designed to control suffering, rather than curative. Death and dying also present challenges to patients and their families which are more acute than is usual in health care because of the finality of the prognosis. It is, thus, much more difficult to disregard the patient's family situation than is commonly the case. These aspects of terminal care confront the established principles of patient autonomy.

First, it is common to withhold from patients information about their diagnosis. The ethical basis of this is suspect. Many commentators suggest that dying patients have a right to know that they are dying. It is difficult to justify deceiving a patient, although it is more legitimate to suggest that unwanted information should not be thrust upon patients.[1] There is also a risk that professionals may refuse to tell their patients in order to protect themselves from the sense of failure.

As Chapters 10 and 11 showed, in general patients have no right to be given all the available information about their condition. Health professionals have a duty to offer responsible care, but as there is controversy about the proper approach to this aspect of terminal care it is unlikely that a claim of negligence for poor counselling could be based on a failure to inform a patient that he or she was dying (see Chapter 10). Access to the patient's notes, which would include the information, could be refused by health professionals who believed that it would seriously harm the patient's physical or mental health to know the true position.[2] The practice of withholding a fatal prognosis from patients is not, therefore, unlawful.

The second common problem which arises is the propriety of informing the patient's relatives of the diagnosis. This may be a problem because the patient does not want them to know. It is also common for relatives to be told

[1] K. C. Calman, 'Ethical Implications of Terminal Care' in M. D. A. Freeman (ed.), *Medicine, Ethics and the Law* (London: Stevens, 1988), 107–19.

[2] Access to Health Records Act 1990, s. 5; Data Protection (Subject Access Modification) (Health) Order 1987, SI 1987 No 1903. See Ch. 11.

even when the patients themselves do not know. The law's approach to both these scenarios raises the same problem. Telling the relatives may be a breach of confidentiality. There will be no problem if the patient consents to relatives being told of the medical situation, but in these cases there can be no such consent. In the first consent is withheld; in the second it cannot be sought because the patient does not know the information to be revealed. The breach of confidentiality will only be legitimate if a paternalistic justification for breach of confidentiality in the patient's own interests exists. As was discussed in Chapter 11 this is problematic. Consequently, the practice of informing relatives without informing the patient may be unlawful.

Dying patients' rights to information about their condition are often, in practice, much reduced in the context of terminal care. The law offers little guidance on the proper approach, and in general follows its usual practice of leaving management to the clinical judgement of the health professionals concerned. The law does offer more detailed principles to govern decisions about when and how death finally occurs. Further consideration needs to be given to the extent to which dying patients have a right to die in the way in which they choose.

Discussion of the right of a patient to die inevitably involves consideration of the concept of euthanasia. Euthanasia means good death, and those who support it contend that in some circumstances it is right to end a life, rather than to continue it at all costs. The circumstances in which euthanasia might be considered can be characterized according to two variables, and these distinctions clarify debate about the relevant law and ethics.

On the one hand the involvement of the patient may fall into one of three categories.[3] First, the patient may choose to die, usually described as 'voluntary' euthanasia. Secondly, the doctor may make a decision on behalf of a patient who has not expressed a view on the matter. This may be because the patient is unable to do so, or because he or she has not in fact done so. This might be described as 'non-voluntary' euthanasia and is probably quite common in geriatric medicine, in that doctors often decide that some patients should not be artificially resuscitated should such assistance be required. Thirdly, there is a category of cases where euthanasia might occur against the wishes of the patient. This could be termed 'involuntary' euthanasia. Few would defend 'involuntary' euthanasia in this sense.

The second way in which euthanasia cases might be classified is on the basis of the involvement of the health professional or other person in control of the patient's care. Here the distinction to be drawn is that between acting so as to cause death and omitting to act so that the death is allowed to occur. These

---

[3] BMA, *Euthanasia* (London: BMA, 1988), para. 5.

cases are usually described as 'active' and 'passive' euthanasia respectively. Most commentators find it easier to justify euthanasia which is passive than that which is active. Not everyone accepts that there is a proper distinction to be made between the two.

A. Active and Passive Euthanasia

As a general principle, people are not legally liable for failing to act, so that a distinction should be drawn between causing death and failing to keep the patient alive. It is true that causing death is illegal. However, it cannot be inferred that passive euthanasia is lawful because there is nothing wrong with failing to act. While that may be true in general terms, the argument cannot easily be applied to health professionals. The usual distinction does not apply when the relationship between the parties obliges them to look after the patient. It is clear that health professionals have such a duty,[4] and are at risk of being prosecuted for manslaughter if their patients die after a negligent failure to treat them.[5] Non-professionals have been found guilty of manslaughter for failing to look after relatives for whose care they have taken responsibility.[6] The real issue in law, therefore, is not whether the euthanasia is active or passive. Passive euthanasia will be treated in the same way as active euthanasia if it happens in breach of a duty to take steps to care for patients.[7] The crucial question is the extent of this duty to act.

Moral theologians from the Roman Catholic tradition have developed a distinction between 'ordinary' and 'extraordinary' means used to keep patients alive. While they would hold that a health professional is obliged to use ordinary means to preserve the life of a patient, they suggest that it is not wrong to abstain from taking extraordinary measures. Skegg has suggested, however, that this approach is alien to English law and proposes a test based on the 'reasonable doctor'.[8] He argued that a doctor only has a duty to carry out acts which all reasonable doctors would carry out. Thus, doctors do not act unlawfully provided that they comply with a practice accepted as proper by a responsible body of the profession.[9] It would follow that a health

---

[4] *Barnett* v. *Chelsea & Kensington HMC* [1968] 1 All ER 1068.
[5] *R* v. *Bourne* [1938] 3 All ER 615, 618.
[6] *R.* v. *Instan* [1893] 1 QB 450; *R.* v. *Stone* [1977] 2 All ER 341.
[7] *Airedale NHS Trust* v. *Bland* [1993] 1 All ER 821, 880–3
[8] P. D. G. Skegg, *Law, Ethics and Medicine* (Oxford: Clarendon Press, 1988), 143–8.
[9] Using the duty of care in negligence, for which see *Bolam* v. *Friern HMC* [1957] 2 All ER 118. This conclusion can also be supported through an examination of the contractual duties of doctors: see H. Benyon, 'Doctors as Murderers' [1982] *Crim. LR* 17–28, 27–8. Benyon's conclusion that

professional has a duty to take positive steps to care for a patient where all reasonable members of the profession would do so, but not otherwise.

This approach was adopted in *Airedale NHS Trust* v. *Bland*.[10] The judges agreed that failing to keep patients alive would be criminal homicide if it were in breach of a legal duty to act so as to sustain their life. They differed slightly when it came to the precise way in which the duties of doctors to sustain life were to be defined, but the differences between the majority of the judges do not seem to be significant. Lord Goff suggested that they were defined in the same way as the duty of care in negligence, so that doctors might withhold or discontinue life support provided that they acted in accordance with 'a responsible and competent body of relevant professional opinion'.[11] Lord Keith argued that the limits of the duty to keep patients alive were reached when 'a large body of informed and responsible medical opinion is to the effect that no benefit at all would be conferred by continuance' with treatment.[12] Lord Browne-Wilkinson stated that doctors were only obliged to sustain their patients' lives when it was in their interests to be kept alive. He recognized that the acceptability of doctors' assessments of their patients' interests should be measured against the range of responsible medical opinion.[13] Thus, in his view:

> where the responsible doctor comes to the reasonable conclusion (which accords with the views of a responsible body of medical opinion) that further continuance of an intrusive life support system is not in the best interests of the patient, he can no longer lawfully continue that life support system. . . . Therefore he cannot be in breach of any duty to maintain the patient's life. Therefore he is not guilty of murder by omission.[14]

The implications of this position are that it would not be unlawful to allow a patient to die, providing that at least one responsible body of professionals would find the decision acceptable. One judge in the *Bland* case, Lord Mustill, was concerned that defining the obligations of doctors to provide life-sustaining treatment by reference to responsible professional opinion alone left too much to clinical judgement.[15] In his view the decision to be made was not medical but ethical, and there was no logical reason why the views of doctors should be decisive on ethical matters. However, as all the judges agreed that it was not in Tony Bland's interests to be kept alive, it was unnecessary for Lord

doctors are employed to exercise their clinical freedom is reinforced by the reluctance of the Court of Appeal in *Thake* v. *Maurice* [1986] 1 All ER 497 to imply that doctors' contractual duties differ from those under the law of negligence.

[10] N. 7 above.

[11] *Ibid.* 871 (see also 868), adopting the test from *Bolam* v. *Friern HMC*, n. 9 above. For discussion of this test see Ch. 7.

[12] *Ibid.*, 861.   [13] Applying *F* v. *W. Berkshire HA* [1989] 2 All ER 545.

[14] *Airedale NHS Trust* v. *Bland*, n. 7 above, 882–3.   [15] *Ibid.*, 894.

Mustill to explain exactly what test he would apply. In *Frenchay NHS Trust* v. *S* the Court of Appeal emphasized that the judge should make his or her own mind up about where the best interests of the patient lay, not merely defer to the consultant's opinion.[16] This seems closer to Lord Mustill's position, than to that of the majority. There was no detailed discussion of the speeches in *Bland*, and it is unlikely that a court would be keen to find a doctor criminally liable for taking a different view from that later reached by a court. In the *Frenchay* case the court was able to examine the matter in advance, and there was therefore no question of the doctors being prosecuted.

It follows from these legal principles that passive euthanasia is acceptable provided that it would be supported by a responsible body of professional opinion. Doctors and nurses who decide responsibly not to resuscitate patients would therefore be acting legally. The reasonable professional test cannot determine matters when active steps are taken, however. Here the law is clear, in that intentional killing is criminal, although the exact scope of the crimes in question needs further consideration.

B. The Law of Homicide

Any person who intentionally kills another may be prosecuted for murder or manslaughter. There are no special rules for health professionals permitting them to kill their patients.[17] Murder will be appropriate where the killer acted intending to kill or do serious harm. People intend to kill or do serious harm if they foresee that this is virtually certain to be the result of their actions.[18] Manslaughter will be the charge where the intention of the killer is less specific. Consequently, anyone who deliberately ends the life of another, as in active euthanasia, is guilty of murder.

A difficult question arises where the health professionals provide treatment that they know will shorten the life of their patient. The main example is where drugs are used at a dosage which will have the result of bringing the patient's death nearer. The professional knows what the result will be, but nevertheless the courts have held that in some circumstances he or she may be acting properly and would not be guilty of murder. A further problem is raised concerning whether turning off a life-support system should be

---

[16] [1994] 2 All ER 403, 411–13.

[17] *R.* v. *Adams* [1957] Crim. LR 365; *R.* v. *Arthur* (1981) 12 BMLR 1, 5; Skegg, n. 8 above, 122–31. The *Arthur* case is discussed in Ch. 17.

[18] *R.* v. *Moloney* [1985] 1 All ER 1025; *R.* v. *Hancock* [1986] 1 All ER 641; *R.* v. *Nedrick* [1986] 3 All ER 1.

classified as killing the patient. This will be considered separately later in the Chapter.

In *R. v. Adams*[19] a doctor was accused of deliberately increasing the dosage of opiates used as pain relief in order to end the lives of patients who had left him money in their wills.[20] The judge summarized the legal position as follows:

> If the first purpose of medicine—the restoration of health—could no longer be achieved, there was still much for the doctor to do, and he was entitled to do all that was proper and necessary to relieve pain and suffering even if the measures he took might incidentally shorten life by hours or even longer.

Having been directed in this way the jury acquitted the doctor.

This direction was based on the argument that in such cases the doctor's actions would not cause death; death would result from the illness itself. In addition a second implicit argument was that the doctor would lack the relevant criminal intention. If the intention was to relieve suffering then there was a lawful excuse for the administration of the drugs despite the incidental effect of shortening the patient's life. This is sometimes called the doctrine of double effect, whereby a good primary motive is seen to outweigh an undesirable, but known, secondary result. Although the basis of this statement of the law can be criticized,[21] it is unlikely that a future judge would depart from this approach. In *R. v. Cox*[22] the judge directed the jury to consider what the primary purpose of the doctor had been. He had administered a lethal dose of potassium chloride to a dying patient. The expert evidence showed that this drug had no pain relieving properties, and that it was clear that the dosage given would be fatal. This might have been taken to suggest that the doctor could not have believed that he was acting to remove the patient's pain. Dr Cox chose not to give evidence. The jury convicted him.

These principles indicate that the administration of drugs which hasten death will be lawful providing that three tests are satisfied. (1) The patient must be terminally ill. It is unclear how close to death the patient need be, and this is not always known with any certainty.[23] However, the patient must already be dying if it is to be argued that the illness, not the drugs, was the cause of death. (2) Prescribing the drugs must be 'the right and proper treat-

---

[19] N. 17 above, 773.

[20] See P. Devlin, *Easing the Passing: Trial of Dr John Bodkin Adams* (London: Faber, 1986) for a detailed account of the case by the judge in the trial.

[21] e.g. G. Williams, *The Sanctity of Life and the Criminal Law* (London: Faber & Faber, 1957), 289–91; Skegg, n. 8 above, 135–9.

[22] (1992) 12 BMLR 38. The charge was attempted murder, because the body had been cremated before a post-mortem could be carried out.

[23] Calman, n. 1 above.

ment'. This appears to mean that it must be treatment accepted as proper by a responsible body of the profession. In 1990 a prosecution against a doctor was dropped when it became apparent that some doctors supported the use of the drugs he had administered, despite the fact that the predominant opinion was that they were not appropriate.[24] (3) The motivation for prescribing the drugs must be to relieve suffering. Otherwise the shortening of the patient's life would not be 'incidental' to the prescription, but its primary purpose.

C. Mercy Killing

When people brings a patient's life to an end because they believe it to be the kindest thing to do, their actions are considered by the law to be homicide.[25] Many believe this to be a harsh rule, and there have been calls for a special defence of mercy killing. However, the Criminal Law Revision Committee has rejected this option,[26] although the issue continues to excite controversy.[27] It is unclear how significant the problem is. Clearly, the fact that mercy killing is a criminal offence encourages secrecy. It is also possible that cases of mercy killing often do not reach the courts because the authorities decide not to prosecute.[28]

Evidence on the course of prosecutions shows that 'mercy killers' are usually convicted of manslaughter rather than murder. In the period 1982 to 1991 (inclusive) the police coded twenty-four homicide cases as mercy killings.[29] In most of them, the alleged killers were spouses, parents, or children of the deceased. No proceedings were taken in three of these cases. Two prosecutions resulted in acquittals. There were sixteen convictions for manslaughter (although the original charge had been murder), one for infanticide, and one for murder. In the remaining case, the suspect died before proceedings were concluded. The special circumstances of mercy killings are likely to be taken into account in sentencing.[30] In the cases previously mentioned, only three of

---

[24] 'Doctor is cleared of murdering patient', *Independent*, 16 Mar. 1990.

[25] *Airedale NHS Trust* v. *Bland*, n. 7 above, 890.

[26] Criminal Law Revision Committee, *Offences Against the Person* (London: HMSO, 1980, Cmnd. 7844).

[27] J. Horder, 'Mercy Killings—Some Reflections on Beecham's Case' (1988) 52 *Journal of Criminal Law* 309–14; J. A. Laing, 'Assisting Suicide' (1990) 54 *Journal of Criminal Law* 106.

[28] For an old study on prosecution policy in the 1960s, see W. L. Parry-Jones, 'Criminal Law and Complicity in Suicide and Attempted Suicide' (1973) 13 *Med. Sci. & Law* 110–19. The current position of the Crown Prosecution Service is explained in its evidence to the House of Lords Select Committee on Medical Ethics, HL Paper (1993–4), 28–III, 79–84.

[29] Select Committee on Medical Ethics, Oral Evidence, HL Paper (1993–4), 28–II, 18, 25.

[30] R. Leng, 'Mercy Killing and the CLRC' (1982) 132 *NLJ* 76–8.

the convicted killers went to prison (although two received suspended prison sentences). Most were put on probation (twelve). The remaining conviction resulted in a conditional discharge.

D. Assisting Suicide

Suicide has traditionally been regarded by the Christian tradition as sinful, and until 1961 suicide was a crime at common law. Clearly, successful suicides could not be prosecuted. However, as suicide was in principle criminal and attempting a crime is illegal, attempting suicide was also criminal. This was not helpful to the care of persons who attempt suicide. Section 1 of the Suicide Act 1961 abolished the crime of committing (and therefore also attempting) suicide. This should not necessarily be taken as a statement that society now approves of suicide,[31] but it certainly removes one source of pressure on patients.

The removal of the criminal stigma attached to those who attempt suicide was accompanied by concern that suicide should not be encouraged, and section 2 of the 1961 Act created an offence of assisting suicide. This offence is made out when 'a person aids, abets, counsels or procures the suicide of another, or an attempt by another to commit suicide'. There were thirty-one convictions for assisting suicide in the ten-year period between 1982 and 1991.[32] Despite the fact that the interpretation of this section has come before the courts, there is still some confusion as to exactly what is required to establish the offence.[33]

In *A. G. v. Able*[34] the Attorney General sought a declaration that a booklet published by the Voluntary Euthanasia Society (VES, formerly known as 'Exit') was illegal under the Suicide Act. The booklet began by indicating that the Society disapproved of hasty decisions about suicide, but went on to describe a number of ways in which 'self-deliverance' might be achieved. The Attorney General had evidence that the booklet was associated with at least fifteen cases of suicide within eighteen months of its publication. It was argued that the fact that the VES felt it necessary to discourage ill-considered suicides indicated that it must have been aware of the risk that people might use the information to commit suicide. It was therefore contended that it was committing the offence of assisting suicide under section 2 of the 1961 Act.

---

[31] See *R. v. Inner W. London Coroner, ex p. De Luca* [1988] 3 All ER 414.
[32] N. 29 above, 18.
[33] K. J. M. Smith, 'Assisting Suicide—The Attorney-General and the Voluntary Euthanasia Society' [1983] *Crim. LR* 579.
[34] [1984] 1 All ER 277.

The court held that, in order to prove the allegations, three things had to be shown: (a) that the accused knew that suicide was contemplated, (b) that he or she approved or assented to it, and (c) that he or she encouraged the suicide attempt. In the case itself, publishing the booklet was not necessarily illegal because the third requirement was not made out in relation to any specific death. However, the judge suggested that if it were sent to someone with a note suggesting that the information contained in it be used to commit suicide this would be illegal. Consequently, giving someone pills saying that they should be taken to end his or her life would be an offence.[35] So, too, is putting people in touch with someone you know will help them end their lives.[36] An offence under section 2 may be committed even if no actual attempt at suicide is made. A person who attempts to encourage another to commit suicide can therefore be guilty, even if unsuccessful.[37]

It can be seen from this discussion that a health professional who helps a patient to take his or her own life is likely to commit a criminal offence. Even explaining how it might be done will be illegal if the professional knows that it would encourage the patient to go ahead. Making drugs available knowing that the patient is likely to take a fatal overdose would also be a crime. However, Lord Goff has stated that a patient does not commit suicide by refusing treatment, and that there could therefore be no prosecution of health professionals for assisting suicide if they respect such a refusal.[38]

E. Voluntary Passive Euthanasia

Under the general law of consent no-one may touch a competent patient without his or her agreement (see Chapter 10). Consequently, where a patient refuses treatment it follows that it cannot lawfully be administered. On this basis voluntary passive euthanasia is permissible under English law. This view of the law would be incorrect only if health professionals had an overriding obligation to keep patients alive. A general obligation to keep the patient alive would not in itself suffice as it would conflict with the patient's right to refuse treatment. For voluntary passive euthanasia to be unlawful the health professional's obligation to keep patients alive must outweigh that right.

At one stage this was indeed the position taken by the courts. In *Leigh* v. *Gladstone* a suffragette prisoner was fed, against her wishes, whilst on hunger

---

[35] *R.* v. *McShane* (1977) 66 Cr. App. R 97.
[36] *R.* v. *Reed* [1982] Crim. LR 819, discussed in *A. G.* v. *Able* [1984] 1 All ER 277, 286.
[37] *R.* v. *McShane*, n. 35 above.
[38] *Airedale NHS Trust* v. *Bland*, n. 7 above, 866. See also *Secretary of State for the Home Department* v. *Robb* [1995] 1 All ER 677 (FD).

strike.[39] The court held that the prison doctor was justified in feeding her because it was 'the duty . . . of the officials to preserve the health and lives of the prisoners'. This case is generally regarded as no longer good law. So far as it can be applied to those who are not prisoners it is probably dependent on the existence of the crime of suicide.[40] If attempting suicide were illegal, overriding the patient's consent could be justified as a step taken to prevent the commission of a crime.[41] However, the crime of suicide was abolished by the Suicide Act 1961, and this justification for an overriding obligation to keep patients alive cannot now be sustained. In relation to prisoners, in *Airedale NHS Trust* v. *Bland* Lord Keith stated that the force-feeding of a hunger striker would be unlawful,[42] and there has now been a case in which a court has declared that a prisoner must be permitted to starve himself to death provided that he has the legal capacity to refuse artificial feeding.[43]

The suggestion that English law requires life to be sustained whatever the circumstances is now untenable. The earliest cases concerned the selective treatment of neonates (see Chapter 18). In *Re C* the Court of Appeal approved a proposed course of treatment which was not aimed at keeping a ward of court alive at all costs.[44] There the baby was dying and all that could be done was to postpone death for a brief period. In *Re J* the Court of Appeal went further and permitted doctors to allow a child to die even though he might have lived for some years with intensive intervention.[45] In *Re R* it was held that antibiotics and cardio-pulmonary resuscitation could be withheld from an adult with very profound mental and physical disabilities.[46] In *Airedale NHS Trust* v. *Bland* the House of Lords held that artificial feeding could be withdrawn from a patient in a persistent vegetative state (see section H below).[47] These decisions would sit uneasily with an overriding and absolute obligation to maintain life. The suggestion that such an obligation exists has been expressly rejected by the House of Lords.[48]

It now appears that a doctor would not be entitled to disregard a refusal of treatment made by a competent patient.[49] The only exceptions are where the patient is under 18, when the parents may authorize treatment,[50] and possibly where a pregnant woman is about to give birth.[51] Consequently, for

---

[39] (1909) 26 TLR 139.

[40] G. Zellick, 'The Force Feeding of Prisoners' [1976] *Public Law* 153.

[41] S. 3, Criminal Law Act 1977.   [42] N. 7 above, 861.

[43] *Secretary of State for Home Department* v. *Robb*, n. 38 above.

[44] [1989] 2 All ER 782.   [45] [1990] 3 All ER 930.   [46] [1996] 2 FLR 99.

[47] N. 7 above.

[48] *Ibid.*, 861 (Lord Keith), 866 (Lord Goff), 882 (Lord Browne-Wilkinson), 891 (Lord Mustill).

[49] *Re T* [1992] 4 All ER 649, 661, 668; *Airedale NHS Trust* v. *Bland*, n. 7 above, 860, 866; *F* v. *W. Berkshire HA*, n. 13 above, 566. For discussion of the earlier case law, see Skegg, n. 8 above, 110–16, 155–7; I. Kennedy, *Treat Me Right: Essays in Medical Law and Ethics* (Oxford: OUP, 1988), 349–63.

[50] See Ch. 12.   [51] See Ch. 17.

example, it is not legitimate to force a blood transfusion on a Jehovah's Witness even if he or she would die without it (special problems arise in connection with children: see Chapter 12). Kennedy has argued that this right to refuse treatment is in practice a precarious one, as it can be nullified by classifying the patient as incompetent to take such a decision.[52] Once a patient is incapable of taking a decision, health professionals can provide treatment if they judge it to be in the patient's best interests.[53] Thus, health professionals may effectively override patients' objection to care by deciding that they are incompetent and then judging the care to be in their best interests.

F. Living Wills

If patients are entitled to exercise this limited control over their care, the question is raised as to the validity of decisions taken before they reach the terminal stages of their lives. Some patients wish to make advance declarations of their desire to die and thus give a prospective refusal of consent to treatment in defined circumstances.[54] Such advance declarations are sometimes called anticipatory decisions or living wills and are becoming more common in the United Kingdom. The Terence Higgins Trust has issued a model aimed, although not exclusively, at those who are HIV positive. Another model, pioneered in Canada, has also been published in Britain.[55] The BMA believes that indications of patients' wishes in this form may be helpful, especially as a means of encouraging discussion.[56]

No court has yet had to determine the validity of an anticipatory decision actually made by a patient who is now incompetent. There are, however, important indications of what a court would do. It is necessary to distinguish between two types of advance directive. One type involves a statement of patients' wishes, with the intention that those caring for them will put the instructions into effect. The other type seeks to ensure respect for the patient's feelings by appointing a person to take decisions as a proxy.

In a report published in 1988, the BMA argued that, in English law, living wills would be ineffective.[57] This view was based on the fact that the Enduring Powers of Attorney Act 1985 applies only to the administration of property.

[52] Kennedy, n. 49 above, 331–48.   [53] *F* v. *W. Berkshire HA*, n. 13 above.

[54] See J. Montgomery, 'Power Over Death: The Final Sting' in D. Morgan and R. Lee (eds.), *Deathrites: Law and Ethics at the End of Life* (London: Routledge, 1994), 37–53; K. Stern, 'Advance Directives' (1994) 2 *Med. L Rev.* 57.

[55] W. Molly and V. Mepham, *Let Me Decide* (London: Penguin, 1993).

[56] BMA, *Advance Statements about Medical Treatment* (London: BMA, 1995).

[57] BMA, n. 3 above, para. 271.

Save for the provisions of the Act, powers of attorney lapse when the person creating them becomes incapable of understanding them.[58] However, this can only apply to the second type of advance declaration. Powers of attorney are not relevant to a living will, or that part of a living will that merely records the wishes of a patient. A power of attorney provides authority for the attorney to act on behalf of the person who creates it. The argument put forward by the BMA is correct, but it only applies to cases where patients have nominated others to consent on their behalf.

There are good reasons to believe that the other type of living will is valid in English law. The enduring validity of a consent is routinely assumed in the context of surgery. Consents do not become invalid when a patient becomes unconscious under anæsthesia. So too, consent to surgery, at least in the NHS, is given without knowing who will perform the operation or exactly when. The patient gives consent some period in advance of the operation itself, usually evidenced by signing a consent form. No-one would suggest that this is ineffective. The consent remains effective until revoked.

The problem with advance statements of intent is created by the fact that the patient may very well have lost the capacity to revoke an earlier decision. It is therefore necessary to decide whether the patient is to be taken to have changed his or her mind. Where the circumstances have been foreseen by the patient, there seems no reason to believe that the advance declaration is ineffective.[59] Consequently, a precisely expressed declaration of refusal of consent to treatment in circumstances which have arisen would seem, on general principles, to be valid in English law. Consent to treatment in advance will similarly be valid, but it will not be binding in the sense that it determines what care the patient receives. This is because, as with competent patients, professionals cannot be forced to offer inappropriate care. Patients may veto specific treatment, but not require it.

This interpretation of the law is supported by the comments of Lord Donaldson in *Re T*.[60] He indicated that a competent refusal of treatment could bind doctors, even after a patient ceased to be competent to take a decision, provided that it covered the situation that had arisen. The case concerned a young woman who had earlier refused a blood transfusion, but whose life was now at risk if she did not receive one. The initial refusal had been based on advice that a transfusion was unlikely to be necessary. Lord Donaldson said that the doctors could not assume that she would have changed her mind and accepted a transfusion, but they should consider

[58] *Drew* v. *Nunn* (1879) 4 QBD 661, *Re K* [1988] 1 All ER 358.

[59] Skegg, n. 8 above, 116; Age Concern/Centre of Medical Law and Ethics, KCL, *The Living Will: Consent to Treatment at the End of Life* (London: Edward Arnold, 1988), 35–7.

[60] N. 49 above; see commentary by A. Grubb (1993) 1 *Med. L Rev.* 84–7.

'whether at the time that the decision was made it was intended by the patient to apply in the changed situation'.[61] If it was intended to apply and it was clear that the patient wished to choose to risk death then Lord Donaldson found that the doctors would be obliged to respect her wishes. However, on the facts, he found that her decision had been based on the misapprehension that there were other effective procedures available, and therefore it was not a decision that it was better to die than have a transfusion. This meant that the earlier refusal was no longer applicable.

Although the *Re T* decision did not concern a refusal of treatment contained in a document, the principles that Lord Donaldson outlined would apply equally to written refusals. Indeed, he supported his reasoning by reference to a Canadian case that did concern a documentary refusal of a blood transfusion.[62] The case can therefore be taken as a strong indication, although not a clear ruling, that a clearly defined refusal of treatment in a living will made by a competent patient will be binding upon doctors. Similar indications were given by the House of Lords in *Airedale NHS Trust* v. *Bland*.[63] Lord Keith stated that a patient's right to refuse treatment 'extends to the situation where the person, in anticipation of his . . . entering into a condition such as PVS [persistent vegetative state], gives clear instructions that in such event he is not to be given medical care, including artificial feeding, designed to keep him alive'.[64]

There may also be difficulties over the degree to which a living will records an informed decision. In *Re T* Lord Donaldson recognized that there is a public interest in 'upholding the concept that all human life is sacred and that it should be preserved if at all possible'.[65] This public interest gives rise to a presumption in favour of saving the patient's life. Thus, if there is any doubt whether the patient really understood what he or she was doing, or over the scope of a refusal of life-saving treatment, it will be deemed to be invalid. The presumption can, however, be rebutted. Both Parliament (in the Abortion Act 1967) and the courts (see Chapter 18) have accepted that sometimes the suffering involved in living outweighs the value of mere existence. Thus, it cannot be argued that allowing patients to die is never in their best interests.

If a living will is valid, then it is binding, and treatment against its provisions is unlawful. This draconian effect may well persuade the courts to limit the recognition they give to such documents, because they will effectively make it criminal to save life. However, where a living will has been found to

---

[61] N. 49 above, 662; see also 664.

[62] *Malette* v. *Shulman* (1990) 67 DLR (4th) 321. [63] N. 7 above.

[64] *Ibid.*, 860; see also Lord Goff at 865. However, see also the more cautious comments of Lord Mustill at 892.

[65] N. 49 above, 661.

be invalid, it may still play a significant role in influencing the care the patient receives. In the absence of a patient's decision, the health professional must take a decision as to where his or her best interests lie. Where patients have expressed a view that they would rather be allowed to die than to have life sustained when its quality was poor, this must be a strong indication of where their best interests lie. Consequently, it seems that, while a vaguely-expressed advance declaration would not force health professionals to abstain from treatment, it would make it more difficult to justify continuing. Again, the law remains unclear and ultimately the best interests of the patient are a matter for professional judgement.

Lord Donaldson indicated that where the situation in which doctors find themselves falls outside the scope of the patient's refusal, 'they have both the right and the duty to treat him in accordance with what in the exercise of their clinical judgment they consider to be in his best interests'.[66] This is an application of the decision of the House of Lords in *F* v. *W. Berkshire HA*,[67] which set out the general principle that, where a patient was incapable of consenting, the health professionals should act in the patient's best interests. In difficult cases, it may be appropriate to take the matter to court to be resolved.[68]

There is considerable interest in clarifying the law relating to living wills. In 1993, a bill on the subject was introduced into the House of Lords.[69] Progress on the bill was halted when the Select Committee of the House of Lords on Medical Ethics was set up, with living wills within its terms of reference. The Law Commission has published proposals for legislation validating some anticipatory decisions, and for the appointment by both patients and the court of proxies empowered to take health-care decisions.[70] However, the House of Lords Select Committee took the view that living wills were to be encouraged, but that it would be preferable for the health care professions to develop a code of practice rather than to legislate (as the BMA has now done).[71] The committee was less convinced that the appointment of proxies would be useful.[72]

---

[66] N. 49 above, 663.   [67] N. 13 above.

[68] Lord Donaldson encouraged this practice in *Re T*, n. 49 above.

[69] Medical Treatment (Advance Directives) Bill (HL Bill 73).

[70] Law Commission, *Mental Incapacity*, Law Comm. No 231 (London: HMSO, 1995). The Government has announced that it does not plan to legislate on the basis of these proposals, but to consult further.

[71] BMA, n. 56 above.   [72] HL Paper (1993–4), 28–I, 54–6.

G. Withdrawal of Life-sustaining Care

The final aspect of terminal care which must be considered concerns the decision to withdraw life-sustaining treatment.[73] It may become desirable to cease prolonging life for a number of different reasons. It may be thought that the patient is in fact already dead and artificial ventilation is doing no more than keep an empty shell of a body mechanically working. If this is an accurate assessment then turning off the ventilator cannot be unlawful. This will usually depend on the acceptance of the brain-death criteria, which were discussed in Chapter 19. As was suggested there, it seems that the law leaves the doctor to establish the point of death. Thus if the doctors responsible for the patients' care decide that they have died applying the usual criteria then artificial ventilation can lawfully be ended. This was accepted in *Re A*[74] where the judge was asked to decide whether a child on life support was dead. He accepted that where the accepted tests established brain-stem death, the child was dead for legal purposes and that it would not be unlawful to turn off the life support. The health professionals caring for the child were free to disconnect the ventilator if they thought it appropriate to do so. As the child was already dead, turning off the machine could not be said to be the cause of death.

If the patient wishes to turn off the life support and is physically able to do so, then the position is equivalent to voluntary euthanasia. The patient is entitled to refuse treatment, and health professionals may not turn the machine back on without consent. This has already been discussed earlier in the Chapter. If the patient is physically incapable of carrying out the wish to turn off mechanical life support the analogy is less clear. If professionals were to do what the patient asked, would it merely be a case of refusal of treatment or would it be an action causing death? If it is properly analysed as the latter then the issues are apparently the same as those raised by voluntary active euthanasia, which is not permissible in English law.

The legal position can be deduced from consideration of the situation in which a health professional begins to administer a drug by injection or to take a blood sample. If, in the course of the procedure, the patient objected to its completion then continuing it would be unlawful. The patient is entitled to change his or her mind and withdraw consent. This analogy suggests that a patient's refusal to accept continued artificial life support should be

---

[73] See generally Kennedy, n. 49 above, 349–63; Skegg, n. 8 above, 161–81; P. D. G. Skegg, 'The Termination of Life-support Machines and the Law of Murder' (1978) 41 *MLR* 423–36, but note that these discussions were written prior to the case of *Airedale NHS Trust* v. *Bland*, n. 7 above.

[74] [1992] 3 Med. LR 303.

recognized on the same basis as voluntary passive euthanasia. It seems, therefore, that health professionals are not only permitted to turn off life support when a patient demands it, but are required to do so.

A counter-argument to this analysis is that the action of a professional in turning off the machine would be assisting in the patient's suicide. This is illegal (see section D above). However, the conclusion that such an act is assisting suicide can be avoided by a number of routes. Some commentators argue that this can be avoided by classifying the health professional's conduct as an omission.[75] If this is legitimate, then no criminal act will have been committed. Kennedy argues that turning off the life support does not actually assist the suicide; it enables the patient to decide whether to choose treatment or death, but does not offer encouragement for either choice.[76] Lord Goff has suggested that the patient would not in fact be committing suicide anyway, and has made it clear that he believes that there is no risk of liability for assisting suicide.[77]

Commonly, however, the patient is not able to express a view as to the continuance of treatment. Here, the health professionals have to decide whether continued treatment is appropriate. Once again the law is not clear. The implications of the law governing euthanasia suggest that life support may be ended in accordance with a responsible decision by the professionals involved that this is the best way forward. They are obliged to act in the patient's best interests, but it has been shown that this does not mean that life should be preserved at all costs. As with drugs hastening death, it is the patient's underlying condition which causes death. The mechanical support merely postpones it. There is, therefore, no causal link between the death and the decision to turn off the life support. It has already been argued that health professionals will not have a duty to save their patient's life unless no reasonable doctor would allow the patient to die. If the decision that continued life support is inappropriate is taken responsibly, no such duty will arise.

This analysis of the law is consistent with the decision of the House of Lords in the case of *Airedale NHS Trust* v. *Bland*.[78] That case did not concern mechanical life support. The patient, Tony Bland, was in a persistent vegetative state. He could breath unassisted, but required artificial feeding. He was not conscious, and it was found that there was no prospect of improvement. The House of Lords rejected any distinction between the provision of food and water and other aspects of care. They upheld a declaration that it would be lawful to discontinue all life-sustaining treatment for Tony Bland, and to

---

[75] Skegg, n. 8 above, 169–79.   [76] Kennedy, n. 49 above, 341–3.

[77] *Airedale NHS Trust* v. *Bland*, n. 7 above, 866. See also *Secretary of State for the Home Department* v. *Robb*, n. 38 above.

[78] N. 7 above.

refrain from further treatment except for the sole purpose of enabling him to die peacefully in dignity.

Their lordships rejected contentions that following this course would have constituted a criminal offence. They argued that the withdrawal of treatment must be treated as an omission. Any other interpretation would discourage doctors from embarking on a course of treatment when the prognosis was poor, because deciding not to start would always be an omission. Given that it was a case of an omission rather than an act, there would be criminal liability only if there was a legal duty to act. The judges differed slightly on the way in which the duty of doctors to offer care to their patients was determined (see section A above). However, they all agreed that in Tony Bland's case there was no duty to continue with care because it would not be in his interests to do so.

H. Patients in a Persistent Vegetative State

Patients in a persistent vegetative state (PVS) continue to breath unaided, their eyes can open but they do not see, they cannot hear, they are incapable of voluntary movement and cannot feel pain, they cannot communicate in any way. The condition is irreversible. The *Bland* case concerned the particularly difficult situation where the patient is in a persistent vegetative state, and there is no indication of his wishes about the continuation of life-sustaining treatment when there is no hope of recovery. The House of Lords indicated that such cases should be brought to court for consideration prior to the withdrawal of treatment. The reasons given for this requirement were that the nature of PVS was uncertain, and that there was therefore scope for disagreement amongst relatives and professional staff. Bringing cases to court cannot be strictly necessary, because the only jurisdiction available to the courts is to make a declaration. This states whether or not a course of action would be legal, but it cannot make something legal that would not already have been permitted without judicial intervention.[79] Thus, taking a PVS case to court would reassure the doctors that they were acting properly, but it would not alter the legal position in any way.

However, the House of Lords emphasized that its approval of the withdrawal of treatment from Tony Bland should not be taken as indicative of its stance on any other factual situation. Tony Bland's case was an extreme one, in which there was no significant disagreement amongst the expert witnesses. Bringing subsequent cases to court, to be heard with the benefit of extensive

[79] The process is discussed in more detail in relation to the sterilization of those with learning difficulties in Ch. 16.

independent investigations by the Official Solicitor as the patient's guardian *ad litem*, was seen as a way of developing broader judicial guidance. It is possible that privacy for the patient may be maintained, even after death in order to ensure that there is no disincentive for invoking the court's jurisdiction.[80]

A number of cases have followed *Bland*.[81] In *Frenchay NHS Trust* v. *S* it was suggested that the courts need not in fact be involved in every PVS case, and that the expected independent investigations may not always be necessary.[82] The court noted that there would be some cases where there was an acute emergency, requiring a decision in minutes or hours, when it would be wholly impractical to involve the court. There would also be others, slightly less urgent, where it was acceptable that there was no independent assessment of the patient's condition, even though there was an opportunity to involve the court.

The *Frenchay* case itself came into this second category. The Court of Appeal found that it was not significant that there was no independent clinical assessment of the patient, some doubt whether the agreed diagnostic protocols for PVS had been followed (the diagnosis having been made after four months, not twelve, as advised by the BMA), and some signs that might have been interpreted as inconsistent with a diagnosis of PVS. Their lordships accepted the judge's finding that it was in the patient's interests to be permitted to die, and that determined the matter. Importantly, they seem to have diverged when explaining the role of the judge. Sir Thomas Bingham MR seems to suggest that the court should review the reasonableness of the doctors' decisions and be wary of substituting their own views. However, Waite LJ clearly stated that the judge must reach an independent view of the patient's best interests, overriding medical opinion if necessary.

Following these decisions, the Official Solicitor issued a Practice Note, giving guidance on seeking court consideration of PVS cases.[83] It notes that a diagnosis of PVS should not be considered as settled for at least twelve months, following RCP guidance. It emphasizes that the views of the next-of-kin should be made known to the court. A subsequent decision permitted the withdrawal of treatment even when the patient's mother (although not his wife) objected to withdrawal.[84] The judge emphasized that the ultimate responsibility lay with the doctor, not the family. The latter's views had to be

---

[80] *Re C* [1996] 1 FCR 605 (FD). There may be some tension here with the less generous approach taken in relation to publicity for cases involving children: see Ch. 12.

[81] See *Swindon & Marlborough NHS trust* v. *S, Guardian*, 10 Dec. 1994, summarized and discussed by A. Grubb at (1995) 3 *Med. L Rev.* 84–6, and a further case involving an 81-year-old woman reported as a news item in the *Independent*, 19 June 1995.

[82] N. 16 above.

[83] *Practice Note (Vegetative State)* [1996] 2 FLR 375.

[84] *Re G* [1995] 2 FCR 46.

considered, but they did not operate as a veto. The Practice Note also advises that the patient should be represented by the Official Solicitor, and any previously expressed views would need to be considered.

I. Administrative Aspects of Death

Once the patient has died, the law provides an administrative framework to ensure the proper collection of data on the causes of death, and safeguards against wrong-doing through the jurisdiction of the coroner. The first step in this process is the obligation of doctors who attend patients during their last illnesses to sign a death certificate in a prescribed form, stating the cause of death to the best of their knowledge. They must then send that certificate to the registrar, and give notice of the certificate to the nearest relative or other 'qualified informant', such as the occupier of the house in which the deceased died, a person present at the death, finding the body, or causing its 'disposal'.[85] The qualified informant must register the death with the registrar, usually within five days.[86] The registrar uses this information to collate mortality statistics.

In certain cases, it is necessary to pass information to the coroner so that an inquest can be held.[87] In such cases, no post-mortem should be carried out without the coroner's consent.[88] The legal duty to inform the coroner of deaths within this category falls on the registrar, not the doctor certifying death. However, this does not prevent a doctor doing so. The registrar is specifically obliged to inform the coroner of deaths that occur without the attendance of a doctor during the last illness, or during an operation, or while the effects of an anæsthetic persist.[89] Coroners must hold inquests where there are reasons to suspect that there has been a violent or unnatural death, or a sudden death due to an unknown cause.[90] The inquest may proceed without a jury unless the circumstances of the death indicate that there may

---

[85] Births and Deaths Registration Act 1953, s. 22. See ss. 16 and 17 for the definitions of qualified informant.

[86] Births and Deaths Registration Act 1953, ss. 16–18.

[87] The standard work on the jurisdiction of coroners is *Jervis on Coroners* (London: Sweet & Maxwell, 1993). See also P. A. Knapman and M. J. Powers, *Casebook on Coroner* (Chichester: Barry Rose, 1989) and D. R. Buchanan and J. K. Mason, 'The Coroner's Office Revisited' (1995) 3 *Med. L Rev.* 142–60.

[88] Anatomy Act 1984, s. 4(5).

[89] Registration of Births and Deaths Regulations 1987, SI 1987 No 2088, r. 41.

[90] Coroners Act 1988, s. 8(1). Inquests are also necessary in relation to deaths in prison or police custody. They are not considered here, as being outside the scope of health care law.

be a continuing risk to the health and safety of the public.[91] In other cases, coroners have a discretion to hold jury inquests if they choose. Inquests are usually held in public,[92] with witnesses being examined by the coroner and interested parties.[93] However, witnesses are not obliged to answer questions if they may incriminate themselves.[94]

The function of the coroner's inquest is to establish the cause of death, not to apportion blame. However, it is natural for relatives who believe that a patient may have died due to failures in professional care to use the evidence given at an inquest, and the verdict delivered, in support of a quest for compensation, particularly as the cost of an inquest is borne by the public purse, making it a cheap way of gathering information. To this extent, inquests may be significant in relation to subsequent malpractice claims. From the perspective of the health professionals, this may be exacerbated by some of the inquest verdicts that can be given.

Technically, there is no prescribed list of such verdicts, but the notes to the forms used for reporting the results of inquests indicate the expected range.[95] The feeling that inquests are sometimes, in practice, used to apportion blame comes partly from decisions where the cause of death is found to be unlawful killing, clearly indicating wrongdoing. However, some verdicts can also be supplemented by a finding that the cause of death was aggravated by lack of care. These are natural causes, want of attention at birth, industrial disease, and drug dependency or abuse. Where a tag of lack of care is attached, it clearly reflects badly upon those responsible for the deceased's care. They may be health professionals. Other possible verdicts include suicide and accident or misadventure.

J. Disposal of the Body

The rules governing burial and cremation are outside the scope of health-care law. However, there are two provisions relating to disposal of corpses that should be noted here. The first is that there are restrictions on the disposal of the bodies of those who have died with notifiable diseases under the Public Health (Control of Disease) Act 1984. These require the isolation of the corpse, prohibit the holding of wakes over the body, and permit doctors to

---

[91] Coroners Act 1988, s. 8(3). There are other circumstances where juries are mandatory relating to deaths in police custody or prison, and certain accidents and poisonings where there have been reporting requirements to the government or health and safety inspectorate.

[92] Coroners Rules 1984, SI 1984 No 552, r. 17.   [93] *Ibid.*, r. 20.   [94] *Ibid.*, r. 22.

[95] *Ibid.*, Sch. 4, Form 22.

prevent the removal of a body from hospital.[96] Some or all of these restrictions have been extended to a number of conditions, including AIDS, meningitis, viral hepatitis, measles, mumps, rubella, whooping cough, scarlet fever, and tuberculosis.[97]

Secondly, there may be a question whether the body may be used for anatomical examination: dissection for the purpose of teaching or research. This may happen if the deceased had made a written request that his body might be so used, or had made an oral request to the same effect during his last illness in front of two witnesses.[98] In the absence of such a request, then it may still be legitimate to use a body provided that the deceased or any surviving spouse or relative is not known to object.[99] These provisions are essentially the same as those relating to the use of organs for transplantation, and the same requirement exists that reasonably practicable enquiries are made to ascertain whether there is any objection. The question whether organs might be used for transplantation may also arise. This was discussed in Chapter 19.

K. Conclusion

English law's approach to euthanasia can be said to be one of partial support for passive euthanasia, although this partial support is a result of the application of general principles rather than special rules designed to deal with the problems of terminal care. In theory a patient has a right to voluntary passive euthanasia, in that professionals may not provide life-saving treatment against his or her wishes. This right can be evaded by classifying the patient as incapable of taking such a decision. Non-voluntary passive euthanasia (such as non-resuscitation) is permissible provided that a reasonable body of practitioners would approve that course of action in the circumstances. In some cases, even involuntary passive euthanasia would be permissible because professionals have no duty to provide treatment which they regard as inappropriate.

Active euthanasia is prohibited by the law of homicide, although proper palliative care which shortens life will be permissible if carried out under the principles set out in *R. v. Adams*.[100] Assisting in voluntary active euthanasia is illegal under the Suicide Act 1961. Withdrawing life-sustaining care is classified by the law as passive, rather than active, euthanasia and will only

---

[96] Public Health (Control of Disease) Act 1984, ss. 43–5.

[97] See s. 10 of the Act and the Public Health (Infectious Diseases) Regulations 1988, SI 1988 No 1546, Sch. 1.

[98] Anatomy Act 1984, s. 4(1),(2).   [99] *Ibid.*, s. 4(3).   [100] N. 17 above, 773.

constitute a criminal offence where there is a legal duty to continue care. The position in relation to life support can be summarized as follows. If the patient is clinically dead, then life support can be terminated. Where the patient is capable of expressing a view, or has done so in advance, that view should be respected even if it is expected to result in death. Where the patient is not able to decide whether artificial ventilation should continue then the matter appears to be one for professional judgement. Provided there would be support from responsible professionals for withdrawing life support, then it may legally be done. Special considerations arise in relation to PVS patients, and such cases should, at present, normally be taken to court before treatment is withdrawn.

Index